ALPHABETICAL LIST OF CHAPTERS

LITIGATION SERVICES HANDBOOK

LITIGATION SERVICES HANDBOOK

The Role of the Accountant As Expert Witness

Edited by

PETER B. FRANK

Price Waterhouse
Los Angeles, California

MICHAEL J. WAGNER

Price Waterhouse
Los Angeles, California

ROMAN L. WEIL

Graduate School of Business
University of Chicago
Chicago, Illinois

WILEY

JOHN WILEY & SONS

New York • Chichester • Brisbane • Toronto • Singapore

This publication is designed to provide accurate and authoritative information in regard to the subject matter covered. It is sold with the understanding that the publisher is not engaged in rendering legal, accounting, or other professional service. If legal advice or other expert assistance is required, the services of a competent professional person should be sought. *From a Declaration of Principles jointly adopted by a Committee of the American Bar Association and a Committee of Publishers.*

Library of Congress Cataloging-in-Publication Data:

Litigation services handbook: role of the accountant as expert witness / [edited by] Peter B. Frank, Michael J. Wagner, Roman L. Weil.

p. cm.

Includes bibliographical references.

ISBN 0-471-60206-X

1. Forensic accounting—United States. I. Frank, Peter B. II. Wagner, Michael J. III. Weil, Roman L.

KF8968.15.L57 1990

347.73′67—dc20

[347.30767] 89-28522

CIP

Printed in the United States of America

10 9 8 7

FOREWORD
An Adversarial Process

There are few more intense and lonely experiences for a certified public accountant than, as an expert witness, facing a talented attorney determined to minimize or destroy the credibility of direct testimony during cross-examination.

The expert is required to demonstrate a thorough knowledge of the relevant fields of learning while answering questions with reasonable promptness and precision despite the complexities and ambiguities of the technical matters involved. During testimony no opportunity is granted for extensive deliberation or consultation with other experienced associates. The intensity of the situation is heightened by the knowledge that the outcome of the case frequently affects the economic welfare of the client and the reputation of the expert witness and the witness's firm. At such times, it appears that the situation is tilted in favor of the cross-examiner who may have other accounting experts and qualified legal and technical staff assisting him, as well as extensive files of analytical data and the luxury of time to test the effectiveness of the questions to be used in cross-examination.

Under such circumstances, the certified public accountant may question the decision to accept the assignment to testify as an expert. However, with experience and complete preparation for the assignment, the expert witness soon realizes that the rigors of cross-examination apply as well to the cross-examining attorney and that cross-examination may be used as a weapon by either participant dependent upon the relative state of preparedness by each party in the drama. Further, the stimulation of pitting one's knowledge, background, and opinions against persons determined to prove the inadequacy of one's testimony makes the challenge one that will be long remembered.

Usually the initial reaction of the expert witness upon concluding testimony is one of relief that a difficult experience has been ended. However, if the trial results are favorable and the expert has contributed to the outcome, there is a feeling of elation rarely experienced in other types of assignments.

FRANCIS C. DYKEMAN

Francis C. Dykeman is the former managing partner of litigation services at Price Waterhouse and a pioneer in this field. He is the author of *Forensic Accounting: The Accountant as Expert Witness*.

PREFACE

Increasingly, CPAs and other financially oriented professionals offer litigation services to lawyers. The lack of reference materials for these professionals who confront new types of cases or new roles to play motivate this collaborative work—*Litigation Services Handbook.*

The editors selected authors who are highly regarded professionals offering litigation services. Each of the authors has substantial expertise in separate facets of this field, and we asked them to provide the reader with insights from experience developed over years of practice.

The *Handbook* comprises six parts. Each part addresses a distinct practice area or a specific set of functional tools and techniques for the practitioner. Part One describes the litigation environment; its nine chapters consider issues that transcend the type of lawsuit or the case-specific issues being addressed. Part Two, Chapters 10 through 18, deals with various types of civil cases in which CPAs are often asked to assist. Each chapter covers issues typical of a particular cause of action.

Although CPAs do not regularly handle criminal matters, a complete litigation services handbook for practitioners must describe the roles that CPAs play in these types of cases. Part Three of the book has two chapters on criminal case issues often addressed by CPAs. CPAs often handle marital dissolution or family law cases. Part Four, Chapters 20 through 24 (and the Appendix at the back of the book), explain some of the more typical analyses and problems encountered by litigation services professionals when dealing with a marital dissolution.

A frequent engagement for CPAs, and many other types of litigation services practitioners, is to be an expert on financial damages. Part Five of the book, Chapters 25 through 31, addresses many of the common types of damage studies performed in litigation, describing some of the unique problems and challenges faced by the damage expert. The final section of the book, Part Six, Chapters 32 through 34, deals with tax issues in marital dissolution cases, settlements and judgments, and tax fraud cases.

This book is written for any practitioner in litigation services. Although aimed at CPAs, this book offers concepts and methods to other skilled professionals: economists, business school professors, management consultants, and engineers, among others.

The editors intend the book to be free of sex-biased pronouns, and the use of *he* or *him* does not mean male but is a reference to a professional, either male or female.

The editors acknowledge the cooperation and patience shown to us by all of our contributing authors. The authors accepted our editorial changes and different writing styles with the belief that our greater view of the entire book and its contents put us in a position to know what to cut and what to leave in each chapter. Although we have edited each chapter, the intellectual content remains that of the chapter's author alone. As with any profession, differences in approach, emphasis, and philosophy exist among CPAs and others who work in this field. The editors believe that the positions expounded by the individual authors are either logical or have a degree of support, but they are not necessarily the position or beliefs of the individual editors.

The editors also acknowledge two individuals who most clearly helped to get this collaborative effort completed: Debra Asakawa made the first pass at suggesting changes to the chapters as submitted by the individual authors; Lynne Trueblood was responsible for organizing the effort, controlling manuscripts, and facilitating the progress of the book.

PETER B. FRANK
MICHAEL J. WAGNER
ROMAN L. WEIL

January 1990

ABOUT THE EDITORS

Peter B. Frank, a Price Waterhouse partner, is the firm's National Chairman for litigation services. He also serves on the firm's Policy Board (board of directors). His experience includes auditing and management consulting for industry, government, and Japan-based international businesses on such matters as strategic planning, information systems design and implementation, valuations, and cost systems design. He has testified as an expert witness in numerous litigation proceedings on issues of damages and liability, with particular emphasis in antitrust and intellectual property matters.

Mr. Frank is a Certified Public Accountant and a Certified Management Consultant. He is a member of the MAS Executive Committee of the American Institute of CPAs, the Institute of Management Consultants, and the California Society of CPAs, where he serves on its Litigation Services Committee.

Mr. Frank is treasurer and a founder of the Los Angeles-Guangzhou (Canton) Sister City Association and co-founder and board member of the Foundation for People. His articles have appeared in *Los Angeles Lawyer*, *Today's Executive*, and *The American Intellectual Property Law Journal*. He has co-authored *Bernacchi on Computer Law: A Guide to the Legal and Management Aspects of Computer Technology* (Little, Brown, 1986), and, with Mike Wagner, the AICPA *Guide to Litigation Services* (1986), and is on the editorial board and a contributing author to *Valuing Businesses and Business Interests*.

Mr. Frank holds a BS degree in economics (1965) and a MS degree (1966) in accounting from the Wharton School of the University of Pennsylvania and resides in Los Angeles with his wife, Eleanor, and daughter, Vanessa.

Michael J. Wagner earned his undergraduate degree in engineering from the University of Santa Clara in 1969, a Masters in Business Administration from U.C.L.A. in 1971, and his Juris Doctor degree from Loyola University at Los Angeles in 1975. He is a licensed attorney and CPA in the State of California, and is also a Certified Management Consultant.

A partner in the litigation services department of Price Waterhouse in Century City, California, Mr. Wagner is the author of ten other publications dealing with the litigation services field. He has participated as an expert or consultant in more than 100 litigations and has testified over 40 times in court or in deposition. His primary areas of expertise are in the computation of commercial damages or the valuation of businesses.

Mr. Wagner is an arbitrator for the American Arbitration Association and the National Association of Securities Dealers, and is currently serving on the Management Advisory Services Practice Standards and Administration Subcommittee for the

AICPA, the Litigations Services Committee (Past Chairman), and the Governmental Relations Committee for the California Society of CPAs. He is also a member of numerous professional organizations.

He resides in Pacific Palisades, California, with his wife Jolon and their four children, Devin, Reid, Teresa and Ross.

Roman L. Weil received his BA in economics and mathematics from Yale University in 1962. He received his MS in industrial administration in 1965 and PhD in economics in 1966, both from Carnegie-Mellon University. He joined the faculty at the University of Chicago in 1965, where he has held positions in mathematical economics, management and information sciences, accounting, and in the Law School. He has been a CPA in Illinois since 1973 and a CMA since 1974. He has also served on the faculties of the Georgia Institute of Technology, Stanford University, and New York University Law School, and as editor or associate editor of several publications, including *The Accounting Review*, *Communications of the Association for Computing Machinery*, *Management Science*, *Journal of Accounting and Economics*, and *Financial Analysts Journal*.

He has co-authored or co-edited three professional reference books for McGraw-Hill and several textbooks for Holt, Rinehart and Winston. His articles have appeared in *Barron's* and the *Wall Street Journal*. He has served as principal investigator for the National Science Foundation on various research projects.

He was a member of the Advisory Committee on Replacement Cost Accounting at the Securities and Exchange Commission, and served on two task forces at the Financial Accounting Standards Board. He is a member of the Financial Accounting Standards Advisory Council.

A member of the American Accounting Association, the American Institute of Certified Public Accountants, the Illinois Society of Certified Public Accountants, and the Institute of Management Sciences, he served on the Accounting Accreditation Committee of the American Assembly of Collegiate Schools of Business.

Mr. Weil has been a consultant to the U.S. Treasury Department, the Internal Revenue Service, and the Securities and Exchange Commission, and has testified as expert witness or consultant in a variety of litigation matters involving accounting principles, business valuation, damage estimation, regulatory issues, and taxes.

CONTRIBUTORS

ROBERT K. ATHY is a shareholder and vice president of West, Johnston, Turnquist & Schmitt, Accountancy Corporation. He has served as a consultant and expert witness in a variety of litigation matters. Athy is a lawyer and a CPA.

CAROL T.F. BENNETT is a management consultant in the Houston office of Price Waterhouse. She holds a PhD in economics and specializes in consulting for the banking industry and in conducting economic analyses for litigation matters, business valuations, and restructuring. Bennett has been a university instructor, a bank vice president and an economist.

DAVID L. BLACK is a partner in the firm of Schultze & Wallace, Inc., Sacramento, California. He has instructed several courses in business litigation and financial statement analysis and is a co-chairman of the Litigation Services Committee in the Sacramento chapter of the California Society of CPAs.

RICHARD S. BRAUN is a vice president and principal of Houlihan, Lokey, Howard & Zukin, Inc., Los Angeles. He is a frequent lecturer on business and security valuation topics. Braun is a senior member of the American Society of Appraisers and chairman of the Valuation Advisory Committee of the ESOP Association of America. He has testified numerous times on valuation issues in Superior Court and U.S. District Court. Braun earned a BS in business from Montclair State College and an MBA from Harvard Business School.

BRIAN P. BRINIG is both a CPA and an attorney who limits his financial consulting practice to the valuation of going business concerns and economic damages analysis. He is president of the Financial Analysts Society of San Diego and has qualified as an expert witness in the California superior courts and bankruptcy courts on many occasions.

GREGORY M. BURKE, CPA, is a director with the John Waddell Accountancy Corporation in Sacramento, California. He practices extensively in taxation and litigation support emphasizing complex business interruption cases. A former Internal Revenue agent, Burke has published articles on taxation, as well as litigation support services. He is a member of the California Society of CPAs and the AICPA.

M. JAMES CALL is a management consultant in the Los Angeles office of Price Waterhouse. He has had extensive experience in developing sales and profit projections for new products and new businesses and but-for projections as a damage analyst and expert witness. Call is an executive member of the American Marketing Association and a member of the American Sociological Association.

SUSAN E. CARROLL is a CPA with Howard Reece Sheppard in Corona, California. A graduate of California State University at Fullerton, she has been involved in litigation services work for over 10 years.

SHERYL L. CEFALI is a senior associate in the firm Houlihan, Lokey, Howard & Zukin, Inc. She has a BA from the University of California at Santa Barbara and an MBA from the University of Southern California. She has managed engagements covering a broad spectrum of valuation issues including ESOPs, litigation support, solvency, and estate and gift tax for clients ranging in size from small closely held concerns to major NYSE corporations and governmental agencies.

JOHN J. COSTELLO is a senior audit partner and head of the Litigation Support Department at Ernst & Young in Los Angeles. He is a member of the American Institute of CPAs, the California Society of CPAs, the American Arbitration Association, the Board of Arbitrators of the National Association of Securities Dealers, Inc., and the Pacific Stock Exchange.

HAROLD R. DILBECK is a professor of finance at California State University, Long Beach, and chairman of Harold Dilbeck Accountants, Inc. He has authored articles in the areas of finance and accounting. His practice includes analysis of and expert testimony on valuation of business and professional enterprises.

RONALD L. DURKIN is a partner in the accounting firm of Neilson, Elggren, Durkin & Co. He is a former special agent of the FBI where he spent over 10 years investigating criminal violations. He is a certified fraud examiner and received his master's degree in business administration.

ELIZABETH A. EVANS is an economist/lawyer at Lexecon Inc. She has an MBA in accounting and finance from the University of Alabama. She is also a CPA and CMA. Evans specializes in performing lost profit or valuation analyses and has extensive experience in applying cost-based predatory pricing tests and "failing firm/failing division" merger defenses.

NEILL W. FREEMAN, CPA, is a member of the firm of Freeman & Mills, Inc., a consulting firm that offers investigative services in the areas of accounting, finance, business, and trade practices. He has provided expert testimony in state and federal courts, and in arbitration, on accounting and auditing matters, business valuations, contract damages, lost profits, business procedures, and business and trade practices. He has served as court-appointed expert in state and federal courts and as special master in the federal court system.

DONALD L. GURSEY is a senior partner at Gursey, Schneider & Co. He has authored numerous articles and lectured on the tax aspects of a marital dissolution, business valuations, tracing, commingling, and apportionment. He is currently the chairman of the Litigation Services Committee of the California Society of CPAs and is the tax editor for the *Family Law News*, a California State Bar publication.

DAN J. HALL is a tax partner at Coopers & Lybrand in San Francisco. He is a CPA as well as an attorney and is a frequent speaker on tax topics in the Bay Area as well as a frequent instructor in the firm's national training courses.

ABRAM E. HOFFMAN is a principal in the economics practice at Price Waterhouse, located in Washington, DC. He has testified in the areas of antitrust liability and damages and consults in the areas of economics, finance, and statistics. Hoffman received his doctorate in managerial economics from the Harvard Business School.

DALE R. HURD is the director of litigation services at the Los Angeles office of Kenneth Leventhal and Company. He holds a PhD in economics from the University of California and has extensive experience in consulting and testifying about damages claims. In addition to being an author and speaker on the topics of economics and finance, Hurd also teaches courses in business forecasting. He frequently acts as arbitrator in disputes involving violations of the Securities and Exchange Code and is a member of the AAA, NASD, and NYSE arbitration panels.

RICHARD I. JANVEY is a litigation partner at Janvey, Berglas & Gordon in New York City. He is a graduate of the University of Chicago School of Law and was formerly an associate general counsel with Arthur Young & Company.

JEFFREY H. KINRICH is a partner at the Los Angeles office of Price Waterhouse. He has degrees in mathematics, statistics, and finance and specializes in litigation damages computation. He is a CPA and was the winner of the Elijah Watts Sells Silver Medal and the Forbes Gold Medal for his performance on the CPA examination.

STEPHEN H. KNOWLTON, Houston, is the partner-in-charge of the Price Waterhouse Reorganization & Litigation Services Group in the Central and Great Lakes region. He is also the firm's national director of Bankruptcy/Restructuring Services. He has testified more than 30 times in California, Texas, Louisiana, New York, and Oklahoma. Knowlton is a CPA, certified management consultant, and a member of the American Arbitration Association.

VICTOR A. LEVI is the founding partner in the firm of Levi, Jones & Bertozzi, Accountants, Inc. He is a frequent lecturer and speaker at accounting and bar functions and has authored "The Use of Substituted Assets in California Property Settlement Agreements," published by the California Society of CPAs. In addition to being a CPA, Levi has JD and MBA degrees from Golden Gate University.

O. KIT LOKEY is president of and principal in the valuation and investment banking firm of Houlihan, Lokey, Howard & Zukin, Inc., Los Angeles. He has authored numerous publications in the area of business and securities valuation.

Lokey is a past member of the Litigation Services Committee of the California Society of CPAs, a past member and officer of the Business Valuation Committee of the American Society of Appraisers and the Valuation Advisory Committee of the ESOP Association of America. He has a BS in engineering and an MBA in finance and operations management from UCLA and is also a CPA in California.

VINCENT J. LOVE is Ernst & Young's National Director of Litigation Support Services, responsible for managing the firmwide practice of providing expert witness and consulting services to litigators. His special areas of expertise include investigative auditing, professional malpractice work, damage analysis, and Securities Act cases. Love has been with Arthur Young since 1967 and is a CPA and chartered bank auditor.

GRANT W. NEWTON, CPA, CMA, PhD, is a professor of accounting at Pepperdine University. He is the author of *Bankruptcy and Insolvency Accounting* and *Bankruptcy Taxation* (with Gilbert D. Bloom), published by John Wiley & Sons, Inc. Newton lectures frequently for professional groups and CPAs on bankruptcy-related topics.

JEFF C. PARMET is a partner at Price Waterhouse, Washington, D.C., where he specializes in document management for complex litigation. He is a frequent speaker and author on the subject of using computer technology in document-intensive litigation. Parmet is a member of the State Bar of California.

ROSEANNA L. PURZYCKI is a tax manager at Gursey, Schneider & Co. She has authored articles on the tax aspects of a marital dissolution and was a member of the faculty of the Graduate School of Business at the University of Michigan where she lectured on tax and accounting.

CATHY PARTMANN RAVANO, CPA, is a member of the firm of Freeman & Mills, Inc., a consulting firm that offers investigative services in the areas of accounting, finance, business, and trade practices. She has provided expert testimony on these subjects in state and federal courts and in federal bankruptcy court and has served as a court-appointed mediator in the state court system. Ravano has also testified in marital dissolution and corporate dissolution proceedings on tracing, appropriation, commingling, and business valuations. She was formerly the associate dean of the Graduate School of Taxation, Golden Gate University.

D. PAUL REGAN, MS, CPA, is director-in-charge of the Litigation Services Group of Hemming Morse, Inc., CPAs. He has testified on numerous occasions as an expert witness in construction-related litigation in federal and superior courts as well as before the American Arbitration Association.

RICHARD Z. SCHATZ is the head administrator of the Litigation Support Services Department and a principal in the firm of Seiler & Company, CPAs, San Francisco office. His extensive forensic financial services experience in both private practice and with Seiler & Company encompasses over 25 years.

MELVIN A. SCHILLER is the managing partner at Jones, Schiller & Company. He is considered one of the pioneers in forensic accounting and has authored many articles and given seminars over a span of many years about the CPA's role in marital dissolutions. Schiller is a charter member of the Litigation Services Committee of the California Society of CPAs.

DAVID G. SCHULTZE is a partner in the firm of Schultze & Wallace, Inc., Sacramento, California. He is a frequent lecturer on matters of business litigation and business valuations. Schultze is a past chairman of the Litigation Services Committee in the Sacramento chapter of the California Society of CPAs.

HOWARD R. SHEPPARD is a certified public accountant. He graduated from Northwestern University in 1946 with a bachelor of science degree in business administration and has spent 42 years in private, governmental, and public accounting. Sheppard is widely experienced as a consultant and expert in litigation matters.

ALAN SILVERMAN is a partner in the San Francisco offices of Coopers & Lybrand. He has worked as a consultant and expert witness in business litigation since 1973. Silverman has authored several articles on damages and expert testimony. He is a certified management consultant and a member of the Litigation Services Committee of the California Society of CPAs.

JAMES A. SPIELMANN, CPA, is a member of the firm of Freeman & Mills, Inc., a consulting firm that offers investigative services in the areas of accounting, finance, business, and trade practices. He has provided expert testimony in court and arbitration proceedings on accounting and auditing matters, business valuations, contract damages, lost profits, business procedures, and business and trade practices.

HENRY STOTSENBERG is a CPA and a member of the Litigation Services Committee of the California Society of CPAs. He has specialized in forensic and investigative accounting for the past twenty years in Southern California.

GEORGE G. STRONG, Jr., is a partner in the litigation services group at Price Waterhouse, Los Angeles. He holds both a JD and an MBA degree. He has provided consulting services and expert testimony on economic and financial issues in many litigations. Strong is an attorney, a CPA, a CMC, a member of the American Arbitration Association and is a licensed U.S. Customshouse broker.

RONALD J. SUTTER is a partner of Steres, Alpert & Carne, a San Diego, California, CPA firm. He serves on the state Litigation Services Committee of the California Society of CPAs and is a member of the board of directors of the Association of Insolvency Accountants. Sutter principally practices in the troubled business/bankruptcy area.

MARSHALL W. TAYLOR, a graduate of Harvard College and Law School, is a partner in the Los Angeles area tax law firm of Taylor, Simonson & Winter.

Previously, he was a senior trial attorney with the Office of Chief Counsel of the Internal Revenue Service.

MICHAEL G. UELTZEN, CPA, is the managing director of John Waddell Accountancy Corporation in Sacramento, California. He practices extensively in the firm's audit practice and provides litigation services with an emphasis on complex business interruption cases. He is past chairman of the Litigation Services Committee and the Accounting Principles and Auditing Standards Committee of the California Society of CPAs and is a member of the AICPA.

WILLIAM E. WECKER is a professor in the Graduate School of Management, University of California, Davis. He has authored numerous publications on statistical theory and methods.

JAMES H. WEST is a shareholder and president of West, Johnston, Turnquist & Schmitt, Accountancy Corporation. He has extensive experience as an expert witness. West is a past director of the California Society of CPAs and a past president of the San Diego Chapter of that group.

RICHARD S. WILKOLASKI is a partner in the firm and the Litigation Support Services Department administrator for Seiler & Company, CPAs in San Francisco and Redwood City, California. His more than 20 years of experience in accounting, taxation, management, and litigation support services has been accumulated while working with local, regional, and national CPA firms.

JOHN D. ZANTE is president of his CPA firm, Zante and Co., in San Francisco, and is active in California and the San Francisco Chapter CPA Committees. He has participated in numerous speaking engagements for California Continuing Education of the Bar and the California CPA Foundation related to marital dissolutions, business valuation, and commercial damages.

CONTENTS

PART TWO COMMERCIAL/CIVIL CASES—UNIQUE CONSIDERATIONS

PART THREE CRIMINAL CASES—UNIQUE CONSIDERATIONS

PART FOUR FAMILY LAW/MARITAL DISSOLUTION CASES

PART FIVE DAMAGES

PART ONE

THE LITIGATION ENVIRONMENT

1

THE ROLE OF THE CPA IN LITIGATION SERVICES

Peter B. Frank, CPA, CMC
Michael J. Wagner, JD, CPA, CMC
Roman L. Weil, PhD, CPA, CMA

INTRODUCTION

Rationale for the Book

The need for the certified public accountant (CPA) to act as an expert witness and consultant to litigating attorneys has grown even more than litigation in the last decade. Ten years ago, few CPAs offered litigation-related services; now, a large number devote much of their practice to this area.

A seminal work in this field, *Forensic Accounting* (Dykeman, 1982), is an excellent introduction to litigation. Our purpose in this book is to provide a more current reference for CPAs involved with typical litigation cases and to explore in greater depth specific technical and case-specific tools.

Although this book is not a complete reference source, it does address the roles commonly played by CPAs in litigation. The book provides practical advice from experienced practitioners who have extensive experience in litigation services.

The Role of Experts in Litigation

Over time, the role of experts has expanded in the American jurisprudence system. Originally, courts allowed expert testimony only when the facts were too complex for an average juror to understand. The Federal Rules of Evidence have liberalized this rule. Rule 702 covers "Testimony by Experts" and states:

> If scientific, technical, or other specialized knowledge will *assist* the trier of fact to understand the evidence or to determine a fact in issue, a witness qualified as an expert by knowledge, skill, experience, training, or education, may testify thereto in the form of an opinion or otherwise. (Emphasis added)

The emphasis is on the phrase "assist the trier of fact." The rules no longer require that the subject matter of the expert's testimony be beyond the ordinary person's understanding. The only criterion that must be met is that the testimony will help the trier of fact.

Rules 703 through 705 of the Federal Rules of Evidence also relate to expert testimony. Rule 703 allows an expert in reaching his opinion to rely on otherwise inadmissible facts or data if they are "reasonably relied upon by experts in the particular field in forming opinions or inferences upon the subject." Experts can, for example, rely on hearsay evidence under certain circumstances.

Rule 704 allows experts to give an opinion on the issue to be ultimately decided by the trier of fact. (The only exception relates to an alleged criminal's mental state.) An expert can give an opinion on such issues as liability or the amount of damages.

Rule 705 allows an expert witness to express an opinion without previously disclosing the underlying facts or data. The rule requires only that these data be disclosed during cross-examination.

Thus, the federal courts have liberalized the rules as to what an expert witness can do. In our specialized world, this is reason enough to encourage the use of experts in litigation.

General Role of CPA in Litigation

Why a CPA? Lawyers use CPAs in litigation for the same reasons that CPAs are widely retained as business advisors. Lawyers need quality advice when litigating, and CPAs offer this service because they give advice in the real world to real companies with real problems. Juries seem to understand and respect this practical experience. Because accounting is the language of business, accountants can often clarify business transactions and explain the records reflecting them to lawyers, judges, and the jury. Because accountants generally have quantitative skills, they are often useful in undertaking and performing the quantitative analyses necessary to develop the technical evidence required in complex commercial cases.

The Tasks CPAs Undertake

CPAs often compute the plaintiff's (or cross-plaintiff's) monetary loss resulting from the defendant's (or cross-defendant's) legal wrong. In addition, CPAs sometimes address the business issues in a case. CPAs with suitable experience often consult and/or testify on issues involving marketing, economics, and industrial engineering.

CPAs can organize and synthesize large amounts of data. Hence, many lawyers rely on CPAs to review large collections of documents to extract, store, and analyze information relevant for discovery and trial.

The General Process

Lawyers for the party involved in litigation normally interview and retain the accountant. The retention usually occurs after the filing of the complaint, but before trial. During the pretrial period, the CPA consults with the lawyers. The CPA may assist in discovery by educating the lawyers as to the types of business records to ask for, drafting interrogatory and deposition questions, as well as suggesting requests for document production.

Once information is received, CPAs often analyze it and explain its relevance. During discovery, CPAs may reach opinions based on their analyses of the facts and data collected. If these opinions are helpful to the trial issues, CPAs may be designated as expert witnesses and testify at trial as to their opinions.

Once a lawyer designates the CPA as an expert witness, the CPA may have to appear and testify at a deposition where the opposing party's lawyer will test the CPA's expertise and probe for the bases of the CPA's opinions.

Description of the Federal Court System

District Courts. The federal system's trial court is known as a district court. To qualify as a plaintiff in a federal case, the plaintiff must either raise a question of federal law, or diversity of citizenship must exist between the plaintiff(s) and the defendant(s). This means that at least one of the defendants must reside in another state. If all the parties in a litigation reside in the same state, no federal jurisdiction exists based on diversity of citizenship. For a case to be filed in federal court, the amount in controversy must exceed a stated amount ($10,000 as of 1988).

After establishing jurisdiction, the case can proceed in federal court. Once the federal court has taken jurisdiction, state law claims can also be tried in the federal case. During the case, if all the federal issues are resolved, it is possible for the federal court to direct the state claims to a state court for resolution.

The federal system has 11 circuits, plus the District of Columbia. The geographic organization of the federal system is:

District of Columbia Circuit: Washington, DC

First Circuit: Maine, New Hampshire, Massachusetts, Rhode Island, and Puerto Rico

Second Circuit: New York, Connecticut, and Vermont

Third Circuit: New Jersey, Pennsylvania, Delaware, and Virgin Islands

Fourth Circuit: Maryland, Virginia, West Virginia, North Carolina, and South Carolina

Fifth Circuit: Texas, Louisiana, and Mississippi

Sixth Circuit: Tennessee, Kentucky, Ohio, and Michigan

Seventh Circuit: Illinois, Indiana, and Wisconsin

Eight Circuit: Arkansas, Iowa, Minnesota, Missouri, Nebraska, North Dakota, and South Dakota

Ninth Circuit: California, Arizona, Nevada, Oregon, Washington, Idaho, Montana, Alaska, Hawaii, Guam, and Northern Mariana Islands

Tenth Circuit: Colorado, Kansas, New Mexico, Oklahoma, Utah, and Wyoming

Eleventh Circuit: Alabama, Georgia, and Florida

Within each state in each circuit there is a separate district court. In larger states, there may be more than one district court. For example, in California there are four judicial districts including Northern, Central, Southern, and Eastern. Likewise, in New York there are four judicial districts including Northern, Southern, Eastern, and Western.

The plaintiff selects the district where the case will be filed subject to the restriction that one of the parties must reside in the district.

Federal Court of Appeals

The federal circuit courts hear appeals from district court decisions.

The trial court jurisdiction dictates the appeals court jurisdiction. A federal court of appeals will accept appeals only from district courts in its circuit, with certain specified exceptions such as appeals involving patent cases. A party has an absolute right to appeal a district court decision only to the appropriate court of appeals.

The U.S. Supreme Court

A party must first have a decision from the federal court of appeals before petitioning the U.S. Supreme Court to review the decision. A party has no absolute right of appeal to the Supreme Court. The Supreme Court accepts only cases with relevance for all United States citizens. If the issue affects only the immediate parties, the case has little chance to be heard unless a question of law needs clarification. Frequently, different circuit courts of appeal decide a matter of law differently. If clarification of the law is deemed important enough, the Supreme Court will decide the case.

"Special" Federal Courts

Tax Court. When an entity has a tax dispute with the federal government, that entity can decide where to litigate the dispute. Because federal law is at issue, the entity can file in a federal district court. There is also a special tax court that exists only to resolve disputes between the Internal Revenue Service and taxpayers.

The complex tax laws often require federal judges with training and experience in resolving tax disputes to resolve these matters expeditiously. The procedural requirements for filing in tax courts differ from those in district courts. The taxpayer should consult with an experienced practitioner to explore the advantages and disadvantages of each of the possible courts.

Patent Court of Appeal. The federal government has preempted state authority and made the patent law strictly federal; although the patent laws themselves are not difficult to understand, the subject matter of patents can be extremely complex. Federal district courts hear patent issues. Appeals from district court decisions on patent cases do not go to the corresponding circuit court of appeal, but to the United States Court of Appeals for the Federal Circuit in Washington, DC.

State Courts

Like the federal system, state court systems have trial courts, courts of appeals, and a supreme court to handle final appeals. State court systems usually have several different types of trial courts, and the nomenclature varies considerably from state to state.

Courts of Limited Jurisdiction. These state trial courts have a limit as to the amount of damages that can be collected or the subject matters upon which they can decide. An example of a court of limited jurisdiction is a small claims court. Small claims courts may not permit attorneys to represent the litigants and will limit the amount of possible award. For example, the maximum amount awardable may be $2000. Many courts of limited jurisdiction cannot hear felony cases. Only civil and criminal misdemeanor cases can be heard.

Courts of Unlimited Jurisdiction. These courts are the states' general purpose trial courts. They are the equivalent of the district courts in the federal system. These courts handle cases involving major issues, whether for large monetary damages or for felony matters in criminal cases. The CPA involved in state court most often works in these courts.

"Choice" of Courts

A plaintiff can sometimes choose the court in which to file a lawsuit. If there are only state law issues but a diversity of citizenship exists between the plaintiff and one of the defendants and the amount in controversy exceeds the necessary level, then the plaintiff can file in either state or federal court. If the plaintiff decides to file in federal court, often more than one federal court may be a proper venue (location) for the trial.

A plaintiff must consider many factors before deciding which court to file in. The judges' reputations, existing law, and the length of wait to trial are factors. The number of jurors necessary to reach a verdict may differ and be important to the plaintiff, as may be the record and apparent attitude of the related appeals court. Deciding which court to file in is often derogated as "forum shopping," an attempt to find the court that will be the friendliest to the plaintiff's position.

Applicable Rules Governing a Litigation

Evidence. All judicial systems have rules of evidence. The current Federal Rules of Evidence, as part of the United States Code, were enacted effective July 1, 1975, and amended in April 1983. Rules of evidence insure fairness in administering justice. Both sides to a litigation know the rules of admissibility of evidence and must abide by these rules.

If a party does not follow rules of evidence, the evidence will be inadmissible at the trial. The judge rules on objections to the admissibility of evidence. Mistakes in evidentiary rulings, if material, are grounds for reversal of the trial court decision.

CPAs who offer litigation services should become familiar with the rules of evidence of the trial court systems in which they work. Article VII of the Federal Rules of Evidence deals with "opinions and expert testimony" and was discussed briefly, earlier in this chapter. Article IX addresses "authentication and identification" of evidence. These rules usually affect the work of forensic accountants.

The rules of evidence in state courts vary. Many follow the Federal Rules of Evidence, but some do not.

Procedure. Courts differ in their methods of operation. *Procedure* is the set of formal steps that guides the judicial process between the filing of the complaint and the culmination of the trial and appeals. It is the machinery or process by which litigants resolve their disputes.

Criminal and civil courts differ significantly in their procedures. This book emphasizes civil cases, so only civil procedure is discussed. As with evidence, there are formal rules governing procedure. These rules are set down by statute in each state and by the United States. These rules set out the particular discovery devices that can be used and when they can be used. Later, this chapter explains the typical discovery tools and their use. In addition to controlling discovery, the rules of civil procedure explain the requirements to be met by the pleadings and other legal motions made before the court. The order of trial and the process of appeal are also addressed.

One important rule of civil procedure affecting CPAs and other financial experts governs the discovery permitted of experts and consultants in a litigation. Federal Rule of Civil Procedure 26(b)(4) governs the discovery permitted in federal cases and is described later in this chapter in the section entitled "Typical Roles Played by the CPA."

Local Rules. Local court rules supplement the rules of civil procedure in both the federal courts and some state courts. The rules of civil procedure do not cover all situations at the detailed level some judges prefer. Therefore, some judges supplement them with additional procedures to be followed in their courts.

Failure to follow the local judge's special rules can cause delay, and the court may refuse to accept legal filings. A CPA who practices before a particular court and becomes familiar with the local rules can assist his client in meeting local requirements.

Alternative Dispute Resolution

The judicial court system is slow and expensive. The large number of cases filed relative to the supply of judicial resources is just one reason. The rights to extensive discovery and the difficulty in scheduling attorneys' time add to the delay. As a result of the cost and delay in the court system, other methods of dispute resolution have been become accepted. Three of the most popular are discussed here.

Arbitration. Arbitration is the most widely used method of alternative dispute resolution. It is the submission of a dispute to one or more unofficial persons who will resolve the dispute privately. The procedures can be set by law, contract, or agreement of the parties. The result can be either final or subject to appeal. Arbitration procedures have been established through such bodies as the American Arbitration Association and the National Association of Securities Dealers.

Minitrials. The minitrial, an innovative approach to dispute resolution, resulted from a businessman's (Ronald Katz, then CEO of Telecredit) attempt to involve the business people up front in the resolution of the dispute. The idea is to have an early, short trial, usually no longer than a day, where both sides present their cases to senior persons, such as each party's CEO, who can settle the matter. The process is nonbinding and nothing from the proceeding can be used in a subsequent trial on the issues in dispute.

No formal rules of procedure or evidence need be followed. Each lawyer presents arguments either in the form of statements or by use of a few witnesses. Once both sides have had the opportunity to hear the best arguments for each side the decision makers discuss the case, without any lawyers present, in an attempt to resolve the dispute.

The Center for Public Resources has become the most well-known sponsor of this process, which has proven most successful where an individual is appointed to conduct the proceeding as a facilitator or pseudojudge. This person may be a retired judge or an experienced person from industry. He has no power to decide the matter but does ask questions and does meet individually with and lead the discussion between the two parties after the hearing, emphasizing his own view of the strengths and weaknesses in each side's case.

The Center for Public Resources* has an extensive list of individuals who are qualified to serve in the role of facilitator. The minitrial has proven most successful in disputes where a commercial settlement is feasible.

Mediation. Mediation has been most successfully applied in marital dissolution cases. A mediator is someone who will interpose between two or more parties in dispute for the purpose of reconciling their differences. A mediator will assist the parties in recognizing the strengths and weaknesses of their respective positions and the positions of the opposing parties. The mediator may also suggest compromises and strategies to resolve the dispute.

Like a minitrial, this process is nonbinding. No decision is made unless it is agreed upon by the parties. The process itself greatly assists compromise and settlement.

* Center for Public Resources, Inc., 366 Madison Avenue, New York, New York 10017. Telephone: (212) 949-6490. Fax (212) 949-8859.

DESCRIPTION OF THE LEGAL PROCESS

Overview of a Lawsuit

This section gives a brief overview of the steps in a typical litigation, which ends in a trial. The expert who understands this structure can better fit his work into the process.

A litigation comprises five major sections: pleadings, discovery, trial, the outcome, and appeal.

Legal Pleadings

Complaint. The complaint is the first pleading by the plaintiff in a civil case. The plaintiff sets out what actions (or inactions) he is complaining about. The complaint will always contain a list of the defendants who are being sued, the name of the court in which it is filed, the laws and legal theories under which the plaintiff is seeking relief, and whether a jury is demanded.

Jurisdictions differ on the amount of detail to be included in the complaint. Some courts require the plaintiff to list all known material facts on which he relies to support his claims. Other courts require minimal disclosure of facts in the complaints because discovery has not yet taken place; in effect, the only requirement is to notify the defendant that a lawsuit has been filed.

Demurrer. A defendant who believes that the plaintiff has not met the legal standard of making a proper complaint may file a demurrer. This pleading disputes the sufficiency in law of the complaint (or other pleading). A demurrer states that even assuming the facts alleged by the plaintiff are true, no cause of action exists that imposes any legal liability on the defendant. The demurrer states that no issue of law needs to be decided and requests the court to dismiss the complaint.

This device usually has the effect of cleaning up the complaint (or other pleading) because when the court agrees with the position of the defendant, it permits the plaintiff to amend the complaint to make it sufficient.

The demurrer forces the plaintiff to be more precise in his pleading and provides time for the defendant to respond to the complaint. It also may eliminate, at the outset, tangential or nonmeritorious claims.

Answer. The answer by the defendant responds to the plaintiff's complaint. Normally, the defendant will admit the allegations in the complaint with which he agrees and deny the allegations with which he disagrees. The defendant may also plead affirmative defenses, which will preclude the plaintiff from prevailing, based on the facts pled in the complaint.

The answer may also contain a cross-complaint in which the defendant will make claims upon the plaintiff (cross-defendant) to which the plaintiff will have to answer and defend at trial. Generally, an answer is required to be filed within a short time of receipt of the complaint (20 to 30 days unless an extension is granted).

Discovery

Discovery takes place in the time between filing the original pleadings and the trial. Discovery is the attempt to ascertain the other parties' facts and theories. This is the period during which most expert work is performed. The expert collects all necessary facts, analyzes them, develops any assumptions, and reaches all conclusions.

Various legal tools are used in discovery, and the lawyer may use any or all of them as aids to the expert in performing his services. A brief description of the major discovery tools and their uses follows.

Interrogatories

Interrogatories are written questions from one party served on the opposing party, who must answer the questions in writing, under oath. Interrogatories help obtain information about the opposing party when little if anything is known about it. The CPA's special knowledge of business or a particular industry can help in constructing questions to develop a thorough understanding of an organization's systems, documentation, files, and structure. For example, the nature and extent of the opposing party's financial reporting and management information systems are possible areas of inquiry. The names and titles of officers or principals in the business also can be obtained for further discovery of their files.

Requests for Production of Documents

A request for production of documents requires one party to provide documents it holds relevant to issues in the case. These requests usually follow interrogatories. They must be specific, or the opposing party will not produce the documents, even when the request makes clear the information sought. Therefore, the request needs to state exact titles of reports, which can be culled from the information already obtained through interrogatories or depositions.

The party responding to the request does not usually copy the documents and send them to the requesting party. Instead, it makes the documents available at the responding party's business or its attorney's offices. The requesting party is then given the opportunity to review the documents and decide which ones to copy at its own expense.

The requesting party's attorney will often want the expert CPA to review financial and other business documents produced by the opposing party. The CPA can help in identifying the relevant documents and in insuring that they are copied. (Copying costs during discovery can be quite high.) In addition, the CPA and the attorney will review the documents copied, so costs will increase as the number of documents discovered increases. A knowledgeable CPA can significantly reduce unnecessary copying (and subsequent review costs) by identifying the types of financial and business records that are necessary to prove the issues and by helping the attorney be selective during the initial review of documents offered by the opponent.

Requests for Admissions

A request for admission seeks the opposing party's verification of information as fact. The request must be relevant to the litigation. Verifying the information as fact is usually adverse to the interest of the party making the admission.

Admissions help narrow the factual issues to be litigated at trial. Any agreed facts by both parties prior to trial do not have to be proved at trial, which can decrease the time for trying a case. Judges like admissions. The CPA can suggest the types of facts within his area of expertise that the opposing party could admit prior to a civil litigation trial. The CPA can also assist the attorney in developing arguments about why certain business facts should or should not be admitted prior to trial.

Depositions

A deposition is the oral testimony of a witness questioned under oath by an attorney. It is transcribed by an official reporter whose written record can be used in court.

The CPA Giving a Deposition. When a CPA is retained as an expert witness, the opposition's attorney usually takes the CPA's deposition in order to comprehend the CPA's background and the bases for the opinions in the case. Often the deposition affords the only opportunity prior to trial for the attorney to question the expert in depth. The attorney uses the deposition to size up the CPA as a trial witness, determine his strengths and weaknesses, and develop a comprehensive understanding of his opinions, studies, and analyses. Some experienced attorneys omit the deposition, in part, because it can educate the expert. A deposition may allow an expert to test theories or approaches and then correct them as needed for the trial.

Questions at the deposition usually cover all work performed by the CPA, including rejected analyses, blind alleys, and information obtained, but not used. In addition, the deposition can be used to narrow the scope of the CPA's testimony at the trial because anything said at the deposition can be used to impeach the CPA's credibility at the trial. The CPA's testimony in the deposition and at the trial must be consistent.

The taking of depositions of experts in federal cases is covered by federal rules of evidence and is not an absolute right of the opposing party. Usually, agreement by both sides or direction of the court is required to obtain an expert's deposition.

The CPA Helping an Attorney Take a Deposition. Although the only person who can ask questions at a deposition is the attorney, a CPA can be a valuable assistant to the attorney during the examination of business people, particularly those in the financial or accounting areas. Frequently, the attorney asks the CPA for assistance at a deposition of the opposition's expert. The CPA knows the language of business, including state-of-the-art terminology, and can usually detect a witness's uninformative answer or sign of weakness that the attorney might miss. The CPA can suggest additional questions to the attorney by passing notes or by discussions during breaks in the deposition. In this way the CPA can help identify an inconsistency, suggest a follow-up question, or expose a flaw in testimony. The CPA has no right to attend another expert's or party's deposition. Normally the attorneys will agree on attendance policy for all depositions.

Even when the CPA is not present at the deposition, the attorney often will request the CPA to draft questions that the CPA would like to have asked. These questions have two aims: (1) to clarify what the opposing expert did in his analysis and (2) to point out problems, inconsistencies, and errors in the analysis.

Some lawyers believe it is unwise to alert the witness to analytical flaws at the deposition. They prefer to hold this information for use at the trial. Others believe that the deposition can be used to point out the weaknesses in their opponent's case, thus encouraging settlement or, at a minimum, forcing the expert to correct his presentation for use at the trial.

Subpoenas

A subpoena commands a person to appear in court. The subpoena ad testificandum commands a person to appear and testify as a witness. The subpoena duces tecum commands a person to produce documents to the court that are then designated as evidence.

The subpoena is frequently the only method of obtaining information from third parties not related to the litigation. A recipient of a subpoena who refuses to cooperate can be found in contempt of court and jailed.

A party, including the CPA expert, may object in court to a subpoena, thus requiring a hearing on the relevance and propriety of materials demanded. An expert CPA who objects to a subpoena for documents might create a conflict between the CPA and his client that can delay the trial and generate costly legal fees. Occasionally, however, the CPA must object, when a subpoena requests irrelevant documents or materials related to other clients. Often the opposing attorneys compromise on how much they will try to discover from the CPA experts and thereby avoid issuing subpoenas or filing objections.

The opposing counsel may wish to "fish" through the records of other nonparty clients of the CPA using the subpoena and deposition process. CPAs need to be careful not to violate Rule 301 of the AICPA Rules of Professional Conduct, which require the CPA to maintain client confidentiality. Because the CPA has a duty to comply only with a validly issued subpoena, he may find it necessary to test the subpoena's validity before revealing confidential client information.

The Trial

Opening Statements. After the jury has been picked, assuming a jury trial, the attorneys for both sides make their opening statements. (However, the defendant may choose to delay his opening until the time he begins presenting his case.) Each attorney explains the issues of the case as he views them, the conclusions the trier of fact should reach on these issues, and the evidence to be presented.

An effective opening statement should provide an overview of the story that the attorney intends to prove. This is time to educate the trier of fact about the entire case. Although the opening statement is not evidence, many believe most cases are won or lost on opening statements.

Plaintiff's Case. The plaintiff carries the burden of proof at trial and must meet the standard either of a "preponderance of the evidence" (civil case) or of "beyond a reasonable doubt," depending upon the type of case. The plaintiff presents his case first. Evidence is normally admitted through witnesses and the normal process of examination is as follows.

Direct Examination. Direct examination is the first examination of a witness by the attorney for the party who is calling the witness. During this question and answer session, the plaintiff must introduce the evidence that proves his case.

Formal rules of evidence apply, and evidence that does not meet the standards set by these rules may be objected to by the opposing party and excluded from admission into evidence by the court.

Normally, leading questions are not permitted on direct examination. These are questions that suggest to the witness the answer the questioner wants. A leading question could put words into the mouth of the witness.

Cross-Examination. Cross-examination is the first examination of a witness by the attorney for the opposing party. It immediately follows the end of direct examination. The opposing side will try to discredit the witness or to obtain evidence favorable to its case.

In principle, cross-examination is limited to issues raised in the direct examination of the witness. If the attorney for the opposing side wishes to raise other issues, he must call the witness as an adverse witness in his own case and then conduct direct examination. Some judges, however, allow fairly wide cross-examination, particularly of an expert witness.

Cross-examination rules permit leading questions. In addition, prior deposition or other testimony or writings of the witness may be read into the record in an attempt to impeach the witness.

Redirect Examination. This is examination that immediately follows cross-examination of a witness. It is limited to issues brought up on cross examination. If a matter was forgotten on direct examination, it cannot now be raised for the first time unless it can be shown to be related to issues raised in the cross-examination.

Recross-Examination. This is examination that immediately follows redirect examination and is limited to issues raised in the redirect examination. The scope of recross is normally narrow.

Defendant's Case

The plaintiff will present all of his witnesses and exhibits before the defendant puts on his case. When the plaintiff rests, it is now the defendant's turn to put on all of his witnesses. The process of examination is exactly the same as described before for the plaintiff's case.

If the defendant believes that the plaintiff has not proved his case, then the defendant may not directly put in a case. Rather, the defendant makes his case through cross-examination and recross-examination of the plaintiff's witnesses. This is not easy to do effectively because most of the plaintiff's witnesses will be hostile to the defendant's positions.

Plaintiff's Rebuttal Case. After the defendant rests his case, the plaintiff has a chance to rebut the defendant's case. This is done through witnesses and documents just like the prior description of phases of the trial.

The scope of rebuttal will be limited to issues raised in the defendant's case. Rebuttal is not an opportunity for the plaintiff to put in brand new evidence.

CPAs are often involved in rebuttal when the defendant has sufficiently discredited the plaintiff's damage theory or study so that a revised damage study must be presented to address the problems raised by the defendant.

Defendant's Surrebuttal Case. Some jurisdictions permit the defendant to respond to issues raised by the plaintiff's rebuttal case. This response is called *surrebuttal* and is restricted to issues raised in the plaintiff's rebuttal case.

Other jurisdictions do not allow surrebuttal or leave it to the judge's discretion as to whether it is allowed or not.

Closing Arguments. Once both sides have rested, the plaintiff will make his closing arguments first, followed by the defendant. Such arguments are not evidence in themselves, but the attorney will summarize the evidence and try to persuade the trier of fact why he should prevail.

Post Trial Briefs and Findings of Fact. The attorneys will often be asked by the judge to file briefs summarizing what points the lawyers think they proved and the relevant law to be applied to the case. This assists the judge in writing his opinion, if it is a bench trial (i.e., a trial heard only by a judge, not a jury).

These briefs contain suggested findings of fact and conclusions of law. CPAs sometimes assist the lawyer in drafting this portion of the brief, particularly the part summarizing the CPA's testimony. The findings of fact are limited to the evidence admitted in the trial. The facts must be part of the record in the trial. New evidence or objectionable evidence is not permitted.

Types of Outcomes

Verdict. The verdict is the decision rendered by a jury (or a judge in a bench trial) in a trial. It is the formal decision or finding made by a jury and reported to the court upon the matters or questions submitted to them at trial. The verdict may be general or special. In a general verdict, the jury finds in favor of the plaintiff or defendant on all issues generally. In special verdicts, the jury decides only the facts of the case and leaves the decisions of the application of the law up to the judge. A special verdict results from the jury being asked to make separate decisions as to different issues in the case. This is normally done through interrogatories to the jury.

Judgment. A judgment is the official decision of the court as to the rights and claims of the litigants. It is the verdict of the jury if it is accepted by the court. If not, the judge can make a judgment notwithstanding the verdict, as explained later. It is the decision of the judge if he is the trier of fact.

Opinion. If the judge makes the judgment, he will often state the reasons for his decision and his understanding of the application of the relevant law. This writing is often reported and becomes part of the basis for court-made law in our judicial system.

Occasionally one side or the other asks the judge to rule on part or all of the case even before the trial commences. In this situation, the party moving for such a summary judgment suggests that even if all the facts alleged by the opponent are true, no triable issue of law exists. That is, the facts on their face do not violate the laws or legal rights asserted by the opponent. Recent court decisions encourage the use of summary judgments to reduce the time taken up by a trial.

However, summary judgments are often overturned on appeal because the party who lost the case did not have its day in court.

Directed Verdict. A directed verdict is requested by the defendant at the close of the plaintiff's case, when the defendant believes the plaintiff has not proven its case either factually or as a matter of law. If the judge grants the directed verdict, the case is over, and the defendant does not have to present its case.

Judgment Notwithstanding the Verdict. In a jury trial, the jury decides the case and renders a verdict. Before the verdict is accepted by the court, the losing party may request, or the judge may volunteer, a decision that is contrary to the verdict rendered by the jury.

In effect, the court does not accept the verdict of the jury and renders an opposite decision. This is called a judgment non obstante verdicto or (JNOV).

Appeal

A losing party in a trial who believes that an error has been committed at the trial can appeal to a superior court to reverse the decision of the lower court. The appeals court is not the forum for a new trial. The appeals court will accept the record of the original trial court and decide if there was any legal error in the record or the reasoning of the lower court.

The appeals process has a defined procedure. It is much more oriented to analysis of the law rather than facts, so CPAs are rarely asked to provide services during appeals.

TYPICAL ROLES PLAYED BY THE CPA

Expert Witness

An expert witness is retained to render an expert opinion at trial. This expert opinion usually relates to business issues with which the CPA is familiar because of special education, training, or work experience. This knowledge or expertise is not possessed by the trier of fact and so the opinion of the CPA expert will assist the trier of fact in reaching a decision.

The CPA is retained by one party and is identified to the opposing party as an expert witness. Once the CPA is so identified, all work performed by the CPA related to the litigation potentially is discoverable. The CPA should conduct the engagement from the outset with the assumption that all his work is discoverable by the opposing party.

Consultant

The CPA as consultant is hired strictly to advise the attorney about the facts, issues, and strategy of the case. The CPA is not retained to testify at trial or to render an expert opinion. The work of the CPA generally will be protected by the attorney workproduct privilege. That means this work is not discoverable by the opposing party.

The work of a consultant will often include analyzing the opposing expert's work and providing arguments to his attorney on how best to discredit the other expert's work. The work may also include investigations into the strengths and weaknesses of your client's case and how best to represent these facts at trial.

Trier of Fact

The CPA may be asked to decide certain facts in a dispute. This might be by court appointment or by agreement of the parties. This role is often described as one of a *special master*. In effect, the CPA will act in this function as the judge and jury.

The special master will be requested where there are difficult accounting issues that can be properly understood only by a CPA. The judge may appoint the CPA to help him decide these issues. Likewise, the parties may want to agree on one individual to make these decisions in an effort to get an informed decision or just to save expenses.

SERVICES TYPICALLY PERFORMED BY CPAs IN LITIGATION SERVICES ENGAGEMENTS

Discovery Assistance

Business litigation often depends on documents to prove or disprove an issue at trial. As a result, voluminous document discovery and production is undertaken.

Business records of a financial nature are crucial to a number of issues in most cases. CPAs can assist in finding, understanding, and explaining the information from these types of documents.

The knowledge of the types of documents that normally exist in managing a business is important so that precise requests for production of documents can be made. This knowledge also helps the lawyer to assess the responsiveness of particular productions and in understanding what other documents might exist.

Depositions of financial and management people often relate to technical business issues. Attorneys need help in understanding the real issues and in the formulation of effective questions. Because technical people will often answer questions in jargon and terms of art, the attorney may need assistance in understanding the answer and developing follow-on questions. CPAs can assist in this area.

Information about the opposing experts is essential for effective cross-examination and rebuttal of the opposing expert's opinion. When the expertise involves business, CPAs can assist lawyers in analyzing the expert's work and articulating the strengths and weaknesses of the support for the expert's opinions.

Proof of Business Facts

Evidence to support a position taken at trial must be based on facts. In commercial litigation, these facts generally must be obtained from the business records of the companies involved. In addition, information may also be obtained from industry and market sources. CPAs are familiar with these sources of information and can assist the lawyers in obtaining, authenticating, organizing, and explaining this information.

Opinion testimony can be based on either facts or assumptions. Assumptions are usually based on facts or presumptions from facts. In either case, a proper foundation must be laid as to the source of the information. CPAs can help to develop these facts by collecting the relevant business or industry data to support various experts' opinions.

Computation of Damages

Calculation of damages is a common task performed by CPAs in commercial litigation. An entire section of this book covers this subject.

There are a number of types of damages—such as actual losses and expected, but lost, profits—and methods to compute them. The type of damages to be computed is a fact question, but the law may restrict or limit recovery of certain types of damages. In addition, the type of recovery permitted may be limited by the causes of action in the pleadings.

The CPA should communicate with the attorney so that both understand the type of damages the CPA is attempting to calculate and the method the CPA is using to make the computation. Otherwise, a calculation of damages may be inadmissible for some factual or legal reason.

One type of recovery is the actual losses incurred. This form of restitution applies in fraud cases. A common method used to calculate actual losses is the out-of-pocket measure of damages that is computed as the difference between what the plaintiff paid for something and the actual value received.

Another common type of recovery is the expected profits from a proposed contract or deal. This is often measured by a benefit-of-the-bargain approach that is a typical method of computing damages in contract disputes.

Lost profits are typically claimed in business litigation. These can be measured by the shortfall between the plaintiff's actual earnings and the earnings that would have occurred "but for" the illegal actions of the defendant. This can be computed as the difference between "but for" profits and actual profits.

Most damage analysis requires the use of assumptions and projections about what would have happened if certain behavior of the defendant were different.

Development of Strategy

CPA litigation consultants can suggest approaches to the business issues in the case. The best trial lawyers do not necessarily have the experience and insights in business issues that CPAs have as a result of their business consulting.

The lawyer needs independent analysis of the positions he believes he must prove in order to win the case. The CPA can help the lawyer spot errors and devise different approaches, perhaps using different facts. Although the CPA hired as a consultant is an advocate, he should remain objective and independent. These qualities are most useful to his client.

Document Management

CPAs are frequently experts on management information systems and computer systems. Such CPAs are qualified to help attorneys in collecting, organizing, and summarizing the large volume of documents often used in a business case. Usually complex and sophisticated computer systems are employed to manage the large databases of documents that are created.

Small cases, where automated document retrieval systems are not cost justified, still need some system for document retrieval. The CPA can help organize the documents by issue in the case so that relevant evidence can be located. Both manual and automated document management systems are covered in some detail in a later chapter.

GAAP/GAAS Rules and Compliance

Only CPAs are qualified to render opinions as to generally accepted accounting principles (GAAP) and generally accepted auditing standards (GAAS). Such issues arise when the accuracy of financial statements is questioned.

GAAP and GAAS come up when an accounting firm is being sued for violating these standards by a plaintiff alleging harm by his reliance on the accuracy of the financial statements. The accountant's liability is covered in a specific chapter in this book.

GAAP issues also arise when litigation is filed related to the purchase or sale of a business and the accuracy of the prior financial statements is questioned. GAAP issues may also arise in any damages computations that rely on financial statements.

NEED FOR INDEPENDENCE

CPAs are held in high esteem as professionals, in part because of their independence. Independence should not be abused in the litigation process. The CPA expert witness should never impair his judgment by becoming an advocate for his client. His lack of objectivity easily may become apparent, thus damaging his client's case and his own reputation.

Conflicts of Interest

The CPA must investigate possible conflicts of interest before accepting a litigation engagement. He must check all parties to the litigation to ascertain if they are current or past clients of the CPA or his firm. Even when no direct conflict of interest exists, the CPA usually does not accept an engagement directly contrary to the interests of another existing client. Frequently, in civil litigation, many persons and entities are named as defendants. The CPA should be wary of working for one defendant when another defendant is a client. A problem can arise if the plaintiff proves joint damages because then the defendants will no longer be united in trying to defeat the plaintiff but will dispute who owes which portion. The defendants will cross-complain against each other in an attempt to escape the ultimate payment of damages. At this point, the CPA could be in the embarrassing position of opposing a current client.

Whether a conflict arises in a litigation engagement against a former client must be resolved on a case-by-case basis. Factors to consider include the length of time since the party was a client, the confidential information the CPA possesses that may become an issue in the litigation, and the issues of the case.

The CPA discloses all current and former relationships with all parties to the litigation to the inquiring lawyer, even though the CPA has concluded there is no conflict of interest. The lawyer and the client have the right to make their own determination about conflicts.

Who Is the Client?

The CPA retained to perform a litigation services engagement has two potential clients. The first is the law firm. The second is the party to the lawsuit. If the work of the CPA consultant is to be protected from discovery, he must be working for the lawyer. If the CPA is hired by the disputant, the attorney workproduct privilege will not apply nor will the attorney–client privilege that protects only communications between a client and the client's attorney.

If the lawyer wants to use the CPA as a consultant only or wishes to protect the CPA's work from discovery until designation of the CPA as an expert witness, then the lawyer must have a client relationship with the CPA. If this is not important, then the CPA can be hired directly by the party.

Some lawyers want the attorney workproduct privilege and yet do not want the responsibility to pay the CPA's fees. Such lawyers will ask the CPA to send bills directly to the party and may ask the CPA to sign a retainer agreement expressly disclaiming any recourse against the lawyer for payment of the CPA's bills. The lawyer needs to understand the risk of losing the attorney workproduct privilege with this type of arrangement.

The CPA may consider both the lawyer and the party to be clients. Most CPAs recognize that the party is the person ultimately responsible for the payment of his fees. The CPA, at the risk of losing the engagement, may insist that the lawyer be equally or solely responsible for fees.

FEE ARRANGEMENTS

Most litigation services engagements are billed like other management consulting engagements. Fees are based on hours, standard hourly rates, and out-of-pocket expenses. Work may also be performed for a fixed fee.

Contingent Fees

There has been a prohibition against the charging of contingent fees in litigation services engagements (Rule 402 of the AICPA Rules of Professional Conduct). Most state boards of accountancy have similar rules prohibiting contingent fees. Texas has recently dropped its ban on contingent fees. The AICPA has suspended enforcement of its ban on contingent fees pending the outcome of litigation with the Federal Trade Commission, which is disputing the ban on contingent fees and commissions as a restraint of trade. However, state rules still take precedence.

An expert witness working on a contingency basis is not independent; opposing counsel is likely to impugn the testimony of an expert whose compensation depends on the outcome. Nonexpert consultants need to decide on the wisdom of accepting contingent arrangements where legal but need not be deterred by ethical issues.

A CPA may be retained by an attorney who works under a contingent fee arrangement with his client. The attorney may wish the expert to work under a similar arrangement.

Retainers

The CPA may require a retainer in some litigation services engagements. If a retainer is to be effective in protecting the CPA's billing, it should be held as security for payment of the final bill. Experience shows that unfavorable outcomes often lead to unpaid bills.

Both parties are usually unhappy with the final outcome of marital dissolution actions. The paying spouse feels that too much has been lost, and the receiving spouse feels that too little has been obtained. Many CPAs who practice in the marital dissolution field always require a retainer.

The CPA would be wise to inquire as to the client's ability to pay if the litigation is unsuccessful. If the client will not be able to pay in this situation, then the CPA should obtain a retainer against the final bill. Otherwise, the CPA will be working involuntarily on a contingent fee basis.

STANDARDS

Few written standards guide the CPA in a litigation services engagement. Standards that the CPA expert witness must follow include the rules of evidence and rules of procedure of the particular court in which the CPA is appearing as a witness. There may also be local rules of the court and individual judge's rules that may affect the CPA's conduct.

OPINION TESTIMONY

Expert Opinion

Expert opinion is testimony by a person qualified to speak authoritatively because of special training, skill, study, experience, observation, practice, or familiarity with the subject matter. Expert knowledge is not possessed by laymen or inexperienced persons. State or federal rules of evidence define the scope and nature of expert opinion testimony.

CPAs are experts on accounting matters and may, depending on training and experience, be expert in the application of economic, financial, statistical, or econometric techniques. A CPA may, based on work in that industry, be expert on the practices of a particular industry.

Audit Opinion

Only rarely does a litigation services engagement call for an attest opinion. Although an audit opinion is an expert opinion, it differs from an expert witness opinion given at trial.

The opposing lawyer may try to confuse the trier of fact by muddling audit opinions with expert opinions. The lawyer might ask whether the CPA performed an audit and can render an audit opinion. When the CPA says "no," the attorney might attempt to suggest that the CPA can have no expert opinion because he has no audit opinion.

SKILLS COMMONLY REQUIRED OF CPAs

Auditing

The investigative skills required by the audit function are frequently used in litigation services engagements. Examples include investigation of fraudulent transactions, reconstruction of financial statements, and development of cash flow statements.

Financial Analysis

Development and analysis of financial ratios often aid in understanding the causes of business problems experienced by a litigant. Ratio analysis may also be modified to derive the assumptions as to what would have happened but for the alleged legal violation.

CPAs in litigation often carry out present value analyses, capital market theory applications, and business valuations.

Economic Analysis

CPAs trained in economics may perform both macro- and microeconomic analyses in a litigation services engagement. These roles are played by both economists and accountants and are discussed in depth in a later chapter.

Marketing Analysis

Much marketing analysis is based on the collection of quantitative data. CPAs can help collect and assess the required data. Examples might include the number of competitors in a particular market or computation of the market share of each participant based on sales.

Statistics

Some CPAs are familiar with statistical techniques as a result of their auditing and consulting backgrounds. Statistical sampling and regression analysis are used in auditing. Litigation services engagements can require these same tools. Sampling is done when analysis of an entire population is too time consuming or expensive to accomplish. Regression analysis is used in projecting sales, establishing cost relationships, or in analyzing other causal relationships.

Cost Accounting

The calculation of damages sometimes requires cost accounting skills. In any case where the plaintiff is a multi-line product manufacturer or service provider, allocating common costs to each product line affected by the defendant's actions will be necessary.

CONCLUSION

This chapter provides an overview of the litigation process and terminology the CPA faces when acting as an expert witness or consultant in a litigation. The rules and procedures both of the CPA's profession and of the legal process govern the work and approach followed by the CPA. A vast quantity of tasks are required in preparing a complex commercial litigation for trial. The CPA brings to bear his training and expertise in an adversarial proceeding where his conclusions will be challenged closely. The balance of this book discusses in depth the specific types of cases and approaches the CPA will face in this dynamic environment.

2

PROFESSIONAL STANDARDS IN A LITIGATION SERVICE ENVIRONMENT

Michael G. Ueltzen, MBA, CPA

The author acknowledges the contributions from the California Society of Certified Public Accountants Litigation Services Committee in discussing the concepts of professional standards in a litigation service environment. He thanks the following for their efforts: Lee Baly, a director with Hemming Morse in San Mateo, California, and David Coburn, a partner with Arthur Andersen in San Francisco, helped develop a discussion paper on conflicts of interest. Howard Sheppard, a CPA from Corona, California, assisted by Don Glenn, a principal with Glenn & Dietler, Walnut Creek, California, helped develop a discussion paper on reporting standards. He also acknowledges as a source the AICPA's Management Advisory Services *Technical Consulting Practice Aid No. 7—Litigation Services*, by Michael J. Wagner and Peter B. Frank, 1986.

INTRODUCTION

The CPA renders a professional service in litigation and must recognize that professional standards apply in all such engagements. CPAs are often asked during cross-examination whether they performed an audit, review, or compilation and whether the work conformed to auditing and professional standards. The opposing attorney may also ask if any professional standards specifically address the CPA's analysis. If the CPA answers "no" to these questions, the attorney might argue the credibility of the testimony.

RESPONSIBILITIES OF A LITIGATION SERVICE PRACTICE

CPAs offering litigation services must abide by two sets of rules. First, they should adhere to the AICPA's professional standards and their state's board of accountancy rules and regulations, and they must ascertain which professional standards apply to the litigation service being rendered. Secondly, CPAs must follow legal standards. The broad standards encompass certain principles, including serving the public interest, integrity and objectivity, and exercising due care in conducting services. A CPA must adhere to these high standards when rendering any professional service, whether it is auditing, tax, consulting, or litigation.

The AICPA has done little until recently to address litigation practice standards. Wagner and Frank (1986) prepared the *Technical Consulting Practice Aid No. 7*, published by the Management Advisory Services (MAS) of the AICPA and entitled *Litigation Services*. This reference categorizes litigation as a consulting rather than an audit service; the AICPA's Statement on Standards for MAS provides, however, little guidance on reporting and other professional standards.

In the fall of 1989, the AICPA issued two interpretations of existing standards related to litigation services. The first interpretation defines litigation services as a MAS service and states that MAS standards must be followed in the conduct of a litigation services engagement. The second interpretation is of the attestation standards. This interpretation exempts litigation services from the attestation standards except where the CPA expresses a written conclusion about the reliability of a written assumption that is the responsibility of another party and this conclusion is for the use of others who have no opportunity to analyze and challenge such work. Some state CPA organizations have formed committees to address litigation services, including the applicable accounting professional standards and the legal concepts that must be adopted in providing litigation consulting services.

Litigation Services; Terminology and Rules of Evidence

The CPA involved in litigation services must recognize that some common terms have specific meanings for lawyers and judges. The term *litigation services* commonly refers to the services provided by a CPA that encompass those accounting and consulting skills used to assist the attorney or client in a legal or regulatory environment.

Litigation services are sometimes referred to as *forensic accounting*. Although not incorrect, forensic accounting is a broader term, referring to any accounting used in a court of law. Forensic accounting includes the application of accounting principles, theories, and disciplines to actual or hypothetical facts at issue in a legal dispute and the application of any branch of accounting to the purpose of the law.

In providing litigation services, a CPA may have one or both of two roles. A "consultant" differs from an "expert witness." Services of an expert witness are usually provided as a designated expert in a proceeding. The CPA will be subject to the rules of evidence and other rules of the applicable jurisdiction. The expert witness's workproduct will likely be available through discovery to the opposing side. Rule 702 of the Federal Rules of Evidence addresses the concept of testimony by experts as follows:

> *Rule 702—Testimony by Experts.* If scientific, technical or other specialized knowledge will assist the trier of fact to understand the evidence or to determine a fact in issue, a witness qualified as an expert by knowledge, skill, experience, training or education may testify thereto in the form of an opinion or otherwise.

Rule 702 allows expert testimony whenever it will "assist" the trier of fact. The former rule was much more restrictive. It required that expert testimony be "necessary" for the trier of fact to understand the issues in trial. This liberalization of the rule allowing expert testimony has dramatically increased the use of experts.

Only an expert witness may provide an "expert opinion." In the legal environment, expert testimony is rendered by a person who is qualified to speak authoritatively by reason of his special training, skill, study, experience, observation, practice, or familiarity with the subject matter under consideration. This expert knowledge is knowledge not possessed by ordinary laymen or inexperienced persons. The scope and nature of expert opinion testimony is defined within the applicable state or Federal Rules of Evidence.

Rule 704 of the Federal Rules of Evidence specifies that an expert may render an opinion on the ultimate issue, as follows:

> *Rule 704—Opinion on Ultimate Issue.* Testimony in the form of an opinion or inference otherwise admissible is not objectionable because it embraces an ultimate issue to be decided by the trier of fact.

Again, this rule like Rule 702 has expanded the use of experts. Prior to this rule, the trier of fact had the sole responsibility to decide the ultimate issue in the case. Now, an expert can render an opinion on how he believes the trier of fact should decide this issue.

To the extent a CPA renders an expert opinion, two additional federal rules must be considered. Rule 703 identifies the bases of opinion testimony by experts, as follows:

> *Rule 703—Bases of Opinion Testimony by Experts.* The facts or data in the particular case upon which an expert bases an opinion or inference may be those perceived by

> or made known to him at or before the hearing. If of a type reasonably relied upon by experts in the particular field in forming opinions or inferences upon the subject, the facts or data need not be admissible as evidence.

This rule permits an expert to rely on hearsay. It is an exception to the hearsay rule. The only requirement is that the information is the type that experts in the field normally rely upon.

Further, the CPA may be compelled under Rule 705 to disclose facts or data underlying his expert opinion.

> *Rule 705—Disclosure of Facts or Data Underlying Expert Opinion.* The expert may testify in terms of opinion or inference and give his reasons therefore without prior disclosure of the underlying facts or data, unless the court rules otherwise. The expert may in any event be required to disclose the underlying facts or data on cross-examination.

Some attorneys engage a CPA to provide consulting services. The term *consultant* has a special meaning in litigation and encompasses those services other than expert testimony provided to an attorney. The attorney may assert a work–product privilege over the CPA's work product. Consequently, the CPA consultant may never become known to the opposition, so that the opinions, discussions, workpapers, and impressions may not be discovered by the opposing party. Consultants in larger, more complex cases are hired as such early in the engagement, with no expectation that they will testify at trial. If the case is large enough, an attorney may believe that it is cost justified to have one CPA firm as a consultant and another CPA firm to provide expert testimony. In some cases, the CPA may be engaged as a consultant and later in the proceedings be declared an expert. A law firm may retain several consultants and name only one as an expert. Obviously, the CPA should develop an understanding with the client as to whether the engagement is as an expert witness, a consultant, or both.

Guidelines for a CPA Involved in a Litigation Service Practice

Because CPAs are recognized for their competence, integrity, and objectivity, they must recognize the legal concepts (such as conflicts of interest) and professional standards (such as objectivity) that guide litigation services.

General Responsibilities: Competency. CPAs embarking on their first litigation engagement may find themselves ill-equipped, ill-prepared, and lacking foundation for some of their opinions. The attorney retaining the CPA may not be able to evaluate the CPA's abilities and capabilities. Accounting professional standards require that the CPA—and any staff members assisting in the engagement—have competence in the subject matter. A CPA uncertain of competence for the engagement should not accept it.

Objectivity. The CPA must recognize the difference between objectivity and independence. In a desire to please the attorney, a CPA may be tempted to render opinions that favor the client. Professional ethics require the CPA to maintain integrity and objectivity and, as an expert witness, not to take any position that may impair objectivity. As a consultant, the CPA may resolve doubt in favor of the client, so long as the position can be supported. Any opinions and positions taken by an expert in previous cases can become a matter of inquiry. For example, the CPA should not testify in a matter involving an accounting principle from a position inconsistent with one previously taken. Opposing counsel could quickly cast doubt upon the CPA's credibility.

Conflict of Interest. The legal profession recognizes that a person rendering professional services should not have any conflicts of interest, and the CPA must also adopt this principle. A conflict of interest exists when current or prior relationships affect a CPA's ability to evaluate objectively and present an issue independently. Conflicts may arise from (1) the CPA's ethical obligation to preserve client confidences or (2) other relationships that may affect the CPA's ability to present an issue for the client.

Confidentiality. The CPA brings to the courtroom all of his prior experience and knowledge of clients and their practices, operations, and trade secrets. The CPA should not disclose information obtained during other professional engagements except with the client's consent or pursuant to an appropriate legal proceeding. Experience in similar cases enables the CPA to render expert opinions, but the confidential information obtained in previous engagements must be protected. Ordinarily the CPA will not need to disclose any confidential information but must recognize the dual responsibility to be both truthful and honest while preserving past and present clients' confidential information.

If a CPA relies on specific information obtained in an unrelated client engagement and uses that information as the basis for his opinion, then it is possible that a judge will require the expert to disclose the source of the information. If the CPA refuses, the judge may preclude use of the testimony because discovery could not be taken on the basis of the expert's opinion.

Contingent Fees. Both the law and professional standards prohibit CPAs from accepting contingent fees or commissions in serving as an expert witness. A contingent fee may be appropriate in some consulting assignments. Consider, for example, a CPA engaged in cases after a marital dissolution and property agreement have become final. An attorney and a CPA can be engaged via a contingent fee to locate undisclosed assets. The attorney and client recognize at the outset that the CPA shall serve only as a consultant, not as an expert witness.

Engagement Letter. The CPA should consider whether an engagement letter is appropriate in a litigation service engagement. Some CPAs believe that an engagement letter may be too restrictive and limit the areas of testimony. The CPA should at a minimum reach an oral agreement with the attorney regarding the services to be rendered.

A letter generally describes the engagement's scope and limits the use of data or reports prepared by the CPA. The scope should identify the nature of the services and whether such services include an audit or review. The letter should restrict use of the CPA's workproduct to the case and prohibit distribution to others. Most engagement letters specify hourly rates and fees and call for reimbursement of out-of-pocket costs. Some letters require a retainer, which is applied only to the final billing. The letter may also specify that any costs the CPA firm incurs for legal counsel during or after the case be reimbursed. The engagement letter might also address the possibility that the client may change attorneys, giving the CPA the option to withdraw, the return of original documents, and a statement of no warranty or prediction of results.

An engagement letter benefits both the CPA and the attorney, setting forth a mutual agreement on the engagement's terms and each party's responsibilities. The CPA's insurance carrier may require one. The *Technical Consulting Practice Aid* published by the Management Advisory Services Division includes a sample engagement letter that may be adapted to a particular engagement (see Exhibit 2.1).

Fieldwork. Initial meetings between the CPA and the client/attorney will deal with many of the CPA's general responsibilities as discussed in the previous section. The fieldwork usually requires most of the CPA's time, although engagements vary from a simple analysis requiring a few hours to a complex antitrust matter requiring many consultations over an extended period. The CPA's responsibilities are the same, whatever the engagement's size. Work should be properly planned, and assistants, if any, should be properly supervised. Sufficient evidential and relevant data should support the opinion expressed, and CPAs should not misrepresent facts nor subordinate their judgment to others.

CONFLICTS OF INTEREST

Overview

A CPA with current or prior relationships affecting the ability objectively to evaluate and present a client's position has a conflict of interest. The CPA should avoid engagements that involve conflicts of interest. Conflicts arise from the CPA's ethical obligation to preserve client confidences or from other relationships that may affect the CPA's ability to present a client's position. The CPA may also decline an engagement based on perceived conflicts or business considerations.

Before accepting litigation engagements, CPAs should evaluate their existing and past relationships, if any, with all known parties to the action for potential conflicts of interest. This evaluation should include opposing parties, other potential parties, and their respective counsel. As the engagement progresses, CPAs should remain sensitive to the possibility of conflicts of interest arising and should evaluate any such conflicts as if they had been identified prior to accepting the engagement.

In evaluating conflicts, the CPA should disclose to the attorney client situations that could raise a conflict question even though the CPA has concluded otherwise.

EXHIBIT 2-1. SAMPLE ENGAGEMENT LETTER

CPA & Company
Anytown, USA

September 4, 19XX

John Smith, Esq.
Smith, Smith & Jones
100 Courthouse Way
Anytown, USA

RE: *Vending Operator, Inc., v. State*

Dear Mr. Smith:

This letter constitutes a retainer between the law firm of Smith, Smith & Jones and CPA & Company under which we will provide such consulting services as you or your client, State, may require in connection with the above-mentioned litigation. We have been retained as consultants only; however, we understand and accept that we may be requested to furnish judicial testimony.

We will submit monthly bills to you, payable within XX days, which will be based on our standard hourly rates for this type of consulting plus out-of-pocket expenses that may be incurred on your behalf. We will meet with you to define tasks in advance and estimate the cost of each task before incurring any substantial fees for a task.

(optional clause for a retainer)

Our customary practice in litigation consulting engagements is to receive a retainer of $XXX before beginning work. We will hold this retainer and apply it to the final bill for this engagement.

This agreement will become effective as soon as you sign and date it and the enclosed copy as indicated. Please forward the copy to us.

Sincerely,

____

(Name and Title)
CPA & Company

Accepted by ____________________
Date ____________________

Before accepting an engagement, the CPA should disclose to the attorney any prior or existing relationships with all parties.

Multioffice CPA firms have a particularly difficult time ascertaining whether a conflict of interest exists. The information maintained by a national CPA firm normally identifies past and present clients, but before accepting an engagement, any CPA may wish to explore the following:

What law firm is retaining me?

What law firm will represent the opposing side?

Who are the known and potential plaintiffs and defendants?

Are they past, present or potential clients? Do the plaintiffs and defendants have any significant business relationships with my past, present, or potential clients?

The following discussion presents several situations that may raise conflicts of interest and illustrates the diversity of such situations. The nature of litigation engagements requires that conflicts of interest be identified early, preferably before the CPA accepts the engagement. Situations that present any questions of conflicts should be discussed with the client's attorney to permit evaluation.

Simultaneous Conflicts.

Assume that a CPA has worked with clients in the travel industry for several years. Current engagements include non-attestation and consulting services with Airline A, a national carrier. Consulting services provided for A included evaluating marketing strategies to assist management with industry deregulation. Recently Commuter B, a start-up, has filed suit against Airline A, alleging predatory pricing by Airline A in Commuter B's market area, thereby causing economic losses to Commuter B. Because of the CPA's expertise and reputation in the airline industry, Commuter B asks the CPA to help prepare its claim for damages. Should the CPA accept this engagement?

Ethics Rule 301[1] of the AICPA reads in part: "A member shall not disclose any confidential information without the specific consent of the client." Has the CPA been privy to sensitive client information in providing Airline A with consulting services? If Commuter B's lawsuit addresses the subject of this consulting service, the CPA should consider whether accepting this engagement would compromise Airline A's confidences. Rule 301 suggests that with Airline A's consent, the CPA could accept the engagement; however, obtaining such consent could be difficult. Airline A would have to be advised as to the CPA's prospective engagement with B to make an informed decision. Such a communication would require the litigator's approval and could pose problems in adequately describing the engagement to A without compromising the litigator's desire for confidentiality of his trial preparation plans on behalf of B.

Consider a different situation in which a CPA (the "tax CPA") provides Company A only tax advice and tax compliance reporting. Company B asks a "litigation CPA" in another office of the tax CPA to help develop its damage case against Company A. The case involves matters totally separate from the tax engagement. Should the litigation CPA decline this engagement because of a conflict of interest?

The litigation CPA with no prior access to confidential information relating to the matter in litigation may conclude that no conflict exists. The tax CPA's engagement should, however, be disclosed to Company B's attorney. Early disclosure allows Company B's attorney to consider this issue before retaining the litigation CPA.

The litigation CPA may also wish to consider the engagement's effect on the tax CPA's relationship with Company A. The CPA may disclose to Company A that the litigation CPA has been retained by Company B if Company B's attorney approves such disclosure. The litigation CPA may not have a conflict of interest but may decline the engagement for business considerations.

Consider the circumstances in which the CPA has completed a consulting engagement regarding Airline A's marketing plan and has no ongoing relationship with A. Subsequently, Commuter B approaches the CPA for assistance in its lawsuit. Would the lack of an ongoing relationship permit the CPA to accept the engagement with B?

Rule 301 is not limited to current clients. A practitioner must have a client's full confidence to adequately provide assistance. To preserve this relationship, the profession assures clients that information gained during an engagement will not be disclosed to others without the client's consent. To be meaningful, this assurance must continue beyond the particular engagement, and thus the CPA must consider whether the litigation engagement would create a conflict.

Clearly, multioffice CPA firms face more difficult problems in monitoring conflicts of interest. Conflicts increase from not only the number of offices and clients but also from the variety of services these firms offer. With more offices and clients, multioffice firms may need a computer-based system under the control of a single individual to identify relationships posing potential conflicts of interest.

Preliminary Interview with Prospective Clients

When a prospective client approaches a CPA regarding a litigation engagement, the client or attorney will typically give the CPA sufficient information about the case to assist in identifying the parties and opposing counsel as well as the key issues in dispute. In describing the matter, the potential client may communicate confidential information to the CPA. Assume that the CPA is not retained by this prospective client but is subsequently approached by the client's opposition. Should the CPA decline the subsequent offer of an engagement to protect the confidential information received previously?

The accounting profession has not addressed this question. However, a California State Bar Standing Committee on Professional Responsibility and Conduct addressed the issue for California attorneys. The committee concluded that a prospective client from whom an attorney obtains confidential information during an initial interview is a client nonetheless, and the attorney cannot use the information. Although questions of conflicts of interest for attorneys differ from those of accountants, this rule may provide a guide to appropriate conduct for the CPA. This ruling provides aggressive lawyers with an opportunity to foreclose the participation of potential experts by contacting them and disclosing minor bits of confidential information. To avoid the problem, CPAs will want to limit the information received from lawyers before being officially retained and inform the inquiring lawyers that they are following this approach.[2]

Joint Representation

Joint representations occur when both opposing parties engage a single CPA for assistance in resolving issues that are a part of their dispute. Given the adversarial nature of these engagements, the CPA should consider the relationship with the parties and the role to be played before accepting such an engagement. Consider the following example.

A CPA has provided a full range of services to a married couple for several years. The husband is a principal in a closely held business to which the CPA has provided tax advice and accounting services. In a dissolution action, the couple ask the CPA to help them with accounting and valuation aspects of the property settlement. Can the CPA accept this engagement?

Case law and legal ethics restrict a lawyer's ability to represent both parties in a dispute. Although the advocate role that a lawyer plays differs distinctly from the objectivity expected of an accountant, the CPA is unlikely to be able to advise both parties to a divorce adequately, given a prior relationship with both. Two issues merit consideration in making a decision. First, as part of the prior engagement with the couple, the CPA may have received confidential information from one of the parties. Accepting the joint engagement could compromise the confidential nature of these communications. The second issue relates to the appearance of objectivity. Often the CPA firm has a more significant economic relationship with the earning spouse. This economic relationship could unwittingly affect the firm's willingness to commit resources to develop both spouses' claims equally. At the very least, it may raise questions of an appearance of lack of objectivity.

The nature of the prior relationship must govern the decision. If no prior relationship existed with the couple or the prior relationship was limited, the CPA might accept the engagement. The CPA should nevertheless consider the dispute's adversarial nature as an inherent risk in joint representation. The CPA might best act as a court-appointed accountant to provide insulation from the assignment's adversarial nature. The CPA should completely disclose to both parties any prior relationship between the CPA and any party and identify the scope of the tasks to be performed.

The CPA should consider the same factors before accepting engagements in which two clients with potentially differing interests may ask for common assistance. Borrowers and lenders as well as buyers and sellers pose other joint representation situations.

Simultaneous Consultations

Conflicts may also arise when a CPA is simultaneously engaged to work for and against the same law firm in different cases. Consider the following situation.

Counsel A has retained Expert A to assist Plaintiff A by valuing an apartment building. Defendant B's attorney in this matter is Counsel B1. Prior to Plaintiff A's case going to trial, Counsel B2 approaches Expert A regarding the valuation of income property for Defendant C. Counsel B2, a partner with Counsel B1, is unaware that Expert A is a consultant or expert opposing Counsel B1's case. Does

Expert A have a conflict of interest in this situation? In terms of Rule 301, no confidential client communications are involved.

This question of conflicts is more of a problem for counsel rather than an ethical question for the expert witness. However, the CPA should be aware of the potential for problems in such circumstances and should fully disclose such relationships to counsel before accepting an engagement.

REPORTING STANDARDS

In 1985 and 1986, the Auditing Standards Board (ASB) of the AICPA issued several statements on standards that exempted litigation engagements from standards regarding financial forecasts and projections, attestation, and GAAP. In 1989 the Auditing Standards Board issued an intrepretation of the attestation standards related to litigation services.

Financial Forecasts and Projections

In 1985 ASB of the AICPA issued a Statement on Standards for Accountants' Services on Prospective Financial Information.[3] The Statement on Standards recognized for the first time that litigation services should be handled differently and sometimes be exempt from the statement established by the ASB. The statement identified such engagements as follows:

> This Statement does not provide standards or procedures for engagements involving prospective financial statements used solely in connection with litigation support services, although it provides helpful guidance for many aspects of such engagements and may be referred to as useful guidance in such engagements. Litigation support services are engagements involving pending or potential formal legal proceedings before a "trier of fact" in connection with the resolution of a dispute between two or more parties, for example, in circumstances where an accountant acts as an expert witness. This exception is provided because, among other things, the accountant's work in such proceedings is ordinarily subject to detailed analysis and challenge by each party to the dispute. This exception does not apply, however, if the prospective financial statements are for use by third parties who, under the rules of the proceedings, do not have the opportunity for such analysis and challenge. For example, creditors may not have such opportunities when prospective financial statements are submitted to them to secure their agreement to a plan of reorganization.[4]

Attestation Standards

In 1986 the ASB of the AICPA also approved a new Statement on Attestation Standards and defined such an engagements as "one in which the practitioner is engaged in issuing or does issue a written communication that expresses a conclusion about the reliability of a written assertion."[5] Again, the ASB exempted professional services that would not be considered an attest engagement including "engagements in which a practitioner is engaged to testify as an expert witness in accounting, auditing, taxation or other matters, given certain stipulated facts."[6]

In late 1989, the Auditing Standards Board (ASB) of the AICPA issued an Interpretation of Attestation Standards: Applicability of Attestation Standards to Litigation Services (Section at 9100).[7] The purpose of this interpreation is to clarify the language in the Statement on Standards for Attestation Engagements (SSAE) (at § 100.02) that gave certain examples of litigation services engagements that would not be considered attest engagements as defined by SSAE.

In the interpretation, the Auditing Standards Board states that litigation services engagements are exempt from the requirements of SSAE when the engagement involves a pending or potential formal legal or regulatory proceeding before a "trier of fact" in connection with the resolution of a dispute between two or more parties. The reason for the exemption is that the accountant's work in such a proceeding is ordinarily subject to detailed analysis and challenge by each party to the dispute.

The only times that the SSAE applies to litigation services engagements is when the accountant is engaged to perform a service in accordance with the Statements on Standards for Attestation Engagements or when others will receive the written work of the accountant and under the rules of the proceeding do not have the opportunity to analyze and challenge the work of the accountant.

In the exemption for litigation services engagements in the SSAE, the ASB used an example of the type of engagement that was exempt from SSAE. This example used the term *stipulated facts*. The interpretation explains what the ASB meant in paragraph 2.f of SSAE in their use of the term *stipulated facts*. This paragraph stated that "engagements in which a practitioner is engaged to testify as an expert witness in accounting, auditing, taxation, or other matters be given certain stipulated facts." In this paragraph, the ASB meant the term *stipulated facts* to mean facts or assumptions that are specified by a party to the dispute that serves as the basis for the development of the accountant's expert opinion rather than its legal meaning of facts agreed to by all the parties to the dispute. So, *stipulated* really means *assumed*.

Finally, the interpretation addesses the question of whether an accountant can testify on the issue of solvency as an expert witness. The ASB has concluded that as long as the accountant is involved with pending or potential formal legal or regulatory proceedings before a "trier of fact" in connection with the resolution of a dispute between two or more parties, he can render an expert opinion related to solvency. Thus, Interpretation of Attestation Standards: Responding to Requests on Matters Relating to Solvency (at § 9100.28–.41) is not applicable.

Application of Generally Accepted Accounting Principles

In July of 1986 the ASB of the AICPA approved the standards set for an accountant in public practice, relative to the reports on application of accounting principles. Once again, the ASB recognized an exemption for CPAs involved in litigation support engagements, as follows:

> This Section does not apply to an accountant ("continuing accountant") who has been engaged to report on financial statements, to engagements either to assist in litigation involving accounting matters or to provide expert testimony in connection with such litigation, or to professional advice given to another accountant in public practice.[8]

Management Advisory Services—MAS Interpretation of MS Section 11.01

In late 1989, the AICPA issued the first Interpretation of the MAS Standards. Applicability of Statements on Standards for Management Advisory Services to Litigation Services (MAS Interpretation of MS Section 11.01)[9] states that litigation services are a form of management advisory services to which the Statements on Standards for Management Advisory Services apply.

Even though the matter in question that the accountant is testifying about relates to accounting, audit, or tax situations involving the litigants, the member is serving in a consulting capacity.

The AICPA has decided that the standards that should be followed in a litigation services engagement are the Statements on Standards for Management Advisory Services and the AICPA Code of Professional Conduct, including Rule 102 on Integrity and Objectivity.

In a litigation engagement, the information and conclusions reached by a CPA are closely scrutized, analyzed, and cross-examined by the opposition. CPAs must understand that their opinions will receive the close attention of counsel and, in most instances, an opposing expert or consultant.

CPAs must ensure that anyone using their reports or workpapers understands why they were prepared or has the right to depose or cross-examine with respect to them. A CPA should prevent a third party who is unaware of the litigation from relying on the reports; such a person would be unable to gain a full understanding of or challenge the underlying assumptions.

The CPA who renders services to the court in an official capacity must conform to the court's reporting requirements. Examples would be as a receiver in bankruptcy or in probate matters. When the CPA renders consulting services in disputes not before the court and the CPA was engaged by a client who is not an attorney, then all standards of reporting should be adhered to as required by the AICPA and the relevant state boards of accountancy.

Wagner and Frank (1986; see Note 10) recognized that expert witnesses use both oral testimony and written reports in presentations. They note that:

> There are no specific elements for reports in litigation services engagements, because the form and content are closely controlled by the lawyer retaining the CPA. However, the CPA would insist that his conclusions and analyses not be misrepresented by the form or content of the presentation.[10]

As a consultant, the CPA's work product usually receives attorney–workproduct privilege.

Other Matters. CPAs may also provide two other forms of written statements.

1. *Affidavits.* An accountant providing litigation services may submit an affidavit, which is a written statement of fact, signed and sworn to before a person having authority to administer an oath. An affidavit usually supports a motion before the court.
2. *Declarations.* A declaration is an unsworn written statement, usually including a statement that the testimony would be the same if made under oath. Whether an affidavit or a declaration is used is a decision for the attorney to make. They are interchangeable for many uses, and custom in a particular court or jurisdiction usually controls which is used.

Special Reports. The CPA not involved before a trier of fact and not protected by the workproduct privilege should follow the guidance provided through statements on auditing standards as well as statements on standards for accounting and review services (SSARS). In a compilation or a review service, the applicable SSARS should be consulted. If a special report is required, SAS No. 35 and SAS No. 62 (AU Sections 622 and 623) will normally guide the CPA as to the appropriate reporting standards. The professional literature applies to auditors' reports in connection with the following:

1. Financial statements that are prepared in accordance with a comprehensive basis of accounting other than generally accepted accounting principles.
2. Specified elements, accounts, or items of a financial statement.
3. Compliance with aspects of contractual agreements or regulatory requirements related to audited financial statements.
4. Financial information presented in prescribed forms or schedules that require a prescribed form of auditor's report.

AU Section 622 applies to agreed-upon procedures applied to specified elements, accounts, or items of a financial statements.

WORKPAPERS

A CPA in a litigation engagement will generate workpapers or analyses documenting opinions. The workpapers and analyses do not follow a prescribed format. The Federal Rules of Evidence require the CPA to identify the bases of opinion (Rule 703) and disclose the facts or data underlying the opinion (Rule 705).

All materials prepared, notes, calculations, correspondence, and materials referred to by an expert witness may be made available to opposing counsel. If the CPA is serving as a consultant, the attorney will probably be able to assert a workproduct privilege and all such workpapers may never be produced and analyzed by opposing counsel. The CPA and the attorney should understand the CPA's role at the outset.

Once the CPA's role has been defined, the CPA should be aware that notes of meetings may include preliminary opinions, draft schedules, and reports; when final versions are prepared, retention of the preliminary workproduct may be unnecessary so long as the CPA can trace the final conclusions and opinions back to source documents.

Lawyers, as a matter of professional principle, will not instruct an expert witness to destroy notes, files, and outdated work. Many experts keep "lean" files, retaining only the absolute minimum. This procedure reduces the problems caused in comprehensive discovery but may cause the witness extra work to become familiar again with items once learned and since forgotten or to recreate discarded work, again deemed useful. Such extra work can generate extra costs for the client, but most lawyers prefer that procedure. The CPA expert who maintains "lean" files should announce to the lawyer a policy of not keeping notes and extensive files, giving the lawyer an opportunity to object, rather than waiting for the lawyer to suggest such a policy.[11]

CONCLUSIONS

The CPA's professional standards and rules require that we undertake only those engagements in which we possess professional competence, that we exercise professional care, adequately plan and supervise our engagements, and obtain sufficient relevant data. For all these reasons, a CPA involved in a litigation support engagement should carefully review the relevant professional standards and the appropriate legal standards in providing services.

APPENDIX: AICPA CODE OF PROFESSIONAL CONDUCT

Membership in the American Institute of Certified Public Accountants is voluntary. By accepting membership in the AICPA, a certified public accountant assumes an obligation of self-discipline above and beyond the requirements of laws and regulations.

These Principles of the Code of Professional Conduct of the American Institute of Certified Public Accountants express the profession's recognition of its responsibilities to the public, to clients, and to colleagues. They guide members in the performance of their professional responsibilities and express the basic tenets of ethical and professional conduct. The principles call for an unswerving commitment to honorable behavior, even at the sacrifice of personal advantage.

Section I—Principles

Article I—Responsibilities. In carrying out responsibilities as professionals, members should exercise sensitive professional and moral judgments in all of their activities.

Article II—Public Interest. Members should accept the obligation to act in a way that will serve the public interest, honor the public trust, and demonstrate commitment to professionalism.

Article III—Integrity. To maintain and broaden public confidence members should perform all professional responsibilities with the highest sense of integrity.

Article IV—Objectivity and Independence. A member should maintain objectivity and be free of conflicts of interest in discharging professional responsibilities. A member in public practice should be independent in fact and appearance when providing auditing and other attestation services.

Article V—Due Care. A member should observe the profession's technical and ethical standards, strive continually to improve confidence and the quality of services, and discharge professional responsibility to the best of the member's ability.

Article VI—Scope and Nature of Services. A member in public practice should observe the principles of the Code of Professional Conduct in determining the scope and nature of services to be provided.

Section II—Rules Applicability

The bylaws of the American Institute of Certified Public Accountants require that members adhere to the Rules of the Code of Professional Conduct. Members must be prepared to justify departures from these Rules.

Independence

Rule 101. A member in public practice shall be independent in the performance of professional services as required by standards promulgated by bodies designated by Council.

Integrity and Objectivity

Rule 102. In the performance of any professional service, a member shall maintain objectivity and integrity, shall be free of conflicts of interests, and shall not knowingly misrepresent facts or subordinate his or her judgment to others.

General Standards

Rule 201. A member shall comply with the following standards and with any interpretations thereof by bodies designed by Council.

A. *Professional Competence.* Undertake only those professional services that the members of member's firm can reasonably expect to be completed with professional competence.

B. *Due Professional Care.* Exercise due professional care in the performance of professional services.

C. *Planning and Supervision.* Adequately plan and supervise the performance of professional services.

D. *Sufficient Relevant Data.* Obtain sufficient relevant data to afford a reasonable basis for conclusions or recommendations in relation to any professional services performed.

Compliance with Standards

Rule 202. A member who performs auditing, review, compilation, management advisory, tax, or other professional services shall comply with standards promulgated by bodies designated by Council.

Accounting Principles

Rule 203. A member shall not (1) express an opinion or state affirmatively that the financial statements or other financial data of any entity are presented in conformity with generally accepted accounting principles or (2) state that he or she is not aware of any material modifications that should be made to such statements or data in order for them to be in conformity with generally accepted accounting principles, if such statements or data contain any departure from an accounting principle promulgated by bodies designated by Council to establish such principles that has a material effect on the statement or data taken as a whole. If, however, the statements or data contain such a departure and the member can demonstrate that due to unusual circumstances the financial statement or data would otherwise have been misleading, the member can comply with the rule by describing the departure, its approximate effects, if practicable, and the reasons why compliance with the principle would result in a misleading statement.

Confidential Client Information

Rule 301. A member in public practice shall not disclose any confidential client information without the specific consent of the client. This rule shall not be construed (1) to relieve a member of the member's professional obligations under Rules 202 and 203; (2) to affect in any way the member's obligation to comply with a validly issued and enforceable subpoena or summons; (3) to prohibit review of a member's professional practice under AICPA or state CPA society authorization; or (4) to preclude a member from initiating a complaint with or responding to any inquiry made by a recognized investigative or disciplinary body.

Members of a recognized investigative or disciplinary body and professional practice reviewers shall not use to their own advantage or disclose any member's confidential client information that comes to their attention in carrying out their official responsibilities. However, this prohibition shall not restrict the exchange of information with a recognized investigative or disciplinary body or affect in any way compliance with a validly issued and enforceable subpoena or summons.

Contingent Fees (as of January 12, 1988; currently being revised)

Rule 302. Professional services shall not be offered or rendered under an arrangement whereby no fee will be charged unless a specified finding or result is attained or where the fee is otherwise contingent upon the finding or results of such services. However, a member's fee may vary depending on the complexity of services rendered.

Fees are not regarded as being contingent if fixed by courts or other public authorities or, in tax matters, if determined based on the results of judicial proceedings or the findings of governmental agencies.

Acts Discreditable

Rule 501. A member shall not commit an act discreditable to the profession.

Advertising and Other Forms of Solicitation

Rules 502. A member *in public practice* shall not seek to obtain clients by advertising or other forms of solicitation in a manner that is false, misleading, or deceptive. Solicitation by the use of coercion, overreaching, or harassing conduct is prohibited.

Commissions (as of January 12, 1988; currently being revised)

Rule 503. The acceptance by a member in public practice of a payment for the referral of products or services of others to a client is prohibited. Such action is considered to create a conflict of interest that results in a loss of objectivity and independence.

NOTES

1. *AICPA Professional Standards* (Vol. 2), § ET 100.
2. The editors of the *Handbook* are aware of a major case in which lawyers for one side contacted many experts, gave them each tasks that turned out to be trivial, but effectively foreclosed the experts from working for the other side.
3. *AICPA Professional Standards* (Vol. 1), § AU 2100.02.
4. Ibid., § AU 2100.03.
5. Ibid., § AU 2010.01.
6. Ibid., § 2010.02(f).
7. *AICPA Professional Standards* (Vol. 1), § AT 9100.
8. Ibid., § AU 625.
9. *AICPA Professional Standards* (vol. 2) § MS 11.01.

3

DISCOVERY AND THE ROLE OF THE CPA

Henry Stotsenberg, CPA

INTRODUCTION

The CPA can play an important role in the discovery phase of financial and commercial litigation. A thorough knowledge of discovery is essential in providing competent litigation services. Nearly every litigation assignment involves some form of discovery. Trials are often won or lost by the quality of pretrial discovery. Although a CPA's expert testimony can greatly influence a litigation's outcome, the testimony's quality has its foundation in and stems from how well the CPA contributed to discovery, particularly in business and financial litigation. This chapter presents aspects of discovery that relate to the CPA providing expert consultant services to attorneys.

DEFINITION, TIMING, AND IMPORTANCE OF DISCOVERY

Definition

Black's Law Dictionary defines discovery in part as "the ascertainment of that which was previously hidden. . . ." For the CPA, this means the investigation of financial and accounting information, assets, or values that were previously unknown; the disclosure of previously hidden financial and accounting information, assets, or values.

Timing

Discovery normally occurs after the filing of a complaint or lawsuit and before final trial preparation. Discovery is a set of pretrial procedures governed by rules. Chapter 1 provides further perspective of how discovery fits into the overall judicial process.

Better Trial Preparation

Effective trial preparation always includes discovery. Effective discovery provides an informed picture of the facts. As information is discovered, issues and contentions are revised or discarded and new ones developed. The more the information, issues, and contentions relate to financial, commercial, or accounting matters, the more important is the CPA.

Effective Settlement Tool

Discovery can also aid settlement. Most lawsuits settle, never advancing beyond the discovery phase. The CPA's work during discovery in business and financial litigation can affect whether a litigant prevails during settlement. A CPA, knowledgeable and competent in discovery, will provide the client with an advantage in settling the litigation.

Protects Evidence

During the discovery, the CPA can help to preserve and protect the financial and business records and evidence. The CPA can assist with locating, authenticating, and identifying financial or business records that may be needed at trial. Some CPAs provide document control services for the attorney, particularly when there are many documents. The CPA should learn the document retention policies of the parties to a litigation. Critical documents may be destroyed through inadvertance if not protected by proper discovery orders.

Exposes Retractions of Testimony

Occasionally, a witness may attempt to retract important testimony given during discovery. Subsequent retraction of well-documented testimony can be difficult. When the testimony involves business and financial matters, the CPA can assist the attorney by documenting and matching the original testimony with subsequent revisions.

Needed for Expert Discovery

A CPA can assist with discovery either as a consultant to the attorney or as a designated expert who may testify as an expert witness, or both. The workproduct, findings, and opinions of a CPA designated as an expert witness generally become discoverable during the discovery phase. A CPA can often help the attorney discover and examine the workproduct, findings, and opinions of the adversaries' designated CPA and economic expert witnesses.

UNDERSTANDING DISCOVERY DEVICES

Discovery enables a litigant to ascertain facts from an adversary and from others who are not parties to the litigation. Several discovery devices are available, and certain rules and procedures must be followed. Discovery rules vary among the states; this chapter focuses on the federal rules, some of which may differ from their state counterparts. The better the understanding of discovery devices, the better the CPA can assist the attorney in the discovery/pretrial phase.

The federal rules (as do some state rules) intend to promote discovery prior to trial with minimal court intervention. The rules permit pretrial discovery of *any matter* helpful in trial preparation that is not privileged. The purpose of discovery is to allow all parties to a litigation to be aware of all the facts, contentions, and legal theories of all the other parties to the litigation. Ideally this means there will be no surprises at trial, and the possibility of settlement will be enhanced with complete information as to the strengths and weaknesses of each parties' positions. (This chapter explains privileged communications later.) The available discovery devices most relevant to the CPA litigation expert are as follows:

1. Depositions
2. Requests for production of documents
3. Interrogatories and responses to them
4. Requests for admissions

5. Pretrial settlement conferences
6. Subpoenas

The following briefly describes these discovery devices.

Depositions

Depositions are the most prevalent discovery device and may be taken any time after the lawsuit is filed. A deposition is an interrogation made under oath and is ordinarily produced orally with attorneys from both sides present asking questions. It comprises an examination and cross-examination of the witness under oath. A court reporter usually transcribes questions and answers. Depositions can—under strict rules—be videotaped. Transcribed depositions are expensive, and videotaped depositions even more so. A witness may be compelled by subpoena to provide a deposition. Depositions are most widely used because they offer the opportunity for spontaneous investigation.

Requests for Production and Inspection of Documents (Subpoena Duces Tecum)

Any litigant may request the other litigant to produce designated documents for inspection or copying. Litigants may also request entry to property to inspect an operation. Such a request is called a subpoena duces tecum. The request can be made as soon as the lawsuit is filed and served on the defendant. The request must specify the items to be inspected and the time, place, and manner of the inspection. A third party not a party to the action may also be served a notice for production of records to be inspected. It is the responsibility of the requesting party to arrange for copying any of the produced documents.

Interrogatories

Interrogatories are written questions to be answered under oath and are served by one party of the litigation upon the other party. Interrogatories usually place a burden on the answering party to carry out an investigation to derive answers to the questions. In the event business records are needed to answer interrogatories, the respondent can answer by referring to the records without producing the record. The questioning party must, however, be given the opportunity to examine and copy the records, if not already produced. Interrogatories should be clear and specific; otherwise the responding party can easily object to ambiguous or irrelevant questions. The answering party typically has 30 days to respond, and the responses usually are drafted by the attorneys. Thus spontaneity is lost, and nonresponsiveness is gained.

Request for Admissions

One party may request that any other party admit the authenticity of any relevant document or the truth of any relevant matters of fact. Copies of documents may accompany the request. Failure to respond to a request is usually deemed an admission. This discovery device is highly favored by the judiciary as it speeds up a trial. Authentication of documents and introduction of evidence to prove obvious facts is avoided.

Pretrial Settlement Conferences

Judges sometimes hold informal settlement conferences with the litigants and their attorneys. The conferences are usually discretionary with the court and are not called unless they are expected to have genuine value. Some jurisdictions mandate these conferences to encourage settlements. These conferences are not themselves discovery devices, although they go hand in hand with discovery. These conferences can reveal the results of discovery, thereby promoting settlement, or the judge's inquiries may lead to further admissions.

Subpoenas

Subpoenas require a witness to appear and testify (subpoena ad testificandum) or to produce a document (subpoena duces tecum). The CPA should understand the process and the nature of the business records to be produced. Expert witnesses testifying at the deposition pursuant to a subpoena duces tecum may have to bring books, documents, or other items that they or their subordinates considered during the preparation of the expert testimony. The subpoena duces tecum should specify the exact documents to be produced. Often no testimony is given, and the deposition involves only the production of records, which usually occurs at the party's place of business.

Informal and Independent Discovery

Often facts can be ascertained and records obtained without using any of the formal devices described. For example, records from a client–litigant may be available to form a basis for additional discovery. A CPA may assist in locating the records and ascertaining the relevant information.

In addition, information may be collected even before the litigation is filed. This discovery may be the basis for deciding whether to file the lawsuit. Potential litigants, unaware that a lawsuit is pending, are much more cooperative when asked for information about their operations before a lawsuit is filed than afterward.

OTHER MATTERS RELEVANT TO DISCOVERY

The Adversarial Process

Litigation is an adversarial process. The adversarial process assumes that each litigant will have competent advocates presenting their version of facts most favorable to them. The CPA's role is not one of an advocate unless the CPA is retained to be a consultant in the litigation. In this role, the CPA should help the attorney prepare his case in the best way for the mutual client. When the CPA is an expert witness, a standard of objectivity will best serve the CPA and the client. The CPA has a professional duty during discovery to use special knowledge and training to help the attorney develop the client's most favorable case.

Privileged Communications

Only privileged documents are exempt from discovery. Some information sought may not be discoverable due to privilege, which protects certain types of communications. The more notable examples are lawyer–client relations, attorney work-product, husband–wife relations, and trade secrets. Individual tax returns are privileged documents in some jurisdictions. Sometimes a CPA may assist an attorney with only discovery and case strategy, not as an expert witness; such assistance becomes privileged, undiscoverable as attorney workproduct. CPAs hired as consultants are duty bound to keep their workproduct confidential unless instructed otherwise by the attorney or the trier of fact.

Not all CPA workproduct is privileged and protected from discovery. The CPA should know what is discoverable and what is not. *All workproduct of the CPA who is identified as an expert witness—including work done during the discovery phase—may become discoverable.* Once a CPA advances from consultant to expert witness, all the CPA's workproduct, writings, and workpapers are subject to discovery. This includes all work done prior to being hired as a consultant, even for an existing client. Separating what is discoverable from what is not becomes difficult when the client has been a nonlitigation client of the CPA expert. For this reason, another CPA is often hired exclusively for the litigation to avoid the problems inherent in isolating privileged CPA workproduct from discoverable workproduct.

THE IMPORTANCE OF THE CPA

The CPA can serve an attorney during discovery in business and financial litigation. Only a few trial attorneys understand business, financial, and accounting issues or have the inclination to address them. Yet discovery may be the most critical phase of financial and business litigation. The quality and magnitude of the disclosures and ascertainment of financial and accounting information during discovery may determine the litigation's outcome. CPAs' knowledge of financial, business, accounting, information systems, and related records and documents qualifies them to know *what* and *where* to investigate. A CPA's expertise and discipline in auditing provides the knowledge of *how* to investigate. If the CPA's expertise is competently applied during discovery, the attorney can focus on the law, procedures, strategy and liability, and less on analyzing financial records and documents.

CPA ASSISTANCE DURING DISCOVERY

The CPA's primary responsibility in discovery is to assist attorneys and follow their direction. The CPA need not be independent and unbiased. The CPA serving as a consultant only (not as an expert witness) assists with discovery and other matters with the objective of prevailing in the litigation. The CPA's responsibility is to the attorney and litigant–client. However, the CPA who is not responsible and objective provides a disservice to the attorney and the litigant–client.

A difference exists between being a consultant for discovery only and being an expert witness. A CPA testifying as an expert witness should be objective and unbiased.

The CPA can perform various services in assisting the attorney during discovery. Some of the more prominent are as follows:

1. Assisting in preparing expert testimony of the expert witnesses retained by the attorney.
2. Identifying for production documents and records thought to exist.
3. Analyzing documents, records, and facts, including summaries.
4. Indexing of documents.
5. Identifying issues and contentions.
6. Preparing questions and documents for and assisting during the taking of depositions.
7. Drafting interrogatories, answers, and requests for admissions.
8. Preparing for pretrial and settlement conferences and negotiations.

Preparing for Expert Testimony

The CPA actively involved during discovery who can present expert testimony is likely to be more credible. An expert witness with insufficient knowledge of the facts supporting an expert opinion can be devastated on cross-examination. The expert witness who actively participates in discovery and document analysis is likely to be better prepared than one who does not. The CPA who assists the attorney during discovery will lay the foundation for competent expert testimony, particularly during cross-examination. But the work of the expert is usually all discoverable. In some cases, a trade-off must be made between privilege and preparation. Thorough preparation of an expert may destroy privilege. When the CPA is not to provide expert testimony, he can assist the attorney develop testimony for other witnesses. On particularly sensitive issues, the CPA can clarify and explore avenues prior to the expert's involvement.

Production of Documents and Records

Ordinarily, the earlier the CPA assists in production of documents and records the better. Gaining access to records in bitterly fought litigation takes time. The production of records usually comes in waves and in response to a subpoena duces tecum. Subsequent notices to produce documents will be based on what was discovered as a result of prior notices. One should begin the process early.

Not many trial attorneys know how to accurately identify accounting and financial records in a production request. Requesting "all business and accounting records" is nearly useless. A CPA will be qualified to identify the exact business records that a production notice should request, based on the issues of the case, in the following areas:

1. General ledger, journals, trial balances, journal entries and subsidiary records, charts of account.
2. Balance sheets, profit and loss statements, cash flow statements, statements of charges.
3. Internal financial statements, audited financial statements, compilations, reviews, budgets, management reports.
4. Corporate, individual, and partnership returns.
5. Pension and profit sharing plan reports.

The list can be extended. The initial production requests are important and will affect the progress of discovery. One must accurately and specifically describe the records requested to ensure that all relevant facts and information are discovered.

Analysis of Documents, Records, and Facts

Analysis should begin as soon as possible because it often leads to requests for additional documents. Skillful trial attorneys will use a CPA to analyze business, financial, and accounting records and will draw on any insights and ideas resulting from the analyses. Occasionally, the CPA will receive permission to enter a business place to investigate records. The CPA can expertly perform the investigative accounting, which may closely resemble auditing.

Indexing of Documents

Another critical service is recording and comparing the produced documents to those requested. In bitterly fought litigation involving numerous records, one can easily lose track of whether the opposition properly responded to the several production notices. This is important for the following reasons:

1. A court order to produce certain records does not assure that the records will be produced. You need to identify any missing document. The burden is on your side to bring to the court's attention any missing documents and the other side's nonresponsiveness to the subpoena. This problem is compounded with informal document production that includes oral responses.

2. You should maintain a record of claims by the other side that documents do not exist or are missing. If the document is later produced at trial, you need to know that the opposition denied early access to it. In a case with numerous documents and intense combat, one can easily forget, without a record, whether the other side has properly responded to a notice to produce.

3. A record of requests and productions will also chart the other side's responsiveness. This may affect whether the other side will have to bear the cost to complete discovery and whether your side may be granted continuances necessary to analyze records produced late. Responsiveness can be measured by records

produced or not produced; or listed as nonexistent, then later produced; and the time lapse between the request and the response.

4. The CPA should record not only what was requested and received but from whom. Subpoena duces tecum can be served on the litigants or others not a party to the action, such as bankers, CPAs, employees, stockbrokers, competitors, pension plan trustees, and general partners. The attorney will need to know *who* produced certain documents and which subpoena the documents were in response to.

As records are produced, one should review them to ascertain what was received and how they compare with the request. The CPA may be asked to gather the documents and, initially, group them according to each subpoena or request.

Identifying Issues and Contentions

As discovery progresses, advocates must revise, drop, or add issues and contentions. A CPA actively involved in discovery and analysis may be able to assist the trial attorney to draft suggested issues and contentions related to the business issues, after gaining understanding of the litigation and the direction the attorney wishes to take. Sometimes the CPA expert is well positioned to suggest ideas for a different approach to a case. Thorough analysis can unearth new approaches to the case. Because the CPA expert will be more intimate with the information in business litigation, the CPA has a responsibility to propose changes in direction for the attorney.

Assisting with Depositions

Many trial attorneys prefer to have a CPA at their side at depositions, particularly when the opposing expert CPA is testifying. Experts' depositions normally occur before trial. The CPA can help the attorney develop a line of questioning for the deposition; the CPA can also take notes and assist with questions during the deposition of the opposing CPA. The litigation's subject matter may make the CPA more effective in recognizing the importance of certain responses, obfuscations, use of jargon, and in suggesting follow-up questions. Also, the CPA can immediately review any documents presented at the deposition and formulate new questions.

Drafting Interrogatories and Answers and Requests for Admissions

Drafting useful interrogatories and answers as well as requests for admissions is difficult. Unless interrogatories are skillfully drafted, the answers may be useless, nonresponsive, or misleading. As answers are received, the CPA should match the answers to the questions and evaluate the other side's responsiveness.

Conversely, the CPA is often asked to assist in preparing draft answers to the other side's interrogatories involving accounting, business, and financial matters.

Pretrial Settlement Conferences and Negotiations

As most cases settle, pretrial discovery proceedings and settlement conferences, in effect, become the trial. The CPA expert can skillfully assist the attorney during this litigation phase. A thorough analysis of the information and a coherent presentation for the negotiations could favor your client's position in settlement negotiations. Settlement negotiations are informal; the absence of courtroom procedures or restrictions allows you to help in an interactive fashion.

ORAL AND WRITTEN REPORTS

Written reports should be prepared only in response to the attorneys' request. Reports may present the status of a part of the litigation or could summarize the expert's opinion or conclusion that will be given in testimony at trial. If an attorney requests a written report, the CPA should advise the attorney that it may be best not to prepare the report until it is required. In the meantime, an oral report should suffice. Once the CPA is identified as an expert witness, *all* writings generally become discoverable. It may be difficult to explain a change in opinion at trial if preliminary opinions were written and subsequently discovered by the opposing side. Therefore, the CPA must use care in what is committed to writing, especially conclusions and opinions until they are final. Some practitioners feel that it is better, if possible, to proceed through discovery and into the trial without written reports.

4

DOCUMENT MANAGEMENT OF LARGE CASES

Jeff C. Parmet, JD

This chapter addresses issues facing the CPA–consultant when called upon to assist lawyers in litigation involving many documents. Although other chapters focus on organizing accountants' documents, this chapter deals with problems lawyers face when organizing "evidentiary" documents. In this discussion, "evidentiary documents" means client and adversary business records obtained through the discovery process. This discussion also treats the organization and retrieval of deposition and trial transcripts and special issues involving organization of "attorney workproduct," that is, legal documents arising out of attorney efforts on the case.

On large, protracted cases, the volume of attorney research and writing alone can present significant organization, storage, and retrieval problems.

THE BIG CASE PARADIGM

Although document management techniques apply to cases of all sizes, the genesis of "litigation support," an information science discipline, lies in several large cases filed in the early 1970s.[1] The Multidistrict Litigation (MDL) Statute,[2] enacted in the late 1960s, contributed significantly to the growth of document-intensive litigation. Only mainframe computers existed then, and they had higher costs.

Although the improved price/performance ratio for computer technology has fueled substantial growth in the application of computer document control of smaller cases, the "big" case still most readily justifies computerization. The practitioner who is thoroughly familiar with this environment can help the attorney client, who is generally unsophisticated technically, to improve document handling.

Although one cannot easily define a *big* case, it typically has one or more of the following attributes:

High exposure
Large document volume
Complex issues of fact and law
Protracted time frame
Coordination

High Exposure

Often referred to as "you-bet-your-company" cases, big litigation involves high stakes. The defendants in *U.S. v. IBM*,[3] *U.S. v. AT&T*,[4]and more recently, *Pennzoil v. Texaco*,[5] to name a few, all faced, if they lost, the dismantling of their companies. The big case, however, is not limited just to government antitrust actions and corporate takeover battles. Recently, mass tort litigation has replaced declining governmental antitrust activity as the leading arena for staging multibillion dollar litigation. Cases involving Agent Orange, Dalkon Shield, asbestos, tobacco, and DES have been large.

Common disasters also frequently result in big litigation. Recall the American Airlines DC10 crash in Chicago, the Hyatt Hotel skywalk collapse in Kansas City, the Hilton Hotel fire in Las Vegas, the Dupont Plaza hotel fire in Puerto Rico, Union Carbide's ill-fated plant in Bhopal, India, and the Three-Mile Island disaster. Not surprisingly, these tragedies resulted in massive litigation.

Securities and fraud cases occasionally, such as Penn Central, Equity Funding, OPM Leasing, and the Hunt brothers, are examples of big cases, though disasters of a different sort.

Finally, the growing number of environmental cases, fueled by the "Superfund," has spawned a number of significant toxic tort, cleanup, and insurance coverage cases.

Large Document Volume

Big cases also involve large document volumes resulting from the trends toward open discovery. Document management is not a problem if the documents are few, even if the stakes are large. Nor is it a problem if a large volume of documents exists where only a few are known to be relevant, assuming one can identify them at the outset. More than one litigator has commented, "There are only 10 important documents in this case. If only I knew which 10."

Although one cannot identify an exact number of documents needed before classifying a case as "big," serious management and control problems usually arise in the 30,000 to 50,000 document range. Modern complex litigation can involve several million documents.

Complex Issues of Fact and Law

Big litigation tends to be complex. In a disaster case, every physical component and every subsystem is examined. In a product liability case, the product's history from design and testing to marketing will be studied. In a securities case, each transaction may require tracing. In an antitrust case the defendant's conduct over a period of decades may be scrutinized. In each of these situations, litigation counsel will need to assemble factual histories. Business documents and the recollection of witnesses provide the principal sources of these facts.

Protracted Time Frame

Big cases typically last at least 3 to 5 years. The IBM antitrust litigation[6] lasted nearly 11 years. Much of the litigation mentioned still exists in one form or another and may continue well into the 1990s.

Coordination

Big litigation frequently has a national scope. If cases are pending in multiple locations, counsel must coordinate litigation activities that may be occurring simultaneously in other jurisdictions. If several parties are joined on the same side of a case, co-counsel for each party must ensure they are following consistent strategy.

Mass tort litigation presents the most extreme coordination problems. Here, effective case management demands that a consistent position be taken in discovery, which may be repeated for each case. Effective management also requires proper document control, as an inadvertent failure to produce a single responsive document in one case can have repercussions for the entire litigation.

COMPLEX LITIGATION

These factors, taken together, tend to complicate things for counsel charged with the responsibility for bringing or defending the action. Hence the notion of "complex" litigation.

In complex cases, both sides use numerous professionals with diverse qualifications. A typical case team might include lawyers, paralegals, computer professionals, economists, investigators, engineers, statisticians, technical experts, accountants, consultants, and subject company staff. Many lawyers may have diverse duties: interviewing fact witnesses, writing and responding to discovery requests, preparing trial exhibits, coordinating support staff, and trying individual cases. Complex cases frequently involve several hundred people. Most work is done under court-imposed time pressure.

Fortunately, the opposing side probably has similar difficulties. The side that better organizes its information assets has a tactical advantage. By helping counsel improve control over access to information from and about evidentiary documents, the CPA can provide valuable service.

USES OF DOCUMENTS IN LITIGATION

To understand the requirements of managing voluminous documents effectively, one should know how documents are used in complex litigations. Usage varies by type of case and whether the client is the plaintiff or defendant. Some typical uses include the following:

- Identify persons with knowledge of any fact relevant to issues in the case
- Prepare for an opponent's deposition
- Ensure that clients called as witnesses are fully aware of and prepared for all issues likely to be raised
- Prepare factual chronologies
- Review prior testimony for consistent or inconsistent statements
- Collect data for quantitative or financial analyses

COMPONENTS OF A DOCUMENT MANAGEMENT PROGRAM

The CPA consultant can help in planning and implementing a successful document management program in several areas.

Project Planning and Budgeting

Early in litigation, the client must formulate a strategy for prosecuting or defending the action. This strategy should take into account the cost of pursuing the desired result. In big-stakes litigation, expenditures typically bear a proportionate relationship to potential risk or recovery amounts. Legal fees associated with big document cases can be enormous, a large percentage of which can be attributed to document review and control. Document management expenditures for copying, microfilming, and computer systems alone can be millions of dollars and involve a dozen or more service providers. The litigation support system may cost 3 percent of exposure amounts. The company's reluctance to spend large sums tends to diminish when important legal precedents or criminal convictions hang in the balance.

Before undertaking a large document management project, one should discuss the expected costs and establish a realistic control budget. In protracted litigation, the budget should be updated periodically to reflect changed circumstances and experience. Proper planning can prevent unrealistic expectations, disappointment, and unnecessary delays. The CPA can help counsel prepare cost estimates, evaluate alternative approaches, and establish cost control mechanisms. Exhibit 4-1 displays a pro forma budget for a hypothetical document management project.

Document Control

An effective document management program involves two major components: the documents and information contained in or about the documents. The distinction

EXHIBIT 4-1. DOCUMENT MANAGEMENT SYSTEM SUMMARY COST ESTIMATE (July 1990–December 1991 [$000])

Task Description	1990	1991	Total
Project planning and control			
Project planning	$ 25	$ 5	$ 30
Project administration/management	40	30	70
Legal oversight	42	20	62
Document acquisition and control			
Inventory	15	—	15
Screening	50	18	68
Numbering	15	7	22
Reproduction and depository	65	40	105
Database design and development			
System design	15	—	15
Procedures development/documentation	15	5	20
Document processing	300	80	380
Transcript processing	20	40	60
System maintenance			
Database administration	25	30	55
Database storage	15	25	40
User training and support			
User training	8	10	18
Search and retrieval	30	70	100
Trial support	—	40	40
Total	$680	$420	$1,100

is important. The chapter first addresses issues of control over the physical documents, involving the more mundane tasks of locating, reviewing, and producing pieces of paper. A later section discusses issues relating to managing key information in or about the documents.

Perhaps the most important document control issue arises in pretrial discovery. Liberalized discovery rules, most notably Rule 26(b)(1) of the Federal Rules of Civil Procedure[7] and comparable state rules, permit each party to request documents from the other, primarily though depositions, interrogatories, and document production requests. Generally, any document relevant to an issue in the case is discoverable, unless a claim of privilege applies. Documents, themselves not relevant, that point to relevant information are discoverable.

This simplified explanation of complex rules of civil procedure provides only a basic lesson. Discovery is often the major, if not sole use of a document management system. At the outset, one must decide how to:

- Control production so that only relevant, nonprivileged documents are produced and so that none are omitted (defensive discovery)
- Track every document that has been acquired (offensive discovery) or produced (defensive discovery)

Establishing a control system to meet these and similar needs involves identifying, screening, numbering, reproducing, and archiving potentially relevant documents. Each of these tasks, which is relatively straightforward in cases involving few documents, presents a logistical challenge in bigger cases. The following sections provide more discussion of each such task.

Identifying Document Sources. Begin by ensuring that all potentially relevant documents are located, identified, and inventoried.

When locating documents, consider all potential document sources. These typically include corporate business records (both the client's and opponent's), third party, records, public domain records, prior cases, and the attorney's own files. The primary focus will be on business records. Depending on the nature of the case, one should first look at the active files from key executives, department managers, engineers, scientists, and other potential witnesses. Inactive files, generally located in company record centers, must be included and can yield important documents. Computer files are often sought to obtain quantitative data, but they are increasingly housing nonquantitative information as well and should not be overlooked as a potential source.

As sources of potentially relevant documents are identified, the files should be inspected to ascertain the departments, custodians, media types, and the volume of documents to be screened. A written "File Survey" should summarize this information. Exhibit 4-2 contains a pro forma file survey for a hypothetical case.

Although their approach may sometimes be less than systematic, attorneys and paralegals undertake these and similar tasks on every big case. By instilling the discipline of quantifying and scheduling the data collected as to volume, source, and types of documents identified during this stage, the CPA can play an important role in preparing for subsequent stages of the document management system.

Screening. Screening involves culling relevant documents from the universe of potentials. Winnowing those that require the attorney's detailed review presents a major challenge. Overinclusion can result in a morass of irrelevant information that one will have to deal with throughout the litigation, together with the cost, delay, and frustration that follows. Underinclusion can result in loss of pertinent information, risk of embarrassment to client and lawyer alike, and even sanctions.

Screening helps to strike a balance between over and underinclusion. This task is complex because the focus of a case changes as it proceeds. Issues that seem minor initially may become critical later, and new issues may arise. To avoid rescreening, counsel should err toward overincluding.

Develop written screening guidelines that define selection criteria before document screening. Screening guidelines should be designed to avoid subjective judgments that vary from reviewer to reviewer and from day to day. No matter how many lawyers and paralegals are to screen the documents, if the document population is large enough, there will not be enough time to read every page. For these reasons, screening criteria should be objective and at a high level. For example, if the case covers events occurring over a specific time period, the criteria should define the relevant date ranges. If the case does not involve financial transactions, certain types of financial records may be omitted. One can usually identify other document types for inclusion or omission altogether. The criteria, once drafted, should be tested for clarity and reliability.

One must not only properly prepare the screening criteria but also ensure that the criteria are consistently applied. This typically involves a quality control review program that often employs statistical sampling techniques.

Prepare a file-by-file inventory during the screening stage. This inventory, or "Screening Log" will contain more detailed information about reviewed documents than the higher level file survey. The Screening Log—such as the one shown in Exhibit 4-3—should record which files have been reviewed, by whom, on what date, and whether relevant material was selected. The log should also describe each selected file's contents.

Because it directly affects project cost, screening is a critical step in an effective document management program. Document management costs are directly proportional to the number of documents selected. Therefore, eliminating irrelevant documents through screening will avoid wasting subsequent processing costs.

Approach to Screening. The selected screening approaches depend, of course, on the case. The following lists several screening criteria that have consistently proven useful:

- Relevance—Screen based on whether each document (or file) is relevant or potentially relevant to the issues of fact. To avoid rescreening, err toward overinclusion. Develop case specific, objective relevance criteria. Test the criteria first by screening a small sample. Refine the criteria, as appropriate. When screening begins, separate documents into three "piles" (1) clearly relevant, (2) marginally relevant, and (3) not relevant. The "not relevant" pile can be ignored whereas the "clearly relevant" pile will be copied for further

EXHIBIT 4-2. FILE SURVEY

Attorney–Client Privelege | Attorney Workproduct

Person/position K. Blackburn, Director

Location Administration Bldg., Room 325

Department Regulatory Affairs

Contact S. Smith

Attorney/paralegal L. Bowers

Date survey conducted 7/5/87

Time spent on survey 4.5 Hours

Storage Unit Type	No. of Units	Storage Unit Type	No. of Units
Standard file drawer	75 drawers	Microfiche drawer	3
Lateral file drawer	14 drawers	Audio/video	
Desk file drawer	7 drawers	DP tapes	2
Open shelves		Data discs	

Index	Paper (Inches)	Microfilm/ fiche	Audio/ Video	DP Cards	DP Tapes	Data Disc
1. EPA Applications	240					
2. Product Registration	850	102				
3. Product Patent Information	600					
4. EPA Permits	50					
5. Regulatory Research	311			3	2	
6. Product Labels	40	50				
7. General & Miscellaneous	170					
Total	2261	152		3	2	

Item	Units of Measure
Paper or Reports	Inches—Measure linear inches in file drawer or box
Audio- /Videotapes	Minutes of recording
Data processing Cards	Inches (same as paper or reports)
Data processing Tapes	No. of reels
Data Disc	No. of documents
Microfilm	No. of documents & film size
Microfiche	No. of documents

Attorney/paralegal comments: ______________________________

____

____

EXHIBIT 4-3. SCREENING LOG (ATTORNEY WORKPRODUCT)

BOX NUMBER: ______ CUSTODIAN: ______ DATE: ______

DEPARTMENT: ______ TITLE: ______ REVIEWER: ______

FOLDER TITLE	COPY	INCLUDE	QUESTIONABLE	EXCLUDE	ID NUMBER
Title: ______ ______ Brand: ______ ______ Chemical Name: ______ ______ Document Dates: ______ ______	______ All ______ None ______ Marked Only	Product Label: ______ Product Application: Corn ______ Soybean ______ Wheat ______ Product Testing: Chemistry ______ Efficacy ______ Residue ______ Toxicity ______ Methodology ______	Regulatory Research ______ Application for Registration ______	Administrative ______ Financial ______ Planning ______ Competitive ______	Include: ______ Questionable: ______ Pages: ______

review and processing. One may decide to process the "marginally relevant" pile at a lesser priority or copy and "mothball" until needed.

- Privilege—The attorney–client privilege may shield communications between lawyer and client, including those between company executives and inhouse or outside counsel, from discovery. Privileged or not, such documents should be screened if relevant. The screening logs can include a notation as to privilege status. Even if shielded from discovery, the court may wish to review privileged documents, and it will almost certainly want a detailed list of any such documents withheld.
- Trade Secret—Documents dealing with proprietary company information and secrets are perhaps the most sensitive of all. A major problem arises when such documents clearly relate to a document request but are not privileged communications between attorney and client.

The classic example would be a request for the formula for Coca-Cola in a suit alleging patent infringement. In such instances, the court may allow production but would usually do so subject to a protective order to prevent the information's dissemination beyond the specific case. The screening logs should also note trade secret documents.

Importance of Document Retention Policy. Too often litigation attorneys bemoan a client's practice of saving too many documents for too long. Most people tend to keep every piece of paper that crosses their desks. This paper proliferation is exacerbated by people's tendency to send a copy of every document to almost everyone having anything to do with a matter. The resulting monumental buildup of ammunition awaits ignition in subsequent litigation.

Document retention policies and practices are currently the focus of attention among corporate general counsel. Although destroying documents that are the subject of current litigation is unlawful, one may routinely dispose of documents according to an approved companywide *document retention policy*. Companies should implement such programs. Of course, they must follow the dozens of federal and state laws that mandate retention requirements for various businesses and document types. An ounce of prevention in this arena can avoid expensive cures later.

The Dilemma of Duplicate Documents. Copies of the same document frequently turn up during screening. One may often identify 20 or 30 copies of the same document within managers' files of a large company. A document's listed recipients may account for some of the copies, but recipients often make "blind" copies for others. These recipients also make copies, and on it goes. No recipient can be ignored because a major legal issue frequently involves who saw the document and, by inference, knows of its contents.

Another duplicate document problem relates to "marginal notes." Comments that a recipient writes on a document can be telling because they convey the recipient's state of mind. For example, if the document relates to a proposed new company pricing policy later alleged to be predatory, a comment written by an executive that merely says "concur" can be relevant. Can one say that this document is a duplicate of the others, given the marginal note? The obvious answer suggests why no duplicate can be ignored completely.

If a document request asks for all copies of a particular document, how can every duplicate be located with certainty? Because the duplicates came from different files, they need to be listed together. This problem, and others like it, can best be handled with a computer, as discussed in the last section of this chapter.

Numbering. Perhaps the most significant step for maintaining control over a document collection is numbering. Generally, every page of every document selected in the screening process should receive a unique, identifying number. Unique document identification facilitates control, simplifies storage and retrieval, and satisfies production requirements in most courts.

Carefully design the numbering system. Designated prefixes can be assigned for separate collections based on source or case. Random sequential numbering is simplest because it avoids having to decide which prefix applies to a given document. Many lawyers prefer the no-prefix approach because in an adversary's hands the document number will reveal nothing about its source.

Numbers can be applied to the documents using either a "Bates"-type of stamp or a computer-printed gummed label. Certain microfilming equipment can also automatically apply a number to the film. To avoid the appearance of "gaps," one must carefully ensure that every number within a series is accounted for.

Some attorneys prefer to number only produced documents or to renumber documents before production to avoid gaps in the numbers. They argue that gaps raise unnecessary questions. This tactic is perhaps overly conservative. Most courts will accept the explanation that all documents were numbered for control purposes but that some were not responsive and, therefore, were not produced.

Reproduction. Big cases usually require much document copying. Opponents will not surrender their original documents to an adversary for very long and, with the possible exception of archived files, active client company files must be returned promptly. Thus one must find and implement a way to copy selected documents.

Tasks that one takes for granted in a normal office environment can become problems in "big" litigation. Consider making two copies each of 10 million pages of documents in 3 months. If each machine operator can disassemble, copy, and reassemble 5000 pages per day, 4000 machine days would be required. This means that 15 machines would have to work 24 hours a day, 7 days a week to complete the job on schedule. This assumes no breakdowns.

Where should this work be done? Few lawyers would send 10 million pages of documents to the local "Sir Speedy" for copying. Consequently, special arrangements have to be made for personnel and equipment. As with every step in the document processing pipeline, one must implement exact procedures and quality control standards to ensure accuracy and consistency.

How Many Copies? Generally one should make one control copy and as many working copies as counsel needs. Additional working copies can later be made from the control copy. This assumes that originals will no longer be readily available. Most courts accept clean copies of documents in place of originals.

Alternative Image Storage Systems. Although this chapter does not intend to exhaustively examine the field of micrographics and more sophisticated electronic imaging systems, some comments concerning their role in litigation support are appropriate.

Micrographics. In large cases, one should use microfilm—not as a substitute for hard copy but to supplement it. Microfilm has many advantages. It is easier and cheaper to store, ship, and reproduce than hard copy. To illustrate, a 10-million-page document collection can be stored on about 4000 rolls of microfilm, each averaging 2500 pages or "frames." Two microfilm file cabinets would store these rolls. On the other hand, the hard copy equivalent requires approximately 5000 shelf-feet of file space (at 2000 pages per linear foot). This translates to higher facilities costs that will accumulate throughout the life of a case.

To avoid the calamitous consequences of a fire at the archive, one should maintain a backup set of the entire document collection at a separate location. The cost of replicating the hard copy archive, however, even at 5 cents per page, would be $500,000! This might well discourage even the most security-conscious client from making a backup set. Because microfilm is relatively cheap to reproduce (under $10.00 per roll), cost is less likely to prevent one from making a backup copy of the collection.

Microfilm also ensures that document integrity will not be lost because pages cannot be removed from a roll of film and become misplaced. Contrast this to hard copy where misfilings occur routinely, resulting in irretrievable pages.

Pages can also be retrieved faster from microfilm. With the aid of computer-assisted microfilm retrieval readers (CAR systems) and reader/printers, a requested "page" can be retrieved, reviewed, optionally printed, and refiled without the operator leaving the work station. A job that would take several minutes manually can be accomplished in seconds using microfilm.

Despite the advantages of microfilm, attorneys accustomed to working from hard copy are unlikely to change their habits. Therefore, one cannot expect litigators easily to surrender paper document collections and replace them with microfilm or other paperless imaging systems. The client should, nonetheless, be advised that hard copy and microfilm can coexist and that each has its place in document management.

Optical Disk. Recent advances in high-capacity disk storage technology now make it practical in certain cases to store document images digitally. This process requires that each page be "scanned" using a cameralike scanner, whereas microfilm involves a more conventional camera that films each page. Once stored digitally, images can be indexed and recalled at computer speed, much faster than can be achieved using microfilm readers and roll film. Comparing microfilm to disk storage is analogous to comparing the time required to find a particular song on a cassette tape, which requires rewinding it to the point where the song begins, and the much faster method of finding the same song on a compact disk, which can be directly (i.e., randomly) accessed.

Both technologies produce a single hard copy in roughly the same time and with the same quality. Printing from microfilm involves a paper copier, almost identical in design to those used to copy standard documents. Printing from the disk involves a now-standard laser printer. But higher volume copying, such as of an entire roll of microfilm, can be done very quickly using copy flow equipment.

Digital storage has not yet replaced its analog counterpart on microfilm. Nor is it likely to for several more years. Although disk storage costs are declining rapidly, storing images on disk rather than microfilm is still more costly. Most experts view this situation as temporary and believe that optical disks will become more widespread for storing large document collections.

Establishing a Document Archive. Housing a large document collection requires attention to several key issues:

- How should the documents be organized?
- Who should have access?
- Where should the archive be located?
- How much space is needed?
- What other facilities (e.g., copiers, microfilm reader/printers) are required on the premises?

Of course, the needs of each case will vary so that these questions cannot be answered here, but the practitioner should resolve these and similar issues early in the planning phase.

File Organization. Document files may be organized physically in one of several ways:

- By source
- Alphabetically by author
- Chronologically
- By document identification number

Each organization method has advantages, depending on how counsel will use the documents. For example, one can more easily prepare fact chronologies if the documents are already filed by date. One can also more easily assemble author indexes if the documents are filed alphabetically by author.

Each organizational approach also has its limitations. Because lawyers invariably need to access files in several different ways, the choice of one filing scheme inherently limits accessibility by others. To overcome this problem, litigators have traditionally created several files, each organized differently. As document-intensive litigation increased, this approach became increasingly inefficient. In response to this growth, lawyers began applying indexing techniques resembling those of most libraries.

One copy of the document is filed and card catalogues or printed indexes prepared to cross-reference the date, author, source, or any other search criteria to the document's physical location. The filing system can be as simple as the Dewey Decimal System, so long as a reliable index exists. Exhibits 4-4 and 4-5 provide examples of chronological and author indexes, respectively.

EXHIBIT 4-4. CHRONOLOGICAL INDEX: 1985 PESTICIDE-B REPORTS BY DATE

Date: 07/21/88 PAGE: 1

Document Number	Document Date	Author	Title
002281-002834	850314	Kendall, R.T.	Residual Efficacy of Pesticide-B
428923-428986	850315	Studley, D.D.G.	Environmental Effects of Pesticide-B
521100-521159	850329	Munson, A.A.	Fate of Pesticide-B in Mammals
062971-062991	850507	Crawley, A.G.	Short-Term Exposure to Pesticide-B
775428-775435	850529	Thompson, J.E.	Study of Residual Toxicity of Pesticide-B to Humans
925721-925732	850811	Wilcox, E.D.	Pesticide-B: Residue in Wheat
927011-927022	850811	Wilcox, E.D.	Pesticide-B: Residue in Wheat
063721-063778	851212	Woodward, R.	Teratogenic Study of Pesticide-B

Although indexes represent a significant step forward in improving document access, computer software developed recently has extended this concept. A card catalog index limits the researcher to only one criterion (e.g., author, date, title) at a time. Today, search criteria can be combined into computer queries such as: AUTHOR-Jones *and* DATE between January 15, 1982 *and* June 30, 1988, *and* TITLE contains "toxicity." In a few seconds, this search might identify the three documents contained in a collection of over a million. Even with a good manual index system, the same search could require days.

This example provides a glimpse of the tactical advantage that a well-designed computer retrieval system provides. In a document-intensive case, hundreds of similar "needle-in-the-haystack" searches may be needed quickly. Experienced litigators know that such a task would require an enormous effort to manually cull through the thousands of potentially relevant documents in search of the relevant few.

Security Concerns. The CPA practitioner will probably encounter the question of who should have document access. The opportunity for unauthorized access can create problems nearly as serious as the fact of it. Not only is legal privilege involved, but a lost or misplaced document can, and has, caused untold embarrassment to more than one corporate counsel.

One should therefore limit the number of people with access to the documents. Identification badges are typically issued to those permitted access to document storage areas. Archive rooms should be lockable, or documents should be stored in lockable cabinets. Fire alarms and sprinklers should be standard. An off-site backup copy or microfilm copy of the entire collection should be made to protect against a catastrophic fire or flood.

Attorneys and staff who remove documents should follow sign-out procedures. Thus, every document should be accounted for at all times. The practitioner can assist counsel by implementing controls and procedures that will ensure document accountability.

EXHIBIT 4-5. AUTHOR INDEX: 1985 PESTICIDE-B DOCUMENTS BY AUTHOR

DATE: 07/21/88 PAGE: 1

Author	Document Number	Document Date	Document Type	Title
Brooks, J.D.	112105-112108	850107	Letter	Toxicity of Pesticide-B to Mammals
Brooks, J.D.	112786-112786	850202	Graph	Efficacy Levels 3, 6, & 9 Months after Application
Crawley, A.G.	062971-062971	850507	Report	Short-Term Exposure to Pesticide-B
Kendall, R.T.	002279-002280	850527	Letter	
Kendall, R.T.	002281-002384	850314	Report	Residual Efficacy of Pesticide-B
Munson, A.A.	521100-521159	850329	Report	Fate of Pesticide-B in Mammals
Nash, J.S.	007534-007538	850705	Memo	
O'Hara, T.	325607-325607	850719	Table	Chemical Properties of Pesticide-B
Studley, D.G.	428921-428922	850329	Letter	
Studley, D.G.	428923-428986	850329	Report	Environmental Effects of Pesticide-B
Sunstreet, M.K.	429521-429522	85040	Letter	
Thompson, J.E.	775428-775435	850529	Report	Study of Residual Toxicity of Pesticide-B to Humans
Wilcox, E.D.	925721-925732	850811	Report	Pesticide-B: Residue in Wheat
Wilcox, E.D.	927011-927022	850811	Report	Pesticide-B: Residue in Wheat
Wilcox, E.D.	925920-925920	850903	Letter	
Woodward, R.	063721-063779	850212	Report	Teratogenic Study of Pesticide-B

Facilities Requirements. Normally documents and support staff are housed in facilities separated from the law office's ongoing operations. This might be in temporary space established specifically for the litigation or in a permanent litigation support facility. In establishing such a facility, one should plan for adequate space for offices, secretaries, document storage, coding activities, conference rooms, supplies, staging areas, and comfort facilities. One also needs to provide for equipment including furniture, shelving, security, telephones, telex, fax, copiers, microfilm readers, and computers. The overall project plan should include a space and equipment plan, and the project budget should include space and equipment costs.

Information Control

So far this chapter has addressed the first major component of an effective document management program: control over the documents. This section discusses the second major component: control over information contained in or about the documents. An attorney's information requirements about the documents in a case will vary substantially, depending on the nature and issues of each case.

Litigation support experts have lumped standard needs into several broad information categories. These categories include control information, bibliographic information, subject matter information, and usage information.

The following provides a general discussion and examples of these categories. This section is by no means exhaustive, and the reader should refer to the bibliography at the end of the chapter for supplemental sources.

Control Information. Control information is not information contained in documents but rather describes the documents' attributes: source, identification number, and type.

Source. Knowing where each document came from is extremely important in understanding its contextual significance in a case. This information may also be necessary to establish a chain of custody or to authenticate a document before it can be admitted into evidence. Therefore, one must ensure that the source of each document has been consistently and accurately recorded.

Source information can simply be the name of the party or other source who produced the document. For documents produced from client files, the custodian's name should be recorded. The custodian's department and title when the document was produced can also prove very useful. If the document came from a records center, the records center's file locator should be recorded. This information can enable counsel to track the document's original source using the records center's own tracking system.

Identification Number. Every page of every document selected as potentially relevant should have a unique identifying number. This number is an extremely important piece of control information and will be used repeatedly throughout the litigation to uniquely identify the document. Every list of documents prepared during the case will contain the document identification number, or doc id. If the document archive is organized by doc id., which most frequently occurs, this control number will provide the key to locating any document in the archive.

Type. Case preparation typically involves collecting and analyzing documents according to their common characteristics. Correspondence, invoices, blueprints, regulations, board minutes, and budgets are examples of documents with particular characteristics in common, referred to as document "types."

"Get me the board minutes for ABC Company during 1986"; "Let me see the invoices from XYZ Company for amounts over $1000"; and "Prepare a chronological list of correspondence from Jones to Smith" are all examples of attorney document requests. In document-intensive litigation, each of these requests would require an extensive effort to complete unless "document type" had been recorded in advance.

Bibliographic Information. Bibliographic information includes information contained on a document's face such as its date, author, addressee, and title.

Date. A document's date decides its significance in the context of a particular case. When was the representation made, contract executed, transaction posted, notice sent, or pricing change implemented? The answer to these questions and hundreds like them is often central to the factual issues.

Name. Who wrote, approved, or received each document provides evidence not only of who was responsible for various acts or omissions but also who had knowledge of the alleged actions. Consequently, the names of authors, addressees, and even document recipients should be systematically recorded. The person's title and organization affiliation when the document was written can be equally valuable.

Of course, many people may have reviewed a document, even though their names do not appear on it. Because of the tendency to make many copies of a document, duplicates can appear almost anywhere. The identity of "blind"-copy recipients may be ascertained from the document's custodian. Names identified in a document's body are also important to record. These "mentioned names" can lead the researcher to sources of additional information, including other documents, that may yield relevant facts.

Title. A document's title enables identification without the readers having to summarize its contents. Just as a library's "title card catalog" provides a means of identifying items of interest, document titles provide a means for quickly searching for documents of potential relevance.

Subject Matter Information. A document's factual content is perhaps most important. A successful lawyer must understand and analyze the factual and contextual significance of all documents relevant to each issue in a case. Preserving the results of this factual analysis is one of the most important purposes of a document management system.

Developing subject classification systems require an expert's services. Case subject matter should be organized into a hierarchical scheme, or "taxonomy." Subject codes will then be recorded to the extent needed to define the document's content.

Designing a taxonomy and the time and labor required to extract subject matter can be the most expensive aspect of a litigation support system. Subject matter capture is inherently subjective. For these reasons, subject matter capture may be reserved for critical documents only.

Usage Information. Attorneys frequently need to create lists of:

- Documents produced
- Documents used as exhibits
- Privileged documents withheld

In mass tort actions, more than one case has turned on an attorney's success or failure in ensuring consistent document productions. It is, therefore, essential in such cases that detailed records be kept each time a document is produced, withheld, or used as an exhibit.

The reader should realize by now that control, bibliographic, subject matter, and usage information will all be easier to record and retrieve with computers, the focus of the remainder of this chapter.

Use of Computers

The underlying principles of document and information control are the same whether one uses computers. However, a well-designed computerized document retrieval system enables one to do things that a manual system cannot. But at what cost? Do the benefits warrant the expense and additional management and technical complexity introduced by computers? This is a threshold question that lawyers must answer before committing resources.

Justification for Computerization. Costs associated with developing a computerized document management system must be assessed alongside the alternative costs of manual systems. If the "big" case characteristics are present, a computerized approach will probably be cost effective. Specifically, the higher the exposure, the larger the document volume, the more complex the issues of fact and law, and the longer the expected time frame, the easier to justify computerization.

For large cases, the costs of managing documents manually can equal or exceed costs for computerizing. Retrieving needed documents quickly and accurately may not be possible manually. Most lawyers involved in legal research have benefited from the enhanced speed and thoroughness of computerized retrieval through services such as LEXIS and WESTLAW. The tactical advantage offered by similar systems for retrieving documents over an opponent who is not computerized may, in some cases, outweigh considerations based purely on cost alone.

The computerization decision should weigh the costs of both alternatives and consider the intangible factors.

Database Development. Once one decides to computerize, database development can begin. The lawyers, system users, and technical experts must define the proposed system's structure and content. Key questions to resolve immediately include the following: How much information contained in and about each document will be needed? Will subject matter capture be necessary, or will bibliographic information suffice? What hardware and software will be used? Who will create the database?

Full-Text Databases. The litigation team must decide whether the computer database should store a document's full text or only bibliographic and/or subject matter information. Generally, one records encoded information on the database for ordinary business documents and the full text for testimony. Testimony requires full text because the lawyer needs to know what a witness actually said. Full-text retrieval software allows searches similar to LEXIS and WESTLAW, except that the database contains case-related documents, not judicial opinions, regulations, and statutes.

Full-text transcript processing is increasing. Many court reporters record depositions using computer-aided devices and can provide a magnetic tape or disk of the transcript just as easily as the hard copy. Because this requires minimal intellectual processing, the full-text transcript can be made available on the database more rapidly than can a transcript digest.

The full-text database presents several disadvantages. First, the greater storage requirements place a bigger strain on system capacity. Second, database management software cannot accommodate full-text retrieval, so one must use specialized, full-text software. Third, one cannot easily find important subjects that the text identifies indirectly. Finally, unless enhanced to make explicit, vague references to pronouns and dates will impair search recall. For example, "She alleged . . ." must be enhanced to "She (KELLY, JE) alleged . . ."; "The next day . . ." must be changed to "the next day (900312). . . ."

Despite these drawbacks of full text, the advantage of locating any witness's testimony on any subject in seconds is certainly appealing. Consequently, these systems are experiencing an unprecedented popularity.

Document Coding. The coding process extracts information from documents and records this information in a structured way for database entry. This process captures control, bibliographic, subject matter, and usage information, depending on the document's importance. Coding guidelines dictate which types of documents to code and how to code each type.

One typically uses a coding form to record the information. Exhibit 4-6 displays a sample document coding form. After review, the coding form is keyed into the database, that is, run through the software's database creation programs. The result is a searchable database containing document *surrogates*. Properly done, the result will provide a fast and accurate means to locate any document based on its relevance to a particular search.

Resource Alternatives. Organizing a litigation support project requires assembly of the following: (1) hardware and software to process and store the information; (2) legal and technical professional staff resources to review and process documents; and (3) project management personnel. Depending on cost, availability, and other factors, several sources can provide these resources: law firm, litigant, vendors, and consultants.

Hardware. Although a mainframe computer was once the only litigation support option, minicomputers and microcomputers now offer the same capabilities but with smaller capacity. Microcomputers currently can handle on the order of 10,000 documents, but only a limited number of users can access the database. Minicomputers can generally support several concurrent users and databases on the order of 100,000 documents. Cases with over 100,000 documents will almost certainly require a mainframe.

To ascertain the hardware requirements, one must develop reliable projections of current and anticipated document volumes. A few law firms have sufficient hardware capacity to handle the big case. If the law firm cannot supply the needed hardware, two alternatives are available. One could use a time-sharing service that specializes in litigation support. Exhibit 4-7 lists some well-known full-service litigation support vendors.

An alternative to using vendor resources is the litigant itself. Large corporations often have excess computer resources that they can dedicate to litigation needs and at substantially less cost than outside service bureaus. Client data processing departments, however, usually lack litigation support expertise. To adequately serve lawyers' needs, the project must have a high level of expertise and priority dedicated to it. If the client cannot commit the needed level, the project should use outside resources.

Software. Many software options are available for handling document storage and retrieval needs, whether the project uses a micro-, mini-, or mainframe computer. Unless the client has already invested in a particular type of software, counsel may ask the practitioner to recommend one.

The number of options complicates software selection. Therefore, the practitioner must become familiar with the basic features and functions of document management software to advise counsel of the most appropriate choice for the particular case.

Some of the more important software features to consider include the ability to:

- Operate on a variety of hardware systems
- Handle full-text and encoded information
- Produce customized reports for display or printing
- Enter and validate data on-line or in batch mode
- Permit the user to easily use and learn the system
- Secure files, records, and fields from unauthorized access
- Perform proximity, key word, and root searching
- Add, modify and delete information efficiently

Exhibit 4-8 lists several popular litigation support software packages.

Staff. Finding the needed project staff can be the most challenging aspect of implementing a document management system. A very large case could require hundreds of screeners, coders, reviewers, data entry operators, and file clerks to process potentially millions of pages of documents in a relatively short (6 months or less) time. Even with strong management, this becomes difficult.

EXHIBIT 4-6. DOCUMENT CODING FORM

Confidential — Attorney Workproduct

DOCUMENT CODING FORM

Document ID number: [ ][ ][ ][ ][ ][ ] — [ ][ ][ ][ ][ ][ ]

Document date: [ ][ ][ ][ ][ ][ ]

Attachment range: [ ][ ][ ][ ][ ][ ] — [ ][ ][ ][ ][ ][ ]

Document type:

Contract	________	Memo	________
Financial	________	Minutes	________
Form	________	Notes	________
Graphics	________	Printout	________
Invoice	________	Proposal	________
Legal	________	Published	________
Letter	________	Report	________
List	________	Specifications	________
Manual	________	Telephone Record	________

Marginalia present: Y

Privilege status:

Privileged & confidential	________
Attorney workproduct	________
Document under seal	________

Author/affiliation:

Recipient/affiliation:

Copyee/affiliation:

(*Exhibit continues on p. 78.*)

EXHIBIT 4-6. *(Continued)*

Title:

Subject Codes:	Chemistry ______	Product A ______	
	Efficacy ______	Product B ______	
	Residue ______	Product C ______	
	Administrative ______	Product D ______	

EXHIBIT 4-7. FULL-SERVICE LITIGATION SUPPORT VENDORS

Vendor Name	Address	Telephone
Acumenics Research & Technology	9990 Lee Highway Fairfax, VA 22030	703-359-6300
American Legal Systems (ALS)	475 Park Avenue South 7th Floor New York, NY 10016	212-213-0550 800-221-3075
Aspen Systems Corp.	1600 Research Blvd. Rockville, MD 20850	301-251-5329 800-545-2327
ATLIS	6011 Executive Blvd. Rockville, MD 20852	301-770-3000 800-638-6595
C.A.C.I. Inc.	3030 N. Clarendon Blvd. Suite 200 Arlington, VA 22201	703-522-3133 703-841-4598
Compulit Inc.	200 Alta Dale SE Ada, MI 49301	616-676-3400
Document Automation Corp. (DAC)	101 Lakeforest Blvd. Suite 310 Gaithersburg, MD 20877	301-590-8140 800-776-1028
Electronic Data Systems Corp. (EDS)	13600 EDS Drive Herndon, VA 22071	703-742-2073
The Gottlieb Group	876 South Windsor Blvd. Los Angeles, CA 90005	213-938-2889
Legal Information Technology Group	12121 Wilshire Blvd. Suite 920 Los Angeles, CA 90025	213-207-2666
The Litidex Centers	7887 Katy Freeway Houston, TX 77024	713-688-0700 800-548-4339
Litigation Systems, Inc.	164 Rollins Avenue Suite 300 Rockville, MD 20852	301-231-0004
Quorum Systems	8100 34th Avenue South P.O. Box 0 Minneapolis, MN 55440-4700	612-853-6504 800-328-4454
TechLaw Systems, Inc.	14500 Avion Parkway Suite 300 Chantilly, VA 22021	703-818-1000 800-TEC-HLAW

The law firm's paralegals and clerical staff, if available, and temporary hires can provide staff resources. Litigation support vendors also offer another good source of document processing and management staff.

Litigation Support Vendors. Several litigation support vendors provide document and data-processing services on a case basis (see Exhibit 4-7). If carefully managed, these vendors can provide a cost-effective solution.

EXHIBIT 4-8. TABLE OF COMMONLY USED LITIGATION SUPPORT DATABASE SOFTWARE PACKAGES

Software	Vendor	Location	Micro	Mini	Mainframe
ask Sam	ask Sam Systems	Perry, FL	×		
BASICS	Information Dimensions, Inc.	Columbus, OH		×	×
BRS/Search	BRS Information Technologies	Latham, NY	×	×	×
Discovery	Data Dynamics Corp.	Mesa, AZ	×		
INMAGIC	Inmagic, Inc.	Cambridge, MA	×	×	
INQUIRE	InfoData Systems, Inc.	Falls Church, VA			×
Micro LS/Microtext	Document Automation Corp.	Wilkes-Barre, PA	×		
STAIRS	IBM	Atlanta, GA			×
TEXTBANK	Group L Corp.	Herndon, VA	×		
Text DBMS	Data Retrieval	Milwaukee, WI		×	
ZyIndex Plus	Zylab Corp.	Chicago, IL	×		

The vendor industry is highly competitive. The practitioner should pay particular attention to the following factors when helping counsel evaluate and select a litigation support vendor:

- *Quality*—An acceptable standard of coding accuracy should be established at the outset. Most vendors are willing to warrant a 95 percent accuracy level. To achieve this level, the vendor must have an effective quality control program. The advisor should ensure that the vendor meets this standard, and the contract should provide for appropriate independent acceptance testing. Failure to achieve an acceptable accuracy level can diminish both the search recall (ability to find relevant documents) and precision (ability to avoid irrelevant documents).
- *Schedule*—The vendor should commit to a mutually agreeable project schedule that may need to be changed if circumstances so dictate. Contractual provision should include penalty assessments if the vendor misses critical deadlines, as the litigation's success may depend on vendor timeliness.
- *Management and Experience*—Vendors advertise their ability to stay on schedule and within budget. Meeting this representation depends on the experience and effectiveness of the vendor's management team. Therefore, vendor selection should weigh heavily the proposed team's commitment and credentials.
- *Price and Payment*—Most vendors will agree to fixed unit pricing for document processing activities, whereas time and materials pricing is customary for management staff. Despite the *pricing* method, *payment* should be tied to performance. Because the two most critical performance measures are timeliness and accuracy, a good vendor contract will reward quality work completed on schedule, while penalizing tardy, error-prone performance.
- *Software*—Most vendors use one of the software packages shown in Exhibit 4-8. Because software differences are, to a great extent, a matter of trade-offs, software is normally not a primary vendor selection criterion. However, in circumstances that dictate, for example, compatibility with certain hardware or other databases, the vendor's software choice may be determinative.

Databases for Legal Workproduct. During lengthy litigation, the number of filings, memos, and legal documents can grow into the thousands, and become as burdensome to manage as the evidentiary documents. Computers can significantly improve access to pleadings, memoranda, deposition outlines, witness interview notes, regulatory materials, and other legal workproduct.

A workproduct database, in addition to servicing the document control function, can be used to synthesize and disseminate attorney analysis, case dockets, and general strategy. Over time, as more and more materials are added, memories fade, and staff turnover increases, the workproduct database will become the institutional memory of the case.

Developing a workproduct database involves the same control, coding, and database creation issues as that of the evidentiary document database. One must implement screening, numbering, and microfilming and decide the type of coding or full-text treatment to be followed. Staff and machine resources must be deployed to perform the needed processing functions.

Once implemented, a workproduct database can save duplicative research, decrease redrafting time, and improve the consistency of legal positions. Attorney efficiency and effectiveness should increase with a well-conceived and implemented workproduct management system.

Benefits and Uses. A major benefit of a litigation support system results from the very process of developing it. With a team available to systematically screen, review, and organize the documents, counsel can focus on case preparation rather than bogging down in a paper morass. However, a litigation support system does not free counsel from reviewing the documents. Rather, it enables counsel to review them in a more orderly way, that is, by selectively locating from the *universe* of documents those that respond to a particular inquiry.

Assume that the litigation support system is built. Now what? The following demonstrates some practical applications that will help the litigant obtain a good return on the investment.

Index Listings. With most document management software, each *field* of information coded is stored in a separate computer *index* that can be displayed or printed. Thus, an *author* index yields an alphabetical list of all authors; a *subject code* index lists all subject codes, and so forth. Typically, such indexes also list the number of documents in which the term appears:

Name	Docs
Abrams, J.	67
Adams, H.	7
Akers, W.	23
Akkers, W.	1
Alen, S.	3
Allen, S.	120
Anderson, J.	49

Indexes and understanding document mix and content are a prerequisite to formulating good searches. The indexes will also highlight apparent mistakes, as the example here demonstrates. This provides an excellent tool for identifying and correcting certain types of database errors.

Witness Preparation. When preparing a witness for testimony, an effective technique is to identify and review documents that the witness authored or received. When preparing for an examination, counsel must also know which documents an adverse witness wrote or read. A database search will accomplish this in seconds, and a report can be printed by date or topic.

Production History. This chapter previously discussed how the litigation support system can keep track of produced documents. Reports optionally can be printed by source (party acquired from) or, in a multiple production action, by the party that requested the produced document. One can separately list documents withheld (either for reasons of privilege or nonresponsiveness).

Fact Chronologies. Case preparation commonly involves factual chronologies, either for a particular witness or for a particular topic. Database records do not have to store only information about actual documents. Records can be created for key facts. Millions of seemingly unrelated facts can then be tied together by sorting them on dates, subjects, and names.

Transcripts. The full text of testimony can be context searched. Searches can be limited to particular witnesses or expanded to include all witnesses. This technique can be useful for locating corroborating or impeaching testimony.

Another effective device is to print lists of witnesses who have testified and on what date(s). By entering completed and expected depositions, the system can provide control reports indicating who has testified and who has yet to testify.

By enhancing the transcript with subject codes, testimony can be searched and printed by topic. Some lawyers like to reorganize the entire transcript according to their case outlines.

If the case involves many system users, the transcript database can serve as a central repository, avoiding the need to make and distribute many copies. Each user would have on-line access to the entire transcript collection and could print all or part of any transcript locally.

Interrogatories. Interrogatories, like depositions, lend themselves to full text treatment. A lawyer responding to an interrogatory can use the database to match up interrogatory questions with prior responses, helping to ensure consistency. With equal efficiency, the database can be used for research in drafting interrogatories.

NOTES

1. *United States v. IBM*, 58 F.R.D. 556 (S.D.N.Y. 1973).
2. See 28 USC 1407 authorizing establishment of a Multidistrict Litigation (MDL) Judicial Panel. Two of the early cases brought under this statute involving computer usage include *In Re Petroleum Products*, 393 F.Supp. 1081 (D. ML 1975); and *In Re IBM Peripherals*, 77 F.R.D. 39 (N.D. Cal. 1977). The MDL statute enabled federal courts to transfer to a single district a number of cases pending in different districts where they shared common questions of fact.
3. *United States v. IBM* 58 F.R.D. 556 (S.D.N.Y. 1973).
4. *United States v. AT&T*, 642 F.2d 1285 (D.C. Cir. 1980).
5. *Pennzoil Co. v. Texaco, Inc.*, No. 84-05905 (Tex. Dist. Nov. 19, 1985).
6. *United States v. IBM*, 58 F.R.D. 556 (S.D.N.Y. 1973).
7. Fed. R. Civ. P. 26(b) (1) expressly authorizes a discovering party to inquire about "the existence, description, nature, custody, condition and location of any books, documents, or other tangible things."

BIBLIOGRAPHY

Amon, J.L., and N. Marcoux, "The Cornerstone of Automating Litigation: Good Manual Systems," *Legal Administrator* 42 (Spring 1983).

Bayer, B.D., "Microcomputer Litigation Aid: 3 Approaches," *National Law Journal* (August 26, 1985).

Block, M., "Use of Alternative Databases Grows for Litigation Support," *National Law Journal* (June 16, 1986).

Bush, J.W., ed., *Computers & Litigation Support: New Approach to Information Management* (Harcourt Brace Jovanovich, 1979).

Cabot, H.R., and L.J. Hoffman, "Using Litigation Support Systems," 23 *Arizona Bar Journal* 14 (August–September 1987).

Canning, B., "Automating Document Management," *Office Administration & Automation* 51 (April 1985).

Clewes, V.L., "Transcript Automation Is Aid to Trial Lawyers," *Legal Tech Newsletter* (October 1986).

Cwiklo, W.E., ed., *Computers in Litigation Support* (Petrocelli Books, Inc., 1979).

———, "Image Management Systems in Litigation Support," 13 *Legal Economics* 54 (November–December 1987).

Drucker, P.F., "How to Measure the Benefits of a Computerized Information System," 3 *Law Practice Management* 39 (May 1987).

DuBowe, J.S., "Automating Litigation Support: A Litigator's Primer," *American Bar Association Journal* 1118 (September 1982).

Emerson, J.D., "Litigation Management Support Systems," *Legal Economics* 49 (September–October 1983).

Fennell, W., "Litigation Support: How to Get the Best of What's Around," 5 *of Counsel* 7 (July 1986).

Goldberg, L.R., "The Use of Computer-Based Evidence in Litigation," *St. Louis Bar Journal* 43 (Summer 1985).

Harmon, D.E., "Put a Handle on Large Trials (with Small Computers)," *Legal Economics* 59 (May–June 1985).

Harrington, W., "Full-Text Transcripts Can Now Be Stored Easily," *National Law Journal* (July 28, 1986).

Haynes, S.L., *Computers and Litigation Support* (Law & Business, Inc./Harcourt Brace Jovanovich, 1981).

Jerome, R., "How to Develop a Successful Litigation Support Capability," *National Law Journal* (March 2, 1987).

———, "Subject Matter Control in Litigation Support," *Legal Tech Newsletter* (November 1985).

Kinney, E.H., *Litigation Support Systems: An Attorney's Guide* (Callaghan & Company, 1980).

Krueckeberg, J.H., "A Litigation Filing System," *Legal Economics* 38 (September–October 1984).

Martin, C., "A Simple Litigation Support System with dBase III," *The Lawyer's PC* (August 1, 1985).

Mednick, H., "The Computer Is Litigation Management's Biggest Gun," *Canadian Lawyer* 31 (April 1984).

Meltzer, C.A., "Automation that Supports Litigation," *National Law Journal* (June 22, 1987).

Norris, G.L., "Personal Computers and the Litigation Firm," 46 *The New Bulletin of the Iowa State Bar Association* 16 (June–July 1986).

Parmet, J.C., and J.W. Davidson, "Document Management Options for PC's Increase," *National Law Journal* (February 2, 1987).

———, "Software Options for PC Litigation Support," 4 *Legal Tech Newsletter* 3 (June 1986).

"Preparing Products Liability Cases," 72 *American Bar Association Journal* 69 (May 1, 1986).

Poirier, C.J., G.C. Robb, and J.R. Mosher, "Computer-Based Litigation Support Systems: The Discoverability Issue," 54 *University of Missouri Kansas City Law Review* 3 (1986).

Potash, S., "Litigation Support for Small Law Firms," 71 *American Bar Association Journal* 68 (March 1985).

Quinn, J.W., "Document Management is Key to Litigator's Success," *Legal Times* (August 29, 1983).

Schneider, A.H., "Turning to Automation in Litigation," *National Law Journal* (June 16, 1986).

Siemer, D.C., and D.S. Land, *Wilmer, Cutler & Pickering Manual on Litigation Support Databases* (John Wiley & Sons, Inc., 1987).

Snyder, P.S., "Stop Playing Hide and Seek with Your Documents," *American Bar Association Journal* 54 (April 1, 1986).

Strong, K.D., *Retrieval Systems for Lawyers* (American Bar Association, Section of Economics of Law Practice, 1980).

Thorpe, V., "How to Measure Quality in Your Litigation Support System," 6 *Legal Administrator* 50 (September–October 1987).

vom Baur, F.T., and W.M. Simmons, "How to Manage the Big Case without Computers," *Practice Lawyer* 45 (January 1983).

Young, J.H., M.E. Kris, and H.C. Trainor eds., *Use of Computers in Litigation* (American Bar Association, 1979).

LIST OF CASES

Pennzoil Co. v. Texaco, Inc., No. 84-05905 (Tex. Dist. Nov. 19, 1985)
In Re IBM Peripherals, 77 F.R.D. 39 (N.D. Cal. 1977)
In Re Petroleum Products, 393 F. Supp. 1091 (D.ML 1975)
United States v. AT&T, 642 F.2d 1285 (D.C. Cir. 1980)
United States v. IBM, 58 F.R.D. 556 (S.D.N.Y. 1973)

5

THE ART OF TESTIFYING

Brian P. Brinig

INTRODUCTION

Testifying, unlike the practice of accounting, does not involve precision. Rather, as an art, success requires knowing the setting and the tactics of the litigation process. This chapter will arm you with that knowledge. It examines the role of an expert witness and offers instruction for testifying at a deposition and at trial. The chapter identifies several techniques to employ during cross-examination to protect your analysis and conclusions.

The author thanks Michael W. Prairie for helping prepare a draft outline for this chapter.

THE STATUTORY SCHEME AND THE ISSUE OF ADMISSIBILITY

When an expert witness testifies, legal questions about that testimony may arise. Rules 702–706 of the Federal Rules of Evidence govern the testimony of expert witnesses in the federal courts. Although most states have similar rules, always check the specific rules that will apply to your testimony.

Like other evidence, expert testimony must be "admissible." In federal courts, expert testimony is admissible if it "will assist the trier of fact to understand the evidence or to determine a fact in issue" (Rule 702). The trial judge decides whether expert testimony meets this standard, and the judge possesses broad discretion on the issue (*Caisson Corp. v. Ingersoll Rand Co.*, 622 F.2d 672 (3d Cir. 1980)). Most states follow the federal approach to admissibility.

DEPOSITIONS AND THE EXPERT'S ROLE

Importance of Depositions

A deposition involves an examination of a witness under oath by the attorney of the party requesting the deposition. A court reporter records the testimony and produces a written transcript. Generally, a deposition's purpose is to elicit information relevant to the lawsuit from a witness.

The deposition is an important tool in the pretrial discovery process. Most business litigation settles prior to trial, and the decision when—and on what terms—to settle often turns on the evaluation by both sides' attorneys of the testimony and demeanor of the deposed individuals.

The Expert's Role

An expert witness may play two critical roles in the deposition process. The first occurs when counsel is preparing to depose the opposing expert. The expert will almost always be more knowledgeable than counsel about the issues to be raised at your counterpart's deposition, so you can provide assistance. The expert should review the following areas with counsel: (1) background, experience, and reputation of the opposing expert; (2) weaknesses, if any, in the method and analysis used by the opponent's expert in reaching an opinion, such as neglecting a critical step in the analysis or failing to review an important financial record; and (3) questions to ask the expert.

The expert's second role in the deposition process occurs when being deposed. The key to performing professionally is a thorough and thoughtful preparation, including a critical review with counsel of the planned testimony. During this review, counsel may cross-examine the testimony; this exercise can uncover potential weaknesses. Do not prepare a report or reduce any of your conclusions to writing unless counsel specifically directs you to do so. The other side may be able to obtain written documents that may record only preliminary conclusions and use them for impeachment.

Ten Commandments for Effective Depositions

The following suggestions will significantly increase the probability of a successful deposition.

1. *Always tell the truth, but answer only the question asked.* Do not volunteer information. If asked, "Do you know the time?" Respond, "Yes," not 10:30 A.M. Avoid long, narrative answers. The more topics you raise in an answer, the more questions the examining lawyer is likely to ask.

2. *Think before answering.* That provides time to formulate an appropriate response, and for counsel to analyze the question and raise objections to it. Beware of an examining lawyer who attempts to develop an informal, but rapid, questioning style that may be designed to elicit answers without careful thought. Be wary also of an examiner's casual, friendly, or flattering manner that may cause you to lower your intensity.

3. *Never answer a question you do not understand.* If a question is unclear, ask the examining lawyer to repeat or rephrase it or have the court reporter read the question back. Do not be bashful; the burden is on the examiner, *not* you, to frame unambiguous and intelligible inquiries.

4. *Do not guess or speculate.* If you do not know the answer to a question, say so. If you are unsure of your answer, qualify the response by "approximately" or a similar expression. Beware of the hypothetical question. Before answering one, make sure the examining attorney has specified all essential assumptions.

5. *Do not bring notes, diagrams, books, or other written material to the deposition unless a subpoena or your attorney requires you to do so.* If asked to testify about any documents or other exhibits, take the time to review them carefully before answering questions about the items.

6. *Listen carefully to each objection made by your lawyer.* Counsel may be trying to alert you to a trick question or to some other problem with the inquiry. If counsel directs you not to answer a question, follow that instruction, even if the examiner threatens you with sanctions for failing to respond.

7. *Do not argue or become angry or hostile with the examining attorney.* Such a reaction communicates a lack of confidence that may be exploited at trial. It also may alert the examining lawyer to weaknesses in your theories or conclusions.

8. *Even if a question calls for a "yes" or "no" answer, ask to explain your response if you feel a qualification or explanation is required to complete your answer.* Do not worry, though, if the examiner's question suggests a lack of understanding about the subject matter of the inquiry. It is not your job to educate the opposing attorney. Your attorney will decide whether clarification is necessary.

9. *Be wary of questions that involve absolutes, such as "Have you identified ALL of the documents you reviewed?" or "Are there ANY other facts you relied upon?"* When asked such a question, always try to qualify your answer in case you have overlooked a pertinent document or fact.

10. *Do not memorize your answers before the deposition.* Provide a direct and factual response to each question. You will be a much more effective witness.

DIRECT EXAMINATION

If a case does not settle during the discovery phase, you will need to testify under oath at the trial. When you testify, you will be asked questions by your attorney during the "direct examination" portion of your testimony. Most of these questions will focus on your qualifications, the scope of your assignment, the method(s) you used, and your conclusions.

Procedural Rules

When you testify as an expert, you should be aware of several procedural rules that affect your testimony. For example, Rule 703 provides that an expert witness may base testimony on matters "perceived by or made known to him [or her] at or before the hearing . . . that is of a type that reasonably may be relied upon by an expert in forming an opinion upon the subject to which his testimony relates." Under this rule, an expert can answer a hypothetical question because it is deemed to be "made known to him [or her] at or before the hearing" See *Teen-Ed, Inc. v. Kimball Int'l, Inc.*, 620 F.2d 399 (3d Cir. 1980). CPAs generally do not rely on hypotheticals during direct examination; opposing counsel often employs the hypothetical on cross-examination, however, to test—and try to defeat—an expert's assumptions and analysis.

Rule 703 also provides that the data that form the basis for an expert's opinion do not have to constitute admissible evidence. Thus you may base an opinion on hearsay evidence (out-of-court statements made by those who will not testify) (*United States v. Sims,* 514 F.2d 147 (9th Cir. 1975)). This rule is especially important if you testify about a business valuation. Valuation work usually involves talking with individuals involved in a similar trade or business, and typically none of them will be testifying.

Rule 705 gives trial judges the right to require experts to state the basis for their opinions before testifying. CPAs regularly base their expert opinions upon the examination of various financial records and certain assumptions. The trial judge often invokes Rule 705 to require an expert, before testifying, to provide detailed information concerning these items.

Qualifying the Expert

Before you can testify as an expert, you must be "qualified" in that capacity. Attorneys sometimes refer to the qualification process as "laying a foundation," which means they ask the expert a series of questions designed to establish the witness's credentials.

In federal court, a witness is qualified to testify as an expert "if he [or she] has special knowledge, skill, experience, training, or education" on the subject on which the witness will speak (Rule 702). The trial judge has the discretion to decide whether a particular witness qualifies as an expert and a higher court can reverse the judge's decision only for an abuse of that discretion (*Garbincius v. Boston Edison Co.*, 621 F.2d 1171 (1st Cir. 1980)). Most states follow the same approach.

An expert's qualifications must relate to the subject about which the expert expresses an opinion (*Reno-West Coast Distribution Co. v. Mead Corp.*, 613 F.2d 722 (9th Cir. 1979)). Most CPAs are qualified to testify as experts on a wide range of subjects, including the results of an audit and whether financial statements were prepared according to generally accepted accounting principles, damages, and valuation.

An expert does not have to be employed in the trade or profession to which the proposed testimony will relate. If the expert's knowledge about the subject of the proposed testimony is inadequate, however, the trial court judge may exclude the testimony. Thus a court may refuse to accept a CPA's testimony regarding a business valuation, for instance, if the witness lacks sufficient valuation experience.

Establishing Credibility through Qualification

In qualifying an expert, an attorney establishes the witness's credibility. The outcome of business litigation can hinge on which side has established greater credibility for its expert. The relevance of the expert's credentials are usually given much weight by the trier-of-fact when assessing the expert's opinion.

When qualifying an expert witness, the attorney usually will ask questions that cover several key areas: (1) education, including any honors or awards received; (2) professional credentials; (3) employment experience, with particular emphasis on its connection to the issues of the case; (4) academic affiliations; (5) publications and lectures; and (6) previous qualifications as an expert witness.

To make the qualification process as effective as possible, you should consider formulating specific questions that the attorney can ask you. Proceeding in this manner will produce a consistent and organized credentials presentation superior to that which will result if the attorney is merely given a copy of your resume and left to draft questions without your assistance.

The precise scope of qualification testimony in a case will vary, depending on the type of case and the trial's circumstances. Both you and counsel should be prepared to condense the planned testimony if either of you sense the judge is becoming impatient or the jury is bored.

After presenting qualification testimony, counsel should ask the judge for a ruling that you qualify as an expert (Rule 702). Although the law may not require such a ruling, many trial tacticians believe it creates a positive psychological effect in your client's favor.

Scope of Assignment

After establishing your qualifications, counsel normally will ask you about your involvement in the case. The inquiries will include such issues as who retained you, what investigation or analysis you were asked to perform, and when you began and concluded your work. You will also be questioned about the basis for your compensation (e.g., hourly rate, flat fee) and whether you have any financial interest in the outcome of the case. Finally, you will be asked to confirm that no one suggested a certain conclusion to you in advance.

An important aspect of this phase of your testimony is the extent of the investigation or analysis you carried out. Be prepared to provide a detailed description of each step you took. Your testimony must convince the judge or the jury that you considered all significant factors.

Methodology

In addition to describing your investigation or analysis, you should testify about the method that you employed. Your testimony should present an overview of the analytic methods available to you. You also should justify the methodology you selected and cogently explain your rejection of alternative approaches.

Testifying about methodology can trap the unwary. You should provide enough information to support the path you have chosen. But you want to avoid detailed explanations of economic theories. A trial is an inappropriate forum for such digressions, which invariably confuse or bore a courtroom listener. In addition, an expert who delves into complicated theories may open the door to a rigorous and frequently devastating cross-examination by opposing counsel.

Techniques for Testifying about Methodology

Like most professionals, CPAs usually are comfortable testifying about "hard data," such as an established formula that produces black-and-white calculations. But analyses routinely involve "soft data" issues, and many experts find themselves uncomfortable when offering such testimony. Fortunately, you can take several steps to increase your comfort level—and your effectiveness—during this portion of your testimony.

Step 1: Acknowledge weaknesses. Every expert opinion involves some weaknesses, which the expert presumably considers and incorporates into the opinion. Tactically, one should take the "offensive" by disclosing weaknesses during the direct portion of your testimony, rather than having them exposed "defensively" during cross-examination.

In evaluating your opinion, you must pay attention to two types of weaknesses. The first are the "real" weaknesses, those inherent in the method selected. Examples include (1) the inability to investigate important information; (2) the inaccuracy of financial information; (3) the lack of confirming, external data; (4) the choice of one method to the exclusion of others; and (5) errors in calculations.

The second type of weaknesses are the "asserted" ones, those an opposing party's attorney will raise no matter what method you used. These weaknesses include the alleged imprecision of your conclusions, the argument that comparable data is insufficiently comparable, and supposed statistical impurities in outside studies. Opposing counsel will probably also argue that you should have chosen a different analytic method, that your analysis should have been more thorough, and that your conclusion might have been different.

Step 2: Plan carefully. An expert should work closely with the client's attorney in developing the strategy for direct examination. One option is to have the attorney ask general questions—"how" and "why"—that call for narrative answers. This option offers the experienced expert witness an opportunity to turn that arena into an impressive economics class. This tactic has a risk, however—in that an attorney relinquishes control of the examination. In addition, the trial court judge may disallow some answers—perhaps important ones—as nonresponsive to the questions posed.

Another approach is to use specific questions calling for relatively narrow responses. For this technique to work, the attorney must be well versed in the nuances of the expert's field and thoroughly understand the expert's analysis.

Whatever the selected approach, the key to success is thorough preparation and agreement between the expert and counsel about the course both will follow. In addition, both must be willing to modify approaches during the trial if rulings from the bench dictate an adjustment in strategy.

Step 3: Take control. An expert witness should not hesitate to take control of some aspects of the case. Be circumspect, however, when doing so. Experts may intimidate many attorneys who are reluctant to disclose their lack of knowledge because they fear the loss of their clients' confidence. A good expert shares control with an attorney without denigrating or antagonizing the latter.

Step 4: Maintain a professional demeanor. *How* you conduct yourself at trial is no less important than what you say. No matter how sophisticated or complicated your financial analysis, you must explain it in a straightforward and understandable manner. Do not appear condescending to the judge or the jury. Avoid any trace of arrogance. And at all times be willing to concede uncontroverted facts and graciously acknowledge errors.

CROSS-EXAMINATION

During cross-examination, the opposing side interrogates you. Exercise extreme caution because the opposing attorney will try to discredit your testimony by exposing and exploiting each weakness disclosed during direct examination.

Procedural Rules Governing Cross-Examination

The scope of cross-examination can be extremely broad. You may be questioned about qualifications and any other matter raised on direct examination. A judge may even permit cross-examination that extends beyond the scope of direct examination (Rule 705). However, the cross-examiner cannot try to discredit your testimony by questioning you about the content of any scientific, technical, or professional treatises or journals, unless you considered those sources in reaching your opinion, or they have been admitted into evidence (*see Bobb v. Modern Products, Inc.*, 648 F.2d 1051 (5th Cir. 1981)).

Survival Tactics for Cross-Examination

Many of the "10 commandments" for testifying at a deposition apply to cross-examination. In addition, the following techniques will make cross-examination easier:

- No substitute exists for good preparation. Nothing is easier to defend than a carefully developed position.
- Before your cross-examination, question your assumptions and explore alternative positions. The cross-examiner certainly will do so.
- Study the opposing expert's analysis. When formulating questions to ask you, opposing counsel will rely on that analysis.
- Frequently an examiner will compound a series of facts or premises into a question or a series of questions asking for a simple "yes" or "no." If you can not answer the question that simply, say so and shift the burden back to the lawyer to frame a proper question, one that can be simply answered or permits a fair explanation.
- Answer only the question asked. Offering additional information gives the cross-examiner an opportunity to use that information against you.
- Become familiar with the examining attorney's background, skills, and tactics.
- Be yourself, but be sensitive to negative habits that may distract from the quality or credibility of your testimony, such as averting your eyes when asked a difficult question.
- Be polite. Generally, it is more effective to answer questions in a pondering or reflective manner than defensively.
- Avoid the appearance of bias or untrustworthiness. Certain facts or arguments will contradict any economic position. Do not hesitate to acknowledge these realities if challenged by the examiner.
- Do not hesitate to concede an error. However, do not accept an opposing lawyer's unfavorable characterization of your testimony, such as the following:
  - "So, you just *picked* a number?"
  - "So, your study *isn't accurate* then, is it?"
  - "So, after this *brief, informal interview*, you decided. . . ."
- Do not overstate your opinion. An extreme or absolute position is easy for a cross-examiner to discredit.

Cross-Examining the Opposing Expert

You can offer valuable assistance when counsel is preparing to cross-examine the opposing expert. You can critique your counterpart's opinion by identifying erroneous facts and assumptions and you can suggest cross-examination questions.

Some lawyers want you to sit at the counsel table during cross-examination, if local court rules permit it. But one should carefully consider this practice because your presence may create an appearance of advocacy that will detract from the credibility of your testimony and outweigh whatever other tactical advantages your attendance might produce. Counsel's sufficient preparation should usually eliminate the need for your presence during cross-examination.

CONCLUSION

As an expert witness, you are ethically bound to analyze objectively the business and economic issues before you, and you should never alter your conclusions merely to advance a client's interest. You also have a duty to the client, however, to meaningfully and effectively testify about your work and conclusions.

LIST OF CASES

Bobb v. Modern Products, Inc., 648 F.2d 1051 (5th Cir. 1981)
Caisson Corp. v. Ingersoll Rand Co., 622 F.2d 672 (3d Cir. 1980)
Garbincuis v. Boston Edison Co., 621 F.2d 1171 (1st Cir. 1980)
Reno-West Coast Distribution Co. v. Mead Corp., 613 F.2d 722 (9th Cir. 1979)
Teen-Ed, Inc. v. Kimball Int'l, Inc., 620 F.2d 399 (3d Cir. 1980)
United States v. Sims, 514 F.2d 147 (9th Cir. 1975)

6

USES OF CHARTS AND GRAPHS: PROOF AT TRIAL

Alan Silverman

THE VALUE OF VISUAL AIDS

Acme Apparel, a retailer of women's clothing, has five stores in shopping malls in a major metropolitan area. One store was in the Westside Mall. The owner of the Westside Mall began reconstructing the common areas of the Mall in February of Year 1. The project took several months.

In Year 2, a dispute arose between Acme and Westside concerning nonpayment of rent. Westside eventually sued for back rent and Acme countersued, claiming that the construction in the first half of Year 1 had disturbed the traffic patterns and caused Acme's business to decline.

The author thanks Virginia R. Sargent, President of Courtroom Graphics, for her contributions to this chapter.

Westside's trial counsel hired a CPA to testify as an expert witness on damages claimed by Acme. In order to measure the impact of reconstruction on Acme's sales and profits, the CPA needed a yardstick against which to compare the performance of Acme's Westside store. The other four Acme stores were in the same metropolitan area and subject to the same economic conditions, and so it was decided to use those stores as the yardstick. The CPA prepared the schedule in Exhibit 6-1 from Acme's accounting records, showing monthly sales for Year 0 and Year 1 for the Westside store and the other four stores.

It is difficult for a trained accountant, let alone an untrained juror, to detect any pattern or derive any conclusion from the data in Exhibit 6.1. However, if these sales figures are plotted in two line charts, as in Exhibit 6-2 and Exhibit 6-3, patterns emerge.

From these charts the CPA was able to infer the following:

1. There *was* a decline in sales in Acme's Westside store during the first half of Year 1, compared to a similar period in Year 0.
2. The decline appeared to be corrected after the completion of construction in August Year 1.

But the charts also showed:

3. The sales pattern in the other four stores was remarkably similar to the Westside store, even though the scale of the chart is obviously different.
4. The decline in sales started in October and November Year 0, *before* the construction started. December Year 0, usually the best month of the year for retailers, was only marginally better than August Year 0.

These charts led the CPA to suspect that Acme's sales problem was not unique to the Westside store and was caused by something other than the construction. In order to substantiate this suspicion, the CPA then looked at the quarterly sales of women's apparel at other stores in the Westside Mall and compared those to the sales at Acme's Westside store. The results were presented in bar charts as in Exhibits 6-4 and 6-5.

These two bar charts clearly indicated that the sales decline suffered by Acme's Westside store in the fourth quarter of Year 0 was not experienced by other stores in the same mall selling similar merchandise.

By using all four charts, the CPA was able to testify at trial that

- Whatever problem Acme had started 3 or 4 months *prior* to the construction.
- The problem was also experienced at other Acme stores in other malls.
- The problem was not experienced by other stores selling women's apparel in the Westside Mall.

The charts helped not only in the analysis of the data, but also helped present a complex set of facts to the jury.

The expert witness did not need to explain what had caused the sales decline, only that it was obviously not for the reasons alleged. Indeed, Acme's counsel

EXHIBIT 6-1. ACME APPAREL (MONTHLY SALES DATA)

Acme Apparel

Monthly Acme Apparel Sales Data (1982 to 1983) Westside Mall Store Source: Acme Apparel General Ledger			Monthly Acme Apparel Sales Data (1982 to 1983) All Stores except Westside Mall Store Source: Acme Apparel General Ledger						
Monthly	Year	Westside Store Sales	Monthly	Year	Store A	Store B	Store C	Store D	Total
Year 0									
J	1982	$17,222	J	1982	$23,062	$15,307	$18,626	$41,539	$98,534
F	1982	$19,623	F	1982	$39,492	$20,220	$18,172	$41,958	$119,842
M	1982	$21,163	M	1982	$43,395	$26,809	$22,708	$49,074	$141,985
A	1982	$33,349	A	1982	$43,390	$23,736	$27,735	$46,577	$141,517
M	1982	$35,942	M	1982	$35,700	$25,420	$32,830	$50,119	$144,069
J	1982	$39,435	J	1982	$52,018	$26,069	$42,408	$54,972	$175,466
J	1982	$26,623	J	1982	$31,006	$20,689	$32,498	$46,103	$130,297
A	1982	$43,726	A	1982	$42,634	$38,730	$47,116	$106,687	$235,168
S	1982	$40,348	S	1982	$47,263	$44,535	$45,658	$102,420	$239,876
O	1982	$17,268	O	1982	$34,063	$18,675	$23,176	$40,502	$116,416
N	1982	$17,858	N	1982	$37,331	$19,437	$24,667	$47,563	$128,998
D	1982	$46,337	D	1982	$106,409	$42,050	$58,042	$115,698	$322,198
Year 1									
J	1983	$13,091	J	1983	$27,743	$16,945	$18,566	$42,597	$105,851
F	1983	$16,410	F	1983	$25,739	$22,232	$19,076	$48,008	$115,056
M	1983	$22,742	M	1983	$31,173	$21,267	$23,340	$58,006	$133,806
A	1983	$19,495	A	1983	$20,811	$23,661	$22,293	$47,050	$113,815
M	1983	$18,100	M	1983	$30,799	$23,931	$26,115	$46,820	$127,664
J	1983	$27,191	J	1983	$35,543	$35,143	$31,179	$83,114	$184,979
J	1983	$27,153	J	1983	$23,876	$26,628	$23,832	$78,923	$153,259
A	1983	$38,852	A	1983	$24,490	$43,248	$35,242	$136,787	$239,767
S	1983	$44,719	S	1983	$29,818	$40,358	$40,673	$130,330	$241,179
O	1983	$34,906	O	1983	$51,818	$27,354	$29,811	$71,218	$180,201
N	1983	$46,816	N	1983	$86,465	$44,136	$48,033	$103,427	$282,061
D	1983	$104,778	D	1983	$195,082	$94,719	$111,101	$234,357	$635,260

EXHIBIT 6-2. ACME APPAREL—WESTSIDE STORE

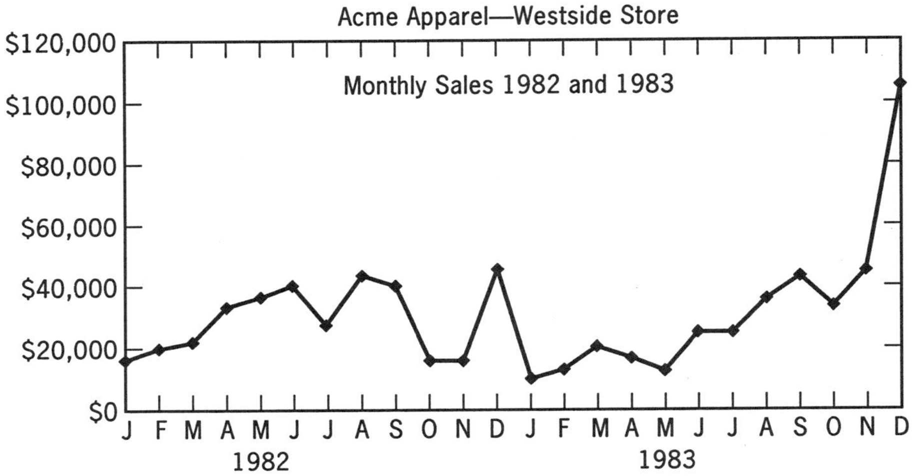

EXHIBIT 6-3. ACME APPAREL SALES—EXCEPT WESTSIDE STORE

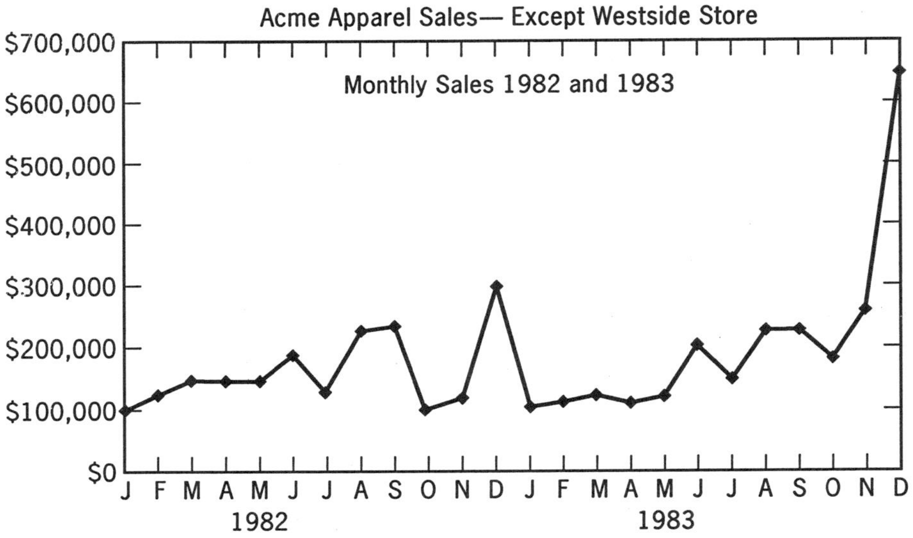

EXHIBIT 6-4. WESTSIDE MALL WOMEN'S APPAREL SALES

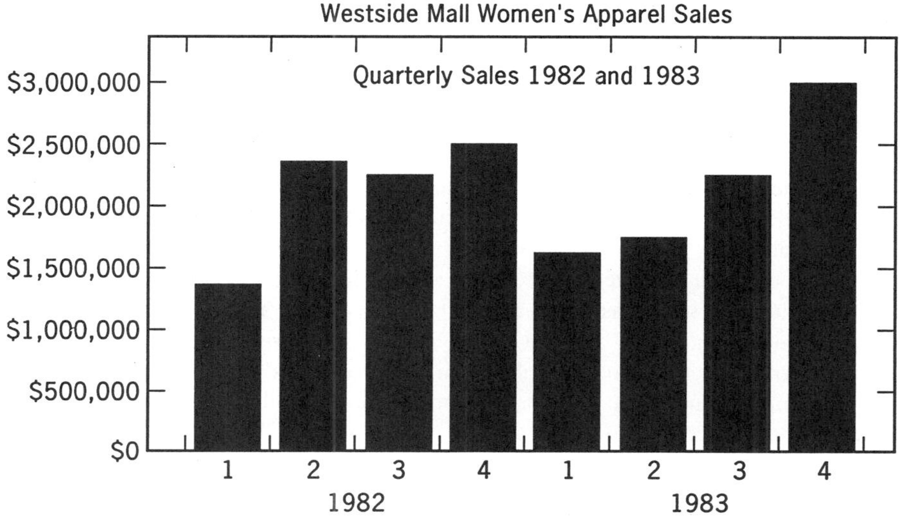

EXHIBIT 6-5. ACME APPAREL SALES—WESTSIDE STORE

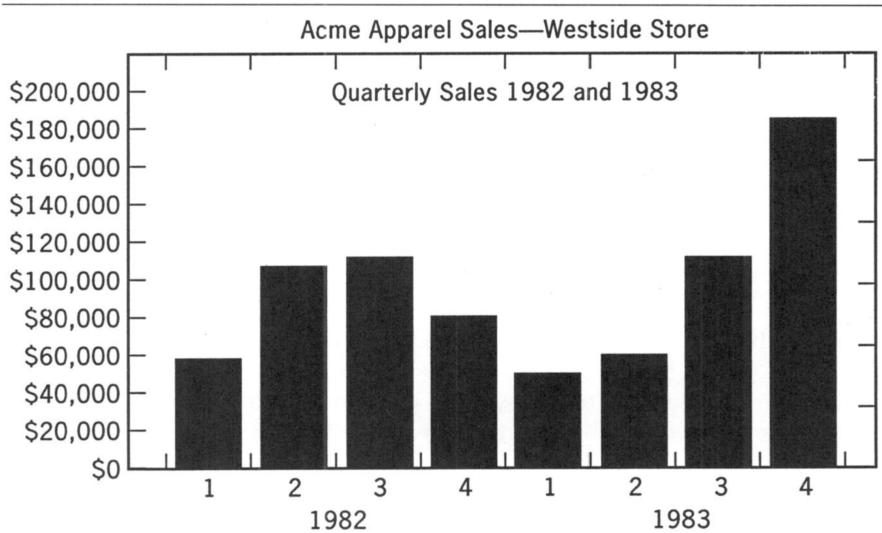

convinced the judge that the CPA's experience in retail merchandising did not qualify him to explain the decline and that he should not be allowed to speculate as to the cause. Nevertheless the jury dismissed Acme's claim.

REASONS FOR USING VISUAL AIDS

As in the preceding example, when the CPA acts as an expert witness, he is placed in the position of explaining financial facts to the court and perhaps to the jury. The facts may be very complex and the issues sophisticated. These facts and ideas must be communicated to people who may have no financial or accounting training. Although some cases will be tried before a judge and the judge may have a general understanding of business, many cases will be tried before a jury. There is no way of predicting the level of education or business experience of the jury. The CPA must assume that the jury has no financial training and *be prepared* to present the evidence accordingly.

Psychologists suggest that our minds can remember and recall visual images better than the written or spoken word. It seems well accepted that retention is further enhanced by exposure to a variety of media.

Studies have been conducted that showed that visual aids significantly increased the rate of group consensus. Decisions could be reached in a first meeting more often with visual aids.

One has only to consider the impact of television or look at popular magazines to realize that we receive much of our information visually. Jurors are accustomed to sophisticated visual presentations but not to complex verbal presentations. The CPA should consider using charts or graphs whenever it is necessary to explain statistical or numeric data, especially to illustrate trends. Charts will help show relationships and make the testimony more interesting. In addition, they act as an outline for the testimony, providing cues. This can help develop the confidence of the witness and make the presentation more relaxed.

Charts and graphs will reduce confusion, make abstract ideas more concrete, add interest, change the pace and will remain in the jury's minds long after the witness has gone. They can also be very useful as a communication vehicle between the CPA and the lawyer, the lawyer's client, and even during settlement negotiations. Charts are easily used by lawyers in their summations or final arguments to the court.

ADMISSIBILITY OF CHARTS AND GRAPHS

The CPA might use one of two types of charts or graphs at trial. The first type is used just to illustrate or explain verbal testimony (illustrative exhibits). The second type is offered as evidence of the truth or what it portrays (substantive exhibits). Only substantive exhibits may be received into evidence and allowed into the jury room.

Illustrative exhibits are routinely received by courts to help illustrate or clarify complex testimony. Because they are offered for illustrative purposes only and are not admitted into evidence, they need not be exact as long as they are a fair representation and any inaccuracies are made known to the court. If the judge decides they are helpful in understanding the testimony, they can be used. The judge can exclude them if they are potentially misleading or confusing.

Substantive exhibits or *demonstrative exhibits* must meet a higher standard. Their admissibility is controlled in part by Federal Rule of Evidence 611 (1) that provides:

> The court shall exercise reasonable control over the mode and order of interrogating witnesses and presenting evidence so as to (1) make the interrogation and presentation effective for the ascertainment of truth, (2) avoid needless consumption of time, and (3) protect witnesses from harassment or undue embarrassment.

This gives the judge much discretion in admitting exhibits.

By 1986, 30 states had adopted evidence codes similar to the federal rules, so the federal rules should provide guidance in most circumstances.

The admissibility of *substantive* charts and graphs is further controlled by Federal Rule of Evidence 1006 that states:

> The contents of voluminous writings, recordings, or photographs which cannot conveniently be examined in court may be presented in the form of a chart, summary or calculation. The originals, or duplicates, shall be made available for examination or copying, or both, by other parties at reasonable time and place. The court may order that they be produced in court.

In order for a chart or graph to be admissible as evidence it must satisfy the following.

1. It must be a fair and accurate representation of the underlying data.
2. The underlying data must be sufficiently voluminous to make it inconvenient for the court to examine it.
3. The underlying data itself must be admissible as evidence.
4. The underlying data must have been produced to the other side.

Judges have much discretion in interpreting these criteria. For example, a judge may admit a chart with a *minor* inaccuracy, providing opposing counsel has had a chance to examine the witness about the chart and does not object. The voluminous data requirement has been very liberally interpreted with as few as 10 documents meeting the test. However, the admissibility of the underlying data is strictly enforced.

The only possible exception to the admissibility of the underlying data is allowed by the Federal Rule of Evidence 703. This rule allows the expert to rely on data usually used by experts in the field, which data itself may not be admissible. An example might be a table of interest rates taken from a Department of Commerce publication.

Substantive exhibits must be authenticated by the testimony of the CPA, although he need not actually prepare the chart, as long as the witness supervised its preparation. The CPA must be able to verify all calculations personally and must be able to identify all underlying data. (For further discussion of admissibility, see Joseph, 1987.)

TYPES OF VISUAL AIDS

Blackboard

This is the most commonly used and abused form of visual aid in the courtroom. It has many disadvantages.

1. It is not easy to write legibly on a blackboard without much practice.
2. Reading a blackboard from a distance is difficult.
3. Advance preparation is not practical.
4. The cross-examining attorney can easily change charts.
5. No permanent record can be taken into the jury room.

Flip Chart

Flip charts are also commonly used but are difficult to read from a distance. They can be prepared in advance, possibly by a professional artist. They can be taken into a jury room. Colors can provide emphasis and interest.

Overhead Transparencies

Overhead transparencies offer several advantages.

1. They are low in cost and quick to produce; most copy machines are capable of generating overheads.
2. They are easy to change.
3. They are easy to transport.
4. The projected image can be much larger than a blackboard or flip chart.
5. The courtroom lights need not be turned off.
6. It is possible to use color to highlight specific areas.
7. Hard copies can be made on paper to introduce into evidence. Multiple copies can be made for judge, reporter, and opposing counsel.
8. Transparencies can be produced directly on a plotter as output from a computer graphics program (see later comments).

If the witness wishes to use transparencies it is wise to visit the courtroom before testifying and experiment with the location of the screen, the projector, and the focus.

Enlargements

Documents or charts can be photographically or xerographically enlarged. Photographic enlargement provides better quality, but at a higher price. The enlargements can be mounted on foamboard to make them light but stable. A typical enlargement would be 36" × 48." Enlargements can be used in the jury room but have the disadvantage of being difficult to transport and not easy to change.

Microcomputers

There are many graphics software programs available for popular makes of microcomputers. Laser printers or plotters produce professional quality charts directly from the computers.

If the CPA testifies very often, it could be worth investing in the hardware and software necessary to produce graphic exhibits. Plotters and laser printers are not expensive. A plotter is able to produce colored output. It is also useful to have a color monitor on the computer. Dot matrix printers do not produce output of sufficient courtroom quality. Plotters can produce graphs directly on transparencies for projection in the courtroom.

In choosing a graphics package, there are a number of considerations.

1. Is it compatible with existing hardware?
2. Will it be necessary to add extra memory, disk storage, or a color monitor?
3. Can the graphics package accept input directly from the calculation program being used without rekeying?
4. Which printers and plotters does it support?
5. How easy is it to learn?
6. How flexible is it in accommodating changes?
7. Can the user change scales and easily override any default options?
8. How flexible are the labeling, titling, and annotating features?
9. Does the vendor offer good support by telephone?

It is usually not possible to answer these questions by just reading brochures. It is necessary to try the packages on a typical chart.

The microcomputer has the advantage in producing trial exhibits that, once the original arithmetic has been done, the exhibits can be produced with very little extra cost, time, and effort. Last minute changes, inevitable in expert testimony, can be accomplished quickly and cheaply. Charts of the quality shown earlier in this chapter can be produced with no artistic skill.

DEMONSTRATIVE EXHIBIT SPECIALIST

Graphic exhibits are visual communication tools, intended to persuade a judge or jury of the validity of the opinions presented by the expert witness. Most CPAs have not spent much time studying visual communication. Although it is possible to prepare extremely effective charts using a microcomputer, not all CPAs have the equipment or skill to do so.

The preparation of effective graphics involves an understanding of style, color, balance, clarity, and impact. If the CPA does not feel comfortable in producing graphic exhibits, then the attorney should add a specialized graphic artist to the trial team as early as possible.

There are graphic artists who specialize in producing demonstrative evidence for the courtroom. Enquiries of lawyers and other witnesses will help identify such specialists. A good courtroom artist can provide creative ideas that will make the testimony more effective. For a complete discussion of graphic exhibits, see *The Demonstrative Evidence Sourcebook* (1985), by Douglas Filter.

TYPES OF CHARTS

Line charts are best for showing trends and comparing trends over time. This technique was used in the first two sales charts for Acme Apparel to show similar sales trends (Exhibits 6-2 and 6-3).

If more than one line is drawn on the same chart, use different colors to distinguish the lines and use a legend to describe the meaning of the color. Transparent overlays should also be considered in presenting comparison of trends. This technique was actually used with the Acme Apparel charts with striking effect.

In another case, the two line charts, Exhibit 6-6, were used to illustrate a dramatic change in the behavior of a bank account in October 1981, the month in which a fraud started. In this case the line charts emphasize differences rather than similarities. The start of the fraud appears as an "earthquake."

Bar charts are best used for comparing similar items for different time periods as in Exhibits 6.4 and 6-5. Cluster bars or grouped bars are helpful in comparing different items for similar time periods. For example, the two separate bar charts in Exhibits 6-4 and 6-5 could have been shown on one cluster bar chart (Exhibit 6-7).

Stacked bars are good for comparing the size of constituent parts of a whole. The sales of Acme Apparel in the Westside Mall could have been displayed as a part of the total sales of women's apparel in the mall, by using a stacked bar as shown in Exhibit 6-8.

Pie charts can also be used for a similar purpose but have the disadvantage of not showing a scale. For this reason, it is usual to supplement the chart with labels indicating the size of the various slices. Exhibit 6-9 shows an example.

Tables can be a problem to present as graphic exhibits. Most of the charts described before are used to display information that probably appears in the CPA's workpapers in tabular form. For all of the reasons previously discussed, it is usually more persuasive to present the numeric data in graphic form. However, there are some situations when it is important for the court to focus on the numbers themselves. It is best to highlight only the key numbers to draw the particular attention of the court, while presenting all of the data for the sake of the integrity of the exhibit. Graphic display software on personal computers now allows this with relative ease.

Exhibit 6-10 was designed to focus attention on a comparison of two critical columns of dates which were not adjacent in the original table.

EXHIBIT 6-6. DAILY BANK BALANCE

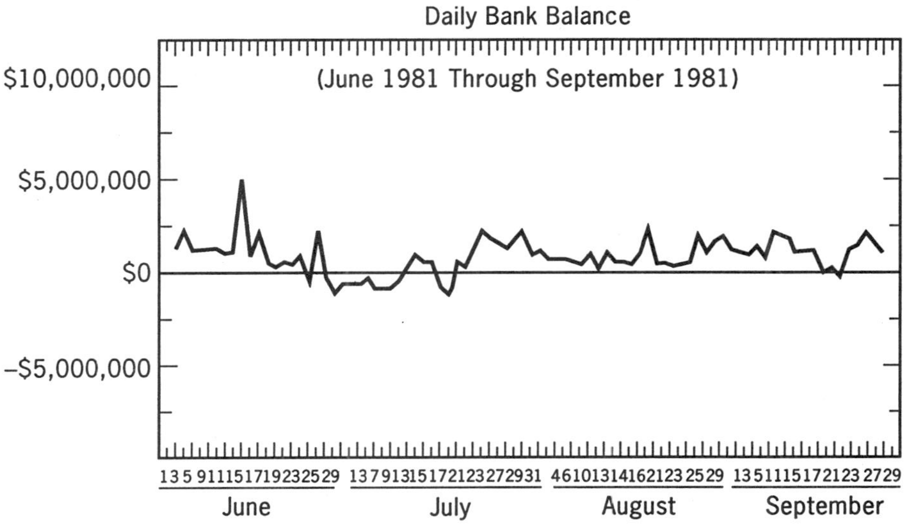

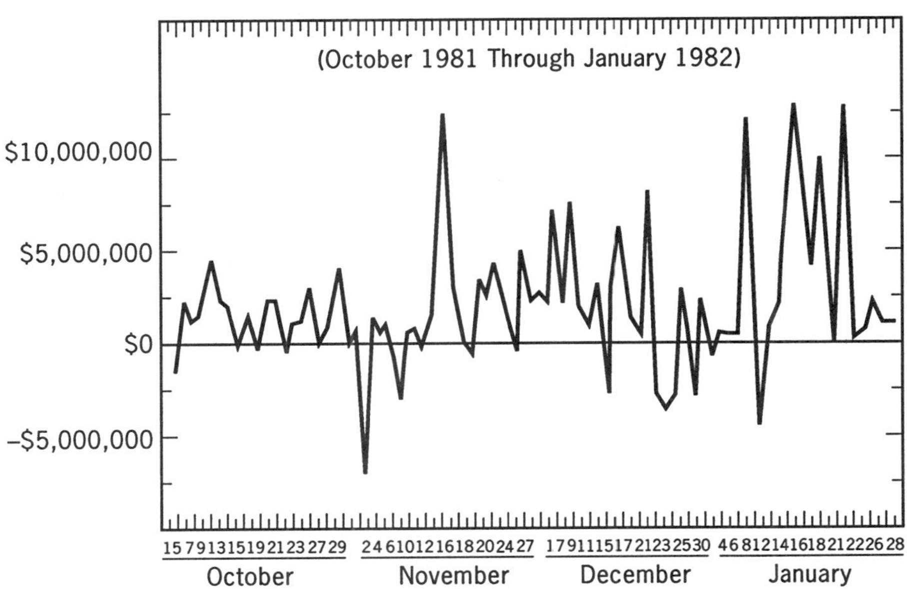

EXHIBIT 6-7. WESTSIDE MALL—QUARTERLY SALES—WOMEN'S APPAREL

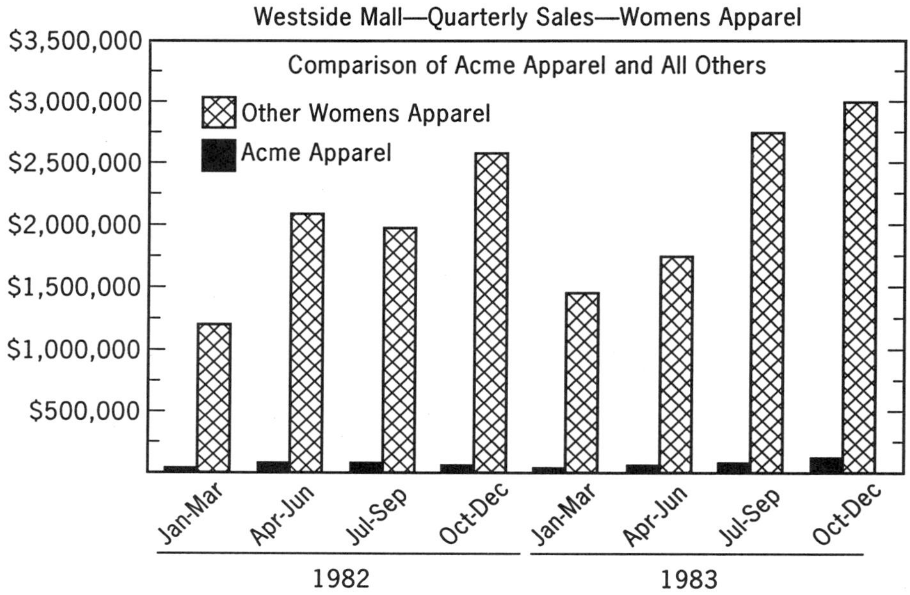

EXHIBIT 6-8. WESTSIDE MALL—QUARTERLY SALES—WOMEN'S APPAREL

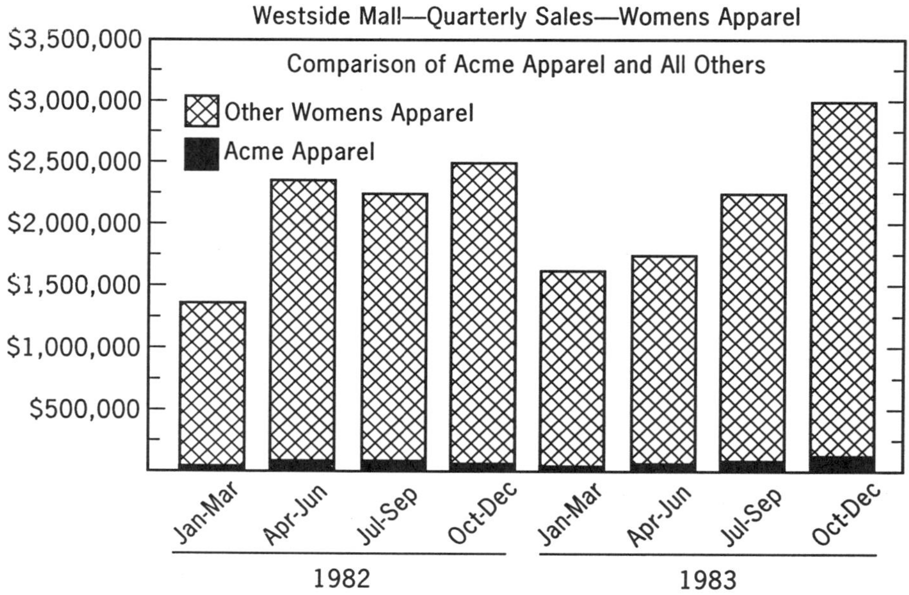

EXHIBIT 6-9. WESTSIDE MALL—ANNUAL SALES—WOMEN'S APPAREL COMPARISON OF ACME APPAREL AND ALL OTHERS

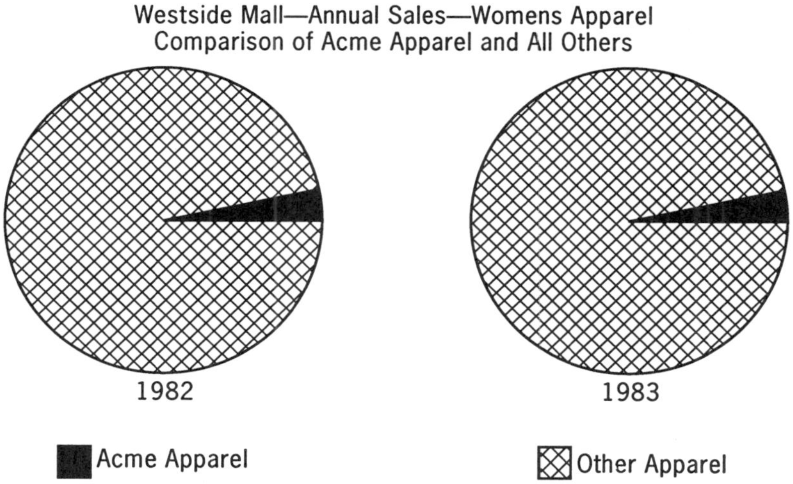

EXHIBIT 6-10.

Date Check Paid	Date Check Issued
12/10/81	12/9/81
12/11/81	12/9/81
12/11/81	12/9/81
12/11/81	12/9/81
12/11/81	12/9/81
12/11/81	12/9/81
12/11/81	12/9/81
12/11/81	
12/14/81	12/9/81
12/14/81	

Receipt Number	Date Check Issued	Date Check Paid	Check Number	Receipt Amount	Check Number	Date Check Issued	Amount of check
10675	12/7/81	12/10/81	1341	107,800	21798	12/9/81	107,276.00
10687	12/8/81	12/11/81	1351	357,700	21802	12/9/81	357,301.50
10688	12/8/81	12/11/81	1360	573,300	21803	12/9/81	572,807.00
10689	12/8/81	12/11/81	1362	958,440	21804	12/9/81	957,947.00
10690	12/8/81	12/11/81	1361	590,940	21805	12/9/81	590,447.00
10691	12/8/81	12/11/81	1359	846,720	21086	12/9/81	846,227.00
10692	12/8/81	12/11/81	1355	200,900	21807	12/9/81	504,162.00
10707	12/8/81	12/11/81	1358	303,800			
10696	12/8/81	12/14/81	1374	539,000	21809	12/9/81	538,327.00
	12/10/81	12/14/81	1400				

PRACTICAL TIPS

Simplicity. Effective charts are simple. Eliminate things that are not absolutely necessary. If the chart is still too complicated, consider breaking it into two or more charts.

Accuracy. To be admissible, the exhibit must be an accurate representation of the underlying data. Particular attention should be paid to the scales and the size relationships of elements being compared. Graphic exhibits are prepared for their impact on the jury. This impact will be dissipated if the exhibit becomes the focus of a courtroom dispute between attorneys. (Of course, if it is then admitted, the jury may pay even more attention to it.)

Consistency. A series of charts should be consistent in style and format. Use the same type style and size for labels and headings. Make the scales consistent from chart to chart. If a color is used to illustrate an element in one chart, use the same color to describe the same element in all charts.

Visibility. Make sure your charts are large enough to be viewed by a jury across a large courtroom. Prepare sufficient copies of your charts on 8½″ × 11″ paper, so that they may be distributed to the judge, opposing counsel, the court reporter and the jury (if permitted). If a 40″ × 60″ exhibit is allowed to be taken into the jury room, it is a good idea to have a copy for the judge's book.

EXHIBIT 6-11.

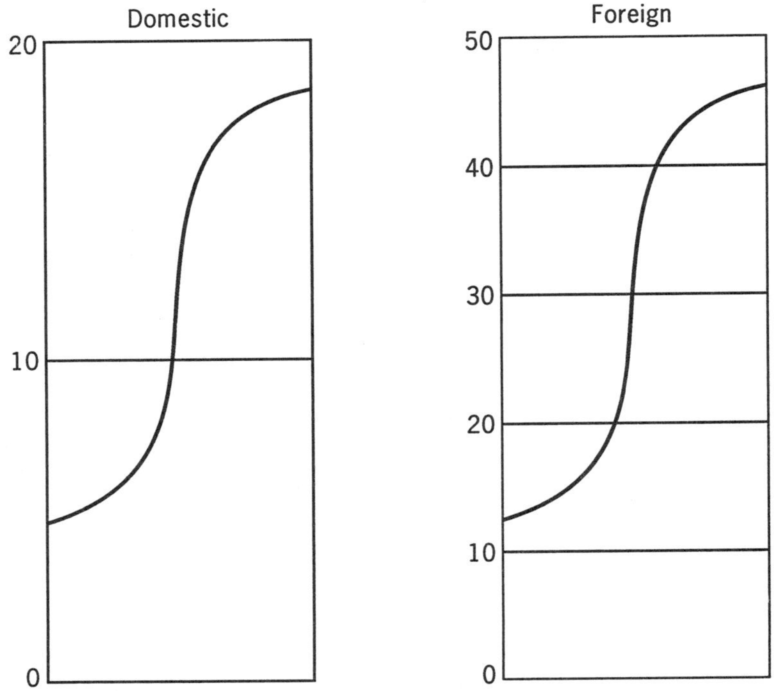

EXHIBIT 6-12.

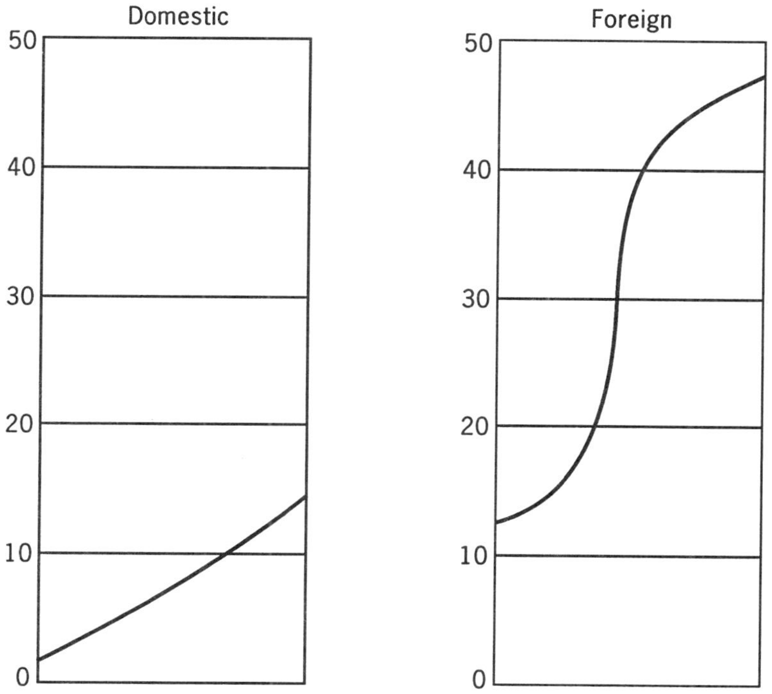

Scales. One of the most common reasons for objections to the admissibility of charts is the use of misleading scales. For example, Exhibits 6-2 and 6-3 are the same overall size, but one has a scale that is six times greater than the other. This might be considered misleading, but in the case the lines were compared merely to illustrate a similar trend and not to compare absolute size. On this ground, they were admitted. However, the charts in Exhibit 6-11 would probably not be admitted. They would be better replaced by those in Exhibit 6-12.

Omission of zero in a scale may distort the presentation of facts. This may be avoided as shown in Exhibit 6-13.

The use of color. Color is very useful to differentiate elements on a chart, and to provide a link between similar elements on several charts. It can also be used for emphasis.

Using too many colors on one chart can be confusing. Three or four colors are a practical maximum. The most important element should have the brightest color. Basic colors such as red, blue, green, and yellow are most conservative and tend to be more credible than such colors as purple or orange. Bright colors tend to be associated with strength and happiness, whereas dark colors evoke weakness and negative feelings.

EXHIBIT 6-13. DIVIDEND GROWTH—SIX YEAR COMPARISON ($ MILLIONS)

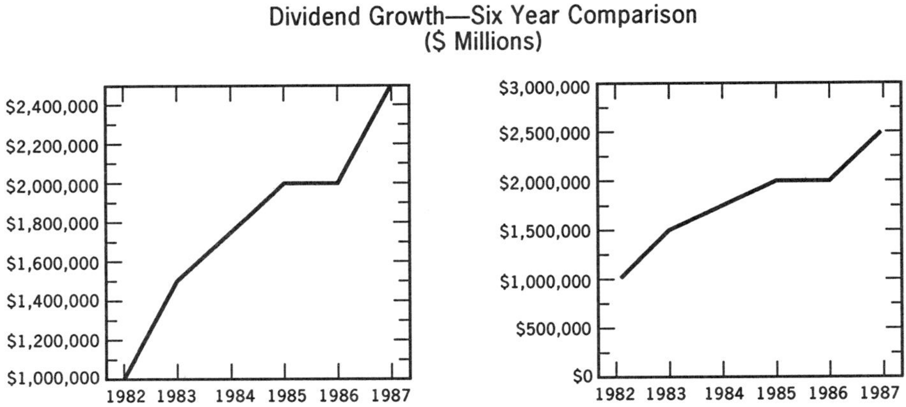

Personal computers make it very inexpensive and quite easy to produce colored exhibits in the CPA office. Plotters attached to personal computers cost very little and are able to generate multicolored charts quickly, using data from most popular spreadsheet programs. The charts can be drawn on paper to be given to the judge, opposing counsel, the court reporter, and the jury (if permitted). The same chart can be drawn directly on a transparency for projection to the jury. Any changes to the numbers in the spreadsheet will automatically generate a revised exhibit in minutes.

BIBLIOGRAPHY

Filter, D., *The Demonstrative Evidence Sourcebook* (Staffort-Hart Publications, 1985).
Joseph, G. P., *Modern Visual Evidence* (Law Journal Seminars Press, 1987).

7

WHERE TO GET THE DATA

Howard R. Sheppard, BS, CPA
Susan E. Carroll, BS, CPA

INTRODUCTION

One task for accountants in litigation engagements is to find information necessary to prepare a damage analysis, calculate lost profits, value a business or professional practice, and form an opinion for testimony. The task is to find appropriate information that the litigant's business records do not usually contain but that the accountant needs for the issues involved. Such information includes industry data, capitalization rates, representative salary and earnings data, industry financial ratios, economic data that affect the business cycle, minority discounts, and blockage adjustments.

For example, in a business valuation matter, U.S. Treasury Department Revenue Ruling 59–60 sets forth eight fundamental factors to consider when valuing a going concern. At least three of these factors require "outside" information sources.

1. The economic outlook in general and the condition and the outlook of the specific industry in particular.
2. Whether the enterprise has goodwill or other intangible value.
3. The market price of stocks of corporations engaged in the same or a similar line of business whose stocks actively trade in a free and open market, either on an exchange or over-the-counter market.

This chapter discusses various information sources that may aid the accountant who is searching for data to develop and authoritatively support opinions or conclusions. The chapter provides a guide of where to look rather than an exhaustive listing of every data source published.

GENERAL INFORMATION ABOUT SOURCE DATA

When an accountant testifies before a trier-of-fact, the testimony's subject matter may vary as widely as the entire international business and economic environment. Consequently, the accountant must learn many facts and statistics relating to the subject and issues of the case.

Two basic source books provide an excellent road map to discovering additional data and information that may relate to the accountant's litigation engagement: *Encyclopedia of Business Information Sources* (Koek et al., 1988) and *Where to Find Business Information* (Brownstone and Carruth, 1982).

The *Encyclopedia of Business Information Sources* is a bibliography of more than 1100 business subjects that cites the following sources for each subject:

General works
Abstract services and indexes
Almanacs and yearbooks
Bibliographies
Biographical sources
Directories
Encyclopedias and dictionaries
Financial ratios
Handbooks and manuals
Online databases
Periodicals and newsletters
Price sources

Research centers and institutes

Statistics sources

Trade associations and professional societies

Other sources

One or more of the following online information vendors provide many of the "online databases" mentioned before:

BRS Information Technologies
1200 Rte. 7
Latham, NY 12110

DIALOG Information Services
3460 Hillview Ave.
Palo Alto, CA 94304

SDC Information Services
2500 Colorado Ave.
Santa Monica, CA 90406

Where to Find Business Information (Brownstone and Carruth, 1982] lists approximately 5000 publications published in English throughout the world. The book emphasizes current business information. The authors have divided the book into three sections: Source finder, listing the publications by subject in alphabetical order; a publishers' index of over 1500 worldwide publishers; and a sources of business information of titles arranged alphabetically.

Selection of Data

Selecting data requires judgment and depends on the litigation issues involved. One should consider the following types of questions while selecting data:

1. Can one easily understand the data?
2. Does a data summary exist that provides a description of the detail?
3. Are the data from a reputable source?
4. Are the data consistently prepared over time?
5. Do the data clearly illustrate the point or position to be portrayed?
6. Are the data current?
7. Do sufficient data exist to form an opinion?
8. How were the data obtained?
9. Can one use the data in court?
10. Are the data from a confidential source and if so, is written permission necessary for their use?
11. Is the data source biased? For example: An accountant may have various clients' records from which to generate a database. Does this "internal" source (assuming the clients give written authorization to use the information) taint the data as biased according to the court?

12. When several sources of the same information exist, which should be used? For example, different private sources of lawyer income and expenses are available for valuing a law practice. Reputation of private data sources is of paramount importance. One can learn the standing of such private publishers through inquiry to other forensic experts experienced in the subject or by referring to other cases.

Reliability of Data

If the expert witness is to maintain credibility, the supporting data's reliability should be unimpeachable. Government publications provide the most acceptable data in court. Where government sources are not available, studies by private organizations may provide the next best source. Whereas some of these data may be considered hearsay, the accountant, as an expert witness, may rely on private sources in forming an opinion if they are the types of data normally relied upon by accountants. If the data have been seriously challenged in any forum, one should carefully consider whether to use them.

Admission of Data

If the accountant has been declared an expert witness, the accountant may use any data source in forming an opinion. However, one should note the Federal Rules regarding an experts' information sources. An article titled "Rules of the Game," from *Management Focus* sets forth the following with respect to experts' sources of information:

> Sources of expert information—Federal Rule 703 describes the permissible bases upon which expert testimony may be founded: a.) Information acquired through firsthand observation. b.) Facts observed by, or presented to, the expert witness at the trial or at the hearing. c.) Data that were considered by the expert witness outside of court. Rule 703 permits an expert to rely upon facts that are not admissible in evidence if they are of a type reasonably relied upon by experts in the field. The rule has two requirements: (1) the data must be the type that experts in the field normally rely upon, and (2) such reliance must be 'reasonable'; that is, the data must be trustworthy. The determination of whether particular data from which an expert formed his opinion were 'of a type reasonably relied upon by experts in the particular field' is left to the discretion of the trial judge. Where the court finds that the expert relied upon materials only for purposes of litigation (for example, he would not have used them in his normal work in the field), or that such materials are not customarily relied upon by experts in that particular field, or, in any event, that such reliance would be unreasonable because the materials are not trustworthy, the testimony should not be allowed. The factors bearing upon the determination of whether an expert's reliance on inadmissible material is unreasonable were summed up by the court, in one case, as follows:
>
> 1. The extent to which the opinion is pervaded or dominated by reliance on materials judicially determined to be inadmissible, on grounds of either relevance or trustworthiness.

2. The extent to which the opinion is dominated or pervaded by the expert's reliance upon other untrustworthy materials.
3. The extent to which the expert's assumptions have been shown to be unsupported, speculative, or demonstrably incorrect.
4. The extent to which the materials on which the expert relied are within his immediate sphere of expertise, are of a kind customarily relied upon by experts in the field in forming opinions or inferences on that subject, and are not used only for litigation purposes.
5. The extent to which the expert acknowledges the questionable reliability of the underlying information, thus indicating that he has taken that factor into consideration in forming his opinion.
6. The extent to which reliance on certain materials, even if otherwise reasonable, may be unreasonable in the peculiar circumstances of the case. It can be added that if, for example, an inadmissible document were one of a myriad of sources consulted by an expert, and if it were clear that the expert recognized and took into consideration the questionableness of that lone source, the opinion would likely be admissible. If, on the other hand, the expert's opinion were so dominated or pervaded by reliance on materials that were excluded for reasons bearing on their reliability, or if his opinion were rife with similarly unreliable unsupported conclusions, having no support in the record, that opinion must also be excluded. In short, it is a balancing process. An expert's opinion may rely upon the opinions of other experts. Furthermore, the reliability of opinions contained in published treatises, periodicals, or pamphlets and, in fact, the admissibility of such opinions can be established through the testimony of the expert himself.[1]

Data Usage

An expert witness must understand the accuracy and reliability of supporting data. The opposing party may know of an inaccuracy or deficiency in the data and devastatingly cross-examine to weaken the witness's credibility, opinions, and conclusions.

Data in litigation engagements support conclusions, pinpoint issues, provide comparability, provide a measuring stick, estimate relationships, reflect trends, show industry standards, provide the basis for charts and graphs and provide background information of a particular industry or segment of the economy that will help the accountant testify knowledgeably about the issues involved.

Geographical Data

Geographical data may vary from a worldwide scope to a limited area of one community. The attorney/client usually will furnish the accountant with enough information as to the geographical area relevant for the litigation. Subjects requiring data on a geographical basis include population trends, building activity, salary and income data, cost of living, cost price index data, interest rates, agricultural statistics, production statistics, and sales data. Many United Nations and U.S. government publications report by geographical areas and provide fine detail. State and local governments and agencies also maintain many records on a geographical basis. For example, the valuation of a medical practice may require geographical data on medical doctors' income to calculate goodwill. If the practice is in a metropolitan area in a midwestern state, such data are published in *Socioeconomic Characteristics of Medical Practice* (AMA Center for Health Research, 1987). If the practice is in a small community, one may need to contact a local CPA, hospital, clinic, or medical association as an additional data source for comparability of income or salary data.

Specialized Industries

Most industries that represent a significant factor in the gross national product usually maintain data through an association or similar organization. These associations may be national, state or regional, or local. The accountant should ask the client whether such special industry associations or groups exist and whether data are available from such organizations.

The *Encyclopedia of Associations* (Gale Research Company, 1986) includes the names of associations for specialized industries. Many of these associations collect and publish data from members about the industry, business, or profession they represent. Data for specialized industries are discussed later.

Originals versus Photocopies

Original documents are always preferable for use in court; originals admitted into evidence, however, will not be returned to the owner. The development of quality photocopy equipment in the last several decades has made photocopies acceptable in many courts.

Whenever one desires to use photocopies, the accountant should ascertain as early as possible through counsel whether the court will accept photocopies, rather than waiting until trial testimony to find that photocopies will not be admissible.

When the quality of an original is such that even the best photocopy equipment has difficulty reproducing an acceptable copy, most often the original must be used; the alternative would be a wet process photo. For enhancement or enlargement, engage a professional photographer.

GROWING NUMBER OF COMPUTER DATABASES

One can choose from hundreds of computer databases covering a large range of subjects; the only problem is in knowing what is available. The following references list databases available with information on the type of database, the content and source of information, and the vendor.

1. *Directory of Online Databases* (Cuadra and Elsevier, 1987). This quarterly directory includes the individual databases arranged alphabetically, and indexes by subject, producer, and telecommunication.

2. *The Computer Data and Database Source Book* (Lesko, 1984). This book describes itself as "a complete encyclopedia of all commercial and public sources of information for use with any computer." The book divides the databases into commercial, government and public data sources. The last section explains how to access public data which is often free.
3. *Complete Guide to Dial-Up Databases* (Datapro Research, 1985). This directory includes a profile of online services suppliers, a description of databases in alphabetical order, a subject index, and also user ratings of information retrieval services and time-sharing services.
4. *Using Litigation Databases* (T. Kiley, 1987). This publication explains how to access a particular database, who maintains each database, the years a database covers, and the total number of records.

How to Access Database Information

One can access many databases by using a personal computer in conjunction with a modem connected to an outside telephone line. For information on accessing a specific database, refer to the database reference books noted before that list the address and phone number of each database publisher. AICPA members can access the AICPA's entire online tax and accounting library that includes the following databases: FEDERALTAXLAWS, NAARS, NEXIS, GENFED, BNKG, BKRTCY, FEDSEC, STATES, and VIEWPT. One can also access databases through computer facilities at local law or university libraries.

FINANCIAL DATA ON PUBLIC COMPANIES

The accountant's litigation engagement may involve a publicly or privately held company or companies. Often data of publicly held companies become useful in both types of situations. Data on publicly held companies are widely published in various mediums and contained in extensive databases. The following sources may help one find the data needed.

Securities and Exchange Commission

All companies issuing securities that meet the following criteria must file Form 10-K, Form 10-Q, and Form 8-K with the Securities and Exchange Commission:

1. The securities are traded on a national securities exchange, or
2. The securities are traded over the counter, and the total assets exceed $1 million, or there are over 500 or more stockholders at any fiscal year end.

The Securities and Exchange Commission publishes these reports daily in the SEC *Digest* that also includes major commission announcements, rule-making actions, court and administrative decisions, and the registration statements filed under the Securities Act of 1933. Databases such as Disclosure II then compile these data for easy reference.

Form 10-K. The company must file this annual report with the Securities and Exchange Commission within 90 days after the close of the company's last fiscal quarter.

Form 10-Q. All registrants who file Form 10-K with the SEC must file Form 10-Q for each of the first three fiscal quarters within 45 days of each quarter's end.

Form 8-K. Form 8-K reports significant events that may affect a company's future or the value of its securities. The following events are considered significant, and a Form 8-k must be filed within 15 days after the event occurs:

1. Changes in control of the registrant
2. Acquisition or disposition of a significant amount of assets other than in the ordinary course of business
3. The appointment of a receiver of the registrant in a bankruptcy or similar proceeding
4. Changes in the registrant's certifying accountant
5. Any event the registrant deems to be of material importance to security holders

Moody's

Information compiled by Moody's from the reports filed with the Securities and Exchange Commission is available through Moody's printed service or through the DIALOG computer database.

Moody's Manuals. This subscription service includes an annual hard-bound manual, news reports issued twice weekly, and the *Complete Corporate Index* published in June, September, and October of each year. The service, available at many local libraries, contains analysis of over 22,000 corporations and institutions. The service comprises of the following seven manuals:

Moody's Bank and Finance Manual
Moody's Industrial Manual
Moody's International Manual
Moody's OTC Industrial Manual
Moody's Public Utility Manual
Moody's Transportation Manual
Moody's OTC Unlisted Manual

The *Complete Corporate Index* alphabetically lists every corporation and institution included in the service and lists the manual, volume number, and page that contains that entity's data.

Databases. Moody's produces three databases that one can access through the DIALOG online service. *Moody's Corporate News—International* contains business news and financial information on about 3900 public and private corporations in about 100 countries. *Moody's Corporate News—U.S.* contains business news and financial information on about 15,000 public and private U.S. corporations. Financial data are taken from annual reports and include manufacturers, banks, savings and loans, insurance companies, real estate companies, investment trusts, public utilities, and shipping companies. *Moody's Corporate Profiles* contains descriptive and financial information on over 3600 publicly held U.S. companies. Sources include corporate annual and quarterly reports, news releases, proxy statements, prospectuses, stock exchange bulletins, and news and trade journals. These services are updated weekly, and most cover from 1983 to the present.

Standard & Poor's

Standard & Poor's offers eight computer accessed databases and corresponding printed subscription services:

Standard & Poor's Blue List. This service is available through Interactive Data Corporation and contains data on current municipal bond offerings including ratings by Standard & Poor's and Moody's. This corresponds to data in Standard & Poor's Blue List.

Standard & Poor's Corporate Descriptions Online. This service is available through DIALOG and provides descriptive and financial information on over 9000 publicly held U.S. corporations. This information is included in the Standard & Poor's Corporation Record printed service. The computer database service is updated weekly.

Standard & Poor's Economic Report. This service is accessed through NewsNet, Inc., and contains analyses of the U.S. economy, interest rates, and the money and bond markets. The information is updated monthly.

Standard & Poor's General Information File. CompuServe Information Service is the vendor for this service and users pay a small surcharge for each profile. This service offers profiles of descriptive and financial information on 3000 major U.S. publicly held corporations. Information is updated weekly.

Standard & Poor's Industry Financial Data Bank. This service is available through DRI and contains over 2000 monthly, quarterly, and annual time series that describe the financial position of some 100 industry groups. Industry data include sales, earnings per share, dividends per share, book value, depreciation, and other information. These data are also published by Standard & Poor's in the *Analysts Handbook*, *Current Statistics*, and *Outlook*. The computer database contains information from 1946 to the present.

Standard & Poor's News Online. This service is also available through DIALOG and contains the full text of financial news stories related to any of more than 10,000 leading corporations. Sources include company releases, reports to the SEC and stockholders, leading newswire services, and the like. The computer database covers June 1979 to the present and is updated daily. The corresponding printed service is S&P's Corporation Records publications, Daily News and Cumulative News.

Standard & Poor's Register—Biographical. This service, available through DIALOG, contains biographies of approximately 72,000 prominent business executives and directors of publicly and privately held companies with over $1 million or more in sales that are listed in *Standard & Poor's Register—Corporate*.

Standard & Poor's Register—Corporate. This service, available through CompuServe and DIALOG, contains descriptive information on approximately 45,000 publicly and privately held corporations. This service is updated quarterly.

Walker's

Walker's Manual is a printed service covering only public corporations and financial institutions headquartered in the 13 western states. The manual is published annually with monthly supplements. The manual contains descriptive as well as financial information on the companies and includes alphabetical, geographic, and standard industrial classification indexes.

Stock Prices

Wall Street Journal. The *Wall Street Journal* publishes daily stock information for the previous trading day including the number of sales, the high selling price, the low selling price, the closing selling price, and the change in closing sales price. The *Journal* includes the American Stock Exchange, the New York Stock Exchange, NASDAQ (National Association of Security Dealers Automated Quotation) Over-the-Counter-stocks, Other Over-the Counter-stocks, foreign markets, and selected stocks from other markets. Other markets include the Toronto, Montreal, Midwest, Pacific, Philadelphia, and Boston exchanges. Foreign markets include London, South African Mines, Switzerland, Tokyo, Amsterdam, Hong Kong, Frankfurt, Brussels, Milan, Paris, Stockholm, and Sydney.

Other Sources. Historical stock prices and current prices are available through various computer-oriented companies such as Dow Jones Quotes—Dow Jones News/Retrieval Service, Quotdial—Autoron Systems, Inc., Vu/Quote–Vu/TEXT Information Services, ADP One Quotation Service, and the Center for Research in Securities Prices of the University of Chicago. Local stockbrokers can also provide current stock prices.

Computer Databases

The following computer databases compile the information on a timely basis from the Form 10-Ks, Form 10-Qs, and Form 8-Ks and make that information available to the public for a charge. The databases are sometimes available from more than one vendor and many have per inquiry pricing.

Disclosure II. Developed by Disclosure, 5161 River Road, Bethesda, MD 20816. Telephone (301) 951–1300. This database is updated weekly from reports filed with the SEC, annual reports to shareholders, registration statements of new registrants, and tender offer/acquisition reports. The database includes information on over

9700 publicly owned companies that must file forms with the SEC. Features include per inquiry pricing, training sessions and inclusion in DIALOG, Dow Jones Retrieval, CompuServe, and ADP Network Services.

ADP Financial System One Quotation Service. This service provides quotes on securities and commodities from national and regional securities markets, options, over the counter, and commodities exchanges in the United States and Canada.

GOVERNMENT SOURCES AND PUBLICATIONS

U.S. Federal Government

The following books provide help in locating government data on a particular subject.

Guide to U.S. Government Publications (Androit, 1977). This publication is an annotated guide to publications of the various government departments. The book provides an alphabetical list of publications within each department and an index to all publications.

Monthly Catalogue of U.S. Government Publications, U.S. Superintendent of Documents. This publication is available at many public libraries.

Bureau of Labor Statistics. The BLS is the government's principal fact finding agency in labor economics. The bureau's many publications include the following:

1. *Area Wage Surveys.* These annual studies include not only office workers but also professional and technical, maintenance, and power plant and custodial and material movement occupations.
2. *Employment and Earnings Statistics for States and Areas.* Annual publication.
3. *Handbook of Labor Statistics.* Annual publication.
4. *National Survey of Professional, Administrative, Technical, and Clerical Pay.* Annual publication.
5. *Monthly Labor Review.* This publication contains all current BLS statistical series covering employment, labor turnover, earnings and hours, consumer and wholesale prices, work stoppages, and productivity. The data date from 1915.
6. *Bureau of Labor Statistics Catalog* of publications, bulletins, reports, releases, and periodicals. Published semiannually.
7. Consumer price index and the CPI detailed report, consumer price index, U.S. city average and selected areas. Published monthly.

Federal Reserve System. The Federal Reserve system controls the banking industry and publishes many banking-related periodicals. The following lists some of those publications:

1. *Federal Reserve Bulletin.* Published monthly, this bulletin presents articles of general and special interest, policy, and other official statements issued

by the Federal Reserve Board and statistical information relating to domestic financial and business developments and to international financial developments.

2. *Summary Report, Assets and Liabilities of Member Banks*. Published at least three times a year.
3. Other reports on member banks including *Member Bank Loans*, *Member Bank Income*, and *Deposits, Reserves, and Borrowings of Member Banks*.
4. *Business Indexes*. Published monthly, this report contains summary tables for various data including industrial production, utility output, employment, and department store sales.
5. *National Summary of Business Conditions*. Published monthly.
6. *Interest Rates*. Interest rates charged on selected types of financial instruments such as commercial paper, finance paper placed directly, bankers acceptances, certificates of deposit, bank prime loans, discount window borrowing, corporate bonds, treasury bills, treasury constant maturities, state and local bonds, and conventional mortgages. The data are available on a weekly, monthly, and annual basis. Certain data can be obtained on a current basis by telephone.
7. *Consumer Credit*. Published monthly.
8. *Crop Report*, by Federal Reserve districts.
9. *U.S. Government Securities Yield and Prices*. Published weekly.

Department of Commerce. This department publishes data on a wide variety of subjects from the *Federal Meteorological Handbooks* to *Export Control, Quarterly Reports*. The department has indexed these publications in the *United States Department of Commerce Publications*, first published in 1952 and supplemented annually. The following briefly lists additional Department of Commerce publications.

1. *Statistical Abstract of the United States*. Published annually since 1878, this abstract is the standard summary of statistics on the social, political, and economic organization of the United States. The appendix to this publication includes a guide to sources of statistics and a guide to state statistical abstracts.
2. *Domestic Commerce*. Published monthly.

Bureau of the Census. The Census Bureau is the largest general-purpose statistical agency of the U.S. government. The bureau collects and publishes statistics for 12 major subject areas:

Population
Housing
Retail trade
Wholesale trade
Service industries
Manufactures
Transportation
Construction

Agriculture
Governments
Mineral industries
Foreign trade

The frequency of the availability of these data range from the weekly survey of retail trade to the population and housing census conducted every 10 years. The publications provide statistics for differing geographic areas, ranging from city blocks to the entire nation.

Standard Industrial Classifications. The *Standard Industrial Classification Manual* (SIC) was developed to help the government facilitate comparability of statistics describing various segments of the economy. Individual business firms and trade associations now use SIC to classify customers and suppliers in market research. Standard & Poor's provides an index by SIC code for classification of the corporations included in that series. Various publications, such as Dun & Bradstreet's *Key Business Ratios*, use the SIC number for accumulating data.

When searching for data relating to a particular industry or segment, the accountant can usually find the SIC code on the litigant's federal income tax returns. If the tax returns are not available, then a description of the business activity will usually indicate a classification from the published SIC list.

State, County, and City Publications and Statistics

State and local entities also maintain various statistics. Some counties publish an annual *County Progress Report* that includes various economic statistics. These reports are compiled from state labor reports, bank research reports, and county agency data. Other counties may have the same data available but publish the data on a request-only basis.

Personnel Reports. Most states' employment agencies maintain the following statistics:

1. The number of people employed and unemployed by specific areas of the state.
2. The number of wage and salary workers by industry per county and the estimated annual pay per employee.

Another information source is State Income Tax Boards that publish annual reports with data on the number of returns in specific adjusted gross income brackets by county and the median income by county.

The economic or personnel department of a specific county or city may also compile additional statistics on wages and personnel.

Economic Trends. State Statistical Research and/or Consulting Divisions, Boards of Equalization, or similar departments or agencies maintain statistics on total sales by type of business and the number of outlets by county. For example, the statistics may track the number of sporting goods stores annually in a particular area and the total retail sales by those stores.

The county's auditor–controller or assessor may publish data on the total assessed valuation by jurisdiction per fiscal year. One can also find these data in chamber of commerce publications.

Data on a city's estimated population, which is more current than the census data, may be found in state finance department records and chamber of commerce publications or county reports. One should investigate these sources if the litigation relates to assessed valuation, population, or related matters.

Agricultural Reports. State and county governments usually maintain—through their weights and measures department, agricultural division, or similar department or agency—data on the agriculture industry. These data are usually published annually in a crop or agriculture statistics report. One should always know the time period covered in these reports. Such information may be on a crop year, fiscal year, season basis, calendar year, or pool year where cooperative organizations are involved.

Business Activity Reports. The chamber of commerce in many cities can provide information on business directories, demographic materials, industrial site information, retail booklets, and economic profiles. Although the city or county supplies the data for these reports, the chamber reports often combine all these data in a convenient package.

Building Permits. One should contact the city and/or county building department to find where the statistics on the number of building permits issued and the valuation are published.

INDUSTRY DATA—GENERAL

In many types of cases, the accountant may find the following data useful:

1. Industry sales volume
2. Selling prices
3. Profit percentages
4. Costs of doing business
5. Accounts receivable collection periods
6. Inventory turnover rates
7. Salary and wage information
8. Market prices of similar business sales
9. Industry standards
10. Capitalization rates

The following publications and information sources should help the accountant find these data:

Annual Statement Studies—Robert Morris Associates

The *Robert Morris Annual Statement Studies* have been published continuously since 1923, and records on some industries are available from 1917. The information is based on standard balance sheet and income statement data for approximately 28,000 customers of member banks of Robert Morris Associates.

The *Statement Studies* are organized into separate industries in manufacturing, wholesaling, retailing, and services by SIC Code, and within each industry the statements are grouped according to asset size as follows: under $250,000, $250,000 to less than $1,000,000 and $1,000,000 to less than $10,000,000, and over $10,000,000.

The statements in these four size classes are then combined into the all-sizes tabulation. Each item on the balance sheet and income statement is reported as a percentage, with total assets and total sales, respectively, equaling 100%. The bottom of each page lists total sales and total assets in dollar amounts to enable one to recast all the figures into dollars. Various ratios are also provided.

Almanac of Business and Industrial Financial Ratios

The *Almanac of Business and Industrial Financial Ratios* (Prentice-Hall, 1987), compiles financial performance data on U.S. firms in 181 lines of business and industry, rating small, medium, and large companies by 22 key financial factors and is an aid for financial analysis, business planning, investment decisions, market research, report writing, and many other purposes. The *Almanac* provides a basis for comparing a company's performance by the 22 indexes of financial performance, from cost of operations to ratio of retained earnings to net income. One can identify areas of financial strength or weakness relative to competitors. The *Almanac* contains performance charts for major industry and lines of business organized by 16 broad classifications generally corresponding to the government's SIC codes: manufacturing, construction, mining, communications, transportation, utilities, wholesale trade, retail trade, banking, real estate, and other major sectors of economic activity. These large groupings are subdivided into 78 smaller categories, which in turn are broken down into the 181 types of industries.

Dun & Bradstreet—Key Business Ratios

Dun & Bradstreet publishes statistics on over 800 lines of business based on a computerized financial statement file containing data on over 800,000 publicly and privately held companies. The more than 800 lines of business are defined by the U.S. Standard Industrial Classification system and are listed by a four-digit SIC code. They cover all the major industries: manufacturing, retailing, wholesaling, mining, construction, and others. The key business ratios are reported in four size ranges by net worth for each SIC Code. This report lists the median and the upper and lower quartiles of the following 14 business ratios:

1. Current assets to current debt
2. Net profit on sales

3. Net profits on tangible net worth
4. Net profits on net working capital
5. Net sales to tangible net worth
6. Net sales to net working capital
7. Collection period
8. Net sales to inventory
9. Fixed assets to tangible net worth
10. Current debt to tangible net worth
11. Total debt to tangible net worth
12. Inventory to net working capital
13. Current debt to inventory
14. Funded debts to net working capital

Accountant's Index—AICPA

The AICPA's annual *Accountant's Index* supplement is a bibliography of accounting literature and a comprehensive index source of reference accounting literature. AICPA members may borrow a copy of the publications listed in the *Accountant's Index* by contacting the AICPA library.

The AICPA Journal of Accountancy publishes an index to its current articles in the June and December issues.

New York Times Index

The *New York Times* provides a computer database available through Mead Data Central that contains the full text of all its news and editorial material from June 1980 to the present.

Handbook of Small Business Valuation Formulas

The *Handbook of Small Business Valuation Formulas* (Desmond and Marcello, 1987) is a guide to rule-of-thumb formulas, which one may consider along with other valuation methods for business valuation related to sale, purchase, or merger, gift and estate tax planning, employee stock ownership plans, eminent domain, insurance planning, and litigation. The handbook includes rules-of-thumb for 20 types of business:

1. Accounting and bookkeeping practices
2. Apparel stores
3. Auto body shops
4. Automobile dealerships
5. Bicycle shops
6. Building material retailers
7. Coin-operated and full-service carwashes

8. Cocktail lounges
9. Coffee shops
10. Coin-operated laundries
11. Dental practices
12. Funeral services and mortuaries
13. Gasoline service stations
14. Grocery stores
15. Insurance agencies and brokers
16. Manufacturers' sales agencies
17. Newspapers (weekly)
18. Travel agencies
19. Veterinary practices
20. Video rental and sales shops

Financial Studies of the Small Business

Financial Research Associates publishes financial ratios for small firms. Heretofore, most published financial data have been compiled from larger firms. This report includes only companies with total capitalization under $1,000,000. The data come from over 25,000 financial statements. Over 1000 independent CPA firms, geographically dispersed across the country, contribute data to the study on an ongoing basis. The reports present the data by asset size for various retail, wholesale, service, contractor, professional, and manufacturing businesses. The asset size ranges are as follows: $10,000 to $100,000; $100,000 to $250,000; $250,000 to $500,000; and $500,000 to $1,000,000.

INDUSTRY DATA—SPECIFIC INDUSTRIES AND PROFESSIONS

Socioeconomic Characteristics of Medical Practice

This American Medical Association publication helps in valuing medical practices. Data tables contain six sections:

1. Weeks and hours of practice
2. Utilization of physician services
3. Hospital utilization by physicians
4. Fees for physicians' visits
5. Professional expenses of physician
6. Physician net income after expenses before taxes

The data for each of these categories are organized by medical specialty, geographical area, type of practice, and age group.

The 1987 edition includes six new studies on medicine's socioeconomic environment:

1. Provision of charity care by physicians
2. Trends, variations and the distribution of physician earnings
3. Physician involvement with Medicare
4. Third party reimbursement and physician fees
5. Physician responses to competition 1980–1987
6. Medical professional liability and claims

Socioeconomic Characteristics of Medical Practice is published annually by the American Medical Association, P. O. Box 10946, Chicago, Illinois 60610-0946.

Survey of Law Firm Economics

Altman & Weil, Inc. Management Consultants (P. O. Box 472, Ardmore, Pennsylvania 19003) publishes this annual survey. Both law firms and valuation experts extensively use this publication that reports the characteristics of participating firms in the survey, ratio of associates to partners to shareholders, ratio of paralegal assistants to lawyers, starting salary offers, gross receipts, total expenses, average income per lawyer and per earner, hourly rates and fees for different types of legal services, annual client hours worked, earnings and compensation of lawyers, staff, value of unbilled time, time written off, and related matters.

Much of the lawyer-related information is identified by the year the lawyer began practicing, the region where the practice is located, the law firm's size, and the community's population.

Altman & Weil also publishes a survey of salaries for the in-house counsel of corporations and institutions. This report arranges the information by position, classification, region, industry and years in practice.

The Lawyer Statistical Report

The American Bar Foundation (Chicago, Illinois) publishes lawyer statistics on law firm income and related matters that may prove useful in lawyer marital dissolution cases.

The American Almanac of Jobs and Salaries (Wright, 1984)

This annually updated almanac lists the salaries for a wide variety of occupations. The information was derived from statistics provided by professional organizations or publications directly involved in a particular field. The following subdivisions show the variety of occupations that this almanac includes:

Public payroll
Entertainment industry
Professional occupations

- Science and technology
- Key white-collar jobs
- Jobs and salaries in representative businesses
  - Advertising
  - Airlines
  - Banking
  - Brokerage firms
  - Department store
  - Hotels and motels
  - Insurance industry
  - Magazine
  - Newspaper
  - Publishing house
  - Railroads
- Jobs and salaries in some big unions
  - Health care industry
  - Workaday world
  - Building trade workers
  - The office staff
  - Machining occupations
  - Material movement workers
  - Mechanics and repairers
  - Restaurant workers
  - Barbers and beauticians
- Special groups
  - Farmers and farm workers
  - Fitness experts
  - Agents, auctioneers, brokers
  - Writers
- Sports

Census of Service Industries

The law requires that the Department of Commerce conduct a Census of Service Industries at 5-year intervals for the years ending in 2 and 7. The 1982 census covered the following service industries as defined in the SIC manual:

- Hotels, rooming houses, camps, and other lodging places
- Personal service
- Business services

Automotive repair, services, and garages
Miscellaneous repair services
Amusement and recreation services, including motion pictures
Health services, except hospitals
Legal services
Selected educational services
Social services
Noncommercial museums, art galleries, and botanical and zoological gardens
Selected membership organizations
Miscellaneous services

All large and medium-sized firms and all firms known to operate more than one establishment are mailed questionnaires. For small firms, the department uses data from existing administrative records of other federal agencies. The collected data were divided into three categories: size of establishment, size of firm, and legal form of organization. The collected data show the receipts, the number of individual proprietorships, the number of partnerships, the annual payroll, and the first quarter payroll. The data are published in the following reports:

- Establishment and Firm Size
- Capital Expenditures, Depreciable Assets, and Operating Expenses
- Geographic Area Series
    - United States
    - Individual State
    - Standard Consolidated Statistical Area
    - Standard Metropolitan Statistical Area
    - County
    - Place
- Hotels, Motels, and Other Lodging Places
- Motion Picture Industry
- Miscellaneous Subjects
    - Advertising Agencies
    - Commercial Photography, Art, and Graphics
    - Management, Consulting, and Public Relations Services
    - Automotive Repair
    - Offices of Physicians
    - Offices of Dentists
    - Legal Services
    - Engineering, Architectural, and Surveying Services
    - Accounting, Auditing, and Bookkeeping Services

Statistics of Income—Business Income Tax Returns

The Department of the Treasury, Internal Revenue Service, annually compiles the data from the tax returns filed and publishes the statistics by industry. For businesses, these statistics were published in *Statistics of Income: Business Income Tax Returns* for the years 1957–1976. Since 1976, the same data have been published in two separate publications: *Statistics of Income, Sole Proprietorship Returns*, and *Statistics of Income, Partnership Returns.* For sole proprietorships, the statistics show the total number of returns, business receipts, depreciation, rent paid deduction, interest, payroll, and net income or loss. The data appear separately for businesses with income and for all businesses.

The partnership publication distinguishes between partnerships with income and all partnerships. The data include each line item on the front of the partnership return including business receipts, rents received, cost of sales, salaries and wages, taxes, and depreciation.

Statistics of Income is published for individual returns, corporation returns, fiduciary tax returns and estate tax returns.

Computerized Databases

The following databases may help one find data and information:

1. *Management Contents Database.* Developed by Information Access Company, 11 Davis Drive, Belmont, CA 94002. This database provides current information on various business and management topics to aid individuals in business, consulting firms, educational institutions, government agencies or bureaus, and libraries in decision making and forecasting. Articles from approximately 500 U.S. and international journals, proceedings, and transactions are fully indexed and abstracted to provide current information in accounting, decision sciences, finance, industrial relations, managerial economics, marketing, operations research, organizational behavior, and public administration.
2. *ABI/INFORM Database.* Developed by Data Courier, Inc., 620 S. 5th St., Louisville, KY 40202. Telephone (502) 582-4111, Telex 204235. This database provides worldwide business and management information from 1971 to present. Information may be found by business issue, topic or term, company name, author, or date of publication.

   The file contains abstracts of over 500 business and management publications including 140 foreign publications. Its full range of industry-specific coverage includes the following functional areas: accounting and auditing, economics, EDP systems and information science, finance and management, law and taxation, management science, marketing, advertising, sales promotion, and human resources.
3. *Congressional Information Services (CIS) Database.* Developed by Congressional Information Service, Inc., 4520 E-W Highway, Suite 800, Washington, DC 20014. Telephone (301) 654-1550. The CIS database is the machine-readable form of the Congressional Information Service's Index to Publications of the

United States Congress. CIS provides current, comprehensive access to the contents of all congressional working papers published by the nearly 300 House, Senate, and joint committees and subcommittees each year. These hearings, prints, reports, documents, and other special publications record the vital investigatory, oversight, and legislative analysis activities of Congress. Hearings' publications contain not only transcripts of testimony from public and government witnesses but also a wealth of exhibit reports, statistical data, and articles. Other publications contain the reports of specially commissioned studies, analyses of federal legislation and activities, and compilations of background materials concerning a broad range of issues.

4. *National Criminal Justice Reference Service Database* (NCJRS). National Criminal Justice Reference Service, Box 6000, Rockville, MD 20850 (301) 251-5500. The NCJRS database covers all aspects of law enforcement and criminal justice from police, courts, corrections, juvenile justice, community crime prevention, criminal justice system, fraud, and waste and abuse in government programs. Documents include both U.S. and international research reports, published papers, books, articles, and audiovisual presentations. Topics range from preliminary research to detailed descriptions of successful programs.
5. *Legal Resource Index Database.* Developed by Information Access Corp., 362 Lakeside Drive, Foster City, CA 94404. Telephone (800) 227-8431. This database provides cover-to-cover indexing of over 660 key law journals and five law newspapers plus legal monographs and government publications from the Library of Congress MARC database. It indexes articles, book reviews, case notes, president's pages, columns, letters to the editor, obituaries, transcripts, biographical pieces, and editorials. The database includes relevant law articles from Magazine Index and National Newspaper Index.
6. *ADP.* Automatic Data Processing, Network Services Div., 175 Jackson Plaza, Ann Arbor, MI 48106. Telephone (313) 769-6800. ADP produces various financial databases available on a subscription basis through its on-line service. The following briefly describes the available databases.
   a. *FX (Foreign Exchange).* This database, updated daily, includes currency exchange rates on over 35 currencies, interest rate data on Eurocurrency, London Interbranch Offer Rate, and the domestic money market and gold and silver prices.
   b. *SCAN200.* This service contains over 375 time series of historical and forecast data of key importance in business trend analysis. Townsend-Greenspare & Co. provides the forecasts, and the historical data date from 1947. This service is updated daily.
   c. *U.S. ECON.* This series contains over 25,000 time series on the U.S. economy that include bank reserves, construction, consumer prices, employment, farm prices, motor vehicles, retail sales and inventories, and numerous other areas. Most data are from 1947 to present and come from various sources, including the Bureau of Economic Analysis, Bureau of Labor Statistic, Moody's Investor Service, National Association of Mutual

Savings Banks, U.S. Department of Agriculture, and *The Wall Street Journal*.

7. *Data Resources, Inc. (DRI).* 24 Hartwell Ave., Lexington, MA 02173. Telephone (617) 863-5100. DRI provides econometric forecasting and associated services to analysts in industry, finance, and government. This service provides access to a vast quantity of historic and predictive information stored as time series in DRI databases and access to software developed by DRI professionals for use in financial reporting, econometric modeling, policy analysis, and corporate planning. DRI consultants also conduct research projects for clients such as building a general forecasting model for a company or preparing a detailed analysis of a specific industry. Database access includes U.S. economics national and regional databases, international economics databases from Canada, Japan, and Europe, international and domestic energy databases, securities industry databases, and various industrial databases on agriculture, forest products, defense economics, insurance, steel, and automotive news. These services are available through DRI's DRINET, or via the Uninet and Tymnet networks.
8. *NEXIS.* Marketed by Mead Data Central, Inc., P.O. Box 933, 9393 Springboro Pike, Dayton, OH 45401. Telephone (800) 227-4908. This database contains the full text of stories from 14 leading general and business newspapers, 43 magazines, 13 wire services, and 52 newsletters. The database replicates the entire text of the primary source and nearly every word or phrase is searchable. NEXIS updates this service continuously, and only subscribers can access it.
9. *AICPA.* The AICPA offers two databases, National Automated Accounting Research System (NAARS), and Accountants. Both databases are accessed on a subscription basis, although NAARS can also be accessed on an individual basis for a fee by calling the AICPA.
   a. NAARS, available through Mead Data Central, Inc., P.O. Box 933, 9393 Springboro Pike, Dayton, OH 45401. Telephone (800) 227-4908. This database comprises three main files; the annual reports file, proxy file, and accounting literature file. The annual reports file contains financial statements from over 4200 annual reports for companies traded on the New York and American Stock Exchanges and over the counter. The proxy file contains elements of proxy statements from selected companies. The accounting literature file contains the full text of various accounting literature, including Statements of the Accounting Principles Board, Statements on Auditing Standards, publications from the Financial Accounting Standards Board, SEC Accounting Series Releases, and International Accounting Standards Committee pronouncements. This service is updated weekly and annual reports are available back to 1972.
   b. *Accountants.* This service, available through ORBIT Search Service, cites business and finance literature with emphasis on accounting, auditing, data processing, financial reporting, investments and securities, management, and taxation. This service corresponds to the printed *Accountant's Index* and contains both international and domestic articles from over 300 periodicals, books, pamphlets, and government documents. About 3500 records

are updated each quarter, and the information dates from 1974 to the present.

10. *Predicast, Inc.* 11001 Cedar Ave., Cleveland, OH 44106. Telephone (800)321-6388. Predicast produces various databases accessible through DRS and DIALOG.

   a. PTS Annual Reports Abstracts. This computer database contains statistical and textual data for over 3000 companies in the United States and selected international companies. The financial tables from company reports show details about sales, profits, capital expenditures, assets, and exports. Textual abstracts describe products, market shares and strategies, major lines of business, and other details. The service is updated monthly.

   b. PTS F&S Indexes. This database covers both domestic and international company, product, and industry information. This database also contains the Source Directory that provides online access to a comprehensive bibliography of more than 5000 publications cited in Predicasts publications.

   c. PTS International Forecasts. This computer database contains abstracts of published forecasts with historical data for all countries (excluding the United States). Information is extracted from more than 1000 international sources, including annual reports to foreign governments, statistical reports of industries and trade associations of foreign countries, publications of the United Nations, and other international publications.

   d. PTS Marketing and Advertising Reference Service. This computer database contains information pertaining to the marketing and advertising of consumer products. The abstracted information comes from more than 70 sources that include trade publications, business journals, and industry journals.

   e. PTS New Product Announcements. This computer database contains the full text of press releases from all industries covering announcements related to products, focusing on new products and services. The press releases are obtained directly from the vendor, and the company contacts and phone numbers are included for further reference.

   f. PTS Prompt. This computer database abstracts information regarding acquisitions, capacities, end uses, environment, international trade, market data, new products, production, regulations, and technology from thousands of newspapers, business magazines, government reports, trade journals, bank letters, and special reports throughout the world.

   g. PTS U.S. Forecasts. This computer database contains abstracts of published forecasts for the United States from trade journals, business and financial publications, key newspapers, government reports, and special studies.

   h. PTS U.S. Time Series. This computer database contains two subfiles—*Predicasts Composites* and *Predicasts Basebook*. *Predicasts Composites* contains time series based on historical data from 1957 and projects data for 1990 for population, GNP, per capita income, employment, production or usage of major materials, products, energy, and vehicles, detailed construction, industrial production, and price series. The *Basebook* contains annual data from 1957 to date for about 47,000 series on U.S. production, consumption, prices, foreign trade, agriculture, mining, manufacturing, wages, and end-use distribution for many types of industries, products and services.

OTHER SOURCES

Banks and Bank Research Departments

Some banks in major cities have research departments that compile a variety of statistics on such subjects as building permits, residential and business valuations, and per capita income. These data may not be available to the general public.

Chambers of Commerce

Even when a city's chamber of commerce does not maintain particular data, it may have reports prepared by local and county agencies on economic, building, sales information, and major manufacturers for the city.

Law Libraries

Law libraries house information about damages, lost profits, and related matters previously adjudicated. The library contains the full text of any published decisions of federal and state courts, the tax court decisions, and the IRS publications, including the letter rulings. Some libraries also subscribe to Lexis or Westlaw.

University Libraries

University libraries can be invaluable. Often they are government depositories and have copies of many of the government publications noted in this chapter. The libraries also have reference books regarding databases and may have access to some of the database services. Some libraries can identify the nearest library owning a publication that they do not.

Brokerage House Reports

Brokerage houses can provide current information on publicly traded businesses. In addition to current stock prices, they can often provide current financial data on selected companies and estimated earnings on those companies, information on current interest rates, statistics on foreign currencies, and historical graphs. Many brokerage houses publish weekly and monthly reports.

ASSOCIATIONS AND PROFESSIONAL ORGANIZATIONS

Associations, institutes, and professional organizations can provide a wealth of data. Sometimes these organizations are reluctant to provided proprietary information based on surveys of members; however, one can usually obtain data by paying for the information or publication. If the data is obtained from a member of the organization, the accountant needs to obtain permission to use or reproduce the data. Many organizations have free publications lists.

An excellent source of the names of professional associations, academies, and institutes is the U.S. Treasury Department IRS publication listing of nonprofit organizations. The *Encyclopedia of Associations* provides another source for association information.

PRIVATE SOURCES OF DATA

Data from private sources are usually the most difficult to obtain. For example, information about professional salaries, for use in a professional practice valuation in a particular local area, is confidential information that accountant–bookkeepers and CPAs are reluctant to divulge.

Nongovernment entities conduct surveys for particular industries and have become a private source of data. One can usually obtain these surveys only by direct purchase from the publisher at a cost of $75 or more for 1 year of data. A helpful source is the *Encyclopedia of Business Information Sources*, Gale Research Company, Book Tower, Detroit, MI 48226. The bibliography contains 22,000 citations covering more than 1100 business subjects. The citations include abstract services and indexes, almanacs and yearbooks, bibliographies, biographical sources, directories, handbooks and manuals, periodicals and newsletters, trade associations, research centers, and institutes. Examples of specific business subjects include federal budget, building contracts, the building industry, the iron and steel industry, and accounting. For example, the *Encyclopedia* cites the following information sources for the iron and steel industry: five directories, the *Iron and Steel Dictionary*, two online databases, five periodicals and a newsletter, six statistical reports, and eight trade associations and professional societies.

MAGAZINES, ARTICLES, PAPERS, JOURNALS, MONOGRAPHS

Because most hard-cover publications relating to litigation require a year or more to prepare and publish. One finds the most current information and data in magazines, articles, papers, journals and monographs. The annual *Accountant's Index* (AICPA) provides information on these types of publications.

Computer databases such as NEXIS have the most current and comprehensive access to various articles. The *Magazine Index* and the *Newspaper Index* published by Information Access are quarterly updated computer databases available at local libraries.

Some magazines print an annual or semiannual index of their current articles.

IRS PUBLICATIONS

The Internal Revenue Service publications, although intended to help prepare tax statements, offers valuable guidelines for valuation.

Bulletin F

The IRS issued Bulletin F in 1942 to set depreciation guidelines for tax returns. The rates are based on useful lives for specific industries and the tangible assets in that industry. For example, under the agricultural industry, the useful life of a snow fence is 8 years, a wood fence is 15 years, and a woven wire fence is 15 years.

This bulletin is obsolete for tax return purposes; however, it is a good outside source for estimating useful lives in valuation matters. Many technological developments have occurred since Bulletin F's publication in 1942. These developments made equipment obsolete that, although in good physical order, has little or no value in the market place. When using *Bulletin F*, one needs to be aware of an item's technological sophistication. Volume 1 of the 1981 *Commerce Clearing House Standard Federal Tax Reports* contains *Bulletin F.*

Revenue Rulings

A revenue ruling is an official IRS interpretation of the tax laws, related statutes, tax treaties, and regulations. These rulings are published weekly in the *Internal Revenue Bulletin* and annually in a bound volume, the *Cumulative Bulletin.* Two widely referenced rulings dealing with business valuations are Revenue Rulings 59-60 and 69-608.

Letter Rulings

The IRS issues private letter rulings to individual and corporate taxpayers who request information on the tax consequences of various proposed transactions. These rulings were originally confidential, but all rulings requested after October 31, 1976, are public information. A ruling cannot be used as a precedent by anyone except the taxpayer requesting the information, but it may guide a taxpayer with identical circumstances as to the possible tax treatment.

Internal Memoranda

The IRS publishes three types of internal memoranda: General Counsel Memoranda (GCM), Technical Memoranda (TM) and Action on Decisions (AOD). Prentice-Hall in its P.H. Internal Memoranda of the IRS Service and the Commerce Clearing House in its IRS Positions Service contain these memoranda.

The Office of Chief Counsel to the IRS prepares GCMs in connection with the review of proposed revenue rulings, technical advice memoranda, and proposed private letter rulings. The assistant commissioner of the IRS uses these memoranda to formulate a position.

The Legislation and Regulations Division of the Office of Chief Counsel drafts TMs to help decide whether to issue a proposed Treasury decision or regulation and what its substantive content should be.

The Tax Litigation Division of the Office of the Chief Counsel prepares AODs and directs them to the Chief Counsel whenever the IRS loses cases in the Tax Court, Federal District Court, Court of Claims, or U.S. Court of Appeals and recommends that the commissioner should either "acquiesce" or "nonacquiesce" in the court's decision.

CASES

Previous cases dealing with the same issues can provide much information about acceptable damage calculation methods, ratios, damages theories, presentation techniques, successful exhibits, charts, diagrams, and the like. The published opinions sometimes contain enough information about the case to indicate whether the accountant should seek additional information from the attorneys of record or the parties to the case. Most cases are not appealed and therefore do not have published opinions. When a published opinion does not exist but the case is significant to the present case, one can obtain copies of the court's unpublished opinion from the court clerk for recent cases. Older cases are not ordinarily available from the court, and one may have to contact the attorneys of record.

To find the cases, counsel for the client may provide a list of citations, copies of the decisions, or refer the accountant to a computerized search service.

Federal

The federal court system comprises the Supreme Court, 12 circuit courts, and 94 district courts. The Bureau of National Affairs publishes the decisions weekly in *U. S. Law Weekly*. This service also includes an index based on the docket number and the topic. The county law library should offer this service.

State

The decisions of the state supreme courts and appellate courts, the structure of which varies among the states, are usually reported in attorney-targeted newspapers. Superior courts' (lower county courts) decisions can be obtained directly from the court clerks.

Westlaw and Lexis

Westlaw (developed by West Publishing Company, 50 West Kellogg Building, P.O. Box 3526, St. Paul, MN 55165) and Lexis (Mead Data Central, Inc.) are two online databases that contain the full text of U.S. federal laws, regulations, executive documents, and federal court decisions. The data's time span varies by source, with the earliest information from 1754. Both services have auxiliary databases on various subjects, including the following:

Admiralty
Bankruptcy
Communications
Delaware and federal corporation law

Energy
Environmental
Labor and government
Military
Securities
State database
Transportation

Each service also has databases unique to its system. For example, Lexis has a patent, trademark, and copyright database not available from Westlaw, and Westlaw has a criminal database unique to its system.

These services may be available on a per inquiry basis for occasional use at law libraries. Many law firms subscribe to the service.

Pleadings

Although copies of pleadings can be obtained from the court, certain courts have eliminated filing depositions, interrogatories, and similar discovery documents.

PROFESSIONAL CONTINUING EDUCATION COURSES

The American Institute of CPAs, New York City, and various state societies offer excellent courses on many accounting-related subjects. These courses not only fulfill continuing education requirements, but they also keep accountants abreast of the profession's latest developments. Most courses provide a course book for study and use that can often be an excellent source for accounting matters involved in litigation. Accountants engaged to assist or testify in marital dissolution cases, business valuations, and many other types of litigation will find the course books a valuable reference.

EXPERTS AND PERSONS KNOWLEDGEABLE IN THE INDUSTRY

Experts and persons knowledgeable in the industry often share their experience and information regarding source data for litigation purposes. In addition to accountants, these experts include economists, engineers, lawyers, consultants, and business executives.

The National Forensic Center, 17 Temple Terrace, Lawrenceville, NJ 08648 is an excellent source reference for the names of such persons.

A few state CPA societies have formed litigation services committees that prepare discussion papers that are available to society members. The committee usually comprises accountants with extensive litigation experience.

AMERICAN ARBITRATION ASSOCIATION

The American Arbitration Association serves the needs and interest of corporations, law firms, unions, and trade associations that use alternative systems to resolve disputes as well as the professional involved in alternative dispute resolution (ADR) as a neutral, counsel, or teacher. The association publishes a quarterly magazine containing articles by scholars and practitioners on labor, commercial, construction, accident claims, and international arbitration. It also publishes the following:

Arbitration Times—quarterly newspaper
Lawyers' Arbitrational letter—quarterly magazine targeting attorneys
Arbitration and the Law—annual summary of significant arbitration developments
Punch List—construction industry newsletter
Study Time—quarterly newsletter
Summary of Labor Arbitration Awards—monthly publication
Arbitration in the Schools—monthly summary
Labor Arbitration in Government—monthly reporting service
New York No-Fault Arbitration Reports—monthly summary
Forum New York—quarterly newsletter

The association maintains the Eastman Arbitration Library that is the largest library of its kind in the nation and offers a full range of research and reference services. The fully computerized library contains more than 10,000 books, periodicals, clip materials, and microforms providing comprehensive coverage in the field of dispute resolution. Students and others seeking information not readily available elsewhere may also use the library's general facilities. The American Arbitration Association has 33 offices and has certified more than 60,000 arbitrators over the last 61 years. In 1987, approximately 53,000 cases were filed with the American Arbitration Association.

In 1986, the association began a computer based listing of information on approximately 600 ADR organizations in the United States and abroad with national, international, regional, and local interests. These ADR organizations use one or more of the following dispute resolution techniques:

Arbitration
Mediation
Conciliation
Rent-a-Judge
Minitrials

The directory maintains current data on agency name, address, country, telephone, telex, cable, telefax, executive director, founding date, staff size, local served, functions and objectives, types of disputes administered, ADR techniques utilized, publications issued, and rules of procedure employed. One can contact the reference desk at 212/484-4127; telex: 12463; telefax: (212) 765-4874. The publications department publishes a catalog of books, periodicals, films, videotapes, rules, pamphlets, and reprints.

PRACTICING LAW INSTITUTE

The Practicing Law Institute (PLI) is a nonprofit organization that provides continuing education to the legal community. The classes cover many legal subjects using the following methods:

Program

The institute presents programs in major cities around the country on topics, like accounting for lawyers and bankruptcy. These programs are also available on audiocassette.

Course Handbooks. The institute uses course material to develop handbooks that are available to the public. The Westlaw System began carrying the information from these handbooks in December 1987.

Hardbound Books. The institute publishes approximately 1500 hardbound books annually.

Miscellaneous. Programs are also available via satellite and videocassette. PLI's annual report contains an appendix that lists the materials, including books and course handbooks, available to the public.

SPECIALIZED INDUSTRY MANUALS

Many specialized industry manuals are available. The *Encyclopedia of Business Information Sources* (Gale Research) lists some of the manuals available for the industries that it explores and also the trade associations that may be contacted for additional information as to manuals and handbooks. The AICPA's library has available for loan to its members many accounting manuals on specific industries. The *Accountant's Index* lists all the publications available through the AICPA library. The *Encyclopedia of Associations* (Kock and Martin, 1988) also lists the names and addresses of over 21,000 national and international nonprofit trade and professional associations that one can contact regarding information for a specific industry.

OTHER MATTERS

Graphic Presentations

Depending on the size and nature of the case, the accountant may prepare graphic exhibits or, with counsel's concurrence, hire a graphics specialist to prepare exhibits for the accountant's use in presentations before a trier-of-fact. Graphic presentations may be prepared manually or by use of one of the many programs available on personal computers. The *Handbook of Graphic Presentation* (Stanton and Schmid, 1979) presents many different ideas that the accountant can use to portray complex sets of numbers in an easily understood visual manner.

Climatological Data

Climatological data is useful in some litigation matters, particularly construction delay claims. Contractors' bids usually assume normal weather delays. Some courts have established a 10-year average to define normal weather; only abnormal weather delay is compensable or deserving of a time extension to the contractor. Delays other than inclement weather may cause the construction phase scheduled to occur during the summer months to fall into a winter period, thus causing further delays because of weather conditions not contemplated in the original contract. In such a situation, the court must decide who is responsible for the delay. Climatological data can be obtained from several sources, such as:

National Climatological Data Center, Federal Bldg., Asheville, North Carolina 28801

Local airport climatological data

U.S. Air Force Climatological Data

Minority Interest-Discount Rate

When valuing a minority interest, in a closely held stock or business, one often applies a discount factor because a ready market seldom exists for such an interest or restrictive covenants may be placed on the sale of such stock or partial business interest.

The *Federal Tax Valuation Digest* (Bishop and Stryker, 1987) lists discounts for various types of business. This publication lists the type of business, business form (i.e., corporation, partnership, trust, etc.), the factors considered and the rate position taken by the government (IRS), the parties to the action, and the rate decided by the court.

Other sources include brokers and consultants that deal with the type of business activity involved.

Consumer Price Index (CPI)

The Consumer Price Index (CPI) published by the U.S. Department of Labor, Bureau of Labor Statistics, measures the average change in prices over time in a fixed market basket of goods and services. The Bureau of Labor Statistics publishes CPIs for two population groups: (1) a CPI for all urban consumers (CPI-U) that covers approximately 80 percent of the total noninstitutional civilian population and (2) a CPI for urban wage earners and clerical workers (CPI-W) that represents about half the population covered by the CPI-U. The CPI-U includes, in addition to wage earners and clerical workers, groups such as professional, managerial, and technical workers, the self-employed, short-term workers, the unemployed, and retirees and others not in the labor force.

The CPI is based on prices of food, clothing, shelter, and fuels, transportation fares, doctors' and dentists' fees, drugs, and the other goods and services that people buy for daily living. Prices are collected in 85 urban areas across the country from about 4000 food stores, 24,000 rental units, and 28,000 establishments—department stores, hospitals, filling stations, and other types of stores and service establishments. The index includes all taxes directly associated with the purchase and use of items. Prices of food, fuels, and a few other items are obtained every month in all 85 locations. Prices of most other commodities and services are collected every month in the five largest geographic areas and every other month in other areas. Prices of most goods and services are obtained by personal visits of the bureau's trained representatives. The bureau mails questionnaires to obtain public utility rates, some fuel prices, and certain other items.

In calculating the index, price changes for the various items in each location are averaged together with weights that represent their importance in the spending of the appropriate population group. Local data are then combined to obtain a U.S. city average. The bureau publishes separate indexes by size of city, by region, for cross-classifications of regions and population-size classes, and for 28 local areas. Area indexes do not measure differences in the price level among cities; they only measure the average change in prices for each area since the base period.

NOTE

1. *Management Focus*, July–August 1982, pp. 12–13.

BIBLIOGRAPHY

A Factual Survey (Corona, California Chamber of Commerce, 1988).

Almanac of Business and Industrial Financial Ratios, Leo Troy, ed. (Prentice-Hall, Inc. 1987).

Altman & Weil, Inc. *Survey of Law Firm Economics* (Altman & Weil Publications, Inc., 1987).

American Bar Foundation, *The Lawyer Statistical Report* (American Bar Foundation, 1988).

American Institute of Certified Public Accountants, *Accountant's Index* (AICPA, 1987).

AMA Center for Health Research, *Socioeconomic Characteristics of Medical Practice* (American Medical Association, 1987).

Androit, J., *Guide to U.S. Government Publications* (Documents Index, 1977).

Bishop, J.A. and C.H. Stryker, *Federal Tax Valuation Digest* (Warren, Gorham & LaMont, 1987).

Brownstone, D.M. and G. Carruth, *Where to Find Business Information* (John Wiley & Sons, 1982).

Business Economic Division, Dun & Bradstreet, *Key Business Ratios* (Dun & Bradstreet, 1987).

Cuadra and Elsevier, *Dictionary of Online Databases* (Cuadra Associates, 1987).

Datapro Research, *Complete Guide to Dial-Up Databases* (Datapro Research Corporation, 1985).

Desmond, G., and J. Marcello, *Handbook of Small Business Valuation Formulas* (Valuation Press, 1987).

DIALOG Database Catalog, 1987 (DIALOG Information Services, 1987).

Encyclopedia of Associations, K.E. Kock and S.B. Martin, eds. (Gale Research Company, 1988).

Encyclopedia of Business Information Sources (Gale Research Company, 1988).

Financial Studies of the Small Business, K. Goodman, ed. (Financial Research Associates, 1987).

Industrial Sites (Corona, California Chamber of Commerce, 1988).

Kiley, T., *Using Litigation Databases* (John Wiley & Sons, 1987).

Lesko, M., *The Computer Data and Database Source Book* (Avon Books, 1984).

Moody's Corporate News—International (Moody's Investor's Service, published annually).

Moody's Corporate News—U.S. (Moody's Investors Service, published annually).

Moody's Corporate Profiles (Moody's Investors Service, published annually).

Hess, Jr., Dr., *Fast Facts Online Search Strategies for Finding Business Information* (Dow Jones–Irwin, 1986).

Progress Report (Orange County Board of Supervisors, 1987).

Robert Morris, *Annual Statement Studies* (Robert Morris Associates, 1987).

"Rules of the Game," *Management Focus* (Peat, Marwick, Mitchell & Co., July–August 1982) pp. 12–13.

Stanton, C.F. and S.E. Schmid, *Handbook of Graphic Presentation* (John Wiley & Sons, 1979).

U.S. Department of Commerce, Bureau of the Census, *1982 Census of Service Industries-California* (U.S. Government Printing Office, 1982).

U.S. Department of Commerce, Bureau of the Census, *Statistical Abstract of the United States* (U.S. Government Printing Office, 1986).

U.S. Executive Office of the President, Office of Management and Budget, *Standard Industrial Classification Manual, 1972* (U.S. Government Printing Office, 1972).

U.S. Department of the Treasury, Internal Revenue Service, *Statistics of Income Bulletin* (U.S. Government Printing Office, published annually).

Walker's Manual (Walker Corporation, 1986).

Wright, J.W., *The American Almanac of Jobs and Salaries* (Avon Books, 1984).

8

INTERACTION BETWEEN ACCOUNTANTS AND ECONOMISTS

Elizabeth A. Evans, JD, CPA, CMA

INTRODUCTION

Although the other chapters in this book will assist a litigation expert in analyzing a case's issues, this chapter will acquaint accountants and lawyers with a group of professionals whose skills are complementary—economists. An economist's qualifications are more difficult to define than those of an accountant; there is no national board similar to the AICPA that certifies a person as an economist. One can make certain generalizations, however, about economists regardless of their academic achievement.

Economists are trained to understand the structure and performance of the economic entity being examined. Industrial organization economists, for example, know about competitive industries, oligopolies, and the like and once they analyze the industry-specific data they will be able to forecast likely behavioral patterns. Labor economists will be familiar with the market for human capital and factors relevant to the earning power of an individual and occupations. Financial economists will understand how the capital markets work. All will use their knowledge to establish a logical framework within which to evaluate the actions of the parties to the lawsuit.

Economists are also familiar with sources of government or other publicly available data. They know where to find the data and what biases the data may have. Finally, many economists know how to use data to devise and test hypotheses using statistical techniques and thereby create empirical proof for theories.

These skills complement those of accountants. Accountants know how financial statements and general business records are derived. They also understand the data supporting financial statements and business records and their limitations. They know how to obtain, organize, and document data. They may bring their own analytic abilities to the task. Most importantly, from auditing, consulting, or tax preparation experience, an accountant will have the firm-specific knowledge about the entity that the economist may not possess.

Every expert witness is aware that in litigation there are at least two sides that exist to every case. One side's expert will attempt to prove that the other side's expert's assertions are untrue, his assumptions are unfounded, and his reasoning is flawed. As a result, experts sometimes obtain the assistance of others whose knowledge is not duplicative, but complementary in order to buttress their opinions. Economists and accountants have skills that are uniquely complementary. Accountants may perform analyses that are based explicitly or implicitly on certain assumptions; economists can test and prove the correctness (or falseness) of the assumptions. Similarly, economists may have hypotheses to test their theories about the manner in which the entity works; accountants provide the correct data for the tests or do the computations involved, or both. Of course, many experts are highly trained in several disciplines and have the combined expertise of accountants, economists, and statisticians.

PARTICULAR STRENGTHS OF ECONOMISTS

This section focuses on the areas in which economists have had specific training that is not easily duplicated. Among these areas are economic modeling (often using regression techniques), defining markets and understanding price theory and implications of market risk.

Economic Modeling

Economists are often familiar with regression techniques, one use of which is to model what would have happened but for certain events. In fact, an entire branch of economics–econometrics–applies statistical methods, of which regression analysis is one, to the study of economic data and problems. Regression analysis is a statistical technique that develops an equation depicting the relation among variables and then uses that equation to predict.[1] For example, if an expert needs to predict the sales that a firm would have made but for the defendant's actions, he may use a regression analysis that models the relationship between the firm's sales and other relevant factors (e.g., total industry sales) over a control period preceding the defendant's actions to predict what sales would have been in the absence of those actions. Similarly, if an expert needs to estimate how a stock would have performed but for some event, a financial economist may predict this by performing a regression analysis that relates an investment in the firm's stock to an investment of the same size in a portfolio of stocks in the same industry or in the market.[2]

The regression analysis also provides other relevant information such as the statistical significance of the relation among the variables, the degree of explanation afforded by the equation, and the ability to construct confidence intervals around the estimate. Thus the technique not only provides predictions, but also explicitly describes the strength or stability of the prediction.

Assume that an expert has constructed an equation that models the sales of Firm A as a function of total industry sales. Now the expert would like to know whether the sales of Firm A and the total industry sales have a strong relationship, that is, whether this variable helps explain the movement of the firm's sales. By examining the *t*-statistic, an economist can ascertain whether the variable has explanatory power and whether it is statistically significant. The economist can also check the coefficient of determination (often called the *R*-squared) to determine the amount of the change in the firm's sales that is explained by the total industry sales. Finally, an economist understands that although the regression results are often the best possible, the results are not "100 percent" accurate. Nevertheless, the economist can be sure that "95 times out of 100" the true measure will lie within a certain interval around that regression estimate and can construct this "confidence interval."

Although regression analysis produces an unbiased estimate, certain data relations can occur that obscure or overemphasize the estimates. The most common are heteroscedasticity, autocorrelation or serial correlation, multicollinearity, and nonlinear relationships. (See Pindyck and Rubinfeld, 1981, and Chapter 28.)

Market Definition

While market definition is most often associated with antitrust analysis, it may arise in cases such as breach of contract or patent infringement or any case where the measure of damages is the plaintiff's lost profits (or the defendant's ill-gotten gains). Analysis of the relevant market divides into two areas: the product market and the geographic market. In defining the relevant product market, one must include not only the specific product in the case at hand but also those products that consumers may substitute (demand-side substitution). One must also identify both the firms that currently make the relevant product(s) and the firms that could switch to manufacturing the relevant product(s) (supply-side substitution). Similarly, in defining the geographic market one must include not only the areas currently served by the firms that make the relevant products, but also the areas from which firms would ship if a supracompetitive (or patent monopoly) price were imposed (Posner and Landes, 1981).

Although it may sound like common sense to identify the relevant product and its substitutes, some factors cannot be incorporated into market definition analysis on a "gut feeling" basis, for example, the effect of price differences between products. Economists, however, can test empirically for a market definition in a way that accounts for these relevant factors. First, they can estimate the change in the quantity sold of a product that will occur if the price of that product changes (own-price elasticity). Second, they can estimate the change in the quantity sold of a good when the price of another good is changed (cross-price elasticity). These estimates are useful tools of market definition: If a 10-percent increase in the price of Product A produces a 20-percent decrease in the quantity sold of Product A and a 15-percent increase in the quantity sold of Products B and C, a market defined as Product A alone may well be too narrow, and one should consider including Products B and C in the market definition. On the other hand, if a 10-percent decrease in the quantity sold of Product A has no (or only a small) effect upon the sales of Products B and C, the relevant product market may be Product A alone.

The geographic market may be tested empirically by correlating the prices of the products in different areas. Correlation analysis is a technique that measures the strength of the relationship between two variables, neither of which can be singled out as the cause of the other.[3] Economists have found that the prices of products that are in the same geographic market will tend to be strongly correlated. That is, if the price in Area A and the price in Area B tend to move together, they are probably in the same geographic market (Stigler and Sherwin, 1985).

Price Theory

Another area of economics important for litigation is price theory. Through observation of prices over long periods of time, economists have discovered that certain markets behave in certain patterns. The most common of these markets are competitive (many sellers of a good and its close substitutes), monopoly (one seller of a good without close substitutes), oligopoly (few sellers of a good and its close substitutes), cartel (a group of firms acting in concert), and monopsony (a firm with monopolistic buying power) markets. For example, economists have observed that in a competitive market, firms cannot raise significantly the price above the competitive level without decreasing their total revenues and profits, whereas a monopolist who can prevent entry can raise price profitably. Although most people associate price theory with antitrust and regulation cases, it may be important in any case where an expert must estimate a firm's behavior in the absence of the injurious conduct. For example, in a breach of contract case, the tools provided by price theory may help ascertain whether subsequent sales were replacement sales for the breached amount or additional sales that would have occurred anyway.[4]

Market Risk

Many empirical studies require that capital market risk be considered.[5] For example, in a present value analysis, an expert discounts cash flows to a specific date, and the discount factor the expert uses should reflect in some cases the market and industry effects of each period. Economists are experienced in estimating the appropriate discount rate.

Financial economists often use the Capital Asset Pricing Model (CAPM) to estimate the appropriate discount rate. The CAPM model defines the return of a firm as the risk-free rate of return (usually measured by the return on short-term T-bills) plus the difference between the return on the market and the risk-free rate of return (otherwise known as the risk premium) times the firm's beta (the measure of the firm's market risk) (Brealey and Myers, 1988, pp. 139–140). A financial economist using the CAPM could develop a discount factor for the present value analysis that would incorporate not only the effects of cash flows occurring in different time periods but also the return that the market and this firm experienced, so that an expert could more precisely measure what an expected cash flow occurring in Time Period 6 would be worth in Time Period 0.

Another type of market risk with which financial economists are trained to deal is the effect of leverage (or debt). The presence of debt that must be paid before the stockholder receives any return makes the stockholders' investment relatively riskier. The discount factor for a firm's assets, thus, will differ from the discount factor for the firm's equity by the amount of risk represented by debt (Brealey and Myers, 1988, p. 185). The financial economist understands this distinction, how to change one to the other, and which one will be applicable to the case being analyzed.

PARTICULAR STRENGTHS OF ACCOUNTANTS

The accountant also has strengths that others would find difficult to duplicate. Among these are the understanding of generally accepted accounting principles (GAAP), the way in which the underlying data were used to produce a financial statement (whether for internal or external use), cost estimation, effects of income taxes, and how best to present the results in an understandable fashion.

GAAP

One of the accountant's most important assets is the understanding of the generally accepted accounting principles used to prepare accounting statements for public use. Much empirical data used in lawsuits come from these statements. If the economist or other expert does not understand how a number was derived or what it represents, that expert may base an empirical study on a set of assumptions that does not apply to the case, or he could simply use the wrong data altogether.

Although the list is long, the following highlights some of the areas nonaccountants understand the least.

The least understood area is, of course, one of the most difficult: consolidation of financial entities. After a subsidiary is consolidated with the parent, an economist may need an accountant's expertise to unravel the consolidation to measure unreported items: the amount the parent paid for the subsidiary, the book value of the subsidiary's assets prior to consolidation, the amount of goodwill on the subsidiary's books prior to consolidation, the intercompany transfers, the effect of the subsidiary's being a foreign operation, and so forth. The accountant must understand these items for both the pooling and purchase methods. Of course, consolidations are even more complicated when the parent's ownership is less than 100 percent.

An accountant must be able to explain valuation bases of assets under generally accepted accounting principles. An economist may plan to use balance sheet data over a period of years to perform an empirical study. An accountant must be able to explain when historical cost data have been used and when they have not. For example, if a firm's holdings of marketable securities are being studied, the accountant may have to ascertain whether the financial statements use a cost or market basis and whether a continuous series of data valued on the same basis is available.

When studies of a firm's sales are performed, an accountant may need to explain the effects of revenue recognition at times other than the time of sale. This is especially true when the firm is involved with long-term construction contracts, installment or consignment sales, or special-order merchandise.

Inventory studies have two problematic areas: the valuation of inventory (acquisition cost, current cost, lower-of-cost-or-market and standard cost) and cost-flow assumptions (specific identification, LIFO, FIFO, and weighted average). The economist may need to understand that although LIFO more accurately measures the cost of goods sold, it less accurately measures the inventory amount on the balance sheet in periods of inflation or deflation. The opposite principles apply to FIFO. Even an economist who understands the basics of LIFO is probably unfamiliar with the intricacies of dollar-value LIFO, gross-margin method, and dollar-value retail method LIFO.

Regarding capital assets, the accountant is knowledgeable about the differences in valuation of purchased and self-constructed assets, as well as the valuation of costs subsequent to acquisition (e.g., repairs and maintenance, moving, replacement and improvement, and additions). Depreciation is another potential area of confusion. To the economist, depreciation simply means the decline in an asset's ability to produce future cash flows. The accountant, however, knows it is not that simple. Two partially offsetting processes affect an asset's change in value: reductions in the asset's value arising from physical use or technological obsolescence and unanticipated holding gains (or losses). Only the former process is always recognized in GAAP financial statements.

Economists often do not understand contra accounts. Although assets such as accounts receivable and property, plant, and equipment have contra accounts, each contra account has a different purpose. The allowance for doubtful accounts helps estimate the recoverable value of accounts receivable, but the contra account "accumulated depreciation" serves another purpose entirely. Moreover, an economist may need to know that whereas tangible assets have a separate contra account, intangible assets do not. Yet the nonexistence of a contra account should not be interpreted to mean that intangible assets are not amortized in much the same manner as tangible assets are depreciated.

An economist who has mastered the relatively simple process of accounting for marketable securities may not be familiar with the methodology used for investments in securities, especially when the investment is in equity securities and represents a minority—but controlling—interest. Generally, an interest in the equity securities of a firm is valued as part of a portfolio in financial statements using the lower-of-cost-or-market (LOCOM) method discussed previously. However, in some cases the economist may be dealing with an investor who uses the equity method to report his interest on his financial statements. The bottom line, of course, is that the balance sheet figure for an investment reported by the equity method is neither the cost that the investor paid, nor is it the investment's market value. Instead it is a mixture of the original cost paid by the investor increased by the investor's share of the firm's profits earned since the time of the investment less the dividends paid to the investor. An economist, moreover, may not know that this investor's income statement will report revenue equal to the increase in this investment, without receiving cash or tangible gain from it.

Bonds are another financial instrument with complicated accounting conventions that may play an important role in empirical studies. The reporting requirements differ depending on whether the bond is an asset (investment) of the firm or a liability (debt). An economist studying a firm's bond investments may not realize that the amount listed on the firm's balance sheet is the present value of the bonds' face value and the expected interest payments (evaluated at the effective interest rate on the purchase date, unadjusted for subsequent interest rate changes) and not the face value of the bonds. Furthermore, the income statement's interest expense for the bond debtor is probably not the interest paid.[6] When bond discounts and premiums and their amortization are considered, an economist may need an accountant's help to calculate the market or face value of what is owed by a firm or even owned by a firm.

Yet another source of mystery to a nonaccountant are pension plans, whose terminology includes such phrases as *normal cost*, *sweetening*, *actuarial liability*, *vesting*, *defined benefit*, *defined contribution*, *fully funded*, *partially funded*, *contributory*, and *noncontributory*. For an economist, the most important fact concerning pension plans and other postemployment benefits may be that a firm's obligations may not appear—or at least not appear in total—anywhere in the financial statements.

Understanding Uses of Accounting Data

An accountant understands how the underlying data are used to create financial statements for both internal and external use, and he may need this knowledge to restate or recreate lost financial records. For example, the issue in litigation may relate only to one division or one product line of a firm. An accountant would ascertain which income streams and assets belong to the entity or product line of interest.

Overhead or common cost allocation is another area in which the accountant's understanding of an entity's underlying data is critical. An accountant preparing an internal report on a division's profitability may have included some allocation of corporate overhead costs. The expert witness, on the other hand, may be interested in the opportunity cost associated with a division's actual overhead expenditures. An accountant can ascertain exactly what overhead costs to include in the witness' study. For example, an accountant preparing an internal division profit report may have attributed one-fifth of total overhead to the division because the division sales were one-fifth of total sales. For the litigation study, however, perhaps only the salary of the division's vice-president should be included because the remaining corporate staff would be working (in fact, did work explicitly) on other divisions anyway.

Most accountants understand the issues of transfer pricing and the various methods that firms use to ensure that the overall effect of buying decisions is to earn profits for the firm as a whole (not necessarily for a single division). In many litigation studies, one may wish to use the market price as the transfer price, particularly when the case focuses on a single division. Here accountants can use their understanding of the underlying financial data to ensure that pricing is restated, if necessary, to reflect market prices (if they can be ascertained).

Some of the litigation studies performed by economists and accountants are enhanced by cash-flow analyses (e.g., the "failing firm" analysis in a merger context). Most firms historically did not present a straightforward cash-flow analysis of their operations, although they now present a statement of cash flows (see *SFAS No. 95*). Accountants, with their understanding of the underlying financial data, can make the required modifications to create a cash-flow statement for a division or a single product line from historical financial statements.

Cost Estimation

Cost estimation requires an understanding of how the underlying data are used in a financial statement. Often expert witnesses are interested in costs that vary with production or sales whereas, at the same time, they need to identify (and possibly ignore) the fixed costs. The accountant's prime concern should be to understand the data needed for the expert's study. For example, if the case requires an analysis of incremental costs, the fixed and variable cost definitions may differ from those used in financial reports. Thus, a study of whether the company made more (or lost less) entering into a new market than it would have otherwise may require that the cost of new equipment purchased for this expansion be considered incremental even though the accountant normally views such costs as fixed.

Income Taxes

In many litigation studies, the expert must consider the effects of income taxes. Although economists know when to consider taxes, they generally have no expertise in calculating these tax effects. The accountant should be particularly sensitive to whether the economist wants to use the average tax rate, the marginal tax rate, the effective tax rate, or even the marginal effective tax rate. For example, a firm's weighted-average cost of capital calculation includes the marginal corporate tax rate, whereas a firm's adjusted present value and adjusted cost of capital uses the effective tax rate (Brealey & Myers, 1988, p. 451).

Presentation of Analysis

Finally, an accountant can assist an economic expert in presenting a litigation report or testimony. Often an economist's findings can best be presented to the court as pro forma financial statements constructed by an accountant. Economists make certain assumptions or estimates in their studies and may need to illustrate how these different assumptions or estimates affect the outcome. A sensitivity analysis presented by an accountant that slightly varies the assumptions in several studies may allow the parties to appreciate which assumptions are the most critical.

SPECIFIC AREAS OF INTERACTION

There are numerous areas of interaction in litigation between accountants and economists, thus the remainder of this chapter will be restricted to a discussion of three: lost profit measurement, antitrust analysis, and securities laws analyses. Moreover, because other chapters in this book discuss these topics at length (e.g., Chapters 10, 28 and 30), this chapter focuses primarily on the economic implications of the analysis that a litigation expert may encounter.

Measurement of Lost Profits

Whether the cause of action is a breach of contract, copyright or patent infringement, violation of antitrust laws, and the like, the general damage measure is the profits that the plaintiff would have realized "but for" the defendant's actions, less the plaintiff's actual profits. Another way of stating this is incremental sales (or revenues) less incremental costs. Although lost profits may be measured in many ways, most measures combine the knowledge of business and financial records with economic assumptions about the relevant industry.

Incremental Sales or Revenues. The first step in a lost profits study is to determine the amount of lost revenues or sales units that are caused by the defendant's actions. Four common approaches to measuring this amount are (1) "before and after," (2) forecast of sales, (3) yardstick and (4) market share.

The "before-and-after" approach compares the plaintiff's sales level "before" the defendant's wrongdoing with the plaintiff's sales level "after" the defendant's wrongdoing; the difference between the two levels represents the lost sales. This approach implicitly assumes that the plaintiff's business volume was affected only by the defendant's wrongdoing; otherwise the volume would have been the same. This approach, however, may underestimate lost sales for a plaintiff whose sales were increasing prior to the defendant's actions. Conversely, if the plaintiff's business was declining during the "before" period, such an assumption may overestimate lost sales. To effectively use such an approach, an expert will often include a market analysis in the lost-profits study. For example, an industrial organization economist might conclude that the industry was a mature, stable one during the period under question and that the plaintiff's sales level probably would have been unchanged but for the defendant's actions.

Instead of the "before-and-after" approach, an expert might forecast "but for" sales by using a variety of tools such as regression (or other statistical) analysis and then subtracting the actual sales to estimate the lost sales. This approach requires that the expert's model (or equation) adequately predict the sales and withstand an attack on the ground that the control period over which the equation is estimated contained events that would bias the results; also the regression equation must not be biased by heteroscedasticity, autocorrelation, etc.[7] The model should also consider all important industry factors that affect the sales of the plaintiff's products. For example, the sale of products used in constructing oil rigs may be affected by the price of oil. The omission of a significant factor may invalidate the expert's results or make these results seem less credible to a judge and jury. An economist can help ensure that all relevant factors are considered and that the model includes the significant ones.

A third common measure is the yardstick approach in which the expert gathers an index of firms similar to the plaintiff's firm and compares the plaintiff's performance to the index's performance. This approach assumes that but for the defendant's actions, the plaintiff would have performed as well as the yardstick. Using an index sometimes can be inappropriate, however, because of underlying biases in the data. If the plaintiff firm is small or large relative to the firms in the index, the results may not be accurate. For example, if the firm being analyzed was very large, and the damage inflicted by the defendant caused it to lose market share, small firms that acquired those shares might appear to be growing even if the market was not.

The fourth common measure of the plaintiff's lost sales is based on the plaintiff's market share during the period prior to the defendant's wrongdoing. Here the expert must not only define the relevant market but also ensure that the market was relatively stable during the relevant time period. Numerous entrances or exits of competitors could undermine the use of this measure. Also, the trend of the plaintiff's market share should be examined because, if the plaintiff's market share varies greatly over the period before the defendant's actions, this measure may be unreliable. As discussed previously, many economists are trained in such market definition and structure analysis.

In some breach of contract cases, the expert may be able to start by assuming that the lost sales are those represented by the breached contract. The next step, however, is to determine whether actual sales during the period of breach were additional sales that would have occurred anyway or were replacement sales for the breached amount.

For example, if the plaintiff's market were perfectly competitive, the expert should assume that the plaintiff is selling at the level justified by cost considerations and capacity. Even a plaintiff who could sell more would not—unless he were willing to use higher cost capacity or to invest in extra capacity, a consideration we will ignore for now. In other words, the seller can get all the customers he wants. Now a customer breaches his contract. In a perfectly competitive market, the expert should assume that the seller could find another customer to take the breaching buyer's amount. The only compensation due the plaintiff would be the difference in the two buyer's prices—if any such difference existed (Goetz and Scott, 1979). On the other hand, assume that contracts are long term, buyers are few, and the seller has extra capacity. Now one of the plaintiff's buyers breaches, and subsequently the plaintiff makes sales to a new buyer (or additional sales are made to a present buyer). Here one may argue that the new sales do not replace the breached amount and that the full amount of the breached contract should be considered as lost sales (Goetz and Scott, 1979). Without first analyzing the plaintiff's market, an expert's conclusions may be vulnerable to an attack.

In addition to the direct damages owed to the plaintiff, consequential damages may also occur. To the economist, this is a natural concept. If damage awards purport to make the plaintiff whole (i.e., to restore the plaintiff to the position he would have been in but for the defendant's actions), the damage claim must encompass every phase of the plaintiff's business affected by the defendant's actions. For example, if a buyer breaches a contract for Product A—which is a joint product of Product B—and the breach causes the plaintiff to alter its production of Products A and B, the breach could also cause damages related to Product B. Another situation where consequential damages may arise would be a breach affecting the sales of a complicated machine that also affects the subsequent sales of replacement parts or maintenance service for the machine. To ascertain whether consequential damages have occurred whenever the plaintiff has an integrated facility requires that the same type of market definition and structure analysis discussed previously be conducted not only for any primary product but also for the joint or co-products.[8]

An expert's most difficult proposition to establish, of course, will be the lost sales or revenues for a newly established or never-established business. Courts now hold that damages to such businesses can be awarded provided they have been proven with "reasonable certainty" (Dunn, 1987, pp. 217–231). As a result, the expert may need to ascertain how the plaintiff's market was structured. If the plaintiff's market contained many small firms or a few large ones, an expert should know where a firm of the plaintiff's expected size would fit along this spectrum. If the plaintiff would have been a small competitor in a market comprised chiefly of large competitors, the plaintiff's expert must be able to refute arguments that his client would not have had the size to have been viable in such a market. Other factors that should be considered are ease of entry and stability of existing firms in the industry. If the plaintiff asserts that its firm would have had an advantage over other competitors because of a patent or other new process but for the defendant's actions, the expert must make some reasonable assumption regarding the length of time the benefits conferred by the patent or new process would last.[9] Regardless of the method used to estimate the plaintiff's lost sales, the expert should have some economic underpinning of his assumptions.

Incremental Costs. Once the expert estimates the amount of lost sales, the expert's work is only half complete. From these lost revenues the expert must now subtract the costs that would have been incurred to achieve these revenues. Such an analysis may consider many different cost measures: marginal, incremental, variable, average, and direct. Marginal cost is the cost of producing one additional unit. If a firm produces and sells a new product, the related new or changed costs are called incremental. Average cost is the total cost divided by the number of units produced. Variable costs are those that change as the activity (or production) level changes. Direct costs are the costs of the direct material and direct labor incurred in producing a product. These definitions are taken from Davidson et al. (1985, pp. 901–907). The expert must decide which cost measure is relevant for the particular case. For example, a variable cost estimate may be applicable only over a certain range of production (called the relevant range). If the estimated lost sales units would increase the production level outside the relevant range, the use of the variable cost estimate may be incorrect.

The relevant cost measure may differ, of course, depending upon whether the business is expanding or contracting.[10] If the business is expanding and the amount of lost sales units would take production past the plaintiff firm's present limits, the expert should consider including the capital costs of investment in new capacity or new equipment as a cost in the lost-profit analysis. If the expert is using incremental costs, he should include such costs and should also make reasonable assumptions concerning the timing of the investments.

Regardless of the measure used, the expert should consider carefully the time period over which to measure costs. Over a long enough time period, almost all costs are variable—over a short enough time period, costs may be largely fixed. Sometimes the appropriate time period will be straightforward (e.g., the duration of the defendant's wrongdoing). In other cases the expert will generally find that as the appropriate time period shortens, the indirect costs items that should be subtracted from the lost sales revenues to estimate lost profits become fewer. In any event, the expert who ignores this issue may get the wrong answer even though all other assumptions in the analysis are correct.

An expert estimating costs for a firm that would have sold more units but for the defendant's actions should consider the possibility of economies (or diseconomies) of scale. If the number of lost units is large, the cost savings that could be achieved at that production level could be quite large. A study using only current costs could underestimate the plaintiff's damages. Similarly, a startup firm may have a higher cost structure because of learning-curve effects than a firm that has been in business for some time.

Other Considerations. If an expert is using dollar amounts in his regression analysis and the regression analysis is being done over a multiyear time period, the expert may often deflate the underlying data to constant dollar values prior to performing the analysis. Failure to perform the analysis in real, instead of nominal, terms will sometimes create or accentuate a trend. Having decided to deflate the underlying data by an index, the expert should carefully choose the appropriate index. Deflating different variables often requires the use of more than one index.

The use of the wrong index, of course, might also invalidate the expert's results.

As the expert is completing his lost profit calculations, he should decide whether to calculate the damages on a pretax or after-tax basis. Because a lost profits award is taxed, some experts believe that the award should be calculated on a pretax basis.[11] This advice, however, may lead to an over- or underestimate of damages by its failure to recognize changes in tax rates. An alternative method is to calculate the award on an after-tax basis and then "gross up" the damage amount by the current tax rate (i.e., divide the after-tax damages by one minus the current tax rate). For example, suppose the plaintiff would have made $100 on a pretax basis during Year 1 and had he earned that money in Year 1 he would have paid $46 in federal income taxes. (This example ignores present-value and state-tax issues.) Thus the plaintiff would have had $54 more but for the wrongdoing of the defendant. The plaintiff's case is finally tried in Year 7, after the marginal corporate federal income tax rate has dropped to 34 percent. If the plaintiff is awarded the pretax $100 in Year 7, he will pay only $34 in federal taxes and on an after-tax basis will have $66, $12 more than the amount needed to make him whole. On the other hand, had the award been made on the "grossed-up" amount of the plaintiff's lost profits on an after-tax basis, the plaintiff would have received $82 ($54/(1-0.34)), paid $28 in taxes, and have $54 left. In this example the plaintiff would have benefitted had the damage award been paid on a pretax basis. Conversely, the plaintiff would not have been made whole if the tax rate had increased.

If an expert has used a discounted-cash-flow analysis to evaluate the plaintiff's lost profits, he will need some interest rate to bring those cash flows forward to the time of the trial from the base point of the analysis. (This assumes that the jurisdiction or particular cause of action permits prejudgment interest.) At the very least, this interest (or discount) rate should reflect the value his money has lost due to inflation. This measure, however, will not compensate the plaintiff for the opportunity costs of the use of his money. This refers to the fact that had the plaintiff not been denied the use of the damage amount, he would have invested it in some enterprise (perhaps in stock, perhaps in the performance of the plaintiff firm) and would have received a return on this amount.

Many experts suggest the use of some nominal interest rate (e.g., 3-year U.S. Treasury security rates). Other experts suggest the plaintiff's cost of capital, that is, a measure of the opportunity cost to the plaintiff (of course, at this point the defendant may argue that consequential damages are being sought). A better measure, however, may be the defendant's borrowing rate. Here the plaintiff's claim should be regarded as an investment (albeit an involuntary one) in the defendant.[12]

Antitrust

Another litigation area that heavily relies on economic analysis is antitrust law. In both liability and damage issues, economic analysis plays such an important role that any study failing to consider the economic aspects of the case would be virtually useless in court or administrative hearings. For an expert to have performed certain calculations is not meaningful; the expert should know what economic concepts those numbers represent and how they fit into the present antitrust framework.[13]

Mergers. The principal concern of the Department of Justice (DOJ) is to prevent mergers that create or enhance market power. Market power is the ability of a firm (or group of firms) to raise price above the competitive level for a significant time period. The DOJ has stated that a price increase of 5 percent for 1 year in most contexts will constitute a "small but significant and nontransitory" increase in price.[14] The firm (or group of firms) possessing market power can raise prices without losing so many sales that the price increase becomes unprofitable by restricting output (Posner and Landes, 1981).

Merger analysis first defines the relevant product and geographic markets. As discussed previously, the study must include not only firms directly competing with the parties involved in the merger but also firms producing substitute products and firms that would enter the market or expand their current output should the merged firm impose a supracompetitive price.[15] The DOJ defines the relevant market as all firms that, should they act in concert, would be able to profitably impose a "small but significant and nontransitory" price increase.[16] Note that if the analysis excluded firms that make substitutes for the merged firms' product, a restriction in output resulting in a supracompetitive price would appear on paper to be profitable. In reality, however, because customers would switch to the competitively priced substitutes, the supracompetitive price level would not be profitable. This same reasoning applies to the omission of firms that would enter the market if a supracompetitive price were imposed.

Having defined the relevant product and geographic markets, the expert should now measure the concentration within the markets to ascertain whether the transaction will fall within a "safe harbor" under the DOJ's guidelines. A common concentration measure (also cited in the DOJ's guidelines) is the Herfindahl–Hirschman Index or HHI. With this measure, the percentage share of each firm is squared and then the sum is compared to preestablished cutoff points.[17] Judgment is involved, however, even in a calculation as simple as this. Market shares can be measured on the basis of sales (either dollars or units), shipments, production, capacity, or reserves.[18] The correct measure depends upon the economic facts of each case. Once the HHI for the correct market has been determined, the expert knows that it is unlikely the DOJ will challenge the transaction if the postmerger HHI is below 1000, or if the postmerger HHI is between 1000 and 1800 and the merger would produce an increase of less than 100 points, or if the postmerger HHI is above 1800 and the merger would produce an increase of less than 50 points.[19]

Even if the HHI concentration measure suggests that the merger could reduce competition, other considerations exist. The primary reason mergers are challenged is the fear of collusion, that is, that the number of firms will be so few that they could easily act in concert as one giant firm. There are recognized factors, however, that facilitate or prevent collusion among a group of firms. Factors facilitating collusion include: fewness of firms, barriers to entry, homogeneous product, demand inelasticity, level of industry profits, industry social structure, and sealed bidding (availability of price information) (Brozen, 1982; Hay and Kelley, 1974). Factors that make collusion difficult include: irregularity and infrequency of orders, high fixed costs, low transportation costs, frequent technological change, and variations in production costs. (Brozen, 1982; Hay and Kelley, 1974). An expert may show that, even though the concentration levels within the relevant market would normally be considered high, collusion is unlikely because the gains from cheating on a collusive agreement would be great because of the presence (or absence) of the factors discussed.[20]

The expert should also consider whether reasons exist for this merger other than the purchase of a competitor's exit. The expert should investigate whether the merger will increase output. If concentration within the relevant market is great, an expert may consider whether the merger of the third and fourth largest firms should be allowed to produce an effective competitor to the industry giants that are the first and second largest firms. The expert should not neglect, moreover, to perform efficiency studies that will document economies of scale and scope between the merging firms.

Finally, when the expert estimates damages in cases alleging that a merger violated the antitrust laws, the expert's damage measure must be causally linked to the anticompetitive acts cited in the complaint. In *Brunswick Corp. v. Pueblo Bowl-o-Mat, Inc.*, 429 U.S. 477 (1977), the plaintiff's damage measure was the profits it would have made had the defendant not acquired certain bowling centers and these centers gone into bankruptcy instead. The Supreme Court vacated the lower court's judgment for the plaintiff on the ground that this damage measure bore no relationship to the antitrust injury of which the plaintiff complained. The plaintiff would have suffered these injuries had the acquired centers obtained refinancing or been acquired by a nonobjectionable party. (*Ibid.*, pp. 487–488.) Thus an expert on damage issues should show that the damages relate to those acts that injure competition, not merely to acts that injure a competitor.

Failing-Firm Defense. The failing-firm defense relates to merger analysis; however, because it involves such extensive financial analysis, this defense is discussed separately. The economic premise for this defense is that an otherwise objectionable merger should nevertheless be allowed if the firm to be acquired would otherwise go out of business. In this case, even a sale to a dominant firm is preferable to removing capacity. The caveat to this defense is that the owners of the firm or division to be acquired must have sought and found no other buyers who would continue to run the business. The best financial analysis will nonetheless fail if a less objectionable buyer can be found.

Assuming that the shopping requirement has been met, the expert must investigate whether the firm or division to be acquired was losing so much money that the present owners will close it rather than continue to incur these losses. First, one must examine the future of the firm or division and estimate whether the future will differ from the recent past. Is competition increasing or decreasing? Is demand increasing or decreasing? Do the firm's competitors have a cost advantage that the "failing firm" cannot duplicate? If a market analysis demonstrates that the future will be no different, an expert may find the following rate-of-return experiment useful: Using actual cash flows for a 5-year period and assuming that everything that has transpired within this time period had been known 5 years ago, would the firm's owners have elected to continue operating the business or would they have chosen to exit the business?[21]

A cash-flow-rate-of-return analysis is used rather than accounting returns because cash flows more accurately reflect whether firms generate sufficient revenue to cover variable costs. In the short run, a firm that generates enough cash to cover its variable costs will be able to, and may choose to, remain in operation. The accounting algorithm labels some cash outflows as *operating expenses* and others as *capital expenditures*. Operating expenses are deducted from each year's income immediately. Capital expenditures are depreciated according to a schedule chosen by the accountant and then deducted from income. Thus the accounting return on investment will reflect some cash expenditures made in previous periods and will not reflect some cash expenditures made during the current period. In addition, the reported accounting book value of the assets may not accurately reflect the asset's market value.

The problems associated with using the accounting definition of return on investment can be avoided by using a cash-flow internal rate of return (IRR) that incorporates the market or salvage value of the assets. The IRR is the interest rate "that will make the present value of cash proceeds expected from an investment equal to the present value of the cash outlays required by the investment" (Bierman and Smidt, 1980, p. 30). In other words, the IRR is that discount rate that makes the net present value of the project equal to zero (Brealey and Myers, 1988, p. 78).

The expert can compare the firm's IRR to the rate of return the firm could have earned elsewhere with investments of similar risk to determine whether the firm would have chosen to exit the business at the beginning date of the analysis had the future been known. If the firm's IRR equals the firm's return on an alternative investment of similar risks, the firm neither profited nor lost from its operations. If the IRR is less than the firm's return on alternative investments of similar risks, then the firm would have been better off withdrawing.[22] In the extreme case, if an existing business has a cash flow with a negative IRR, the firm not only made less than it could have earned elsewhere, it diminished the value of its original investment as well.[23] In such a case, obviously the firm would be better off shutting down the business and selling out rather than running the business and continuing to incur losses.

To calculate the IRR of a business, the expert should measure each year's cash flow. Generally, an expert will adjust a firm's financial statements to a cash basis. For example, noncash items, such as depreciation, must be added back to income. The expert will also need to subtract the actual cash spent on capital investment (net of their tax effects). Although the expert will not include any financing effects in the analysis (e.g., interest payments on firm debt), the expert should include a charge for the change in the level of working capital used in operations. The expert's analysis should be done on an after-tax basis because tax effects, such as the use of one division's losses to offset the profits earned by another division, may alter the results of the analysis. The expert may also revise the analysis to remove the effects of extraordinary events, such as investment in a major project or the effects of a recession, to disprove the notion that the underlying business is sound but that a large investment in an unsuccessful project or economic conditions that no longer exist was the cause of the firm's difficulties.

The most difficult part of the IRR analysis is estimating the amounts of the beginning and ending flows. Because the premise under examination is whether the firm would have been abandoned had the future been known, the beginning and ending flows should reflect what the firm could expect to have received upon abandonment 5 years ago and what the firm could expect to receive upon abandonment at present. In other words, what was the value of the assets at their next best alternative use outside the industry in which the assets are currently employed 5 years ago and what is that value today? The expert should ensure that the analysis includes all unrecorded liabilities. For example, unrecorded pension or environmental cleanup costs may be so large that the firm would prefer to continue operating with minimum losses rather than pay the large lump-sum required immediately upon abandonment. Again, these beginning and ending flows should be after-tax because losses associated with writing down assets that can be used to offset the firm's other profits since they are a liquidation benefit.

Finally, if the acquiror is paying more than the salvage value of the acquired firm, the expert may find it useful to provide an analysis of the acquiror's price (e.g., relating price to cost savings that will accrue to the acquiror because of efficiencies). Otherwise the entire analysis may be undermined by questions such as why the acquiror is paying a few million when the assets are worth only one million.

Predatory Pricing. Predatory pricing has been defined as pricing a firm's products below cost with the intent of driving one's competitors from the market and thereafter raising the firm's prices to a supracompetitive level.[24] Predatory pricing constitutes an offense under Section 1 (unlawful restraint of trade) and Section 2 (monopolization or attempt to monopolize) of the Sherman Act and Section 2(a) of the Robinson–Patman Act (destroying competition or eliminating a competitor).[25] Although many courts agree with the stated definition, there is disagreement on exactly what cost measure should be used to calculate "below-cost" pricing in an antitrust analysis.[26]

The most widely used cost standard is that put forth by professors Areeda and Turner in their "Predatory Pricing and Related Practices under Section 2 of the Sherman Act, 88 *Harv. L. Rev.* 697 (1975) and later published as part of *Antitrust Law*, ¶¶ 711–722 (1978).[27] The authors' initial standard was that a price above reasonably anticipated short-run marginal costs is nonpredatory. They recognize that marginal cost data are often unavailable, so that a first approximation price above reasonably anticipated average variable cost should be presumed lawful.[28] Nevertheless, other cost measures have been held relevant to the question of whether the defendant was engaged in predatory pricing.[29] The details of the particular case may determine the relevant cost analysis. Although an average variable cost analysis may be appropriate for a firm already in the market, it may be inappropriate for a new entrant who may have to engage in promotional pricing to gain customer loyalty, a capital asset that a long-time competitor already possesses.

Even when the relevant cost measure has been determined, important aspects of the analysis still remain. For example, if the predatory claims are associated with a single division (or product) of a multidivision (-product) firm, the expert needs to consider joint costs.[30] The time frame over which the firm's costs are analyzed as fixed or variable becomes extremely important: The shorter the time period the fewer the variable costs. Another consideration is whether the expert analyzes costs that vary as production rises and falls within some output range or does the expert measure which costs vary as production falls to zero (going-concern versus shut-down analysis). To a firm that has large costs associated with producing one unit, which do not increase with the production level (zero-one costs), the level over which costs are measured as variable could be depositive of the case.[31]

Important as cost estimation may appear in predatory pricing analysis, market analysis also has an equally, if not more, significant role. For a campaign of predatory pricing to be successful and for its anticompetitive effects to occur, the firm engaging in this behavior must be able to recoup its losses, that is, it must obtain and retain market power. If the firm cannot absorb the market shares of its competitors that have failed, demand will remain for the surviving competitors whose prices are higher and the firm will have injured itself to no avail.[32] Similarly, if barriers to entry do not exist, the firm that has driven all present competitors from the market by predatory pricing will soon find it has yet another set of competitors and that it can not maintain supracompetitive prices for the period of time needed to recoup the losses it has inflicted upon itself.[33]

Securities Laws

Securities cases increasingly show the influence of economic analysis. Many developments have centered around "fraud on the market" cases. In *Basic Inc. v. Levinson*, 108 S.Ct. 978 (1988), the U.S. Supreme Court cited the findings of academic studies that show the price of a widely traded stock reflects all publicly available information about that stock, that is, markets are "efficient."[34]
Thus a plaintiff who can establish that a false, misleading, or omitted statement has affected the stock's price may be entitled to recover the difference between the stock's actual value and "true" value (i.e., the value the market would have reached had the truth about the firm been known).[35] The expert in such cases will consider whether the "true" value of the stock differed from the actual value.

Many academic empirical studies have demonstrated that a significant portion of a stock's price movement is explained by movements in the overall market (Brealey and Myers, 1988, pp. 125–144; Copeland and Weston, 1988, pp. 193–240; Fama, 1976, pp. 41–132). Based on these studies, experts have constructed statistical models (regression equations) that predict stock price movements. Using stock price data from a time period prior to the period of interest, the expert may calculate the relationship between the return on a particular firm and the return on a market index (e.g., S&P 500). This regression relationship (market model) and the actual market return during the period of interest then may be used to predict the particular stock's return. If the difference between the actual value and the predicted value is large enough, the firm is said to have experienced a statistically significant "abnormal" return.

Thus by combining the efficient market theory and the market model, experts can study the effects of information on a stock's price and ascertain whether the effects were material (Fischel, 1982). For example, the expert may compare the actual and predicted return of a firm's stock when information is disclosed to estimate whether any abnormal declines in value occurred relative to the stock's predicted value at the time an alleged falsehood, misstatement, or omission was "corrected." If no abnormal change occurs after the information is publicly disclosed, the information is immaterial, and there should be no liability.

This same methodology can be used to quantify the amount of damages (assuming liability). For example, the plaintiff may allege that certain information was omitted from an annual report and that when the information was publicly released subsequently, the stock price dropped. The expert's analysis might assume that any abnormal negative returns occurring when this information was released were due solely to the release of the information and then estimate what the stock's price would have been had these abnormal negative returns occurred earlier (i.e., when the plaintiff alleges disclosure should have occurred). Under this type of analysis, the plaintiff who owns stock would be entitled to recover only if he bought when the actual price was above the predicted price (or "true" value). On the other hand, a plaintiff who sold the stock in question could recover only if he sold when the predicted price ("true" value) was higher than the actual price. In both cases, the amount of damages would be related to the difference between the actual value and the "true" value. A more complete discussion of damages in securities litigation can be found in another chapter in this book.

NOTES

This paper reflects the author's views and she alone takes responsibility for any errors or omissions.

1. We forego a detailed explanation because there are other chapters in this book that discuss regression analysis. See also Fisher, "Multiple Regression in Legal Proceedings," 80 *Colum. L. Rev.* 702 (1980), for a more complete explanation of the construction and use of regressions.
2. See "Securities Laws" (p. 166), for a discussion of this point.
3. If two variables (e.g., the prices of two products) are strongly correlated and one observes a change in one of the variables, one will expect to see a change in the other. If this change in the second variable is in the same direction as the first, the variables are positively correlated. If the change in the second variable is in the opposite direction, the variables are said to be negatively correlated. If a change in the first variable results in random fluctuating changes in the second, the two variables are uncorrelated and have no strong relationship.
4. See "Measurement of Lost Profits" (p. 157), for a discussion of this point.
5. Capital market risk results from economy-wide factors that generally benefit or threaten all businesses.
6. Only when bonds are issued at par are the amounts of interest expense and interest paid the same.
7. See also the chapters in this book discussing cost estimation and regression.
8. The presence of joint or co-products in the analysis will also have implications for mitigation. Minimizing the losses for one product and minimizing a division's losses may result in two different sets of actions.
9. Most patents have a legal life of 17 years. Their effective life, however, may be less if the market has frequent technological changes or the patent can be easily designed around.

10. See Chapter 29, infra.

11. See Chapter 28, infra.

12. Patell, Weil, and Wolfson, "Accumulating Damages in Litigation: The Roles of Uncertainty and Interest Rates," 11 *J. of Legal Studies* 341 (1982). Note that the defendant's interest rates used to bring the damages to present value should be the effective aftertax rate to reflect the realities of the plaintiff's alternative uses of cash. To do otherwise would have investments in damage claims grow more rapidly than real investments of similar risk. The final amount, or course, should be "grossed up" by the plaintiff's tax rate, as discussed previously.

13. See Rosenfield, "The Use of Economic Analysis in Antitrust and Securities Litigation," 1 *Colum. L. Rev.* 49 (1986), for a detailed discussion of the widespread influence of economics in antitrust analysis.

14. U.S. Dept. of Justice, *Merger Guidelines*, 49 Fed. Reg. 28, 823 (1984).

15. See p. 151, for a discussion of market definition.

16. U.S. Dept. of Justice, supra.

17. A firm that had 10 percent of the market would have an HHI number of 100 ($10 \times 10 = 100$). A market that had 100 firms with a 1 percent share would have an HHI of 100. A market with one firm would have an HHI of 10,000 (100×100).

18. U.S. Dept. of Justice, supra.

19. *Ibid.*

20. See G. Stigler, "A Theory of Oligopoly," in *The Organization of Industry* 39 (1968) for a more complete discussion of modern collusion theory.

21. The choice of a 5-year time period is purely arbitrary. The facts of each individual case will determine the appropriate period to use. If the future appears to differ from the past, the expert will do the same type of analysis, only with projected cash flows. Of course, this experiment may not be as strong as the first because the projected cash flows are less reliable.

22. An expert may find the after-tax return on U.S. government securities to be a useful and conservative benchmark because people may disagree on what return the firm could expect from alternative investments of similar risks. Certainly a firm that earns less than it could from investing in risk-free government securities would be better off withdrawing from its operations.

23. For example, if the IRR is −10 percent, an initial investment of $100 will be worth only $90 at the end of the year.

24. E.g., *Cargill, Inc. v. Monfort of Colorado, Inc.*, 479 U.S. 104 (1986); *Matsushita Elec. Ind. Inc. Co. v. Zenith Radio Corp.*, 475 U.S. 574, 584 (1986). For those readers interested in a detailed analysis of the economic aspects of predatory pricing (and for potential expert witnesses in this area), the following are recommended: R. Bork, *The Antitrust Paradox* 144–160 (1978); Easterbrook, "The Limits of Antitrust," 63 *Tex. L. Rev.* 1 (1984), Easterbrook "Predatory Strategies and Counter-strategies," 48 *U. Chi. L. Rev.* 263 (1981); Koller, "When is Pricing Predatory?," *Anti-trust Bulletin* 283 (Summer 1979); McGee, "Predatory Pricing Revisited," 23 *J. Law & Econ.* 289 (1980).

25. 2 CCH Trade Reg. Rep. ¶ 6500.

26. *Cargill*, 107 S. Ct. at 493 n. 12.

27. *E.g., Bayou Bottling, Inc. v. Dr. Pepper Co.*, 725 F.2d 300 (5th Cir. 1984); *Arthur S. Langenderfer, Inc. v. S. E. Johnson Co.*, 729 F.2d 1050 (6th Cir. 1984); *D&S Redi-Mix v. Sierra Redi-Mix & Contracting Co.*, 692 F.2d 1245 (9th Cir. 1982).

28. P. Areeda and D. Turner, *Antitrust Law* ¶ 711d (1978).

29. P. Areeda and H. Hovenkamp, *1988 Supplement to Antitrust Law* ¶ 711.1c. *E.g., MCI Communications Corp. v. American Tel. and Tel. Co.*, 708 F.2d 1081 (7th Cir. 1983).

30. In *Marsann Co. v. Brammal, Inc.*, 788 F.2d 611 (9th Cir. 1986), the Ninth Circuit held that the relevant average variable cost is that of the items sold at the challenged price, rather than that associated with the production of the total output.

31. Remarks about cost estimation made previously in this chapter are also applicable here.

32. *Cargill*, 107 S. Ct. at 494 n. 15.

33. *Matsushita*, 106 S. Ct. at 1359 n. 15. (Citing Easterbrook, *Limits of Antitrust*.)

34. *Basic Inc. v. Levinson*, 108 S. Ct. at 991 n. 24. See also, *Flamm v. Eberstadt*, 814 F.2d 1169, 1179 (7th Cir. 1987).

35. *Basic*, 108 S. Ct. at 991–992; *Flamm*, 814 F.2d at 1179–80.

BIBLIOGRAPHY

Areeda, P., and D. F. Turner, *Antitrust Law* (1978).

Areeda, P., and D. F. Turner, "Predatory Pricing and Related Practices Under Section 2 of the Sherman Act," 88 *Harvard Law Review* 697 (1975).

Bierman, Jr., H., and S. Smidt, *The Capital Budgeting Decision* (5th ed. 1980).

Bork, R.H., *The Antitrust Paradox* (1978).

Brealey, R., and S. Myers, *Principles of Corporate Finance* (3rd ed. 1988).

Brozen, Y., *Concentration, Mergers and Public Policy* (1982).

Copeland, T.E., and J.F. Weston, *Financial Theory and Corporate Policy* (3rd ed. 1988).

Davidson, S., M.W. Maher, C.P. Stickney, and R.L. Weil, *Managerial Accounting* (2nd edition 1985).

Dunn, R.L., *Recovery of Damages for Lost Profits* (3d ed. 1987).

Easterbrook, F.H., "The Limits of Antitrust," 63 *Texas Law Review* 1 (1984).

Easterbrook, F.H., "Predatory Strategies and Counterstrategies," 48 *University of Chicago Law Review* 263 (1981).

Fama, E., *Foundations of Finance* (1976).

Fischel, D., "Use of Modern Finance Theory in Securities Fraud Cases Involving Actively Traded Securities," 38 *Business Lawyer* 1 (1982).

Fisher F.M., "Multiple Regression in Legal Proceedings," 80 *Columbia Law Review* 702 (1980).

Goetz, C.J., and R.E. Scott, "Measuring Sellers' Damages: The Lost-Profits Puzzle," 31 *Stanford Law Review* 323 (1979).

Hay, G.A., and D. Kelley, "An Empirical Survey of Price Fixing Conspiracies," 17 *Journal of Law & Economics* 13 (1974).

Koller II, R.H., "When is Pricing Predatory," *Antitrust Bulletin* (Summer 1979) 283.

McGee, J.S., "Predatory Pricing Revisited," 23 *Journal of Law and Economics* 289 (1980).

Patell, J.M., R.L. Weil, and M.A. Wolfson, "Accumulating Damages in Litigation: The Roles of Uncertainty and Interest Rates," 11 *Journal of Legal Studies* 341 (1982).

Pindyck, R.S., and D.L. Rubinfeld, *Econometric Models and Economic Forecasts* (2d ed. 1981).

Posner, R.A., and W.M. Landes, "Market Power in Antitrust Cases," 94 *Harvard Law Review* 937 (1981).

Rosenfield, A.M., "The Use of Economic Analysis in Antitrust and Securities Litigation," 1 *Columbia Law Review* 49 (1986).

Stigler, G.J., "A Theory of Oligopoly," in *The Organization of Industry* 39 (1968).

Stigler, G.J. and R.A. Sherwin, "The Extent of the Market," 28 *Journal of Law & Economics* 555 (1985).

U.S. Department of Justice, "Merger Guidelines," 49 *Federal Register* 28, 823 (1984).

LIST OF CASES

Arthur S. Langenderfer, Inc. v. S.E. Johnson Co., 729 F.2d 1050 (6th Cir. 1984)
Basic Inc. v. Levinson, 485 U.S. 224 (1988)
Bayou Bottling, Inc. v. Dr. Pepper Co., 725 F.2d 300 (5th Cir. 1984)
Brunswick Corp. v. Pueblo Bowl-o-Mat, Inc., 429 U.S. 477 (1977)
Cargill, Inc. v. Monfort of Colorado, Inc., 479 U.S. 104 (1986)
D&S Redi-Mix v. Sierra Redi-Mix & Contracting Co., 692 F.2d 1245 (9th Cir. 1982)
Flamm v. Eberstadt, 814 F.2d 1169 (7th Cir. 1987)
Marsann Co. v. Brammall, Inc., 788 F.2d 611 (9th Cir. 1986)
Matsushita Elec. Ind. Co. v. Zenith Radio Corp., 475 U.S. 574 (1986)
MCI Communication Corp. v. American Tel. and Tel. Co., 708 F.2d 1081 (7th Cir. 1983)

9

THE TIME VALUE OF MONEY

Harold R. Dilbeck, PhD, CPA

The author expresses his appreciation to Vernon W. Hunt, Jr., Esq., and Patrick O'Keefe, Esq., for reading and making helpful comments on this chapter.

ATTENTION TO THE TIME VALUE OF MONEY

Although most participants in economic affairs recognize that time is money, the courts remain uncertain.

In the twentieth century, the U.S. Supreme Court has had to assert this simple principle several times. Some lower courts' reluctance to embrace one of the financial world's truths provides accountants with an opportunity to educate and persuade. Alternatively, other courts' acceptance of the time value of money as fundamentally important offers accountants an opening to apply their talents in various litigation settings.

The time value of money arises whenever time passes between an economic cost and an economic benefit. The accumulation point may be in the past, the future, or the present. The accumulation point of most court decisions involving the time value of money is the present: Money due in the past must be accumulated to the present or a prospective sum due in the future must be discounted to the present. This chapter investigates the appropriate rate at which this accumulating or discounting occurs. This rate should reflect risk, inflation, and income tax considerations.

The chapter briefly reviews familiar formulas applicable to accumulating and discounting cash flows, examines the components of the rate of return used for accumulating or discounting, and discusses the need for parity between the rate of return and the cash flows with respect to risk, inflation, and income taxes. The chapter highlights cases where accountants are needed.

BASIC FORMULAS FOR ACCUMULATING OR DISCOUNTING CASH FLOWS

The essential tools are a future value formula, present value formula, and perpetuity formula. Each requires a cash flow amount and an interest rate for each period considered. The first two formulas also require the number of periods. The perpetuity formula assumes an infinite number of periods. This chapter also discusses annuity formulas and a modified version of the perpetuity formula.

Future Value Formula

The future value formula applies when the accumulation point occurs after the occurrence of the cash flow in the litigation. Prejudgment interest for tort actions illustrates this formula's appropriate application: Courts not only allow the plaintiff to recover the value of damages at the time of a past wrongdoing but also recognize that the period between that act and judgment has deprived the plaintiff of the time value of money. The court establishes the cash flow as of some prior date, and the accumulation point is the present. The formula is the following:

$$FV = PMT \times (1 + i)^n$$

where FV is the compound sum of damages plus interest at the accumulation point, PMT is the amount of payment (damages) occurring at the beginning of the first period, i is the interest rate or rate of return per period, and n is the number of periods from the date of the damage assessment to the accumulation point.

EXAMPLE:

$1000 due for damages that were incurred 3 years ago, using an interest rate of 9 percent per annum has

$$\text{FV} = \$1000 \times (1.09)^3 = \$1295.$$

If damages occurred in several prior periods, one must expand the formula in a manner similar to that for the present value formula explained below.

Present Value Formula

The present value formula applies when the cash flows occur after the accumulation point (e.g., time of trial). Damages for lost future wages or profits are examples of such cases. The court ascertains the future cash flows that one must then discount to the present to calculate a lump-sum payment. The formula is as follows:

$$\text{PV} = \text{PMT}_1 \times (1 + i)^{-1}\ \text{PMT}_2 \times (1 + i)^{-2} \ldots \text{PMT}_n \times (1 + i)^{-n}$$

where PV is the value of the future payments discounted to the accumulation point (the present), PMT_1 is the lost wages or profits in Period 1, PMT_2 is the lost wages or profits in Period 2, and so forth through Period n, i is the discount rate, and n is the last period in which losses are expected to occur.

Example
$1000 to be received at the end of Year 1, $800 at the end of Year 2, and $500 at the end of Year 3, discounted at 7 percent has a

$$\begin{aligned} \text{PV} &= \$1000 \times (1.07)^{-1}\ \$800 \times (1.07)^{-2} + \$500 \times (1.07)^{-3} \\ &= \$935 + \$699 + \$408 \\ &= \$2042. \end{aligned}$$

Perpetuities

A perpetuity model is a special version of the present value model: All payments are equal, periodic, and the number of periods approaches infinity. Business valuation cases, where future perpetual earnings are assumed to be equal in every period, commonly use this model. The formula is the following:

$$\text{PV} = \text{E}/k,$$

where PV is the present value of future equal periodic earnings (E), and k is the required rate of return appropriate to the risk contained in the earnings.

Example

Future income of \$1000 per year, discounted at 8 percent required rate of return has a present value as follows

$$PV = \$1{,}000/.08 = \$12{,}500.$$

This perpetuity model does not consider growth or inflation because it assumes constant earnings. An expanded model can accommodate such elaborations:

$$PV = \frac{E_1(1 - b)}{k - br} = \frac{D_1}{k - g}$$

where PV = present value of future earnings
E_1 = earnings in Period 1
b = percentage of earnings retained in the business
r = rate of return earned on additional earnings retained
k = required rate of return appropriate to the risk
g = growth ($b \times r$)
D_1 = dividends in Year 1.

This familiar model assumes dividends will grow at a constant rate equal to $g = br$. If $r = k$, the model simplifies into the perpetuity model, regardless of b's magnitude. For this model to be meaningful, therefore, r must exceed k, which is a disequilibrium condition and, accordingly, suspect in the long term. Moreover, if inflation is introduced and assumed to affect k and r equally, the denominator does not change, and PV does not change. Consequently, this elaborated model has dubious value for expert witnesses because it requires more tutelage for the court and does not add substance over the simpler version.

Annuities

An annuity is a series of equal periodic payments for a specified number of periods. One can express the annuity as a present value or future value and as an ordinary annuity (payment received at the end of each period) or an annuity due (payment received at the beginning of each period). Annuity formulas often appear in structured settlements of personal injury or wrongful death cases, where the defendant makes installments rather than a lump-sum payment. These settlements are private transactions, and information regarding the discount rates used is not available. For this reason, this chapter will not discuss annuity formulas and structured settlements. (For more reading on the formulas and their applications, see Brigham, 1983, pp. 71–76; Weston and Copeland, 1986, pp. 76–79).

The next sections examine the formulas' empirical content: the appropriate rate of return and the need to maintain parity between the cash flows and the rate selected.

ASCERTAINING THE APPROPRIATE INTEREST RATE

A complex set of factors affects market interest rates. Many analysts divide nominal interest rates into components; one can more readily understand why different cases require different rates after reviewing these components. This chapter examines five such interest rate components (Brigham, 1983, pp. 44–53; Weston and Copeland, 1986, 139–158).

The pure rate of interest. This component—also referred to as the "pure productivity of assets"—would exist in a market unfettered by uncertainties and price level changes. The closest observation of this abstraction would be the rate on short-term U.S. Government Treasury bills in periods of stable prices. The unadorned interaction of demand and supply controls this rate.

The maturity premium. The second component, associated with longer term obligations, is the premium for maturity that reflects the risk of committing funds for longer periods. This premium is best evidenced by the premiums on longer term government bonds over Treasury bills in periods of stable prices and expectations of no change in future interest rates.

The inflation premium. The third component compensates the lender for inflation expected over the term of the payments.

The riskless rate of interest includes these components and depends on the elapsed time until the expected cash flow. The maturity premium is not part of the riskless rate because it compensates for market risk of fluctuating interest rates during the term to maturity. One can, however, refer to the riskless rate not as a single rate but as a series of rates varying with maturity.

Two other potential components of observed interest rates are the default and illiquidity premiums. The rates for U.S. Government bonds and bills do not include these premiums, as they do not form part of the riskless interest rate.

The default premium. The default premium reflects the risk of default and consequent loss of principal and accrued interest in the event of the debtor's liquidation or reorganization. Spreads between bonds of differing risk classes—such as U.S. Government bonds, AAA corporate bonds, and AA corporates—indicate the default premium.

The illiquidity premium. The illiquidity premium represents a premium for lack of marketability and the resulting sacrifice of value if disposition becomes necessary, especially if that disposition must occur quickly. The spread between the interest rate earned on a portfolio of first mortgage or trust deed notes compared to that of highly marketable pass-through certificates indicates an illiquidity premium.

Interest rates used in litigation frequently do not sufficiently consider these components. The courts often use statutory rates or risk-free rates that seldom relate to applicable market rates. Courts also frequently use interest rates for debt securities when rates applicable to equity investments may be appropriate, as in breach of contract cases for lost future profits.

CAPITALIZATION OR DISCOUNT RATES FOR EQUITY INVESTMENTS

One must go beyond interest rates to select a rate suitable to ownership interests. Business valuation for estate or other income tax purposes, marital dissolutions, and stockholder or partner disputes requires a rate of return applicable to equity investments, not interest rates for debt securities. The Capital Asset Pricing Model (CAPM) was developed to estimate the required rate of return on equity investments.

The Capital Asset Pricing Model

This model hypothesizes that the required rate of return on a given stock consists of two components in a linear relationship: a riskless component—the riskless rate on short-term debt obligations—and a premium to compensate for risk. This risk premium is analyzed further into two elements: (1) a component for the equity market as a whole and (2) an adjustment for the risk of a given stock in relation to the market. This adjustment for the individual stock is the "beta" coefficient. A beta coefficient of 1.0 signifies no adjustment to the risk premium for the market as a whole and that returns on the individual stock resemble the market returns.

This can be expressed in mathematical terms as follows:

$$k_i = r + b(k_m - r),$$

where k_i is the required return on stock i, r is the risk-free rate, b is the beta coefficient and k_m is the expected return on the market as a whole.

The analyst must estimate the parameters r and k_m and the variable b for the given stock to compute k_i. Beta values are available for traded securities in published statistics. For example, if $r = 3\%$, $k_m = 10\%$ and $b = 1.2$, then $k_i = 11.4\%$. This required rate of return would then be applied to an estimated cash-flow stream to calculate its present value, that is, the value of a share of stock or the value of a company. In using the CAPM model, the analyst must take care to use consistent after- or pretax values as discussed later in this chapter (Brigham, pp. 157–159; Weston and Copeland, pp. 440–445).

The Arbitrage Pricing Model

Financial analysts also use the Arbitrage Pricing Model (APM) to estimate the required rate of return on equity investments. APM is related to an extension of the capital asset pricing model—CAPM. The essential difference is that APM is a multifactor model, whereas CAPM is a single factor model, namely beta applied to the market risk premium. One may express the APM formula as follows:

$$k_i = r + p_1 s_1 + p_2 s_2 \ldots p_j s_j \;,$$

where k_i is the required return on stock i, r is the risk-free rate, p_1 is the risk premium applied to Factor 1 (e.g., industrial production), s_1 is the sensitivity of stock i to Factor 1, and the like (Bower et al., 1984). Among the factors found important in the APM are industrial production, inflation, interest rate term structure and the spread between low- and high-grade bonds (Roll and Ross, 1984)

One can illustrate the model by assuming only two factors, industrial production and inflation. With a risk-free rate of 3 percent, a risk premium of 5 percent for production and 1 percent for inflation and sensitivity factors of 1.2 for production and .8 for inflation, k would equal 9.8 percent [3% + (5%)(1.2) + (1%)(.8)].

The Expert's Judgment

Regardless of the expert's analytical framework, judgment will probably play a larger role in estimating the required rate of return for an equity investment than for interest rates appropriate to debts. Some valuations, moreover, may require preparation on so limited a time schedule or budget that the analyst must apply his judgment without the support of a mathematical model. Court precedent may influence the expert's estimation more than independent financial analysis will, considering the cost of performing the latter and the difficulty of making esoteric models comprehensible to the court. For these reasons, the expert may use the CAPM and APM as a way of thinking about the problem more than as an expository device.

ESTIMATING CASH FLOWS

A critical relationship exists between the cash flow to be discounted or accumulated and the rate of discounting or accumulating. Although this chapter does not discuss how to estimate cash flows, it will address three rules regarding cash flows and the related discount rate:

1. If cash flows include (exclude) income taxes, the discount rate should include (exclude) the effect of income taxes.
2. If cash flows include (exclude) effects of anticipated inflation, the discount rate should include (exclude) anticipated inflation.
3. If cash flows include (exclude) risk, the discount rate should include (exclude) risk.

Parity in Income Taxes

Income tax parity between cash flows and discount rates exists when both are stated either before or after income taxes. For example, if an investment today of \$1000 is expected to return \$1060 before taxes in 1 year, the pretax return is 6 percent. If tax rates are 30 percent, the after-tax accumulation income is \$1042. Only one discount rate will discount \$1042 to a present value of \$1000 and that is 4.2 percent or 6 percent times (1 − .3), the after-tax discount rate.

U.S. Supreme Court personal injury or wrongful death decisions have discussed these parity issues during the past few years. The following highlights several of those cases.

The Supreme Court first addressed the admissibility of evidence and jury instructions regarding income taxes payable on personal injury damage awards in 1980 (*Norfolk & Western Railway Co. v. Liepelt*). The Court permitted evidence regarding the effect of income taxes on the plaintiff's earnings and stated that trial courts should instruct juries that such awards are not subject to federal income taxes. This case implied that after-tax earnings are the appropriate figures to discount. The Court did not discuss the discount rate for this earnings stream (Inga, 1981, pp. 873–79). The Supreme Court did, however, consider the income tax parity issue in a later case: "Moreover, since under *Norfolk* . . ., the lost stream of income should be estimated in after-tax terms, the discount rate should also represent the after-tax rate of return to the injured worker" (*Jones & Laughlin Steel Corp. v. Pfeifer*, p. 537).

In 1983, a California appellate court discussed this issue extensively and reached similar conclusions in reversing the trial court's treatment of income taxes (*Canavin v. Pacific Southwest Airlines*). In this wrongful death action, the jury received evidence on both gross and net future earnings and on rates of return on taxable investments (12¼ percent) and tax-exempt investments (8 percent) (Ibid., p. 523). (The difference in present values between $30,000 per year for 30 years discounted at 12¼ percent and at 8 percent approximates $100,000.)

The jury calculated damages on an after-tax basis and then calculated the present value using the discount rate applicable to taxable investments, thereby double counting the effect of income taxes in the award (Ibid., p. 518). A major point on appeal concerned the trial court's refusal to instruct the jury, in accordance with the plaintiff's request, concerning the need to maintain parity between the cash flow and the discount rate. A damage award that reflects gross earnings should be discounted at the rate earned on taxable investments; for an award that includes after-tax earnings, the discount rate should be the rate earned on tax-exempt investments. The appellate court held this failure to instruct the jury to be reversible error: "The trial court erroneously denied the request and, in fact, gave no legal guidance at all to the jurors on this critically material point" (Ibid., p. 523).

Parity in Inflation

The U.S. Supreme Court in *Pfeifer* required parity in treatment of inflation on both the earnings estimates and the discount rates. The effects of ignoring parity regarding inflation can be illustrated by an example of lost future wages commencing at $30,000 per year after taxes, and increased 5 percent per year for inflation for 30 years. If those future wages are discounted at a 2-percent tax-exempt, noninflationary rate rather than the parity rate of 7 percent, consisting of the 2-percent rate plus the 5-percent inflation premium, the award would be excessive by approximately $738,000.

Parity in Risk

Since *Chesapeake & Ohio Railway Co. v. Kelly*, the Supreme Court has taken the position in personal injury and wrongful death cases that the discount rate applied to estimated lost future earnings should be that "earned on the best and safest investments" (*Kelly*, p. 491, as quoted in *Pfeifer*, p. 537).

> Once it is assumed that the injured worker would definitely have worked for a specific term of years, he is entitled to a risk-free stream of future income to replace his lost wages; therefore, the discount rate should not reflect the market's premium for investors who are willing to accept some risk of default (Ibid., p. 537)

In the absence of further assumptions, this view lacks the appropriate parity. Uncertainty regarding the earnings to be discounted arises not only from the number of years the worker may continue working but from uncertainty about wage increases, income taxes, employment expenses, and the probability of being employed in any given year. A risk-free discount rate can apply only to a risk-free earnings stream to achieve a risk parity that parallels the Court's reasoning on inflation and income taxes. A *risk-free* earnings stream is not identical to an *expected* earnings stream, as the Court's statement implies.

The difference between an expected value and a certainty equivalent, although widely accepted among analysts in finance and economics, remains unrecognized in law. Goetz, for example, uses both terms synonymously: "In deriving an expected value, one converts a possibly very complex set of possibilities into a single value, the certainty equivalent of the prospect being considered" (Goetz, 1984, p. 157).

An expected value represents a weighted average of possible outcomes, each outcome weighted by the probability of its occurrence, which the decision maker supplies. A certainty equivalent represents a fixed and certain amount that the decision maker would exchange for an uncertain expected value. For example, if you had a 50/50 chance of winning $20,000 or nothing at a lottery drawing, your expected value would be $10,000. What amount would you accept before the drawing in exchange for your ticket? A rational, risk-averting person would always accept a guaranteed amount of less than the expected value, say $9000. This amount would be your certainty equivalent of the lottery ticket's expected value. You can translate this idea to your lifetime income: You would exchange each year of expected future income for some guaranteed amount. Only this lower amount should be discounted at the risk-free rate. Each year's expected income would be discounted at a risk-adjusted rate. (For an elaboration of the differences, see Weston and Copeland, 1986, pp. 441–445.)

The courts take the position in personal injury and wrongful death cases that they are dealing with a certainty equivalent earnings stream, when in fact it is an expected value. The following excerpts from the court's opinion in *Pfeifer* illustrate the analysis that is typical in these cases. The court's language in the first paragraph clearly acknowledges they are dealing with expectations and probabilities, that is, an expected value. The second paragraph reveals a conversion from that expectancy to a certainty, to justify the use of the risk-free discount rate. There is, however, no recognition of the need to reduce the cash flow to a certainty equivalent. The cash flow is obtained by multiplying the expected (now assumed certain) worklife by the expected (now assumed certain) wage, and so on, and the result is called a certainty.

> The lost stream's length cannot be known with certainty; the worker could have been disabled or even killed in a different, non-work-related accident at any time. The probability that he would still be working at a given date is constantly diminishing. (p. 781)

> Once it is assumed that the injured worker would definitely have worked for a specific term of years, he is entitled to a risk-free stream of future income to replace his lost

wages; therefore, the discount rate should not reflect the market's premium for investors who are willing to accept some risk of default. (p. 783)

Too large a "slip twixt cup and lip" exists here to be ignored. The difference between expected value and certainty equivalent of lost future income involves more uncertainty than that related to the number of years the worker would have continued employment. Uncertainty also exists regarding future wage and tax rates, to mention the equation's two most obvious terms.

What risk-adjusted rate should one apply to a deceased or disabled worker's future expected earnings? The worker's borrowing rate? The worker's lending rate? The employer's borrowing or lending rate? Neither of these is analytically satisfying. Or should one approach the problem from the other direction and convert the expected earnings to a certainty equivalent, then discount at the risk-free rate? If so, what guidelines do courts have for converting expectations into certainty equivalents? How do expert witnesses develop testimony on this topic?

It is discouraging that this lack of parity persists after the courts have successfully addressed income taxes and inflation. The disparity overstates affected awards. For example, assume that the risk-free, tax-exempt rate is 2 percent, and a 1-percent risk premium is considered applicable to an *expected* future annual stream of $30,000 after taxes for 30 years. The present value of that stream is over $80,000 less when discounted at the parity rate of 3 percent rather than at the 2-percent risk-free rate.

Conclusion

The U.S. Supreme Court knowledgeably guided litigants and courts on parity between cash flows and discount rates involving income taxes and inflation. The inattentiveness to parity regarding risk, however, remains curiously at odds with current thinking among students of finance and economics. One suspects that elementary terms such as *certainty* and *uncertainty* have such diverse meanings across disciplines that more time will pass before the courts recognize parity. Accountants can help improve interpretations on this point by understanding the issues and noting any opportunities for changing attitudes within the judiciary.

TIME VALUE OF MONEY IN LITIGATION

Damages and business valuation calculations often employ time value of money concepts. Damages calculations usually use some interest rate to accumulate or discount cash flows. Business valuation uses a capitalization or discount rate that is either an estimated required rate of return for equity investors or a weighted average of the rates of return required by the firm's debt and equity investors.

The most advanced attention to the time value of money in litigation today relates to lost future wages from personal injury or wrongful death. The Supreme Court first addressed discounting in 1916 (*Kelly*). A 1988 decision deals in new ways with the subject (*Monessen Southwestern Railway Company v. Gerald L. Morgan*, as reported in 88 *Daily Journal* D.A.R. 7133). The lower courts' decisions have twisted and turned a great deal in the interim.

The 1916 *Kelly* case dealt with an injured railway worker who brought an action under the Federal Employers' Liability Act (FELA) to recover lost future wages. The court required discounting to avoid the plaintiff's unjust enrichment because the plaintiff received a lump sum amount rather than payments spread over the years that the wages would have been paid.

The 1988 *Morgan* case involved an injured railway worker who brought a similar action under FELA in a Pennsylvania state court. The trial judge instructed the jury to use a zero discount rate in calculating the award's present value as a matter of Pennsylvania state law, referring to the Pennsylvania Supreme Court's decision in *Kaczkowski v. Bolubasz*, which held that future inflation would be conclusively presumed to equal future interest rates and that state courts in Pennsylvania therefore were not to reduce damages to present worth (88 *Daily Journal* D.A.R. 7135). The U.S. Supreme Court overruled the Pennsylvania courts, referring to the numerous cases following *Kelly* and concluded that the Court has consistently recognized that damage awards in suits governed by *federal law* should be based on present value and that the lower courts erred in instructing the jury that the discount was zero *as a matter of law* (Ibid., pp. 7135–7136). (This chapter reviews these cases in the previous section.)

The chapter's remaining sections address the following types of litigation, which commonly deal with the time value of money:

Damage cases
Future and past damages
Tort damages
Breach of contract damages
Business valuation cases
Federal estate and income tax cases
Other cases

Case examples were selected on the basis of availability of numerical data on rates of interest, discount, or capitalization rates that were in evidence or used by the courts in making decisions. Many more cases discuss the time value of money, but citing the actual numbers used by the courts and recognizing the limited availability of such information enhances this chapter's usefulness to the reader.

DAMAGE CASES

Damages constitute pecuniary compensation for an injury or a wrong sustained from a breach of contract or a tortious act (*Ballentine's Law Dictionary*, 1969). Damages can be divided into two categories: compensatory and other. The latter category includes exemplary, or punitive, damages and nominal damages. Exemplary damages make headlines, but accountants focus almost exclusively on compensatory damages. No California case has reduced damages for pain and suffering to present value; this also appears true for most other states (Johns, 1986 § 1.86).

Although both breach of contract and tort actions seek compensatory damages, they do not share an identical standard for such damages:

> The primary aim in measuring damages is compensation, and this contemplates that the damages for a tort should place the injured person as nearly as possible in the condition he would have occupied if the wrong had not occurred, and that the damages for breach of contract should place the plaintiff in the position he would be in if the contract had been fulfilled. (McCormick, 1935, p. 560)

These legal subtleties affect the cash flow definition and estimation. The parity relationship between cash flows and discount rates means that such distinctions will also affect the discount rate computations. For example, contrast a tortious claim for lost future wages resulting from personal injury to a breach of contract suit on an employment contract. The cash flow from injury-related lost future wages is estimated net of income taxes because the award is not taxable, and the discount rate, correspondingly, should be a tax-exempt rate. The award for lost future wages on an employment contract, however, constitutes taxable income, so the cash flow is estimated before income taxes, and the discount rate reflects income from a taxable source.

Future and Past Damages

The accumulation point for damage actions is the present: the time of judgment. Prejudgment damages (past damages) frequently receive treatment different from future damages regarding the time value of money. Discount rate information for future damages appears scant by comparison. Past and future discount rates are measured with little uniformity both within and between these categories. The following discussion highlights some clusters of frequent behavior and thought.

Future Damages in Tort Cases. The discount rate applied to future damages in personal injury tort cases involving federal law is the investment rate that would make the plaintiff whole without requiring financial expertise. The Supreme Court in the *Kelly* case stated the following:

> We do not mean to say that the discount should be at which is commonly called the "legal rate" of interest. . . . It may be that such rates are not obtainable upon investments on safe securities, at least without the exercise of financial experience and skill in the administration of the fund; and it is evident that the compensation should be awarded upon a basis that does not call upon the beneficiaries to exercise such skill, for where this is necessarily employed the interest return is in part earned by the investor rather than by the investment. (*Kelly*, p. 490)

The states that do not follow federal law either do not discount or use low discount rates indicative of risk-free, after-tax rates. The legal rate does not prevail in most personal injury or wrongful death cases regarding future damages.

Past Damages in Tort Cases. Most tort cases apply the legal rate to past damages. The uncertainty in these cases is whether to award interest separately, which is then usually calculated at the statutory rate (Dobbs, 1973, p. 164). Admiralty law presents a refreshing alternative to this prevailing practice, although the freshness is found in diversity rather than in consistently elevated discussion. Admiralty suits customarily award prejudgment interest, and it is an abuse of discretion to deny interest without an explanation. The interest rate applied in these maritime cases is within the trial judge's discretion, and it is governed neither by the legal rate in the forum state nor by the postjudgment rate established by federal law (Sharpe and Acomb, 1984, p. 7). Some of these courts apply a 6 percent rate (referred to as the admiralty rate) apparently to persuade other courts of uniformity's merit. Others apply the state's statutory rate. Another group applies the market rate for riskless securities, whereas some estimate the plaintiff's borrowing cost. For a thorough review of prejudgment interest in admiralty court decisions, see "Award of Prejudgment Interest in Admiralty Suits," *34 A.L.R. Fed.* 126–270 (1977 and current supplement).

Defendant's Borrowing Rate for Past Damages in Tort Cases. In an article addressing prejudgment interest, Patell, Weil, and Wolfson (1982, p. 362) argue that the defendant's borrowing or debt rate is the proper interest rate for accumulating compensatory damages from the date of injury to the payment date if the litigation claim is marketable. This invigorating view has influenced some admiralty court decisions: *Re M/V Vulcan* 553 F.2d 489 (5th Cir. 1977) (using 12 percent); *General Facilities, Inc. v. National Marine Service, Inc.* 664 F.2d 672 (8th Cir. 1981) (using 15.75 percent); *Consolidated Grain & Barge Co. v Wisconsin Barge Line, Inc.* 522 F. Supp. 842 (E.D. Mo. 1981) (using 10 percent). The admiralty courts also recognize the contrary view; one court refused to use the borrowing rate and applied the statutory rate because the plaintiff offered no evidence that it borrowed any money (*Signal Oil & Gas Co. v. Barge W-701* 468 F. Supp 802 (E.D. La. 1979).

Past and Future Damages in Breach of Contract Cases. The search for something meaningful to say about the appropriate interest rates for past and future damages in breach of contract cases could lead an honest researcher to embellish any findings to maintain an audience. Or the researcher may yield to another temptation: to say that the contract governs the rate, if the contract specifies the rate; otherwise the statutory rate applies (Dobbs, p. 164; McCormick, p. 211). The writer then exits before illustrating this rule with some current cases. The second choice is more appealing. Refer to the later section entitled "Breach of Contract Damages," where the only case we found on point appears to contradict the rule.

Restitution and Judgment Interest. Awards of restitution, which intend to prevent the defendant's unjust enrichment as distinguished from compensatory damages, use more market-oriented interest rates for past wrongs than do tort or breach of contract cases. This is because the defendant, if clever, has earned at least the market rate, which if greater than the statutory or contractual rate would enrich the defendant beyond the claim for compensatory damages, thereby engendering a restitution action (Dobbs, p. 169).

Interest on past damages (prejudgment interest) differs from judgment interest, which accrues from the judgment date until payment. This customary interest is calculated at the statutory rate (Ibid., p. 164).

Tort Damages

A tort arises from general law violation and differs from a breach of contract. Personal injury or wrongful death actions are based in tort law. A major issue in these cases concerns the appropriate treatment of inflation in estimating lump-sum damage awards. A review of the cases provides instruction regarding the courts' attitudes and sophistication regarding the time value of money.

Loss of Future Earnings from Personal Injury or Wrongful Death. The problem of estimating lost future earnings based on real wage growth, income taxes, inflation, and the earning power of money is the same for personal injury and wrongful death actions. The calculation involves the following steps:

1. Estimate the future earnings, considering the past earnings preceding the injury or death, future increases in those earnings based on probable merit increases, general productivity increases, and inflation.
2. Multiply each year's earnings by the probability of employment or, alternatively, extend the stream to the end of the injured's or deceased's expected worklife.
3. Discount each year's earnings to the present to arrive at a lump-sum award.

Such a procedure is essentially the practice today under federal law as outlined in *Pfeifer* (p. 533, Note 8). As noted however, the Supreme Court first considered discounting future wage losses to the present to avoid the plaintiff's undue enrichment as late as 1916. That case followed a long deflationary period in the United States and the Court's view of the discount rate was essentially the riskless interest rate, without allowing for inflation. The inflationary decades following World War II forced the courts to consider inflation's effect in the estimation procedures. The judicial process developed several approaches to the treatment of inflation, including the three outlined next.

Nondiscounting (Total Offset). The first approach can be described as nondiscounting, although one commonly encounters the phrase *total offset*. The approach rationalizes that long-run general productivity for the U.S. economy equals approximately 3 percent that also equals the riskless interest rate. An inflation premium added to the interest rate should also be added to the earnings. If a 4-percent inflation rate were projected, wages would be projected as those at the time of injury or death increased by 7 percent per year to account for general productivity and inflation and would then be discounted at 7 percent per year to reflect a 3-percent riskless real rate of interest and a 4-percent inflation premium. The discounting process, therefore, exactly offsets the wage increase; thus the term *total offset* (Posner, 1977, pp. 146–148).

The supreme courts of Alaska and Pennsylvania have followed variations of this total offset approach (*Beaulieu v. Elliott*; *State v. Guinn*; *Kaczkowski v. Bolubasz*).

Asymmetrical Discounting. For several years, most federal courts commonly ignored inflation in estimating future wages but considered it when discounting those wages. A current market interest rate in an inflationary period includes the inflation premium. Estimating future wages without including an inflationary element results in asymmetry and penalizes the plaintiff (Gross, 1986, pp. 491–492).

Symmetrical Discounting. By the time the Supreme Court considered the *Pfeifer* case in 1983, many circuit courts had rejected the asymmetrical treatment and had opted either for total offset or for explicit consideration of inflation in both numerator and denominator. In *Pfeifer*, the Supreme Court outlined two symmetrical approaches: one in an inflation-free economy and the other in an inflationary economy and concluded that in the latter, inflation should affect both the projected lost wages and the interest rate used for discounting. The Court failed to express a preference for either approach (*Pfeifer*, at 780–789).

Discussion of the Proper Discount Rate in the Pfeifer Case. The *Pfeifer* case includes the following remark: "We are satisfied that whatever rate the District Court may choose to discount the estimated stream of future earnings, it must make a deliberate choice, rather than assuming that it is bound by a rule of state law" (Ibid., p. 553). *Pfeifer's* discussion of the discounting procedure excluding consideration of inflation emphasized several points. First, the need to estimate the discount rate exclusive of inflation, "the real rate of interest," involves considerations that proponents do not often appreciate. The available evidence does not conclusively support the premise of a stable real interest rate (Ibid., p. 548). Furthermore, the real interest rate may or may not include the maturity premium, depending on the assumption one makes regarding how the worker will invest the award: In a series of obligations maturing as the projected earnings would be received or in a series of short term obligations (Ibid., p. 539, n. 23; 542, n. 26). Despite these and other reservations, the Court concluded that "we do not believe a trial court adopting such an approach in a suit under Article 5(b) should be reversed if it adopts a rate between 1 and 3% and explains its choice" (Ibid., pp. 548–549).

Conclusion. Experts may differ as to the measurement of real wages, merit wages, income taxes, and the real interest rate, and the courts have not often explained their views. The courts after *Pfeifer*, where federal law is applicable, may no longer exclude evidence on inflation.

Adjusting Loss of Past Earnings to the Present. The *Pfeifer* case also considered adjusting loss of past earnings to the present. After commenting on McCormick's suggested practice (*Pfeifer*, p. 784, n. 22) of discounting lost future wages to the time of trial and separately calculating the pretrial loss, the Court stated:

> It is both easier and more precise to discount the entire lost stream of earnings back to the date of injury—the moment from which earning capacity was impaired. The plaintiff may then be awarded interest on that discounted sum for the period between injury and judgment, in order to ensure that the award when invested will still be able to replicate the lost stream. (Ibid.)

The Court did not address the appropriate interest rate in calculating prejudgment interest (Ibid.).

A New York case illustrates the leading alternative to the *Pfeifer* approach. In *Shu-Tao Lin v. McDonnell-Douglas Corporation*, the Second Circuit Court of Appeals considered prejudgment interest under New York's wrongful death statute and concluded in that

> although case law on this question is surprisingly scant . . . a wrongful death recovery for lost future income under New York law is thus effectively split into two components: (1) compensation for prejudgment losses, as to which interest is applied at a statutory rate . . .; and (2) compensation for postjudgment losses, which are discounted to present value. . . . (Ibid., pp. 51–52)

The court acknowledged the difference between its approach and that of the Supreme Court in *Pfeifer*, observing that "in cases involving federal law, a specific method has been developed for the computation of the value of lost future income" (Ibid., p. 52, n. 8).

Breach of Contract Damages

Many actions for damages may be brought under tort law or contract law because the cause of action can be construed as both a statute and a contract violation. Given a choice, most plaintiffs' attorneys elect tort actions so the plaintiffs can claim exemplary damages. Professional journals give less attention to breach of contract cases, reflecting fewer precedent-setting cases than those under tort law. The following discussion includes several cases that illustrate the variety of decisions involving the time value of money found under contract law. These cases are not the basis for generalization nor are they exhaustive in scope. They were selected because they are among the few to include details about specific interest rates used in computing present value.

Lost Future Profits or Compensation. One authority, after stating that lost future profits should be discounted to present value, remarks that few cases specifically consider the need to do so (Dunn, 1981, p. 325). The occasional refusal of some courts to discount future earnings is often a failure of proof by the defense. "If defendant does not raise the point, it has been held waived" (p. 325). These remarks imply that the standards in contract cases for using time value of money concepts may be lower than that for tort cases.

In a 1963 breach of contract action that involved selling a one-half interest in a timber business, the ninth circuit affirmed the trial court's finding of the right to recover lost profits over a 15-year period (*Liberman v. Nagel*). These estimated lost profits were discounted to present value at a 4-percent rate. The case reporter does not reveal whether the profits were calculated before or after taxes (and how inflation was treated), but either way, a 4-percent rate for business profits lacks risk parity between the cash flow and the discount rate. An after-tax rate of around 10 percent seems more appropriate. Prejudgment interest, incidentally, was calculated at 6 percent.

In *Daum Development Corp. v. Yuba Plaza, Inc.*, 1970, a California appellate court, in an action for anticipatory breach of contract, discounted future leasing commissions earned but not yet paid, at the legal rate, 7 percent simple interest. The court did not use the 5-percent rate provided for in the contract for interest on delayed payment.

A 1979 second circuit case for breach of contract to relocate sellers of a liquor distributorship (*Lee v. Seagram & Sons, Inc.*) upheld the jury's award for lost future profits. The plaintiff's expert discounted the estimated pretax profits for 10 years at approximately 8.5 percent to equal $549,000. The jury awarded $407,850. Although the defendant emphasized the uncertainty of the profits (the business had not begun or even been located), no testimony was reported objecting to the plaintiff's discount rate that reflected a pretax borrowing rate rather than a pretax return on an equity investment.

In a 1949 California case, *Noble v. Tweedy*, the trial court used the legal rate, 7 percent simple interest, to measure the present value of damages to a tenant attributable to the landlord's failure to complete the building as promised. The appellate court, commenting on the conflicting authority regarding the appropriate rate, did not reverse the use of the legal rate but pointed out that the court did not by implication approve the rate that was used.

A 1974 New York case for damages due to the tenant for the landlord's prohibition against subletting used the 6-percent statutory rate to discount the award to present value (*Passaic Distributors, Inc. v. The Sherman Company*). Another New York case, *Randall-Smith, Inc. v. 43rd St. Estates Corp.*, 1966, also involving landlord–tenant issues, used 5 percent as the discount rate, without explaining why.

Finally, a pioneering 1978 Wisconsin case involving damages arising from breach of contract to loan money, *Bridgkort Racquet Club Inc. v. University Bank*, reversed a lower court's decision by holding that present value applied to the case. Damages were measured by the difference in interest rates on the promised loan (10.25 percent) and the actual loan (11 percent). The appellate court found that the incremental interest should be discounted to present value. No one had raised the issue before, and the court's own prior decision on a similar case did not discuss the matter because the defendant did not advance the argument. The court found only one other case discussing the present value application to breach of contract to loan money (*Financial Federal Savings & Loan Assn. v. Continental Enterprises, Inc.*, a 1976 Florida case). That court, fortunately, also applied the present value concept. The defendant bank, for reasons known only to itself, used a 7-percent discount rate in its present value calculations, rather than the plaintiff's 11-percent borrowing rate.

BUSINESS VALUATION

Accountants are well suited to provide business valuation services in litigation, especially for smaller nonpublic entities. A skilled accountant can analyze the books and records not often understood in detail by other professionals. Subsequent chapters more fully address business valuation; this chapter focuses on the time value of money in valuation procedures. One must observe the need for parity between cash flows and discount rates regarding income taxes, risk, and inflation when valuing a business.

IRS Formula Approach

One increasingly popular approach to business valuation is the formula approach outlined by the Internal Revenue Service in several rulings. The first ruling was issued in 1920 as Committee on Appeals and Review Memorandum 34 (A.R.M. 34, C.B. 2, 31). The memorandum, although disclaiming any ability "to lay down any specific rule of guidance for determining the value of intangibles which would be applicable in all cases and under all circumstances" (Ibid., p. 31), suggests allowing a rate of return on tangible assets at 8 to 10 percent and capitalizing excess earnings at 15 to 20 percent when valuing intangibles. The actual rate used for capitalization within those ranges depends on the risk of the business (Ibid., p. 32). This memorandum has been supplemented, modified, and eventually replaced by a series of rulings issued during the 1960s: Revenue Ruling 59–60, C.B. 1959-1, 237; Revenue Ruling 65-193, C.B. 1965-2, 370; Revenue Ruling 68-609, C.B. 1968-2, 327. These rulings set forth the service's approach for valuing closely held corporate stocks for estate, gift, or income tax purposes.

The approach has two steps: (1) a valuation of tangible assets plus (2) a valuation of intangible assets, principally goodwill. Tangible assets of cash, accounts receivable, inventory, and the like are appraised by whatever means appears suitable, and liabilities are subtracted to arrive at net tangible assets. Valuation of intangible assets involves the measurement and capitalization of "excess earnings." A prevailing industry rate of return, or 8 to 10 percent in the absence of specific information, is applied to the net tangible assets to calculate normal earnings. Excess earnings equal actual earnings less normal earnings. These excess earnings provide the basis for valuing intangibles and are capitalized at rates from 15 to 20 percent to establish such values. Exhibit 9-1 illustrates this approach.

Two observations should be made regarding this formula approach. First, the bifurcated approach to asset valuation reflects the view that earnings attributable to intangible assets have more uncertainty associated with them than earnings from tangible assets and, consequently, should be discounted at a higher rate of return. This estimation technique appeals to economic analysis because mearnings from intangible assets reflect "excessive" earnings that attract competitors to an industry.

Second, the formula's customary application assumes that earnings from both tangible and intangible assets will continue indefinitely at the same amount: The formula is a perpetuity.

Residual Method

A similar approach to business valuation, referred to as the *residual method*, bifurcates the appraisal of tangible and intangible assets differently. The method capitalizes earnings at an appropriate rate of return to calculate the value of the

EXHIBIT 9-1. ILLUSTRATION OF BUSINESS VALUATION UNDER IRS FORMULA APPROACH

Calculation of normal earnings	
Appraised value of tangible assets	$100,000
Required rate of return for business class—assumed	9%
Normal earnings	$ 9,000
Calculation of excess earnings	
Actual earnings	$ 12,600
Less normal earnings computed above	9,000
Excess earnings	$ 3,600
Intangible valuation	
Excess earnings computed above	$ 3,600
Capitalization rate	÷ 18%
Value of intangibles	$ 20,000

business as a whole. The value of intangibles equals the total business value less the appraised value of the assets. Exhibit 9-2 illustrates this method.

Capitalization Rates in Estate and Income Tax Cases

Evidence on capitalization rates actually applied in federal estate and income tax cases appears scant. The *Federal Tax Valuation Digest* (Bishop & Howitt, 1988) lists the following as the only goodwill valuation cases that report information as to the capitalization rates used by expert witnesses or the courts.

Edison International, Inc. v. United States, 10 Cl. Ct. 287 (1986). The court, in this income tax case, had to decide whether the goodwill of Studebaker Corporation of New Jersey upon its formation in 1911 equaled $19 million. One expert for the plaintiff used a capitalization rate of 12.5 percent, and another used 15 percent. A third expert for the plaintiff testified that a 15-percent rate of return would be insufficient to induce investment in the automobile industry at that time. The court found for the defendant and relied on the publicly traded market price per share as a basis for its finding rather than the discounted value of future net cash flow. Evidence of transactions involving similar operations at price/earnings ratios of 2.37

EXHIBIT 9-2. ILLUSTRATION OF BUSINESS VALUATION UNDER RESIDUAL METHOD APPROACH

Actual earnings	$ 12,600
Capitalization rate	÷ 10%
Total value of entity	126,000
Less appraised value of tangible assets	100,000
Residual equals value of intangible assets	$ 26,000

and 2.56 was also introduced, thereby implying a capitalization rate of 40 percent as appropriate to the case. Referring to the plaintiff's approach, the court observed that "the experts' value conclusions are premised so much on subjective assumptions lacking underlying support in the record as to render those conclusions essentially meaningless in the context of this litigation" (Id. at 85121).

The plaintiff's experts appeared to reach for a conclusion to support the plaintiff's position. The case involved a publicly traded common stock. Whenever experts claim their opinions' superiority over that of the market, however meritorious the analytical framework, the opinions must be documented far better than those in this case. When General Motors can buy Cadillac for 2.37 times earnings, when Will Durant allows an option to lapse enabling him to purchase the Ford Motor Company for 2.56 times earnings (because financing cannot be obtained), and when Studebaker's stock is selling below net tangible assets per share, one cannot easily believe that a proper valuation of Studebaker would be 23.6 times earnings resulting in goodwill equal to 35 percent of its total assets.

Seaboard Automotive, Inc. v. Commissioner, 42 T.C.M. (CCH) 529 (1981). This income tax case concerns the purchase price allocation to goodwill and other assets. Two petitioners presented testimony that did not persuade the court; one denied any goodwill, and the other estimated goodwill as one-third of sales. The tax court made its own calculation applying the formula approach of Revenue Ruling 68-609. The court used the ruling's recommended 8-percent rate for the return on tangible assets, citing the company's probable low-risk nature and noting that the ruling was issued about the same time (1968) as the purchase (1971). The court applied the ruling's suggested 15-percent rate to excess earnings to calculate goodwill.

This case presents a classroom example of the application of Revenue Ruling 68-609. Risk is specifically considered, though not carefully explored. The result is to adjust the rate of return on tangible assets downward, to the lowest rate cited in the revenue ruling, to reflect the court's judgment of lower risk. The figure capitalized for excess earnings is excess average net income, that is, excess *after-tax* earnings averaged for a 5-year period. The court used a perpetuity model to capitalize earnings and average excess net income as a simple (not weighted) average. The published case does not discuss inflation or growth.

VGS Corp. v. Commissioner, 68 T.C. 563 (1977). This case involved the purchase and sale of petroleum refineries, service stations, and related equipment. The tax court applied the formula approach of Revenue Ruling 68-609, applying an 8-percent rate of return to net tangible assets and concluding an absence of excess earnings and, therefore, an absence of goodwill. Other evidence included an independent party's appraisal of the tangible assets, which equaled the purchase price.

The formula's straightforward application involved nothing more than an explanatory footnote in the published case.

R.M. Smith, Inc. v. Commissioner, 36 T.C.M. (CCH) 97 (1977). The court valued goodwill by the residual method after calculating the value of patents through estimating cash flows and discounting them to present value. The petitioner's expert witness provided the only explicit comments on present value. This expert appears to have calculated the before-tax royalty income from the patents and discounted that cash flow at a 4-percent rate in a 1970 setting. The court concluded both experts overstated their cases and found its own value without providing details on its calculations, although the general approach and the need to discount cash flows to the present can be inferred from the court's comments.

Applying a 4-percent discount rate to before-tax cash flows from patents seems to lack the required parity on two counts: (1) after-tax cash flows should have been used to equate to an after-tax discount rate and (2) a 4-percent discount rate seems difficult to support for these uncertain cash flows, even if the cash flows were after taxes and noninflationary. The petitioner's expert thus could substantially overvalue the patents and leave nothing for goodwill by disregarding the required parity for taxes and for risk.

Concord Control, Inc v. Commissioner, 35 T.C.M. (CCH) 1345 (1976), 78 T.C. 742 (1982). The government's expert computed substantial goodwill by applying a 7.8-percent return to the company's tangible net assets, measured at *book value* rather than *fair market value*. This calculation resulted in a large excess earnings figure, which was capitalized at 20 percent to estimate goodwill. The calculation used after-tax cash flows, implicitly considered risk, and ignored inflation. The court disagreed with the government's expert and found no goodwill. In a controversial decision, the court allocated part of the purchase price to going-concern value but failed to explain how it made the allocation (1976). On remand from the Sixth Circuit Court of Appeals, the tax court explained that it used a 7.8-percent return on tangible net assets measured at fair market value and capitalized excess earnings at 20 percent (1978).

Apart from the issue of whether this rose smells like goodwill or going-concern value, this case raises two matters of interest. First, the government's expert, applied the 7.8-percent return to Concord's *book* value rather than *fair market value* of its tangible net assets. The expert substantially understated the return on tangible net assets and overstated excess earnings, as the formula approach defines those terms. The court discerned this difference and rejected the approach.

Second, the 7.8-percent rate of return on tangible net assets, which both the government's expert and the court used, was itself derived from book values of some 50 companies. The practice of deriving a rate of return from book values is suspect but did not receive any scrutiny in the case. Book value calculations may be useful at times, but expert witnesses should rely primarily on market-based rates in applying the formula approach.

Samuel S. Schahet v. Commissioner, 18 T.C.M. (CCH) 243 (1959). In this case concerning the sale proceeds for corporate stock, the petitioner argued that part of the proceeds related to intangibles, and the commissioner contended that it was a dividend. The petitioner applied the formula method using an 8-percent return on tangible assets and used a 20-percent rate to capitalize excess earnings. The court accepted the petitioner's calculation.

The petitioner deftly employed the commissioner's weapon and triumphed easily. The court neglected to consider the formula approach's limitations during inflationary and rapid growth periods. The calculations are "straight out of the book."

Northern Trust Co. v. Commissioner, 87 T.C. 349 (1986). This estate tax case related to the valuation of shares in a closely held corporation. The tax court approved one of the methods used by the petitioner's expert described as the "discounted cash flow approach." The expert estimated the cash flow that the corporation could distribute during the next 10-year period "without impairing business operations" and the value of the shares at the end of the 10-year period. He then discounted these cash flows to the present at a 21-percent required rate of return estimated by applying the Capital Asset Pricing Model using the following elements:

Risk-free rate	=	The rate available on 10-year U.S. Government bonds amounting to 6.96 percent.
Market premium	=	6 to 8 percent.
Beta for companies engaged in construction operations	=	1.3 and .95 for railroad supply companies.

An additional discount for unlisted securities of 3 to 7 percent.

This calculation maintains parity between cash flows and discount rates for taxes and risk. The calculation does not specifically address inflation and may lack this parity. The riskless rate on government bonds and the risk premiums may include inflation, although there is no indication whether the increases in cash flow over the 10-year period and beyond reflect inflation in addition to real growth.

This case presents the most sophisticated treatment of parity in goodwill valuations and is more representative of a seminar in a graduate business school than most court valuations. More such discussion would improve the quality of thinking in the courts.

Capitalization Rates or Interest Rates in Other Types of Business Valuation Cases

Business or professional valuations are needed frequently during dissolutions of marriage or of the entities themselves. Valuations of closely held corporations, partnerships, or proprietorships in dissolution proceedings require considerations similar to those of tax cases. A review of many cases, concentrated in California's courts, reveals little evidence regarding specific capitalization rates used for valuation. Many reported cases, moreover, value goodwill, especially in professional practices, by a multiple of monthly revenues (a rule-of-thumb approach) rather than by approaches already discussed (Markey, 1988, ¶ 24.47).

Two cases decided in California's Second District Court of Appeals criticized and rejected the trial courts' sole reliance on use of the price/earnings approach that applies price/earnings ratios of public companies to a closely held corporation's earnings (*In re Marriage of Hewitson*, a marital dissolution case; *Ronald v. 4-C's*

Electronic Packaging, Inc., a corporate dissolution case). The court referred to Revenue Ruling 59-60 in both cases and concluded in *Hewitson*: "Unless there is some statutory or decisional proscription on their use, the factors listed in Revenue Ruling 59-60 [cite omitted] should be consulted and used to evaluate closely held stock" (Ibid., p. 888). The factors are as follows (Rev. Ruling 59-60, p. 238):

(a) The company's nature and history
(b) The general economic outlook and the specific industry's condition and outlook.
(c) The stock's book value and the company's financial condition.
(d) The company's earning capacity.
(e) The dividend-paying capacity.
(f) Whether the enterprise has goodwill or other intangible value.
(g) Stock sales and the size of the block of stock to be valued.
(h) The stock price of corporations engaged in the same or a similar business and which are actively traded in a free and open market, either on an exchange or over-the-counter.

The cases discussed regarding tax matters criticized the use of price/earnings ratios of publicly held companies to value closely held businesses, noting the lack of comparable public companies from which one can develop the price/earnings ratios (*Hewitson*, p. 886; *Northern Trust*, p. 376). The courts expect the expert to be more analytical, to consider all the factors listed in Revenue Ruling 59-60 and not to rely primarily on comparable price/earnings ratios in making the valuation. How the analyst converts these factors into a cash flow and discount rate that can persuade the court remains as uncertain as before the cases were decided.

CONCLUSION

The cases reviewed in this chapter reveal that the courts treat the time value of money unevenly. At one extreme, the U.S. Supreme Court discusses the effects of inflation and income taxes on the discount rate applied to future damages with the erudition of a graduate seminar in economics. At another, courts and legal researchers complain of a lack of precedent on applying present value to, of all things, a contract to loan money. And in many cases, defendants fail to raise the issue of present value, despite its significance and a sympathetic court.

The time value of money *is* receiving more attention. It needs even more. Accountants have an opportunity to be of service to clients, attorneys and judges on this important subject.

BIBLIOGRAPHY

Ballentine, J.A., *Ballentine's Law Dictionary*, 3rd ed., W.S. Anderson, ed. (The Lawyers Co-operative Publishing Company, 1969).

Bishop, J.A., and I.A. Howitt, *Federal Tax Valuation Digest*, 1988 Cumulative Edition

(Warren, Gorham & Lamont, 1988).

Bower, D.A., R.S. Bower, and D.E. Logue, "Arbitrage Pricing and Utility Stock Returns," *Journal of Finance* (September 1984), pp. 1041–1054.

Brigham, E.F., *Fundamentals of Financial Management*, 3rd ed. (Dryden Press, New York, NY, 1983).

Dobbs, D.B., *Handbook on the Law of Remedies* (West Publishing Co., 1973), p. 164.

Dunn, Robert L., *Recovery of Damages for Lost Profits*, 2nd ed. (Lawpress, Tiburon, CA., 1981).

Fisher, F.M. and R.C. Romaine, "Janis Joplin's Yearbook and the Theory of Damages," *Journal of Accounting, Auditing, and Finance*, January, 1990.

Goetz, C.J., *Cases and Materials on Law and Economics* (West Publishing Co., 1984), p. 157.

Gross, D.L., "Calculating Lost Future Earnings Under Federal Law: Courts Must Consider Inflation As Well As The Earning Power of Money," *Arizona State Law Journal* (Summer 1986).

Inga, L., "Damages—A Jury Should Receive Evidence and Instructions Concerning the Impact of Federal Income Taxation on an Award of Damages—Norfolk & Western Railway Co. v. Liepelt, 444 U.S. 490 (1980)," 21 *Santa Clara Law Review* (Summer, 1981), pp. 873–879.

Internal Revenue Service, Committee on Appeals and Review Memorandum 34, A.R.M. 34, C.B. 2, 31.

________, Internal Revenue Code, § 56(g)(4)(i) and (v)

________, Revenue Ruling 59-60, C.B. 1959-1, 237

________, Revenue Ruling 65-193, C.B. 1965-2, 370

________, Revenue Ruling 68-609, C.B. 1968-2, 327

Johns, L.M., *California Damages—Law and Proof*, 3rd ed. (Parker & Sons Publications, Inc., 1986).

McCormick, C.T., *Handbook on the Law of Damages* (West Publishing Co., 1935, reprinted 1975).

Markey, C.E., "Dissolution of Marriage," *California Family Law: Practice and Procedure*, Vol. 2 (Matthew Bender, 1988).

Patell, J.M., R.L. Weil, and M.A. Wolfson, "Accumulating Damages in Litigation: The Roles of Uncertainty and Interest Rates," *Journal of Legal Studies*, Vol. XI (June 1982).

Posner, R.A., *Economic Analysis of Law* (Little, Brown and Company, 1977), pp. 146–148.

Roll, R., and S.A. Ross, "The Arbitrage Pricing Theory Approach to Strategic Portfolio Planning," *Financial Analysts Journal* (May–June 1984), pp. 14–26.

Sharpe, D.J., and R.B. Acomb III, "Damages Recoverable in Collision and Stranding Cases," in R.B. Acomb Jr., ed., *Damages Recoverable in Maritime Matters: An ABA Annual Meeting Symposium* (American Bar Association, 1984).

Weston, J.F., and T.E. Copeland, *Managerial Finance*, 8th ed. (The Dryden Press, 1986).

88 *Daily Journal* D.A.R. 7135

LIST OF CASES

Beaulieu v. Elliott, 434 P.2d 665 (Alaska 1967)

Bridgkort Racquet Club, Inc. v. University Bank, 85 Wis. 2d 706, 271 N.W.2d 165 (1978)

Canavin v. Pacific Southwest Airlines, 148 Cal. App. 3d 512 196 Cal. Rptr. 82 (1983)
Chesapeake & Ohio Railway Co. v. Kelly, 241 U.S. 485 (1916)
Concord Control, Inc. v. Commissioner, 35 T.C.M. (CCH) 1345 (1976)
Concord Control, Inc. v. Commissioner, 78 T.C. 742 (1982)
Consolidated Grain & Barge Co. v. Wisconsin Barge Line, Inc., 522 F. Supp. 842 (E.D. Mo. 1987)
Edison International, Inc. v. United States, 10 Cl. Ct. 287 (1986)
Financial Federal Savings & Loan Assn. v. Continental Enterprises, Inc., 338 So. 2d 907 (Fla. App. 1976) as quoted in *Bridgkort* at 714, n. 7
General Facilities, Inc. v. National Marine Service, Inc., 664 F.2d 672 (8th Cir. 1981)
In re Marriage of Hewitson 142 Cal. App. 3d 874, 191 Cal. Rptr. 392 (1983)
Jones & Laughlin Steel Corporation v. Pfeifer, 462 U.S. 523 (1983)
Kaczkowski v. Bolubasz, 491 Pa. 561, 421 A.2d 1027 (1980)
Lee v. Joseph E. Seagram & Sons, 552 F.2d 447 (2d Cir. 1977)
Liberman v. Nagel, 316 F.2d 214 (9th Cir. 1963)
Monessen Southwestern Railway Co. v. Morgan, 486 U.S. 330 (1988)
Noble v. Tweedy, 90 Cal. App. 2d 738, 203 P.2d 778 (1949)
Norfolk and Western Railway Co. v. Liepelt, 444 U.S. 490 (1980)
Northern Trust Co. v. Commissioner, 87 T.C. 349 (1986)
Passaic Distributors, Inc. v. Sherman Company, 386 F. Supp. 647 (S.D.N.Y. 1974)
R.M. Smith, Inc. v. Commissioner, 36 T.C.M. (CCH) 97 (1977)
Randall-Smith, Inc. v. 43rd St. Estates Corp., 17 N.Y.2d 99, 215 N.E.2d 494, 268 N.Y.S.2d 306 (1966)
Ronald v. 4-C's Electronic Packing, Inc. 168 Cal. App. 3d 290, 214 Cal. Rptr. 225 (1985)
Samuel S. Schahet v. Commissioner, 18 T.C.M. (CCH) 243 (1959)
Seaboard Automotive, Inc. v. Commissioner, 42 T.C.M. (CCH) 529 (1981)
Shu-Tao Lin v. McDonnell Douglas Corporation, 742 F.2d 45 (2d Cir. 1984)
Signal Oil & Gas Co. v. Barge W-701, 468 F. Supp. 802 (E.D. La. 1979)
State v. Guinn, 555 P.2d 530 (Alaska 1976)
VGS Corp. v. Commissioner, 68 T.C. 563 (1977)
Re M/V Vulcan, 553 F.2d 489 (5th Cir. 1977)

PART TWO

COMMERCIAL/CIVIL CASES—UNIQUE CONSIDERATIONS

10

ANTITRUST

Stephen H. Knowlton, CPA
Abram E. Hoffman, DBA
Carol T.F. Bennett, PhD

INTRODUCTION

The U.S. antitrust laws intend to protect consumers from prices higher than would prevail in a competitive market. Nevertheless, historically, few antitrust actions were brought by consumers. Government agencies charged with enforcing the antitrust laws—the Department of Justice and the Federal Trade Commission—or competitors of the firms alleged to be violating these laws generally brought suit. In recent years, however, the government has been relatively quiet, and private cases have predominated. Government actions usually seek to block a proposed merger or change an anticompetitive practice. Private business antitrust suits seek these same remedies, motivated by their private interests rather than the public welfare, and they usually seek treble damages.

Accountants and economists can contribute to resolving antitrust disputes by quantifying allegations. In a world where monopoly is rarely absolute, except as protected by patents or government regulation, antitrust issues are usually matters of degree. The judge and jury must weigh the degree of harm caused to plaintiffs and the public in comparison to the social cost of hindering business judgments by defendants.

Per Se Violations and the Rule of Reason

A per se antitrust violation is an act that is illegal in itself. The plaintiff must prove only that the action has occurred and need not prove specific damage to competition to establish liability. Examples include price fixing, horizontal market division, resale price maintenance, and tying arrangements.

Distinct from the per se rule, the rule of reason looks to the effects of alleged anticompetitive behavior. If efficiency or cost justifications exist for the action, then it may be judged legitimate. Accounting or economics expertise is needed most for antitrust issues tried under the rule of reason.

Quantitative Measures

Quantitative measures that apply to liability and damage issues consist of competitive analysis, market and product definition, business valuation, lost profits estimation, cost analysis, and estimation of price elasticity of demand. Accurate analysis and damage measurement, followed by effective courtroom presentation, are particularly important in antitrust litigation. Liability issues often hinge on the testimony of economists and accountants, and damage issues are expanded by the punitive trebling of actual damages.

Antitrust law is always close to public policy interpretations. A plaintiff usually must prove not only that a company's actions damaged competitor profits but that these actions harmed society as well. The effects on prices and quantities of the product in question often provide the best evidence of anticompetitive impact. Detailed analysis of individual sales transactions, business segment analysis, and overall industry analysis are generally required in addition to comparisons with comparable company statistics and trend data.

The seven sections that follow each present a different type of antitrust action. For each, we first present the relevant law followed by a discussion of issues and economic or accounting analytical techniques.

CONTRACTS AND CONSPIRACIES TO RESTRAIN TRADE

Section 1 of the Sherman Antitrust Act (1890) prohibits combined actions that harm competition.

> Sec. 1. Every contract, combination in the form of trust or otherwise, or conspiracy, in restraint of trade or commerce among the several States, or with foreign nations, is hereby declared to be illegal.

Horizontal Price Fixing

Horizontal price fixing, the setting or stabilizing of prices among competitors, is a per se violation of § 1 of the Sherman Act. As a per se violation, proof of price fixing suffices; liability does not require proof of the economic consequences.

The prohibition against price fixing also includes cases where detailed price information is disseminated to industry members because such arrangements stabilize prices (*United States v. Container Corp. of America*, 393 U.S. 333 (1969)).

Certain industries are more susceptible to price fixing than others. Prices can more readily be fixed in industries with few competitors, undifferentiated products, the ability to hide and enforce collusion, and less sensitivity by buyers to prices. Demonstrating that these conditions do not persist in the industry may help to refute the price-fixing allegation.

Computing damages in a civil price-fixing case commonly involves an analysis of lost profits to businesses that paid an excessive price for their supplies. Evaluating the excess of actual prices over the competitive level involves an analysis of costs of production, any relevant cost trends, and a comparison of prices before and after collusion.

The analyst must also determine the quantities actually purchased at the excessive price and the amounts that would have been sold at a legal price. If the product was purchased for resale, the damage calculation might include lost profits on units that were uneconomic to sell at the fixed price but would have been sold at the fair market price. A similar, but more complicated damage calculation, would be required if the product was purchased as a component within another product, which could have been sold but for the price-fixing action.

Horizontal Market Division

Market division among competitors has consequences at least as damaging to the economy as price fixing because each seller becomes, in effect, a monopolist.

For this reason, market division is also a per se violation of § 1 of the Sherman Act.

Horizontal market division may take the form of a group of manufacturers allocating certain regions or cities to specific producers. Sometimes, the differentiations between procompetitive and anticompetitive effects of market division are vague. In *United States v. Topco Assoc., Inc.*, 405 U.S. 596 (1972), small grocers agreed to purchase private label products cooperatively to better compete with the large chains. They also agreed not to sell within the territories of other Topco members. The district court considered the agreements to be procompetitive under the rule of reason and found for the defendants. The Supreme Court, under the per se rule, reversed the lower court.

As a per se violation, an extreme case of market division does not require quantitative analysis of the liability issues. More ambiguous is the case of a firm that exits from the market, leaving its competitors with a larger share. If two or more firms withdraw from different geographic markets, the pattern may resemble market division. Under these circumstances, quantitative analysis can focus on the cost structure of serving the different markets, profit margins, and expected growth opportunities in the markets. Other indicators are changes in production trends or input costs that might explain the pattern, changes in marketing practices or government restrictions, and the resulting impact on competition. The approach to quantifying damages is similar to that of price-fixing cases.

Group Boycotts and Concerted Refusal to Deal

Group boycotts are agreements among competitors not to deal with a specific supplier or customer. As with other horizontal arrangements, group boycotts are a per se violation of the Sherman Act. The Supreme Court has held irrelevant the argument that the practice may have only minimally affected overall competition, pointing out that concerted refusal to deal can eliminate competitors one by one (*Klor's, Inc. v. Broadway-Hale Stores, Inc.*, 359 U.S. 207 (1959)).

Economic efficiency has been argued as a defense to group boycott allegations. In *United States v. First National Pictures, Inc.*, 282 U.S. 44 (1930), a group of film distributors formed credit committees to evaluate credit worthiness of theater owners and refused to supply films if the owners did not pay deposits and comply with existing contracts. In *Fashion Originators' Guild of America v. Federal Trade Commission*, 312 U.S. 457 (1941), members refused to deal with firms who pirated design styles. Although both cases presented credible economic rationales for the boycotts, the groups were found liable on a per se basis.

Damage calculations in group boycott cases resemble lost profit analyses. Alternatively, the plaintiff can present business valuation analyses before and after the boycott. Expert witnesses for damaged competitors must estimate what reasonable profits or market value would have been but for the group refusal to deal. Existing and potential market share, market growth, cost structure, and profit margins are the basis for estimating damages, which are then trebled.

MONOPOLIZATION AND THE ATTEMPT TO MONOPOLIZE

Section 2 of the Sherman Antitrust Act (1890) prohibits monopolization and attempts to monopolize.

> Sec. 2. Every person who shall monopolize, or attempt to monopolize, or combine or conspire with any other person or persons, to monopolize any part of the trade or commerce among the several States, or with foreign nations, shall be deemed guilty of a felony . . .

The offense of monopolization is the ability to control prices or exclude competition and the deliberate intent to maintain that power, as distinguished from growth or development owing to a superior product, business acumen, or historical accident.

Courts will hold firms liable for attempting to monopolize only if a "dangerous probability of success" exists. The following factors can be quantified to evaluate this probability of success.

- The firm's size in relation to its market. Other things being equal, the larger the market share, the higher the probability of successful monopolization.
- The number and size of the other firms in the industry. An industry with several intermediate-sized firms with some market power will generally be harder to dominate than one with many very small firms.
- Changes in market share over time. An increasing market share indicates greater ability to monopolize.
- The type and intensity of the firm's business practices in combination with the market structure.
- The profit performance of the firm and the industry. Typically, a stagnant or declining industry is easier to monopolize than a growing industry, which attracts more entrants. A successful firm in a weak industry may be engaging in unfair practices, but alternative explanations should be sought.

Geographic Market Definition

Most antitrust suits require the definition of the relevant market, and it is essential in cases alleging an attempt to monopolize. Although firms rarely control products nationwide, firms commonly have some local market power.

> To establish monopolization or attempt to monopolize a part of trade or commerce under Sec. 2 of the Sherman Act, it would then be necessary to appraise the exclusionary power . . . in terms of the relevant market for the product involved. Without a definition of that market there is no way to measure . . . ability to lessen or destroy competition. (*Walker Process Equipment, Inc. v. Food Machinery and Chemical Corp.*, 382 U.S. 172, 177 (1965))

A list of significant factors for geographic market definition follows:

- When prices change simultaneously in two areas without direct cost justification, the two are likely to be in the same market.
- Many product shipments between two locations indicate that they share the same geographic market.
- Transportation costs to deliver goods are an important determinant of the geographic market. Beyond a certain distance from distribution facilities, it is uneconomic for suppliers to compete.
- Geographic (including psychological) barriers may exist among customers who might otherwise travel between competing businesses. For example, businesses may not be competitors if their customers refuse to cross a toll bridge between them.
- International borders may limit an otherwise open market due to customs duties and import restrictions.
- Government restrictions may help to define geographic markets, such as hospital and bank locations allowed by regulatory authorities. In these cases, regulatory documents may have been written to substantiate the geographic definitions when the firms filed applications, and these will generally be available.
- Location of advertising activity indicates where a business considers its market to be.

Product Market Definition

The broader the definition of the product market, the less likely it is to be monopolized. For example, in *United States v. E.I. DuPont de Nemours & Co.*, 351 U.S. 377 (1956), DuPont controlled 75 percent of the cellophane industry. However, because it controlled less than 20 percent of the market for flexible packaging materials, the Court held that it did not possess monopoly power.

The courts have identified the following issues as relevant to product market definition:

- The product's characteristics and uses
- Reasonable interchangeability between the product and its substitutes
- Specialized vendors
- Unique production facilities
- Distinct customers
- Distinct prices
- Sensitivity to price changes
- Industry or public recognition of the market as a separate economic entity.

The substitutability of the product at issue for other related products is an important measure of the relevant market. The cross-elasticity of demand, a technical measure of this, is the degree to which price changes in the product at issue will induce changes in quantity demanded of the other product. If there is little effect, then the products are not substitutes. If a price increase in the relevant product results in a quantity increase in the other product, then they may be substitutes, and hence, competitors. (Products may be complementary if a price increase for one product causes a quantity decrease for the other product, such as cars and tires, but this result is less relevant for antitrust issues.)

- As with many quantitative measures used in antitrust law, the cross-elasticity of demand is arithmetically straightforward. The difficulties are in obtaining and analyzing data on quantities and in separating the price impact from other factors.
- Often factors that cause price increases in one product cause prices to rise for related products. Inflation, government regulation, and input prices may affect unrelated businesses. It is then more difficult to measure the independent impact on quantity demanded of the second product.
- Sometimes a business will use a cost increase faced by a competitor as an opportunity to raise its own price. For example, if the cost of coffee beans rises, the sellers of tea may raise their prices, all with an indeterminate impact on quantity demanded.

Other indicators of product definitions are often industry specific, but the following factors are common to many sectors:

- Government definitions of industries are delineated in Standard Industrial Classification Codes (SIC Codes) with varying degrees of specificity. These SIC definitions provide a consistent basis for industry analysis.
- Surveys of consumer behavior can help define the market. If airline fares rise, nonbusiness travelers may increase bus or automobile usage, or they may travel less.
- International market differences may also affect product definition. For example, in a banking market, deposits are often the basis for determining market domination. However, international banking offices established for loan origination may still be significant competitors.

Potential Competition

Potential competition is significant in analyzing an alleged attempt to monopolize because new entrants into the industry can prevent a firm from maintaining successful monopolization. The existence of monopoly profits will encourage new firms to enter the market.

Market entry can occur in the following ways:

- A firm in the same industry in another geographic market can expand into the market in question. The quantitative issues here involve the transportation costs of distribution from existing warehouses, the market's long-run growth potential, and the relative profit margins of each geographic market.
- A firm in the same geographic market but in a related industry can expand its product line. The issues to be quantified center around the similarity of materials

and labor inputs, any economies of joint production and distribution, and the relative profit margins of the two products.

- Employees of existing competitors can form new businesses. However, large capital requirements, large advertising requirements, or a large minimum scale of business may deter employees from entering competition.
- New entrants could, of course, come from unrelated businesses, but their existence and impact would be more speculative.

In addition to large capital requirements, barriers to entry into an industry can include other factors:

- If product innovations occur frequently in the industry, or technological innovations occur rapidly in the production process, then research and development costs raise the barriers to entry.
- Institutional constraints, such as international trade restrictions, governmental limitations on geographic expansion, and costly regulatory requirements can create barriers to entry.

Essential Facility

Several cases have construed § 2 of the Sherman Act to include cases involving "essential facilities." An essential facility claim alleges that without access to a specific facility, a business cannot be profitable in a market. Facilities have been found to be essential in cases involving professional sports arenas, advertising media, skiing areas, and wholesale marketplaces (*Aspen Skiing Company v. Aspen Highlands Skiing Corp.*, 472 U.S. 585 (1985)).

To substantiate an essential facility claim, the plaintiff must prove the following:

- The facility owners have substantial market power, based on market share data.
- The facility is essential to profitability in the market. An analysis of revenue and cost trends can indicate the impact on profitability if access had once been available.
- The facility owners denied access to the plaintiff without justification.
- The facility cannot be replicated at reasonable cost. Cost estimates of utilizing the best available alternative can be used to quantify this claim.
- The antitrust claim is stronger if the denial of access harms consumers. In *Aspen Skiing*, for example, consumers no longer had access to four ski areas on a common ticket but only the three areas owned by the defendant.
- The allegation is stronger if the plaintiff and defendant are competitors and the defendant has benefitted from denying access to the plaintiff.

Case Study: Attempt to Monopolize

In a case alleging the attempt to monopolize, a hospital in a distinct geographical area had entered a joint venture to provide customers with durable medical equipment and related supplies. The plaintiff alleged that the hospital was using its monopoly over hospital services to control the market for home medical equipment, by offering to arrange for this equipment while the patient was still hospitalized.

The plaintiff argued that the hospital was an "essential facility," without access to which businesses could not profit in this market.

This case hinged on the definitions and the measures of market power already listed, in particular:

- Geographic market definition was important in this case. It was not necessary to assume that the hospital market and the medical equipment market were coterminous because the medical equipment companies delivered the products. Virtually all the competitors advertised in an area broader than the hospital's primary market.
- The parties disagreed on a product market definition. Plaintiff argued that the product was equipment rentals, whereas defendant included sales as well as rentals.
- Prices were restricted by Medicare payment ceilings for most of the market and were not a major basis of competition.
- This industry had substantial potential competition, and there had been several recent entrants of nationwide companies and by former employees of local competitors.
- Market growth potential was good, based on state government forecasts because population growth was projected to be high in the target market.
- Barriers to entry were low if access to the hospital was not determined to be a necessary condition for profitability. There were no regulatory constraints and low capital requirements.
- Market share statistics were not available for all market participants because several competitors were units within national firms without separate data.
- Essential facility allegations centered around the hospital's monopoly as a source of patient referrals. It was, however, possible to quantify the nonhospital referral base such as nursing homes, home health care providers, doctors' offices, community groups, and walk-in business.
- Because the "Certificate of Need" (a form of governmental licensing of hospital facilities) governs establishment of a hospital, the cost of replicating the facility was not an issue.

TYING ARRANGEMENTS AND OTHER EXCLUSIONARY PRACTICES

Section 3 of the Clayton Act (1914) specifies:

> Sec. 3. That it shall be unlawful for any person engaged in commerce . . . to lease or make a sale of goods, wares, merchandise, machinery, supplies, or other commodities,

> whether patented or unpatented, . . . on the condition, agreement, or understanding that the lessee or purchaser thereof shall not use or deal in the goods . . . of a competitor or competitors of the lessor or seller, where the effect . . . may be to substantially lessen competition or tend to create a monopoly in any line of commerce.

Tying Arrangements

Tying arrangements, sometimes known as "monopoly leveraging," are attempts by a business to extend its monopoly in one market into a related market that it does not monopolize. A customer who wants to purchase the "tying" good must also purchase the "tied" good. With a few exceptions, courts have held tying arrangements to be per se antitrust violations.

An early example of tying was IBM's requirement that its tabulator lessees purchase the punch cards from IBM. Sales of the cards measured tabulator usage and thus functioned as a metering device for rental charges, in addition to the fixed rent for the computer. (This arrangement also effectively maximized profit through price discrimination, where heavy users paid less per unit than light users.) The case was decided against IBM (*International Business Machines Corp. v. United States*, 298 U.S. 131 (1936)).

Tying unpatented items to a patented product is also unlawful, such as in the case of films for a patented film projector (*Motion Picture Patents Co. v. Universal Film Manufacturing Co.*, 243 U.S. 502 (1917) overruled *Henry v. A.B. Dick Co.*, 224 U.S. 1 (1912)). Even when no market dominance existed, extending a patent monopoly through tying was deemed illegal per se (*International Salt Co. v. United States*, 332 U.S. 392 (1947)).

Apparent tying arrangements may be more ambiguous in the following instances:

- Technological factors may justify an apparent tie for quality control reasons (*Pick Mfg. Co. v. General Motors Corp.*, 299 U.S. 3 (1936); *Jerrold Electronics Corp. v. United States*, 187 F. Supp. 545 (1961)). If the defendant demonstrates that substandard servicing, software, or expendable components can cause hardware malfunctions, then requiring certain services or products may be legitimate. This argument is more supportable with technologically advanced or higher risk products, and it has often been ineffective. Quantification methods may include analyzing repair costs, quantifying consumer dissatisfaction with the separated products, and showing presence or absence of monopoly profits on the tied product.
- For economic reasons, products that appear to be separate may in practical terms be a single product. Quantifying the costs of eliminating the tying arrangement can sometimes justify the tie. "Economies of joint sales" was the justification alleged in a case where advertisers were required to purchase space in both the morning and evening newspapers if they bought space at all. The defendant argued that rearranging the layout to accommodate one advertiser would have significantly raised the costs to all advertisers, and that, in effect, newspaper space was a single product, not two tied products. The Court agreed (*Times-Picayune Publishing Co. v. United States*, 345 U.S. 594 (1953)). More

recently, the Court held that anesthesiology services are separate from other hospital services, based on practices of separate hiring and separate billing, but the effect was not held to be anticompetitive. (*Jefferson Parish Hospital District No. 2 v. Hyde*, 466 U.S. 2 (1984)).

- Promotional sales are a variation of tying, where purchase of one good enables the customer to purchase another good at an attractive price. Promotional ties are legitimate except where the company has sufficient market power in the tying good to restrain competition in the tied good. In *United States Steel Corp. v. Fortner Enterprises, Inc.*, 429 U.S. 610 (1977), the Court found that U.S. Steel lacked sufficient power in the credit market to force a builder to buy its prefabricated houses at an uncompetitive price. The rule of reason permitted an analysis of market share in the credit markets.

Exclusive Dealing and Requirements Contracts

Exclusive dealing arrangements that substantially lessen competition or create a monopoly may violate § 3 of the Clayton Act. These arrangements give a supplier the exclusive right to a customer's business. A requirements contract mandates that a customer purchase his total requirement of a particular commodity from the same seller.

A pure monopoly will never require an exclusive contract because it is the only supply source. Rather, these contracts often result from product differentiation that creates some monopoly power in an attractive product.

Public policy is concerned with exclusive dealing because it may lead to market foreclosure to competitors. This can occur only when the following conditions are met:

- The manufacturer or seller must have obtained sufficient monopoly power, through product differentiation, to induce its customers into signing exclusive contracts. In this context, an exclusive contract is a substitute for a higher price.
- The retail sales outlets for the product must be limited, or buyers would choose other sources that offered a more diverse product mix. In *Standard Fashion Co. v. Magrane-Houston Co.*, 258 U.S. 346 (1922), the court held that exclusive contracts operating with limited outlets would lead to monopoly.
- The contract period must exceed the industry's normal purchasing period. More frequent contracts would allow for selling opportunities for competitors.

Cases of alleged market foreclosure require that the following factors be considered:

- The percentage of the market foreclosed
- Duration of the foreclosure
- The purchaser's position as a distributor or the final customer
- Increasing or decreasing market share
- Competitors' use of exclusive dealing practices

- The impact on market entry
- The strength of competition
- Any cost or efficiency justifications

Market foreclosure must be shown to affect a sizable share of competition, rather than just involve sizable dollar amounts. However, in *Federal Trade Commission v. Brown Shoe Co.*, 384 U.S. 316 (1966), even a 1 percent market share was deemed sufficient to rule the contracts an unfair trade practice.

Beyond the exploitation of monopoly power, economic reasons exist for exclusive contracts for both the seller and the buyer:

- For sellers, selling expenses may be reduced, price fluctuations may be decreased, market entry may be facilitated, and management may focus more on product promotion.
- For buyers, supplies can be ensured, prices guaranteed, inventory management stabilized, and long-term planning simplified. This can be particularly useful for utilities, such as in *Tampa Electric Co. v. Nashville Coal Co.*, 365 U.S. 320 (1961), where a requirements contract was upheld.
- To quantify the cost justification for such contracts, the analyst can look to the industry's price and quantity fluctuations, inventory carrying costs, necessary product promotion, profit margins on sales, return policies, product obsolescence, importance of warranties, and product loyalty at the retail level.

The following are additional elements of economic evidence for exclusionary contracts, proposed by the Supreme Court in *Standard Oil Co. of California v. United States*, 337 U.S. 293 (1949):

- Evidence that competition flourished despite the contracts. Profitability of other competitors and new entrants in the market indicate that the contract has little affect on market foreclosure.
- The contract length relative to the standard industry practice. Depending on the industry, an exceptionally long contract will indicate that competitors will not have the opportunity to respond to changing economic circumstances.
- The defendant's longevity in the industry. The years when competitors entered the market will help to indicate the purpose for the exclusive contract.
- The degree of market control maintained by the defendant. The defendant's market share and the industry's structure can be used to quantify the degree of market control.
- The product's nature. A high degree of consumer comparison shopping, such as for durable and expensive products, will limit the effectiveness of exclusive contracts between manufacturers and distributors, as consumers search out alternative brands.

Case Study: Requirements Contract

In a case involving fluids used in the drilling industry, the plaintiff alleged that the defendant was preventing customers from dealing with him. The defendant had established a policy that customers who did not purchase all their fluids of this type from him could not buy any from him. The plaintiff, a much smaller company, could not satisfy all his customers' demands. The cyclical and seasonal nature of the business exacerbated the supply problem, and the technical constraints on production limited entry by companies similar to the plaintiff.

Because this was a straightforward case of monopolization, it was settled before trial. The damage estimation was also straightforward.

Sales of the fluid highly correlated with the area's drilling rig count, so actual data on rig counts provided a basis for lost sales estimation. The geographic market was defined as the area that could be served economically by customer truck pickups. The accountant then tabulated the plaintiff's market share before the restraint and assumed no increase. The accountant conducted a cost-per-volume profit analysis, allocating fixed and variable costs according to sales volume. Under this unusual set of circumstances, labor and depletion were fixed costs. Profit margins on lost sales were the basis for damages.

PREDATORY PRICING AND OTHER UNFAIR TRADE PRACTICES

The Federal Trade Commission Act (1914) prohibits an additional range of business practices, which include predatory pricing and vertical restrictions on trade:

> Sec. 5(a)(1). Unfair methods of competition in or affecting commerce, and unfair or deceptive acts or practices in or affecting commerce, are hereby declared unlawful.

Predatory Pricing

Predatory pricing occurs when a firm with market power lowers its price in the attempt to drive existing and potential competitors out of the market, so that it can eventually become a monopolist and receive monopoly profits.

As defined by legal and economic concepts, predatory pricing is determined by whether prices are above or below a relevant cost measure.

- *Average cost* is total cost divided by the number of units produced. Over the long run, prices must exceed average costs for a firm to be profitable.
- *Total variable costs* vary with the number of units being produced. These typically include costs like labor, materials, inventory costs, and utilities. Average variable costs are total variable costs divided by the number of units.
- *Fixed costs* do not vary with units produced or sold over a specific volume range. These typically include certain management costs, depreciation of facilities, and insurance.
- *Long-run variable costs* consider a long enough time frame that almost all costs are variable. Generally, the only costs that remain fixed are depreciation of assets that are not consumed in production, such as buildings; and officer time not spent in the operations at issue.

A simple profit margin analysis does not suffice for ascertaining the existence of predatory pricing because profit maximization may sometimes require pricing below average cost.

- If average variable costs can be covered at the market price, a firm will lose less money by selling at that price than it will by leaving the market. This is because some contribution is made to cover fixed costs, which must be paid regardless of whether goods are being produced and sold.
- Selling at a price below average variable cost can rarely be cost-effective. Prices that are below average variable costs of production may be evidence of predatory intent.
- If prices exceed average variable cost but are below long-run variable cost, then additional evidence of predatory intent may be needed.
- In *Transamerica Computer Co., Inc. v. IBM Corp.*, 698 F.2d 1377 (9th Cir. 1983), the court, although ruling for the defendant, recognized that even prices exceeding average total cost may be predatory, such as price reductions to eliminate rivals.

Cost measurement issues become more complex for multiline companies. Proving predatory pricing for one product line of a multiline company requires appropriate overhead cost allocation. Furthermore, one must ascertain whether a new business line incurs additional expense. If no additional costs were incurred to enter this business, there is no additional incremental variable cost. If there are additional expenses, the cost analysis should allocate incremental variable costs.

For example, a product line may use only 40 percent of a warehouse. If the warehouse would not have been built without this new product line, its costs can be allocated 100 percent to the new product. Thus the analysis must consider the new product's before-and-after impact on costs.

Case Study: Predatory Pricing

In a case involving two major competitors in the building products market, one alleged that the other was pricing below cost. An important indicator of predatory pricing is whether the pricing structure covers the production and operating costs.

To determine the likelihood of liability, it was necessary to review individual sales invoices and related costs of defendant for indications of sales at prices below average variable costs.

Because this was a multiline business, the accountant had to allocate fixed and variable overhead costs among the various lines. The profitability, total costs, and average variable cost of the relevant lines could not be measured without this allocation.

In this case, the general ledger, individual customer invoices, and carefully structured interrogatory and deposition questions were the major sources of cost data. In other cases, internal operating reports, standard or actual cost-accounting reports and tax return information may be the primary sources.

After allocating overhead costs, the product line's selling price was found to be below long-run variable cost but above average variable cost. Other evidence of predatory intent was needed.

It was found that the defendant charged plaintiff's former customers lower prices than were charged to those who had always been customers of defendant. When price discrimination exists concurrently with predatory pricing, it can mask the overall profitability structure and the ability to analyze costs on an overall basis.

In effect, defendant was financing predatory pricing by charging higher prices in different markets. The gross profit margins on sales to new customers were significantly lower than gross margins on sales to older customers.

As in most antitrust matters, it was necessary to define the relevant geographic market, which comprised two cities. A market share analysis was then prepared for the relevant geographic market.

To estimate damages, the market share of the two major competitors was assumed to remain a constant proportion of the total market. For defendant, the market share was adjusted back to the level actually reached before predation.

An assumption was then made to apply the defendant's actual prepredation growth to the market share projections. The defendant's historical market share growth percentage was assumed to continue over the forecast period. For example, if the defendant had experienced a 20-percent market share and 20-percent market growth without predation, then the defendant would have been assigned a 24-percent market share in the next year.

The second part of the damage calculation involved projecting total market sales. Historical sales were compared (via regression techniques) to several indicators of building activity in the area for the past 7 years. Past lost sales for the plaintiff and future total market sales were estimated based on the regression results.

The final damage estimation component was to calculate profits on lost sales on a pretax basis, using incremental rather than average costs. Plaintiff's profit structure, rather than defendant's, was relevant here.

HORIZONTAL MERGERS

Section 7 of the Clayton Act (1914), as amended by the Celler–Kefauver Act (1950), restricts mergers between competitors:

> Sec. 7. That no corporation engaged in commerce shall acquire, directly or indirectly . . . the whole or any part of the assets of another corporation engaged also in commerce, where in any line of commerce in any section of the country, the effect of such acquisition may be substantially to lessen competition, or tend to create a monopoly.

Under the Hart-Scott-Rodino Pre-Merger Notification Act, an acquiring firm with assets or sales exceeding $100 million must report to the Department of Justice (DOJ) and the Federal Trade Commission proposed acquisitions of assets with a value exceeding \$15 million. In 1982, the DOJ issued Merger Guidelines regarding the competitive effects of horizontal mergers. The guidelines focus on market concentration and ease of entry. Any efficiency benefits or other factors receive secondary consideration.

The guidelines set out a five-step procedure for evaluating horizontal mergers:

- Defining a relevant market
- Calculating a measure of concentration
- Evaluating the likelihood of entry
- Considering factors that might affect the likelihood of successful collusion
- Analyzing any efficiency benefits of the proposed merger.

The guidelines define the relevant market as the smallest group of firms that could, if they acted together, profitably raise prices 5 percent above current levels for a year.

The Herfindahl-Hirschman Index (HHI) measures market concentration. Arithmetically, this index equals the sum of the squares of the market shares of the industry firms. For example, in an industry with two firms, with market shares of 90 percent and 10 percent, the index is 8200 (= 8100 + 100). The index is 5000 if the shares are 50 percent and 50 percent.

The Department of Justice considers a market to be highly concentrated if the HHI exceeds 1800 and is likely to challenge mergers that bring the index above this level. A merger that results in an index below 1000 is unlikely to be considered anticompetitive. In the range between 1000 and 1800, a merger that raises the index by less than 100 points is not likely to trigger an antitrust challenge.

Ease of entry is considered in a manner similar to the market definition issue. Entry is considered "easy" if enough new capacity would be brought on line within 2 years of a price increase to render the price increase unprofitable.

The quantitative tools that an accountant or economist can employ in analyzing horizontal mergers include market definition through consideration of demand, supply, and geographic substitution; concentration analysis by means of the Herfindahl-Hirschman Index; quantification of barriers to entry; and analysis of efficiency benefits through cost savings.

VERTICAL MERGERS AND OTHER RELATIONSHIPS

Vertical Mergers

Vertical mergers can significantly benefit both the company and society by creating greater production and distribution efficiencies. Transaction cost savings can result from scale economies of information, management, transportation, and finance. But forward integration, when a firm acquires the market outlets for its goods, generally forecloses opportunities for other sellers. Backward integration, when a firm acquires its supplier, forecloses competition from other supply sources.

In 1982, the Department of Justice issued guidelines defining vertical mergers that it would find objectionable. The primary concern was that vertical integration would increase barriers to entry and significantly hinder competition. The DOJ indicated that it would object to a merger under the following circumstances:

> First, the degree of vertical integration between the two markets must be so extensive that entrants to one market (the "primary market") also would have to enter the other market (the "secondary market") simultaneously. Second, the requirement of entry at the secondary level must make entry at the primary level significantly more difficult and less likely to occur. Finally, the structure and other characteristics of the primary market must be otherwise so conducive to noncompetitive performance that the increased difficulty of entry is likely to affect its performance. (Department of Justice Release, 1982)

Vertical mergers have been prohibited where one of the companies was a regulated natural monopoly. Some experts have expressed concern about the government's ability to contain the monopoly within the framework where it is truly natural. The DOJ specified:

> The clearest example is the acquisition by a regulated utility of a supplier of its fixed or variable inputs. After the merger, the utility would be selling to itself and might be able arbitrarily to inflate the prices of internal transactions. . . . As a result, inflated prices could be passed along to consumers as "legitimate" costs. In extreme cases, the regulated firm may effectively preempt the adjacent market. . . .

Vertical integration may also conceal price collusion. Concentration in the upstream market, as measured by the HHI defined before, is an important indicator of the danger of collusion.

> The Department is unlikely to challenge a merger on this ground unless (i) overall concentration of the upstream market is above 1,800 HHI and (ii) a large percentage of the upstream product would be sold through vertically-integrated retail outlets after the merger.

Price discrimination is also an issue here. If a supplier firm is a monopolist, it can maximize profits by selling inputs to its competitors at one price and to its subsidiary at a lower price. As with all price discrimination, a necessary condition is a differential in elasticity of demand by market segment.

Quantification of the claim that a vertical merger would benefit the economy centers around economies of integration. Market share data may also document the lack of opportunity for abuse.

- Manufacturing interdependence can be demonstrated by analyzing the two entities' cost structures, including transportation costs, utility costs and overhead items that could be combined, and similar labor requirements. Potential improvements in quality control may be documented through evidence on warranty costs due to input failure.

- Management economies can be shown by historical data on fluctuations in input costs and availability, any history of suppliers' inability to perform on contracts, costs of carrying excess inventory due to uncertainty of supplies, data on negotiation and selling expenses, and any evidence of large profit margins in the upstream industry.
- Financing benefits can be documented by efficiencies in borrowing, improvement in credit rating or lowered interest costs, improved prices or liquidity in issuing stock. Economies of finance can also include the merger of a cash surplus company with one needing large capital investments.

Resale Price Maintenance

Resale price maintenance is a form of vertical price fixing and can occur with either a maximum or minimum price.

- Maximum price fixing occurs when the manufacturer establishes a contract with a retailer that the price to the consumer will not exceed a set amount. The benefit to the manufacturer is that the retailer cannot exploit his own monopoly power in a local area. Thus it enhances competitiveness for the product relative to other products. Although maximum price setting offers unambiguous benefits for consumers, it still violates § 1 of the Sherman Act (*Albrecht v. The Herald Co.*, 390 U.S. 145 (1968)).
- Minimum price fixing occurs when a manufacturer establishes a contract with a retailer that the price to the consumer will not fall below a set amount. The manufacturer's primary motivation generally is to ensure that retailers have an incentive to offer adequate product demonstrations. For example, if retailers charge different prices, consumers may go to the higher price retailer for a demonstration, then purchase the product from the lower price retailer. However, resale price maintenance can also enforce a cartel of distributors, who then use the manufacturer's contract to avoid competition among themselves. Minimum price restrictions are a per se violation of the Sherman Act (*United States v. Parke, Davis and Co.*, 362 U.S. 29 (1960)). Federal antitrust laws have replaced state "fair trade" laws that once allowed resale price maintenance.

Other vertical arrangements have ambiguous legality under antitrust laws. Refusing to deal with distributors who do not follow the policy of maintaining prices is not per se illegal. However, aggressive actions to enforce those policies have been deemed illegal (*United States v. Colgate & Co.*, 250 U.S. 300 (1919); *United States v. General Motors Corp.*, 384 U.S. 127 (1966)). If a retailer distributes a product as an agent for the manufacturer, the manufacturer may set the price. But if the agent loses his lease because of noncompliance with the set pricing, the practice may be unlawful (*United States v. General Electric Co.*, 272 U.S. 476 (1926); *Simpson v. Union Oil Co. of California*, 377 U.S. 13 (1964)).

Factors that are to be analyzed in ambiguous cases may include the following:

- The reasonableness of the price suggested
- The business necessity of instituting the program

- The relative roles of the manufacturer and the distributor in serving the customer, such as order taking, billing, and warranties

Exclusive Territories

Product manufacturers commonly assign exclusive sales territories to their distributors, thereby creating a local monopoly in their particular product. These arrangements can include franchises that specify the exclusive territory and are prevalent in such businesses as newspaper distribution.

Territorial division has the effect of reducing competition among retailers of the product and maintaining the retail price. Because the reduced competition is within one brand, rather than among brands, these restrictions are not per se violations, as are the horizontal exclusive territories discussed earlier but are governed by the rule of reason. Where competition among brands is strong, vertical restrictions have few market effects.

Several valid economic rationales exist for exclusive territories, and the interpretation of any one arrangement under antitrust law can be quantified from accounting, general business, and industry documents.

- Exclusive territories resemble resale price maintenance in that they can encourage retailers to adequately demonstrate the product. This was an important consideration in *Continental T.V., Inc. v. GTE Sylvania, Inc.*, 433 U.S. 36 (1977), where applying the rule of reason permitted an exclusive territory arrangement. Sylvania had only a small market share and required aggressive interbrand competition to gain visibility in the market. Information on product demonstration costs and servicing costs, in comparison with profit margins, can help substantiate this claim. Market share data can demonstrate the degree of competition among brands.
- This type of arrangement can capture economies of scale in local distribution. Due to transportation costs, there may be a virtual natural monopoly in providing local goods or services, such as home delivery of newspapers. Even in less extreme cases, such as *Sylvania*, the Court acknowledged that restraints may "promote interbrand competition by allowing the manufacturer to achieve certain efficiencies in the distribution of his products."
- Exclusive territories can help to provide an adequate return on a franchisee's investment, so that quality controls and the value of a franchisor's goodwill will be maintained. Antitrust law has little concern with this issue.

PRICE DISCRIMINATION

Price discrimination involves the charging of different prices to different purchasers without cost or competitive justification. It is illegal only where it has anticompetitive results and thus has been outlawed where businesses are affected and not only consumers.

Section 2 of the Clayton Act (1914), as amended by the Robinson-Patman Act (1936), prohibits price discrimination:

> Sec. 2(a). That it shall be unlawful for any person engaged in commerce, . . . either directly or indirectly, to discriminate in price between different purchasers of commodities of like grade and quality, . . . where the effect of such discrimination may be substantially to lessen competition or tend to create a monopoly in any line of commerce, or to injure, destroy, or prevent competition with any person who either grants or knowingly receives the benefit of such discrimination, or with customers of either of them. . . .

Sellers cannot provide promotional allowances and services to their distributors on a discriminatory basis:

> Sec. 2(e). That it shall be unlawful for any person to discriminate in favor of one purchaser against another purchaser or purchasers of a commodity bought for resale, with or without processing, by contracting to furnish or furnishing, or by contributing to the furnishing of, any services or facilities connected with the processing, handling, sale, or offering for sale of such commodity so purchased upon terms not accorded to all purchasers on proportionally equal terms.

To quantify allegations concerning the provision of services, the analyst can use cost of sales data by type of advertising or promotion in the industry and the degree of disproportionality among purchasers.

Finally, large buyers are prohibited from extracting lower prices from smaller sellers.

> Sec. 2(f). That it shall be unlawful for any person engaged in commerce, in the course of such commerce, knowingly to induce or receive a discrimination in price which is prohibited by this section.

Cases have been brought under this section that involve a company's inducing a labor union to lower its wage rates below those charged to competitors. (Labor unions are generally exempt from antitrust laws, except where they combine with a nonlabor organization.)

In theory, a producer can profit from price discrimination only when purchasers can be separated according to price elasticity of demand. Elasticity of demand measures a buyer's price sensitivity: The higher the elasticity of demand, the more quantity demanded will change as the price changes.

For example, high air fares do not deter much business air travel, but low fares encourage a large amount of leisure travel. Demand for business air travel is relatively inelastic, whereas demand for leisure air travel is highly elastic. Price discrimination allows airlines to capture high prices from one group and large quantities from the other group. If an industry's elasticities of demand are not likely to result in increased profitability from price discrimination, this type of analysis can provide a basis for refuting the allegation.

Cases in which the plaintiff and defendant are in direct competition involve "primary line injury." In *Utah Pie Co. v. Continental Baking Co.*, 386 U.S. 685 (1967), the defendants charged retailers less for pies in the Utah market than in other parts of the country. The Court was concerned that the national companies would use profits earned in other markets to subsidize price decreases in the Utah market. Despite the proconsumer consequences, the Court held that falling prices might lead to lessened competition if some firms withdrew from the market.

Cases in which the supplier sells to competing companies at different prices, thereby altering their competitive positions, involve "secondary line injury." In *Federal Trade Commission v. Morton Salt Co.*, 334 U.S. 37 (1948), the Court held that the defendant unfairly sold salt at discounted prices to large volume purchasers. When not justified by cost differentials, volume discounts are considered pernicious because they enhance the ability of large companies to drive smaller competitors out of business.

If the product at issue is an input to the ultimate product sold, the impact on competition may also depend on its relative importance in the final product's cost structure. Quantifying the impact of price discrimination involves analyzing lost competitiveness and profit margins on resale of the final product.

Another issue emerges when manufacturers sell the same product to different categories of distributors and/or the general public. For example, in *FLM Collision Parts, Inc. v. Ford Motor Co.*, 543 F.2d 1019 (2d Cir. 1976), sales of automobile parts at different prices to different levels of wholesalers, jobbers, and retailers were held to be legal.

Meeting Competition

As specified in Clayton Act § 2(b), a firm may practice price discrimination to meet its competitor's price:

> Nothing herein contained shall prevent a seller rebutting the prima facie case thus made by showing that his lower price or the furnishing of services or facilities to any purchaser or purchasers was made in good faith to meet an equally low price of a competitor.

Evidence that the seller was merely meeting the competition's price does not require absolute price verification but rather a "good faith" belief. The law also permits a wholesaler to reduce prices to one retailer to allow that retailer to meet his competition. This defense does not permit a seller to reduce prices on a discriminatory basis below the competitor's prices.

Data on actual transaction prices and pricing patterns over time by both the plaintiff and defendant can substantiate or refute the claim of illegal price discrimination. However, if prices are shown to be below average variable costs, allegations of predatory pricing are possible.

Cost Justification

Section 2 of the Clayton Act also provides a basis for justifying price discrimination based on costs:

> Nothing herein contained shall prevent differentials which make only due allowance for differences in the cost of manufacture, sale, or delivery resulting from the differing

methods or quantities in which such commodities are to such purchasers sold or delivered.

Prices are to be analyzed net of allowances, rebates, and cash discounts. The following cost differentials have been used to justify price discrimination:

- Freight and delivery cost efficiencies, such as factory versus warehouse delivery
- Inventory expense reductions
- Depreciation of facilities used for one customer or class of customers
- Brokerage allowances passed on to a class of customers
- Manufacturing cost efficiencies, such as off-season production, special orders, or minor variations

Customers may be grouped according to the costs of providing goods or services to them, but the groups must correspond to cost structure and not other variables, such as size or ownership (*United States v. Borden Co.*, 370 U.S. 460 (1962)).

Such cost justifications can be demonstrated by analyses of specific cost items per unit of output, compared with incremental costs at various capacity utilization rates. For example, delivery costs for the average unit can be compared with fully loaded delivery costs. Any cost reductions that are passed on by suppliers can also be quantified.

Other justifications include the product's perishability and obsolescence and discontinuance of the business.

It is not permissible to consider certain types of cost efficiencies and disregard others that are countervailing. It is also improper to justify price discrimination by not allocating overhead costs to certain customers. Overhead items such as marketing, technical service, and warehousing can be allocated on the basis of time spent per call, inches of advertising space, and volume of units held in storage.

BIBLIOGRAPHY

Advisory Committee on Cost Justification, Report to the FTC, (1956), reprinted in H. Taggart, *Cost Justification* 555 (1959).

American Bar Association, Section of Antitrust Law, Monograph No. 4, "The Robinson–Patman Act: Policy and Law," Volumes I and II (1983).

American Bar Association, Section of Antitrust Law, Monograph No. 2, "Vertical Restriction Limiting Interbrand Competition" (1977).

Areeda, P., *Antitrust Analysis* (Boston: Little, Brown & Company, 1974).

Blair, R.D., and D.L. Kaserman, *Antitrust Economics* (Homewood, IL.: Richard D. Irwin, 1985).

Hills, C.A., ed., *Antitrust Advisor*, 3rd Ed. (Colorado Springs: Shepard's/McGraw Hill, 1985).

Posner, R.A., *Antitrust Law: An Economic Perspective* (Chicago: University of Chicago Press, 1976).

Shniderman, H.L., *Price Discrimination in Perspective* (Philadelphia: American Law Institute, 1977).

Sullivan, L. A., *Antitrust* (St. Paul: West Publishing Company, 1977).

United States Department of Justice and Federal Trade Commission, "Merger Guidelines—1982" (Chicago: Commerce Clearing House, June 16, 1982).

LIST OF CASES

Albrecht v. The Herald Co., 390 U.S. 145 (1968)
Aspen Skiing Company v. Aspen Highlands Skiing Corp., 472 U.S. 585 (1985)
Continential T.V., Inc. v. GTE Sylvania, Inc., 433 U.S. 36 (1977)
Fashion Originator's Guild of America v. Federal Trade Commission, 312 U.S. 457 (1941)
Federal Trade Commission v. Brown Shoe Co., 384 U.S. 316 (1966)
Federal Trade Commision v. Morton Salt Co., 334 U.S. 37 (1948)
FLM Collision Parts, Inc. v. Ford Motor Co., 543 F.2d 1019 (2d Cir. 1976)
Henry v. A.B. Dick Co., 224 U.S. 1 (1912)
International Business Machines Corp. v. United States, 298 U.S. 131 (1936)
International Salt Co. v. United States, 187 F. Supp. 545 (1961)
Jefferson Parish Hospital District No. 2 v. Hyde, 466 U.S. 2 (1984)
Jerrold Electronics Corp. v. United States, 187 F. Supp. 545 (1961)
Klor's, Inc. v. Broadway-Hale Stores, Inc., 359 U.S. 207 (1959)
Motion Picture Patents Co. v. Universal Film Manufacturing Co., 243 U.S. 502 (1917)
Simpson v. Union Oil Co. of California, 377 U.S. 13 (1964)
Standard Fashion Co. v. Magrane-Houston Co., 258 U.S. 346 (1922)
Standard Oil Co. of California v. United States, 337 U.S. 293 (1949)
Tampa Electric Co. v. Nashville Coal Co., 365 U.S. 320 (1961)
Times-Picayune Publishing Co. v. United States, 345 U.S. 594 (1953)
Transamerica Computer Co., Inc. v. IBM Corp., 698 F.2d 1377 (9th Cir. 1983)
United States v. Borden Co., 370 U.S. 460 (1962)
United States v. Colgate & Co., 250 U.S. 300 (1919)
United States v. Container Corp. of America, 393 U.S. 333 (1969)
United States v. E.I. DuPont de Nemours & Co., 351 U.S. 377 (1956)
United States v. First National Pictures, Inc., 282 U.S. 44 (1930)
United States v. General Electric Co., 272 U.S. 476 (1926)
United States v. General Motors Corp., 384 U.S. 127 (1966)
United States v. Parke, Davis and Co., 362 U.S. 29 (1960)
United States v. Topco Assoc., Inc., 405 U.S. 596 (1972)
United States Steel Corp. v. Fortner Enterprises, Inc., 429 U.S. 610 (1977)
Utah Pie Co. v. Continental Baking Co., 386 U.S. 685 (1967)
Walker Process Equipment, Inc. v. Food Machinery and Chemical Corp., 382 U.S. 172 (1965)

11

THE ACCOUNTANT'S ROLE IN ARBITRATION

Vincent J. Love, CPA
John J. Costello, CPA

With court calendars typically backed up 5 years or more and with litigation costs rising, many business people resolve their disputes by arbitration. Millions of contracts contain arbitration clauses. The number of commercial and labor cases filed under the auspices of the American Arbitration Association (AAA) has more than doubled in the last decade. In 1986, 15,028 commercial arbitration cases were filed, and the National Association of Securities Dealers reported a 50-percent increase in the number of its arbitration requests.[1] Some believe that today more commercial claims are arbitrated than are tried before a jury.[2]

More and more industries prefer to arbitrate rather than to litigate. In 1987, the Supreme Court strengthened the trend by upholding the arbitration procedure in disputes between brokers and their customers.[3] The banking industry, recently plagued with costly litigation, may also be moving toward arbitration. Blair Reynolds, as chief counsel for the California Bankers Association, recommended that all commercial contracts require arbitration to resolve disputes. Bank of America already requires such clauses in many of its farm and commercial loan agreements.[4] Other industries also find that arbitration keeps costs down. Although more claimants receive awards in arbitrations than in litigations, the amounts are smaller. Arbitration is less popular with plaintiffs than with defendants. Often, however, the litigation costs are so large compared to the size of the claim that the plaintiff elects to arbitrate.

Arbitration is the final and binding resolution of a dispute by one or more impartial individuals. Because the decision is binding, arbitration differs from negotiation, mediation, fact finding, and minitrials—all of which also settle disputes outside the courtroom. In mediation, for example, the third party talks to both sides and helps them negotiate their own settlement; it is more tentative than arbitration, and either party can withdraw at any point. An arbitration is a decision on the facts, and it has legal power that is second only to that of the Supreme Court. Courts of appeal will not review arbitration awards on the merits of the case.

Less formal than trials, arbitrations are often conducted around a conference table, and the rules of evidence do not apply. The AAA favors a panel of three arbitrators, which usually includes a lawyer and someone with industry experience. A sole arbitrator can decide an arbitration. Arbitrators usually have almost complete authority over the entire procedures—rules, documents, evidence, testimony, and cross-examination. Unlike members of a jury, arbitrators are not laypeople and unlike judges, they are not necessarily lawyers. The typical arbitrator is an expert chosen for specialized knowledge of the disputed matter. In business disputes, the arbitrator might be an engineer, a management consultant, an attorney, or an accountant.

Although arbitration hearings are relatively informal, participants usually choose to follow specific rules or are directed to follow them by a contract. They often use the AAA's rules, but many special systems of rules also exist, such as those of the National Association of Securities Dealers (NASD) and the United Nations Committee on International Trade Law (UNCITRAL). Often, arbitrators or panels will set their own rules or adapt a set of rules to their specific needs.

Construction contracts and insurance claims top the list of the AAA's most common type of disputes. Construction agreements have included arbitration clauses since 1871, and the construction industry has since developed special procedures and panels of arbitrators. Most insurance contracts specify that a disagreement will be settled by each side engaging a competent and disinterested "appraiser," as the arbitrator is called in the insurance industry. The two appraisers, who are often accountants, then choose a third to be the "umpire."

Most broker dealer agreements also contain an arbitration clause to resolve disputes about such matters as how the account was handled, whether a trade was made, or when it was made. Many acquisitions and business contracts, notably those with contingent payment terms, require arbitration to settle disputes about the amount due the seller. Arbitrations are also common at the New York and Pacific Stock Exchanges, in divorce settlements, and in other areas.

WHY AN ACCOUNTANT?

The accountant can take one of three roles in an arbitration—consultant, expert witness, or arbitrator. Those of consultant and witness are the same as in a trial. As a consultant or an expert witness, or often both, an accountant helps an attorney sift through business data and prepare a case clearly and simply, so that the panel can understand it.

An expert accounting witness in an arbitration often, however, has to work harder to prove a point. Although a jury is made up of laypeople, an arbitrator is likely to be a CPA, who will challenge and discredit colleagues whose testimony is suspect. An expert who makes a point that is contrary to accepted practice may find that the arbitrator will give less weight to the rest of the testimony. Although showmanship may persuade, it usually displeases an arbitrator.

The third potential role for an accountant, that of arbitrator, is one for which most do not have formal training. In effect, the arbitrator is a judge. Those who are new to this role might find it valuable to observe a judge at trial. CPAs with extensive business experience might qualify as arbitrators. They can become members of the AAA's national panel of arbitrators or the arbitrator panel for the New York Stock Exchange or some other body. In some areas of the country, a person who qualifies by schooling or experience can become an AAA arbitrator just by applying. In other places, a new person has to be recommended by a current member. Usually, a new member must attend a half-day training program before serving on a panel.

Accountants often arbitrate for the New York and Pacific Stock Exchanges, the National Association of Securities Dealers, and other regulatory bodies. CPAs serve as arbitrators in many commercial disputes because they are familiar with various business transactions, they may be experts in particular industries, and they understand the financial aspects of business. The profession is widely respected, and it has clear ethical standards.

Typically, an arbitration concerns a limited number of specific issues. Accountants might be asked to arbitrate an acquisition dispute in which the selling and buying parties disagree as to the accuracy of the financial information. Accountants might have to decide whether financial statements were false and misleading in a specific area. Accountants who are not qualified to arbitrate a particular dispute should disqualify themselves. Thus it is important to ask about the facts of the case before accepting an appointment as an arbitrator.

THE ARBITRATOR'S ROLE

Arbitration is favored by federal law, though a few states have not passed modern arbitration acts. The arbitrator has broad powers, such as setting ground rules and issuing subpoenas for witnesses and records. An arbitrator must make a decision based upon the merits of the case. This involves first ascertaining the truth about the busines situation in question and then deciding on an award. The facts, not the personalities involved nor the presentation of the case, matter. The arbitrator must not be swayed by emotions.

Like a judge, the arbitrator can ask questions to ascertain the facts. This is especially valuable in matters of law. Accountant arbitrators are usually not authorities on the law. An arbitrator can ask the opposing attorneys to explain or to prepare a written brief on the applicable law. An arbitrator should not consult an outside attorney for such advice without permission from both sides.

Fairness and impartiality are as important as competence in an arbitrator. An arbitrator must have no interest in a proceeding's outcome. An arbitrator who discovers a prior personal or business connection with one of the parties should disclose that connection. A close connection requires disqualification. Often, however, the relation will not impugn the arbitrator's neutrality, so that disclosing the connection will satisfy both sides.

Impartiality in an arbitration extends both to fact and to appearance. An arbitrator should not communicate with either party in the absence of the other nor comment unfavorably about a party or a witness or reveal any feelings about the dispute. The arbitrator should apply identical rules to both sides. If the claimant's expert prepares a report, then the respondent's expert must be invited to prepare one. Generally, the claimant reports first; then the respondent is given time to respond.

THE ELEMENTS OF AN ARBITRATION

An arbitration involves little or no discovery. The hearing usually occurs in a conference room, with opposing parties on opposite sides of the table. Common terminology denotes the plaintiff as the *claimant* and the defendant as the *respondent*. The rules are flexible and less formal than in court. At the request of both sides, rules of evidence or civil procedure may be applied. This is the exception, rather than the rule.

Generally, arbitrations do not follow the formal rules of evidence. Many reasons exist for this. The rules of evidence were created to prevent juries from hearing unreliable or irrelevant testimony. Arbitrators being more sophisticated can be trusted to ignore such statements. Also, allowing the parties to vent their emotions in a hearing can help because they may be more inclined to settle, or to cooperate, if they do so. Finally, an award can be legally overtuned because the arbitrator refused to hear or admit relevant evidence; it cannot be overturned because the arbitrator considered irrelevant evidence.

Rules and the Function of the AAA

Though arbitrations generally do not follow formal courtroom rules, lawyers may still refer to them. Of course, there should be a set of rules. The AAA rules are standard, and every arbitrator should be familiar with them. Special cases often have rules, such as those of the NASD. Other industries also have their own rules, and many experienced arbitrators create their own rules.

Besides providing the most widely accepted set of rules, the AAA performs other services for arbitrators. However, not all arbitrations are held under AAA auspices.

The AAA, when involved, assigns each arbitration a tribunal administrator to help the arbitrators manage the case. The administrator handles communication between the parties to set dates for hearings, decide on postponements, exchange documents, or issue subpoenas. The administrator also answers questions about the rules.

Founded in 1926, the AAA has offices in 31 major cities. Besides its arbitration services, the AAA trains, researches, and produces publications valuable to arbitrators, lawyers, and parties in disputes. It maintains a list of 60,000 arbitrators and helps parties choose among them.

Selecting Arbitrators

The AAA, when involved, sends each party lists of qualified arbitrators, allowing the parties 7 days to study the names and eliminate objectionable candidates. The tribunal administrator helps the parties agree upon an arbitrator or a panel, and if the parties fail to agree, the AAA will appoint the arbitrator.

Often, when the AAA is not involved, an arbitrator or the parties agree on an impartial arbitrator. Some insurance and other contracts specify that each party select an accountant in case of a dispute and that the two accountants select a third. Only the independent accountant rules.

Preparation for the Hearing

The AAA, another organization, or the arbitrator consults with the parties to set a time and place for the hearing. A preliminary administrative hearing is often held to resolve procedural matters and to set the ground rules for the hearings. At this time each side can estimate the time it needs to present its case, and the parties can set dates for the hearings.

The preliminary hearing helps the parties narrow the issues, by reviewing their agreement and disagreement. The arbitrator should try to get as much information as possible in writing—contracts, exhibits, briefs, lists of expert witnesses, and their reports. This preparation allows one to understand the dispute ahead of time, so that the hearings can proceed more quickly and efficiently.

Conducting the Hearing

An effective arbitration seems to result from an attitude of cooperation. The arbitration's ambience differs with the personalities of the arbitrators. Some states require that an arbitrator take an oath of office, whereas others do not. Many arbitrators choose to be sworn even when not required.

Some arbitrators do not allow witnesses to be present when other witnesses testify; others allow everyone to attend the hearing. If the arbitrator excludes one side's witnesses, the other's must be excluded well. The room size may govern the number of attendees. One of the reasons many parties select arbitration is to keep the resolution of their disputes private. The arbitrator must respect this desire and exclude all unnecessary persons from the proceeding.

Some arbitrators prefer to swear in witnesses themselves because it is a bit more formal, so that the witnesses know they are expected to tell the truth. Other arbitrators leave the swearing in to the stenographer or tribunal administrator. If a witness does not appear in person but instead submits an affidavit, the arbitrator should want to know why and may subpoena other documents relevant to the testimony in the affidavit. The absence of a witness who lives far away from the location of the hearings may be understandable. The arbitrator might give less credibility to the testimony of absent witnesses.

The general format of a hearing includes opening statements, introduction of documents, examination of witnesses, presentation of exhibits, and final briefs. Customarily, the claimant's case is heard first. If, during the hearing, the parties decide to negotiate directly, the arbitrator should encourage such a discussion but not participate. The neutrality of an arbitrator who participates in a failed attempt at settlement may later be challenged.

Arbitrators generally allow a wide range of evidence in a hearing because they can use their judgment as to what is relevant. Leading questions and hearsay evidence are permitted, but experienced arbitrators understand that direct testimony is generally more persuasive than hearsay and that documents and facts are stronger than arguments alone. Often an arbitrator will not allow hearsay evidence if a witness who can give direct testimony on the subject is scheduled to testify—even though hearsay may be allowed in other instances.

The arbitrator might intervene in certain situations. For example, in disputes between broker dealers and investors, commonly the investor has no representation, so that the arbitrator may want to step in on behalf of the individual. Also, though the rules allow witnesses to be asked leading questions, the arbitrator may have to set limits. Effective arbitrators do not permit lawyers to harass witnesses. Arguments can become quite heated. When two attorneys shout at each other or threaten each other, for example, the arbitrator should attempt to exercise control. Arbitrators have no censure powers, so the arbitrator must be firm but diplomatic.

When witnesses and attorneys appear to stray from the subject, the arbitrator may interrupt and ask the lawyer why the testimony is relevant. At times, the arbitrator may attempt to focus the testimony of a talkative witness. An arbitrator should give the opponent's lawyer a chance to object. The arbitrator might ask the witness to listen to the question and say "yes" or "no" before explaining. Arbitrators can ask lawyers to rephrase difficult questions.

The arbitrator must remain impartial no matter how unpleasant the behavior of a lawyer. The ruling must be based on the facts of the case, not the personalities. The arbitrator should never criticize an attorney's conduct in front of the client. Sometimes, however, the arbitrator may ask the principals to leave and then talk with the attorneys. If the hearing appears to be slipping out of control, the arbitrator can quiet the irrational attorney with such requests as "Mr. Jones, please sit down" or "May we continue the hearing?" or "You are out of order. Please sit down."

An arbitrator should not be tempted to make a decision before having heard all the facts. Even the most experienced arbitrators often agree with parties who testify eloquently, only to change the opinion after hearing the other side.

The Award

Under AAA procedure, the arbitrator has 30 days from the last hearing date or receipt of posthearing briefs to write an opinion. It is best to adhere to the 30-day rule in any arbitration so that the ruling can be made when the evidence is fresh in the arbitrator's mind. Arbitrators should not decide at the hearing but review the facts afterwards. The arbitrator may ask both sides for a posttrial brief summarizing what each believes the evidence shows and why their side should prevail.

The written decision should say who receives the award and the amount. The rules do not require an explanation for the decision. In fact, such as explanation can damage the authority of the award, opening the door to an appeal.

Though mediators often work toward a middle ground, arbitrators generally rule in favor of one party or the other. When however, the facts do not clearly favor one party on all the issues, compromises occur, so that the amount need not be an "all-or-nothing" decision. Experience has shown that arbitrations are more likely than trials to result in some award for the claimant (plaintiff); however, the awards are usually smaller than in trials.

Compensation

The AAA generally sets the compensation for arbitrators in AAA-administered arbitrations. AAA arbitrators usually are not compensated for their time in claims with only one hearing. Compensation at a set AAA daily amount usually begins on the second day of the hearings. Most other arbitration panels also serve without compensation. When the claim is large, complicated, or requires special knowledge, arbitrators often receive fees at their normal rate.

Arbitrators who serve outside the auspices of the usual organizations are free to set the fee after negotiating with both parties. The fee is usually split equally by both parties, but the parties may agree otherwise.

MANAGING A COMPLEX DISPUTE

Complex cases must be well managed. The volume of information and testimony in a large case can threaten the efficiency of the arbitration process. A skilled arbitrator can move along the most complicated dispute at a reasonable speed while giving the parties a fair hearing.

In most arbitrations, the parties will not have had months to refine the issues and to study each other's arguments. The arbitrator must simplify the case as it progresses. Although completing much of the work in advance saves hearing time, delaying the case while every item is being assembled is not productive. The most important consideration is to keep the arbitration moving.

The AAA, when involved in an arbitration, will schedule a preliminary conference before the arbitrators have been selected. At this meeting, which is generally off the record, the AAA's tribunal administrator tries to handle procedural matters. Among the topics that can be covered are document requests, lists of claims, witness lists, and scheduling. An arbitrator who serves as administrator should similarily hold a preliminary hearing.

Once appointed, the panel should meet and choose a chairperson. At the procedural conference, sometimes called a preliminary hearing, the arbitrator meets with the two parties to set the ground rules and to outline the case. The arbitrator sets the tone of the hearings here and asks the two parties to cooperate with one another and to produce evidence rather than conceal it. Each party presents its claims so that they can define more clearly their areas of disagreement. The parties and the arbitrator can decide on information to be exchanged before the evidentiary hearings begin. Each party should provide a list of witnesses and the subject of their testimony. The parties should discuss the anticipated length of the hearings and set up a schedule. In some complex arbitrations, limited discovery is permitted, including depositions.

Scheduling the hearings in a complex case is not simple. Hearings should occur on consecutive days. With many individuals involved, conflicts are inevitable. Nevertheless, the hearings deserve a high priority. Many arbitrators prefer to arrange for only the first few days of the hearings at the initial procedural conference. The time required for the rest of the hearings may become clearer after those sessions.

The arbitrator should ask the parties for reading material that will help in understanding the case. The hearings will move more quickly if the arbitrator becomes familiar with contracts, exhibits, and other documents in advance. Some discovery of documents may be desirable in a large case. To save time, documents should be accepted as authentic unless they are in dispute. Exhibits should be available in advance, numbered either by the attorneys or by the arbitrator.

Major witnesses will testify in person, but less important witnesses can testify via affidavit. Biographical information about witnesses can be submitted in advance, in writing, so that the actual hearings involve only testimony. It is wise for the arbitrator to ask what the expert witnesses are going to say before they testify and to have the written report, if any, provided in advance.

The arbitrator should warn the parties against repetitive direct testimony and cross-examination, and during the hearings, if repetitiveness occurs, he should firmly cut it off. Posthearing briefs assist the arbitrator in analyzing the evidence. Each party should summarize the facts it presented and recommend how the arbitrator should rule. At a final hearing, the arbitrators should be prepared to test the soundness of their understanding and ask searching questions.

SUMMARY

In arbitration, an accountant can be consultant, expert witness, or arbitrator. The first two roles are similar to the parallel roles in a trial. The expert witness accountant in an arbitration has a more demanding task. Unlike a jury, an arbitration panel will probably include a CPA who can challenge the expert's testimony on technical grounds.

Accountants are often arbitrators, a logical choice because of their knowledge of business transactions. As an arbitrator, the CPA is faced with a role that resembles that of a judge: making a legally binding decision based upon the facts.

An arbitration is less formal than a trial. It is typically held in a conference room, and the rules of evidence do not apply. There is little or no discovery; both hearsay evidence and leading questions are permitted, although the arbitrator may give them little weight. The parties will generally cooperate with an arbitrator because failure to do so will harm their case.

Some arbitrations are complex and require careful management. Several steps can be taken to move the hearings forward efficiently, while giving the parties a fair and impartial hearing. A procedural conference can set the ground rules and outline the dispute in advance. The arbitrators can ask for written reports, exhibits, and witness lists before the hearings begin. They can also guide the parties firmly to avoid repetitive testimony.

The American Arbitration Association (AAA) is a private nonprofit organization that offers information, education, and research, as well as practical help for arbitrators. In disputes with which it is involved, the AAA assigns a tribunal administrator, who helps the arbitrators manage the case. The AAA is also the source of the most widely accepted arbitration rules. There are other rules, however, and other organizations that oversee arbitrations, among them, the National Association of Securities Dealers (NASD) and the United Nations Commission on International Trade law (UNCITRAL).

NOTES

1. Lorna Doubet, "Arbitration Trend Tempts Banks," *San Francisco Chronicle* (August 17, 1987).
2. Steven A. Meyerowitz, "The Arbitration Alternative," *ABA Journal, The Lawyer's Magazine*, Vol. 71 (February 1985), pp. 78–80.
3. Bruce Ingersoll, "SEC Proposes New Rules for Arbitrations," *The Wall Street Journal*, September 11, 1987.
4. Doubet, *op. cit.*

BIBLIOGRAPHY

American Arbitration Association, *Alternative Dispute Resolution: A Procedural Guide* (New York: American Arbitration Association, 1986).

American Arbitration Association, *Code of Ethics for Arbitrators in Commercial Disputes* (New York: The American Arbitration Association, 1977).

American Arbitration Association, *A Commercial Arbitration Guide for Business People* (New York: American Arbitration Association, 1985).

American Arbitration Association, *Facts about the American Arbitration Association*. (New York: American Arbitration Association, 1985).

American Arbitration Association, *Commercial Arbitration Rules*. (New York: American Arbitration Association, 1987).

American Arbitration Association, *A Guide for Commercial Arbitrators* (New York: American Arbitration Association, 1985).

Barrett, William L.D. "Arbitration of a Complex Case: Practical Guidelines for Arbitrators and Counsel," *The Arbitration Journal*, Vol. 41, No. 4, December 1986.

Coulson, Robert, *Business Arbitration: What You Need to Know*, 3d ed. (New York: American Arbitration Association, 1986).

McClendon, J. Steward, and Rosabel E. Everard Goodman, *International Commercial Arbitration in New York* (New York: World Arbitration Institute, 1986).

Meyerowitz, Steven A, "The Arbitration Alternative," *ABA Journal, The Lawyer's Magazine*, Vol. 71, February 1985, pp. 78–80.

National Association of Securities Dealers, *Code of Arbitration Procedure*. (New York: National Association of Securities Dealers, 1984).

Poppleton, Allen. "The Arbitrator's Role in Expediting the Large and Complex Commercial Case," *The Arbitration Journal*, Vol. 36, No. 4, December 1981, pp. 6–10.

12

THE TROUBLED BUSINESS AND BANKRUPTCY

Ronald J. Sutter, CPA
Grant W. Newton, CPA, CMA, PhD

INTRODUCTION

A Challenging Area

Troubled business and bankruptcy engagements challenge the accountant who helps a failing business. Such engagements require knowledge of and experience in business management, auditing, and taxation. Reorganizing a business in a bankruptcy proceeding may involve an accountant in the following:

- Business sales or mergers
- Business valuation
- Operational audits
- Forecasts, projections, and business plans
- Litigation services
- Organization and management evaluation
- Fraud or mismanagement investigations
- Determinations of damages
- Special and unusual financial reporting and taxation problems
- General business management activities
- Computer services
- Data management and control services
- Negotiation for or with creditors or other parties
- Other management services

Each case can present problems that differ considerably from those found in a general accounting and tax practice. This chapter indicates where a CPA can provide special services to a troubled business in or outside of the bankruptcy forum.

Bankruptcy as a Specialty

Bankruptcy-related work has become a specialized profession. Bankruptcy has its own court system, laws, language, and fraternity. One must be able to apply the Bankruptcy Code and speak the language of the bankruptcy laws before becoming a bankruptcy specialist. The term *specialist* does not reflect a designated title as a licensed specialist but rather refers to the individual who emphasizes and has experienced in this practice area.

Judges may appoint experienced CPA bankruptcy experts to be trustees, reporting and acting independently of counsel.

A General Overview

This chapter serves only as an introduction to this practice area and does not substitute for complete authoritative research of legal and taxation issues.

Nine details appear in texts on the accounting and tax considerations in reorganization and bankruptcy proceedings. The chapter appendix includes a brief list of reference materials related to troubled businesses and bankruptcy.

The Bankruptcy Code and Rules and Guidelines of the Office of U.S. Trustee are essential tools. Like most laws, the Bankruptcy Code is often amended, thus requiring *continuing* education. This chapter will primarily address issues related to Chapter 7 (liquidation) and Chapter 11 (reorganization) cases under the Bankruptcy Code (Title 11 of the U.S. Code).

THE BEST PLACE TO START

When

The greatest service provided to a troubled business is to prevent its failure. Accordingly, the best time to help is before it petitions for bankruptcy. The bankruptcy system weighs the interest of the debtor, its creditors, and other parties in interest. This can require costly proceedings to establish the facts and appropriate action.

Where

One source of troubled business engagements are clients with cash flow problems who cannot obtain a line of credit with their bankers. Another source is from bankers who refer clients to experts for specialized assistance. Bankers sometimes refer their existing borrowers with financial difficulties. Caveat: Avoid a lender liability assertion that claims that the bank, or you as its purported representative, assumed management control of the bank customer.

Local credit associations provide referrals. Credit association engagements involve arrangements with creditors, which are handled under state or common laws, not through the U.S. Bankruptcy Court system.

Corporate or bankruptcy attorneys provide referrals in the insolvency/bankruptcy arena. The local bar association can provide the names of those specializing in this area. A business person facing severe financial difficulties often seeks an attorney's advice before consulting a financial advisor. This may be because his problems are first brought home by a lawsuit, IRS notice, or concern for personal liability.

How

A CPA who concentrates in troubled businesses is much like a physician. Accordingly, before the CPA can cure an ill, he must first identify it. These steps will help you start:

- Obtain samples of operating management financial reports.
- Obtain *detailed* financial reports for at least the last 5 years.
- Complete an internal control questionnaire.
- Obtain and compare industry operating ratios and statistics
- Obtain information that will enable you to understand the structure (both legal and operational) of the business and its operations, including the following:
    1. Management/organization charts
    2. Operating locations
    3. A brief description of all its business operations (i.e., the product, competition, major suppliers, customers, distribution, etc.)
- Identify the major assets; ascertain their liquidation and market values; determine which assets are pledged as collateral for debts.
- Identify the business segments that provided most of the past profits and cash flow.
- Tour the facilities. Be observant and ask questions.
- Interview the management team individually to ascertain their view of the problems and possible solutions.
- Obtain an aging of the receivables *and* payables.
- Obtain the terms of all leases, loans, and contracts payable.
- Ascertain the status of deposits for taxes with the IRS and state taxing authorities.

Some managements cannot identify impending financial problems. The balance sheet, profit and loss statements, and income tax returns alone are *not* adequate to manage most businesses. Detailed aging reports of receivables could have saved many businesses if they had been available and properly used.

Recognizing the Characteristics

Business failures have many common characteristics. Consider the following typical profile: A person technically competent in his area of expertise, but with little capital or management experience starts a business. The business prospers, but as it grows, it fails to grow in management depth. The owner/manager, confident because of earlier success, will not believe that the company is unable to continue to grow without additional specialized management help such as marketing, production, accounting, and finance. Receivables and payables increase. A bank loan is obtained but quickly becomes inadequate. The company enters high-risk transactions to appear successful. Management neglects accounting records and procedures. Excessive salaries and questionable "perks" (generally personal expenses) continue. The owner/manager is typically the eternal optimist. The company acquires new facilities and equipment. Questionable transactions are recorded, and doubtful receivables are carried without reserves. Payroll taxes go unpaid, and the bank loan is in default. The business ultimately files a bankruptcy petition. The debtor claims that it is the bank's or supplier's fault because they would not increase the loan amount and extend its repayment terms.

BANKRUPTCY—AN OVERVIEW FROM BEGINNING TO END

Alternatives Available to Troubled Businesses

The debtor's first alternatives are to locate new financing or to merge with another company. If neither of these is possible, the debtor may have to seek an arrangement with creditors, either informally (out of court) or through judicial proceedings.

Out-of-Court Settlements. The informal settlement is an out-of-court agreement that usually consists of a time extension (stretch-out), a pro rata cash payment for full settlement of claims (composition), an issue of stock for debt, or some combination of these. The debtor, through counsel or a local credit association, calls an informal meeting of the creditors to discuss his financial problems. The credit association often assists in out-of-court settlements by arranging a meeting of creditors, providing advice, serving as secretary for the creditors' committee, and serving as a disbursing agent under an informal arrangement with creditors.

A credit association is composed of credit managers of various businesses in a given region. The association provides credit and other business information to member companies concerning their debtors, helps make commercial credit collections, supports legislation favoring business creditors, and provides courses in credit management to the credit community. At the creditors' meeting, the debtor describes the failure's causes, discusses the value of assets (especially those unpledged) and unsecured liabilities, and answers the creditors' questions. This meeting must convince the creditors that they would receive more if the business were to continue operating rather than liquidating, and that all parties would be better off if they agreed to an out-of-court settlement.

Creditors' Committee. To facilitate the debtor's work with creditors, a committee of creditors is normally appointed during the initial meeting of the debtor and creditors, providing that the creditors decide to cooperate. The creditors often desire a settlement as much as the debtor does.

No formal procedure exists for forming a committee. Ideally, the committee should comprise four or five of the largest creditors and one or two representatives from the smaller creditors. No legal rules exist for a committee's formation, and each situation is unique. Although smaller creditors often serve on committees, other committees include only larger creditors, either because the smaller creditors lack interest or because the larger creditors dominate. Conflicts of interest may arise when creditors are also competitors.

The debtor's job of running the business while under the creditor committee monitoring is easier if the committee members are friendly to the debtor.

The Committee's Duties. The creditors' committee serves as the bargaining agent for the creditors, monitors the debtor's operations during development of a reorganization plan, and solicits acceptance of the plan once the committee approves it. Generally, the creditors' committee meets immediately to select a presiding officer and counsel. The committee also may engage an independent accountant to review or audit the debtor's books and records.

The creditors' committee will meet to discuss the completed review or audit. If the CPAs report reveals questionable practices, the acceptable settlement amount will increase. A debtor probably will face bankruptcy proceedings under these conditions. Conversely, if the debtor is honest and demonstrates a plan to reverse the unprofitable trends and reestablish the business, the creditors will approve a settlement.

Plan of Settlement. The debtor's accountant and attorney should help the debtor prepare a suggested settlement plan to present and discuss at the first creditors' meeting. Typically only the largest creditors and a few smaller creditors are invited to avoid a group too large to function effectively. No formal guidelines exist for the settlement plan. It may call for a 100-percent payment over an extended time period, cash payments on a pro rata basis for full settlement of creditors' claims, satisfaction of debt obligations with stock, or some combination. A carefully developed forecast of operations, based on realistic assumptions developed by the debtor with an accountant's or consultant's assistance can help creditors ascertain whether the debtor can perform under the plan's terms and operate successfully in the future.

Creditors will accept a plan only if they receive at least as much as they would receive in liquidation. This amount per dollar of claim equals the sum of a forced-sale value of assets, realizable accounts receivable, cash, and prepaid items, minus priority claims, secured claims, and expenses of administration—all divided by the total amount of unsecured claims.

The plan should adequately dispose of all costs of administration, secured claims, and priority claims, including wages and taxes to protect the unsecured creditors. If the debtor's plan includes a cash down payment in full or partial settlement, the payment should at least equal the probable dividend the creditors would receive in Chapter 7 bankruptcy.

Advantages and Disadvantages. The following summarizes some reasons why today's environment encourages informal settlement:

- The out-of-court settlement is less disruptive to a business that continues operation.
- The debtor can benefit from the advice of a committee, especially if some members have considerable business experience but preferably not in the same line of business.
- The informal settlement avoids invoking the Bankruptcy Code provisions, and, as a result, more businesslike solutions can be adopted.
- A settlement minimizes frustrations and delays by resolving problems informally without court hearings.

- The parties can usually reach an agreement much faster informally than in court proceedings.
- An out-of-court settlement usually costs less to administer than a formal reorganization.
- Informal (sometimes called composition) settlements have the following weaknesses:
- A successful settlement plan requires all creditors' approval, and some creditors may not accept a settlement calling for payment of less than 100 percent.
- The debtor's assets are subject to attack while a settlement is pending. (Of course, if a creditor takes legal action, a petition in Bankruptcy Court could be filed.)
- The informal composition settlement does not provide a method to resolve individual disputes between the debtor and specific creditors.
- Executory contracts, especially leases, may be difficult to settle.
- Certain tax law provisions make it more advantageous to file a bankruptcy court petition.
- Priority debts owed to the United States under Rev. Stat. § 3466 must be paid first.

Assignment for Benefit of Creditors

Some states allow a debtor in serious financial difficulties to obtain an assignment for the benefit of creditors. In this procedure, the debtor voluntarily transfers title to its assets to an assignee, who then liquidates them and distributes the proceeds among the creditors. Assignment for the benefit of creditors is an extreme remedy because it terminates the business. This informal liquidation device (court-supervised in many states) requires that all creditors consent or at least agree to refrain from taking separate action. Appointing a custodian over the debtor's assets gives creditors the right to file an involuntary bankruptcy court petition.

Bankruptcy Code Protection

A formal bankruptcy filing is required when suits have been filed against the debtor, and its property is under garnishment or attachment or threatened by foreclosure or eviction.

Bankruptcy Court proceedings usually result when the debtors financial condition makes it impossible to acquire additional funds. When the debtor agrees to bankruptcy court proceedings, the assets' liquidation value often represents only a small fraction of the debtor's total liabilities. If the business is liquidated, the creditors receive only a small percentage of their claims. The debtor is discharged of its debts and is free to start over. The business and all the assets, however, are lost. Normally, liquidation proceedings result in large losses to the debtor, to the creditor, and also the business community. Chapter 7 of the Bankruptcy Code governs liquidation proceedings. The Bankruptcy Code has another option that grants relief to the debtor who will then have enough time to negotiate agreements with creditors. Chapters 11, 12, and 13 of the Bankruptcy Code govern this procedure, referred to as "reorganization" cases.

The Bankruptcy Code and the Bankruptcy Court

Recent History. The Bankruptcy Reform Act of 1978 was passed and signed on November 6, 1978. This legislation repealed the Bankruptcy Act of 1898 and its amendments (including the Chandler Act of 1938) and applies to all cases filed on or after October 1, 1979. The few remaining cases filed before that date are governed by the old law as to the parties' substantive rights and many procedures. Congress passed the Bankruptcy Tax Bill of 1980, effective October 1, 1979. The Bankruptcy Reform Act of 1978 addresses all the bankruptcy court proceedings, except for federal taxes. The 1980 tax bill establishes the procedures regarding federal income taxes.

In July 1984, Congress passed the Bankruptcy Amendments and Federal Judgeships Act of 1984 that changed the bankruptcy court system and several provisions of the Bankruptcy Code. In 1986, Congress again amended the Bankruptcy Code with the Bankruptcy Judges, United States Trustee, and Family Farmer Bankruptcy Act of 1986. This act, among other provisions, expanded the pilot programs using U.S. trustees to all federal districts and added Chapter 12 to help family farmers reorganize.

In 1983, the U.S. Supreme Court submitted to Congress bankruptcy rules that supplement but may not contradict the Bankruptcy Code. These rules, effective August 1, 1983, deal primarily with matters of form, practice, and procedure. These rules prescribe official bankruptcy forms that one must follow, with alterations as appropriate, in filing the petition and other reports that the code or the rules require. For example, the schedules that must be filed with the petition or shortly thereafter should follow the format of Official Form No. 6. In 1987, several revisions were made to the Bankruptcy Rules.

The bankruptcy law appears in Title 11 of the U.S. Code. The code has eight chapters:

Chapter 1	General provisions
Chapter 3	Case administration
Chapter 5	Creditors, the debtor, and the estate
Chapter 7	Liquidation
Chapter 9	Adjustment of debts of a municipality
Chapter 11	Reorganization
Chapter 12	Adjustment of debts of a family farmer with regular income
Chapter 13	Adjustment of debts of an individual with regular income

Chapters 1, 3, and 5 apply to all proceedings under the Code except Chapter 9, to which only specified sections of Chapters 1, 3, and 5 apply. A case under the Bankruptcy Code—Chapters 7, 9, 11, 12, or 13—is referred to as a "Title 11" case.

Bankruptcy Courts. The Bankruptcy Reform Act of 1978 established a bankruptcy court ("the court") in each judicial district with jurisdiction to decide almost any bankruptcy-related matter. This jurisdiction included not only the traditional case matters such as objections to discharge or claim but also affirmative actions against third parties, such as for the recovery of preferential transfers or fraudulent transfer actions. As originally passed, the court also had jurisdiction to hear matters related to antitrust claims, personal injury claims, wrongful death claims, and any other matter related to the bankruptcy case. This authority to settle all case-related claims was restricted, however, first by a Supreme Court decision, then by temporary rules, and more permanently by the 1984 amendments.

The Bankruptcy Amendments and Federal Judgeship Act of 1984 provides that the bankruptcy judge may hear and decide all cases and all "core proceedings" arising in a case that the district court refers to the bankruptcy court. The 1984 act defines "core proceedings" as including the following:

- Matters concerning administration of the estate.
- Allowance or disallowance of claims and determination of exemption claims.
- Counterclaims by the estate against persons filing claims.
- Orders relating to obtaining of credit.
- Orders relating to turnover of property of the estate.
- Proceedings to determine, avoid, or recover preferences.
- Motions to terminate or modify the automatic stay.
- Proceedings to determine, avoid, or recover fraudulent conveyances.
- Determination as to the dischargeability of debts.
- Objections to discharge.
- Determinations of validity, extent, or priority of liens.
- Confirmation of plans.
- Orders approving the use or lease of property, including the use of cash collateral.
- Orders approving the sale of property of the estate.
- Other proceedings affecting an estate's liquidation, or the adjustment, of the debtor–creditor or the equity–security holder relationship. Exceptions are personal injury tort or wrongful death claims that are heard in the district court where the bankruptcy case is pending or where the claim arose, as determined by the district court where the bankruptcy case is pending.

Chapter Selection. The Bankruptcy Code consists of five chapters under which a petition can be filed. An individual may file under Chapters 7, 11, 12, or 13. A partnership or corporation may file under Chapters 7, 11, or 12. A municipality files under Chapter 9. The following sections discuss the general provisions of Chapters 7, 11, 12, and 13.

Chapter 7—Liquidation. Chapter 7 addresses the liquidation of a debtor in financial trouble. It provides for a trustee's appointment, liquidation of the business, the estate's distribution to the creditors, and discharge of the debtor from liability. All persons and entities may file a petition under Chapter 7, except railroads, domestic insurance companies, banks (including savings and loan associations, building and loan associations, credit unions, etc.), and foreign insurance companies and banks engaged in the insurance and banking business in the United States. Although farmers and nonprofit corporations may file voluntary petitions, their creditors may not bring them involuntarily into the bankruptcy court.

The person filing voluntarily need not be insolvent in either the bankruptcy or equity sense; the petitioner must simply have debts. As soon as the court grants an order for relief, the U.S. Trustee will appoint a disinterested person from a panel of private trustees to serve as the interim trustee. A person serving as trustee in an involuntary case prior to the order for relief may also be appointed as interim trustee.

A creditors' meeting called under § 341(a) may elect a trustee if at least 20 percent of the amount of the qualifying claims requests an election. To be eligible to vote, creditors must hold an allowable, undisputed, fixed, liquidated, unsecured claim, cannot have an interest materially adverse to other creditors' interest, and cannot be "insiders." ("Insiders" include relatives of individual debtors and directors, officers, or persons-in-control of corporate debtors.) To elect a trustee, holders of at least 20 percent of the qualifying claims must vote, and the candidate must receive a majority in dollar amount of those voting. If a trustee is not elected, the interim trustee will serve as trustee. Typically, creditors do not elect a trustee, and the interim trustee continues.

In addition to voting for a trustee, the creditors' may also elect a committee of 3 to 11 creditors. Each eligible committee member must hold an allowable unsecured claim. The committee will consult with the trustee regarding the estate's administration, make recommendations to the trustee regarding the performance of his duties, and submit to the court any questions affecting the estate's administration. Unlike Chapter 11 cases where the U.S. trustee appoints creditors' committees, a creditors' committee will not serve in a Chapter 7 liquidation unless the creditors elect one.

Section 723(a) provides that if a partnership's property cannot fully satisfy the claims of the partnership and if a general partner is personally liable, a claim exists against the general partner for the entire deficiency. According to § 723(b), the trustee must seek recovery first from the general partners that are not debtors in a bankruptcy case. The court can order the general partners to provide assurance that the partnership deficiency will be paid or may order general partners not to dispose of their property.

The trustee may, with court approval, operate the business for a short time if this will increase the amount available to creditors. After the estate has been liquidated and the secured claims have been satisfied to the extent allowed, the remaining amount shall be distributed to the claim holders in a specified order. Unless a claim is subordinated under § 510, § 726(a) distributes the balance in the following order:

1. Priority claims as set forth in § 507.
2. General unsecured claims who filed proof of claim on time or those who filed late because of lack of notice or knowledge of the case.

3. General unsecured claims filed late.
4. Allowed secured or unsecured claims, not compensation for actual pecuniary losses, for fines, penalties, forfeitures, or damages suffered by the claim holder.
5. Interest on the preceding claims at the legal rate from the date of filing the petition.
6. Any balance to the debtor.

Section 726(b) provides for claims within a particular classification to be paid on a pro rata basis when the funds do not fully satisfy all the claims of a particular classification. This policy has one exception: If the funds are not available to pay all administrative expenses and part of the administrative expenses related to a Chapter 11, 12, or 13 case prior to conversion to Chapter 7, then those administrative expenses incurred in Chapter 7 after conversion will be paid first. Thus professionals' fees in a Chapter 11 case unpaid at the time of conversion, might not be fully paid if insufficient funds exist for all administrative expenses in a subsequent Chapter 7. After the assets have been liquidated and the proceeds distributed in proper order, the trustee will make a final report and file a final account of the estate's administration with the court. The trustee will then be discharged from further responsibility.

SIPC Liquidation. A special type of liquidation that may require accounting services is a stockbroker liquidation. The Securities Investor Protection Act of 1970, as amended and §§ 741–752 of Chapter 7 of the Bankruptcy Code govern a stockbroker or stock dealer liquidation. The Securities Investor Protection Corporation (SIPC) is responsible for the liquidation of a troubled stockbroker. The membership of SIPC—a nonprofit corporation—comprises all persons registered as brokers or dealers under § 15(b) of the Securities Exchange Act of 1934. Through an annual assessment from its members, SIPC establishes a fund to cover the costs to customers of a stockbroker's liquidation.

As soon as the court issues a protective decree, it appoints a trustee—and an attorney for the trustee—to liquidate the broker or dealer. The trustee and attorney may be associated with the same firm. Usually, the trustee in a SIPC liquidation is an attorney, but accountants have also served in this capacity. The court that issues the protective decree appoints the trustee. The SIPC may appoint itself or one of its examiners as trustee when the unsecured general creditors and subordinated claims total less than $750,000 and the debtor has fewer than 500 customers.

The trustee must satisfy customer accounts promptly and orderly. A stockbroker liquidation satisfies claims in one of two ways. If the records are orderly, the trustee may—with SIPC approval—transfer the customers' accounts to another broker. The trustee may waive or modify the required written statement of claim and enter into an agreement with the broker receiving the accounts to cover shortages of cash or securities in customer accounts sold or transferred. SIPC funds cover any cash or security shortages.

The second approach involves settling the accounts directly with the customers. Each customer receives a claim form, and the stockbroker's records are then compared with the customer's proof of claim. Once these have been reconciled, a check or securities or both is then sent to satisfy the customers' accounts. This approach requires more time than transferring the customers' accounts to another broker; the direct settlement approach is generally used, however, to liquidate small brokers or brokers with poor customer account records.

Chapter 11—Reorganization. Chapter 11 provides the debtor with court protection, allows the debtor (or trustee) to continue operating the business while a plan is being developed, and minimizes the substantial economic losses associated with liquidation. Chapter 11 allows the debtor to use different procedures depending on the nature of the debtor's problems and the creditors' needs. Agreements under this chapter can affect unsecured creditors, secured creditors, and stockholders. A voluntary or involuntary petition can be filed under Chapter 11. Once the involuntary petition is filed, the court may, at the request of a party in interest, appoint a trustee. The appointment is not mandatory, and the debtor may continue to operate the business as if a bankruptcy petition had not been filed, except that certain transactions may be avoided under the Bankruptcy Code. If the creditors prove the petition's allegations, the court enters an order for relief, and the case proceeds in a manner identical to a voluntary case. The Bankruptcy Code provides that a creditors' committee will be appointed in a Chapter 11 case. Chapter 11 proceedings include assessing whether the business (or part of the business) can be reorganized. If not, the business might be sold or liquidated. The current bankruptcy law allows that, if the business should be liquidated, the debtor may propose a plan that would liquidate the business without converting the proceedings to Chapter 7.

In Chapter 11, the debtor will continue operating the business unless a party in interest requests that the court appoint a trustee for specified grounds. A trustee appointment is the exception, not the rule. An order to allow the debtor to continue operating the business is not required

A party cannot solicit a plan's acceptance or rejection from the affected creditors and stockholders unless they receive a written court-approved disclosure statement. Section 1125(b) of the Bankruptcy Code requires that this disclosure statement must be provided before or concurrent with the solicitation. The court must approve the disclosure statement, after notice and hearing, as containing adequate information.

When the business is operated by the debtor-in-possession, the debtor has 120 days after the order for relief to file a plan and 180 days after the order for relief to obtain acceptance before other parties can file a plan. This is sometimes referred to as the "*plan exclusivity period*," and the court may extend these deadlines. After the creditors and the equity holders have approved the plan, the court will hold a hearing to confirm the plan and discharge the debts that the plan does not provide for.

Commencement of Case

A voluntary case begins when a debtor files a bankruptcy petition that constitutes an order for relief resulting in the debtor and the debtor's property being under the court's supervision.

An involuntary petition can also be filed by creditors with aggregate unsecured claims of at least $5000 and can be initiated only under Chapters 7 or 11. If 12 or more creditors hold unsecured claims, at least 3 creditors must sign the petition; if less than 12 creditors are unsecured, a single creditor can force the debtor into bankruptcy. Only one of two requirements must be satisfied for the creditors to force the debtor into bankruptcy:

1. The debtor generally fails to pay its debts as they become due, or
2. Within 120 days prior to the petition, a custodian was appointed, or a custodian took possession of substantially all the debtor's property.

Only an individual, partnership, or corporation can be forced into bankruptcy. Governmental units, estates, and trusts cannot have an involuntary petition filed against them. Section 303(a) provides that neither a farmer nor a nonprofit corporation can be forced into bankruptcy.

If the creditors can prove the allegations set forth in the involuntary petition (or if they are not promptly contested), the court will enter an order for relief, and the case will proceed. If the creditors cannot prove their allegations, the case will be dismissed. To discourage creditors from filing unwarranted petitions, § 303(i) provides that the court may require the petitioners to cover the debtor's costs and reasonable attorney's fees, compensate for any damages resulting from the trustee (if appointed) taking possession of debtor's property, and, if filed in bad faith, for any damages—including punitive—caused by the filing.

The Automatic Stay

A petition filed under the Bankruptcy Code results in an automatic stay of the creditors actions and prohibits any party, with minor exceptions, including unsecured creditors and creditors having a security or adverse interest in the debtor's property, from interfering with the debtor or its property, regardless of the property's location, until the stay is modified or removed. The debtor or the trustee may use, sell, or lease property (other than cash collateral) in the ordinary course of business without notice or hearing if the business has been authorized to operate in a Chapter 7, 11, 12, or 13 proceeding and the court has not restricted the debtor's or trustee's powers in the order authorizing operation of the business.

Section 362(a) lists eight acts and conducts subject to the automatic stay:

1. The commencement or continuation of a judicial, administrative, or other action or proceeding against the debtor including the issuance or employment of process, that could have been commenced before the petition date or would be commenced to recover a claim that arose prior to the commencement of the case in the bankruptcy court.
2. The enforcement against the debtor or against property of the estate of a judgement obtained before the commencement of the case.
3. Any act to obtain possession of property of the estate to exercise control over the property of the estate.
4. Any act to create, perfect, or enforce any lien against property of the estate.
5. Any act to create, perfect, or enforce against property of the debtor any lien to the extent that such lien secures a claim that arose before the commencement of the case.

6. Any act to collect, assess, or recover a claim against the debtor that arose before the commencement of the case.
7. The setoff of any debt owing to the debtor that arose before the commencement of the case against any claim.
8. The commencement or continuation of a proceeding before the United States Tax Court concerning the debtor.

The stay of an act against the estate's property continues, unless modified, until the estate no longer owns the property. The stay of any other act continues until the case is closed or dismissed, or the debtor is either granted or denied a discharge. The automatic stay does not apply against initiating or continuing a criminal action against the debtor, enforcing governmental police or regulatory powers and certain other actions.

Under § 362(d) the court may grant relief, after notice and hearing, by terminating, annulling, modifying, or conditioning the stay. The court may grant relief for cause, including the lack of adequate protection of the interest of a secured creditor seeking relief. Relief may be granted from an act against property under Chapter 11 if the debtor does not have an equity in the property and the property is not necessary for an effective reorganization.

For example, suppose that a creditor holds a first mortgage debt of $100,000 on real property owned by the debtor having a value, estimated by the creditor, of $75,000. The creditor will seek relief from the stay by claiming that the debtor has no equity in the property, that the property is not essential to the debtor's reorganization, or that reorganization is not possible or feasible, and that the creditor should be allowed to foreclose on the property. The debtor will argue the opposite and claim that the value exceeds $75,000.

The parties in interest must consider whether an asset will diminish in value. Often the loan's collateral is the debtor's inventory and accounts receivable. Their value may constantly change because of continued business operatons. "Cash collateral" is the cash generated from selling inventory or collecting accounts receivable. The creditor's collateral must be protected and its use subject to challenge by a "relief from stay" motion before the court.

The use of cash collateral and the related adequate protection is complicated, and often key in a Chapter 11 reorganization proceeding.

Filing Schedules and the Statement of Affairs

"Schedules" are a prescribed form for listing the debtor's assets and liabilities, required by § 521. The schedules list assets at market value and briefly describe the asset and its location. Each individual liability is reported in defined classifications:

1. Creditors having priority (as defined by statute)
2. Creditors holding security
3. Creditors having unsecured claims without priority

For secured claims without priority, the schedules report the related collateral and its market value.

The schedules also note if the claim's status is "disputed", by the debtor. If it is not disputed, the claim is filed for the amount shown on the debtor's schedules. Claims may also be listed as contingent, unmatured, and unliquidated.

The Statement of Financial Affairs (not to be confused with accountants' use of the same term) is a prescribed series of questions concerning the debtor, its business, its financial records, and other historical information.

These reports are filed with the bankruptcy court when the petition is filed or shortly thereafter. They become the basis for inquiry by creditors, a trustee, or other parties in interest. The debtor's accountant often assists in the preparation of these reports.

Employment of Professionals

In Bankruptcy Court proceedings, all professionals must, upon application to the court, obtain an order authorizing their engagement under § 327. The professional should obtain this order prior to commencing services. If work must start before obtaining such an order, it must be obtained shortly thereafter and should request it be "nuncprotunc" (retroactive treatment).

Any engagement that will request payment from the bankruptcy estate must be authorized by the court otherwise, it may reject any compensation requests even though the services were performed.

Engagements that must have the court's authority (excluding services as a trustee or examiner where the order of appointment suffices) include services as accountant or expert witness for the debtor, trustee, or official creditors committee. If a creditor or other parties in interest engage a professional and they agree to pay for services, the fee application process is not applicable.

The application for employment of professionals must disclose all former and current relationships between the accountant and the debtor or any other parties involved.

Under § 330, fees for services may be paid only after submitting detailed applications and the court holds a noticed hearing. The accountant should consider the assistance of attorneys in preparing fee applications. The fee applications contain more detail than required in other areas of professional practice. The fee application should describe specifically the service performed, the date it was performed, the time (sometimes in tenths of an hour), and charges involved. Each individual working on the engagement must provide descriptive and detailed time records. The court, the U.S. Trustee's office, and all parties in interest may challenge the fee application: All compensation must be reasonable, for actual and necessary services rendered, and inadequate time records may be a basis for a reduction or denial of compensation.

Debtor-in-Possession

The management of a Chapter 11 debtor who continues to control and operate the business (as opposed to a trustee) is referred to as the *debtor-in-possession*. Under § 1107, management has a fiduciary responsibility that must be exercised with utmost care, and the creditors' interest must be placed above the best interest of the shareholders.

Many actions of a debtor-in-possession (like those of a trustee) require the court's prior approval. Such actions include setting wages for key management personnel, hiring professionals, obtaining additional capital by way of loans or issuing new equity certificates, pledging assets, and selling assets (other than goods normally held for sale). Counsel should be consulted in all such cases.

Creditors and Equity Security Holders Committees

In Chapter 11, a committee of unsecured creditors is appointed soon after an order for relief is entered. Other creditor and/or equity security holder committees may also be appointed, though this usually occurs only in larger cases. The committees generally consist of the seven largest parties in each class who agree to serve. Under § 1103, the committees monitor the debtor's activities and will be the primary negotiating bodies regarding the reorganization plan. The committee members must act in a fiduciary capacity to benefit all members in their class and not for their individual interest. The official committees may apply to the court for authority to engage professionals to assist them. This offers another opportunity for a CPA knowledgeable in bankruptcy proceedings to provide service.

Surprisingly, the appointed committees are often inactive. An active committee can assist the debtor when a good working relationship exists. This relationship becomes important when the debtor seeks the acceptance of a proposed reorganization plan. Without support, the debtor will have difficulty obtaining a plan's acceptance. Open, truthful, and complete communications between the debtor and the committees help ensure success.

The creditor and equity security holders committee also must actively protect their own interest. All committees must see that adequate controls exist to assure that the debtor's assets are is not dissipated.

Trustee and Examiner

Under § 1104, the bankruptcy court may, after notice and hearing, appoint a trustee for cause. Cause includes . . . "fraud, dishonesty, incompetence, or gross mismanagement of the affairs of the debtor by current management, either before or after the commencement of the case, or similar cause if such appointment is in the interest of creditors, any equity security holders, and other interests of the estate."

If the court does not appoint a trustee, upon request of a party in interest and after notice and hearing, the court

> may order the appointment of an examiner to conduct such an investigation of the debtor as is appropriate, including an investigation of any allegations of fraud, dishonesty, incompetence, misconduct, mismanagement, or irregularity in the management of the affairs of the debtor of or by current or former management of the debtor . . .

The court may appoint an examiner upon request if the court finds such an appointment to be in the best interests of creditors, any equity security holders or other interests of the debtor's bankruptcy estate, or if the unsecured liabilities exceed $5 million.

A trustee becomes the company's chief executive and, like a debtor-in-possession, must file operating reports and seek the court's approval for the sale of assets not in the ordinary course of business. According to § 1106, the trustee also has all the duties of a debtor-in-possession and investigates

> the acts, assets, liabilities, and financial condition of the debtor, the operation of the debtors' business and the desirability of the continuance of such business, and any other matter relevant to the case or to the formulation of a plan [of reorganization]. . . .

and prepares a report of his investigation of the debtor's affairs and its current and past management.

Usually, an examiner only performs an investigation and reports the findings. The court may, however, limit or expand these duties and has recently tended more toward expansion.

A trustee or examiner may be selected from (1) a panel of people who devote most or all of their time as trustees (listed by the U.S. Trustee) or (2) a panel of parties who possess particular expertise in business and financial management. Attorneys and CPAs often fill this role.

A trustee is compensated based on a percentage of monies disbursed. The percentage is set by § 326 (15 percent on the first $1000 or less, 6 percent on the next $2000, and 3 percent on the amount exceeding $3000). The court may award less than the percentage formula. A trustee's compensation depends largely on the case facts and the trustee's ability.

An examiner usually receives an hourly rate as established by the court.

Filing Operating Reports

The court receives monthly operating reports that reflect the financial activities of the bankruptcy estate. The reports detail cash receipts, cash disbursements, and cash position data as well as other financial information in a format prescribed by the U.S. Trustee.

The operating reports provide the key information linkage between the debtor, the court, and the court-appointed committees (i.e., the official unsecured creditors committee).

Liquidation vs. Reorganization

Should the debtor liquidate or try to reorganize? If that question was not analyzed and answered before the debtor filed a petition for relief, it certainly demands top priority after filing a Chapter 11 petition.

EXHIBIT 12-1. A TO Z MANUFACTURING CORPORATION ANALYSIS OF FREE AND PLEDGED ASSETS AS OF DECEMBER 31, 1990

			Assets Pledged as Collateral to Creditors							Summary		
	Book Values	Estimated Liquidation Values	Other Creditors	Last National Bank	Supplier A	Mortgage Company	Finance Company A	Finance Company B	Unencumbered Assets	Total	Partially Secured	Fully Secured
Cash in banks	$13,800	$13,800		$5,500					$8,300			
Accounts receivable	327,500	205,000		205,000								
Allowances for doubtful accounts	(32,000)											
Inventories												
Supplies and spare parts	19,000	7,500							7,500			
Raw materials	34,000	20,000			$15,000				5,000			
Work-in-progress	17,000	4,000		4,000								
Finished goods	47,000	22,500		22,500								
Prepaid expenses	7,500	4,500							4,500			
Other assets	8,500	8,500	$8,500									
Land	70,000	150,000				$150,000						
Buildings	218,500	230,000				230,000						
Machinery and equipment	102,500	58,000					$25,000	$33,000				
Vehicles	58,700	21,000						21,000				
Leasehold improvements	52,000											
Allowance for depreciation	(113,000)											
Notes receivable	75,000	15,000							15,000			
Accrued interest receivable	15,000											
Trademarks and patents	6,000	1,000							1,000			
Total assets	$927,000	760,800	8,500	237,000	15,000	380,000	25,000	54,000	$41,300			
Less assets book value		927,000										
(Loss) on Liquidation		($166,200)										
Centralized debts												
Principal balance			11,500	250,000	13,000	258,400	24,500	73,000		$630,400	$359,000	$271,400
Accrued interest				5,200	400	6,500	900	4,200		17,200	10,300	6,900
Real property taxes						19,000				19,000		19,000
Total collateralized debts			11,500	255,200	13,400	283,900	25,400	77,200		666,600	369,300	297,300
Collateral excess (shortage)			($3,000)	($18,200)	$1,600	$96,114	($400)	($23,200)		$52,900	($44,800)	$97,700

As previously discussed, the debtor's assets are reported at their market value in the Schedule of Assets and Liabilities filed with the court initially. The optimistic debtor usually overstates these "market" values, hoping to reorganize.

Valuing the business as a going concern should be weighted against selling the business or some of its assets. Part of the business may be highly marketable, whereas another portion requires liquidation.

Consider a single product line business operation, for example. Exhibit 12-1 summarizes the value of *specific* assets related, where appropriate, to the *specific* debt for which the asset serves as collateral. These relationships may become controversial, in the eyes of specific creditors.

A debt may be collateralized, but is it fully secured? Consider the situation for Finance Company B in Exhibit 12-1:

Liquidation value of	
Machinery and equipment	$33,000
Vehicles	21,000
Total collateral value to Finance Company B	$54,000
Debt owing to Finance Company B:	
Principal	$73,000
Accrued interest	4,200
Total debt	$77,200
Secured debt	$54,000
Undersecured debt	23,200
Total debt	$77,200

Finance Company B is undercollateralized. In the bankruptcy proceeding, Finance Company B would fall into two separate creditor classifications that probably would not (unless this were a solvency case) be treated similarly in a liquidation or reorganization plan. Note that a collaterized debt is not always fully secured.

Using the information summarized in Exhibit 12-1, one can prepare the debtor's Statement of Affairs, Exhibit 12-2 (not to be confused with the required questionnaire previously discussed). Such an analysis and statement provides an overview of the debtor's liquidation situation and a foundation for a reorganization or liquidation plan. One can modify it for a combination of alternatives. The statement's preparer must understand the debt terms, classifications, their treatment and priorities as specified in the Bankruptcy Code, the documents creating the debt and collateral interest, and the related collateral values.

In this example, what would an unsecured creditor prefer: liquidation with a small return ($.16 on the dollar) or a gamble on a reorganization? To answer that question, the creditor needs additional information regarding the prospects for the debtor's future operation.

The unsecured creditor will compare the liquidation return of $.16 with the uncertain return under the proposed reorganization plan and the likelihood of the debtor's success under the plan.

EXHIBIT 12-2. A TO Z MANUFACTURING CORPORATION STATEMENT OF AFFAIRS AS OF DECEMBER 31, 1990

Assets	Net Book Values	Estimated Liquidation Values	Gain/(Loss) upon Liquidation	Estimated Assets Available for Unsecured Creditors
Assets pledged to fully secured creditors:				
Inventories	$15,000	$15,000	$0	
Real property	247,500	380,000	132,500	
Total		395,000		
Less fully secured debts (contra)		297,300		
Excess available for unsecured creditors		$97,700		$97,700
Assets pledged to partially secured creditors:				
Cash	5,500	5,500	0	
Accounts receivable	295,500	205,000	(90,500)	
Inventories	64,000	26,500	(37,500)	
Other assets	8,500	8,500	0	
Machinery and equipment	71,500	58,000	(13,500)	
Vehicles	26,700	21,000	(5,700)	
Total deducted (contra)		$324,500		

Liabilities and (Deficiency) in Net Assets	Net Book Values		Amounts Unsecured
Liabilities fully secured:			
Mortgage payable	$264,900	$264,900	
Real property taxes payable	19,000	19,000	
Payable to suppliers	13,400	13,400	
Total deducted (contra)		$297,300	
Liabilities partially secured: Payable to bank on line of credit	255,200	$255,200	
Payable to finance companies	102,600	102,600	
Payable to other creditors	11,500	11,500	
Total		369,300	
Less assets pledged (contra)		324,500	
Amount unsecured		$44,800	$44,800

Assets unencumbered:				
Cash	8,300	$8,300	0	8,300
Inventories	38,000	12,500	(25,500)	12,500
Prepaid expenses recoverable	7,500	4,500	(3,000)	4,500
Notes and interest receivable	90,000	15,000	(75,000)	15,000
Trademarks and patents	6,000	1,000	(5,000)	1,000
Leasehold improvements	43,000	0	(43,000)	0
Total		$41,300		139,000
Less debts having priority (contra)				107,500
Assets estimated to be available for unsecured creditors (approximately 16¢/$)				31,500
Estimated deficiency to unsecured creditors				169,300
Estimated gain/(loss) upon liquidation of assets (deducted contra)			($166,200)	
Totals	$927,000			$200,800

Liabilities with priorities:			
Estimated liquidation and other administrative costs	85,000	$85,000	
Wages payable	10,000	10,000	
Payroll taxes payable	12,500	12,500	
Total deducted (contra)		$107,500	
Unsecured liabilities:			
Trade payables	121,000		121,000
Loans from shareholder	35,000		35,000
Total Liabilities	930,100		200,800
Stockholders' (deficiency):			
Common stock issued	1,000	$1,000	
Accumulated (deficiency) at December 31, 1990	(4,100)	(4,100)	
Estimated loss upon liquidation (contra)		(166,200)	
Total stockholders (deficiency)	(3,100)	($169,300)	
Totals	$927,000		$200,800

Proofs of Claims or Interests

A creditor files a proof of claim. An equity security holder of a corporation or a general or limited partner of a partnership files a proof of interest.

A properly filed claim, under § 502, is allowed unless a party in interest objects. If the debtor's filed schedules (in a Chapter 11 case) list the creditor's claim or equity security holders' interest as undisputed and the creditor agrees to the amount and classification (i.e., secured vs. unsecured), this is prima facie evidence of the claim's or interest's validity. In such situations the creditor or equity security holder does not need to file a proof of claim or interest. Every creditor should protect its own interest and file a proof of claim. In a Chapter 7 case, creditors must file a proof of claim. Claims may be disallowed for only specific reasons set forth in the Bankruptcy Code.

Remember that a creditor filing a collateralized claim may have two classes of claim:

- A secured claim to the extent of the related equity (based upon value) in the collateral
- An unsecured claim for the balance

Claims administration provides another significant, but often overlooked, opportunity for the CPA to provide a unique service to a bankruptcy estate by combining computer and auditing skills with bankruptcy law knowledge. Depending on the number of claims and interests involved, such services can be highly valued, and computer resources are essential. Such services may include the following:

- Investigating claims and interests
- Comparing proofs of claims and interests filed with the debtor's books and records and the schedules
- Eliminating duplicate proofs of claims and interests
- Classifying secured vs. unsecured, different equity security interests, reorganization plan classes, or other descriptive categories
- Calculating the voting results to accept or reject a reorganization plan
- Determining amounts allowed, allowable, or disallowed
- Determining amounts to be paid for securities (i.e., stock of a corporation) issued according to a reorganization plan
- Maintaining the claim and interests register and the master mailing list.

Duplicate proofs of claim and interest and multiple classifications of a single proof of claim commonly occur. The accountant should discuss materiality and the extent of investigation with the debtor, trustee or the case attorney before undertaking such tasks.

Conversion or Dismissal of Bankruptcy Petition

When a case converts from one chapter to another, § 348(a) provides that the conversion constitutes an order for relief under the new chapter; the petition's filing date, the commencement of the case, and the original relief order do not change. Conversion from one chapter to another terminates the services of any trustee or examiner serving at the time of conversion.

Conversion from Chapter 7. Section 706 allows the debtor to convert a case under Chapter 7 to Chapters 11, 12, or 13, provided the case was not previously converted to Chapter 7. The court may also convert a case to Chapter 11 after notice and a hearing, when a party in interest requests such action. Section 707 allows the court to dismiss a Chapter 7 case, after notice and a hearing for cause. Cause includes the debtor's unreasonable delay that is prejudicial to creditors, nonpayment of fees or charges, and failure to punctually file the necessary information and schedules as § 521 requires but only if the U.S. Trustee makes such a motion. The court on its own accord or at the U.S. Trustee's request may also dismiss a Chapter 7 petition consisting primarily of consumer debts if the granting of relief would abuse Chapter 7 provisions.

Conversion from Chapter 11. Section 1112 provides that the debtor may convert a case under Chapter 11 to Chapter 7 unless a trustee has been appointed, the case was commenced involuntarily, or the case was converted to Chapter 11 from another chapter and not at the debtor's request. A party in interest or the U.S. Trustee may request the court to convert a Chapter 11 case to Chapter 7 or to dismiss the case (whichever is in the estate's or the creditor's best interest) for cause including the following:

- Continuing losses and absence of reasonable likelihood of rehabilitation
- Inability to implement a plan
- The debtor's unreasonable delay that is prejudicial to creditors
- Failure to propose a plan within the court-imposed deadline
- Denial of every proposed plan and denial of a request for more time to file or modify the plan
- Revocation of a confirmation order
- Inability to consummate a confirmed plan
- The debtor's material default of a confirmed plan
- The plan's termination owing to an occurrence specified in the plan
- Nonpayment of fees and charges

On its own or at the U.S. Trustee's request, the court may convert a voluntary Chapter 11 case to Chapter 7 or dismiss the case (according to the estate's or creditors' best interest) if the debtor fails to file the information and schedules that Section 521 requires.

Classification and Priorities Claims and Interests

Classification. Claims and interests are classified according to § 1122 by their nature, and all claims and interests placed into a particular "class" (a common group) must be substantially similar. The claim's or interest's legal description usually governs its classification. For example, preferred stockholders and common stockholders have different rights and require separate classification. Creditors holding claims collateralized by different property will generally be classified separately.

Priorities. Claims and interests usually receive a priority that does not alter their legal, equitable, and contractual rights. The priority status usually has the following order:

- Collateralized claims to the extent that they are secured but only against the property that is collateral
- "Priority" claims as defined (see later)
- Unsecured claims including undersecured claims
- Equity interests

Section 507 of the Bankruptcy Code creates a special priority category of allowed expenses and claims that have the following order:

a. Administrative expenses and costs of preserving the bankruptcy estate, including compensation for services rendered to the estate after the bankruptcy proceeding begins.
b. Unsecured claims arising after an involuntary case is filed but before an order for relief is entered.
c. Wages earned by an individual within 90 days before the filing date, not to exceed $2,000 per individual.
d. Unsecured claims for contributions to an employee benefit plan related to services rendered within 180 days before the filing date, not to exceed $2,000 multiplied by the number of employees so covered, less:
   i. the aggregate amount paid under (c) and
   ii. the aggregate amount paid by the bankruptcy estate on behalf of the employees to any other benefit plan.
e. Certain unsecured claims of farmers and fisherman, not to exceed $2,000 per individual.
f. Unsecured claims of individuals arising from the deposit of money for the purchase, lease or rent of property, or the purchase of services which were not delivered or provided, not to exceed $900 per individual.
g. The unsecured claims of governmental units, but only for
   i. A tax measured by income or gross receipts for a taxable year ending on or before the petition's filing date and for which a return (if required) was last due (including extensions) within three years prior to filing the bankruptcy petition
   ii. A property tax assessed before the petition's filing date and last due, without penalty, within one year prior to filing the bankruptcy petition.
   iii. A tax collected or withheld in whatever capacity.
   iv. An employment tax on wages, etc., earned from the debtor before the petition's filing date (whether or not paid) for which a return was last due (including extensions) within three years prior to filing the bankruptcy petition.
   v. An excise tax relating to a transaction occurring before the petition's filing date for which a return was last due (including extensions) within three years before filing the bankruptcy petition.

vi. Custom duties on merchandise imported within one year before filing the bankruptcy petition.
vii. A penalty related to the priority claims specified above and as compensation for actual pecuniary loss.

Subordination. The court, under the authority of § 510(c), after notice and hearing, may subordinate a claim or interest. Such subordination, under principles of equity, usually occurs when the claimant, generally an insider, is guilty of inequitable conduct.

Preferences and Fraudulent Transfers

Matters relating to preferences and fraudulent transfers provide another major focus of assistance by CPAs with bankruptcy law knowledge. Detecting and confirming such transactions requires the CPA to identify exactly when the debtor became insolvent and to perform a liquidation analysis. A trustee may void preferences and fraudulent transfers by bringing an action before the court.

Section 547 allows the trustee to void the transfer of the debtor's property as a "preference" under the following conditions:

1. The transfer benefitted a creditor.
2. The transfer was for or on account of an antecedent debt owed by the debtor before such transfer was made.
3. The transfer was made when the debtor was insolvent.
4. The transfer was made on or within 90 days preceding the filing date (or 1 year if that creditor was an "insider" at the time of the transaction).
5. The creditor received more from the transfer than it would have received if the case was in a Chapter 7 liquidation, if the transfer had not occurred, and under other Bankruptcy Code provisions (i.e., under the reorganization plan).

Exceptions to a preference transfer include the following:

1. Contemporaneous exchange for new value
2. A transfer made in the debtor's ordinary course of business
3. The creation of a security interest in property acquired for new value

Section 548 allows the trustee to void the transfer of the debtor's interest in property or any obligation incurred by the debtor, made or incurred within 1 year before filing the bankruptcy petition if the debtor

1. Made such transfer or incurred such obligation intending to hinder, delay, or defraud a creditor or
2. Received less than fair value and
   a. Was or became insolvent from such transaction
   b. Left the debtor with unreasonably small capital
   c. Intended or believed that the debtor would incur debts that the debtor could not repay as they matured.

Discharge of Debts

The extent to which a debt is discharged depends on (1) whether the debtor is an individual or corporation, (2) the chapter under which the petition is filed, and (3) the debt's nature and priority.

Individual Debtors. Section 523 exempts several debts from an individual debtor's discharge. (In bankruptcy, *discharge* refers to releasing a debtor from an obligation.) These debts are exempt from discharge under Chapters 7, 11, and 12, but Chapter 13 has special provisions. The § 523(a) exemptions include the following:

a. A tax with priority under Section 507(a) (2) or (7) or related to a tax return which was not filed or was filed late (and within two years of the petition date) or that was willfully evaded.
b. Debts from which money, property, services or a credit renewal was obtained by false pretenses, false representations or fraud. This includes materially and intentionally false written statements concerning the debtor's financial condition upon which the creditor reasonably relied. Also exempt from discharge are individuals' consumer debts—if more than $500 is owed to a single creditor for "luxury goods or services" incurred within forty days before the order for relief—and cash advances exceeding $1,000 that extend consumer credit under an open-end credit plan obtained by an individual within twenty days before the relief order.
c. Debts which were not scheduled in time to allow creditors to protect their rights, unless they had notice or knowledge of the proceedings.
d. Debts for fraud or defalcation while acting in a fiduciary capacity, embezzlement, or larceny.
e. Alimony, maintenance, or support obligations.
f. Debts due to willful and malicious injury to another entity or its property.
g. Debts for fines, penalties, and forfeitures that are not compensation for actual pecuniary loss payable to a governmental unit except a penalty relating to a non-dischargeable tax or to a tax due which relates to a transaction which occurred more than three years prior to bankruptcy.
h. Most educational loans, unless the loan first became due more than five years before the petition date or an undue hardship would be imposed.
i. Debts from judgments or consent decrees resulting from operating a motor vehicle while intoxicated.
j. Debts owed that were or could have been listed in a prior bankruptcy case, if the debtor waived a discharge or had been denied a discharge for a statutory reason other than the six year limitation.

Section 523(c) provides that the creditor who is owed a debt that might be exempted from discharge as a result of false statements, for fraud, embezzlement, or larceny or for willful or malicious injuries as specified here, must initiate proceedings to obtain the exception to discharge. Otherwise, those debts will be discharged unless the court denies the debtor's entire discharge.

Chapter 7 Cases. Section 727 contains 10 conditions in a Chapter 7 case that will result in denial of a discharge:

a. The debtor is not an individual.
b. Within one year prior to the filing of the petition, the debtor, transferred, destroyed, or concealed—or permitted to be transferred, destroyed, or concealed—any of his property with the intent to hinder, delay, or defraud his creditor.
c. The debtor failed to keep or preserve adequate books of accounts or financial records.
d. The debtor knowingly and fraudulently made a false oath or claim, offered or received a bribe, or withheld information related to the case.
e. The debtor failed to explain satisfactorily any losses of assets or deficiency of assets to meet his liabilities.
f. The debtor refused to obey any lawful order or answer any material questions in the course of the proceedings after being granted immunity from self incrimination.
g. Within one year before filing the petition, the defendant committed any of the above acts related to another bankruptcy case concerning an insider.
h. Within the past six years the debtor received a discharge in bankruptcy under Chapter 13 of the Code or Chapter XIII of prior law unless payments under the plan totaled 100 percent of the allowed unsecured claims or at least 70 percent of such claims under a plan proposed in good faith and ascertained to have been performed according to the debtor's best effort.
i. After the order for relief, the debtor submits a written waiver of discharge and the court approves it.

Only an individual debtor can obtain a discharge in a Chapter 7 case; a partnership or a corporation may not obtain a discharge in a Chapter 7 case. Also, a corporation or partnership liquidating under a plan adopted in a Chapter 11 case would not obtain a discharge. Because a corporation effectively goes out of business as a result of the liquidation, granting a discharge might be unimportant. A corporation, however, may continue to exist, and shareholders may have kept these shells alive to reactivate later for tax reasons or to avoid the costs of creating another corporation. A debtor will be reluctant to use these shells under the current bankruptcy law because the creditors for prebankruptcy debts may attach any assets owned by the corporation. Section 727(c) provides that the U.S. Trustee, a creditor, or the trustee can object to the court granting the debtor a discharge under § 727(a). Subsection (d) provides that on request of the trustee, a creditor, or the U.S. Trustee, and after a notice and hearing, the court may revoke the discharge if:

a. The discharge was obtained through the debtor's fraud and the requesting party did not know of the fraud until after the discharge was granted.
b. The debtor acquired or was entitled to acquire property that is or should have been the estate's property and knowingly and fraudulently failed to report or deliver the property to the trustee.
c. The debtor refused to obey a lawful court order or respond to material questions approved by the court.

Chapter 11 Cases. Section 1141(d) provides that in a Chapter 11 case, a plan's confirmation discharges the debtor from any debt that arose before the plan's confirmation except to the extent that the plan provides for such debt. This discharge occurs whether the proof of claim was filed or deemed filed, whether § 502 allows such claim, or the claim's holder has accepted the plan. Individuals may not discharge a debt of the type listed in Section 523 (previously above).

Plan of Reorganization

A plan of reorganization (the "plan") is the blueprint for satisfying creditors and equity security holders under Chapter 11 of the Bankruptcy Code. A plan may not completely satisfy all creditors and equity security holders because sufficient assets or earning power may not be available to do so.

Provisions. Section 1123 promulgates mandatory provisions for all Chapter 11 plans:

a. Designate classes of all claims and interests;
b. Specify the unimpaired classes;
c. Specify the treatment of all impaired classes;
d. Provide for identical treatment for each claim or interest in a particular class (unless a particular party agrees to a less favorable treatment);
e. Provide adequate means to implement the plan's provisions such as selling certain assets, merging with other entities, modifying contractual terms, curing defaults or issuing the debtor's securities;
f. If the debtor or its successor is a corporation, the plan must prohibit issuing nonvoting equity securities and provide for the seniority of different equity security classes, etc.;
g. Contain provisions which protect when selecting the best interest of creditors and equity security holders and public policy when selecting management of the reorganized entity.

A plan *may* include other provisions:

a. Impair or leave unimpaired any class of claims or interests;
b. Assume, reject or assign executory contracts or unexpired leases;
c. Settle, adjust, retain and enforce any claim or interest belonging to the debtor;
d. Sell all or substantially all of the debtor's assets and then distribute the proceeds to holders of claims and interests of the debtor;
e. Include any other provision which is consistent with the Bankruptcy Code provisions.

Impaired Claims and Interests. Section 1124 states that claims and interests are "impaired" if the holder's legal, equitable, and contractual rights are altered, if the debtor does not cure any defaults and does not compensate for damages. The debtor may pay with a cash equivalent the allowed amount of the claim or interest at the plan's effective date, thereby removing the impaired classification. Payments over time that equal or exceed the claim's present value at the effective date would also be considered unimpaired.

A successful reorganization plan may have to impair some claims and interests, but this may affect the plan's acceptance or rejection, as discussed below.

Developing the Reorganization Plan. Aside from the technical provisions mandated by the Bankruptcy Code, the key question is feasibility: Will the plan really work? The court formally addresses this question at the confirmation hearing. Some practitioners avoid the feasibility issue until the confirmation hearing. The practitioner who properly addresses the issue early in a plan's development will avoid unnecessray time, cost, and frustration later on. Feasibility should be the first major issue studied in a plan's development and an issue openly addressed in the disclosure statement and the plan's approval hearings.

With this in mind, plan development begins by addressing some very basic questions:

1. Where have we (the debtor) been?
2. Where are we now?
3. How did we get here?
4. What do we have to work with?
5. Where do we want to go?
6. How do we get there?

Each question must be addressed from several viewpoints: economic (financial), marketing and managerial.

To answer the questions, take inventory of the information available and generate information not available. The following sources provide information:

1. Prepetition historical financial reports
2. Postpetition historical financial reports
3. Marketing plans (past and future)
4. Business plans (past and future)
5. The current financial position (accrual basis)
6. Investigation reports relating to the performance and capabilities of the individual management team members and the probable causes of bankruptcy
7. The analysis of claims and interests and their designation to specific "classes"
8. The valuation of specific assets
9. The analysis of current and historical financial information
10. The liquidation analysis
11. The debtor's Schedules of Assets and Liabilities and Statement of Affairs (court-required questionnaire)
12. Reports filed by the trustee, examiner, creditor, or equity security holder committees
13. Operating Reports filed since the petition date
14. The Analysis of Free and Pledged Assets (see Exhibit 12-1)
15. The Statement of Affairs (see Exhibit 12-2)
16. A 5- to 7-year cash flow forecast with information on existing product lines
17. Other useful information

Product line information carries particular importance. One or more products (or services) may be unprofitable when considering the assets and debt or capital that they require. Selling or discontinuing such product or service lines may leave the debtor a smaller but profitable business.

With this in mind, one can reuse and present the cash flow forecast for different alternatives. This will then indicate the cash available to service a reorganization plan that itself should be developed with different alternatives, that is, debt restructure by principal reduction or term revisions, or both; lease or contract rejections, conversion of debt to equity, and the like.

The alternative plans should then be analyzed by giving pro forma effect to the current balance sheet in conjunction with the appropriate cash flow forecast over the subsequent plan life (the time required to complete all terms of the proposed plan). Financial projections must also be considered for the period between the current balance sheet date and the plan's expected effective date.

The parties can then select the proposed plan from the alternatives. Such decisions must be a team effort between the debtor and/or trustee, their attorneys and CPAs and the creditor and equity security holder committees.

Remember to be realistic about the proposed plan's feasibility. If it is not feasible, say so now, for you will probably testify to this question.

Disclosure Statement

A "disclosure statement" presents the proposed reorganization plan to the creditors and equity security holders. It resembles a prospectus in its nature and intended use. The Bankruptcy Code does not specify in detail the disclosure's required content, leaving this to the court's discretion. The Bankruptcy Code in § 1125 does, however, define "adequate information" as "information of a kind, and in sufficient detail, as far as is reasonably practical in light of the nature and history of the debtor and the condition of the debtors' books and records, that would enable a hypothetical reasonable investor typical of holders of claims or interests of the relevant class to make an informed judgment about the plan, . . ."

Required disclosures vary for each case, however. The following matters should be considered:

1. Opinions, disclaimers, etc., concerning the statement's content (here lies a special reporting issue for a CPA);
2. A brief description of the debtor and its current business;
3. A description of the proposed management team including individual profiles and current and proposed compensation;
4. A summary of the proposed reorganization plan including a description of the classes of creditors and equity security holders and the treatment the plan affords each class;
5. Disclosure of related parties, affiliates, and major equity security holders under the plan's terms and a description of the transactions which will change the current situation;

6. A liquidation analysis;
7. Special risk factors;
8. Income tax issues;
9. Financial information, including
   a) Historical operating results for pre- and post- petition periods;
   b) Current financial position;
   c) Cash flow forecast for the plan life;
   d) Pro forma effect of the plan and the forecast.
10. A statement indicating the plan's implementation;
11. A brief description of pending legal proceedings;
12. A valuation of the specific assets and the going concern business;
13. Marketing plans;
14. Major postpetition events and transactions including the appointment and reports of a trustee, examiner, and official creditor or equity security holder committees, and
15. Terms of new debt or security instruments issued or to be issued under the plan's terms

The court must approve the disclosure statement after a noticed hearing, before its release. The CPA may testify on matters concerning the disclosure statement's content and adequacy.

Acceptance or Rejection of the Plan

Each claim or interest holder receives a court-approved disclosure statement, the proposed plan, and a ballot. This is the formal solicitation for the plan's approval in accordance with § 1126. Promises, representations, terms of treatment, and the like that the approved plan and disclosure statement do not include are improper and unauthorized, and these documents should state this caveat.

Each claim or interest holder may vote to accept or reject a proposed reorganization plan. The court, however, presumes that an unimpaired class of claims or interests has accepted the plan and does not require their formal solicitation.

A class of creditor claims has accepted a plan if at least two-thirds in amount *and* more than one-half in number of allowed claims accept the plan.

A class of interests has accepted a plan if at least two-thirds in amount of allowed interests accept the plan.

The required vote computations are based on the total claims or interests by each class that actually votes (as opposed to the entire amount and number of allowed claims or interests composing a defined class). The bankruptcy court fixes the voting period when it approves the ballot or performs other related procedures.

For any bankruptcy case with a large number of creditors or equity security holders, CPAs may also mail the voting materials and receive, tabulate, and report the results.

During the first 120 days after a bankruptcy proceeding begins, the debtor has the exclusive right to file a reorganization plan. After that period, other parties in interest may file a plan. Accordingly, the claim and interest holders may simultaneously vote to accept or reject competing plans.

Confirming the Plan

Following the vote for a proposed reorganization plan, the plan's proponent will seek its confirmation by the court. Section 1128 provides that a court hearing occurs after notice to all parties in interest to give them the opportunity to object to the plan's confirmation.

Section 1129 specifies certain requirements before the bankruptcy court confirms a plan:

1. The plan complies with the applicable provisions of the Bankruptcy Code (Title 11, United States Code).
2. The plan's proponent complies with the applicable provisions of the Bankruptcy Code.
3. The plan has been proposed in good faith and not by any means forbidden by law.
4. Payments made or to be made related to the case or the plan are reasonable and have been approved by the court or are subject to such approval.
5. The plan makes disclosure of management or proposed management, insiders and affiliates.
6. Approval of governmental regulatory bodies concerning rate changes is obtained.
7. Each impaired class of claims and interests accepts the plan or will receive or retain under the plan (as of the plan's effective date) an amount not less than the amount such holders would receive or retain if the debtor were liquidated under Chapter 7 of the Bankruptcy Code. This is sometimes known as the "best interest" test.
8. Each class of claims or interests has accepted the plan (or, if unimpaired, is deemed to have accepted the plan).
9. The plan provides for the treatment of "priority claims."
10. At least one class of impaired claims—other than a class held by insiders—accepts the plan.
11. The plan will not likely be followed by the liquidation or need for further reorganization of the debtor or its successor (if not provided for in the plan). This is the "feasibility" test.
12. All fees payable under Section 1930 of the Bankruptcy Code have been paid or provided for.

Notwithstanding requirement Number 8, the court may, under certain circumstances and upon the proponent's request, confirm the plan if the plan does not discriminate unfairly and if the plan is fair and equitable with respect to an impaired class of claims or interests that rejected the plan. This is known as the "cram-down" provision. Section 1129(b) specifies tests for ascertaining whether a plan is fair and equitable.

Postconfirmation Activities

After the court confirms a reorganization plan, it must be implemented. The implementation date is the "effective date of the plan."

This presents another professional service opportunity. For example, if a plan provides for payments equaling some percentage of an allowed claim or the issuance of equity securities based on a formula related to an allowed claim or interest, one can develop a program to make these calculations. Professionals can assist with the accounting and taxation issues related to a confirmed plan.

Upon completing the plan's implementation according to its terms, the plan is "consummated."

INCOME TAX CONSIDERATIONS

The income tax effect of certain transactions during the administration period and of tax assessments related to pre-bankruptcy periods can impose undue hardship on the debtor, who is already in a tenuous financial position. Frequently, a debtor realizes substantial taxable income from taxable recoveries. Net operating loss carryovers and other offsetting tax deductions sometimes do not nullify the income tax effect. Therefore, in addition to ensuring that all statutory tax reporting and filing requirements are satisfied at the due dates, the accountant must identify those tax aspects that will preserve and enlarge the bankrupt's estate.

This section identifies items that the debtor (and, to a limited extend, creditors and other interested parties) should consider in solving the problems of financially troubled companies. Newton and Bloom's *Tax Planning for the Troubled Business* (revised annually) contains a more detailed discussion of these tax issues.

Assessing Tax Liability

Section 505 of the code authorizes the bankruptcy court to assess a debtor's tax liability, if the tax issue was not contested and adjudicated before the bankruptcy case began. The assessment would include any fine or penalty relating to a tax or any other addition to a tax. The bankruptcy court establishes the tax claims allowed under § 502 of the Bankruptcy Code and the dischargeability of the tax under § 523 of the Bankruptcy Code. Section 505 applies to all types of taxes, including income tax, excise tax, sales tax, unemployment compensation taxes, and so forth. Once the bankruptcy court has established the tax liability under § 505, the IRS can assess the tax against the debtor or, if an individual files the petition, against the estate (§ 505(c)). The automatic stay delays collection.

Before the bankruptcy court can establish the estate's right to a tax refund, the trustee must file a claim for the refund and either receive a determination from the

IRS or allow 120 days to pass after filing the claim. If the IRS has not made a determination within 120 days, the bankruptcy court can then establish the estate's right to a tax refund.

A debtor facing a tax liability can request the taxing unit to assess the liability. The tax unit then has 60 days to notify the debtor that an examination will occur. If the tax unit decides to examine the return, it has 180 days from the request date to take action.

If the taxing unit does not notify the debtor that it plans to examine the debtor or does not complete the examination, it has no recourse.

Responsibility for Filing Income Tax Returns—Corporation

The receiver (under state law), trustee (under a Title 11 case), or assignee who possesses title to all or substantially all of a corporation's property or business is responsible to file the income tax return for the corporation exactly as the corporation would. The bankruptcy trustee, while acting on behalf of a debtor's estate, acts as a fiduciary. The trustee does not represent a separate taxable entity apart from the corporation. Regulations § 1.641(b)-2(b) provide that a corporation in bankruptcy is not a taxable entity separate from the person for whom the fiduciary is acting. Hence the corporation's tax return should include income and expenses of a debtor corporation's trustee. The trustee uses the debtor corporation's identification number. The Bankruptcy Tax Act of 1980 added § 1399 to the Internal Revenue Code (IRC) that provides that no separate tax entity results from a corporation commencing a case under the Bankruptcy Code.

A trustee should file a corporate income tax return annually, regardless of whether the corporation has any income, as long as the corporation exists for tax purposes. A corporation existing during any part of the year must file a return. A corporation does not exist after it ceases business and dissolves, retaining no assets, even though state law may consider it as continuing for certain limited purposes connected with concluding its affairs, such as lawsuits. If the corporation has valuable claims for which it will bring suit during this period, it has retained assets and therefore continues to exist. A corporation does not cease to exist if it is turned over to receivers or trustees who continue operations.

Responsibility for Filing Income Tax Returns—Partnerships and Individuals

Whereas well-established procedures exist for corporations, much controversy existed in the past regarding individual and partnership returns. To eliminate the uncertainty as to whether a separate entity was created, the Bankruptcy Tax Act (1980) added §§ 1398 and 1399 to the Internal Revenue Code (IRC).

Partnerships. Section 1399 of the Internal Revenue Code provides that no entity is created when a partnership files a case under the Bankruptcy Code provisions. The trustee must file a partnership information return under § 6031 of the I.R.C. for the period(s) that the trustee operated the business. The legislative committee reports indicate that the trustee has responsibility to file the partnership return, although the statute does not specifically require it.

In a Letter Ruling (8509038), the IRS held that a partnership's trustee must file Form 1065 only for the year that the trustee was appointed and later years. No obligation exists to file Form 1065 for earlier partnership years. The trustee must, however, cooperate with the IRS by providing all relevant tax information he or she may have concerning prior years. This practice area needs definitive rules because of the practical problems that it presents.

Individuals. When bankruptcy proceedings enter into an individual's affairs, a separate taxable entity is created, consisting of the debtor's property before bankruptcy. After the petition has been filed, the bankruptcy estate can earn income and incur expenses. A trustee (or debtor-in possession) administers these transactions for the creditor's benefit. Concurrently, the individual debtor can also earn income, incur expenses, and acquire property that do not become part of the bankruptcy estate. The separate taxable entities for federal income tax purposes occur in bankruptcy cases under Chapter 7 and 11 of Title 11 of the U.S. Code. No new taxable entity is created, however, under Chapter 13 of the U.S. Code. When the bankruptcy court dismisses a bankruptcy case involving an individual, the estate is not deemed to have been a separate taxable entity.

When the individual and bankruptcy estates are separate entities, they must file separate returns. The estate files Form 1041 for the period beginning with the petition filing date or for any subsequent year if gross income exceeds the exemption amount plus the basic standard deduction, or more as required by IRC § 6012(a)(9). The individual files Form 1040, as usual, and reports all income earned during the year. This includes income earned before bankruptcy proceedings but not the estate's income. IRC § 6012(b)(4) requires that the estate's fiduciary file the return. This would be the trustee, if appointed; otherwise, the debtor-in-possession must file the estate's return.

The new act gives an individual debtor the right to elect to close his taxable year as of the day before the date bankruptcy commences. Individuals in either Chapters 7 or 11 proceedings have this election. The taxpayer using this election must divide his taxable year into two "short" taxable years. The first short year's tax liability is collectible from the bankruptcy estate. The tax is considered a liability before bankruptcy and thus payable by the estate. If the estate does not possess enough assets to pay the tax, the remaining liability is not discharged but is collectible from the individual after the case. This election must be made by the fifteenth day of the fourth month after filing for bankruptcy, which is the return's due date without an extension.

Special Rules for Individuals

Section 1398's addition to the IRC suggests for individuals different considerations because a new estate is created under Chapters 7 and 11. The considerations include who—the individual or the estate—must report income and expense items, treatment of transfers between the debtor and the estate, and carryover and carryback of administration, liquidation, and reorganization expenses.

Income and Deductions. Section 1399 of the IRC provides that the estate's gross income for each taxable year includes the debtor's income to which the estate is entitled under Title 11 of the Bankruptcy Code. This does not include any income that the individual earned before the bankruptcy case began. The gross income of the debtor (the individual as opposed to the estate) will include income earned prior to bankruptcy plus any income items that the estate's gross income does not include.

The original bill passed by the House divided deductions and credits between the debtor and the estate. These provisions were subsequently modified to provide that if IRC § 1398(e)(3) regards a deduction or credit as belonging to the bankruptcy estate, the debtor may not deduct the item.

Transfers between Debtor and Estate. A transfer (other than by sale or exchange) of an asset from the debtor to the estate does not give rise to gain or loss recognition, deduction, or credits recapture or income acceleration. Thus a transfer of an installment obligation would not give rise to income under IRC § 453(d). The same nondisposition provisions apply when assets are transferred (other than by sale or exchange) from the estate to the debtor as provided under § 1398(f).

Attribute Carryover to Estate. Section 1398(g) provides that the estate assumes the following income tax attributes of the debtor under Chapter 7 or 11:

1. Net operation loss carryovers under IRC § 172.
2. Capital loss carryovers under IRC § 1212.
3. Recovery exclusion under IRC § 111 (relating to bad debts, prior taxes, and delinquency amounts).
4. Credit carryovers and all other items that, except for the bankruptcy, the debtor would have to consider with respect to any credit.
5. Charitable contribution carryover under IRC § 170(d)(1).
6. The debtor's basis in and holding period for the character of any asset acquired in the debtor's hand (other than by sale or exchange from the debtor).
7. The debtor's accounting method.
8. The debtor's other tax attributes to the extent provided by Treasury regulations. For example, the regulations could allow the estate the benefit of IRC § 341 if the estate repays income the debtor received under claim of right.

Attribute Carryover to Debtor. Upon terminating of the estate in Chapters 7 or 11 cases, the debtor assumes the following:

1. Net operating loss carryover
2. Capital loss carryover
3. Recovery exclusion
4. Credit carryover
5. Charitable contribution carryover
6. The estate's basis in, holding period for, and the character in the estate's hand of any asset acquired (other than by sales or exchange) from the estate
7. Other tax attributes to the extent provided by Treasury Regulations

Carryback of Net Operating Losses and Other Credits Incurred Subsequent to Commencement of Case. IRC § 1398(j)(2)(A) provides that if the estate incurs a net operating loss (NOL)—apart from the loss passing to the estate from the debtor—the estate can carry back its net operating loss to the debtor's taxable years before the year in which the bankruptcy proceeding commenced, as well as to the estate's previous taxable years. An individual incurring net operating losses cannot carry back these losses to the years preceding the Chapter 7 or 11 filing. Similarly, § 1398 allows the bankruptcy estate to carry back excess credits, such as an investment tax credit, to the years preceding the case; it also prohibits the individual from carrying back these credits to the prebankruptcy time period.

Administrative Expenses. IRC § 1398(h)(1) allows the estate to deduct any administrative expense allowed under § 503 of the Bankruptcy Code and any fees or charges assessed under Chapter 123 of Title 28 of the U.S. Code (court fee and costs). This section allows these expenses even though some may not be considered trade or business expenses. Administrative expenses may be disallowed, however, under other IRC provisions, such as § 263 (capital expenditures), § 265 (expenses relating to tax-exempt interest) and § 275 (certain taxes).

The new law allows any administrative, liquidation, and reorganization expenses not used in the current year to be carried back 3 years and carried forward 7 years. The amount carried to any other taxable year is stacked after the net operating losses for that particular year. The unused administrative expenses can be carried back or carried over to only the estate's taxable years. IRC § 1398(h)(2)(D) allows only the estate to deduct expenses that are deductible solely through § 1398(h)(1).

Often administrative expenses are not paid until the bankruptcy proceedings conclude, unless they were considered trade or business expenses. These costs are not deductible until paid, and often income does not exist during the last year of operating the estate to charge these expenses against, which means that these expenses have no tax benefit. To alleviate this problem, the new law provided, as previously noted, for the carryover and carryback provision. Note that the restriction on carryback or carryover of administrative expenses to the estate applies only to those deductions allowed solely by § 1398(h)(1) of the IRC. Thus an expense (even though it is an administrative expense in a bankruptcy case) that would normally be classified as an operating cost can be carried forward to the debtor, once the estate terminates, as an item in the net operating loss carryover.

MINIMIZING TAX AND RELATED PAYMENTS

A debtor in financial difficulty can take several steps to reduce the cash outflow for taxes or to obtain tax refunds.

Estimated Tax. A company with financial problems may, after paying one or more installments of estimated taxes, decide that it should recompute its estimated tax liability. Downward recomputations may show that additional payments are unnecessary. If too much tax was paid, the company can obtain a quick refund by filing Form 4466 immediately after the taxable year ends.

Prior Year Taxes. The IRS allows companies that owe taxes from the previous year to extend the time for payment to the extent that the tax will be reduced because of an expected net operating loss in the current year. This request is made on Form 1138. To quickly obtain a refund of taxes previously paid, the company must file Form 1139. The company must file this form within 1 year after the end of the year in which the NOL occurred and only after it has filed Form 1120 for the loss year.

Pension Funding Requirements. An employer may receive a funding waiver if it can show that substantial business hardship exists and that funding the pension would adversely affect the plan's participants in the aggregate. If the funding cannot be waived, payments may be deferred under Revenue Ruling 66-144.

TREATMENT OF INCOME DURING THE BANKRUPTCY PERIOD

Income Required to be Reported. One does not expect to see positive income during bankruptcy proceedings because insufficient profits have contributed to the insolvency. During the administration of the estate, however, transactions may generate taxable income. The estate must report any income from selling or operating the debtor's assets as it is earned.

A bankruptcy estate may have many income sources. Proceeds will be received from selling or liquidating assets. Rental income may be realized, royalties from patents, dividends from securities, and interest may be accumulated on savings and other deposits of the debtor (or trustee, who may deposit the bankruptcy estate's funds). A debtor who is solvent and not in a Chapter 11 proceeding will recognize income to the extent of the debts forgiven.

Deductions Allowed. In calculating taxable net income, the trustee receives certain deductions. The most common are as follows:

1. The costs of administration in general.
2. The costs of administration directly associated with producing income by the estate, provided that they are construed as ordinary and necessary business expenses.
3. Payments made to priority and general unsecured creditors if such distributions are allocable to a debt associated with an item that the debtor would have deducted. Note that debtors using an accrual basis may have already deducted the expense while the trustee makes actual payment.
4. Payments for priority tax claims incurred before filing the petition, which therefore would have been deductible by the debtor if paid prior to bankruptcy.
5. Net operating loss carryovers.

The taxpayer must, however, be careful in deducting general administration costs. For example, the IRS stated in Rev. Rul. 77-204 that expenses connected with a reorganization are generally not deductible under IRC § 162 because they are capital expenditures that will benefit the corporation in future years. All costs necessary to operate the business are deductible under IRC § 162, as they would have been without the bankruptcy proceeding. Note that professional fees are for help to operate the business profitably and not solely to reorganize the business. This ruling also held that in a liquidation, the expenses incurred to sell assets are not deductible under IRC § 162 but must be offset against the sale proceeds.

Discharging Debts. One major income source in most insolvency and bankruptcy proceedings is debt cancellations. Section 61 lists discharge of debts as subject to tax, and Reg. 1.61-12(a) provides that the discharge of indebtedness may result in complete or partial income realization. Taxable income, however, is not realized if a stockholder cancels a debt owed to him without consideration. The amount canceled results in an additional contribution to capital by the stockholder.

In selecting the form of financial relief, a debtor should consider the tax factors related to a gain on debt forgiveness. The rules for out-of-court proceedings differ from those under the Bankruptcy Code. Amended IRC § 108 provides that income from discharge of debt can be excluded from gross income under any of the following conditions:

a. The discharge occurs in a Bankruptcy Code case.
b. The discharge occurs when the taxpayer is insolvent.
c. The discharge was from farm debt.

The amount excluded because of insolvency provisions, however, cannot exceed the amount by which the debtor is insolvent. Thus in an out-of-court settlement where the debt outstanding is $10 million, the fair market value of the assets is $7 million, and $4 million of indebtedness is discharged, $3 million would fall under Condition 2 (insolvent debt), and $1 million would be taxed as income from debt discharged. Section 108(d) indicates that indebtedness of the taxpayer means debts for which the taxpayer is liable or debts on property owned by the taxpayer such as a nonrecourse mortgage on real property. Thus § 108 affects both recourse and nonrecourse debts.

In bankruptcy or insolvency cases, the debt amount discharged is not considered income; however IRC § 108(b) reduces the tax attributes in the following order:

a. *Net operating losses.* Any net operating loss for the taxable year of discharge and any net operating loss carryover to the year of discharge.
b. *Research credit and general business credit.* Any carryover to or from the taxable year of discharge of a credit under IRC Section 38 relating to general business credit.
c. *Capital loss carryovers.* Any capital loss for the taxable years of the discharge and any capital loss carryover to the year of discharge under IRC Section 1212.
d. *Basis reduction.* The debtor's property reduced according to the provisions of IRC Section 1017.
e. *Foreign tax credit carryovers.* Any carryover to or from the taxable year of discharge of the credit allowed under IRC Section 33.

The foreign tax credit and other credit carryovers (Item b) are reduced 33⅓ cents for each dollar of debt canceled. All other reductions are dollar for dollar. One takes the reductions after establishing the tax for the year of discharge. For net operating and capital losses, the reduction shall be made first from the losses for the taxable year and then from the loss carryovers in the order of the taxable years for which the losses arose. The reduction of tax credits is to be made in the order the carryovers are considered for the taxable year of discharge.

For tax years beginning in 1987, 1988, or 1989, a corporation's alternative minimum taxable income (AMTI) includes one-half of the amount by which its adjusted book value exceeds the AMTI calculated without considering the book income preference. Income from debt discharge is not taxed if the debtor corporation is in Title 11 or is insolvent. Because the corporation's income statement reports income from debt discharge as an extraordinary gain (income), income from debt discharge could in fact increase the corporation's tax liability. Under the new rules of IRC § 382, the net operating loss remains even though § 382(b)(1) restricts its use. The adjustment to net operating losses due to the Title 11 exception covered in § 382(1)(5)(C) that states 50 percent of the gain due to debt discharge (50 percent of the difference between the amount of debt and the value of stock used to satisfy debt) shall be treated as though it were not income. Thus under the bankruptcy exception, the net operating loss is not carried forward and would not be available to absorb future income from debt discharge that may arise when the corporation is in bankruptcy or insolvent.

Election to Reduce Basis First. Section 108(b)(5) allows the debtor to elect to apply, first, any portion of the reduction required due to debt discharge to reduce the basis of depreciable property. The reduction amount cannot, however, exceed the aggregate adjusted basis of depreciable property held by the taxpayer as of the beginning of the first taxable year subsequent to the taxable year of discharge.

Basis Adjustments. As noted before, two conditions exist under which the debtor may elect or be required to reduce the basis in assets:

1. Under IRC § 108(b)(5), the debtor can elect to apply the gain from discharge to depreciable property before reducing net operating losses, capital losses, or other credits.
2. Under IRC § 108(b)(2)(D), the debtor (whether in bankruptcy or insolvent) must reduce the basis in property if net operating and capital loss carryovers and certain tax credits do not absorb these losses.

Future Treasury Regulations will prescribe the order of reduction of assets. Practitioners anticipate that the regulations will generally follow the procedure under Treas. Reg. §§ 1.1016-7 and 1.1016-8 for proceedings under the Bankruptcy Code or for insolvent debtors and under Treas. Reg. §§ 1.1017-1 and 1.1017-2 for solvent debtors. In all cases, the reduction will occur on the first day of the taxable year following the year the discharge occurred.

Limitation on Deduction. The basis reduction for a bankruptcy case or an insolvent debtor cannot exceed the total basis of the debtor's property over the total liabilities immediately after the discharge. This limitation does not apply if the debtor elected to first reduce the basis in property under IRC § 108(b)(5).

Individual's Estate. IRC § 108(c)(7) provides that the estate as the taxpayer, and not the individual, is to make the basis adjustments along with other attribute reductions from debt discharge. Thus the trustee or debtor-in-possession will make the election to reduce depreciable property and not tax attributes. Basis adjustment is to be made as of the first day of the taxable year following the discharge. For example, suppose the estate files its final return for a period ending September 15, 19X6, and basis adjustment is required. Should the individual reduce property as of September 16, 19X6—the beginning of a new taxable year of the estate (if it had to file a return), or January 1, 19X7—the first day of the individual's taxable year? The Senate Report (96-1035, 96th Cong. 2nd Sess. (1980)) indicates that if basis reduction is required owing to debt discharge in the final year of the bankruptcy estate, the reduction is to be made on the basis of assets acquired by the debtor from the estate and at the time acquired. Thus in our example, the basis should be reduced as of September 16, 19X6, and cannot include reduction of other property held by the debtor on September 16, 19X6. Section 1017(c)(1) specifically states that basis of exempt property cannot be reduced. The trustee or debtor-in-possession must make attribute reductions other than basis reduction in the taxable year that the discharge occurred.

Partnerships. IRC § 108(d) applies at the partner level for discharge of debt in a bankruptcy case or a situation out of court involving either an insolvent debtor or solvent debtor (qualified business indebtedness provision). IRC § 1017(b)(3)(c) regards a partner's interest in any partnership (whether or not that partnership's debt was discharged) as a depreciable asset only if a corresponding reduction occurs in the partnership's basis in depreciable property with respect to such partner. Treasury regulations will establish the amount and nature of the reduction in the partner's basis in the partnership interest and assets.

Exchanging Stock for Debt. The courts have generally not required income recognition when an exchange of stock for debt occurs, and IRC § 108(c) of the revised Bankruptcy Tax Bill concurs with this position. In addition to not recognizing income, the debtor will not have to reduce attributes. Also, this provision applies to all debts even though not evidenced by a security. The Deficit Reduction Act of 1984 codified the general rules developed by case law and restricted the exclusion to Title 11 cases and to insolvent debtors. Section 108(e) was amended to provide that if a debtor corporation transfers stock to a creditor to discharge its indebtedness, such corporation shall be treated as having satisfied the indebtedness with an amount equal to the stock's fair market value. This general rule shall not apply to a debtor in a Title 11 case or to the extent the debtor is insolvent. Thus solvent corporations (fair market value of its assets exceed the liabilities) must recognize income from debt discharge on an exchange of stock for debt. Finally, § 108 as amended provides that a stock for debt exchange does not give rise to income from debt discharge under a new workout exception. The effective date for the allowance of this exception, is January 1, 1986, the date on which the amendments to § 382 by the Tax Reform Act of 1986 become effective.

Section 108 provides that if the creditor receives stock for debt that was previously written off as ordinary bad debt deduction, subsequent gain on the stock's sale would be ordinary income to the extent of the loss previously taken. For a cash basis taxpayer, any amount not taken into account by the method of accounting used is to be handled as a bad debt deduction.

Limitations (de minimis cases). In computing the debtor's income from discharging debts, the stock for debt exception will not apply to issues of nominal or token shares or to unsecured debt if the creditor receives less than half the stock that it would receive if all the corporation's unsecured creditors—to the extent their debts are canceled or satisfied with the debtor's stock—received a pro rata amount of the stock issued.

For example, Creditor A held $1000 of unsecured debt against a debtor corporation and in a workout, the debtor corporation fully satisfied $10,000 of its unsecured debt (including the debt to A) by transferring $6000 of its stock to creditors. Creditor A must then receive at least $300 of stock to satisfy its claim (assuming no other property is transferred) for the debtor to avoid recognizing—with respect to the stock issued to A—any debt discharge income and attribute reduction. If Creditor A receives only $100 of stock for its $1000 debt, then the debtor corporation will have a debt discharge income of $900 for the stock issued to Creditor A. If Creditor A receives $300 or more of stock for its $1000 debt, then the debtor corporation will not recognize any debt discharge income for the stock issued to Creditor A.

Purchase-Money Debt Reduction. When the debt arises from a property purchase, the debtor may treat the discharge as a reduction of the purchase price. To be treated this way, the case must not be a Chapter ll case, or the purchaser must not be insolvent, and the reduction would otherwise have been treated as income from a discharge of debt.

Tax Planning. The debtor should consider the tax consequences of any decisions to resolve its financial problems. A Chapter 11 petition may be better than an out-of-court agreement for a company that will be solvent after debt discharge. One should not ignore the tax advantages of issuing some stock to pay obligations as opposed to only cash or notes.

Corporate Reorganization

One way for a corporation in bankruptcy or insolvency proceedings to continue operations is to transfer all or part of its assets to another corporation. This transfer should be structured as one of the tax-free reorganizations described in IRC § 368(a)(1). With a tax-free reorganization, the new entity may be able to assume some of the bankrupt corporation's tax attributes, such as unused net operating losses.

IRC § 371—which provided for tax-free reorganization only for Chapter X reorganization under the Bankruptcy Act or a receivership or similar proceeding—no longer applies, and corporate reorganizations must now qualify under § 368(a)(1).

Tax-Free G Reorganization. The Bankruptcy Tax Act of 1980 adds a new category of tax-free reorganization to IRC § 368(a)(1). The new "G reorganization" includes certain transfers of all or part of the debtor's assets to another corporation pursuant to a court-approved reorganization plan in a bankruptcy case under the new Title 11 of the U.S. Code, or in a receivership, foreclosure, or similar proceedings in federal or state court.

This new section provision eliminates many of the requirements that have prevented financially troubled companies from using the tax-free reorganizations included under the current law. The new G reorganization does not require compliance with state merger laws (as in A reorganizations), does not require that a financially distressed corporation receive only stock of the acquiring corporation in exchange for its assets (C reorganization), and does not require that the former shareholders of a financially distressed corporation control the corporation receiving the assets (D reorganization).

The G reorganization provision requires that the transfer of assets by a corporation in a bankruptcy case and that the distribution of stock or securities of the acquiring corporation qualify under Sections 354, 355, or 356 of the IRC.

Availability of Net Operating Losses

Section 172 provides for the carryback and carryforward of net operating losses (NOL). This provision allows a corporation, in most cases, to carry forward for up to 15 years (9 years for regulated transportation companies) NOLs sustained in a particular tax year and not carried back to prior years. The period was 5 years (7 for regulated transportation companies) for tax years ending before 1976. Beginning with tax years ending in 1976, the taxpayer can elect not to carry losses back (§ 172(b)). Prior to that time, however, to losses had to be carried back to the three preceding tax years first, and if all of the loss was not used against income in prior years, it might then be carried forward. The extent, however, to which the net operating loss can be preserved in bankruptcy and insolvency proceedings depends on how one restructures the debt.

The Tax Reform Act of 1986 includes the annual § 382 limitation that minimizes the effect of tax considerations on the decision to acquire loss corporations by limiting potential loss carryovers to a hypothetical income stream that would have been realized had the assets of the loss corporation's assets been sold at their fair market value and the proceeds reinvested in high-grade securities. Further conditions for loss survival include the coverage of built-in losses, rules governing changes in ownership, and exceptions for bankruptcy debtor corporations.

Net operating loss limitations are considered only when the corporation holding the carryovers changes ownership. IRC § 382 recognizes that an ownership change has occurred when more than half the loss corporation's stock value changes ownership. The use of any NOL resulting from operations before the ownership change in any period after the change is subject to the § 382 limitation. The loss corporation acquired through a taxable purchase can no longer preserve NOLs by simply continuing its historic business.

This limitation now restricts the absorption of any prechange NOL in a post-change taxable year to the fair market value multiplied by the "long-term tax-exempt rate." For example, X Corporation has a net operating loss of $4 million and Stockholder A purchases 60 percent of the outstanding stock for $600,000. The long-term tax-exempt rate is 6 percent. The value of the loss corporation of $1 million ($600,000 ÷ .60) times the long term tax-exempt rate of 6 percent results in a maximum use per year of the net operating loss of $60,000 ($1,000,000 x .06). The § 382 limitation not used in a given year because of insufficient taxable income is added to the limitation for a following year. The key factor in using NOLs is the loss corporation's fair market value. For a taxable stock purchase, this valuation will be relatively simple. When a change in control results, however, from a reorganization in which the purchase price includes stock of a privately held corporation, this valuation will be much more difficult.

BIBLIOGRAPHY

AICPA Professional Standards, Vol. 2, Section MS 11.06. M. J. Wagner and P. B. Frank, 1986, *AICPA Technical Consulting Practice Aid No. 7—Litigation Services.*

Collier Bankruptcy Code and Rules, 1988 (Matthew Bender & Co., 1987).

Collier Bankruptcy Manual, 3 volumes (Matthew Bender & Co., 1987).

Dykeman, F.C., *Forensic Accounting—The Accountant as Expert Witness* (John Wiley & Sons, 1982).

Myers, L.O., *Debtor–Creditor Relations—Manual and Forms* (McGraw-Hill, 1986).

Newton, G.W., *Bankruptcy and Insolvency Accounting Practice and Procedures*, 4th. ed. (John Wiley & Sons, 1989).

Newton, G.W., and G.D. Bloom, *Tax Planning for the Troubled Business* (John Wiley & Sons, 1987).

Pratt, S., *Valuing Small Business and Professional Practices* (Dow Jones-Irwin, 1986).

Robert Morris Associates, *Annual Statement Studies* (1986).

Sulmeyer, I., D.M. Lynn, M. Rush, M.R. Rocheole, and R.J. Mottern, in L.P. King, ed., *Collier Handbook for Trustees and Debtors in Possession* (Matthew Bender & Co., 1987).

13

BREACH OF CONTRACT

Alan Silverman

UNIFORM COMMERCIAL CODE

The Uniform Commercial Code (U.C.C.), together with its commentary and interpretations, generally describes the laws of damages relating to breaches of contract. Pennsylvania first adopted the U.C.C. in 1954, and subsequently all states and the District of Columbia, except Louisiana, have adopted it. Some differences in the code's implementation exist across states, so the CPA should consult with a lawyer

The author would like to thank Kathryn Gustafson of Coopers & Lybrand, San Francisco, for her contribution to this chapter.

before relying on this chapter's guidance, to ensure that the local law agrees with that described here.

A buyer or a seller may breach a contract. The code prescribes different remedies, depending on which party breaches: a seller cannot receive consequential damages (i.e., those losses that result from an act or breach but are not direct and immediate), whereas a wronged buyer may be able to claim consequential damages under certain conditions.[1] The code's language focuses on sales contracts, but this chapter also addresses manufacturing contracts. (A subsequent chapter discusses construction contracts.) This chapter first describes the code, then discusses damages for buyers and sellers in more detail.

SELLER'S REMEDIES FOLLOWING BREACH BY A BUYER

A buyer's breach may occur when a buyer rejects goods, fails to pay for them, or fails to pay on time.

General Remedies—U.C.C. Section 2-703

A breached seller may withhold delivery of any undelivered balance, resell the goods and recover damages as described in § 2-706 or recover damages for non-acceptance as described in § 2-708.

Identification of Affected Goods—Section 2-704

The wronged seller can specify the contract goods that were demonstrably intended for the particular contract, even though the seller did not possess them at the time of the breach. For a manufacturing contract, where the goods are not completed at the time of breach, the manufacturer may use reasonable business judgment in deciding whether to complete the manufacturing and then sell the goods or stop and sell them for scrap.

Resale of Goods—Section 2-706

When a buyer breaches a contract, the seller may resell the goods and recover the difference between the resale price and the contract price, together with any incidental damages allowed under § 2-710, less any expenses saved as a consequence of the breach. The resale must be reasonably shown to have been related to the breach, but the goods need not necessarily have existed at the time of breach or be specifically identified to the contract.

Seller's Lost Profits—Section 2-708

If the damages allowed by the resale provisions do not make the seller "whole," then the seller can claim lost profits ("including reasonable overhead"), plus any incidental damages allowed by § 2-710, with an allowance for costs reasonably incurred and a credit for the proceeds of any resale.

Seller's Incidental Damages—Section 2-710

The wronged seller may recover any reasonable costs or commissions incurred in stopping manufacture or delivery, in transportation, in storage, and any resale costs.

Seller's Damages

Most contract cases involving seller's damages fall into three categories. The first of these involves the sale of commonly used or generic goods. Examples might include commodities such as wheat, wood pulp, and oil or manufactured generic products such as computer diskettes or pencils. When dealing with products such as these, the wronged seller may be able to find another buyer. If a grower has a contract to sell wheat to a breakfast cereal manufacturer and the cereal manufacturer breached the contract, the grower could possibly find another cereal producer or a baker to buy the wheat. The seller's damages would then be limited to the difference in price received for the wheat, plus the incidental costs such as additional storage, sales costs, and commissions and transportation costs.

The second type of buyer's breach case concerns the sale of unique merchandise, which commonly occurs where the contract requires the seller to manufacture a product according to the buyer's unique specifications. Examples include computer disk drives produced by a peripheral manufacturer for a mainframe producer. The product probably is not marketable to another buyer and may even contain the original buyer's name. The seller's damages may be calculated as the profit lost because of the breached sale, plus any incidental expenses. To calculate damages, one must measure the quantity of the product that was not delivered and the "but-for" profit on each unit. If the deliveries would have occurred over a period of time, then the timing of the profit becomes important. In those jurisdictions allowing prejudgment interest, the interest calculation depends on the expected delivery schedule. If the delivery schedule extends beyond the trial or arbitration date, the schedule will affect the discounting of future damages.

The manufacturer whose buyer has breached a contract may also receive incidental damages. These might include the cost of component inventories purchased specifically for production under the contract that cannot be used elsewhere. The incidental costs might also include the cost of terminating employees hired specifically to perform the contract work. The seller must prove that a certain and proximate relationship existed between the incidental expenses and the contract. For example, if the components were commonly used in many products and did not become uniquely identified with the contract goods until late in the manufacturing process, the seller would have to prove that the components were purchased for the contract. The effect of using the component for other products would have to be considered. Similarly, a manufacturer who uses a buyer's breach as an opportune time to train employees in skills unnecessary for the contract but of future value to the manufacturer may have difficulty attributing these expenses to the contract.

The third category of seller's damages involves the seller as middleman—one who buys for resale. The middleman in breach-of-contract cases is sometimes referred to as a lost-volume seller. For example, a bathroom fixtures wholesaler may have a contract to supply bathtubs to a housing tract builder. If the builder breaches the contract and the wholesaler resells the bathtubs to another builder, this might seem to be a simple resale case of the first type. The courts have held, however, that the wholesaler, as a middleman, has or "may have" an unlimited capacity to do business. The bathroom fixture wholesaler might have had the opportunity to supply both the first and the second builder, thereby making two profits. In this case, damages would be calculated not by the difference in profitability of the two sales but by calculating the total lost profit from the first sale. The seller should be prepared to prove, however, that it had the capacity to make both sales.

Calculating damages for a buyer differs from that of a seller in the treatment of consequential damages. The code does not allow the seller to claim consequential damages because the buyer cannot easily foresee the seller's intended use of the contract's profits. For example, the seller might claim that he intended to take the $1 million profit from the contract and use it to fund an acquisition. This acquisition would have resulted in profits of $50 million, and so the breaching buyer owes him $51million rather than $1 million. The U.C.C. will not permit this type of speculation.

However, a wronged buyer may claim consequential damages, as discussed next.

BUYER'S REMEDIES FOLLOWING BREACH BY A SELLER

A seller breaches a contract by failing to deliver in whole or in part.

General Remedies—Section 2-711

A buyer may cancel the contract and recover the price paid for any undelivered goods. Section 2-712 also allows the buyer to "cover" by buying substitute goods.

"Covering"—Section 2-712

The buyer may use reasonable business judgment to buy substitute goods within a reasonable time to replace those not delivered. The buyer may recover any price difference plus any incidental or consequential damages allowed by § 2-715, less any expenses saved. A buyer who fails to "cover" is not barred from other remedies.

Nondelivery or Repudiation—Section 2-713

The measure of damages for nondelivery or repudiation if the buyer did not "cover" is the difference between the contract price and the market price when the buyer learned of the breach, plus any incidental or consequential damages allowed by § 2-715, less any costs saved.

Acceptance of Nonconforming Goods—Section 2-714

If the buyer accepted delivery of goods and subsequently notifies the seller that they do not conform to the contract, the damage is the difference between the value of the goods accepted and the value they would have had if they had been as warranted.

Buyer's Incidental and Consequential Damages—Section 2-715

The buyer can recover incidental damages including expenses incurred in inspection, receipt, transportation, storage, and commissions. For the buyer to recover consequential damages, they must have been reasonably foreseeable by the seller at the time of the contract. Foreseeability is discussed in more detail later.

Buyer's Damages

As with seller's damages, one must consider whether the goods were unique and whether the wronged buyer was a middleman.

If the goods not delivered by the seller were of the type generally available on the market, then the buyer's damages may be limited to the difference between the "cover" price and the contract price, plus any incidental or consequential damages. The "cover" price is a reasonable price paid for substitute goods. If the grower failed to deliver wheat to the cereal manufacturer and the manufacturer bought wheat elsewhere, then the manufacturer would be entitled to any additional price paid for the wheat plus any incidental expenses, such as for transportation. If the buyer could cover by buying replacement goods but fails to do so, the buyer may not be able to recover damages.

If the goods are unique or no available substitutes exist, then the covering remedy is not available to the buyer, and the measure of damage becomes lost profit. This would clearly be the case in the manufacturing contract for disk drives mentioned, where the lack of disk drives may reduce mainframe sales.

The middleman buyer has a situation analogous to the middleman seller mentioned. The middleman buyer can claim total profit lost, not just the difference between the contract price and the cover price paid for substitute merchandise. The courts have typically held that the buyer's resale of the goods has to be reasonably foreseeable by the seller for the total lost profits to be recoverable.

Buyer's Consequential Damages

An example of buyer's consequential damages arises in the case of the disk drive manufacturer selling to the computer mainframe manufacturer. If the seller breaches the contract and the buyer cannot replace the unique disk drives, then a natural consequence is that the mainframe manufacturer would be unable to sell the total computer system, of which the disk drives were part. In this case, the buyer could claim the lost profit on the entire computer system—not just the disk drives.

The courts have held that for the buyer to recover consequential damages of this type, the consequences must have been reasonably foreseeable by both parties as a probable result of a breach, at the time the contract was made. For a detailed discussion of foreseeability and current law, see Dunn, *Recovery of Damages For Lost Profits* (1987).

CONTRACTS INVOLVING FOREIGN CURRENCIES

A breach of contract involving two or more currencies presents damage issues that the courts have not often addressed. These issues become more important as international trade and the variation in currency exchange rate fluctuations increase. Assume that the computer mainframe manufacturer was located in the United States and had entered into a contract with a French manufacturer to purchase disk drives. Both parties knew that the disk drives would be manufactured in France using French labor and that payment for most components and labor would be in francs. However, the contract called for the disk drives to be delivered in the United States and paid for in dollars. If the sales price was $1000 per unit and the buyer had agreed to accept 100 units on January 1, Year 1, then the buyer would have incurred an obligation of $100,000. If the buyer breached the contract and was sued, the seller may have been awarded lost profits of, say, $10,000. If judgment was entered on December 31, Year 2, the award might have been $12,000, allowing for 10-percent simple prejudgment interest. If the exchange rate at the end of Year 2 was 5 francs to the dollar, the French company would have received 60,000 francs. Suppose, however, that the exchange rate on January 1, Year 1, was 10 francs to the dollar. If the contract had not been breached, the seller would have had 100,000 francs profit and so might feel that the damage award plus interest is insufficient. On the other hand, the buyer entered into a contract that called for payment in dollars, thereby placing the currency fluctuation risk in the seller's hands. The court has to choose the date of the breach or the date of the award as the conversion date.

Another school of thought says that if the contract requires payment in dollars and if the action is brought in the United States, then the court need only concern itself with dollars and need not consider what the plaintiff might do with any dollar award. Indeed, it could be argued that this currency fluctuation question would be the equivalent of consequential damages and therefore not allowable to a seller. New York is the only state that seems to have addressed this issue; it has adopted this last position. Although this subject is still unsettled, it is included here so that CPAs looking at international contracts are aware of the potential complications.

NOTES

1. The U.C.C. (§ 2-715(2) states that: "Consequential damages resulting from a seller's breach of contract include any loss resulting from general or particular requirements and needs of which the seller at the time of contracting had reason to know and which could not reasonably be prevented by cover or otherwise, and injury to person or property proximately resulting from any breach of warranty."

BIBLIOGRAPHY

Dunn, R.L., *Recovery of Damages For Lost Profits* (Lawpress Corporation, Kentfield, CA. 1987).

14

BUSINESS INTERRUPTION

Michael G. Ueltzen, MBA, CPA
Gregory M. Burke, CPA

OVERVIEW

Business interruption is a broad concept with a generally understood meaning; yet a survey of accounting, business, and legal literature yields little in the way of a definition. *Black's Law Dictionary*, for example, does not define "business interruption." Although no formal definition exists, for practical purposes *business interruption* can be defined as the disruption of normal business operation resulting from some identifiable event beyond the business entity's control.

Business interruptions arise from various causes, including a subcontractor's failure to perform according to a contract's requirements, a key employee's injury in an automobile accident, a fire, and other acts of nature.

CAUSES OF BUSINESS INTERRUPTION AND THEORIES OF RECOVERY

Business interruptions can be divided into three general categories: (1) a short interruption without permanent loss of continuing business, (2) a longer interruption and/or a permanent loss of continuing business occurs, and (3) permanently suspended operations. Recoverable damages depend partly on the length and severity of the interruption of operations.

Although a broad spectrum of events may interrupt a normal business operation, the recovery of damages in civil litigation involving a business interruption can follow from either statutory law or common law. Under common law, damages may be recoverable under two general legal concepts either singularly or in combination. The two concepts are the *contract* and the *tort*. The distinction between these two concepts is fundamental regarding the recovery of damages because the measure of recoverable damages will differ under each theory. Whereas each recovery theory may bring to bear a distinct measure of damages, the theories may overlap. Breach of contract by a party that deals in bad faith (tortious conduct) is an example.

Determining the relevant recovery theory in a case is obviously a legal question to be decided by competent counsel. An accountant asked to prepare a damage model in a business interruption case should know the proper measure of damages under the theory or theories being pleaded, or the model may fail to meet legal requirements. Such knowledge requires an understanding of the theory or theories under which damages are being sought, the requisite measure of damages, and the underlying facts.

The accountant should also know the statutory provisions that apply to the theories being relied on to avoid potential pitfalls. The California Civil Code, for example, contains provisions that bear upon the recovery of damages. In the area of contracts, the California code prohibits the recovery of speculative, grossly aggressive, or unconscionable damages.[1] The accountant should be aware of the provisions of the Uniform Commercial Code and the Uniform Sales Code that may apply to a given case.

Contracts

Many businesses rely on bank lines of credit to meet short-term financing needs. Consider, for example, a wholesaler who must meet funding needs for seasonal increases in inventory levels. The business may have an established relationship with a bank. The bank promises to extend an existing line of credit at agreed-upon terms to provide the necessary funds to meet the upcoming season's inventory needs as projected by the company's management. The company's accounts receivable and inventory secures the line of credit.

The company orders inventory assuming that the line of credit will be available. As partial inventory shipments are received and the invoices become due, the company draws against its cash reserves, then against the line of credit.

After a change in management, the bank assigns a new loan officer to the company's account. The new loan officer, after reviewing the company's credit history and its current financial position, decides that the company has not been aggressive enough in collecting slow-paying accounts during times of economic difficulties. The bank officer informs the company's management that after subsequent review, advances on the credit line have been denied.

Checks to suppliers bounce, and the delivery of subsequent inventory orders to the wholesaler are suspended. The company has to suspend sales efforts because inventory is not available. Existing customers have to look elsewhere for the goods previously available from the company. Some customers are lost permanently. As news of the dishonored checks circulates among the company's suppliers, favorable credit terms that were previously available to the company are withdrawn, causing an increase in its operating costs. Some suppliers refuse to extend further credit to the company.

To obtain short-term financing so that normal operations can be reestablished, the company management unsuccessfully seeks potential lenders, incurring costs in the process.

This example illustrates how an alleged breach of contract—the bank's failure to provide the promised credit—interrupts normal business operations. Once a party alleges breach of contract, the question arises as to recoverable damages.

Recoverable damages in contract cases include those that are

1. Proximately caused by the defaulting party to the contract
2. Capable of being proven with reasonable certainty
3. Foreseeable as of the time of making the contract.[2]

Assuming that the company described sues the bank for breach of contract and lender liability, the company might seek to recover lost profits from the sale of inventory that could have been purchased if the promised credit had been extended; recovery of the reduction in goodwill due to the permanent loss of continuing customers, earning power, and reputation as well as attorney and expert witness fees attendant to the suit. The company could also sue to recover extra costs resulting from the breach, such as costs incurred to find new financing, and increased operating costs resulting from the breach.

The company would not be entitled to recovery of punitive damages under a strict breach of contract theory because punitive damages are recoverable only under tort theories. Statutory and case law seek to avoid introducing tort questions to contract disputes.[3]

An accountant reviewing or preparing a damage model in a business interruption case involving a breach of contract should bear in mind that asserted damages must be proximately caused by the defaulting party. Similarly, the model must prove the damages with reasonable certainty. The assumptions underlying the model must be reasonable. Data used in the model should be drawn from admissible evidence and should be accurate.

The analysis will stand or fall, given reasonable certainty, on the assumptions' defensibility. The opposing side will emphatically point out any unreasonable or indefensible assumptions.

Tort Theories

A tort is a civil (as opposed to a criminal) wrong, not involving breach of contract. Tort litigation involves principles for recovery in business interruption cases different from those used in contract recoveries. Tort theories fall into three general subcategories: negligence, intentional torts, and strict liability. Each subcategory implies a different measure of damages.

Foreseeability is generally a contract principle, although it may have limited application in tort cases. To recover damages under a tort theory, the plaintiff must show that the incurred damages were within the range of foreseeable harm resulting from the defendant's conduct.[4] The measure of damages in tort litigation involving business interruption is the amount of prospective profits that are (1) reasonably certain to have arisen except for the tort and (2) measurable with reasonable certainty.[5] Proximate cause becomes the guiding principle in tort litigation involving business interruption. Note that punitive damages are available only under tort theories.

From an accountant's viewpoint, the underlying damage model must prove with reasonable certainty the damages being sought. This becomes increasingly important if tort theories are also being pled because punitive damages are often predicated on general damages.

Negligence. Personal injury and property damages cases often rely on the theory of negligence. In personal injury cases, lost profits are generally not recoverable. The measure of damages is the reduction in earning ability resulting from the negligent act.[6] The prohibition against recovering lost profits does not preclude the introduction of evidence of lost profits as proof of lost earnings. The difference is that the negligent act results in injury to a person, rather than to a business. The measure of damages, therefore, must be in terms of the person. This is not to say that a negligent act cannot result in a business interruption. Some authority exists to allow recovery by a corporation for lost profits arising from the negligent injury of a key employee, such as a shareholder active in the business.[7]

The measure of damages in a business interruption caused by damage to or destruction of income-producing property resulting from a negligent act is generally the cost to repair or replace the property and the profits lost during the period required to repair or replace the damaged or destroyed property.[8] Lost profits due to business interruption may not be awarded if the loss could have been mitigated—by using rental or replacement equipment or merchandise, for example. If the damaged or destroyed property is not replaceable within the time necessary to avoid a business interruption resulting in lost profits, such profits are recoverable under the negligence theory if the proof of such losses is not speculative or conjectural.[9]

Intentional Torts

Another class of business interruptions where damages may be recoverable arises when the contract breaches leading to interruptions are caused by intentional tortious conduct. Theories comprising this subcategory of tort actions include interference with a business, unfair competition, fraud, and interference with contracts.[10] Statutory guidelines often apply to this class of tort actions, including the Uniform Commercial Code and various antitrust statutes.

Let us turn our attention to the wholesale company that we addressed earlier. The facts in that example were drawn, in part, from the case of *K.M.C. Co., Inc. v. Irving Trust Co.* 757 F.2d 752 (6th Cir. 1985). A more precise recital of the facts in this case follows.

K.M.C. ("the company") was a wholesale and retail grocery business operating in Tennessee. Its annual gross sales were approximately $100 million. The company had entered into a financing agreement with Irving Trust ("the bank") that provided a $3.5 million line of credit to the company. The line of credit was secured by inventory and accounts receivable. In addition to this security, the company's cash receipts were deposited into a "blocked account" to which only the bank had access. Normally, the company would write checks daily to pay its obligations. If the total checks on a given day exceeded the funds available in the blocked account, the company would contact the bank and request an advance on the line of credit to cover the checks written. This arrangement had existed for 2 years prior to the events to be described.

The company requested an $800,000 advance, which was within its existing credit limit. The bank refused the advance and called the entire line of credit without prior notice to the company. The existing collateral at the time of the denial totaled approximately $12 million.

The evidence indicated that the loan officer who denied the advance and called the line of credit had a personality conflict with the company's president. The bank officer believed that the company should have been more aggressive in collecting slow-paying accounts. The company's president believed in following relatively lenient collection practices, based on the company's 50 years of experience and on his belief that a reasonable collection policy created goodwill among the company's customers.

During this period, the company's owners had been negotiating the company's potential sale. The potential buyer heard of the bank's intention to deny the requested advance. The buyer's attorney spoke to the loan officer, indicating that a party was interested in buying the company but was concerned that dishonoring the company's checks would ruin the company's credit standing with its suppliers and thereby effectively ruin the company.

The bank officer agreed that denying the advance would have serious consequences for the company. The buyer's attorney requested that the loan officer delay the denial of the credit line to avoid damaging the company's value and endangering the sale. The loan officer agreed to delay the denial of the advance because it would not jeopardize the bank's position with respect to the credit extended to the company.

After his statements to the buyer, the loan officer changed his decision and denied advances. The loan officer also called the line of credit. The bank's actions caused the company to cease operations because suppliers, after receiving dishonored checks, required the company to pay cash in advance. The company's assets were liquidated and the proceeds used to satisfy creditors. The line of credit with the bank was satisfied in full.

The evidence indicated that no reason existed to deny the advances requested and that the loan officer's actions were arbitrary and capricious and therefore lacking in good faith. The bank was at all times adequately collateralized, and the company had had no previous difficulties in repaying advances on the credit line. The court awarded damages totaling $7.5 million including punitive damages.

This case illustrates several points. The case contains facts that support both contract and tort theories of recovery. The company's business was interrupted by breach of contract with respect to the line of credit extended to the company. The appeals court upheld the finding that the bank owed the company the duty to notify it of any significant changes with respect to the extension of credit to the company. In addition, the financing agreement's terms effectively gave the bank financial control of the company. Because the bank failed to discharge its duty to notify the company of its decision to deny credit and financially control the company, the subsequent denial was tortious.

Strict Liability. An area of growing interest in business litigation involves actions under the theory of strict liability. *Strict liability* provides that the seller of a defective or dangerous product is liable for the physical harm caused to the user or the user's property by the unreasonably dangerous product.[11] This theory is currently expanding in the area of toxic hazards. To the extent that a business may use hazardous equipment or chemicals, the manufacturers and sellers of such products may be liable to the business for damages, including lost profits, if the property causes physical harm.

The theory of strict liability also extends to the performance of hazardous tasks, such as building demolition. One case on point is that of *Rosenblath v. Louisiana Bank & Trust Co.*, 432 So.2d 285 (La. App. 1983) wherein damages including lost profits were awarded to a retail store whose normal business operations were interrupted by the rupture of a gas line caused by the demolition of a nearby building.

Other Causes

Aside from the types of business interruptions described, most business interruptions are caused by casualty. Most businesses carry insurance to cover the most common casualties. To the extent that insurance coverages are contracts, contract theories of recovery apply to business interruptions covered by insurance.

A common cause of business interruptions is fire to business property. A fire's size or severity can lead to short-term interruptions or to the total destruction of a business. Most businesses carry fire insurance and also insure against those perils that, in management's best judgment, warrant the cost of such coverage.

The accountant preparing or reviewing a claim for damages pursuant to an insurance policy must become thoroughly familiar with the general type of policy and the provisions of the specific policy. Consider a company that suffered an embezzlement of funds exceeding $100,000 over a 2-year period. The company carried a policy indemnifying it against such acts, with a limit of $50,000. During the period of the embezzlement but before the theft was discovered, the company changed insurance carriers. After discovering the theft, the company filed a claim with its current carrier. The accountant's inquiry revealed that the previous coverage was a "per occurrence" coverage in contrast to straight-term coverage, so the company then filed a claim with the previous carrier. Even though the previous policy had expired, the company was entitled to indemnification under its previous policy because it could prove that funds had been embezzled during the period that the policy had been in force. The company could recover from under both policies, and both claims were honored.

Insurance policies are sometimes vaguely worded or silent as to certain items of coverage. This is often vexing to the accountant who is estimating the amount of damages to be submitted under a policy. The accountant may find it necessary to consult with counsel or the insurance company to assist in ascertaining the coverage aspects of a claim.

OTHER CONSIDERATIONS

Availability of Records

For business interruptions caused by a breach of contract, and in most tort cases, the accounting records of the affected business remain intact. These records will provide the best information source regarding the company's financial results for computing the damages incurred by the affected entity. Access to the accounting records may be voluntary, as when the accountant assists an existing client. In litigation, access to accounting records may require discovery. The accountant should be familiar with the rules of discovery applicable to the jurisdiction in which the case is being litigated.

A fire that caused an interruption may destroy a portion, if not all, of the entity's accounting records. These cases require third-party sources of information concerning the company's financial results. Such sources include banks, accountants who have rendered services to the company, the Internal Revenue Service, and lending institutions.

Cyclicality and Seasonality

The accountant estimating damages caused by business interruption must isolate factors that affected the entity's financial results, yet did not cause the interruption. Factors such as cyclicality and seasonality should be analyzed. Long-term cycles or trends may not be evident on an annual basis. A historical perspective must be developed.

Industry publications and business periodicals can provide information about long-term cycles or trends in the industry of the affected business.

Similarly, the accountant reviewing a damage model should look for factors included in the model that did not result from the business interruption. The accountant needs to examine the damage model's underlying assumptions.

Multiple Interruptions

Sometimes a business experiences several causes of interruption concurrently, or in such a manner that the effects overlap. Although separating the effects of each cause of interruption may be impossible, the accountant should attempt to understand the assumption required to disentangle the various effects.

Allocations among Related Entities

When the calculations involve related entities, common costs will need to be allocated among them. In constructing or reviewing a damage model, the accountant must scrutinize bases of allocation as well as the nature of the costs allocated to the affected entity. To estimate the common costs allocations for an entity, the accountant may have to perform extensive tests of the accounting records to understand the allocation basis appropriate to the circumstances. For example, in some situations increased costs allocations will be appropriate, whereas others, a full cost basis will be. The accountant may suspect that costs that should be allocated to an entity are not thereby overstating earnings. The nature and extent of these tests must be balanced against the incorrect or absent allocation's effect on damages. Consider materiality in such matters.

Mitigation

As a matter of law and, for insurance matters, a matter of contractual obligation, the harmed party is obligated to minimize the damages resulting from business interruption. Finding replacement property quickly and avoiding unnecessary costs should be undertaken to minimize damages. In reviewing a damage model or claim for damages, the accountant should be aware of mitigation measures that could have been undertaken as well as those that were undertaken. To the extent that an aggrieved party increases claimed damages by not taking mitigation measures, recovery will be reduced.

New Businesses

The requirement that recoverable damages be provably with reasonable certainty has been held to deny recovery of lost profits related to the interruption of a newly established business.[12] Recent court decisions have softened this holding. The current rule is one of evidence rather than law.[13] If evidence proves with reasonable certainty that the newly established business could show future profits but was prevented from doing so because of the business interruption, lost profits may be awarded. Such evidence might include the past experience of the management or owners of the new business or the results of similar businesses that have been in operation for some time.

INSURANCE IN BUSINESS INTERRUPTION

The causes and types of business interruption can be categorized in several different ways. One might consider a contractual violation to have caused a business interruption; a tort action as a result of fraud, or a personal injury may give rise to a business interruption. Other types of business interruptions result from acts of God, product liability, fire, theft, accident, and explosion. Although insurance companies are frequently involved in such business interruptions, they need not necessarily be involved in the accounting analysis of the loss.

Types of Coverages

A business interruption is normally conceived in insurance contracts relative to some form of catastrophic of catastrophic event such as fire, flood or other hazard against which insurance has been obtained, to the extent that profits have been reduced as a result of the event. Insurance against business interruption originated in England in the 1800s, and was known as "consequential insurance." In this country, it was referred to as *use and occupancy* (U&O) insurance, or as *prospective* insurance being more descriptive of the type of coverages included.

An accountant involved in an insurance claim for business interruption should know that the existing forms of such coverage fall into two general categories: (1) mercantile and nonmanufacturing and (2) manufacturing and mining. Insurance companies recognize that different types of operations require different types of coverages, but from their standpoint, business interruption should not include property damage. In estimating gross earnings, analysts consider the performance of the business preceding the damage or destruction and estimate the performance thereafter had no loss occurred.

Mercantile or Nonmanufacturing Risk

Coverage for nonmanufacturing risk is normally written for a specified amount. The amount is based upon gross earnings, generally defined as

- Total net sales
- Other earnings derived from the operation of the business, less the cost of
  - Merchandise sold including packaging materials
  - Materials and supplies consumed directly in supplying the services sold by the insured
  - Services purchased from outsiders (not employees of the insured) for resale that do not continue under contract

No other costs are deducted in measuring gross earnings.

Normally, the entire payroll is covered, as are other continuing expenses. The accountant should expect that some form of co-insurance exists.

Manufacturing and Mining Coverage

The manufacturing and mining coverage resembles that of mercantile and nonmanufacturing with several adjustments. This coverage defines gross earnings as:

- Total net sales value of production
- Total net sales of merchandise and
- Other earnings derived from the business operations less the cost of
  - Raw stock from which such production is derived
  - Supplies consisting of materials consumed directly in converting such raw stock into finished stock or in supplying services sold by the insured
  - Merchandise sold, including packaging materials, and
  - Services purchased from outsiders (not employees of the insured) for resale, which do not continue under contract

Normally, no other costs are deducted in measuring gross earnings. In a manufacturing entity, finished goods are not usually included in the lost profits calculation, and they have been excluded from many such analyses, assuming that other insurance coverage exists to address those needs. Equally important from an accounting standpoint are two endorsements that a policy may include: (1) an ordinary payroll exclusion endorsement and (2) ordinary payroll–limited coverage endorsement.

Ordinary Payroll Exclusion Endorsement. The ordinary payroll exclusion endorsement excludes payroll expense from business interruption coverage.

Ordinary Payroll–Limited Coverage Endorsement. The ordinary payroll–limited coverage endorsement normally covers ordinary payroll for up to 90 calendar days and covers only those expenses necessary to continue during the business interruption. The insured can modify this endorsement.

Earnings Insurance

The earnings insurance contract covers against loss of earnings caused directly by the perils identified in the policy. It is usually designed for smaller business establishments and is usually not available to manufacturers or larger mercantile operations. The contract is normally written without a co-insurance clause and limits recovery to a fixed dollar amount over a specific time period.

Loss of Income Insurance

The loss of income insurance policy covers the actual business loss sustained by the insured and the expenses necessarily incurred to resume normal business operations. The coverage applies when the loss results from the interruption of business or the untenantability of the premises when the building or the personal property is damaged as a direct result of an insured peril. The actual business loss sustained by the insured shall not exceed: (1) the reduction in gross earnings, less charges and expenses that do not necessarily continue during the interruption of the business; and (2) the reduction in rents, less charges and expenses that do not necessarily continue during the period of untenantability.

The actual business loss sustained shall not include charges and expenses that do not necessarily continue during the interruption of business or during the untenantability of the premises.

Loss of income shall be payable for only such length of time as would be required for the business to resume normal business operations but not exceeding such length of time as would be required to rebuild, repair, or replace such part of the building or personal property as has been damaged or destroyed as a direct result of an insured peril.

Nature and Scope of the Engagement

A CPA may become involved in a business interruption claim through several routes. If a client has suffered a business interruption, the CPA may assist the client in measuring and managing the damages and in submitting information to the insurance company. Some accounting firms serve as intermediaries between an insured and the insurance company neither of which were prior clients. Some accounting firms have developed such an expertise in this area that insurance companies retain them to help review complex business interruption claims. Finally, some insurance policies specify that the insured and the insurance company may each retain an accountant to review the policy and refer any disputes to an umpire. The accountant may also be called upon to confer with both parties and act as an arbitrator in the event of disagreement as to the claim's value. Thus the CPA involved in business interruption claims may play different roles in rendering professional services. See Chapter 11 on arbitration.

LOST PROFITS

Fundamentally, lost profits are measured by the amount that would make the company whole had the business interruption not occurred—the profits that would have been earned had operations not been suspended. The theory that business interruption value does not exist for a company operating at a loss is incorrect. If a company operates at a loss, the lost profit calculation must consider fixed charges and expenses that continue during the business interruption. Other chapters discuss whether lost profits should be measured on an increased cash flow basis or based on accounting accruals, with fully absorbed costs.

EXPERT TESTIMONY

As discussed in other sections of this *Handbook*, expert opinions must be based upon data that are admissible evidence; any assumptions must be reasonable and based upon facts. Most important, written records must be admissible, or testimony based thereon will not be admissible. For a case to be brought to trial, it must be based upon the accountants' professional understanding of the business and their reliance on financial data. The use of graphs helps to portray the impact of the business interruption on the operations of the company.

CONCLUSION

This chapter addresses several different areas of business interruption that are covered in greater depth in other chapters. An accountant involved in business interruption calculations must obtain a copy of the policy to decide how to compute lost profits and what, if any, special provisions exist. In addition, different causes and types of business interruptions exist, including breach of contract, tort claims, acts of God, product liability, fire, theft, accident, and explosion. Special considerations include the factual issues of the claim and legal issues involved in computing business interruption losses. The computation of lost profits must project lost sales and analyze cost savings, including direct costs and overhead. In this environment, the accountant relies not only on accounting principles and auditing standards but also managerial accounting.

NOTES

1. California Civil Code § § 3301 and 3359.
2. *American Jurisprudence*, Volume 22, Damages, § 172, p. 242. See also California Civil Code, § 3300.

3. Isadore Rosenblatt, Ed., *California Attorney's Damages Guide*, 1974, § 1.23, p. 14.
4. Robert L. Dunn, *Recovery of Damages For Lost Profits*, 3d ed., 1987, § 1.18, p. 49.
5. *American Jurisprudence*, *supra*, § 177, p. 252.
6. Dunn, *Recovery of Damages For Lost Profits*, 3d ed., supra, § 3.1, p. 144.
7. Ibid., § 3.2, p. 148.
8. *American Jurisprudence*, supra, § 176, p. 250.
9. Ibid., p. 251.
10. The reader is referred to *Restatement of the Law of Torts*, 2d ed. (American Law Institute, 1965).
11. Ibid., § 402A. See also Dunn, *Recovery of Damages For Lost Profits*, 3d ed., supra, § 3.23, p. 214 et seq.
12. See Dunn, *Recovery of Damages For Lost Profits*, 3d ed., supra, § 4.1 and following for a discussion of the "new business rule" as it applies to recovery of damages for lost profits.
13. Ibid., § 4.2, p. 220.

BIBLIOGRAPHY

American Jurisprudence (Rochester, NY: The Lawyers Cooperative Publishing Co., 1965), Volume 22, Damages.

California Attorney's Damages Guide (Cal CEB 1974).

California Attorney's Damages Guide (Cal CEB 1986), supplement.

Capello, A. Barry, and Frances E. Komoroske, *Lender Liability* (Los Angeles, CA: Parker & Son, 1987).

Dunn, Robert L., *Recovery of Damages For Lost Profits*, 3d ed. (Kentfield, CA: Lawpress Corporation, 1985).

Magee, John H., and Oscar N. Serbein, *Property and Liability Insurance* (Homewood, IL: Richard D. Irwin, Inc., 1967).

LIST OF CASES

K.M.C. Co., Inc. v. Irving Trust Co., 757 F.2d 752 (6th Cir. 1985)
Rosenblath v. Louisiana Bank & Trust Co., 432 So.2d 285 (La. App. 1983)

15

LITIGATION CONSULTING: CONSTRUCTION CLAIMS

D. Paul Regan

THE CONSTRUCTION PROCESS AND CLAIMS

A construction project brings together many entities under contract. These entities are jointly obligated to construct a project to specifications, within a time period, at a specific price or according to an agreed pricing method. The entities involved include the following:

- Owner (or owners' representative)
- Architect and engineer
- Construction manager
- Contractor
- Subcontractors
    - Civil
    - Electrical
    - Mechanical

These entities agree to commit their resources to a complex sequence of interdependent events and transactions. Delays or changes in the scheduled sequence will affect those depending upon its integrity. Changes in the project's scope during its construction, for example, could affect the design professional, the construction manager, and contractor and subcontractors, who each may have to revise labor, materials, equipment orders, and resequence work.

These effects can alter the entities' ability to meet their contractual obligations and to earn a profit on the project. In fact, the ripple effects of unplanned events often generate costs larger than the originally expected profit. The combination of interdependency among parties to a construction project and the dramatic economic impact of disruption makes construction litigation common.

Trends in construction litigation can be seen in the American Arbitration Association's (AAA) statistics. In 1983, the AAA administered 2675 construction cases. In 1988, construction cases increased to 4,940, a 13 percent annual growth rate. Because most of these claims and their related complexities arise from the contractor (or the subcontractor in a pass-through claim or both), this chapter focuses on the contractor's claims against the entities responsible for added costs (usually the owner, sometimes the design professional, or the construction manager).

COMPLEXITY OF CALCULATIONS

Construction litigation generates a variety of different concepts of claims. A project may produce claims for the following types of costs:

- Extra work—the contractor often has many, sometimes hundreds of separate claims for added quantities of labor or materials
- Delays
- Escalation
- Acceleration
- Disruption
- Contractor termination
- Unabsorbed home office overhead
- Cost of capital

These claims frequently result from many separate but interrelated events or transactions.

The financial impact of these events can be complex. Given the complexity of claims arising from construction projects, the contractor can only estimate the damages. The law requires only that the contractor prove a logical connection between liability and the resulting damages, calculated with reasonable certainty. This standard was recently reaffirmed in *Dept. of Transportation v. Guy F. Atkinson Co.*, 187 Cal. App. 3d 25 231 Cal. Rptr. 382 (1986), where the court stated that:

> The difficulties confronting the factfinder and rationale justifying a reasonable approximation of damages in similar cases find cogent expression in a federal decision: ". . . in cases like this, if not in every complex case, it is humanly impossible to trace, find, and specify in detail and quantity in effect, the numerous circumstances which cause or contribute to financial consequences. By such a process the determination of damages by court or jury could be bogged down in almost any case or rendered more inaccurate than a considered judgement appraisal of the combined effect of all actionable elements duly considered by an informed factfinder after elimination of the influence of extraneous causes . . ." (Telex Corp. v. International Business Machines Corp., 367 F. Supp. 258, 308–309, 351 (N.D. Okla. 1973), affd. in part: revd. and remanded on other grounds 510 F.2d 894 (10th Cir. 1975)).

The court in *M & R Contractors & Builders v. Michael*, 215 Md. 340, 138 A.2d 350 (1958) summarized the precision required by plaintiffs when computing and presenting claims:

> Courts have modified the "certainty" rule into a more flexible one of "reasonable certainty." In such instances, recovery may often be based on opinion evidence, in the legal sense of that term, from which liberal inferences may be drawn. Generally, proof of actual or even estimated costs is all that is required with certainty.
> Some of the modifications which have been aimed at avoiding the harsh requirements of the "certainty" rule include: (a) if the fact of damage is proven with certainty, the extent or the amount thereof may be left to reasonable inference; (b) where a defendant's wrong has caused the difficulty of proving damages, he cannot complain of the resulting uncertainty; (c) mere difficulty in ascertaining the amount of damage is not fatal; (d) mathematical precision in fixing the exact amount of damage is not required; (e) it is sufficient if the best evidence of the damage which is available is produced; and (f) the plaintiff is entitled to recover the value of his contract as measured by the value of his profits.

The courts have also addressed the level of imprecision that may prove fatal to the plaintiff. In *Zirin Laboratories Int'l Inc. v. Mead-Johnson & Co.*, 208 F.Supp. 633 (E.D. Mich. 1962), the court concluded that the damages presented must not be based upon "mere speculation, guess or conjecture." The courts have clearly recognized that "especially in sizable construction claims when mathematical precision is impossible" damage computations must reasonably approximate the amounts that the plaintiff is entitled to recover from the defendant (*Joseph Pickard's Sons Co. v. United States*, 532 F.2d 739, 742–743 (Ct. Cl. 1976)).

Complexity of Presentation

The methods used to present construction claims depend partially on the forum. If the matter is before an arbitrator, it may be appropriate to eliminate preliminary exhibits or testimony while presenting more detailed and technical testimony. To a lesser extent, this may also be true with a bench trial. With a jury trial, however, the jury must be presented with all the testimony and exhibits that will allow them to clearly understand the disputed matters, the bases for the opinions, the facts upon which they can properly assess liability, and the resulting damages.

Important elements in presenting construction claims include:

- A team consisting of client representatives, attorneys, accountants, engineers, scheduling, productivity, and other experts must communicate effectively and frequently. The lawyers are responsible for leading this team.
- The contract and related documents should be understood by team members.
- The key project documents (job diaries, meeting minutes, schedules, correspondence, labor records, job cost records) should be understood.
- The claim itself should be summarized for presentation (including the use of graphs) while assuring the trier of fact that the summary fairly represents the thousands of underlying project records.
- Placing the damage calculations on a computer enables the damage witness to respond quickly to changes, if new information or alternatives are appropriate for inclusion in the damage presentation. Because the damage witness is often the last witness for the plaintiff, prior witnesses often present testimony that necessitates adjustment to the claim.

Preparing Claims

No single method of damage calculation applies to every construction project. This chapter illustrates possible approaches for dealing with

- Extra work
- Compensable delays
- Acceleration disruption
- Escalation disruption

Extra work is performed by the contractor under changes in scope by the owner or owner's representative. In claiming costs for extra work, the contractor must show (1) the scope of the extra work, (2) that there was no previous inclusion of the work within the contract by change order, and (3) proper calculation of the added labor, materials, equipment, other costs, and profit. Documents used in pricing extra work include:

- The contract, particularly the changes clause and related pricing provision.
- Related documents identifying the project's scope, added work, and the pricing method.
- Meeting notes, correspondence and other job documents that may address the extra work performed.
- As-built drawings that document actual quantities installed on the project.
- Supporting cost records that validate the actual purchase, receipt, and cost of added quantities.

- Labor and equipment records that document the actual cost of installing the added quantities
- The project's job cost report, which enables timely recognition of extra work's occurrence. This report collects costing information associated with the extra work and facilitates the presentation and pricing of an extra work claim.

Compensable delays occur when another contract party's actions or inactions delay a contractor. The contractor may receive a time extension and damages reimbursement. When excusable delays occur, however, the contractor may receive only a time extension. An excusable delay results from unforeseeable events beyond the owner or contractor's control, fault, or negligence. Unusually severe weather (as compared with reasonably expected weather for the project location during the expected time period) is an example of excusable delay. If a contractor did not receive an appropriate time extension for an excusable delay, the contractor may have incurred damages through acceleration attempts to maintain timetables.

Delays that often call for both a time extension and compensation to the contractor include:

- Failure to provide the contractor site access as scheduled
- Delayed or changed design drawings
- Late delivery of owner-supplied equipment or materials
- Untimely field inspections

Documents Used in Pricing the Impact of Delays. A scheduling analysis representing the project is generally prepared using a computer program that plots the sequence and interdependencies of the project's significant activities. This analysis will reveal the activities' most logical sequence.

Many contracts, particularly for large projects, require identification of a critical path. Once the parties to a contract agree on a specific path, a party failing to perform within it may be liable for others' damages attributable to such failure.

The Critical Path Method (CPM) concepts were recently reaffirmed in *Appeal of Santa Fe Engineers, Inc.*, ASBCA 34, 225, 87-3 B.C.A. (1987) where the Board concluded that

> There is a rebuttable presumption of correctness attached to CPMs upon which the parties have previously mutually agreed. In the absence of compelling evidence of actual errors in the CPMs, we will let the parties "live or die" by the CPM schedule applicable to the relevant time frames . . . under the earlier October CPM, the suspended AHU work was critical and we find that the first eleven days of the suspension entitles the Contractor to an eleven-day extension to the contract completion date. Under the November CPM, the balance of the suspension applied to noncritical work and no time extension is warranted.

A delay claim relies on careful review of the contact and related documents. One clause frequently found in construction contracts reads that "in no event shall any delay or extension of time be construed as cause or justification for payment of extra compensation to the contractor."

The courts have generally upheld these clauses where they have not been coerced (*Peter Kiewit Sons' Co. v. Iowa So. Utilities Co.*, 355 F. Supp. 376 (S.D. Iowa 1973)). However, in the May 1986 New York Court of Appeals case of *Corinno Civetta Construction Corp. v. The City of New York*, 67 N.Y.2d 297, 493 N.E.2d 905, 502 N.Y.S.2d 681 (1986), the court listed four situations in which a contractor may recover delay damages and avoid the application of a broadly worded "no damage for delay" clause:

1) Delays caused by the contractee's bad faith or its willful, malicious, or grossly negligent conduct.
2) Uncontemplated delays,
3) Delays so unreasonable that they constitute an intentional abandonment of the contract by the contractee, and
4) Delays resulting from the contractee's breach of a fundamental obligation of the contract.

When the contractor is entitled to compensable delay damages, the accountant must estimate the related costs. These costs generally arise from extended contract performance, escalation, and acceleration.

Extended contract performance costs usually increase with the passage of time. For example, assume that a delay made it impracticable to remove a tower crane and the compensable delay was 65 days. The contractor would be entitled to 65 days of the crane's rental cost. If the contractor owned the crane, the contract may suggest how to price the delay. Usually rental value is used to price contractor-owned equipment included in a delay claim. The equipment's purchase price and depreciation is not usually relevant because accounting depreciation does not measure the item's value.

In addition to equipment, many other contractor costs are "time sensitive" and compensable:

- Supervisory costs
- Site security
- Certain site overhead expenses
- Weather protection and weather impact costs

Escalation claims require proof that costs incurred in later periods had higher unit prices than the prices that would have existed had no delay occurred. This proof is often more difficult than it may first appear. Escalation claims frequently include labor cost. A delay claim on a large complex project is often a series of many individual delays, and the labor cost generally comprises multiple crafts (electricians, pipefitters, laborers, etc.) with multiple wage levels (apprentice, journeyman, foreman, etc.) within each craft. Computing the incremental labor cost resulting from these multiple delays often requires an approximation. Exhibit 15-1 illustrates one approach to approximating escalation of labor costs.

EXHIBIT 15-1. HMI CONTRACTING: COMPUTATION OF LABOR ESCALATION

(A) Labor Contract Period	(B) As-Planned Hours Distribution	(C) As-Built Hours	(D) Actual Labor Cost	(E) (D/C) Average Labor Cost/Hour	(F) (B × C) Hours Distributed as Planned	(G) (E × F) Labor without Escalation
19X1	15.00%	25,000	$ 1,031,250	$41.25	78,750	$ 3,248,438
19X2	65.00%	195,000	8,517,600	43.68	341,250	14,905,800
19X3	20.00%	255,000	11,883,000	46.60	105,000	4,893,000
19X4		50,000	2,455,500	49.11		
	100.00%	525,000	$23,887,350		525,000	$23,047,238

Assuming that the increasing average labor cost is attributable only to the inflation of wage rates, the escalation claim derived from Exhibit 15-1 is $840,112, which is the difference between the actual labor cost in Column D and the computed labor cost without escalation, Column G.

Acceleration results when a contractor revises the contract schedule to complete the remaining activities in less time than planned. The contractor usually reduces the time span by adding manpower and shifts, increasing overtime and revising work sequences. If the owner ordered the acceleration or if the appropriate authority refused to allow the contractor a proper time extension, the contractor may receive compensation for the additional costs (*Wallace Process Piping Co. v. Martin-Marietta Corp.*, 251 F. Supp. 411 (E.D. Va. 1965) and *Natkin & Company v. George A. Fuller Company*, 347 F. Supp. 17 (W.D. Mo. 1972)).
Acceleration costs include

- Premium portion of overtime and the inefficiencies associated with extended overtime
- Higher wage rates of added shifts
- Vendors' premiums for expedited delivery of materials
- Equipment increases required to support added crews
- Disruptive effects on the work force causing lower productivity
- Extra hours associated with revised work

The contractor's acceleration claim must prove that the owner or owner–representative decided to accelerate. Depending upon the applicable contractual relationships, the owner's representatives for this purpose may include the contracting officer, architect, engineer, or contractor (assuming a subcontractor accelerates). The plaintiff must obtain the applicable correspondence, meeting notes, witness statements, or other notes and records that prove why the project was accelerated.

Disruption of the contractor's work force by the owner or owner representative resulting in reduced productivity is often compensable to the contractor. Disruptions affect the contractor's work force in many ways:

- Uneven labor force levels, including overtime
- Inefficient work force level
- Inefficient sequence scheduling, stacking of crafts (e.g. forcing electricians and pipefitters to work simultaneously in the same location)
- Excessive drawing changes
- Early, late, or out-of-sequence material and equipment deliveries
- Delayed or restricted site access
- Performance beyond contract specifications or tolerances

Analysts frequently ascertain the affected activities, then calculate the affected versus unaffected productivity rate for these activities. The incremental costs associated with the lower productivity experienced in the affected period becomes the core of the contractor's disruption claim, as illustrated later.

An alternative to the affected versus unaffected approach uses the contractor's experience from other projects or uses industry productivity standards. Here the analyst must adjust these productivity measures for those factors unique to the disputed project. Because these adjustments can be difficult to ascertain, using data from within the project itself is generally preferable because both the affected and the unaffected productivity rates reflect the contractor's actual performance on the same project with the same, or many of the same, persons.

Another approach uses research studies that measure the effects of certain types of disruptions. For example, the *Modification Impact Evaluation Guide* issued by the Army Corps of Engineers has studied the effects of crew overloading, crowding, and overtime.

Case Study

This case study assumes the following:

- The project consisted of two identical buildings (Buildings A and B).
- Building A was affected by delayed site access, late, and/or revised drawings, acceleration, and overcrewing and overtime.
- Revised drawings for both buildings increased the lumber requirements by 37,320 board feet for each building. The owner denied that any board feet were added.
- The contractor's labor force was adversely affected by factors that were the contractor's responsibility while installing rough carpentry on both buildings.

The following records provided the information presented in Exhibit 15-2 and the related graphs shown in Exhibits 15-3 through 15-6:

- Hours by building, from time cards prepared daily by the foreman.
- Board feet data from progress measurements taken by contractor personnel.
- Added quantity of board feet data derived by an engineer comparing the as-bid and as-built drawings. (Paid invoices support the as-built board footage delivered to the site; ending inventory and a scrap factor must be considered.)
- The planned bid hours data from the bid and planning working papers.

The graphs typify those presented to support disruption claims. Exhibits 15-3 through 15-6 support the following conclusions:

Exhibit 15-3

- For Building A, the start of rough carpentry is delayed until Week 3, and it does not reach the planned manning level for Week 2 until Week 6.
- Though Building A was expected to be completed in Week 8, manloading reaches its peak in Week 10, and completion occurs in Week 12.
- Building A appears to have been delayed and then accelerated by substantial overmanning.

Exhibit 15-4

- Although rough carpentry of the buildings is equal in scope, the actual hours to perform this work were considerably higher for Building A than for Building B.

EXHIBIT 15-2. P & H CONTRACTOR INC. ROUGH CARPENTRY

Actual Rough Carpentry Manloading

Row Number	Week Number	Total Hours Building A	Total Hours Building B	Total Hours	Building A Board Feet	Building B Board Feet	Building A BF/MH	Building B BF/MH
1	1	0		0				
2	2	0		0				
3	3	95		95	4,094		43	
4	4	189		189	8,106		43	
5	5	236		236	9,822		42	
6	6	473		473	18,610		39	
7	7	473		473	17,576		37	
8	8	567		567	19,354		34	
9	9	567		567	18,610		33	
10	10	3,025		3,025	81,077		27	
11	11	2,741	292	3,033	77,955	11,484	28	39
12	12	1,087	438	1,525	30,913	18,184	28	42
13	13		583	583	0	26,797		46
14	14		729	729	0	35,889		49
15	15		1,458	1,458	0	73,372		50
16	16		1,021	1,021		54,844		54
17	17		729	729		37,484		51
18	18		583	583		28,073		48
19								
20		9,453	5,833	15,286	286,117	286,127		

21			
22			
23	Average board feet (BF) per manhour (MH)	30.27	49.05
24			
25			
26	Added quantity of BF	37,320	37,320
27	Actual manhours required for added BF.	1,233	761
29	(Row 26 ÷ Row 23)		
30	Manhours required for contract work		
31	(9.453–1,233 and 5,833–761,		
32	respectively)	8,220	5,072
33			
34	Manhours required for Building A		
35	assuming Building B productivity	5,072	
36			
37	Manhours lost to disruption	3,147	
38			
39	Cost of manhours lost, including		
40	fringes, before support costs,		
41	overhead, and profit	$78,686	
42			

EXHIBIT 15-3. P&H CONTRACTOR INC., ROUGH CARPENTRY—BUILDING A, BID VERSUS ACTUAL CRAFT HOURS

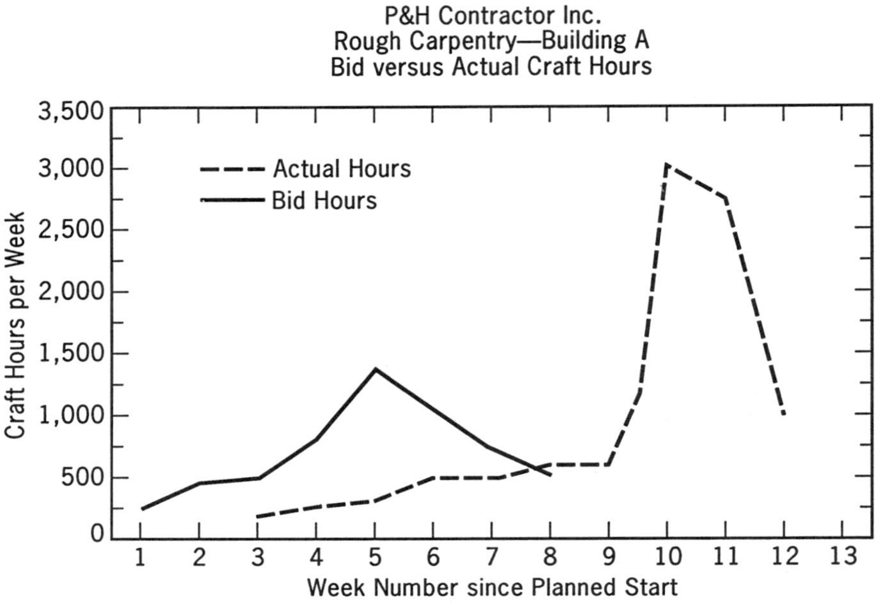

EXHIBIT 15-4. P&H CONTRACTOR INC., ROUGH CARPENTRY—BUILDINGS A & B, ACTUAL CRAFT HOURS

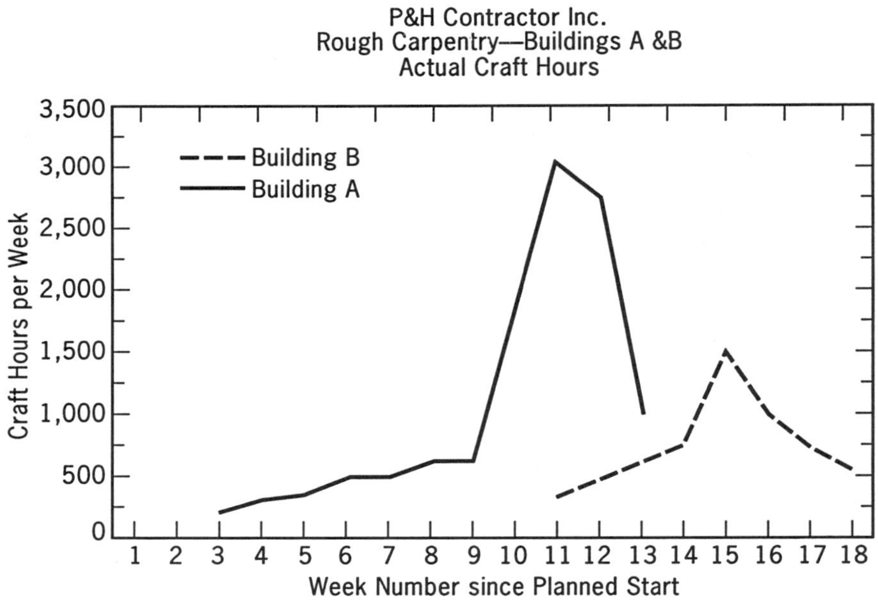

EXHIBIT 15-5. P&H CONTRACTOR INC., ROUGH CARPENTRY—BUILDING B, BID VERSUS ACTUAL CRAFT HOURS

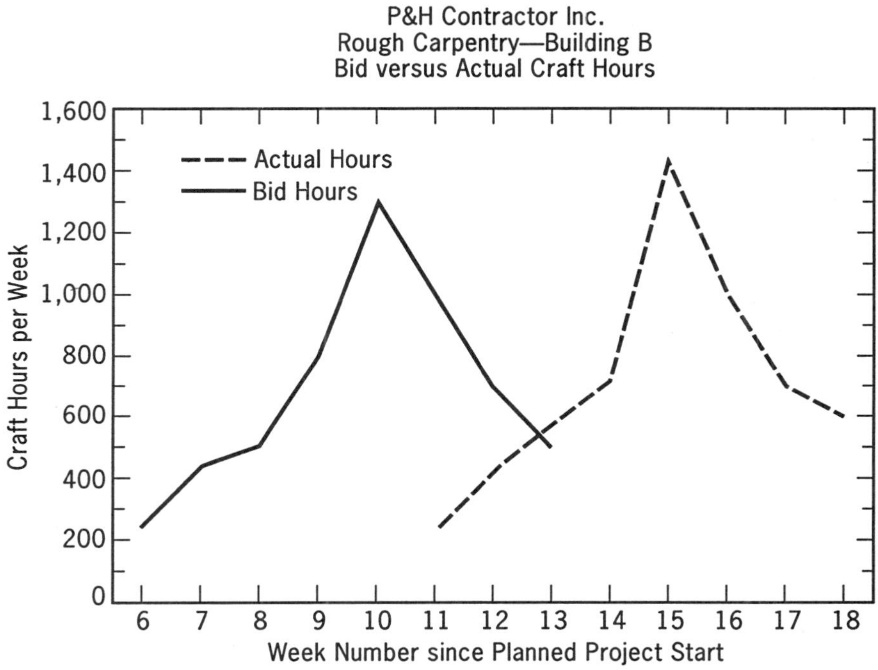

Exhibit 15-5

- The start of rough carpentry on Building B was delayed 5 weeks until Week 11.
- The finish of rough carpentry for Building B was delayed 5 weeks until Week 18,
- The planned and actual manloading are very similar even with 15% more board feet,
- Though this aspect of the project was delayed, it does not appear to have been accelerated (the work was planned and performed over an 8 week period).

Exhibit 15-6

- The contractor's productivity level in Building A began close to bid level but deteriorated rapidly as the activity became severely overmanned (Exhibit 15-6), finishing well below the bid level,
- The contractor's productivity level in Building B began poorly (perhaps the result of a lingering effect of the disruption experienced on Building A) but improved rapidly, finishing well ahead of the bid level.

EXHIBIT 15-6. P&H CONTRACTOR INC., WEEKLY PRODUCTIVITY ANALYSIS, ROUGH CARPENTRY

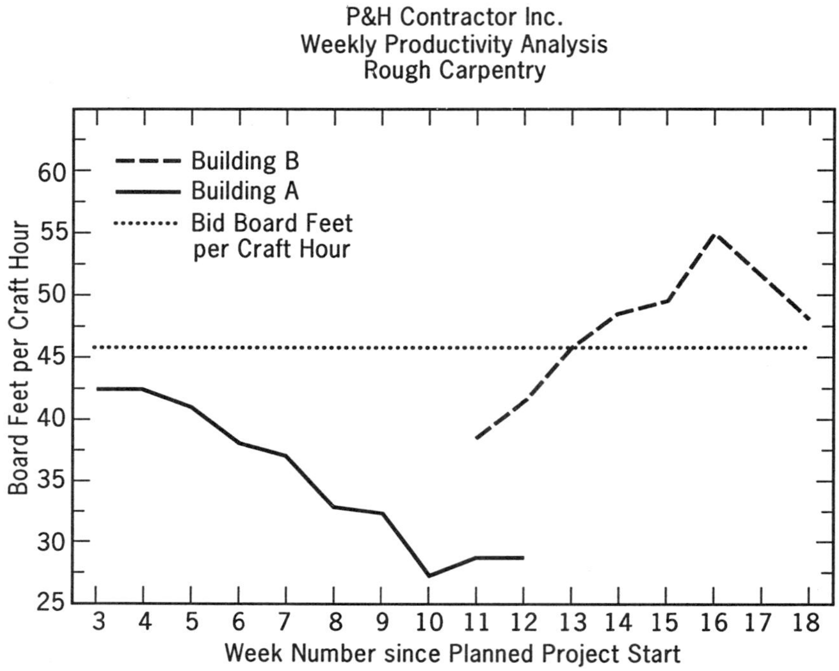

Exhibit 15.2

- Assumes the additional board feet is priced based upon cost (often the contract will apply unit prices or some other specific remedy to extra work). The claim's labor portion would include the actual labor hours incurred by the contractor to install the added quantity of board feet. This exhibit also displays the segregation of hours associated with added scope from the contractor's disruption claim. (Rows 30 to 33)
- The expert assumes that the contractor's experience while installing rough carpentry on Building A provides a reasonable estimate for Building B. Therefore, had the contractor not been disrupted, Building A would have incurred the same hours as that of Building B (ignoring learning curve considerations). Exhibit 15-2, thusly, prices the disruption claim in Rows 33 through 38. To the $78,686 computed on Row 42 of Exhibit 15-2 would be added other incurred costs (site support, overhead, and profit factors) as allowed by the contract. If counsel determines that the contract is not limiting, the claim also would include support costs (e.g., tools, equipment), and other site costs affected by an overmanned and disrupted work force as well as related allocations of the contractor's overhead and profit.

TOTAL COST METHOD

In its purest form, the total cost method computes recoverable damages by subtracting the bid costs (plus profit) from the total actual costs (plus profit). When applying this method to a particular claim, the contractor usually modifies the total costs incurred to account for items such as

- Costs included in change orders and other claim items
- Costs incurred by the contractor that are not recoverable from the owner
- Modifications necessary to the bid's estimated costs

This claim pricing method is described as the "Modified Total Cost" method. Courts have traditionally allowed this approach under the following conditions:

- The nature of the losses make it highly impractical to accurately determine the losses on a specific identification method
- The bid price was realistic
- The actual costs were reasonable
- The contractor was not responsible for the increased costs

Several cases have clarified and expanded the conditions under which the contractor may prepare a total cost claim. In each of these cases, the contractor proved that a recovery was deserved and that it was impossible to prove damages under any other approach.

> Defendant challenges the manner in which these costs were computed by arguing that the commissioner's report erroneously accepts the "total cost" theory expressly rejected by us in *River Construction Corp. v. United States*, 159 Ct. Cl. 254 (1962) and in *F.H. McGraw & Co. v. United States*, 130 F. Suppl. 394 (Ct. Cl. 1955). We are aware that we have on a number of occasions expressed our dislike for this method of computing breaches of contract damages, and we do not intend to condone its use as a universal rule. However, we have used this method where there is no other alternative, since we recognize that the lack of certainty as to the amount of damages should not preclude recovery *J.D. Hedin Construction Co. v. United States*, 347 F.2d 235 (Ct. Cl.[171] (1965)).

If the owner's actions help cause the impossibility or impracticability of the contractor's using other, more acceptable, methods of claim pricing, the courts will be more inclined to accept the total cost method. In *C. Norman Peterson Co. v. Container Corp. of America*, 172 Cal. App. 3d 628, 218 Cal.Rptr. 592 1985), the court stated that where the contractor

> . . . was unable to keep more accurate cost records due to fault on the part of the owner. The trial court made specific findings, supported by the record, that due to the many errors and omissions in the drawings furnished by [the owner], the latter orally instructed [the contractor] to perform numerous changes during the critical shutdown period. The work caused by these changes was complex, and the trial court

> found it was impossible for [the contractor] to keep accurate cost records for each and every change during the shutdown. Thus, unlike in Boyajian and Nichols, the owner's conduct prevented [the contractor] from making a more detailed showing as to how the damages claimed were caused by the breach. Although the total cost theory of proving damages in a contract case is not generally favored, under proper safeguards and where there is no better proof it has been upheld. Under the facts of this case, it was appropriate for the trial court to award damages based on the total cost method.

Dept. of Transportation v. Guy F. Atkinson Co., 187 Cal. App. 3d 25, 231 Cal. Rptr. 382 (1986) has been described as a significant case for the total cost method and the court's willingness to admit its presentation into evidence.

Lost Profits

When a contractor cannot complete a project because of a breach by the owner or a person for whom the owner is responsible, the contractor can recover the lost profits that would have been earned had the project been completed. Lost projects usually are measured as the remaining contract price, less the contractor's incremental costs to complete the project.

Extended Home Office Overhead

On projects that are delayed, the contractor will continue to incur home office overhead without the expected gross margin to absorb these expenses. If the contractor is unable to secure replacement revenue during this period because of the troubles encountered on a project with claims or if the contractor incurs incremental home office overhead because of the extended project, the contractor may be entitled to recover this unabsorbed home office overhead.

Such overhead costs are separate and in addition to indirect site costs that may also have been extended as a result of delays. Home office costs are those that are not allocable to specific projects. If the contractor has incurred home office costs that are specifically identified with a project, an ideal accounting system would capture these costs charged on the related project. However, for certain costs and circumstances, this is not possible or practicable.

The most common method of computing extended home office overhead has become knows as the Eichleay formula *Appeal of Eichleay Corp.*, ASBCA 5183, 60-2 B.C.A. (1960). The mechanics of this formula are not complicated:

Claim amount = Daily home office overhead (daily rate)
times number of days of delay

Where daily rate = Home office overhead allocable to the contract
divided by originally planned number of contract days

The Eichleay formula has fallen in and out of favor with the courts over the years (see *Berley Industries, Inc. v. City of New York*, 45 N.Y.2d 683, 385 N.E.2d 281, 412 N.Y.S.2d 589 (1978) which rejected the Eichleay formula when the contractor presented it without accompanying evidence linking the formula in some way to actual expenditures made during the delay period.

> It is relevant to the application of these principles that, in the case before us now, any increase in home office overhead was not merely hard to measure, but was lacking altogether. True, unlike jobsite overhead increases whose relationship to a particular job will usually be capable of direct proof, the connection between home office overhead increases and delay in a particular project will more often be indirect. But because proof is indirect does not mean it does not exist. Here, there was no showing that the delay caused an increase in home office activity or expense of any kind.

The Eichleay formula has generally fared better in federal courts. In 1984, the Court of Appeals for the Federal Circuit reversed the General Services Board of Contract Appeals in *Capital Electric Co. v. United States*, 729 F.2d 743 (Fed. Cir. 1984) by holding that

> As far as this panel is concerned, we do not believe these procedures should be overruled. They are of such long standing and have been followed in so many decisions of the various boards of contract appeals that such action should more properly be taken by the Congress.

An examination of the Eichleay formula reveals that it calculates an average rather than a precise amount of extended home office overhead for a particular project. Additionally, calculations based upon the facts and circumstances of a particular project are possible. Although it might be appropriate to make such modifications (for example, by using total direct costs rather than revenues to allocate overhead, or by adding the claimed amount to contract billings in computing the allocation), the contractor also should present the calculation exactly as called for by the formula. This caution stems from the position taken by the court in *George Hyman Construction v. Washington Metropolitan Transit Authority*, 816 F.2d 753 (D.C. Cir. 1987). We reject this condition. Except when parties have contracted specifically to use an alternate formula, courts and board of contract appeals have applied the Eichleay formula to calculate the exact amount of recovery for home office overhead costs. The Federal Circuit, for example, has mandated the use of the Eichleay formula in all disputes arising out of contracts involving the federal government.

Because of the love–hate relationship the courts have had over the use of the Eichleay formula, lawyers should guide its use in any particular jurisdiction. Additionally, when using Eichleay in a presentation of extended home office overhead costs, the contractor should demonstrate to the court a linkage to actual home office expenditures made during the delay period or demonstrate that such a linkage is not impossible.

Interest or Cost of Capital

A contractor's interest cost or cost of capital claim is usually dependent upon the terms of the contract, the jurisdiction in which the claim is brought, and the facts and circumstances applicable to the particular project. These include whether there is any linkage between the costs incurred on the project and money borrowed by the contractor to finance these costs in whole or in part. In making these determinations, the contractor must consult with legal counsel to determine whether such a claim can be presented and the specifics of its calculation.

CONCLUSION

Construction claims result from events that modify the contract performance of one or more parties. Coping with these changes successfully will be enhanced by

- Planning and related documentation
- Project documentation that will capture and detect modifications
- Costs records that will capture and account for costs associated with modifications
- Effective communications systems to all parties associated with the changes

With these in place, the long, hard task of calculating and presenting claims for these changes hopefully can be shortened.

LIST OF CASES

Berley Industries, Inc. v. City of New York, 45 N.Y.2d 683, 385 N.E.2d 281, 412 N.Y.S.2d 589 (1978)
Capital Electric Co. v. United States, 729 F.2d 743 (Fed. Cir. 1984)
C. Norman Peterson Co. v. Container Corp. of America, 172 Cal. App. 3d 628, 218 Cal. Rptr. 592 (1985)
Corinno Civetta Construction Corp. v. The City of New York, 67 N.Y.2d 297, 493 N.E.2d 905, 502 N.Y.S.2d 681 (1986)
Dept. of Transportation v. Guy F. Atkinson Co., 187 Cal. App. 3d 25, 231 Cal. Rptr. 382 (1986)
Appeal of Eichleay Corp., ASBCA 5183, 60-2 BCA (1960)
F.H. McGraw & Co. v. United States, 130 F. Supp. 394 (Ct. Cl. 1955)
George Hyman Construction v. Washington Metropolitan Transit Authority, 816 F.2d 753 (D.C. Cir. 1987)
J.D. Hedin Construction Co. v. United States, 347 F.2d 235 (Ct. Cl. 1965)
Joseph Pickard's Sons Co. v. United States, 532 F.2d 739 (Ct. Cl. 1976)
M&R Contractors & Builders v. Michael, 215 Md. 340, 138 A.2d 350 (1958)
Natkin & Company v. George A. Fuller Company, 347 F. Supp. 17 (W.D. Mo. 1972)
Peter Kiewit Sons' Co. v. Iowa So. Utilities Co., 355 F. Supp. 376 (S.D. Iowa 1973)
River Construction Corp. v. United States, 159 Ct. Cl. 254 (1962)
Appeal of Santa Fe Engineers, Inc., ASBCA 34,225, 87-3 BCA (1987)
Telex Corp. v. International Business Machines Corp., 367 F. Supp. 258 (N.D. Okla. 1973), affd. in part: revd and remanded on other grounds 510 F.2d 894 (10th Cir. 1975)
Wallace Process Piping Co. v. Martin-Marietta Corp., 251 F. Supp. 411 (E.D. Va. 1965)
Zirin Laboratories Int'l Inc., v. Mead-Johnson & Co., 208 F. Supp. 633 (E.D. Mich. 1962)

16

DAMAGES ISSUES OF COPYRIGHT, TRADEMARK, AND TRADE SECRET CASES

M. James Call, AM, MBA
George G. Strong, JD, MBA, CPA, CMC

INTRODUCTION

Copyrights, trademarks, and trade secrets are intellectual property rights. These rights have evolved to allow one to profit from one's own efforts by restricting certain kinds of competition: selling unauthorized copies of another's work, offering one's product as being that of another, or using another's trade secrets. These kinds of competition are discouraged by statutes that provide for two types of remedies:

monetary sanctions as redress and nonmonetary sanctions to prevent continued infractions.

Monetary Sanctions

Successful plaintiffs in cases against infringers of intellectual property rights can generally claim two kinds of monetary sanctions as redress: (1) restitution for actual damages suffered as a result of the infringement or (2) the disgorgement of the infringer's profits, or both. Both kinds of sanctions redress the relationship among the parties, bringing each to the position it would have had if the infringement had not occurred.

Exhibit 16-1 presents a simplified illustration of these two claims. The intellectual property owner recovers its damages. (These are the difference between its actual sales and the sales it would have had "but for" the infringement times the difference between its net selling price and its incremental costs of sale.) The infringer also gives up its profits. (These are the infringing product's total sales times the difference between its net selling price and its incremental costs of sales.) Note that the amounts covered by the intersection of the plaintiff's damages and the infringer's profits are recovered only once.[1]

EXHIBIT 16-1. MONETARY REMEDIES FOR COPYRIGHT INFRINGEMENT

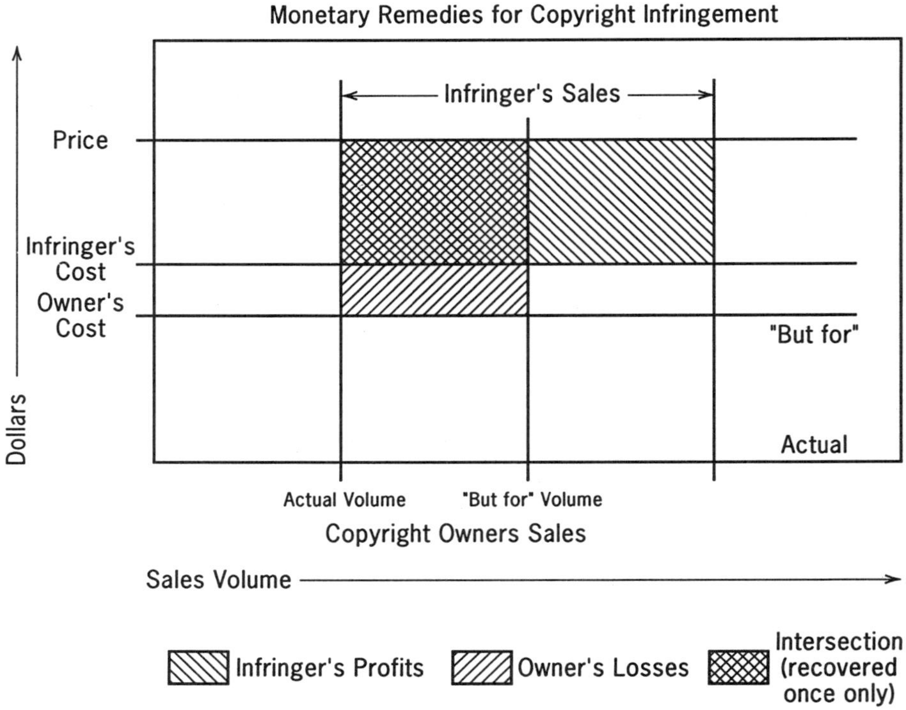

The damages and profits that are the subject of redress are the *economic* damages and profits. These might differ from *accounting* losses and profits that are calculated and reported in conformity with generally accepted accounting principles.

This chapter neither discusses nor critiques the various theories that courts have used to calculate the remedies they impose. The authors assume, however, that courts will continue current trends toward greater sophistication in using marketing and financial experts to understand business situations and ascertain appropriate remedies. The bulk of this chapter, therefore, presents techniques to calculate damages and profits in cases of intellectual property rights infringement.

Beyond the requirements of redress, the law also allows for punitive damages in certain cases of trademark infringement and criminal penalties in some cases of stealing trade secrets.

Nonmonetary Sanctions

Several types of nonmonetary sanctions exist, ranging from temporary injunctions to imprisonment. In applying these sanctions, courts maintain a balance between free and unfettered commercial competition and protection of intellectual property rights.

Courts are also asked to issue orders restraining infringing behaviors and impounding infringing goods.

Legal Issues

As usual in damage claims, the plaintiff must establish the *fact of damage*, that is, that the infringer's actions *caused* the owner's loss. Once this link or *nexus* is established, the court allows greater latitude in proving the *amount* of damages. The damages must, however, be "nonspeculative."

Once liability is established, the plaintiff's claim for a disgorgement of the defendant's profits begins with an estimate of the defendant's relevant sales revenues. The burden then shifts to the defendant to prove which costs should be deducted in calculating its real profits.

Finally, the damages analyst should thoroughly understand the legal principles of both the liability and the damage elements of each cause of action.

- This understanding is useful in knowing how to meet the many threshold causation requirements of the damage elements.
- Also, damage analysts often discover facts or methods that are relevant to the liability claims.

This chapter will, therefore, discuss some of the unique liability and remedy issues associated with each of these intangible property rights before exploring acceptable methods of calculating monetary sanctions for violating these rights. As with monetary sanctions, this chapter neither discusses nor critiques the tests that courts have used to ascertain liability, but will present an overview, with references to selected statutes and case law.

The discussion begins with copyright law and then follows with trademark and trade secret law.

COPYRIGHT

A copyright is, simply, the exclusive right to copy, sell, or display copies of an original work. The original work can be a photograph or a painting, a play or choreography, a musical score or a recording, a chapter in a book or a computer display—any original work that is in a form that could be copied or reproduced.

In the United States, the 1976 Copyright Act grants this exclusive right to copy and sell, and other rights, to an author when the work becomes "fixed" in a "tangible medium of expression" from which it "can be perceived, reproduced or otherwise communicated, either directly or with the aid of a machine or device."[2] The statute does not require registration with the Copyright Office.

The Copyright Act grants exclusively to the copyright owner the specific rights to:

- Reproduce the copyrighted work
- Prepare derivative works based upon the copyrighted work
- Distribute copies of the copyrighted work to the public by sale or other transfer of ownership
- Perform the copyrighted work publicly
- Display the work publicly.[3]

With limited exceptions, those who infringe on these rights without the copyright owner's permission violate the Copyright Act and are subject to various monetary and nonmonetary sanctions.

Legal Standards of Proof

To establish the *fact* of unauthorized infringement, the copyright owner must prove only two things: (1) that the infringing party was aware of the copyrighted work and (2) that the infringing work is substantially similar to the copyrighted work. The copyright owner need not have been damaged to establish that an infringer violated the Copyright Act. The copyright owner need not have been damaged to claim the profits that an infringer has unjustly acquired from the infringement.

Remedies

Once the plaintiff proves unauthorized infringement, the court may award any or all of the following remedies:

- An injunction to stop continuing infringement
- Impoundment and destruction of the infringing articles

- Recovery of actual damages to the copyright owner and any additional profits of the infringer *or* statutory damages
- Costs and attorney's fees.

This section briefly discusses injunctions, impounding, and the financial issues a court might consider in setting statutory damages for copyright violations. It also discusses damage and lost profit considerations unique to copyright issues.

Injunctions and Impounding. The court may issue a preliminary injunction or order the seizing and impounding of infringing goods before a trial when it believes there is a prima facie case for infringement and that the copyright holder will suffer irreparable harm by allowing continued infringement. A prima facie case exists when two elements are shown: copyright ownership and unauthorized copies.

If the plaintiff proves infringement at trial, the court may issue a permanent injunction and order the destruction of the impounded goods.

Actual Damages to the Copyright Owner. Actual damages to the copyright owner may be measured as the market value of the infringed copyrighted work or as the profits that the copyright owner has lost or will lose as a result of the infringement.

Market Value of Copyrighted Work. The parties' prior dealings and the custom in a particular trade or industry have both been used to establish bench marks for the market value of copyrighted works.[4]

Prior dealings would include earlier authorized use of similar copyrighted material and unfulfilled contracts authorizing use of the material in question.

Appropriate trade customs may be offered as evidence through an industry expert's testimony. This testimony would explain the factors that affect market value in the particular industry and how those factors apply to the copyrighted work in question.

Copyright Owners' Lost Profits. Absent an established market value for the copyrighted work itself, the most frequently used measure of actual damages is the profits that the copyright owner has lost as a result of the infringement. The profit measure is the contribution margin on the lost sales—the revenue from the lost sales less the incremental or variable expenses that would have been incurred in generating that revenue. The lost profits calculation, therefore, requires estimating the lost sales and the variable costs.

The case of *Stevens Linen Associates, Inc. v. Mastercraft Corporation*,[5] in which Mastercraft was found to have violated Stevens's copyright on one of Stevens's upholstery fabric designs, illustrates the way one court responded to four different approaches to establishing the fact of damage and estimating the copyright owner's lost sales. The four approaches were based on infringer's sales, customer overlap, copyright owner's own sales projections, and product mix analysis (Exhibit 16-2). Although other courts are not bound by the reasoning of the *Stevens* court, its reactions to each of these techniques is especially interesting because the same trial considered all four of them. Further, because estimating lost sales for all causes of

EXHIBIT 16-2

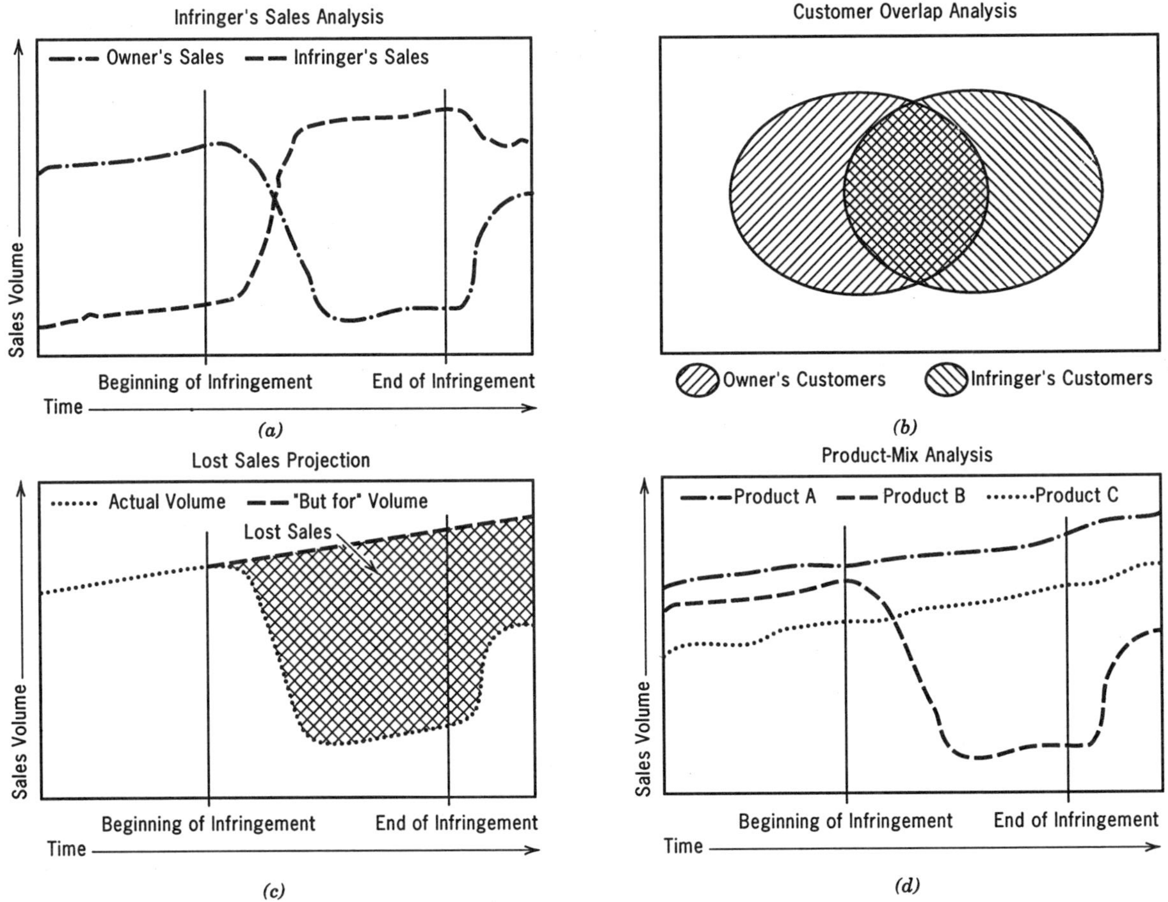
Infringer's Sales Analysis
Owner's Sales
Infringer's Sales
Sales Volume
Beginning of Infringement
End of Infringement
Time
(a)
Customer Overlap Analysis
Owner's Customers
Infringer's Customers
(b)
Lost Sales Projection
Actual Volume
"But for" Volume
Lost Sales
Sales Volume
Beginning of Infringement
End of Infringement
Time
(c)
Product-Mix Analysis
Product A
Product B
Product C
Sales Volume
Beginning of Infringement
End of Infringement
Time
(d)

action is similar for the damages analyst, this illustration is also relevant in trademark and trade secret cases.

Using the *infringer's sales* approach, Stevens claimed that it would have sold all of the copyright-infringing fabric that Mastercraft sold had Mastercraft not infringed on Stevens's copyright. The court rejected this approach because Stevens did not convince the court that the sales of the two parties were *comparable* and that Stevens would have sold as much of the copyrighted product as Mastercraft sold. Specifically, the court rejected this approach because of the relatively large difference between the price Stevens charged its customers for the fabric ($5.40/yard) and the price Mastercraft charged its customers for the fabric ($3.40/yard).

This comparability standard could well extend to other elements of the marketing mix such as customer segments, distribution channels, packaging, and advertising. Failure to consider and adjust for areas of noncomparability might result in unfairly estimating the copyright owner's sales based on the infringer's superior or weaker marketing position. Because this is the simplest and most often used method to prove plaintiff's lost sales, the analyst should carefully consider and affirmatively establish this comparability before accepting the infringer's sales technique.

Secondly, Stevens claimed lost sales by showing that some of its own customers bought some of the infringing product from Mastercraft (the *overlapping customer* method). The court accepted this method and ruled that because Stevens had shown that Mastercraft was selling the infringing product to Stevens's customers, the burden shifted to Mastercraft to prove that it had not diverted sales from Stevens, that customers of the copyrighted product would not have purchased all of their fabric from Stevens if Mastercraft were not offering the infringing design.

Although overlapping sales to customers offers compelling evidence of diverted sales, these estimates rarely measure the exact amount of lost sales. One must also consider the marketing factors mentioned, the specific customers' relative importance to each party, and the basis of competition for business from common customers, as well as other factors.

Third, Stevens used its own *sales projections* and showed that the projected sales exceeded the actual sales of the copyrighted pattern during the infringement period. The court rejected this method because Stevens had not shown that its sales projections were valid.[6]

Where the copyright owner has records of its projected and actual sales for periods prior to the infringement, expert analysis and testimony could show the historical correlation between projected sales and actual sales. This would validate a copyright owner's sales projections as the basis for measuring lost sales. Note that prior projections would not have to be accurate, only that the relationship between projections and actual experience has been stable. For example, if projections routinely exceeded the actual results by 20 percent, an analyst could adjust for this historical bias and provide the necessary validation of projections.

As its fourth approach, Stevens showed how its *product mix* changed when Mastercraft was selling its infringing fabric. Sales of Stevens's original fabric had been growing over five times as fast as its other lines until Mastercraft began infringing. Thereafter, this infringed line grew more slowly than Stevens's other lines were growing, even though overall business was up. In contrast to the "sales projection" method, the court approved the product mix method, apparently finding the appropriate factual basis in the historical comparisons with which to establish the validity of the assumed sales relationships.

As with the other methods of estimating lost sales, expert analysis and testimony showing the mix of sales of different products during infringed and noninfringed time periods and in infringed and noninfringed market segments can provide bench marks for estimating what the mix relationships would have been but for the infringement.

Other factors to consider while estimating lost sales might include changes in the size of the target market for the copyrighted work, sales of competitive alternatives to the copyrighted work, and other more general trends in the market.

The *Stevens* case offers a glimpse of the favored position enjoyed by the "diverted sales" technique. Courts have more willingly awarded damages for plaintiff's losses if a diversion of its sales to the defendant can be shown to have resulted from the infringement. This requires a common customer base.

Obviously, an expert using several different, independently derived estimates of but-for sales presents a more robust opinion to the court. Assaults on one of several methods might not challenge the overall opinion of damages nearly as strongly as if they were focused on the only method employed.[7] This is especially true if the different methods result in relatively close estimates.

Deductible Costs. Once the analyst estimates plaintiff's lost sales, the analyst must estimate the costs needed to generate those lost sales and then subtract those costs from the sales revenues to calculate the lost profits. The costs relevant to this calculation are only those that are both (1) attributable to the infringed product and (2) variable within the range of volume between the actual sales and the but-for sales.

Neither accounting jargon nor a prior court's categorization of a cost as "variable" or "fixed" should prejudice the analysis: any cost, however named, which varies as a function of increased sales should be deducted to the extent that it varies *in the range between the actual sales and the but-for sales*. Exhibit 16-3 shows how a change in sales volume will always increase strictly variable costs. The same change in volume, however, have a different impact on deductable semivariable costs depending on how that cost changes in the specific range of the increased or decreased volume.

Nominal Dollars versus Real Dollars. Because the copyright holder lost the return on the investment of the lost profits, the historical dollar losses should also compensate for the copyright holder's opportunity costs of these lost profits.

Many jurisdictions treat these lost earnings-on-earnings or present value adjustments as "prejudgment interest" rather than as a component of actual damages from lost sales. Further, courts often use the degree of culpability as the test for the recovering these real economic losses. If considered as "prejudgment interest," the rate is often prescribed by statute.

EXHIBIT 16-3

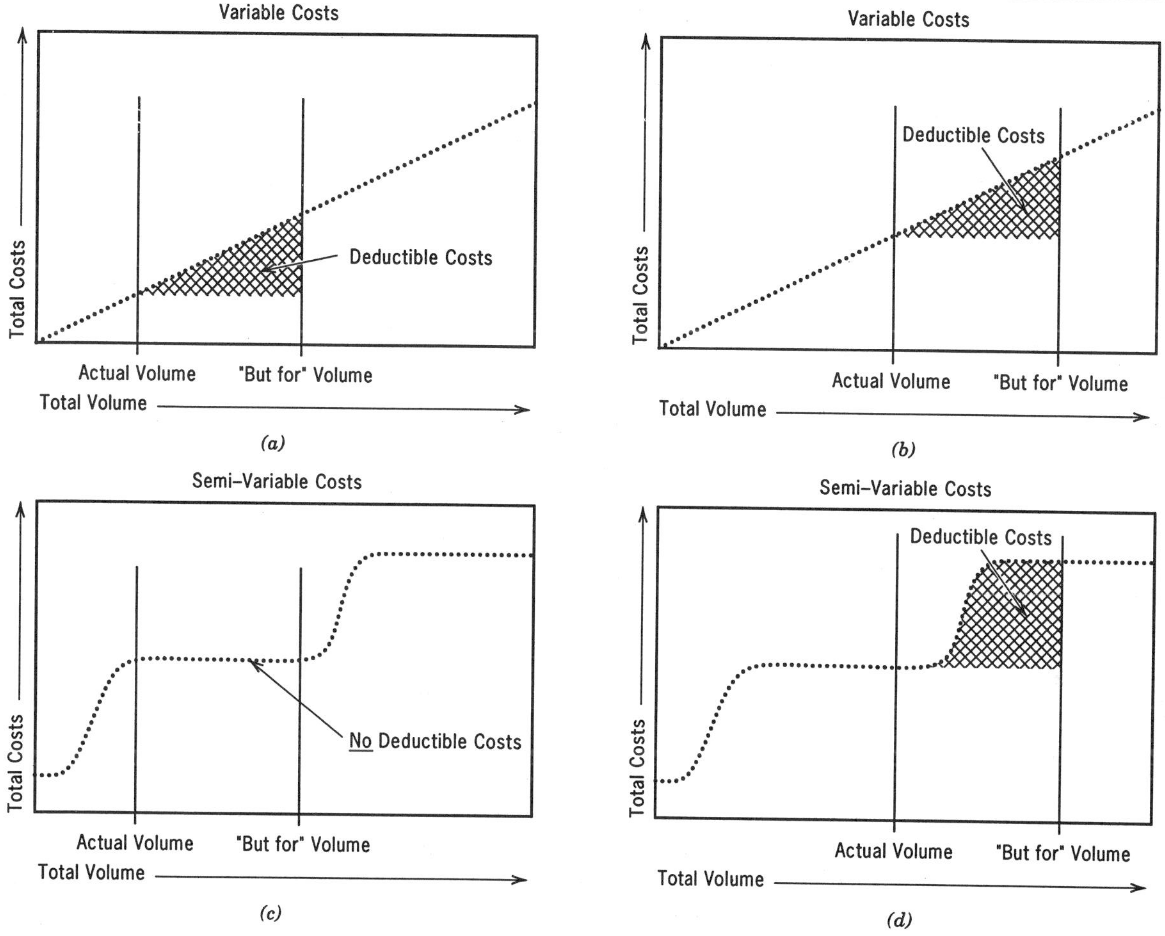

Variable Costs
Total Costs
Deductible Costs
Actual Volume
"But for" Volume
Total Volume
(a)
Variable Costs
Total Costs
Deductible Costs
Actual Volume
"But for" Volume
Total Volume
(b)
Semi–Variable Costs
Total Costs
No Deductible Costs
Actual Volume
"But for" Volume
Total Volume
(c)
Semi–Variable Costs
Total Costs
Deductible Costs
Actual Volume
"But for" Volume
Total Volume
(d)

Copyright Infringer's Profits. Section 504 of the Copyright Act of 1976 also permits recovery of "any profits of the infringer that are attributable to the infringement and are not taken into account in computing actual damages."[8] In this claim, the copyright owner must establish only the infringer's gross revenue. The burden of proof then shifts to the infringer "to prove his or her deductible expenses *and* the elements of profit *attributable* to factors other than the copyrighted work"[9] [emphasis added].

Elements of Infringer's Profit Attributable to Other Factors. Where the plaintiff proves sales of an infringing work, the infringer may apportion some of those revenues to factors other than the infringing work itself. This would be possible, for example, when the infringed work is published in a book with other works, sung as part of an otherwise original musical play, or included as a subroutine of a complex computer program.

The standard for apportioning sales revenue is the contribution of the infringing versus noninfringing factors to the *value* of the work, not simply the amount of the infringing material compared to the amount of material in the whole work. As part of the defense against a claim for profits, an infringer must show the relative contributions of other noninfringing factors to the work's *value*.[10] The infringed software subroutine may be only 10 percent of the lines of codes but represent most of the entire program's *value*. Plaintiff could also argue that, absent the infringement, the infringer would have sold many fewer units than it did. However, in many cases the infringing element will be inextricably intertwined with noninfringing elements. These cases do not accommodate a simple segregation and require more complex apportionment.

Apportioning sales value traditionally has been subjective, often provided by industry expert testimony. Some mathematical techniques exist, however, that might reveal the relative values contributed by various factors, given the appropriate fact pattern. For example, one could demonstrate the effect of several factors on sales in a multiple regression model in which binary indicators (as "dummy" variables) represent each factor's presence and absence. This analysis would be especially meaningful if the whole product was sold for a period of time without the infringing element.[11]

Assuming the model's validity, the coefficient of these dummy variables could be used to estimate (and remove) each factor's influence on sales of the work that included the infringing factor. The analyst should search for bench mark time periods during which the infringing factor was not present and not affecting sales ("clean periods"). Alternatively, the behavior of sales of closely competitive products might provide the appropriate bench mark against which to measure the effect of the infringing factor.

Deductible Expenses. Although the 1976 Act and Committee reports do not define deductible expenses, ample case law has clarified what meets that standard.[12] Generally, the only deductible costs are those that would have been saved but for the production of the infringing work. As with estimating the copyright owner's lost profits, this but-for standard is used to screen all potentially deductible cost items.

Analytic Techniques. The analyst can use several methods to identify deductible costs. Other chapters of this text thoroughly elaborate several of these techniques. This section discusses some of those techniques.

First, one must complete a line-by-line selection of the cost categories that meet the criteria of benefiting the production of the infringing product. The greater the specificity of line items, the more accurate will be the analysis.

Where accounting records are not specific to the individual-product level, as is usually the case with overhead costs, courts have accepted allocating these costs to the infringed work based on the infringed work's share of total sales. For example, in *Aitken, Hazen, Hoffman, Miller, P.C. v. Empire Construction Co.*,[13] defendant divided its overhead expenses by net sales to yield a pro rata share. This share was applied to the infringing sales to yield the "attributable" overhead costs.

The difficulty with this approach is that it measures the *average* cost per sales dollar rather than the *marginal* cost. A better alternative would be to use regression analysis to measure the variability of overhead costs as a function of either all sales or as a function of the smallest sales category encompassing the infringing sales. This approach would better estimate the variable component of overhead costs and conform more to the legal standard of using costs that would not have been incurred but for the infringement.

In spite of this relatively clear standard, however, different courts have reached markedly different conclusions regarding deductible costs.[14] No court, however, is bound by any single procedure.[15] The analyst should be aware of how local courts have ruled.

Also, the infringer must be consistent in the claim for deductible expenses and the claim for apportionment: The analyst cannot deduct expenses for that part of a work that has been eliminated from the sales base.

Finally, the degree of the infringer's culpability may influence both the inclusion of whole categories of expenses and the methods employed. In the *Sheldon* case (noted before), a deduction for income taxes that would otherwise have been included was denied defendants because the court found them to be "deliberate plagiarists."[16]

Statutory Damages. The courts award statutory damages in two situations: (1) where proof of the copyright owner's damages or the infringer's profits is deemed too speculative to support a calculated damage award or (2) where the copyright owner elects to receive statutory damages in lieu of actual damages. This election may be made at any time prior to final judgment being entered.[17]

"The amount [of statutory damages] is determined by the court within the range of a minimum $250 and a maximum of $10,000 per infringement."[18] A "willfully" committed infringement raises the upper limit to $50,000, and, similarly, an "innocent infringer" case reduces the lower limit to $100.[19] The court should consider evidence of the owner's actual losses and the infringer's actual profits in establishing an award number within this broad range.

EXHIBIT 16-4. COMPARISON OF THE CONSEQUENCES OF INCLUDING INCOME TAXES AS A DEDUCTIBLE COST IN DETERMINING PROFITS TO BE DISGORGED BY AN INFRINGER

	Income Taxes Treated as a Deductible Expense	Income Taxes Ignored in Calculating Remedies	
Infringer's profit calculation			
Before-tax profits	$2,000,000	$2,000,000	a
Income taxes	920,000	920,000	b = a * 46%
After-tax profits	$1,080,000	$1,080,000	c = a − b
Amount to be disgorged	$1,080,000	$2,000,000	d = c or a
Income tax credit	496,800	920,000	e = d * 46%
Net cost of disgorgement	$583,200	$1,080,000	f = d − e
Net after-tax effect of infringement and disgorgement	$496,800	$0	g = c − f
Copyright holder's damage calculation			
Before-taxes losses	$1,500,000	$1,500,000	h
Income taxes	690,000	690,000	i = h * 46%
After-tax losses	$810,000	$810,000	j = h − i
Damages claimed	$810,000	$1,500,000	k = h or j
Income tax payable	372,600	690,000	l = k * 46%
Net after-tax recovery	$437,400	$810,000	m = k − l
Net after-tax effect of damage and recovery	$372,600	$0	o = j − m

This rule was used in *Sid & Marty Krofft Television Productions, Inc. v. McDonald's Corporation et al.* where the court awarded statutory damages based on: (1) the number of copyrights involved, (2) the number of infringements, (3) whether the defendants received actual notice, and (4) the amount that should be awarded for each of the various types of infringements. This was done in lieu of awarding the infringer's profits because the court could not ascertain what the sales that resulted from the infringing advertising had been. Without knowing these sales, it found it was impossible to ascertain what the profits from the infringement had been.

The "in lieu" damages were summed from 114 different infringing commercials at $6000 per infringement, 66 different infringing promotional items at $5000 per infringement, and 60 other infringing acts at $50 per infringement. In awarding the $1,044,000, the court rejected the plaintiff's claim that each airing of each of the commercials and each sale of each of the promotional items constituted a separate infringement rather than one part of a single continuous infringement.[20]

TRADEMARKS

The law recognizes that trademarks, trade names, trade dress, and service marks contribute to the public good by (1) identifying the manufacturer or distributor to the consumer and (2) encouraging the trademark owner to increase the value of the products sold under the trademark by granting the owner a limited monopoly in its use.

Although also covered by various common law provisions and state statutes, the primary source of law for trademark and unfair competition is the Lanham Act.[21] Section 43(a) of the Lanham Act prohibits unfair competition, of which trademark infringement is one type. Lanham Act provisions have been used to discourage a wide range of actions that deceive, mislead, or otherwise confuse consumers.

Legal Standards of Proof

A showing of a likelihood of confusion between trademarks or trade dress is enough to support an injunction to prevent continued infringement.

Remedies

Consistent with other causes of action, establishing liability entitles the owner of a trade or service mark to injunctive relief and recovery of actual damages. Sometimes, especially where the mark has been registered with the Patent and Trademark Office, the mark owner may also recover the wrongdoer's profits, attorney's fees, and any other amount that the court finds just.[22]

Injunction and Impounding. As with copyright infringing products, goods bearing counterfeit trademarks are subject to seizure with the court's approval.

In addition to ordering a stop to the unauthorized use of trademarks and trade dress, courts may order an infringer to change the way it identifies itself in business, limit the geography or channels of distribution it uses to reach its customers, or pay for advertising and merchandising to correct customer confusion.

Monetary Remedies. For monetary damages to be awarded, however, a plaintiff must demonstrate damage "by actual consumer reliance on the misleading statement."[23] This is an impact requirement. Many jurisdictions require consumer research among the product's target customers to substantiate a claim of consumer confusion.

Another requisite for monetary damages is a showing of "bad faith", defined in case law as

- Fraud or palming off one's goods as being those of another[24]
- Deliberate intent to cause confusion, mistake, or deceive purchasers[25]
- A wanton and intentionally fraudulent act[26]
- An infringement done knowingly and with callous disregard of the mark holder's rights[27]

Once accomplished, however, plaintiff enjoys a more relaxed standard in proving the *amount* of damages: "A basis for calculating the amount of damages in dollars and cents is a matter of *reasonable inference*."[28] Further, the more directly the trademark owner and infringer compete, the more liberally the courts assess damages.[29]

Plaintiff's Actual Damages. The standard for calculating the trademark owner's actual damages is the profitability the owner would have enjoyed but for the defendant's infringement. A damage claim may include all identifiable and quantifiable ways in which the plaintiff suffered injury, provided they do not double count the same transactions. Elements of injury that the courts have specifically approved in trademark cases include

1. Diverted sales
2. Loss from reduction in price of goods[30]
3. Harm to plaintiff's reputation caused by defendant's inferior reproductions of plaintiff's goods[31]
4. Cost of advertising expense incurred to correct public confusion[32]

Many of these elements are legal categories for which damage claims are supported by similar if not identical methods. These methods calculate only two things: lost profits and added costs. These occur in several manifestations, each of which results in economic damage.

Loss of price on actual sales that the trademark owner made is often overlooked and *not* generally duplicative of damage from lost sales volume. Exhibits 16-5 and 16-6 depict a useful way to illustrate both these damage elements. Exhibit 16-5 illustrates the lost profits resulting from sales lost to a trademark infringer during the damage period: As the number of units sold declines from Q_1 to Q_2, profits decline by the amount in the rectangle Q_1, Q_2, P_1, and C.[33] Exhibit 16-6 illustrates the further effect of lost profits resulting from lowered prices during the damage period: As the price declines from P_1 to P_2, profits decline by the amount bounded by the rectangle P_1, P_2, Q_1 and Q_2.[34]

EXHIBIT 16-5. LOST PROFITS FROM LOST VOLUME

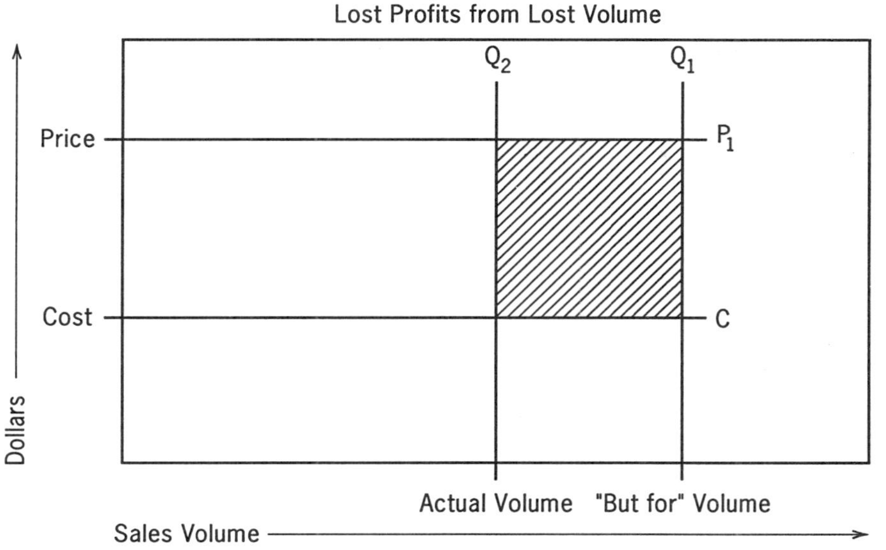

EXHIBIT 16-6. LOST PROFITS FROM LOST VOLUME AND LOWERED PRICE

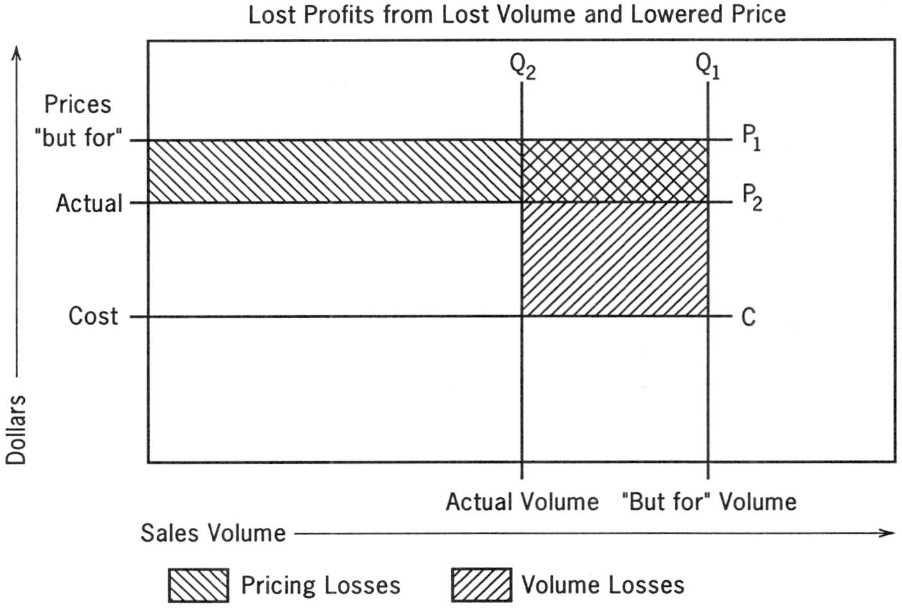

Often, owing to the large number of actual sales, loss from the price impact will exceed losses attributable to diverted units. Also, rarely will cost offsets be necessary because most costs are a function of units produced, not revenue obtained. (Sales commissions and allowances for bad debts are exceptions.)

Methods of Proving Damages. As with copyright cases, lost profits from lost sales is an acceptable claim, if nonspeculative, and may be proven by reference to the infringer's sales of the infringing product.[35] Depending on the facts involved, the courts have considered several methods of proving damages flowing from each of the elements of injury.

The *reasonable royalty* standard has been used to provide a basis for the trademark owner's actual damages.[36] The argument is that, but for the infringement, the mark's owner would have enjoyed royalties from the infringer. This measure is problematic because if the plaintiff is also seeking the infringer's profits, those profits will be reduced by the hypothetical royalty, thus yielding, in total, no net gain to the mark owner. Because defendant's sales are usually more easily proven, only where defendant made no profits does this royalty measure of plaintiff's actual damages seem useful to plaintiff.

The mark owner can also recover any *increased costs* to maintain its sales. As with the damage from price erosion due to infringement, these damages do not generally duplicate the infringer's profit element.

Courts generally avoid using *loss of reputation or goodwill* as a basis for money damages but sometimes accept an estimate of the present value of future lost profits. For this estimate, the analyst must project both sales and costs in the actual and but-for worlds.

Defendant's Profits. As in copyright cases, the trademark owner is entitled to both its actual damages and the infringer's gains but only those gains that are additional to and not duplicative of those captured in the owner's recovery of its lost profits.[37] Generally, plaintiff must prove bad faith or a willful and deliberate infringement as a precondition to recovering defendant's profits.[38]

Calculation. As with copyright, once plaintiff proves the infringing sales, the burden of proof for all elements of related cost shifts to the infringer.[39] The infringer also suffers a rebuttable presumption that attributes *all* profits from sales of goods with infringing content to the infringement.[40] But, if defendant made no profits from the infringing activity, then generally no damages for this element are awardable.[41]

Deductions. The cases addressing trademark infringement have used three methods for calculating the expenses that can be deducted from an infringer's sales.

The *percentage-basis* theory allocates all costs according to the ratio of infringing sales to total sales. This is the cost accountant's "fully loaded" cost concept in which each sale bears its share of all costs, including overhead and fixed costs. This method is often used as a last resort when data deficiencies prevent use of more exact methods.[42] It more appropriately estimates but-for costs in cases of longer time frames and wider ranges of units produced. Although occasionally accepted by courts, it tends to overestimate the but-for costs.

Under the *differential cost* or *marginal cost* theory, defendant can deduct only expenses that vary with the production of the infringing goods. Fixed expenses are not deductible. This method seems to accord more neatly with the but-for model and recreates more accurately the economic world of the defendant but for the infringing sales. Not all courts have adopted this method, however.[43]

Under the *contribution theory* espoused by the *Restatement of Torts*[44] all expenses that "contribute" to the production, including fixed overhead, are deductible. This standard is quite different from the economic concept of "contribution margin"—which results from deducting marginal costs from marginal revenues. It confuses the notion of conferring a benefit with causality. For example, a building may confer a benefit upon and thus "contribute" to a good's production. However, producing one more good will normally not cause the building expense to be incurred or increased. We do not believe, therefore, that this approach recreates the economic world as it would have been but for the infringement.

Note also that cost behavior is a function of time as well as production range. All indirect costs may be fixed for the next hour, but over 10 years almost all may vary. Therefore, analysis of the variability of costs should reflect the damage claim period.

Year-by-Year and Product Compartmentalization. Some courts have curiously set upon 1 year as the appropriate time frame in which to measure profits. They have not allowed losses, as calculated, on a year-by-year basis, to offset profits.[45] Nor are offsets allowed for losses in one infringing product against profits of another infringing product.[46]

Forcing the analysis to be both year-by-year and product-by-product without offsets for losses may exaggerate the differences between allocation methods and their effect on total damages. Furthermore, losses from the early startup years of a product's life cycle will not be offset against profits from later years. Thus, even though a defendant lost money on the infringing product overall, if it made profits in *any* year, defendant might be required to disgorge the profits gained in that year.

Prejudgment Interest. Prejudgment interest has been granted for the period of time from the day of notice of infringement in cases of deliberate and willful infringement; otherwise from the date of entry of interlocutory judgment.[47] Court receptivity to this very real economic loss is increasing.[48]

Treble Damages. The court may award *treble damages*,[49] but this usually requires documentation of bad faith.[50] The possibility of treble damages magnifies the importance of selecting the most appropriate damage claim method according to the available facts.

TRADE SECRETS

A trade secret is generally defined as information that is used in one's business or profession, is not generally known or knowable by persons outside the business, gives one an advantage over one's commercial competitors, and for which one has taken reasonable steps to maintain as confidential. Generally, protected trade secrets include knowledge of proprietary manufacturing processes, chemical formulas, marketing plans, and certain kinds of information about customers.[51]

Trade secret law has evolved from the need to protect an enterprise from losing the competitive advantage gained by developing or acquiring specific information relating to its business, thereby encouraging competition to develop better products and processes.

Unlike copyright and trademark law, this trade secret law comes not from federal statute but the common law and is defined by state regulations and case law.[52]

Legal Standards of Proof

To establish liability, plaintiff must prove both the existence of a legally protectable trade secret and that the defendant had a confidential relationship as an employee or by contract.

Remedies

As with other infringements of intellectual property rights, remedies are available to restore the parties to the position they would have had but for the unauthorized infringement: injunctions to prevent continued use of the trade secrets, recovery of damages, and disgorgement of the defendant's gains. Some jurisdictions also impose punitive damages and criminal sanctions.

Injunctions. As in other areas of the law, courts will grant restraining orders and injunctions to prevent continuing harm to the plaintiff. Trade secret cases, however, rarely result in permanent injunctions. On the theory that the secret information could be developed independently, courts may prevent use of the information for the length of time it would have taken the usurpers to develop the information using generally available information and art.

Recovery of Damages. The standards for monetary damages for trade secrets resemble those applicable to trademark and copyright actions: plaintiff must prove both the fact of damage and a causal connection between defendant's actions and plaintiff's loss.[53] Moreover, where the claim involves the misappropriation of specific customer information, the plaintiff must show diversion of sales to those customers from the owner of the information to the infringer. Often plaintiff must first prove that plaintiff and defendant competed in the same market.

In addition to the typical lost profits model, the expert may calculate the cost of restoring a company to its former level of competitive advantage and the present value of the lost higher profits that that competitive advantage would allow.

Do not overlook the fact that the plaintiff's actual losses always have two aspects: One should consider both lost sales and increased costs when comparing costs and financial position in the actual and but-for worlds. The courts have recognized the following as recoupable added costs caused by violation:

1. Start-up expenses[54]
2. Additional overhead[55]
3. Cost of remedial or mitigation steps[56]
4. Reduction in capital value[57]

Restitution of Profits. As mentioned, the plaintiff is also entitled to restitution equal to the defendant's gains. Where plaintiff has proven the causal link, the claim for restitution is aided by a rebuttable presumption that attributes all of defendant's sales to the theft; the thief carries the burden of proving the extent to which portion its sales were not attributable to the theft.[58]

Deductible Costs. Defendant must prove which costs are deductible, but the standard of variable costs seems well accepted.[59] This is essentially the same task discussed in trademarks. As there, losses from one "accounting period" may not be offset against gains from another.[60] Depending on the facts, selecting different accounting periods could produce widely differing damage amounts. As with trademark infringement, analysis of damages on a year-by-year and product-by-product basis might yield damages where none appeared at the aggregate level.

Defendant, of course, has an advantage here because defendant possesses the detailed accounting records that could support such an analysis. However, the usefulness of this "compartmentalization" approach reinforces the need to secure through discovery the most detailed accounting and operational records available.

Also, costs saved by the trade secret's unauthorized use is gain to the infringer and might be included in the amount to be disgorged.

CONCLUSION: COMMON THREADS

Some common threads exist among the special considerations in calculating damages for copyright, trademark, and trade secret cases.

The first is the ability to recover and thus the need to consider and calculate both the innovator's damages—the lost profits or added costs *and* the infringer's gains—the profits made or costs avoided by the infringer as a result of the illegal behavior.

This dual recovery aspect—unlike that of many causes of action—entitles the plaintiff to a monetary award even if the plaintiff suffered no monetary damage.

Because analysts can more easily prove defendant's gains, proof-conscious attorneys may steer them in this direction. In circumstances involving diverted sales, one might expect much duplication of damages from plaintiff's losses and defendant's gains, and pursuing *only* defendant's gains becomes reasonable. In other cases, however, both aspects should be considered.

Second, this family of torts requires many causation demonstrations not only to prove the fact of damage but also to show what part of a product's value was attributable to either infringing or noninfringing factors. These specialized showings, required to calculate monetary remedies in these causes of action, explicitly weave more liability issues into the damages fabric than many others in business litigation. Thus a greater opportunity exists for liability or causation types of analyses (e.g., regression or time series analysis) and the damages analyst must employ a broader range of financial and statistical skills.

Lastly, these causes of action increase the focus on damages because the burden of proof shifts to the defendant for deductible costs. In most other commercial litigation, plaintiff bears the entire burden of proving all elements of damages. In those cases, the defendant can sit back and critique plaintiff's efforts as a "speculative" claim. No such luxury is possible here. Both parties must enter the fray with positive proof to sustain their independent affirmative burdens.

NOTES

1. The legislative history to section 504 of the Copyright Act of 1976 clarifies this important characteristic of copyright damages: "Where the defendant's profits are nothing more than a measure of the damages suffered by the copyright owner, it would be inappropriate to award damages and profits cumulatively, since in effect they amount to the same thing. However, in cases where the copyright owner has suffered damages not reflected in the infringer's profits, or where there have been profits attributable to the copyrighted work but not used as a measure of damages, subsection (b) authorizes the award of both." H.R. Rep No. 94-1476, 94th Cong., 2d Session (1976) p. 161.

2. 17 U.S.C § 102.

3. 17 U.S.C. § 106.

4. A good example of the market value standard is architectural drawings. Traditionally, the fee is a percentage of the cost of the building and is a measure of the value of the drawings. Unauthorized use of a set of drawings would deprive the architect of the normal fee. [*Aitkin, Hazen, Hoffman, Miller, P.C. v. Empire Construction*, 542 F. Supp. 252 (D. Neb. 1982).]

5. 656 F.2d 11 (2d Cir. 1981).

6. The way in which one court accepted projections as a valid basis for calculating damages is revealing. In *Taylor v. Meirick*, 712 F.2d 1112 (7th Cir. 1983) the court *averaged* the two preceding years sales and used the result as a projection, without growth, for the next 3 years. This conservative approach may illustrate a judicial fondness for both averages and historical data.

7. Another benefit of presenting multiple approaches is the opportunity it gives the court to select the damage approach it deems most appropriate to the level of culpability. After selecting the "overlapping customers" and "product mix" as acceptable methods for calculating lost sales, the *Stevens* court chose the method resulting in the greater damages amount.

8. 17 U.S.C § 504(b).

9. 17 U.S.C. § 504(b).

10. See *Szekely v. Eagle Lion Films*, 242 F.2d. 266 (2d. Cir. 1957).

11. For example, assume a computer program is rereleased with a new infringing subroutine that makes the entire program more powerful and attractive to customers. If the new subroutine is the only change, its impact might be estimated with regression analysis.

12. *Aitken, Hazen, Hoffman, Miller, P.C. v. Empire Construction Co.*, 542 F. Supp. 252, 264 (D. Neb. 1982).

13. Ibid.

14. *Baldwin Cooke Co. v. Keith Clark, Inc.*, 420 F. Supp. 404 (N.D. Ill. 1976); (*Nimmer on Copyright*. 1984, § 14.03(b)).

15. In *Sheldon v. MGM*, 106 F.2d 45 (2d Cir. 1939), the court allocated distribution

costs based on number of movies produced (output measure) and allocated overhead according to the cost of producing each movie (input measure).

16. Income taxes are a variable cost to the infringer; to omit them overstates the infringer's incremental profit. Including them as a deductible cost, however, would allow the infringer to realize an after-tax gain on the infringement, even if all of its after-tax profits are disgorged (see Exhibit 16-4).

Further, income taxes should not be deducted in calculating the plaintiff's lost profits claim because the judgment itself will be taxed. As shown in Exhibit 16-4, if the claim were limited to the after-tax damages, the plaintiff would not be made "whole" after paying taxes on the judgment or settlement.

17. Section 504(c)(1) of the 1976 act.

18. Section 504(c)(1) of the 1976 act.

19. Section 504(c)(2) of the 1976 act.

20. *Sid & Marty Krofft Television Productions, Inc. v. McDonald's Corp.*, 562 F.2d 1157 (9th Cir. 1977).

21. 15 U.S.C. §§ 1051–1127.

22. 15 U.S.C. § 1117. "If the court shall find that the amount of the recovery based on profits is either inadequate of excessive, the court may in its discretion enter judgement for such sum as the court shall find to be just, according to the circumstances of the case. Such sum in either of the above circumstances shall constitute compensation and not a penalty."

23. *Schutt Mfg. Co. v. Riddell, Inc.*, 673 F.2d 202, 206 (7th Cir. 1982).

24. *Carl Zeiss Stiftung v. VEB Carl Zeiss Jena*, 433 F.2d. 686, 717 (2nd Cir. 1970).

25. Ibid.

26. *Fuller Products Co. v. Fuller Brush Co.*, 299 F.2d. 772, 777 (7th Cir. 1962).

27. *Stuart v. Collins*, 489 F. Supp. 827, 831 (S.D.N.Y. 1980).

28. *Borg-Warner Corp. v. York-Shipley, Inc.*, 293 F.2d 88 (7th Cir. 1961).

29. *Donsco, Inc. v. Casper Corp.*, 587 F.2d 602 (3d Cir. 1978).

30. *Obear-Nester Glass Co. v. United Drug Co.*, 149 F.2d 671 (8th Cir. 1945).

31. *Boston Prof. Hockey Assoc. v. Dallas Cap & Emblem Mfg.*, 597 F.2d 71, 75 (5th Cir. 1979).

32. *Big O Tire Dealers, Inc. v. Goodyear Tire & Rubber Co.*, 561 F.2d 1365 (10th Cir. 1977).

33. For simplicity, these exhibits show no change in cost or price as volume changes.

34. Where both volume and price impact are proven, the area P_1, P_2, Q_1, and Q_2 will be counted only once.

35. *Playboy Enterprises v. PK Sorren Export Co.*, 546 F. Supp. 987, 997 (S.D. Fla. 1982).

36. *Carter Products, Inc. v. Colgate-Palmolive Co.*, 214 F. Supp. 383 (D. Md. 1963).

37. In a recent Ninth Circuit decision involving a Lanham Act violation for deceptive advertising, "profits" were more broadly defined to include any economic enrichment. Even though the defendant made no profit, plaintiff was awarded defendant's advertising expenses (for the deceptive material) to deprive defendant of an assumed enrichment to its goodwill that these expenses had created. *U-Haul International Inc. v. Jartran, Inc.*, 793 F.2d 1034 (9th Cir. 1986).

38. *Playboy Enterprises v. PK Sorren Export Co.*, *supra* note 35.

39. *Ibid.*; 15 U.S.C. 1117.

40. *Carter Products, Inc. v. Colgate-Palmolive Co.*, 214 F. Supp. 383 (D. Md. 1944).

41. But see *Otis Clapp & Son, Inc. v. Filmore Vitamin Co.*, 754 F.2d 738 (7th Cir. 1985) that allowed an award of 15 percent of sales even though defendant made no profit. The court states that plaintiff should not be prejudiced by defendant's inefficiency.

42. *Hamilton-Brown Shoe Co. v. Wolf Bros. & Co.*, 240 U.S. 251 (1916).

43. *Century Distilling Co. v. Continental Distilling Corp.*, 205 F.2d 140 (3d Cir. 1953).

44. Section 748 (i).

45. *Duplate Corp. v. Triplex Glass Co.*, 298 U.S. 448, 458 (1936) (patent case).

46. *Carter Products Inc. v. Colgate-Palmolive Co.*, 214 F. Supp. 383 (D. Md. 1963).
47. *Duro Co. of Ohio v. Duro Co. of New Jersey*, 56 F.2d 313, 317 (3rd Cir. 1932).
48. *S.C. Johnson & Son, Inc. v. Drop Dead Co.* 144 U.S.P.Q. (BNA) 257 (S.D. Cal. 1965).
49. Section 35 of the Lanham Act (15 U.S.C. 117).
50. *Playboy Enterprises v. Baccarat Clothing Co.*, 692 F.2d 1272 (9th Cir. 1982).
51. Several states have adopted the definition of the Uniform Trade Secrets Act (1979) § 1 (4): "Trade Secret" means information, including a formula, compilation, program, device, method, technique, or process that "(1) derives independent economic value, actual or potential, from not being generally known to, and not being readily ascertainable by, other persons who can obtain economic value from its disclosure or use, and (2) is the subject of efforts that are reasonable under the circumstances to maintain its secrecy."
52. The Federal Trade Secret Act (18 U.S.C. § 1905, 1948) and the Federal Trade Commission Act (15 U.S.C. § 41, 1914) prohibit disclosure of trade secrets by federal employees who receive such information in their role as federal employees. Further, the Freedom of Information Act (5 U.S.C. § 552, 1946) does *not* require public disclosure of documents containing trade secrets if the appropriate official believes that the information is not of the type that is normally released to the public and would cause significant competitive harm to the trade secret's owner.

Because the Racketeer Influenced and Corrupt Organizations Act (18 U.S.C. § 1961 et seq.) allows recovery to anyone injured by interstate theft, a RICO action might be used to recover damages if trade secrets are stolen and taken across state lines.

53. *Telex Corp. v. IBM*, 510 F.2d 894 (10th Cir. 1975).
54. *University Computing Co. v. Lykes-Youngstown Corp.*, 504 F.2d 518 (5th Cir. 1974).
55. *Grand Trunk Western Co. v. HW Nelson Co.*, 116 F.2d 823 (6th Cir. 1941).
56. *Dozor Agency, Inc. v. Rosenberg*, 218 A.2d 583 (Penn 1966).
57. *DeVries v. Starr*, 393 F.2d 9 (9th Cir. 1968).
58. *Mishawaka Rubber & Woolen Manufacturing Co. v. S.S. Kresge Co.*, 316 U.S. 203 (1942).
59. *Vitex Manufacturing Corp. v. Caribtex Corp.*, 377 F.2d 795 (3d Cir. 1967).
60. *Adolph Gottscho, Inc. v. American Marketing Corp.*, 26 N.J. 229, 139 A.2d 281 (1958).

LIST OF CASES

Adolph Gottscho, Inc. v. American Marketing Corp., 26 N.J. 229, 139 A.2d 281 (1958)
Aitkin, Hazen, Hoffman, Miller, P.C. v. Empire Construction 542 F. Supp. 252 (D. Neb. 1982)
Baldwin Cooke Co. v. Keith Clark, Inc., 420 F. Supp. 404 (N.D. Ill. 1976)
Big O Tire Dealers, Inc. v. Goodyear Tire & Rubber Co., 561 F.2d 1365 (10th Cir. 1977)
Borg-Warner Corp. v. York-Shipley, Inc., 293 F.2d 88 (7th Cir. 1961)
Boston Prof. Hockey Assoc. v. Dallas Cap & Emblem Mfg., 597 F.2d 71 (5th Cir. 1979)
Carl Zeiss Stiftung v. VEB Carl Zeiss Jena, 433 F.2d 686 (2nd Cir. 1970)
Carter Products, Inc. v. Colgate-Palmolive Co., 214 F. Supp. 383 (D. Md. 1963)
Century Distilling Co. v. Continental Distilling Corp., 205 F.2d 140 (3d Cir. 1953)
DeVries v. Starr, 393 F.2d 9 (10th Cir. 1968)
Donsco, Inc. v. Casper Corp., 587 F.2d 602 (3d Cir. 1978)
Dozor Agency, Inc. v. Rosenberg, 218 A.2d 583 (Penn. 1966)
Duplate Corp. v. Triplex Glass Co., 298 U.S. 448 (1936)
Duro Co. of Ohio v. Duro Co. of New Jersey, 56 F.2d 313 (3d Cir. 1932)
Fuller Products Co. v. Fuller Brush Co., 299 F.2d 772 (7th Cir. 1970)
Grand Trunk Western R. Co. v. HW Nelson Co., 116 F.2d 823 (6th Cir. 1941)

Hamilton-Brown Shoe Co. v. Wolf Bros. & Co., 240 U.S. 251 (1916)
Mishawaka Rubber & Woolen Manufacturing Co. v. S.S. Kresge Co., 316 U.S. 203 (1942)
Obear-Nester Glass Co. v. United Drug Co., 149 F.2d 671 (8th Cir. 1945)
Otis Clapp & Son, Inc. v. Filmore Vitamin Co., 754 F.2d 738 (7th Cir. 1985)
Playboy Enterprises v. Baccarat Clothing Co., 692 F.2d 1272 (9th Cir. 1982)
Playboy Enterprises v. PK Sorren Export Co., 546 F. Supp. 987 (S.D. Fla. 1982)
S.C. Johnson & Son, Inc. v. Drop Dead Co., 144 U.S.P.Q. (BNA) 257 (S.D. Cal. 1965)
Schutt Mfg. Co. v. Riddell, Inc., 673 F.2d 202 (7th Cir. 1982)
Sheldon v. MGM, 106 F.2d 45 (2d Cir. 1939)
Sid & Marty Krofft Television Productions, Inc. v. McDonald's Corp., 562 F.2d 1157 (9th Cir. 1977)
Stevens Linen Associates, Inc. v. Mastercraft Corporation, 656 F.2d 11 (2d Cir. 1981)
Stuart v. Collins, 489 F. Supp. 827 (S.D.N.Y. 1980)
Szekely v. Eagle Lion Films, 242 F.2d 266 (2d Cir. 1957)
Taylor v. Meirick, 712 F.2d 1112 (7th Cir. 1983)
Telex Corp. v. IBM, 510 F.2d 894 (10th Cir. 1975)
U-Haul International, Inc. v. Jartran, Inc., 793 F.2d 1034 (9th Cir. 1986)
University Computing Co. v. Lykes-Youngstown Corp., 504 F.2d 518 (5th Cir. 1974)
Vitex Manufacturing Corp. v. Caribtex Corp., 377 F.2d 795 (3d Cir. 1967)

17

PATENT INFRINGEMENT DAMAGES

Peter B. Frank, CPA
Michael J. Wagner, JD, CPA

INTRODUCTION[1]

Patterson Co., a manufacturer of video cassette recorders (VCRs), developed a new recording head that greatly increases playback quality. The company obtained a patent on the recording head, and its VCR sales grew rapidly. Looking to cash in on Patterson's success, Imitator Co. developed a similar recording head and introduced a competitive VCR. Imitator's sales soared, cutting into Patterson's share of the new market.

When it realized what had happened, Patterson sued Imitator for patent infringement and won a court judgment affirming its patent and halting Imitator from making, selling, and otherwise using Patterson's patented recording head. But like most patent holders, Patterson is seeking compensation for its lost profits, as well as the injunction. The court must now hear evidence to decide how much money Patterson will get.

Collecting substantial damages in a hypothetical case such as *Patterson Co. v. Imitator Co.* depends on the quality of proof to demonstrate the patent owner's total loss. This proof may require inquiries using many of the business disciplines of industrial engineering, management science, marketing, operations research, organizational behavior, finance, accounting, and statistics. A patent case typically requires a working knowledge of some or all of these disciplines to establish evidence of lost profits or the amount of reasonable royalties.

A patent is a legally protected right to exploit an invention. Patents are granted to the inventor or patentee by the U.S. Government Patent Office, upon application, and proof that the invention (process, machine, manufacture, or composition of matter) is novel, useful, not anticipated by prior art, and nonobvious to one possessing ordinary skill in the relevant field. The patent filing also will identify the applications to which the protection applies. Patents generally run for 17 years from the date of grant and are not renewable. During that period the patentee, or his licensee, is the sole person allowed to make, use, or sell the product in the United States. Thus the ownership of a patent imparts a potential economic benefit that is exploited either by sales of the product or licensing of the patent. If the patent is infringed, the patentee may claim damages equal to either the profits from sales lost or from royalties not obtained.

This chapter first describes the analytical tasks required to satisfy the standards of proof for lost profits. The accounting issues in the patent owner's computation of lost profits on sales that would have been made absent the infringer's unlawful behavior are discussed. Patent infringement cases require special considerations for the revenue component of lost sales; the cost component calculations, however, resemble those of other business litigation damages. For this reason, this chapter will focus on lost revenue calculations, and we refer the reader to other chapters in this text for notes on the related cost calculations. For simplicity, we discuss the issues in terms of Imitator's unlawful sales, although the patent laws cover unlawful manufacture, use, or sale. The analytical problems generally are similar.

The chapter then presents the issues surrounding the computation of a reasonable royalty payable to a patentee like Patterson for the infringer's unlawful manufacture, use, or sale of the patented produce. A patent holder is entitled to either lost profits, or, if not reasonably quantifiable, no less than a reasonable royalty. In developing its case, a patent holder will typically provide evidence of both lost profits and reasonable royalties, usually arguing for the larger of the two.

LOST PROFITS

Standards of Proof

Patent law provides that the patent owner is entitled to the profits he would have earned on the patented article but for the infringement. The standard of proof for lost profits in a patent case, in practice, may be somewhat more stringent than in, say, an antitrust case. A convincing showing that the patent owner would have made some or all of the sales taken by the infringer is required. Because the law allows the use of the alternative reasonable royalty standard when lost profits cannot be shown without speculation, courts may not allow the latitude found in other lost profits damage areas.[2]

Estimating Lost Sales

Infringer's Sales. In measuring a patent owner's lost profits, one must first calculate the volume of patented items sold by the infringer. This is not always an easy or straightforward task, depending upon the type of accounting records kept by the infringer. (The law apparently places the burden on the infringer to maintain adequate records of infringing sales. Thus the patentee may be given considerable latitude in estimating infringer's sales, absent clear records.) Many companies' records do not segregate infringing from noninfringing sales. This occurs, for example, where the product's patented feature—such as a new recording head on a VCR—normally is not used to differentiate products in a company's line.

The individual invoices, if copies have been retained, can be used to calculate the infringing product's total sales when no summary sales reports provide the information needed to compute the extent of infringing sales. However, this is a time-consuming, laborious, and expensive process, and the individual invoices may be ambiguous sources for infringing sales information. Unless the invoice defines unambiguously the products sold, it may be impossible to ascertain whether the products were infringing. For instance, an invoice for a VCR probably would not identify the recording head separately.

Another potential source for calculating the infringing sales amount may be the infringer's production records. Sometimes production records include more detail than sales records. One must use care with this approach, however, and not assume that all infringing items produced were sold. Estimates of quantity sold as opposed to manufactured may be made by evaluating the quantity of infringing goods currently in inventory and by obtaining records of returns, free goods, and other dispositions of production. Creativity may be required to reasonably estimate infringing sales; for example, look at purchases of unique components or warranty records.

The Patent Owner's Lost Sales. Not all of the Imitator's sales of patented items may be lost by Patterson. Some of the infringer's customers, for instance, might buy only from Imitator, and Patterson may not have been able to break those customer loyalties. Or some customers may be unwilling to purchase from Patterson because of unfavorable past dealings, its reputation, service, or other factors.

In addition, Imitator may have expanded demand for the patented recording head beyond the market facing Patterson as a single source. This may be from the infringer's superior marketing capability, additional advertising expenditures, different distribution channels, or simply different geographic locations. Perhaps Imitator sold the infringing product at a discount and expanded sales by obtaining a price-sensitive segment not served by Patterson.[3] The market's expanded portion that the infringer garnered and the patentee could not reach does not represent lost sales to the patent owner. (These sales may be subject to a royalty claim, however. But it is not likely that both lost profits and reasonable royalty damages will be applied to sales in a particular market over the same period of time.[4])

Capacity Considerations. After measuring Patterson's potential lost sales, the question remains whether Patterson had the capacity to produce and sell the additional units of the patented product.

The patent owner's actual capacity and its level of utilization during the infringement period should be studied. Many manufacturing companies maintain records of capacity utilization. Alternatively, a study of the manufacturing process might help identify key or bottleneck resources. The analysis should study actual utilization of these resources against their practical capacity. Production cycles and peaks as well as use of extra shifts also merit consideration. As production facilities and processes become more complex and flexible, measuring the capacity to produce a particular product becomes more difficult. With the increasing use of robotics, computer control, and more complicated machinery, production runs are becoming shorter, and particular production lines and machines can make several different products. Consequently, one cannot easily measure the economic effect of dedicating a production line to one particular product. The decision to manufacture a particular product may affect the costs and the ability to make and sell other products.

Even without any existing capacity to produce some or all of the infringer's sales, the patent owner might show it could have or would have expanded its manufacturing capacity to meet the additional sales.

This hypothetical expansion of capacity might, however, be viewed as more speculative. Evidence to rebut the charge of speculation may include a history of plant expansions to meet sales demand, contemporaneous cost analysis of required plant expansion, and sufficient financial ability to pay for the capital expansion. Also, the patent owner's strategic and operating plans and budgets might reveal discussions of capacity expansion during the infringement period, or, better yet, capacity adjustments not made because of the presence of the infringer.

If Patterson's history shows a pattern of capacity expansions over time as demand expands, this evidence may support an argument that, but for the infringement, capacity and sales would have expanded. Conversely, a patent owner's capacity constraints during periods of high demand might show a reluctance to expand capacity.

Of course, one should also consider the nature of the particular industry. If the industry is cyclical, then firms may be reluctant to expand to meet all demand.

The Correct Unit Price. To establish lost revenue, Patterson must identify unit prices. Typically, the plaintiff's damage study refers to prices that the infringer charged. This initially makes intuitive sense because these prices reflect actual transaction prices accepted by customers in the real world.

Circumstances, however, may lead to a different but-for price. If the infringer received a higher price because of added value (e.g., its recording head resists wear better), the patent owner should not claim the premium attached to this feature. The patent owner's and infringer's terms of sale (e.g., credit and warranties), that is, the product's total package price, must be compared. If the infringer's price exceeds the patentee's (owing to added value), the but-for unit price may differ from the infringer's actual price.

Patterson might argue that but for the infringement it would have had higher prices because Imitator's competition depressed actual prices for both parties. Under this theory, the patentee, Patterson, also has lost revenues on its actual sales because competition forced it to sell at prices below what it could have realized.[5]

For example, suppose Patterson claims in the but-for world a higher sales price than the actual price both it and Imitator charged. Patterson has not only the lost sales of the units sold by Imitator but also lost revenue on the sales it did make. The actual quantities Patterson sold, however, may no longer be relevant. Generally, as prices increase, fewer units are sold. Consequently, one must analyze the responsiveness of quantity demanded relative to prices charged for the patented product to ascertain whether a higher price would have had any negative effect on volume sold. In economics, this is called the price elasticity of demand. The analysis would also study noninfringing alternatives (i.e., substitute goods) and their ability to affect the patentee's price and quantity sold. An econometrics and accounting expert may be able to perform a price elasticity study, if appropriate data are available, to measure the relationships between price and quantity.

Estimating Costs

We stated previously that cost calculations in a patent infringement case resemble those of most other litigations. Therefore, we refer the reader to other chapters in this volume for a full discussion and will list here briefly some issues that an expert should consider.

One needs to include only the variable or incremental costs that arise from the incremental sales. This requires characterizing costs as fixed or variable and identifying the fixed and variable components of semivariable costs. One often uses regression analyses (which can be constructed to mathematically relate cost to output), engineering studies (which painstakingly scrutinize the actual relationship between volume and costs), and account analyses (line-by-line categorization of chart of accounts) for this purpose.

One must avoid naively analyzing a company's financial statements without first making adjustments. Most companies use absorption accounting, which allocates a portion of fixed manufacturing overhead to the cost of each unit produced, muddling the distinction between fixed and variable costs. Also, the company's time horizon (inherent in the financial reporting system) may not be appropriate for the litigation; differing time horizons affect the characterization of costs as fixed or variable.

Multiproduct companies may have substantial common costs that are allocated to individual products. The identification of incremental costs associated with the infringed product obviously is complicated in this situation and requires careful analysis.

REASONABLE ROYALTY

Case Law Guidelines

Arriving at a reasonable royalty for a patented device involves an analysis of accounting, economic, financial, statistical, marketing, and business considerations. These cannot be segregated; the best evidence of a reasonable royalty rate depends upon all these disciplines.

Patent law awards a claimant like Patterson no "less than a reasonable royalty for the use of the invention by the infringer. . . . The court may receive expert testimony as an aid to the determination of . . . what royalty would be reasonable under the circumstances."[6]

What constitutes a reasonable royalty in the absence of actual arms-length bargaining between the patentee (Patterson Co.) and the would-be licensee (Imitator Co.) is a matter of much dispute. Solid analytical formulas do not exist, and typically the two parties to the dispute will be far apart on a reasonable royalty rate. Patent case law provides little enlightenment on the analytics of establishing a rate.

The cases that address the issue generally indicate that the royalty rate should reflect what a willing buyer and willing seller would have negotiated at the beginning of the infringement period. Ascertaining the rate thus requires constructing a conceptual set of hypothetical negotiations.

A significant case on the subject is *Panduit Corp. v. Stahlin Bros. Fibre Works, Inc.*, 575 F.2d 1152 (6th Cir. 1978). *Panduit* states that a reasonable royalty is an amount that a person who wants to manufacture and sell a patented article would be willing to pay as a royalty and still be able to sell the item at a reasonable profit. *Panduit* states that the royalty rate is that which would have been established at the beginning of infringement.[7] The court in *Panduit* also refers to the *Georgia-Pacific* case.[8] In *Georgia-Pacific*, the court laid out 15 factors deemed pertinent to its decision on a royalty rate. We first discuss the last factor, which gives shape to most of the remaining fourteen.

Hypothetical Negotiations

Georgia-Pacific's broadest criterion for an equitable royalty rate relates to hypothetical negotiations:

> 15. The amount that a licensor (such as the patentee) and a licensee (such as the infringer) would have agreed upon (at the time the infringement began) if both had been reasonably and voluntarily trying to reach an agreement; that is, the amount which a prudent licensee—who desired, as a business proposition, to obtain a license to manufacture and sell a particular article embodying the patented invention—would have been willing to pay as a royalty and yet be able to make a reasonable profit and which amount would have been acceptable by a prudent patentee who was willing to grant a license."[9]

This criterion assumes that a reasonable royalty would be set at the rate the parties would have arrived at had they, at the outset of infringement, agreed instead upon a license. Conceptually, this factor—hypothetical negotiations—melds the other factors in *Georgia-Pacific* (discussed later) and, therefore, is a sound basis, absent a directly comparable proxy rate, for suggesting the appropriate reasonable royalty rate.

The court in *Panduit*, however, cautions that the fiction of a negotiation should not be carried too far:

> The setting of a reasonable royalty after infringement cannot be treated . . . as the equivalent of ordinary royalty negotiations among truly "willing" patent owners and licensees. That view would constitute a pretense that the infringement never happened. It would also make an election to infringe a handy means for competitors to impose a "compulsory license" policy upon every patent owner.[10]

The court further pointed out that

> Determination of a "reasonable royalty" after infringement, like many devices in the law, rests on a legal fiction. Created in an effort to "compensate" when profits are not provable, the "reasonable royalty" device conjures a "willing" licensor and licensee, who like Ghosts of Christmas Past are seen dimly as "negotiating" a "license." There is, of course, no actual willingness on either side and no license to do anything, the infringer being normally enjoined . . . from further manufacture, use, or sale of the patented product.[11]

In *Panduit*, the court resolves this conundrum by referring to the factors set out in the *Georgia-Pacific* case and suggesting that one also consider the licensee's profits. Apparently the hypothetical negotiation approach is valid but must be tempered in some undefined manner by hindsight.

Simulating a Negotiations Environment

In a set of negotiations, each party usually sets boundaries for itself: The patent owner identifies a rate below which it would be "unwilling" to license, and the licensee sets an amount above which it could not pay. Normally the boundaries must overlap to some degree to strike a deal. Of course, in an infringement case, a "deal" will be struck in any case. If no overlap can be established, then this method of suggesting a rate may prove nondefinitive.

Because a rate is to be established as if the parties met at the time of infringement, the analysis must consider how each party at that time viewed the market, the expected profitability of the patented item, and other benefits. This requires a good bit of discovery of each party's records and opinions as of the time of first infringement. Ideally, discovery would reveal reliable projections, memoranda, market research, competitive analysis reports, project evaluation techniques, and decision factors such as rates of return and hurdle rates that measure the percentage profitability that a company desires to earn. Also, any documents that suggest either party's view of the invention's value would be important. One might search relevant trade journals, newspapers, and business periodicals to reconstruct the product's outlook. As the cases have pointed out, a relatively high contemporaneous valuation may be inferred on the part of the infringer from its very act of infringement. In the simulated negotiations, the parties will make such calculations for both sides to establish the range in which the negotiations would occur.

When considering the hypothetical license, the patent holder should consider the benefits of a license, not the fact of infringement. Licensing can expand the total market available for the invention, particularly if the licensee has access to customers to which the patent owner does not. Licensing can reduce risks associated with building the capacity necessary to exploit the total market, particularly in a cyclical industry. Licensing also may expand the product's total market by creating demand through advertising and marketing efforts carried out by more than one company. The patent owner may want to set a precedent for licensing in case it needs its competitors' patented technology in the future. Licensing gives the licensor a financial advantage over its competitors because royalties increase the licensor's profits and decrease the infringer's profits. Finally, licensing may dissuade others from developing inventions that could make the patented item obsolete.

The patent owner, however, may have reasons not to license its technology—it forfeits the legally sanctioned near monopoly to produce and sell the invention. The ability to extract high profits may be economically advantageous, especially if the advance over other products is so significant that it practically eliminates competition.

From the licensee's perspective, a license reduces the risks associated with attempting to invent a similar product without infringing and reduces the time necessary to get to market with a substitute product. But a licensee loses control over the product, ceding technological leadership to the patent owner. And, as mentioned, royalties may reduce profits.

A license has a double impact on the licensee's profits in relation to that of the patent holder (assuming similar market level prices and quantities for the licensee and the patent holder). A 5 percent royalty adds approximately 5 percent of revenue to the licensee's costs and an equivalent amount to the patent owner's profits. Therefore, with sales evenly split, the licensee suffers a competitive disadvantage equal to 10 percent of sales compared to the patent holder.

The two parties must evaluate these and other considerations, including cost projections, to establish hypothetical negotiating postures.

It may be obvious that "the opinion testimony of qualified experts" (*Georgia Pacific's* fourteenth factor)[12] is necessary to ascertain the royalty rate that would result from this hypothetical negotiating environment. Although some instances may call for an expert to state an opinion about "the rate" based solely on expertise and experience, the expert's testimony generally will need a basis in fact and analysis. More specifically, *Georgia Pacific* lists assumptions and analyses in its remaining 13 factors that an expert must address. The following discusses these factors.

Similar Licenses of the Patentee or Licensees

Georgia-Pacific's first two factors suggest that where arm's-length negotiations for the same or similar inventions exist, the rates established in those proxy negotiations should be a guide for establishing the reasonable royalty for the product in issue.

1. The royalties received by the patentee for the licensing of the patent in suit, proving or tending to prove an established royalty.
2. The rates paid by the licensee for the use of other patents comparable to the patent in suit.[13]

The proxy license must involve not only a similar invention but also similar terms and conditions to the patent in issue before applying the proxy rate. One can easily compare the rates if the terms are similar. If the proxy license provides for a percentage royalty paid over the same length of time as the patent in issue, then the rates might be applicable. However, if the proxy license provided for a lump sum payment, a translation into an applicable royalty rate is necessary. A lump sum royalty yields any number of royalty rates, depending upon the assumptions used.

For example, a lump sum of $500,000 might imply a royalty rate of 5 percent of net cash receipts from the patented article if the lump sum was negotiated based upon projected Imitator sales receipts of $2,300,000 annually for 6 years. The present value, at 10 percent annually, of this estimate of receipts is $10 million, which compared to a $500,000 lump sum payment yields an implied royalty rate of 5 percent.[14] Assumptions underlying this translation are the discount rate and the period and amount of annual expected receipts. As these assumptions change, the royalty rate changes. Other factors present in the proxy license affect the calculation, such as a cap on total royalties to be paid, royalties that vary as sales increase, and payment timing terms.

Difficulties arise when using another licensee's rates as a proxy if the conditions are not similar. Is the license comparable in terms of what has been conveyed to the licensee; that is, does it include technical support, trademarks, updates—and so forth? These conditions tend to raise the value of the license and thus increase the royalty rate.

Does the proxy license provide for territorial or market restrictions? Is the licensee in the same market position as Imitator is to Patterson? For example, the proxy licenses might pertain to geographic territories in which the patent owner does not operate, thus suggesting the proxy rate would be lower than that demanded of the infringer. Or the licensee may have access to market segments or customer groups that the patentee could not reach otherwise, possibly because the licensee is selling the patented product at different price points or through different channels than the patentee. This condition also tends to decrease the royalty rate that the patent owner could demand.

Thus in suggesting existing licenses as proxies for the rate that should apply to the litigated case, an analysis must consider whether the patent owner would expect a different rate from the infringer based upon differences in terms and market conditions between the proxy and the infringement cases.

Commercial Considerations

The third, fourth, fifth, and seventh factors suggested by the court in *Georgia-Pacific* set forth commercial considerations (such as those discussed with the first two factors) in selecting the appropriate royalty rate.

3. The nature and scope of the license, as exclusive or non-exclusive; or as restricted or non-restricted in terms of territory or with respect to whom the manufactured product may be sold.
4. The licensor's established policy and marketing program to maintain his patent monopoly by not licensing others to use the invention or by granting licenses under special conditions designed to preserve that monopoly.
5. The commercial relationship between the licensor and licensee, such as, whether they are competitors in the same territory in the same line of business; or whether they are inventor and promoter.
7. The duration of the patent and the term of the license.[15]

These four factors raise fact, or descriptive, issues and must be evaluated to judge if other license royalty rates apply to the infringed product. If similarities exist between an actual license and the hypothetical license, the actual royalty rate can be a starting point to ascertain the appropriate hypothetical rate.

The fourth factor, already quoted, raises many difficult questions, beyond the scope of this chapter, in assessing an appropriate royalty in hypothetical negotiations for a party whose policy it is to never enter into such licenses. The patent owner's previous licensing history is one of the better indicators of the hypothetical rate; the lack of such history adds significant challenges. Courts may tend to believe that a company's historical refusal to license should justify a higher rate than one that hypothetical negotiations would suggest.

In *Santa Fe-Pomeroy, Inc. v. P&Z Company, Inc.*,[16] the plaintiff did not have a practice of licensing and had intended to profit from its lawful monopoly without licensing. The district court found that with the unusual facts of this case, "particularly where the patent holder did not license his patented process, a reasonable royalty equated to expected profit is a satisfactory reasonable approximation."[17] We take issue with this decision as a general proposition and note that, as discussed previously, even one that has not previously granted a license often licenses for something less than expected profit: A potential licensee may have a larger distribution system, licensing reduces risks (e.g., those related to expanding capacity) and may dissuade others from research and development that could obsolete the patented item. Further, it seems to be a rare situation where a licensee could be expected to pay a royalty equivalent to 100% of the profit it would earn from the products.

Effect on Sales of Other Products

Georgia-Pacific's sixth factor deals with "the effect of selling the patented specialty in promoting sales of other products of the licensee; the existing value of the invention to the licensor as a generator of sales of his non-patented items; and the extent of such derivative or convoyed sales."[18]

That the patented article may generate sales of other products may be true for the infringer and/or the patent owner. For example, Imitator's sale of the infringing VCRs might have switched follow-on purchases of service, repairs, and new replacement models from Patterson. Related product sales may also benefit from the patented item's availability. The sales force, for instance, may be able to use the patented item as a door opener and then successfully promote the company's remaining product line. For example, Patterson may also manufacture video cameras, and a sale of a VCR may lead to a sale of a video camera as well.

Quantifying the effect on the patent owner of the lost sales of other products complicates the analysis. First, one must demonstrate that such a relationship exists. Then the analysis must encompass the profits of not only the patented items but also the related items. Lastly, a fair royalty might consider not only the sales and profits of the patented item but also the profitability of related products and services that are expected to follow directly from the sales or availability of the item.

If the patented item leads to sales of other products and services, empirical evidence gathered from studies of historical sales performance should prove the nexus. The analysis should include both the infringer and the patent owner because each may have different relationships that would lead to differing beliefs about a reasonable royalty rate.

Clearly, one needs to collect the accounting information on sales by product, preferably in unit volume terms. The analysis requires a thorough understanding of the marketing and sales programs, techniques, and relationships. Interviews or depositions should lead the marketing people to identify their perception of product interrelationships. Analyses of historical data will confirm or contradict the beliefs of the in-house people.

The simple case would see parallel movement in the sales volumes of the patented article and the related products. One should, however, examine to verify that other independent factors are not causing the volume increases. For example, sales of related products may increase because of changes in demand, general growth in sales, new product introductions, or growth in the economic sector served by the related products. Service sales may grow rapidly, for instance, because consumers own more nonpatented units than previously. Thus one must ascertain with reasonable certainty that the sales of related products are caused primarily by the patented item's sales. Tools commonly employed to perform this analysis include graphical analysis of sales performance and regression analyses.

With a causal link established, the profits resulting from sales of all related articles must be identified to calculate lost-profits damages, discussed earlier, or an appropriate reasonable royalty rate.

Established Profitability of the Patented Products

Georgia-Pacific's eighth factor notes the relevancy of "the established profitability of the product made under the patent; its commercial success; and its current popularity."[19]

Profit on the product and the derivative sales should be calculated as described earlier. To establish a reasonable royalty, the primary focus should be the projected profits of the infringer and the patent owner at the time of first infringement. The time of first infringement is the time that the hypothetical license negotiations would occur. The product's expected profitability is the assumption that each party would bring to the negotiation.

If one or both of the parties misunderstood the patent's value, however, their expectation at the date of the hypothetical negotiation may not be relevant. The court might assume that both parties have full knowledge of the patent's extent and value. Of course, full knowledge does not imply both parties have identical knowledge, perfect foresight, or similar assessments of the likely sales and profits. It also should not presume that each party has perfect knowledge of the benefits and detriments that each could bring to exploit the invention. This concept of the extent of knowledge is often subjective and intensely argued at patent infringement trials.

Projected Profits. The courts have established that a reasonable royalty can consider the patent holder's expected profit. The *Panduit* case states that when "the patentee's business scheme involves a reasonable expectation of making future profits by the continuing sale to the purchaser of the patented machine, of supplies to be furnished by the patentee, which future business he will lose by licensing a competitor to make the machine, this expectant loss is an element to be considered in retroactively determining a reasonable royalty."[20]

Several points warrant mention in relation to the *Panduit* case. The court requires that a company like Patterson should make a showing that it had planned to make follow-on sales, such as video cameras, video cassettes, and servicing of VCRs in order for it to claim that the profit on these related items should be considered in establishing a royalty rate. The court states that there must be a reasonable expectation of profits.

The court also clearly indicates that what is to be considered is the loss of "expectant" profits, not the infringer's actual profits or the ex post calculation of the patent owner's lost profits. Of course, absent a basis for estimating projected profitability, one may have to use actual lost profits as a guide to estimated profits as of the date of infringement.

Although both *Panduit* and *Georgia-Pacific* indicate that the patent owner's profitability is a factor, it alone should not control the choice of a royalty rate.

Considerable uncertainty or unacceptable speculation may cloud the patent owner's profitability forecast. Otherwise, the inquiry would have ended when the patent owner's lost profits damages have been estimated.

Available Substitutes. The patent owner's estimate of lost profits is relevant for computing the reasonable royalty because it represents a theoretical maximum that the patent holder could demand as a royalty. But that maximum would be reduced to the extent a "noninfringing alternative" exists. Suppose another product is available as a close substitute, a VCR with a traditional recording head, for instance. Then one could assume that the patent owner's profits would be smaller relative to the case where a close substitute does not exist. Of course, what constitutes a close alternative will be controversial in most patent cases.

The *Panduit* case suggests that a substitute may look more viable in hindsight when defending an infringement suit than it looked when the defendant decided to infringe:

> The "acceptable substitute" element . . . must be viewed of limited influence where the infringer knowingly made and sold the patented product for years while ignoring the "substitute." There are substitute products for virtually every patented product; the availability of railroads and box cameras should not of itself diminish royalties payable for infringement of the right to exclude others from making the Wright airplane or the Polaroid camera.[21]

One must consider an infringer's substitute and its effect on a product line's projected profitability. Several questions, however, exist. Is the substitute already in production, or would it require substantial development to be ready for the market? Does the infringer have a market image and customer base, or is it using the credibility of the patent owner's product to develop a market niche for itself? The overriding analytical question is whether the infringer using the substitute product could have garnered for itself the same unit sales performance, by time period, as it did using the patent owner's product.

Calculating the Infringer's Incremental Profits. An infringer's profits equal incremental revenues less incremental costs arising from sales of the patented product. Typically, the patented product represents an improvement over the infringer's existing product. Thus any calculation of incremental costs normally would include the overhead, or period costs, that the new invention absorbs as it displaces the previous product. An acceptable method for estimating these costs is to consider what Imitator would look like if it did not produce the infringing VCR recording head. The company would either shed overhead and period costs[22] or would instead produce another product using some or all of its existing overhead structure. Thus, although not conceptually different from the calculations related to the patent owner's lost profits, the calculations of the infringer's profits from infringement could well differ from patentee's lost profits.

For example, suppose Imitator makes two products, a compact disk player and an older technology VCR. Its VCR has now become obsolete by Patterson's invention.

Imitator's sale of compact disk players (CD) is independent of the sale of both its obsolete VCR and the new patented product. Each of the CDs and the VCRs sell for $1000 and have variable costs of $500. The two products together contribute $1000 to offset a joint overhead or period cost of $900. Profits are thus $100.

	VCR & CD
Sales ($1,000 × 2)	$2,000
Variable costs ($500 × 2)	(1,000)
Contribution	1,000
Period costs (overhead)	(900)
Profit pretax	$ 100

If Imitator exits the VCR business entirely and only sells CDs without shedding its period costs, the income statement will show a loss of $400.

	CD only
Sales ($1,000 × 1)	$1,000
Variable costs ($500 × 1)	(500)
Contribution	800
Period costs (overhead)	(900)
Loss pretax	($ 400)

Now assume that instead of leaving the VCR business, Imitator agrees to license Patterson's invention and to pay a royalty of 20 percent of the sales price. Imitator's income statement will now show a loss of $100.

	VCR & CD
Sales ($1,000 × 2)	$2,000
Variable costs ($500 × 2)	(1,000)
Royalty (20% × $1,000)	(200)
Contribution	800
Period Costs (overhead)	(900)
Loss pretax	($100)

Obviously looking only at sales less variable costs, in this case $500 for the VCR, to compute the funds available to pay as a royalty can lead to a result that projects a loss to the infringer.

This oversimplified example shows how critical it is to properly identify those costs that are truly incremental to the analysis. The appropriate analysis would consider the financial effect of the alternatives available to the infringer.

One alternative for the infringer would be to exit the business entirely. Assume a pro rata share of overhead, or period costs could then be eliminated. For Imitator, this would be $450. Further, assume that Imitator had an investment in capital at current value of $600, which could be 50 percent liquidated. Imitator's profits would fall to $40 plus whatever could be earned on the $300 of freed resources, say $10, for a total of $60. This is $40 less than the original profit of $100.

	CD only
Sales ($1,000 × 1)	$1,000
Variable costs ($500 × 1)	(500)
Contribution	500
Interest on capital freed-up	10
Period costs (½ eliminated)	(450)
Pretax profit	$ 60

Under those assumptions, the patent technology is worth at most $40 to Imitator, and a royalty of some portion of the $40 could be paid.

A second alternative would be to continue selling the predecessor technology. Assume this would require a 4 percent price discount to maintain projected sales levels. Again, this would reduce profits, in this case by $40; thus the infringer would be in a position to pay a portion of this reduction of $40 as a royalty.

A third alternative would involve the production and sale of an acceptable substitute. Assume this substitute would be equivalent from a market standpoint but would require additional manufacturing costs of $30, thus lowering profits by that amount. The infringer would thus be in a position to share with the patent owner the $30 cost differential as a royalty.

Analyzing all the alternatives available would lead to an identification of the "next best alternative." This should then form the basis for a decision on the proper royalty from the infringer's perspective.

Discounted Cash Flow Models. The discussion here proceeds under the simplifying assumption that the profit from each alternative falls in an equal manner in each year. The real world is rarely as straightforward as this. Fortunately there a technique—the "discounted cash flow" model—which supports the analysis after lifting this simplifying assumption. Using a discounted cash flow approach allows an analyst to incorporate a large variety of differences between the investigated alternatives. Each alternative is viewed as a project, and all of the associated cash flows are identified and arrayed across time. One then calculates present values for each alternative. The difference between net present value of the patented product and that of the infringer's next best alternative identifies the pool of dollars available to be shared with the patent holder as royalties.

Rule-of-Thumb Approaches. We have discussed some factors that the infringer and the patent holder must consider when answering *Georgia-Pacific's* question about the patented product's profitability. One final technique bears mentioning because it has its proponents, and it reflects the business reality of setting royalty rates. This approach proceeds from the same sort of profit analyses we have discussed. A realistic projection as of the date of infringement of the pretax profits to the infringer is prepared and aggregated over a realistic number of years. This available profit pool is divided by a rule-of-thumb formula between the licensor and licensee.

This rule of thumb is judgmental and depends upon experience in negotiating royalties. One well-known negotiator advocates a "25% rule" (Goldscheider, 1984). The rule states that a percentage, averaging 25 percent, of the available profit pool will go to the patentee (licensor) as a royalty and leave 75 percent of the profit pool to the licensee. The rule is described as a starting point for setting the appropriate rate; raising or lowering the percentage "depending on the qualitative and quantitative contributions of the respective parties" (Goldscheider, 1984, p. 198) and on the terms of the license to be agreed upon. Using one of our previous examples, the profit pool available for sharing would be \$100. If a 25-percent sharing formula were viewed as appropriate, the patentee would enjoy a 2.5% royalty rate (\$15 royalty divided by the \$1000 sales price). The licensee would generate profits of \$75.

Utility and Advantages of the Patented Article

The ninth factor from *Georgia-Pacific* defines the descriptive analyses that must be done in a patent case to identify the improvement in the art and the benefits of the invention. It focuses on the utility and advantages of the patent property over the old modes or devices, if any, that had been used for working out similar results.[23]

This type of an analysis should provide some ranges for a reasonable royalty. To the extent that the new art is an improvement over prior technology, an economically measurable benefit will exist: higher prices, lower manufacturing or distribution costs, an enlarged market through a shift in demand, or some combination.

The analysis will quantify these benefits as the difference in profits to the involved parties with or without the patented article. This maximum profit will then be shared in the form of a royalty on the new product's sales. As previously stated, one useful tool for this analysis would likely be a discounted present value study of the profit stream from the new product and from the replaced technology. If done carefully, the differences between the two competing technologies can be quantified and expressed as a percentage. For example, if the patented VCR recording head reduces manufacturing costs by \$50 per unit and the average sales price is \$1000, then at a maximum, the royalty will range up to 5 percent.

Alternatively, the new features may allow the product to command a higher price in the marketplace. Also, assume that no shifts will occur in sales volume expectations between the old and the newer products. Again, we see a clear track toward estimating the maximum royalty that could be paid. Assume that the price increase is \$100 over the existing price of \$1000 (and no costs change). The maximum rate then would be 9.1 percent—a \$100 increase in profits divided by a new sales price of \$1100.

Of course, a more complicated issue arises if the new product, with its better feature complement, shifts sales away from companies employing the older product without the added features. The analysis in this situation can proceed in several ways. Conceivably, a shift in volume could be overcome through pricing. That is, some price relationship would exist between the new and the old product that would maintain the historical market shares. Once identified, the price difference acts the same as a price increase, and royalty rates are established as described in the preceding paragraph. An alternative proceeds on the basis of quantifying the loss of sales volume to the new technology, assuming a license is not negotiated. The calculation would consider the lost profits from the lost sales volume as a boundary for the royalty rate. The net present value approach would likely be required to translate these prospective losses into a royalty rate.

Of course, combinations of all factors discussed are possible, but any analysis should consider if feasible the boundary established by the next best alternative, discussed earlier. At some royalty rate, the licensee would redeploy its assets and energies to a totally different venture to generate a higher rate of return than it could obtain by making the patented product and paying a high royalty rate.

Several other factors complicate the analysis. The first is the issue of leads and lags. Leads and lags refer to the time period required for an adjustment to occur. Our discussions so far have assumed that all adjustments in the market occur at the date of the infringement or date of establishment of the reasonable royalty rate. The world may not respond so quickly. Changes in prices and market shares occur over time. Also, perfecting an adequate substitute could take time, thus allowing the patent owner to obtain market share and position before its competitor has a viable alternative. These timing considerations must enter the analysis of differences in economic flows between the patented technology and the next best alternative. The net present value tool is ideal for amalgamating the effects of changing assumptions on cash receipts and payments at different times.

A second complicating factor, however, is not so neatly dealt with—the issue of uncertainty. Because, in concept, the analyses we have been discussing are prospective analyses as of the date of infringement, all the estimates are by definition uncertain. However, the degree of uncertainty may vary for each estimate. For example, suppose Patterson's patented recording head is clearly superior in the market, and Imitator has no alternative product currently available. Suppose further that Imitator believes it could have designed around the patent, using technology and designs already available to it, and marketed its own variant with the same profitability and without losing market share. (Of course, as *Panduit* suggests, the courts would tend to view such a claim skeptically.) Even accepting Imitator's claim, one must consider the uncertainty of this alternative's success as compared to the potential successful sales of the patented article. Although the defendant may claim that the patented article offers little or no benefit, other than some lead time over an alternative that does not yet exist, such a claim would be viewed with some skepticism. The risks or uncertainties associated with the alternative would seem to exceed those related to the patented product.

Analytical tools exist to deal with this problem. We have discussed the use of discounted present value techniques to measure the net benefit of one alternative over another. Our prior discussions did not include the selection of discount rates for such calculations. The discount rate brings future cash flows to a present cash value.[24] The inference has been that one would use the same rate for all alternatives. However, one approach to dealing with the variance in risks among the cash flows is to use differing discount rates. A measure of market-level risk might be obtained by analysis of publicly traded companies in the same industry as the patent owner or infringer. The flows arising from the patented technology might be discounted at the corporate borrowing rate or the corporate rate of return on investment. The substitute technology may be much more risky and thus might be discounted at a higher rate to allow for the greater risk. The analyst's task is to identify and support the selected rates.

Invention's Benefits to the User

Georgia-Pacific's tenth factor states that "the nature of the patented invention; the character of the commercial embodiment of it as owned and produced by the licensor; and the benefits to those who have used the invention"[25] will help establish the royalty rate.

Basically, such an analysis should identify whether a pricing advantage adheres in the new item as a result of either a cost advantage in its production or superior performance over competitive products. Such an advantage might lead to a higher sales demand for the invention over alternative technology. This benefit could be quantified to suggest a reasonable royalty rate.

Value to the Infringer from the Invention's Use

"The extent to which the infringer has made use of the invention; and any evidence probative of the value of that use."[26]

Value arises from the infringer's profits on the sale of the product and from the related effects, if any, on the infringer's sales of other products, its business image, or other benefits. Of course, the infringer's profits do not necessarily provide the amount of a reasonable royalty. As discussed previously, one must evaluate the profits in comparison to the next best alternative available to the infringer to ascertain the amount available as a royalty. Only the difference in profit between sales of the patented item and the next best alternative is relevant to the royalty amount that the infringer should pay.

Customary Rate

The twelfth factor in *Georgia-Pacific* specifies the identification of a royalty rate customary to the particular business as a solution to picking a reasonable royalty rate: "the portion of the profit or of the selling price that may be customary in the particular business or in comparable businesses to allow for the use of the invention or analogous inventions."[27] Clearly, this "proxy" rate provides a market-tested, "real-world" negotiated solution. One must take care, however, to assure that the purported real rates apply to the hypothetical negotiations issue. Questions to consider include the following:

1. Is the invention truly comparable in utility and technological advancement to that reflected by the customary or proxy rate?
2. Is the life remaining on the proxy license similar to that of the infringed item?

3. Are the two parties in each case in similar circumstances such that one could reasonably expect the proxy rate to have resulted from a negotiation between the infringer and the patent owner?
4. Are the relative markets reasonably comparable?
5. Typically, a negotiated license might include not only rights to the invention but also know-how, trademark, updates, drawings, technical assistance, and cross-licenses. The infringement is more similar to a "naked" license that grants only the use of the patent. As a result, the proxy rate may not be applicable in the infringement if any of these other rights are present.[28]

Profit Apportionment

The final item that we list from *Georgia-Pacific* relates more to lost profits rather than reasonable royalty:

> 13. The portion of the realizable profit that should be credited to the invention as distinguished from non-patented elements, the manufacturing process, business risks, or significant features or improvements added by the infringer.[29]

This ruling prevents a patent owner with, say, five significant patents on a single product from collecting lost profits several times over from an infringer. Although this may be conceptually sound, in practice the data are rarely available to make the computation. Identifying an analytical approach for separating the profit into its constituent elements is very difficult. One could also argue that where the patented attribute caused the buyer to purchase the product, the patent owner has lost the entire profit—even that amount attributed to noninfringed parts—because of the infringement. Generally, an analyst is led back to one of the approaches we discussed earlier about comparison to alternatives and calculations of incremental costs and profits in order to apportion profits.

Alternatively, technical experts could offer their judgments on the patented features' relative importance. This approach has several flaws, most significant of which may be the difficulty in introducing such subjective testimony as evidence. The other difficulty is that in making such qualitative judgments, each expert may bring differing assumptions on the importance and benefit of each product feature. Thus the subjective approach, in reality, only masks the underlying analytical assumptions that should be set forth for the trier of fact to evaluate.

NOTES

1. A prior version of this chapter appeared in Vol. 15, No. 4 of the *American Intellectual Property Law Association Quarterly Journal*, 1987.
2. See *King Instruments Corp. v. Otari Corp.*, 767 F.2d 853, 863 (Fed. Cir. 1985); *Hartness International, Inc. v. Simplimatic Engineering Co.*, 819 F.2d 1100, 1112 (Fed. Cir. 1987); *Hanson v. Alpine Valley Ski Area, Inc.*, 718 F.2d 1075, 1078 (Fed. Cir. 1983).
3. If Patterson is forced to meet the lower price, price damages might also be justifiable.

4. *Smith International, Inc. v. Hughes Tool Co.*, 229 U.S.P.Q. (BNA) 81, 92–93 (C.D. CA 1986).

5. See *Pfizer, Inc. v. International Rectifier Corp.*, 218 U.S.P.Q. (BNA) 586 (C.D. CA 1983).

6. 35 U.S.C. § 284

7. *Panduit Corp. v. Stahlin Bros. Fibre Works, Inc.*, 575 F.2d 1156 (6th Cir. 1978).

8. *Georgia-Pacific Corp. v. United States Plywood Corp.*, 318 F. Supp. 1116, 1120 (S.D.N.Y. 1970), *modified and aff'd.*, 496 F.2d 295 (2d Cir. 1971).

9. Ibid., p. 1120; see also *Santa Fe-Pomeroy, Inc. v. P & Z Co., Inc.*, 569 F.2d 1084 (9th Cir. 1978).

10. *Panduit*, supra, p. 1158.

11. Ibid., p. 1159.

12. *Georgia-Pacific*, supra, p. 1120.

13. Ibid.

14.

Year	*Receipts*	*10% Present Value (Rounded)*
1	$ 2,300,000	$ 2,100,000
2	2,300,000	1,900,000
3	2,300,000	1,700,000
4	2,300,000	1,600,000
5	2,300,000	1,400,000
6	2,300,000	1,300,000
	$13,800,000	$10,000,000

$500,000 divided by $10,000,000 = 5%

15. *Georgia-Pacific*, supra, p. 1120.

16. *Santa Fe-Pomeroy, Inc. v. P&Z Company, Inc.*, 569 F.2d 1084 (9th Cir. 1978).

17. Ibid. p. 418.

18. *Georgia-Pacific*, supra, p. 1120.

19. Ibid.

20. *Panduit*, supra, p. 1163.

21. Ibid., p. 1162 n. 9.

22. Period costs, within a defined volume range, are those incurred through passage of time as opposed to the volume of activity. For example, many accounting department costs are period costs.

23. *Georgia-Pacific*, supra, p. 1120.

24. See Note 13 for an example of discounting cash flows; Goldscheider (1984, p. 198) for further information on this subject and the chapter in this volume dealing with interest rates.

25. *Georgia-Pacific*, supra, p. 1120.

26. *Ibid.*

27. *Ibid.*

28. See generally Goldscheider, Chapter 23, for a discussion of these five factors.

29. *Georgia-Pacific*, supra, p. 1120.

BIBLIOGRAPHY

Goldscheider, R., *Technology Management Handbook* (Clark Boardman, 1984).

LIST OF CASES

Georgia-Pacific Corp. v. United States Plywood, F.2d 295 (2d Cir. 1971)
Hanson v. Alpine Valley Ski Area, Inc., 718 F.2d 1075 (Fed. Cir. 1983)
Hartness Int'l, Inc. v. Simplimatic Engineering Co., 819 F.2d 1100 (Fed. Cir. 1987)
King Instruments Corp. v. Otari Corp., 767 F.2d 853 (Fed. Cir. 1985)
Panduit Corp. v. Stahlin Bros. Fibre Works, Inc., 575 F.2d 1152 (6th Cir. 1978)
Pfizer, Inc. v. International Rectifier Corp., 218 U.S.P.Q. (BNA) 586 (C.D. Cal. 1986)
Santa Fe-Pomeroy, Inc. v. P & Z Co., Inc., 569 F.2d 1084 (9th Cir. 1978)
Smith International, Inc. v. Hughes Tool Co., 229 U.S.P.Q. (BNA) 81 (C.D. Cal. 1986)

18

PROFESSIONAL LIABILITY

James A. Spielmann, CPA

LITIGATION EXPLOSION INVOLVING ACCOUNTANTS

Both the number of lawsuits and the amounts awarded to plaintiffs are climbing. The number of federal civil actions filed annually since 1960 has increased more than fivefold. By 1985, 8 million lawsuits were pending in state and local courts—about 1 lawsuit for every 20 adult Americans. A 1987 Rand Corporation analysis of civil jury awards shows significant increases over the previous 25 years. The average malpractice jury award in Cook County, Illinois, increased by a factor of 20 between 1960 and 1984.

Malpractice suits directed toward accountants have followed this trend. More lawsuits have been filed against members of the accounting profession in the past 15 years than in the entire previous history of the profession. The number of lawsuits reported to the special investigations committee of the American Institute of Certified Public Accountants (AICPA), SEC practice section, increased throughout the 1980s. Judgments and settlements of lawsuits against the former Big Eight accounting firms have amounted to more than $200 million since 1980.

Professional liability insurance premiums are escalating, coverage is shrinking, and many carriers have discontinued offering coverage. Insurance premiums for the largest CPA firms have increased approximately fivefold since 1984, whereas coverage has been cut in half and deductibles substantially increased (Mednick, 1987, p. 119).

A number of factors have contributed to the significant increase in litigation against accountants since the 1960s. From a sociological perspective there has been a heightening of the public's expectations of independent accountants and their work and a far greater willingness on the part of investors and creditors who relied on that work to file suit against the accountant for losses. The public perceives the accountants as guarantors of the accuracy of the company's financial statements. The accountants often are looked to for their substantial resources and are sued, primarily because of their ability to pay, regardless of their culpability (Sullivan et al., 1985, pp. 131–132).

The litigation explosion may reflect increasing general distrust of experts and traditional authority figures. Growth in the number of lawyers is a factor. For every perceived injury, somewhere there is an attorney prepared to file a claim.

Developments within the legal system, discussed later, have also enhanced the prospects of plaintiffs. These trends tend to feed on themselves. Massive verdicts receive wide publicity and provide more incentive for plaintiffs and their attorneys to initiate additional lawsuits (Amhowitz, 1987, p. 359).

COMMON CAUSES OF CLAIMS AGAINST ACCOUNTANTS

Pratter (1983, p. 12) cites the following nine common causes of claims against accountants: tax services, audit services, accounting services, client counterclaims, defalcations, third-party claims under various federal and state securities laws, business and investment advice, breach of fiduciary duties, and management consulting services.

Tax Services

Based on AICPA Professional Liability Insurance Plan statistics, tax services generate more civil damage suits against accountants than any other practice category. Tax services give rise to claims that range from allegations that an accountant is responsible for late filing of returns or for underpayment of estimated tax obligations to claims based on Internal Revenue Service (IRS) disallowance of treatment advised by the accountant as reported on a tax return prepared by the accountant.

The IRS has a variety of penalties it can assess against tax practitioners. It can suspend or disbar tax practitioners from practicing before it. It can obtain an injunction to prohibit further preparation of tax returns by the accountant.

Erroneous tax return preparation exposes the tax practitioner to civil liability to the client for IRS penalties and interest and in some cases for income taxes.

In instances where the accountant failed to warn about inherent risks of a successful IRS challenge or specific risks involving a specific transaction, the accountant may be held liable for the resulting taxes, penalties, and interest.

Accountant involvement in tax shelters poses risk exposure to civil damage suits based on allegations of (1) violation of state "blue sky" laws, (2) violation of federal securities laws, (3) common law negligence, or (4) breach of common law fiduciary duty (*The CPA Journal*, March 1986, p. 72).

Audit Services

The second most frequent cause of claims results from the performance of audit services. The accountant engaged to perform an audit essentially investigates, gathers, and analyzes data for purposes of drawing inferences and reaching conclusions that are presented in the form of an opinion or report.

The courts tend to measure an independent accountant's potential legal liability from the perspective of the accountant's various duties as enumerated in the technical and ethical standards of the profession. A duty considered to be essential and virtually inviolate is the duty of independence. Failure to follow generally accepted accounting principles (GAAP) or generally accepted auditing standards (GAAS) is considered to be strong evidence of professional negligence as is failure to adhere to the practitioner's own in-house audit procedures manuals.

A practitioner engaged to perform nonaudit services may be held liable for failing to follow professional standards if some audit procedures were performed in the overall performance of the nonaudit services.

The independent accountant's duty (as often perceived by the public) to detect fraud or inquire into suspicious circumstances or abnormal activities can give rise to claims by client and third parties.

Accounting Services

Accounting services generally involve allegations of improper execution of an engagement to provide financial statement review or compilation services. These services form the basis for what probably is the third most frequent cause of claims.

Many accounting services claims are based on the improper assumption that an audit was performed. These claims can often be reduced if the accountant can substantiate that an audit was neither contemplated nor performed and if the substantive differences between audit and nonaudit engagements can be explained to, and understood by, the plaintiff.

Since 1978, accountants have been required to follow the Statement on Standards for Accounting and Review Services No. 1 (SSARS 1) in the performance of financial statement review and compilation engagements. Not all of the standards contained within SSARS 1 are clearly defined, particularly as to the scope of a review engagement. This uncertainty has increased the accounting profession's exposure to liability.

Client Counterclaims

Client counterclaims to accountants' fee collection suits are a frequent cause of claims against practitioners. The most effective deterrent to these claims is for accountants to bill for services promptly and regularly in order to minimize the later need to file suit for unpaid fees.

Defalcations

Claims are frequently filed relating to a perceived failure of an accountant to detect embezzlement or other defalcations during an engagement. Claims based upon client–employee dishonesty often include allegations that the accountant has recommended or approved the hiring of the employee or had failed to communicate to the client that its internal control system was inadequate.

Securities Laws

Securities-related claims are probably the most feared type of third-party claims against accountants because they usually involve significant monetary liability and defense costs.

Civil liability to third parties under the federal securities acts is discussed in detail elsewhere in this chapter.

Business and Investment Advice

These claims often are related to advice given in connection with business acquisition or divestitures and the preparation of financial statement projections. Also involved is a rapidly expanding services area in which the accountant provides advice to businesses and individuals on such things as a suitable mix or portfolio investments. Recipients of those services who suffer financial loss may be inclined to seek recovery of their losses from the accountant.

Breach of Fiduciary Duties

With the addition of actuaries on the staffs of many accounting firms, claims filed against accounting firms for breaches of pension plan fiduciary responsibilities under ERISA may increase.

Management Consulting Services

These types of claims allege that the consulting advice given was not correct or appropriate in the circumstances. To the extent an accounting firm uses nonaccountant specialists to render services subject to claims, the care with which the specialists were selected and their level of expertise will be open to scrutiny.

LIABILITY TO CLIENTS

An accountant's liability to clients is based on the concept of privity and on the law of torts. Privity refers to the direct contractual relationship between the parties. The law of torts relates to wrongful acts that injure another's person, property, or reputation (Sullivan et al., 1985, p. 132). A breach of contract occurs when, for example, the accountant issues an unqualified opinion without performing an examination in accordance with professional standards. The accountant is also liable to the client under tort law for negligence.

Ordinary negligence is the failure to exercise due professional care. For accountants, due professional care requires adherence to professional standards. Gross negligence is the absence of even slight care. Fraud involves direct or intentional misrepresentation or omission of a material fact.

Most claims brought against accountants by clients have been based on allegations of negligent misrepresentation. Often the accountant's failure to detect a defalcation has been the primary cause of a negligence finding against the accountant.

CIVIL LIABILITY TO THIRD PARTIES UNDER COMMON LAW

An independent accountant is usually liable for ordinary negligence to primary beneficiaries as well as to foreseen third parties. A primary beneficiary is any party the accountant specifically knows may rely on the accountant's opinion. Foreseen third parties are any reasonably definable class of persons the accountant might reasonably expect to rely on such opinion. Liability for gross negligence and fraud applies to all third parties, including foreseeable third parties (defined as an unlimited class of persons not identified by the independent accountant who may foreseeably be expected to rely on the accountant's opinion).

Traditionally, in the absence of liability based upon a statute such as the federal securities acts, an accountant could be held liable to third parties only for fraud. The first case to test the privity of contract concept was *Ultramares v. Touche Ross*[1] in 1931.

In that case the plaintiff, without the defendant's knowledge, had relied on financial statements opined on by the defendant accountant to make loans to a company that later became insolvent. The New York Court of Appeals upheld the dismissal of a negligence count because of the absence of privity.

The *Ultramares* decision became the basis for common law negligence actions throughout the United States for many years. Prior to 1965, most third-party plaintiffs bringing suit against independent accountants were unsuccessful, even in instances in which specific third parties were known by the accountant to be recipients of the accountant's report.

In 1965, the American Law Institute interpreted the law of negligent misrepresentations by professionals to third parties to apply to a limited group of persons, known as foreseen persons, whom a defendant expects and intends to influence (Sullivan et al., 1985, p. 136). This is in contrast to an unlimited foreseeable class of persons. The foreseen class concept was accepted in a 1968 federal court decision, *Rusch Factors, Inc. v. Levin.*[2] In this case the accountant was held liable to the third-party plaintiff, a lender of the client. The plaintiff had specifically requested the accountant's report and thus was a primary beneficiary. The court's decision, however, extended liability for ordinary negligence to foreseen and limited classes of persons in addition to the plaintiff–lender.

In 1983 in *H. Rosenblum, Inc. v. Adler,*[3] the New Jersey Supreme Court ruled that an independent accountant has a duty to reasonably foreseeable but unidentified third-party users who may rely on financial statements for various business reasons. Thus, in some jurisdictions, the accountant's liability for ordinary negligence may be extended to reasonably foreseeable third parties.

In addition to negligence actions, third parties may sue accountants for fraud. Fraud actions require the plaintiff to prove some form of knowledge by the accountant of the falsity of a representation. This knowledge is known as scienter. Depending upon the jurisdiction, scienter may be established by proof of actual knowledge of the falsity of a representation, lack of knowledge of the truth of a representation, and/or a reckless disregard for the truth or falsity of a representation.

CIVIL LIABILITY TO THIRD PARTIES UNDER THE FEDERAL SECURITIES ACTS

Any accountant who examines and reports on the financial statements of a company whose securities are publicly traded is subject to the various provisions of the federal securities statutes, including their liability provisions. The principal provisions of the acts that have determined the accountant's civil liability are Section 11 of the Securities Act of 1933 (1933 Act) and Section 10(b) and related Rule 10b-5 of the Securities Exchange Act of 1934 (1934 Act).

1933 Act

The 1933 Act regulates initial public offerings of securities and includes provisions intended to protect purchasers of securities. An accountant may be held liable to unnamed third-party purchasers of registered securities under Section 11 of the 1933 Act for misrepresentations or omissions of material facts in the registration statement. Ordinary negligence is a sufficient basis for liability.

The accountant is held to a due diligence standard of care. The accountant must perform a reasonable investigation up to the effective date of the registration statement leading to a belief that the financial statements contained therein are neither false nor misleading.

The plaintiff need only prove the existence of a material misstatement or omission but does not need to prove reliance on the financial statements containing such misstatement or omission.

A defense to a § 11 action requires showing that a reasonable investigation has been performed and that the accountant had reasonable grounds to believe, and did believe, that the financial statements were true and not misleading as of the effective date of the registration statement.

If the accountant is held liable but can prove that factors other than the misleading financial statements caused the plaintiff's loss, then any amount of loss relating to such other factors is not recoverable from the accountant.

1934 Act

The 1934 Act regulates continuous open-market trading of securities following an initial public offering and includes provisions intended to protect both purchasers and sellers of securities. The 1934 Act requires companies whose securities are publicly traded to file periodic reports with the SEC, some of which include annual audited financial statements.

Section 18 of the 1934 Act imposes liability on the accountant for filing a false or misleading statement. Under § 18, an accountant can avoid liability by proving that the accountant acted in good faith and had no knowledge of any such false or misleading statements.

The majority of civil cases against accountants have been brought under Section 10(b) and Rule 10b-5 that states, in part, that

> It shall be unlawful for any person—(a) to employ any device, scheme, or artifice to defraud, (b) to make any untrue statement of a material fact or to omit to state a material fact necessary in order to make the statements made, in light of the circumstances under which they were made, not misleading, or (c) to engage in any act, practice, or course of business which operates or would operate as a fraud or deceit upon any person, in connection with the purchase or sale of any security.

There is no good-faith defense under § 10(b) and Rule 10b-5. In contrast to both § 18 of the 1934 Act and § 11 of the 1933 Act, under Rule 10b-5 the burden of proof that the accountant acted fraudulently is with the plaintiff.

The 1976 United States Supreme Court decision in *Ernst & Ernst v. Hochfelder*[4] clarified that, under § 10(b) and Rule 10b-5, a showing of fraudulent conduct or recklessness is necessary to establish that an independent accountant breached the duty to disclose. Therefore, an accountant's liability to unforeseen third parties under the 1934 Act is basically the same as under common law at the time of *Ultramares Corporation v. Touche Ross*.

The Court also ruled in *Hochfelder* that § 10(b) applies to conduct involving elements of scienter. Under § 10(b) the courts have held that a showing of reckless actions evidencing a lack of concern for the truth will satisfy the scienter requirement.

CRIMINAL LIABILITY AND OTHER SEC SANCTIONS

Willful or intentional violations of the federal securities acts may also subject accountants to criminal penalties (monetary fines and/or imprisonment) under § 24 of the 1933 Act and § 32 of the 1934 Act. No motive need be proved, and no personal gain is required to be shown.

Accountants are also subject to civil injunctive proceedings and administrative (Rule 2(e)) proceedings available to the SEC. In an injunctive proceeding, the SEC must prove to a court both that a violation of the securities laws has occurred and also that there is a reasonable likelihood that future violations will occur if an injunction is not imposed.

Although Rule 2(e) proceedings usually are conducted in private hearings, they are always publicized by the SEC in the form of Accounting and Auditing Enforcement Releases. Such publicity can significantly impact an accountant's practice.

DEFENSES AGAINST LIABILITY

The best defense against legal liability for both accounting firms and individual practitioners is attained by strict adherence to the technical and ethical standards of the profession. Policies and procedures should be established to ensure that all engagements are performed by staff that understand the client's business; that they are systematically planned, supervised, and reviewed; and that all work performed is carefully and completely documented. All staff assigned to an audit engagement must be aware of possible audit red flags. Also, the use of engagement letters and second-partner reviews should be considered.

Although the following discussion is largely stated in the framework of an audit engagement, much of it is applicable to the variety of nonaudit services rendered to clients by accountants.

Understand the Client's Business

In all engagements, the accountant must understand the client's business and its complex business transactions. It is important that the client's accounting for business transactions reflects the substance of the transactions and not simply the form of the transactions. Partners and other supervisory staff need to understand the business in order to plan the work. Less experienced staff need to understand the business to be able to carry out the detailed work in an effective and efficient manner.

Adequate and Timely Planning, Supervision, and Review

It is important for a planning process to take place and that it include timely participation by all members of the engagement management team, including adequate involvement, when appropriate, by tax, management consulting, and industry specialist personnel. The planning process should be documented in the engagement workpapers.

Supervision and review are essential elements of managing an engagement because the ultimate responsibility for forming and expressing an opinion on the financial statements rests with the engagement partners and cannot be delegated. Supervision involves monitoring and directly reviewing the work performed to ensure that it is completed in accordance with the detailed engagement plan. Questions raised during the review process should be resolved prior to completing the engagement and issuing the report.

Careful and Complete Documentation

The accountant's report on a client's financial statements should be supported by a full and complete record of the work performed. Specifically, be sure to document the evaluation of the client's computer facilities as an integral part of the examination. All substantive points should be addressed in properly dated management representation letters.

Carefully review representations contained in legal representation letters. Follow up confusing or incomplete responses with client officials and attorneys. Be sure that legal representation letters are properly dated.

Be sure that appropriate audit work is completed and that the work performed and conclusions reached on significant accounting and disclosure matters are documented fully in the workpapers.

Complete a subsequent events review through the issuance date of the report. Be sure that all workpaper review lists have been cleared and all audit program steps are signed off. Remove from the workpaper files all completed review lists, outdated financial statement drafts, and any other obsolete material.

Audit Red Flags

The accountant performing an audit must be alert for and recognize danger signals, or audit red flags, and also must formulate and execute appropriate audit responses to any such red flags. Examples of red flags include business operating difficulties such as rapidly deteriorating operating cash balances, insufficient working capital, and inadequate lines of credit.

Particular attention must be paid to unusual transactions such as leasing transactions and off-balance sheet financing, interest expense reduction schemes, significant related party transactions, and substantial fourth quarter adjustments.

Improper revenue recognition continues to be one of the single most frequent causes of SEC enforcement actions. Audit procedures must be designed to identify unconventional practices and unusual sales arrangements. Accountants must be alert to material contingencies, extended terms, rights of return, bill and hold arrangements, consignment arrangements, and improper cutoffs. The practitioner must audit transactions and not rely solely on management representations. Documents must be examined that substantiate the client's procedures.

Other warning signals to watch for include uncorrected material weaknesses in internal control systems, lack of management cooperation, and lack of documentation to support recorded transactions.

Engagement Letters

An effective defense against legal liability is the use of engagement letters. Not only is this essential on all audit engagements, but it should be seriously considered in connection with any engagement involving one or more of the full spectrum of services that accountants perform.

Although not required by current professional standards, engagement letters should be used to avoid misunderstandings about the accountant's responsibility for discovering errors, fraud, defalcations, and illegal acts, and to remind clients of the inherent limitations of an audit. Many accountants request clients to sign and return a copy of the letter to indicate their acceptance of and agreement with its contents (Sullivan et al., 1985, p. 128)

Second Partner Reviews

Many accounting firms require that all financial statements be reviewed by a second partner before an audit report is released. Second partner reviews are required on audits of SEC clients if the accountant is a member of the SEC practice section of the AICPA Division for CPA Firms. The second partner should focus on how all significant matters were resolved and documented during the engagement. The second partner should be satisfied that the financial statements and related audit report comply with professional and firm standards. The accountant's report should not be released until all questions raised by the second partner have been satisfactorily resolved. If such a review is performed, it should be documented in the workpapers.

ROLE OF THE FORENSIC ACCOUNTANT

In disputes involving claims against accountants, the services of an accounting expert hired by plaintiff's counsel differ very little from those of an accounting expert engaged by defendant's counsel. In both circumstances, the forensic accountant conducts a postaudit review to determine whether actual performance conforms with established professional and firm standards.

As in the case of other types of commercial litigation discussed in other chapters of this *Handbook*, the forensic accountant can assist the attorney throughout the litigation.

During discovery, the forensic accountant assists counsel in preparing written interrogatories and requests for documents. In addition to requesting copies of audit workpaper files, the accountant should consider requesting access to defendant accountant's proprietary forms, programs, checklists, firm procedures manuals, time and billing files, and personnel files, including evaluations of staff assigned to the engagement that is the subject of the litigation.

The forensic accountant typically conducts a postaudit review of the working papers produced. Issue files may be prepared supported by selected workpapers and witness files based on documents prepared or reviewed by a particular staff member assigned to the engagement under review. The objective is either to demonstrate compliance with professional and firm standards or to show deviation of actual performance from such standards.

The forensic accountant can play an important role in assisting counsel in preparing for, and taking of, depositions of defendant accountants. During the deposition, the witness usually is asked about the extent and details of the witness' participation in the examination at issue and also about selected workpapers and other documents.

By reviewing the engagement workpapers and other documents and observing the deposition testimony of witnesses, the accounting expert is able to essentially reconstruct selected portions of the engagement. For example, if the appropriateness of a company's inventory accounting policies were central to the lawsuit, then the forensic accountant would need to thoroughly investigate this area. The following types of questions are only some of those that would require answers. How was audit risk assessed? Were the audit procedures employed adequate when considered in light of the perceived risk? Was the inventory portion of the engagement adequately staffed? How many hours were budgeted versus actually expended? Were adjustments recommended by the staff performing the work but passed by a higher level reviewer?

If the accounting expert concludes that the defendant accountant was negligent in the conduct of an audit engagement, then counsel will probably require a determination of the monetary extent to which the financial statements at issue were impacted.

Although this discussion of the forensic accountant's role is largely stated in the context of an audit engagement, the overall approach and tasks to be performed are also generally applicable to claims against accountants involving various other nonaudit services.

ARBITRATION AS AN OPTION FOR RESOLVING CLAIMS AGAINST ACCOUNTANTS

> The modern jury system, current tort law and the practicalities of litigation under the rules of procedure make trial by jury an expensive process fraught with uncertainty that a fair decision will result. Especially troublesome in this regard are the complex cases involving sophisticated financial concepts, which are often beyond the understanding of the average juror. CPAs must therefore assess the probability to exposure even to claims that appear totally without merit simply because their factual or legal positions may be misunderstood or even arbitrarily rejected by lay jurors. (Banick and Broeker, 1987, p. 125)

Arbitration, discussed in detail elsewhere in this volume, may provide an attractive alternative for resolving claims against accountants. Arbitration usually is significantly less costly and less time consuming in its demands on the defendants and witnesses. A significant advantage of arbitration is the elimination of the uncertainties associated with the determination of a complex dispute by an unsophisticated jury. The factors of emotional sympathy for the plaintiff and general emotional hostility to professionals are significantly reduced in arbitration. The risk of a jury's returning a verdict that far exceeds actual losses may be substantially eliminated by arguing the case before arbitrators who usually possess extensive business experience. Finally, extensive and time-consuming discovery is generally not permitted in arbitration.

The reader should be aware of the possible negative factors in arbitration. Rigid adherence to case or statutory law is not required. Also, courts require that evidence be legally admissible and considered in accordance with legal principles; both parties lose this protection in arbitration. Arbitrators are not required to state the bases for their decisions, which are final and binding on the parties, unless otherwise specified. Finally, the opportunity for judicial review of an arbitrator's decision is extremely limited.

The pros and cons of using arbitration should be carefully weighed by accountants and their counsel. In order to afford the opportunity for its use, accountants may consider the use of written agreements with their clients that provide for arbitration to resolve future disputes.

NOTES

1. *Ultramares Corp. v. Touche*, 255 N.Y. 170, 174 N.E. 441 (1931).
2. *Rusch Factors, Inc. v. Levin*, 284 F. Supp. 85 (D.R.I., 1968).
3. *H. Rosenblum, Inc. v. Adler*, 93 N.J. 324, 461A.2d 138 (1983).
4. *Ernst & Ernst v. Hochfelder*, 425 U.S. 185 (1976).

BIBLIOGRAPHY

Amhowitz, Harris J., "The Accounting Profession and the Law: The Misunderstood Victim," *Journal of Accountancy* (May 1987), pp. 356–367.

Banick, Richard S., and Douglas C. Broeker, "Arbitration: An Option for Resolving Claims Against CPAs," *Journal of Accountancy* (October 1987), pp. 124–128.

Collins, Stephen H., "Malpractice Prevention and Risk Management," *Journal of Accountancy* (July 1986), pp. 52–58.

The CPA Journal, March 1986, p. 72.

Mednick, Robert, "Accountants' Liability: Coping with the Stampede to the Courtroom," *Journal of Accountancy* (September 1987), pp. 118–122.

Pratter, Gene E.K., "Accountants' Professional Liability," The Society of Chartered Property & Casualty Underwriters, *Professional Liability: Impact in the Eighties*, 1983, pp. 9–21.

Sullivan, Jerry D., Richard A. Gnospelius, Philip L. Defliese, and Henry R. Jaenicke, *Montgomery's Auditing* (10th ed.) (John Wiley & Sons, Inc., 1985), pp. 128–160.

Weiss, Stanley H., "An Introduction to Concepts of Accountants' Liability," *The CPA Journal* (July 1987), pp. 24–30.

LIST OF CASES

Ernst & Ernst v. Hochfelder, 425 U.S. 185 (1976)
H. Rosenblum, Inc. v. Adler, 93 N.J. 324, 461 A.2d 138 (1983)
Rusch Factors, Inc. v. Levin, 284 F. Supp. 85 (D. R.I., 1968)
Ultramares Corp. v. Touche, 255 N.Y. 170, 174 N.E. 441 (1931)

PART THREE

CRIMINAL CASES—UNIQUE CONSIDERATIONS

19

CRIMINAL CASES AND THE INVESTIGATIVE ACCOUNTANT

Ronald L. Durkin, CPA, MBA

Other chapters of this book discuss civil litigation. *Civil* actions enforce, redress, or protect private rights; *criminal* actions, the subject of this chapter, enforce laws forbidding acts committed or omitted against the state. The government, rather than a private individual or entity, brings these actions.

Accountants participate primarily in civil cases. This chapter discusses the accountant's criminal litigation services, an area foreign to most of the profession. Although civil actions will continue to outnumber criminal actions, the growing incidence of white-collar crime provides opportunity for the profession to develop expertise in criminal actions.

THE IMPACT OF WHITE-COLLAR CRIME IN THE ACCOUNTING PROFESSION

What Is White-Collar Crime?

The sociologist Edwin Sutherland coined the term *white-collar crime* in 1939. Sutherland studied crimes committed, not by the poor or the pathological, but by "respectable" individuals of social standing. Scholars have defined a white-collar crime as a nonviolent act perpetrated by an individual, acting alone or with others, who uses entities or organizations to obtain money or property from others through deceit, concealment, or a violation of trust. White-collar crimes include political and public corruption, fraud against the government, bank fraud, fraud by wire, tax fraud, computer fraud, and mail fraud.

Who Investigates White-Collar Crime?

This chapter discusses only federal investigative agencies but note that states also have their own agencies. State courts adjudicate state crimes, except when they link to federal crimes (see RICO Act violations, discussed later).

The Federal Bureau of Investigation (FBI) pursues most federal white-collar crime violations. The Internal Revenue Service (IRS) also plays an important investigative role in fraud cases. Within their statutory limits, the IRS's ability to gather financial data and reconstruct scenarios from a sketchy set of facts makes this agency a potent weapon against white-collar crime. The Criminal Investigative Division of the Treasury Department investigates tax fraud cases.

The U.S. Postal Service also has its own investigative arm, the postal inspectors, as do the U.S. Customs Department and the Secret Service. The postal inspectors concentrate on mail fraud cases and occasionally share investigative responsibility for these violations with the FBI.

Other federal agencies infrequently encounter white-collar crime and, not having their own investigative arms, refer criminal matters to the Department of Justice (DOJ). The referral role of the Securities and Exchange Commission (SEC) will be significantly increasing. Correspondingly, the ramifications for vigilance by the accounting profession will also increase.

Traditionally, the SEC has administered federal securities laws and regulated financial reporting. The SEC can impose sanctions ranging from suspension of stock trading to fines and other penalties. Over a 5-year period ending August 1986, the SEC took enforcement action against more than 110 public companies and 40 accountants or CPA firms or both. In October 1987, the National Commission on Fraudulent Financial Reporting issued a report recommending that the SEC and DOJ expand criminal prosecution of fraudulent reporting. The DOJ's small staff constrains its efforts, especially in complex white-collar crime cases requiring years to resolve. Nevertheless, the commission stressed the urgency of more prosecutions, and it recommended that they become a higher priority for the DOJ, fueled by more SEC referrals. It further recommended that the SEC educate the DOJ about the seriousness of fraudulent reporting.

The DOJ has actively prosecuted crimes within the SEC's purview. The DOJ, through the FBI, has contributed heavily to combatting the sophisticated skills of white-collar criminals with its own equally sophisticated measures. J. Edgar Hoover, at the beginning of his administration, staffed the bureau with special agent accountants who not only had the skills to interpret, probe, and translate financial data for submission in court but also matched the criminals' organizational skills.

Recently, accountants who are not employed by the FBI or other federal agencies have also investigated criminal allegations. These independent CPAs devote their professional expertise to clients in criminal matters. Those who frequently practice in this area gain expertise in what is referred to as *investigative accounting*.

What Is Investigative Accounting?

Investigative accounting operates as part of substantive law, which governs whether evidence is sufficient to prove a criminal violation. Substantive evidence proves a fact in issue, as opposed to evidence that discredits a witness.

An investigative accountant (IA) explores the facts of a case without assumptions and searches for answers to questions, keeping in mind possible criminal motives. Criminal motives are useful in understanding why crimes are committed. White-collar crime cases most frequently involve economic motives. Murder cases, on the other hand, may involve motives other than those of an economic origin. Terrorism, for example, generally involves ideological rather than economic motivation.

The IA interviews witnesses, gathers evidential documents and pieces together elements necessary to prove a crime. In order to prove a crime, two essential elements are necessary. The "actus reus," or criminal act, must be tied to the "mens rea" or criminal intent. Criminal intent is demonstrated by showing "guilty" knowledge on the part of the person or persons suspected of wrongdoing.

Upon completion of the investigation, the IA prepares a report detailing the results. The report usually contains a summary of the facts (predication), a list of the witnesses interviewed, a summary of their testimony, copies of documents (originals are maintained for later introduction at trial), a chronology of events, and any schedules or exhibits the IA feels are necessary. An experienced IA knows what substantiation is necessary and how it should be presented in court.

This reporting process presupposes awareness of procedural law as well, which entails the admissibility of evidence according to the procedures prescribed for obtaining the evidence. To be admissible in a court of law, evidence must have been obtained legally.

Accountants often become criminal investigators by happenstance. Internal and external auditors, who in the course of business discover fraud, become IAs. The new vigilance of the SEC/DOJ suggests these episodic instances of investigatory assignment by ordinary accountants will increase. Traditionally, independent CPAs and their firms have been unenthusiastic about accepting work as investigative accountants in criminal cases. Because of this, they have not acquired the investigative techniques necessary to become valuable expert witnesses in criminal cases.

Many CPAs do not wish to be associated with an alleged criminal as an expert IA defense witness. Nevertheless, criminal cases have increasingly demanded the accounting profession's attention, even before the National Commission on Fraudulent Financial Reporting made its recommendations. The following sections explain situations that accountants typically encounter in criminal cases and suggest conduct that may safeguard the accountant's professional integrity and independence.

AN OVERVIEW OF INVESTIGATIVE ACCOUNTING CONDUCT

What Do External and Internal Auditors Need to Know?

Both external and internal auditors need to behave in an informed way when they discover fraud, either through their own auditing or through an informant who has volunteered allegations. (A list of steps required to be followed appears later.) The external and internal auditors' roles and recommended conduct do differ, however.

The External Auditor. To understand how the external auditor "accidentally" becomes an investigative accountant, one must first comprehend the auditor's role in a normal audit as that of expressing an opinion on a company's financial statements. The accepted standards of a normal audit suppose that the supporting documents are valid.

The American Institute of Certified Public Accountants (AICPA) (*Codification of Statements on Auditing Standards* (1985), the International Auditing Guidelines No. 1, § 8001, Objective and Scope of Financial Statements), discusses the auditor's responsibility when the audit circumstances veer from the normal[1]:

> In forming his opinion on the financial statements, the auditor carries out procedures designed to obtain reasonable assurance that the financial statements are properly stated in all material respects. Because of the test nature and other inherent limitations of an audit, together with the inherent limitations of any system of internal control, there is an unavoidable risk that even some material misstatement may remain undiscovered. However, any indication that some fraud or error may have occurred which could result in a material misstatement would cause the auditor to extend his procedures to confirm or dispel his suspicions.

The external auditor should be alert to indicia of a lack of management's forthrightness. Such a perception may be the initial or only indication of potential fraud, signaling the need to shift focus into investigative accounting. The auditor may, however, also be contacted by a person leveling an allegation.

If factors indicate fraud or material misstatement, the auditor should perform modified or additional auditing procedures. The latter usually involves the following investigative accounting techniques designed to detect irregularities.

Interview Percipient Witnesses. An accounting investigation of fraud matters is usually predicated upon certain allegations. Of course, early in the process, legal counsel should become actively involved. The IA must first ascertain whether the allegations have merit. This process is facilitated by the receipt of a signed statement from the witness (accuser) who initially brought the allegations. A signed statement is a written narrative of the allegations that is signed by the witness under penalty of perjury. The signed statement is important to the investigation because it provides some protection against lawsuits brought by those who are the targets of the investigation. If the accuser refuses or is reluctant to sign a statement reflecting the allegations, the IA should obtain all pertinent information from the witness and attempt to corroborate the allegations wherever possible.

The interview of percipient (knowledgeable) witnesses should ascertain all pertinent details such as the exact dates, times, persons involved, business records, pervasiveness of the fraud, and how the witness learned of the fraud scheme. These answers can be obtained by asking the following questions:

1. *Who* is involved in the alleged fraud?
2. *What* fraud has occurred, if any?
3. *When* did the fraud allegedly occur?
4. *Where* did it happen (including in which documents)?
5. *How* was the alleged fraud perpetrated or carried out?

Allegations that appear to have merit must be pursued. The accountant should consider carefully which client management representative to tell about the allegations and their merit.

If management will not respond to discussions or limits the investigative audit's scope, the auditor may suspect that management is a party to the fraudulent activity. In either case, the auditor should withdraw from the engagement. Prior to departing, however, the auditor should instruct management (in writing) to notify all parties relying on the company's financial statements that they are no longer reliable. The auditors should take positive action with respect to the fraud, even when another accountant completes the full investigation. Failing to act will invite civil liability and may be construed as a conspiratorial omission by the auditor acting with the alleged perpetrator. This may result in criminal charges against the auditor. For public companies, the auditor must file an 8-K report with the SEC and the board of directors detailing any disagreements with management and giving reasons for withdrawal from the engagement.

The Internal Auditor. As a monitor of a company's daily operations, the internal auditor is well positioned to detect and investigate suspicious or fraudulent acts. An internal auditor who learns of fraud should take specific investigative steps.

If the suspicion stems from another person's allegations, the internal auditor must first interview the accuser to ascertain if the allegations have merit.

Second, if a fraud has been established, the internal auditor must notify appropriate management officials. Because the auditors work for the firm, they should exercise care in observing the normal reporting relationships and procedures. If the person to be apprised of the allegations is suspected in the fraud, the auditor should take alternative procedures to protect the information sources and reports.

If the allegations have merit, the internal auditor should conduct the accounting investigation and prepare a report detailing the investigation's results, with the documented support of any conclusions. Management should review this report for appropriate action.

Management may, alternatively, ask the external auditor or an independent accountant with investigative expertise to conduct an investigation. This investigation would normally reconstruct the fact scenario through the interview process.

Whether the investigation starts from the discovery by an external or an internal auditor, a third-party auditor ideally serves as an independent investigator. The investigation could be presented as a "follow-up" on management letter items during the audit, or it could be disguised by an audit term such as *interim work*. Some guise should be used because, if client personnel realize that the accountants are investigators, their stress level as witnesses will rise, causing defensiveness and impairing their cooperation. They are, however, usually accustomed to the activities of independent auditors. By behaving in a normal audit fashion, the investigators can develop a better rapport with potential witnesses.

Bullish Corporation, a Practical Example

Bullish Corporation is a growth-oriented company that syndicates limited partnership interests in commercial real estate properties throughout the United States. Each limited partnership acquires an office building, renovates it, and leases space to commercial tenants. The partnership agrees that the limited partners receive any tax advantages, cash flow from the property, and the potential for appreciation in property values.

Bullish has been syndicating limited partnerships for over 5 years and has nearly doubled in size every year. Mr. Wayne Principal, founder and general partner of all Bullish limited partnerships, has added employees at nearly the same rate. In the fifth year of operation, he installed an internal auditing department to ensure that internal controls were being followed and that the accounting and other related departments were functioning as designed. Because Principal hoped that Bullish would have nationwide scope, he engaged a national CPA firm to audit Bullish.

In the sixth year, Principal's wife, Deanna, discovered that Wayne had been living two lives, maintaining a separate residence with another woman. She vowed to get even with Wayne. Over the past 5 years Deanna had discovered that he had been depositing large sums of money in foreign bank accounts while spending large amounts on personal items. During that period, he acquired a new house, three new cars, and other real estate properties.

She knew that Wayne and an old schoolmate, Don Friend, were working together, but she was not certain of the details. She believed that Friend gave fictitious invoices to Bullish for construction work that was never performed. She also knew that the limited partnerships bought the properties from companies owned or controlled by Principal—at suspiciously high prices.

Deanna called the accountant responsible for the Bullish audit engagement, Todd Partner. She told him the facts, as she understood them.

As the external auditor, Partner attested to the fairness of the financial statements. If Deanna's allegations were true, not only were the financial statements not fairly presented, but legal issues could also arise, such as civil liability to investors and others who relied upon the financial statements. There might be criminal action. Todd Partner decided to expand the audit's scope to ascertain whether the allegations had substance.

After examining the appropriate records and gathering other evidence, Partner ascertained that sufficient documentation existed to support Deanna's allegations. After confronting Principal with the facts, Partner demanded, by a letter, that Principal immediately notify all limited partners and others who received the audited financial statements that they should no longer be relied upon. The letter also urged that all previously issued financial statements be amended to include the fraud's effect and all appropriate disclosures.

Naturally, Principal denied the allegations and refused to acknowledge the demands. Instead, he summarily fired Partner and quickly started a search for a replacement auditor. Partner subsequently learned that a local CPA firm accepted the engagement and began issuing audited financial statements on Bullish. The FBI eventually entered the investigation and subsequently indicted Principal and Friend for criminal violations of the RICO statute (discussed later in this chapter).

Procedures List

Partner's actions after receiving Deanna's call were as follows:

1. Partner obtained a signed statement from Deanna containing all pertinent details, especially her answers to the who, what, where, when, and how questions listed earlier. He also maintained original interview notes.
2. He interviewed other knowledgeable witnesses and obtained their signed statements.
3. He examined all transactions between Bullish, Friend, and other affiliated entities.
4. He prepared a schedule detailing all of the preceding transactions listing dates, services performed, and amounts charged.
5. He examined all entries to the construction account and vouched to supporting documents.
6. He conducted a physical inspection of all buildings constructed by Friend.
7. He listed all checks to cash, financial institutions, and checks payable to Friend, Principal, and all affiliated entities.
8. He prepared a schedule listing all bank accounts for Friend and Principal and entities through examination of the checks. (The backside of all checks provided this information.)

After completing these steps, Partner, on advice from the firm's legal counsel, wrote a report.

OVERVIEW OF CRIMINAL CASES: THE CPA AS ADJUNCT

RICO

In 1970, Congress enacted the RICO statute [Racketeer Influenced and Corrupt Organizations Statute (RICO)(Title 18, U.S. Code, §§1961–1963)] to combat organized crime. If convicted under its criminal provisions, an individual faces a maximum imprisonment of 20 years or a possible $25,000 fine, or both, and forfeits any interest in real or personal property acquired or maintained in violation of § 1962. This statute, one of the government's most powerful tools, has also affected individuals and businesses not associated with organized crime. Among its provisions is the plaintiffs' opportunity to recover treble damages plus attorney fees under the statute's civil provisions for injury to business or property.

The statute's § 1962 describes prohibited activities. The section prohibits one from investing profits illegally derived from a "pattern of racketeering activity" that acquires, establishes, maintains, or controls a business enterprise. It also disallows conducting or participating in a business enterprise through a pattern of racketeering activity or conspiring to violate any of the RICO provisions.

The statute describes several "predicate acts" prohibited by state and federal law as racketeering activity. The state crimes range from murder and drug dealing to bribery and extortion. The federal crimes range from bankruptcy and securities fraud to mail fraud and fraud-by-wire. To obtain a racketeering conviction, the government must prove that at least two of these acts were committed within 10 years. Accountants deal most often with the statute's forfeiture provisions that allow the government to confiscate property. The defendant may ask accountants to counterinvestigate to demonstrate that the business is legitimate, with a view to refuting the government's position. Because racketeering profits are usually "laundered" through business enterprises, the investigation and counterinvestigation focus on the flow of funds.

Occasionally, the government overzealously pursues recovery of legitimate assets under the statute's forfeiture provisions. In these circumstances, the accountant should perform sufficient investigative accounting to identify the fund's sources and disbursements. Because this analysis may be presented in court, the accountant, prior to accepting this type of engagement, should perform a due diligence investigation of the business enterprise and its principals.

For example, assume that profits from a securities fraud are laundered through wire transfers to Company A. Meanwhile, other individuals unrelated to the criminal activity have acquired an interest in Company A. The government attempts to confiscate Company A and its assets under the theory that it was acquired with illegal profits. The accountant could show that the legitimate investors were not associated, either financially or otherwise, with the fraud perpetrators.

Bankruptcy Fraud

(Title 18, U.S. Code, §§ 151-155; Title 11, United States Code (Bankruptcy Code), Section 548(a)(1).

Accountants called into bankruptcy cases by trustees, examiners, or creditors' committees may be involved in fraud investigations. The investigating accountant takes action similar to that of the FBI and IRS in that each traces funds, locates assets, and interprets business transactions, looking not only for civil but also criminal fraud.

Sections 152 and 153 of Title 18 discuss the concealment of assets and the fraudulent appropriation of property from the debtor's estate. These sections also apply to any false oaths or declarations and to any false claims made against the estate. Section 548(a)(1) of the Bankruptcy Code addresses the trustee's powers to void fraudulent transfers, when the debtor had an actual intent to defraud creditors.

To illustrate, a debtor makes a significant cash transfer to an undisclosed, related company. The monthly operating statements filed with the U.S. Trustee's Office does not list this transfer. To show intent to defraud, the investigative accountant must demonstrate a pattern of activity sufficient to establish that this is not merely an oversight by the debtor.

Tax Fraud

(Title 26, U.S. Code, § 7201 (Tax Evasion); § 7206 (Fraud and False Statements))

Criminal tax fraud, described in Title 26 of the U.S. Code, usually requires willful tax evasion where intent to defraud can be demonstrated. Other criminal violations—such as filing of false or fraudulent statements or documents with a federal agency or department (Title 18, § 1001)—are usually charged in connection with tax fraud cases. The defendant asks accountants to demonstrate lack of willful intent; this requires examining these statements and documents to ascertain whether they were fraudulently filed.

Wire Fraud

(Title 18, U.S. Code, § 1343)

The FBI uses the fraud-by-wire statute as a principal tool in combatting white-collar crime. It addresses any "wire" use, including radio and television communications, to obtain money or property through fraudulent pretenses.

Both electronic funds transfers and telemarketing as an advertising tool provide fertile ground for the white-collar criminal. Accountants become involved through their involvement with clients who are either defendants or victims of the fraud scheme. In either case, the accountant usually focuses on the flow of funds rather than statements made by the defendants.

"Ponzi" or "pyramid" schemes are the most common fraud-by-wire cases. A Ponzi scheme is a fraud that lures investors to part with money or property to recover something of increased value later. (The Bullish Corporation is an example.) The scheme requires increasing numbers of investors whose cash goes in part to preceding investors whose claims must be satisfied to maintain the basis for continued perpetration of the fraud. Though some Ponzi schemes appear legitimate and carry on for several years, disgruntled investors eventually file complaints with the FBI or other investigative agencies. As in all criminal cases, the investigating accountant focuses on intent to defraud.

Other Related Cases

Bank fraud (Title 18, § 1344), securities fraud (Title 15, § 78), fraud against the government, and political and public corruption cases—although they do not fall within any specific title of the U.S. Code—also may require investigative accounting services.

NOTE

1. In 1988, the AICPA issued a new standard (No. 53) that expanded the auditor's responsibility to design the audit to provide reasonable assurance of detecting errors and irregularities that are material.

BIBLIOGRAPHY

American Institute of Certified Public Accountants, *Codification of Statements on Auditing Standards*, Number 1-49 (AICPA, 1985).

Bernstein, G.L., "On the Brink of a New Era," *Journal of Accountancy* (September 1985), pp. 150–161.

Black, H.C. (M.A.), *Black's Law Dictionary*, 5th ed. (West Publishing Co., 1979).

Bologna, G.J., *Corporate Fraud, the Basics of Prevention and Detection* (Butterworth Publishers, 1984).

______, and R.J. Linquist, *Fraud Auditing and Forensic Accounting, New Tools and Techniques* (John Wiley & Sons, 1987).

Collins, S.H., "Spotlight to Shine More Brightly on Accounting Profession, Warn SEC Officials at AICPA Conference," *Journal of Accountancy* (April 1985), pp. 55–57.

Dykeman, F.C., *Forensic Accounting: The Accountant as Expert Witness* (John Wiley & Sons, 1982).

Federal Criminal Code and Rules (West Publishing Co., 1986).

Gill, E.K., "The VIP Crook," *The National Notary* (November 1987), pp. 10–12, 25.

Herzog, A.S., and L.P. King, Collier pamphlet ed., *Bankruptcy Code, Part I*, 1987.

Lynch, G.G., and D.L. Goelzer, "Enforcement Actions in Accounting: With Special Consideration of 'Good Soldier' Issues," SEC and Financial Reporting Institute Conference, May 14, 1987, pp. 1–63.

Mednick, R., "The Auditor's Role in Society: A New Approach to Solving the Perception Gap," *Journal of Accountancy* (October 1985), pp. 70–74.

Minow, N.N., "Accountants' Liability and the Litigation Explosion," *Journal of Accountancy* (September 1984), pp. 71–86.

Munger, Tolles, & Olson, "Civil RICO Litigation after Sedima and Cianci: Trap or Bonanza?," ABTL Panel, February 10, 1986, pp. 1–35.

Newton, G.W., *Bankruptcy and Insolvency Accounting, Practice and Procedure*, 4th ed. (John Wiley & Sons, 1989).

Palmrose, Z.V., "Litigation and Independent Auditors: The Role of Business Failures and Management Fraud." *Auditing: A Journal of Practice & Theory*, Vol. 6, No. 2 (Spring 1987), pp. 90–103.

Report of the National Commission on Fraudulent Financial Reporting (October, 1987).

Seidler, L.J., and D.R. Carmichael, *Accountants' Handbook*, 6th ed., Vol. 1 (John Wiley & Sons, 1981).

Stern, R.L., "In Whom Do We Trust," *Forbes* (April 25, 1983), pp. 38–40.

Sumutka, A.R., "Questionable Payments and Practices: Why? How? Detection? Prevention?" (American Institute of Certified Public Accountants, Inc., 1979).

Sutherland, E.H., and D. Cressey, "Learning and Transmitting Criminal Behavior," Reprinted from E.H. Sutherland and D. Cressey, *Principles of Criminology*, 7th ed. (Lippincott & Co., 1966), pp. 74–81.

20

FRAUD AND EMBEZZLEMENT

David G. Schultze, CPA
David L. Black, CPA

THE ACTS OF FRAUD

The term fraud encompasses a broad range of illegal acts ranging from employee embezzlement to bribes and the violation of regulatory rules. This chapter focuses on five areas of fraud for which a certified public accountant would be retained to investigate and assist counsel within a litigation environment.

Management Fraud

The auditing profession faces public scrutiny as a result of highly publicized business failures. Most of these failures occurred because of a lack of good management, economic circumstances, and other conditions unrelated to fraud. Many investors, writers, and regulators, however, attribute the failures to fraud and question why the auditors did not detect it. This perception has prompted the accounting profession to devote much attention to what it terms *management fraud.*

Management fraud, as defined by the accounting profession in Statement on Auditing Standards (SAS) No. 16, is "deliberate misrepresentation by management which results in the distortions of financial statements."

The auditing profession often uses the term *irregularities* that is defined by the SAS as

> intentional distortions of financial statements by management, sometimes referred to as management fraud or misappropriation of assets, sometimes referred to as defalcations. Irregularities in financial statements may result from the misrepresentation or omission of the effects of events or transactions; manipulation, falsification, or alteration of records or documents; omission of significant information from records or documents; recording of transactions without substance; intentional misapplication of accounting principles; or misappropriation of assets for the benefit of management; employees or third parties.

Management Diversion of Profits and Misappropriation of Assets

Managers can often divert the profits of an otherwise profitable transaction and misappropriate assets for their own use. Some managers frequently have special knowledge of a potentially profitable transaction unknown to others and could use this knowledge to their advantage. The kickback scheme is an example of this type of fraud.

Employee Embezzlement

Employee embezzlement generally involves the circumvention of internal controls. Frauds by nonmanagement employees generally convert cash or other assets for the employee's own use. Employee fraud is generally easier to detect than that of a member of management. The embezzlement is more likely to occur under weak internal controls, such as an accounting department with no separation of duties.

Fraudulent Misrepresentation to Regulatory, Administrative, and Taxing Authorities

This area of fraud encompasses false or misleading reports to agencies such as the Internal Revenue Service. This fraud is more subjective than an employee embezzlement scheme; its detection or defense requires the accountant to possess strong technical and analytical skills.

Fraudulent Misrepresentations to Business Associates

Intentional misrepresentations in contract negotiations, but transfers with the intent to defraud, and the issuance of fraudulent commercial paper all fall within this category. The penalties for some of these business-related frauds are addressed in the Uniform Commercial Code.

THE ACCOUNTANT'S ROLE

Audit of Financial Statements in Accordance with Generally Accepted Auditing Standards

The Statement on Auditing Standards (SAS) No. 53, *The Auditor's Responsibility to Detect and Report Errors and Irregularities* supersedes Statement of Auditing Standards No. 16 and is effective for years beginning after December 15, 1988. The new SAS requires that the audit be designed to *detect* material errors and irregularities that affect the financial statements. This contrasts with SAS No. 16 that required that the engagement only *search* for irregularities that could be material to the financial statements. The following summarizes auditor responsibilities under the new SAS:

- Design audits to detect material errors and irregularities. But the new statement recognizes that because of the characteristics of certain irregularities, an audit may not detect a material irregularity.
- Conduct preliminary assessment of the risk of material irregularities and the likelihood of management misrepresentation.
- Exercise due care and professional skepticism to achieve reasonable assurance that material errors and irregularities will be detected.
- Be assured that the audit committee or others with equivalent responsibility are adequately informed about irregularities.
- Render an adverse opinion on the financial statements if they are materially affected by an irregularity and are not revised.
- Disclaim an opinion on the financial statements and communicate findings in writing to the board of directors when an audit's scope has been restricted with respect to a possible irregularity.

This statement also recognizes that the auditor may have to disclose irregularities to parties outside the entity.

Retention to Detect Management Diversion of Profits and Misappropriation of Assets and Employee Embezzlement

The accountant may be retained for various reasons to conduct a fraud investigation; the retaining party may suspect a member of management or an employee of diverting assets or profits for his own use. This engagement requires the accountant to use a hybrid of auditing, accounting, and consulting skills. The accountant should also be innovative and maintain a skeptical attitude.

If the alleged defalcation is an employee embezzlement, planning for detection is simplified by procedures discussed in this chapter. An embezzlement committed by a member of management generally requires more planning to detect.

Fraudulent Misrepresentations to Regulatory, Administrative, and Taxing Authorities

In cases concerning fraudulent misrepresentation to governmental authorities, the accountant supports the defense attorney and acts as expert witness. In a tax fraud case, for example, the accountant will help counsel develop the taxpayer's defense. He must first analyze the client's books and records with an eye for possible problem areas—such as understatement of inventories, omitted items of income, fictitious or double invoicing, falsification or inflation of expenses, or fictitious wages. He must also verify the accuracy of the government's computation. The attorney may also ask the accountant to develop technical defenses based on accounting principles. Also, the accountant should be present at the counsel table during the trial to help the trial attorney prepare the technical phases of this examination and cross-examination of other witnesses. If the accountant will also be a witness, the impact on the trier of fact of seeing the accountant at counsel table should be considered.

Fraudulent Misrepresentations to Business Associates

The accountant retained as the result of a misrepresentation to a customer, supplier, or business associate generally ascertains the misrepresentation's nature and extent and calculates the lost income and damages.

For a more thorough discussion of assessing damages or lost income, review Chapters 25–31 of this *Handbook*.

METHODS OF FRAUD DETECTION

The fraud engagement requires a specialized program designed for discovery. Unlike an audit conducted under generally accepted auditing standards, the materiality concept does not exist. Generally accepted accounting principles are of no concern unless the fraud led to the misstatement of financial statements.

Management Embezzlement

Detecting an embezzlement committed by a member of management generally requires that the investigator understand the company. The investigator should review any information related to the industry such as trade journals, financial surveys, and company brochures. Comparative information can be obtained through services such as Dun & Bradstreet and interviews with other companies in the industry. Several years of financial statements are then analyzed to highlight trends and identify questionable areas. For example, a notable increase in bad debt expense or other write-offs may indicate a kickback scheme and slow collections may signify embezzlement.

Interviewing other company personnel is certainly beneficial. This may not be possible however, if the investigation is confidential.

The investigator should scrutinize any related party transactions to determine their propriety. Members of management can sometimes divert profits by contracting with a related entity at less-than-favorable terms.

The investigator should perform the following initial steps to identify related party transactions:

- Read the minutes of Board of Directors' meetings
- Review names of the company's known related parties
- Review major transactions for indications of previously undisclosed relationships
- Consider if any transactions are not being recorded
- Review significant or nonroutine transactions

Employee Embezzlement

The most common types of employee embezzlement are false payroll, false vendors, check kiting, lapping and inventory schemes.

In the *false payroll* scheme, the perpetrator creates a fictitious employee and then cashes the "employee's" payroll check. This procedure will also create false tax deductions for the payor that give rise to tax fraud. One technique useful in detecting a false payroll scheme is the examination of social security numbers. The Social Security Administration may have not issued the fictitious employee's social security number. The first three digits of the social security number are assigned by geographic area. Reviewing the employee personnel files and residency history may indicate a discrepancy.

Another rather simple technique is listing employees who have elected life or health insurance coverage. Rarely will the perpetrator do so because of the cost involved.

A third procedure is to observe the employees receiving their checks on payday. This procedure, usually done on a surprise basis, helps detect any extra checks dishonestly produced or checks written to fictitious payees to be picked up by the perpetrator.

In the *false vendor scheme*, the perpetrator forms a fictitious entity that invoices the company and receives payment. Another form of accounts payable fraud is the alteration or manipulation of valid invoices. These types of fraud may be detected by the following:

1. Watching for photocopied invoices in the files. These may reflect alterations that include different discount terms, increased payables, and altered locations for shipment of inventory.

2. Reviewing the files of new vendors to determine their validity.
3. Examining the reverse side of cashier's checks for deposit and endorsement date.
4. Reviewing monthly statements for the purchase of cashier's checks and checks made payable to cash.
5. Reviewing increases in payables for legal, accounting, and other professional services, which services may be performed over a lengthy period.

The *check kiting scheme* involves transferring cash from one bank to another and improperly recording the transfer. The check kiter takes advantage of the time period or "float," that is, the number of days between a check deposit and a funds collection.

The check kiting scheme is most easily detected by scheduling bank transfers near the end of a period and requesting cut-off bank statements.

The *lapping scheme* is somewhat more complicated and difficult to detect. Under this scheme, the perpetrator steals from one customer's account and covers the theft by applying to that account later collections from another customer. Lapping usually occurs when the same employee opens the mail and schedules receipts, prepares the deposit slips, makes the bank deposit, and posts the books.

The perpetrator may not be able to take time off from work because the scheme often involves hundreds of accounts and requires constant manipulation. Accordingly, the investigator should review the employee vacation records to see if vacation is taken in accordance with company policy. The scheme may be detected by comparing the details of name, amount, and date on remittance advises with the cash receipts journal and duplicate deposit tickets.

The *inventory scheme* can take many forms, but the most common types are employee pilferage and the purchase of inventory for cash or its equivalent.

Under the latter scheme, the perpetrator pays cash for the inventory, and consequently the perpetual inventory does not increase and the related sales are not recorded. For example, the manager of a chain appliance store may purchase televisions for cash and pocket the sales proceeds. This type of fraud is difficult to detect because no entries appear on the books. One method of detection is to review the vendor's invoices for unrecorded purchases. A surprise inventory count compared to the perpetual records may also disclose unreported inventory. The investigator can also compare freight cost as a percentage of inventory cost; an increasing percentage may indicate unrecorded delivered inventory.

The pilfered inventory may be discovered with a surprise inventory count compared to perpetual records. Also, a purchase recorded on the books with no receipt at the receiving dock could indicate theft at the receiving dock.

An increasing cost of sales percentage may also indicate inventory pilferage.

Fraud Indicators

The following list indicates management or employee involvement in fraud and red-flag areas for further investigation.

1. A high rate of employee turnover, particularly in a department that would be privy to company financial information. This high rate, such as in the accounting department, might signify that management fires staff before they discover fraud. It might also indicate collusion within the accounting department to commit a fraud and then subsequently resign.
2. An extravagant life-style, poor investment decisions, and other factors can cause an employee to fall into debt. When this situation occurs, the employee may then illicitly obtain funds through fraud.
3. Excessive charges in bad debts and other write-offs may indicate a kickback scheme.
4. Transactions with no business or economic purpose may indicate a scheme to benefit solely the employee.
5. A bribe is sometimes recorded as a sale of assets, whereas, in reality, possession is maintained.
6. Loans to managers and employees may not be recorded in the proper loan amounts and instead be hidden in another asset category. This may signify disguised compensation or a bribe to the employee.
7. An excessive number of corporate checks bearing second endorsements, if unusual, may indicate several schemes including payroll fraud.
8. An excessive number of checking accounts with no apparent purpose may indicate a check kiting scheme.
9. Serially numbered documents are always an integral part of internal control. The refusal to use this method should be questioned.
10. In a bankruptcy situation, review all new payables that occurred prior to the bankruptcy filing. False accounts payable is one method of removing cash from the soon-to-be-bankrupt company. A bargain inventory sale is another method of generating quick cash. A common scheme, when recording the false payable, is to have the outside party file a lien against the company's fixed assets so the transaction will appear legitimate.
11. An inventory shortage may indicate fictitious purchases, unrecorded sales, or employee pilferage.
12. A declining or usually small increase in cash or credit sales could mean that some sales are not recorded.
13. Slow collections can mask an embezzlement.

Computer Fraud

The use and understanding of electronic data processing by the perpetrator can simplify the mechanics of embezzlement, thereby allowing one to misappropriate and conceal larger sums.

The documentation available in EDP systems may differ considerably from that of manual systems. Also, EDP systems often consolidate several functions that would normally be segregated in manual systems. Those developments present problems both for evaluating controls and collecting suitable evidence.

A resource available to the fraud investigator is the computer audit software programs designed to audit in EDP environments. The programs allow the investigator to select exceptional transactions and accounts for examination, compare data for correctness and consistency, and perform mathematical and clerical functions.

These functions can be categorized as follows:

1. *Selection*—items may be selected from a data file statistically or according to specified criteria. For example, biweekly payroll checks over $5000 could be selected.
2. *Comparison*—matches records on two files or items on a file may be matched with data obtained in other tests. For example, inventory test counts could be matched to perpetual records.
3. *Calculation*—specified fields within a record may be added, subtracted, multiplied, and divided. In addition, records within a file may be summarized.

Most national accounting firms have developed software to audit in an EDP environment and maintain a staff of computer audit specialists. It may be necessary to retain their service on more complex engagements.

THE LEGAL ENVIRONMENT

The following laws address fraudulent activities nationwide. This book does not consider the penalties for fraudulent activities that vary from state to state. Chapter 19 of this *Handbook* discusses civil versus criminal fraud.

Securities Act of 1933

The Securities Act of 1933, sometimes known as the "truth in securities law," provides investors with financial and other information concerning securities offered for public sale; it also prohibits misrepresentation and other fraudulent acts in the sale of securities. The act's principal provision requires that an issuing company file a registration statement with the Securities and Exchange Commission (SEC) before marketing securities to the public.

The Security Exchange Act of 1934 was passed to establish a permanent office to administer the 1933 act and to provide current information on previously registered securities.

The Foreign Corrupt Practices Act of 1977

This act requires a system of internal accounting control as defined in SAS No. 1, § 320. The act was stimulated by the discovery that several hundred corporations had made illegal foreign and domestic bribes and political contributions. Although most of those payments circumvented existing accounting controls, the accounting control requirement was introduced at the SEC's request.

Uniform Commercial Code

The UCC, enacted by all states but Louisiana, addresses fraudulent activities. A major provision of the UCC provides that a party to a sales contract who brings a cause of action against the other party for material misrepresentation or fraud may use any of the code's remedies for nonfraudulent breach (2-721).

BIBLIOGRAPHY

Allen, B., "Embezzler's Guide to the Computer," *Harvard Business Review* (July–August 1975), pp. 79–89.

Baker, D.W., M.J. Barrett, and L.P. Ruddle, "Top-Management Fraud: Something Can Be Done Now!" *The Internal Auditor* (October 1976), pp. 25–32.

Dunn, R.L., *Recovery of Damages for Lost Profits* (Lawpress Corporation, 1987).

Elliott, R.K., and J.J. Willingham, *Management Fraud-Detection and Deterrence* (Petrocelli Books, Inc., 1980).

Fink, R.S., "The Role of the Accountant in a Tax Fraud Case" *The Journey of Accountancy* (April 1976), pp. 42–48.

Glick, R.G., and R.S. Newsom, *Fraud Investigation Fundamentals for Police* (Charles C Thomas, 1974).

Kpanick, H., "Responsibility and Detection in Management Fraud" *CPA Journal* (May 1976), pp. 19–23.

Levy, M.M., "Financial Fraud: Schemes and Indicia," *Journal of Accountancy* (August 1986), pp. 72–78.

Liebtag, B., "Fraudulent Financial Reporting," *Journal of Accountancy* (August 1986), pp. 72–78.

McCullough, W.W., *Sticky Fingers—A Close Look at America's Fastest Growing Crime* (AMACOM, 1981).

Moran, F.J., *Preventing Embezzlement* (U.S. Small Business Administration).

Pennington, W.J., "Embezzling: Cases and Cautions," *The Journal of Accountancy* (July 1964), pp. 47–51.

Richter, M.J., "Shrinking the Embezzlement Loophole: Some Observations on Weak Audit Procedures," *The Practical Accountant* (October 1985), pp. 67–70.

Wells, J.T., "White-Collar Crime: Myths and Strategies," *The Practical Accountant* (August 1985), pp. 43–45.

Willingham, J.J. and D.R. Carmichael, *Auditing Concepts and Methods* (McGraw-Hill, Inc. 1979).

PART FOUR

FAMILY LAW/MARITAL DISSOLUTION CASES

21

CHILD AND SPOUSAL SUPPORT AWARDS

John D. Zante, CPA

Spousal and child support awards are generally based on the court's evaluation of the estimated cash available for spending by each spouse. Therefore, the court needs data sufficient to assess an appropriate support award. This chapter reviews the relevant considerations for child support and spousal support. The first two sections of this chapter provide an overview of statutory and case law in various states. The third part specifically applies to California. The chapter appendix includes a sample Spendable Income Report generally required of the expert to present to the court. Spousal and child support tax implications are analyzed in a later chapter.

CHILD SUPPORT

Introduction

In a dissolution or separation proceeding, the court may order either one or both parents to financially support a minor or dependent child.

Mutual Obligation. Both parents have mutual responsibility to support and educate their child. Such support must reflect the child's circumstances, considering each parent's earnings or earning capacity.

Dependent Child. The term *dependent child* applies to *minor child* and may also extend to an adult child who cannot work. Such consideration generally requires proof of a physical or mental handicap. The term *minor child* may include adopted, illegitimate, and unborn children.

Statutory Authority

Uniform Marriage and Divorce Act. The Uniform Marriage and Divorce Act [§ 309] permits the court to order one or both parents to pay a reasonable and necessary amount to support a minor dependent child.

Relevant factors to consider are the financial resources of the custodial parent, the noncustodial parent, and even the financial resources of the child. Other factors include the standard of living the child would have enjoyed had the marriage continued and the child's emotional and physical needs.

Amendments. The Child Support Enforcement Amendments of 1984 required each state to furnish guidelines by October 1, 1987, for the trier-of-fact assessing child support awards. The guidelines replaced the subjective criteria previously used. As of December 31, 1987, 34 states had adopted child support guidelines.

Statutory Guidelines

Minimum Support. Some states require the courts to order minimum child support conforming with the amount of AFDC (Aid to Families with Dependent Children). In those states, the minimum award may be reduced only in exceptional circumstances, reflecting the parents' lack of adequate disposable income.

The court may consider the savings generated by shared custody, calculating each parent's share accordingly.

Discretionary Support. In addition to or in lieu of the minimum support award, the court may award child support based on the factors identified in the Uniform Marriage and Divorce Act or other guidelines established by the state, or both. The following lists the most common factors considered when setting child support:

Need. The child's support must be compatible with the parents' station in life. This includes basic necessities such as food, clothing, medical costs and may include supplemental items such as special education costs, special medical costs, and child care costs.

Ability to Pay. The court considers the parents' relative financial positions when setting the award. Under special circumstances, when the obligor spouse deliberately attempts to suppress income, the court may consider the parent's earning capacity rather than actual earnings. However, the court may consider legitimate reasons for lower income such as illness or age.

Definition of Income. The states have varying guidelines as to what income includes. Some states consider gross income, whereas others consider disposable or net income. Differences exist as to the expenditures included in assessing disposable income. Some states offset the value of the custodial spouse's nonmonetary time devoted to the child against the custodial spouse's income when setting child support.

Other Factors. Child support from a previous marriage may be considered, whereas all states generally ignore the earning capacity of a child's separate estate. Additionally, income of a new cohabitant spouse of the obligor spouse may be considered when establishing the obligor spouse's ability to pay.

Types of Child Support Awards

Form of Payment. Commonly, a cash payment is made pursuant to a court order that provides for assignment of the obligor spouse's wages to the custodial spouse. Such assignment occurs when the obligor spouse falls into arrears in child support payments. Other payment methods include payment of medical costs, special education costs, or payment to a creditor in discharge of a minor's debt.

Modification. Inflation, increased education, costs, and the increased expenses incurred as the child grows older may substantiate modifying and increasing the award. Changes in the parents' income level may also justify an increase or decrease in the award.

Termination. Generally, child support liability terminates when the child attains the age of majority, currently 18 years. This may vary if the child is still a student. Child support may terminate prior to the child's attaining the age of majority if the child marries, enters the armed services, or receives a judicial declaration of emancipation from the court.

Role of Consultant/Expert

A consultant or expert is retained in these matters to assist counsel for one or both spouses in calculating the applicable amount of estimated child support based on the statutory guidelines. To assist counsel, the consultant must have a working knowledge of the statutory guidelines and their application.

Expert Witness. In addition to possessing the necessary skills required of a consultant, the expert witness must also be proficient at preparing a report to help the trier of fact ascertain an equitable child support award. The expert needs to conduct proper discovery to detect understatement of income or overstatement of expenses in order to measure the spouses' correct disposable income.

SPOUSAL SUPPORT

Introduction

Spousal support, also referred to as alimony or maintenance, provides a spouse with funds to accommodate his or her reasonable needs consisting of clothing, food, shelter, and other necessities.

Origin of Support. The alimony concept is a product of English common law, which prohibited divorces and a wife's ownership of property. Thus alimony represented the husband's continuing obligation to support his wife. This concept has survived in states with community property and common law jurisdictions.

Current Trend. Each state currently provides some form of alimony based on factors established by state statute or based on the court's discretion.

Statutory Authority

Uniform Marriage and Divorce Act. The Uniform Marriage and Divorce Act permits the court to order spousal support when the spouse seeking maintenance lacks sufficient property to sustain his or her reasonable needs and does not earn sufficient support through employment (Uniform Marriage and Divorce Act, § 308(a)).

Effect of Cohabitation. Alimony may be modified or terminated if the obligee spouse openly lives with a member of the opposite sex. In 1986, 12 states still subscribed to this standard. (*Family Law Reporter*, p. 400i–ii).

Issue of Fault. Most states no longer consider fault or marital misconduct a necessary issue in determining spousal support. By 1986 seven states continued to consider the issue of fault (*Family Law Reporter*, p. 400i–ii).

Relevant Factors

Statutory Factors. In 1986, 30 states still had statutes specifying factors for a court to consider when setting alimony. These factors resemble those listed in Section 308 of the Uniform Marriage and Divorce Act (*Family Law Reporter*, p. 400i–ii). Other states give the courts discretion in ascertaining the need for alimony or maintenance payments. The following factors may influence the court's decision:

1. *Financial resources.* The obligee spouse's resources, including apportioned marital property, spouse's ability to meet his or her needs independently and the amount received for child support (Uniform Marriage and Divorce Act, § 308(b)(1)).
2. *Rehabilitative factor.* The time necessary for the obligee spouse to acquire sufficient education or training to enable the finding of appropriate employment (Uniform Marriage and Divorce Act, § 308(b)(2)). The duration of support may be set, subject to possible modification, approximating the time needed

to obtain employment. Thereafter, the initial spousal award would be reduced or terminated accordingly.

3. *The standard of living*. Established during the marriage.
4. *Duration of the marriage*.
5. *Age and the physical and emotional condition of the spouse* seeking maintenance.
6. *Ability of the obligor spouse to meet his or her own needs while meeting those of the obligee spouse* (Uniform Marriage and Divorce Act, § 308(b)(3)–(6)).

Statutory Guidelines. Some states have adopted guidelines to assess the amount of spousal support. In California, most counties refer to the California Guideline Schedule or a variant thereof in estimating spousal support.

Although these schedules may help establish temporary spousal awards, they are not the only guides used to estimate permanent support. (*In Re Marriage of Burlini*, 143 Cal. App. 3d 65, 191 Cal. Rptr. 541 (1983); *In Re Marriage of McNaughton*, Cal. App. 3d 845, 194 Cal. Rptr. 176 (1983)).Although *temporary* support guidelines intend to maintain preseparation living conditions, permanent support is intended to provide financial assistance based on the standards listed. Temporary support usually lasts 1 to 5 years until the assets are liquidated or valued and any other complex financial aspects of the marriage are settled. The accountant should consult with counsel as to the state's law and customs regarding such variances.

Types of Spousal Awards

Typical Orders. Spousal support can take various forms such as (1) payment tied to earnings of either spouse, (2) payments for a fixed period, (3) step down orders (i.e., decreasing payments amounts), (4) payments for a contingent period (subject to a contingency such as death, remarriage, or change of economic circumstances), (5) payment of in-kind consideration such as payment of obligee spouse's liabilities, and (6) lump sum awards.

Rehabilitative Alimony. By 1986, 25 states had adopted a form of rehabilitative alimony. Rehabilitative alimony either limits alimony for a certain duration or provides courts with a statutory guideline regarding the time necessary to enable a party seeking support to find appropriate employment (*Family Law Reporter*, p. 400i–ii).

Role of Consultant/Expert

Consultants/expert witnesses must understand the relevant statutory and case law. They must also understand the interrelationship of child support and spousal support. Expert witness services include discovery necessary to ascertain spouse income and a report or testimony before the trier-of-fact regarding equitable spousal support. Spousal support controversies appear to require more frequent court testimony than do disputes involving only child support.

Consultant services include tax planning, assessment of spousal income, and related child support matters.

SPENDABLE INCOME REPORT

Scope of Report

The Spendable Income Report provides the judge with each party's disposable income in order to evaluate the appropriate level of spousal and child support. A properly prepared report helps the judge assess equitable spousal and child support awards.

The judge is the report's principal user. Both counsel may also use the report to agree on temporary spousal and child support, thereby avoiding a costly formal hearing.

Period of Report

Temporary Award. The report may address temporary spousal or child support or both. When the economic circumstances of either party change, the accountant may need to update the report before the award becomes permanent.

Permanent Award. This report updates the report prepared for temporary support—assuming that one exists—to reflect the parties' changed economic circumstances, inclusive of the property distribution.

Report's Objective

To facilitate the judge's evaluation, the report should include all financial data that a judge needs to render a decision. In California, judges rely heavily on information from each party's Income and Expense Declaration. The Spendable Income Report appended to this chapter has a format similar to the Income and Expense Declaration.

Income and Expense Declaration. Each spouse prepares a four-page California Judicial Form, listing sources of monthly income and expenses based on historical and projected information. The documents are signed under penalty of perjury and are subject to cross-examination.

Spendable Income. The first page summarizes both the monthly income and required deductions (detailed on the second page) to compute Net Monthly Disposable Income (herein referred to as spendable income).

Required Deductions. Required deductions comprise federal and state taxes, including income and employment taxes. Other deductions include typical payroll deductions, such as health insurance premiums, mandatory union dues, and mandatory retirement and pension fund contributions. Deductions also include court-ordered child and spousal support paid to another party unrelated to the current proceeding.

Discretionary Deductions. The declaration also includes expenses that are considered discretionary with respect to type or amount, such as food, clothing, shelter, travel, and entertainment.

Although these amounts are not considered in calculating spendable income, one should not erroneously assume that the judge will ignore these items when evaluating the support award. It appears, however, that judges consider these items more often for temporary awards than for permanent awards.

Levels of Support. The report should indicate spendable income based on varying levels of spousal and child support. In practice, using more than five variables invites confusion. The report appended to this chapter (see Exhibits 21-1 and 21-2) considers four levels of spousal and child support based on four disposable income amounts.

Zero Support. The first column assumes zero spousal and child support. This helps the judge assess the disparity in spendable income between the parties before support payments and helps the judge evaluate the dollar and tax rate change in the award granted.

California Guidelines. The second column reflects San Francisco's support guidelines based on the income level and required deductions shown in the report. Most California counties refer to the California Guidelines or variant thereof to estimate support. Although temporary spousal awards may reflect these guidelines, permanent support awards reflect other information as well.

Set Spendable Amounts. The report's third column attempts to estimate the amount of spousal support (excluding child support) that would provide the same spendable amounts for the parties as the second column. This approach may afford a tax planning element for the parties and therefore should not be overlooked when presenting the spendable income report.

California Guidelines—Optimized for Tax Considerations. The fourth column uses spousal and child support amounts that reduce income taxes and increase spendable income from that of column 2. Although the amount of monthly cash spendable by the Smiths is small ($13), tax savings could be substantial in another set of circumstances. Accordingly, every report should consider tax planning.

In practice, a report may reflect more or fewer alternatives than those included in this example. A presentation may also contain different line items.

Elements of Report

An accountant usually needs from one-half of a day to a week to prepare a spendable income report, depending on the difficulty or ease of discovery. Tax planning and spreadsheet software will help identify optional dollar amounts for the variables.

Ideally, the report should present a one-page financial summary for each spouse. Footnotes may indicate information sources or contain detailed calculations. Judges have found footnotes useful when an extended time lapse occurs between the hearing and final support evaluation. Such an approach may also defuse the testimony of an unprepared opposing expert.

Income. The income number will be more credible if it is based on the IRS definition of Adjusted Gross Income (AGI) and if it is comparable to the AGI of previous years' tax returns.

Business Income (Loss). Business income (loss) amount is usually difficult to assess. Ideally, it should be assessed immediately after a business valuation. Without a business valuation, one should use several years of historical income or loss data, heavily weighting recent years' results. If business income substantially declines after separation, discovery should include: a review of and comparison with industry data to ascertain whether an internal expansion has occurred; a review of unusual expense increases that might include personal legal costs, payroll costs for a girlfriend, or purchases of unnecessary equipment and extended vacations.

Passive Income (Loss). Previously, the obligor spouse often invested in tax shelters to minimize available cash flow as well as spousal and child support payments. The current, tougher tax laws associated with passive activities will limit this practice. When assessing available cash for support, however, one must consider the new tax effects associated with passive activity losses (PAL).

To assess each party's PAL, the prior year's tax return is most likely to be an accurate estimate for the future, although one may find helpful data in the 2 or 3 preceding years' tax returns.

Other Income (Loss). Actively managed rental property appears most commonly in the category for other income (loss). Usually, the prior year best predicts the future year's expected cash flow. Individuals owning older properties often ask the consultant for advice regarding refinancing.

Cash Adjustments. The next section of the report contains all adjustments required to convert taxable income to expected cash flow. Accordingly, the section includes nontaxable income and losses. For temporary spousal support, this section includes depreciation on business assets. For temporary and permanent spousal support, this section includes depreciation for investment assets subject to appreciation, such as buildings.

Required Expenditures. Taxable income equals the expected income (discussed before), less expected itemized deductions. For presentation purposes, the expert should detail the itemized deductions and tax basis as shown in Notes G and Note H, respectively, of the sample report. An expert using tax planning software should provide a hard copy of the calculations to the court for further support.

Spendable Cash. To help the court to evaluate the report, also include separately stated amounts for Annual Cash Spendable, Monthly Cash Spendable, Cash Spendable Percentages, and the Federal Tax Brackets.

APPENDIX

In Re Marriage of Smith
Estimated Cash Spendable
Table of Contents

TO: ______
ATTORNEY AT LAW
SAN FRANCISCO, CALIFORNIA

RE: THE MARRIAGE OF SMITH

The accompanying tables for John Smith and Mary Smith are based on information obtained from records and documents including the Income and Expense Declarations provided to us by representatives of both the Petitioner and Respondent. Any inaccuracy in the data used is necessarily reflected in these tables.

The accompanying tables were prepared by us pursuant to the request of ______ Attorney at Law, solely to facilitate a suitable support agreement in the marital dissolution of John Smith and Mary Smith and are not to be used for any other purposes.

San Francisco, California

December 15, 1987

EXHIBIT 21-1. JOHN SMITH, ESTIMATED CASH SPENDABLE BASED ON ASSUMED LEVEL OF SPOUSAL SUPPORT, DECEMBER 15, 1988

Column	(1)	(2)	(3)	(4)
	Assumed Level of Monthly Spousal Support			
Spousal Support	$0	$3,904	$11,163	$5,487
Child Support	0	4,456		3,481
Income				
Salary and wages (Note A)	$222,000	$222,000	$222,000	$222,000
Interest/Divided income (Note B)	10,000	10,000	10,000	10,000
Business income (loss) (Note C)	40,833	40,833	40,833	40,833
Passive income (loss) (Note D)	(26,000)	(26,000)	(26,000)	(26,000)
Other income (Loss) (Note E)	(3,800)	(3,800)	(3,800)	(3,800)
Spousal support	0	(46,848)	(133,956)	(65,844)
Subtotal	243,033	196,185	109,077	177,189
Cash Adjustments				
Child support	0	(53,472)	0	(41,772)
Passive income (loss) (Note D)	13,500	13,500	13,500	13,500
Other income (loss) (Note E)	27,500	27,500	27,500	27,500
Cash income	284,033	183,713	150,077	176,417
Required Expenditures				
Federal income tax	44,498	32,601	10,516	26,972
State income tax	14,850	10,493	2,392	8,726
Social security tax	3,379	3,379	3,379	3,379
State disability insurance	263	263	263	263
Mandatory deductions	0	0	0	0
Cash expenditures	62,990	46,736	16,550	39,340
Annual Cash Spendable				
John Smith	$221,043	$136,977	$133,527	$137,077
Mary Smith (from Exhibit 21-2)	$82,365	$168,056	$167,743	$168,124
Monthly Cash Spendable				
John Smith	$18,420	$11,415	$11,127	$11,423
Mary Smith	$6,864	$14,005	$13,979	$14,010
Cash Spendable Percentages				
John Smith	73%	45%	44%	45%
Mary Smith	27%	55%	56%	55%
Federal Tax Bracket				
John Smith	28%	28%	28%	33%
Mary Smith	15%	28%	33%	33%

EXHIBIT 21-2. MARY SMITH, ESTIMATED CASH SPENDABLE BASED ON ASSUMED LEVEL OF SPOUSAL SUPPORT, DECEMBER 15, 1988

	Assumed Level of Monthly Spousal Support			
Spousal support	$0	$3,904	$11,163	$5,487
Child support	0	4,456	0	3,481
Income				
Salary and wages (Note A)	$25,000	$25,000	$25,000	$25,000
Interest/dividend income (Note B)	36,500	36,500	36,500	36,500
Business income (loss) (Note C)	0	0	0	0
Passive income (loss) (Note D)	(2,000)	(2,000)	(2,000)	(2,000)
Other income (loss) (Note E)	(3,800)	(3,800)	(3,800)	(3,800)
Spousal support	0	46,848	133,956	65,844
Subtotal	55,700	102,548	189,656	121,544
Cash Adjustments				
Child support	0	53,472	0	41,772
Passive income (loss) (Note D)	4,500	4,500	4,500	4,500
Other income (loss) (Note E)	27,500	27,500	27,500	27,500
Cash income	87,700	188,020	221,656	195,316
Required Expenditures				
Federal income tax	2,125	12,897	38,745	18,358
State income tax	470	4,327	12,428	6,094
Social security tax	1,877	1,877	1,877	1,877
State disability insurance	263	263	263	263
Mandatory deductions (Note F)	600	600	600	600
Cash expenditures	5,335	19,964	53,913	27,192
Annual Cash Spendable				
Mary Smith (To Exhibit 21-A)	$82,365	$168,056	$167,743	$168,124
Monthly Cash Spendable				
Mary Smith	$6,864	$14,005	$13,979	$14,010
Federal Tax Bracket				
Mary Smith	15%	28%	33%	33%

EXHIBIT 21-3. REMARRIAGE OF SMITH, ESTIMATED CASH SPENDABLE, NOTES TO STATEMENTS

A. *Salaries and wages—$222,000 & $25,000*

The taxable bonus and salary of the Petitioner (John Smith) is based on an average of compensation earned for the recent two years derived from the closely held corporation, Apex, Ltd.. Salary of the Respondent (Mary Smith) is based on her current salary derived from her teaching position. Respondent's earnings from special tutoring were based on an average of compensation earned for the recent two years.

	Petitioner	Respondent
Apex, Ltd.		
Bonus	$ 40,000	
Salary	182,000	
San Francisco College		$23,500
Tutoring fees		1,500
Total Salary and Wages	$222,000	$25,000

B. *Interest/dividend income—$10,000 & $36,500*

Investment income consisting of interest and dividends is derived from the following sources:

		Petitioner	Respondent
Separate property cash accounts dated 9/30/87		$32,000	$17,710
Estimated interest rate		7.00%	7.00%
Subtotal		2,240	1,240
Community property cash accounts dated 9/30/87	$107,425		
Estimated market interest rate	7.00%		
Subtotal	$ 7,520	3,760	3,760
Separate property note receivable to equalize property division dated 11/30/87	$300,000		
Actual interest rate	10.00%		
Sub-total	$ 30,000		30,000
Taxable Interest		6,000	35,000
Dividend income:			
Taxable—Per IRS Form 1040	3,900		1,400
Add dividend exclusion	100		100
Interest/Dividend Income	$10,000		$36,500

C. *Business income—$40,833*

Apex, Ltd. was distributed to the Petitioner in the final distribution of community assets on November 30, 1987. Business income expected to be derived from the Petitioner in the form of undistributed profits from Apex, Ltd. is based on information obtained from the business valuation, detailed as follows:

EXHIBIT 21-3. *(Continued)*

	Adjusted Net Income	Weighing Factor	Total
Fiscal year ending			
October 31, 1985	$40,000	1	$ 40,000
October 31, 1986	35,000	2	70,000
October 31, 1987	45,000	3	135,000
Subtotal			245,000
Weighting factor			6
Average undistributed profits			$ 40,833

Information in support of adjusted net income is included in a separate report. Adjusted net income was increased for excessive depreciation and amounts contributed in behalf of the Petitioner to a profit sharing plan. Effective with the property division on November 30, 1987, the Petitioner was owner of 100% of the outstanding stock.

D. *Passive income (loss)—$(26,000) & $(2,000)*
Income and loss from partnerships is based on the following information derived primarily from the 1986 individual income tax returns:

Taxable Income (Loss)	Petitioner	Respondent
Partnership A	$10,000	$10,000
Partnership B	(15,000)	(15,000)
Partnership C	(25,000)	
Partnership D	(35,000)	
Subtotal	(65,000)	(5,000)
Passive loss adjustment (1986 Reform Act)—calendar year (1988)	39,000	3,000
Taxable Income (Loss)	$(26,000)	$ (2,000)
Cash income (Loss)		
Partnership A	$ 2,500	$ 2,500
Partnership B	0	0
Partnership C	(5,000)	
Partnership D	(10,000)	
Cash income (Loss)	$(12,500)	$2,500
Difference between taxable/Cash Income (Loss)	$ 13,500	$4,500

E. *Other income (loss)—$(3,800)*
Distribution of community property includes a commerical building to be held in co-tenancy by both the Petitioner and Respondent. Expected rental income from the commercial property to be earned by each the Petitioner and Respondent is based on the following detail:

(Exhibit continues on p. 412.)

EXHIBIT 21-3. *(Continued)*

	Taxable income	Cash flow
Expected monthly rental	$132,000	$132,000
Expected expenditures		
Depreciation	60,000	
Insurance	3,000	3,000
Mortgage Payments:		
Interest	65,000	65,000
Principal		5,000
Other Expenses (5%)	6,600	6,600
Property taxes	5,000	5,000
Total Expenses	139,600	84,600
Net	$ (7,600)	$ 47,400
Co-tenancy Interest	$ (3,800)	$ 23,700

F. *Mandatory deductions—$600*
Mandatory deductions in the form of union dues are withheld from the monthly paychecks paid to the Respondent spouse. The amount of dues are based on the December 1987 monthly dues and annualized at $600.

G. *Deductions*
We have applied itemized deductions based on the 1986 individual income tax returns, detailed as follows:

	Petitioner	Respondent
Medical	$	$ 3,000
Taxes:		
Real estate	8,000	4,000
Other	263	185
Interest:		
Mortgage	50,000	25,000
Other	15,000	5,000
Contributions	5,000	2,000

H. *Income taxes*
Income taxes have been computed using the 1988 Federal and California tax rates. A filing status of single with four exemptions has been used for the Petitioner and a filing status of head of household with two exemptions for the Respondent.

LIST OF CASES

In Re Marriage of Burlini, 143 Cal. App. 3d 65, 191 Cal. Rptr. 541 (1983)
In Re Marriage of McNaughton, 145 Cal. App. 3d 845, 194 Cal. Rptr. 176 (1983)

22

MARITAL DISSOLUTION: PROFESSIONAL GOODWILL AND RELATED INTANGIBLES

Victor A. Levi, JD, MBA, CPA

INTRODUCTION

Professional goodwill results from reported court decisions. As a rule, these decisions are from courts of appeal that have either upheld or overturned the trial courts' findings. Professional goodwill, therefore, is not a static concept but is ever changing in each jurisdiction. As with any subject dependent upon case law, one cannot treat the material in this chapter as the current state of the law in any jurisdiction. The accountant must consult with his or her client attorney on the current case law to treat this subject intelligently. This chapter guides the accountant, retained in a marital dissolution matter, in determining the existence and value of professional goodwill.

The chapter deals with the goodwill of sports figures, celebrities, and business executives. Finally, the chapter concludes with a look at unusual goodwill problems including the value of professional licenses and education.

DEFINITIONS OF PROFESSIONAL GOODWILL

This chapter uses the term *professional* to mean members of occupations licensed by state or state authorized agencies. This group includes doctors, dentists, lawyers, accountants, architects, engineers, chiropractors, acupuncturists, and other similar occupations. Frequently licensed but excluded from the designation as "professional" are barbers, court reporters, and the like. Other callings that could be termed professionals include certified financial planners, real estate appraisers, dental laboratory technicians, and almost any self-employed person or owner–employee of stock in a closely held corporation in which capital is not the primary income-producing factor.

Goodwill, a future economic benefit, need not be an accounting asset, and although it may be transferable, the amount is difficult to measure.

> Goodwill may be properly enough described to be the advantage or benefit, which is acquired by an establishment, beyond the mere value of the capital, stock, funds, or property employed therein, in consequence of the general public patronage and encouragement, which it receives from the constant or habitual customers, on account of its local position, or common celebrity, or reputation for skill or affluence, or punctuality, or from other accidental circumstances or necessities, or even from ancient partialities or prejudices (J. Story, *Commentaries on the Law of Partnerships*, § 99 at 170 [6th ed. 1868]).

Lord Eldon was more succinct: "The goodwill, which has been the subject of sale, is nothing more than the probability, that the old customers will resort to the old place" (*Cruttwell v. Lye*, 34 Eng.Rep. 129, 134 (Ch. 1810)).

Accounting goodwill is the excess of an acquired firm's cost over the fair market value of the net assets. The economics of goodwill relate to the value of good customer relations, a well-respected business name, and so on that result in greater than normal earning power.

The major elements of professional goodwill are (1) location (see *Spaulding v. Benenati*, 57 N.Y. 2d 418, 442 N.E.2d 1244, 456 N.Y.S. 2d 733 (1982). *In re Marriage of Asbury*, 144 Cal. App.3d 918, 193 Cal. Rptr. 562 (1983); *In re Marriage of Lukens*, 16 Wash. App. 481, 558 P.2d 279 (1976)) and (2) reputation (*Dugan v. Dugan*, 92 N.J. 423, 457 A.2d 1 (1983)). The former is important because we usually seek professional services within a small geographical area; the latter for the reasons enunciated by Justice Story and Lord Eldon. In *Wisner v. Wisner* (129 Ariz. 333, 631 P.2d 115 (1981)), the husband, a surgeon, argued that he could have no goodwill because he had no repeat patients. Not so, said the court, because the referral base of physicians provides the repetitive business, which supports the finding of goodwill.

All businesses with goodwill have "going-concern value," but the reverse is not necessarily true. Two definitions are commonly used and are not necessarily consistent. *Going-concern value* (versus liquidation or exit value) reflects the assumption that the business is an operating entity, perhaps exhibiting synergistic effects. Or, as stated by one court, going-concern value equals "the amount by which the value of the assets as a whole, assembled together for the conduct of a business, exceeds the aggregate value of the separate items of property" (*In re Marriage of Sharp*, 143 Cal. App.3d 714, 192 Cal. Rptr. 97 (1983)).

HISTORY OF PROFESSIONAL GOODWILL IN COURT

The first case dealing with professional goodwill in a domestic relations setting was *Mueller v. Mueller* (144 Cal. App.2d 245, 301 P.2d 90 (1956)), which involved a dental laboratory. The court, in reviewing prior cases wherein no goodwill was found, stated:

> Where a person acquires a reputation for skill and learning in a particular profession, as, for instance, in that of a lawyer, a physician, or an editor, he often creates an intangible but valuable property by winning the confidence of his patrons and securing immunity from successful competition for their business, and it would seem to be well settled that this is a species of good-will which may be the subject of transfer. (At 251 citing 24 Am.Jur. 808.)

Mueller was followed by other California cases (*Golden v. Golden*, 270 Cal. App.2d 401, 75 Cal. Rptr. 735 (1969) and *Todd v. Todd*, 272 Cal. App.2d 786, 78 Cal. Rptr. 131 (1969)) that found goodwill values in medical and law practices.

California, as a community property state, treats goodwill as a community asset to be divided as part of the marital property.

Texas, although a community property jurisdiction, took a different approach regarding small professional practices in *Nail v. Nail* (486 S.W.2d 761 (Supreme Ct. Tex. 1972)) wherein the Court stated:

> His goodwill did not possess value or constitute an asset separate and apart from his person or from his individual ability to practice his profession. It would be extinguished in the event of his death, or retirement, or disablement, as well as in the event of the sale of his practice or the loss of his patients, whatever the cause.

Dr. Nail's goodwill was not community property, said the court. This position was followed in *Austin v. Austin* (619 S.W.2d 290 (Tex.App. 1981)) and *Depner v. Depner* (478 So.2d 532 (La. App. 1985)).

Texas took a different posture with larger professional organizations. In *Finn v. Finn* (658 S.W.2d 735 (Tex. App. 1983)), the husband was a senior partner in a Dallas law firm. The court found that goodwill existed independent of the professional spouse's personal ability and that it had commercial value.

These findings of the existence of goodwill, obtained in the community property state courts, were unobtainable in the courts of common law states, which looked solely to the title of property. Courts in common law states assigned the practice, without charge, to the practitioner as separate property (*Closson v. Closson*, 30 Wyo. 1, 215 P. 485 (1923)).

As the use of and statutory authority for "equitable distribution" spread among the common law jurisdictions in the 1960s, the courts in those jurisdictions began to recognize and value professional goodwill. Representative cases are *In re Marriage of White*, 98 Ill. App.3d 380, 424 N.E.2d 421 (1981); *Stern v. Stern*, 66 N.J. 340, 331 A.2d 257 (1975) and *Nehorayoff v. Nehorayoff*, 108 Misc.2d 311, 437 N.Y.S. 2d 584 (1981); and *Hanson v. Hanson*, 12 Fam. L. Rep. (BNA) 1596 (Mo. Ct. App. W. Dist. 1986).

Under community property statutes, a marital interest in property runs only to property acquired during marriage. However, under the "equitable distribution" doctrine, the courts can award marital property, legally owned by one party, to the other at the time of the marital breakup. The marital partnership concept, ingrained in community property law, provides the basis for the theory of equitable distribution.

See the Appendix to this book for a categorization by state of the property approach taken in marital dissolutions.

VALUATION METHODOLOGY

Even the courts that have found goodwill to exist have left open a variety of methods to measure its value. Depending on the case, the court will allow any reasonable method (*In re Marriage of King*, 150 Cal. App.3d 304, 197 Cal. Rptr. 716 (1983)). As a result, the court records contain several methods, each depending upon its particular case's circumstances.

Most methods assume that goodwill is indicated by prices paid to acquire practices, for example, (1) sales of the particular practice (*In re Marriage of Fortier*, 34 Cal. App.3d 384, 109 Cal. Rptr. 915 (1973)); (2) withdrawal rights in partnership agreement (*In re Marriage of Fonstein*, 17 Cal. 3d 738, 552 P.2d 1169, 131 Cal. Rptr. 873 (1976)); and (3) sale of an interest in a law practice (*In re Marriage of Lopez*, 38 Cal. App.3d 93, 113 Cal. Rptr. 58 (1974)).

Two theories exist concerning the benchmarks for the value of personal goodwill. One theory, that only the "sale value"—that is, the market price agreed by a willing buyer and seller—properly measures goodwill. Under this theory, one might exclude the value of law practice goodwill from this method because the Canons of Ethics prohibit the sale of goodwill, so it cannot be separated from the person or persons who generated it. (See *Geffen v. Moss*, 53 Cal. App.3d 215, 125 Cal. Rptr. 687 (1975)). Opponents reject this concept, claiming sale values frequently reflect a discount, recognizing the risk of patient/client transfer from one professional to another, whereas such is not a factor in marital dissolution, when the owner spouse continues to operate his or her business. But, one could argue that if it cannot be separated, then it is not goodwill but merely human capital.

Proponents of this alternative theory claim the value of community goodwill is not necessarily the price that a willing buyer would pay for such goodwill. They assert that exigencies attend marriage dissolution such that the market price might be less than a hypothetical, unseen "true" value of goodwill (*In re Marriage of Foster*, 42 Cal. App.3d 577, 117 Cal. Rptr. 49 (1974)). However, some practices, such as psychoanalytic and psychiatric, entail such close personal relationships between practitioner and patient that there is little possibility of patient transfer. Under this theory, the practice will have goodwill if it exhibits something called "superior earnings." Of course, the difficult measurement and conceptual problem of "superior" earnings remains.

The provisions limiting marketability contained in partnership/professional corporation agreements have been both accepted and rejected by various courts. They have been rejected as nonbinding upon the nonprofessional spouse by the courts (*In re Marriage of Slater*, 100 Cal. App.3d 241, 160 Cal. Rptr. 686 (1979); *In re Marriage of Morris*, 588 S.W.2d 39 (Mo. 1979); *In re Marriage of Fenton*, 134 Cal. App.3d 451, 184 Cal. Rptr. 597 (1982)). In opposition, they have been accepted as binding in *Stern v. Stern*, supra; *Hertz v. Hertz*, 99 N.M. 320, 657 P.2d 1169 (1983) and *Stolowitz v. Stolowitz*, 106 Misc.2d 853, 435 N.Y.S.2d 882 (1980).

Whatever theory of goodwill value is used by a given jurisdiction, the valuation expert ultimately bases goodwill measurements upon formulas. Sometimes these formulas are based on standards developed by practice brokers and others. As an example, general dental practices may change hands for 40 percent of annual gross practice income (see *A Guide for Your Practice*, Santa Clara County [California] Dental Society 1986); accounting practices have sold for prices from 75 percent to 100 percent and 125 percent of the annual gross revenue (*Mitchell v. Mitchell*, 152 Ariz. 317, 732 P.2d 208 (1987)). Other formulas accepted by the courts include multiples of a month's collections on accounts receivable (*Foster*, supra; and percentages of gross and net income (*Mueller*, supra).

Be aware that it is difficult to apply a single-factor formula, such as one based on gross revenue, to a variety of professional activities. Therefore, these approaches have limited credibility unless industry practice (i.e., transactions) supports their use. Possibly the most common formula for valuing goodwill is the "capitalized excess earnings" method. This formula contains several subjective inputs that an "expert" accountant must justify based on his experience and training.

First, the expert must determine the subject's actual professional earnings. This task requires an analysis of the professional's reported income and, more important, expenses for some reasonable time period, generally 5 years (see, for example, Revenue Ruling 68-609, 1968-2 Cum. Bull. 327 as one authoritative voice). Extraordinary results, either high or low, should be rejected if their inclusion distorts the analysis.

Adjustments must be made, where necessary, to include only the elements of a professional's income that are common to all similar practitioners. This removes personal income and expenses from legitimate business costs in order to obtain a picture of the actual earnings generated in the professional practice. Nonpractice income such as interest and excessive expenses in any discretionary category such as auto, travel, and entertainment must be eliminated. Dues and membership expenses should be reviewed as should insurance, repairs and maintenance, salaries and wages, and noncurrent asset accounts. Retirement plan contributions for the professional should be eliminated as an expense, as should his salary, in the case of a professional corporation.

If the professional is a member of a partnership or a multi-owner professional corporation, removing personal expenses is more complicated. One must review all agreements between the professionals and analyze income and expense accounts to measure the professional's actual income.

Having measured the professional's actual income, next compare the professional's adjusted income with that of his or her peer group. Some courts, *Dugan v. Dugan*, supra, have suggested that the comparison should be made with employed professionals, similarly educated and experienced. The rationale to this approach is that the employee has no goodwill, and a comparison of this group with the subject will produce true "excess earnings."

One difficulty in using available salary data is that they infrequently allow one to identify the experience level of salaried professionals. Moreover, many salaried professionals are younger, with less experience, or employed by governmental units, with different retirement benefits, working hours, and entrepreneurial incentives than the independent professional whose practice is at issue. Factors other than goodwill can cause some individuals to earn more than the averages; examples are inborn talent, hard work, and family connections.

Others believe that the proper comparison is with the professional's peers. James T. Friedman argues in his article, "Professional Practice Goodwill: An Abused Value Concept," 2 J. Am. Acad. Matrimonial Law 23 at 26 (1986), that "entrepreneurial drive and acceptance of income uncertainty increase the replacement cost of the professional who is willing to risk self-employment."

Surveys of the earnings of professionals self-employed or employed by professional corporations can provide appropriate data. If the survey is sound, professionals at both ends of the economic spectrum may be included, and the data can be used to calculate "excess earnings." One must be prepared, of course, to establish that such summary data result in an average compensation that does not also include a measure of goodwill.

The analyst must select a survey carefully. A survey of a firm's own clients in a particular profession might be attacked on the grounds of independence and might not be admitted by the court because the opposition has no opportunity to cross-examine the testimony. However, surveys regularly performed for the American Medical Association and the American Dental Association, if properly used, have received almost "judicial notice" by the courts. (Judicial notice is a legal concept that allows a court to accept something as a fact without independent proof thereof.)

Courts generally treat surveys skeptically, and so the expert should present data closely related to the subject professional in terms of age, experience, hours worked, geographical locale, practice setting (urban, rural, etc.), and practice size. No survey will match perfectly. For certain specialties (particularly medical), surveys may be unobtainable. (The appendix at the end of this chapter lists some sources for surveys of various professions and their specialties.)

Surveys are also often out of date. Most courts allow updating using the change in relevant price index between the survey date and the current date.

One could combine survey data to make it more responsive to the need. For example, suppose a survey of professionals reports by ages and practice sizes. Assume one wishes to combine these data to develop comparable income for a professional aged 45 in a practice group of 15. A qualified statistician might be able to perform this calculation in a manner acceptable to the local courts, if sufficient data are available about the survey size and methodology.

If a comparison of survey data with the adjusted earnings of the professional produces no excess earnings, then the professional enjoys no measurable goodwill in either the economic or accounting sense.

Going Concern Value

Some cases may require the measurement of a practice's going-concern value. Several courts have suggested that such a value would, at a minimum, equal start-up costs. To calculate such costs involves pricing out a list of costs typically incurred in starting a professional practice. This list can be simple, but should include the following:

1. Value of investigating, negotiating for, and leasing the office space used by the professional so long as the existing lease has some reasonable term before expiration.
2. Value of installing telephones and other specialized equipment together with the cost of moving furniture, equipment, library, and the like to the occupied space.
3. Value of stationery, other paper goods, and supplies normally on hand at any time.
4. Value of hiring and training support staff.
5. Value of current client/patient files.

The economic value of a "below-market" lease is not included in the preceding, but should be treated as a separate item in valuing the practice. The net value of tangible practice assets generally represents another marital asset that is considered separately from goodwill in the marital estate.

If the analysis reveals "excess earnings," one additional item warrants discussion. Many writers on the capitalized excess earnings method require a reduction of excess earnings by a calculated return on practice net assets. This recognizes that a portion of professionals' earnings represents a return on capital employed in the practice. However, as most professionals employ assets in their practices, such a return may already be encompassed in the peer group average and thus arguably not part of the excess, as measured.

Assuming that "excess earnings" have been found, the next step is to ascertain the consistency of excess earnings over the study's 3 to 5 year period, rather than rely on just 1 year's calculation. It may be appropriate to "inflation adjust" the earlier year's amounts by a relevant price index, perhaps giving greater weight to more current data.

Capitalization Multiplier

Last, one must ascertain the proper "capitalization" multiplier. This multiplier is the number of years that one can reasonably project excess earnings to continue, given the frailty of human existence, practice risks, clientele and referral source turnover, and other elements. Certain factors have been enumerated as requiring consideration in determining the capitalization multiplier: the practitioner's age, health, past earning power, professional reputation in the community as to judgment, skill, knowledge, and comparative professional success. One must also consider the nature and duration of the professional's business as a sole practitioner or as a member of a partnership or professional corporation to which the professional has made a proprietary contribution (*In re the Marriage of Lopez*, supra).

A more recent case, *In re Marriage of Rives*, 130 Cal. App. 3d 138, 181 Cal. Rptr. 572 (1982), required consideration of the professional's (here a beekeeper) expressed desire to retire, coupled with his age.

Few guidelines or empirical bases point to a proper capitalization multiplier. Whereas a multiplier as high as 10 has been used for commercial enterprises (but not for domestic relations purposes), a multiplier of 5 seems to represent the maximum rate for professional goodwill. Looking to the factors set forth in Lopez and using a "normal" multiplier of 3 times earnings for a sole practitioner (*Dugan v. Dugan*, supra), one can understand how the rate adjusts to reflect age, health, the presence of partners to carry on the practice in the event of illness or injury, and even a near-term planned retirement.

Valuing professional goodwill is a significant undertaking requiring the skills, training, and qualitative judgment of an accountant. One court stated that "for goodwill to be found in a case of this sort, competent, informed and *expert* testimony should be offered to establish that the value of the personal services is less than the net income of the practice." (*Levy v. Levy*, 164 N.J. Super. 542, 397 A.2d 374 (1978) (emphasis added)).

Some jurisdictions do not recognize professional goodwill in marital dissolutions. Those jurisdictions prefer to compensate the other spouse, when appropriate, with spousal support. Examples of these are: *Depner*, supra; *Matter of Marriage of*

Fleege, 91 Wash. 2d 324, 588 P.2d 1136 (1979); *Holbrook v. Holbrook*, 103 Wis. 2d 327, 309 N.W.2d 343 (1981); and *Powell v. Powell*, 231 Kan. 456, 648 P.2d 218 (1982)).

BEYOND GOODWILL

No discussion of professional goodwill would be complete without discussion of trends in the treatment of goodwill of members of large professional organizations, the potential goodwill of athletes, celebrities, and business leaders, and the interest of a spouse in a professional degree and license.

LARGE PRACTICE GOODWILL

Special consideration possibly should be given to the professional goodwill of members of large professional organizations, such as the international accounting firm.

Some analysts believe that a threshold inquiry should be made as to whether the professional occupies a position in his organization that lends itself to a finding of goodwill.

To find professional goodwill, current practice requires self-employment or a proprietary interest in a professional corporation. (Others, outside of this narrow category, may have goodwill.) Some business community members and sports figures command compensation levels far greater than that of their peers and are not charged with a measure of goodwill upon marital dissolution. Why does this double standard exist? It appears to flow, not from any concept of superior earnings, but rather from the individual's ability to control his or her destiny.

If a board of directors or a sports-related injury can terminate an individual's compensation, no court has, to date, found goodwill to exist. The individual's lack of control appears to be the reason.

This same argument might be advanced for members of large legal, accounting, architectural, and similar firms that are operated more like corporations than like small professional organizations. Although each member of the firm may have some proprietary interest in the entity's net assets, these interests are often measured in miniscule percentages—frequently less than 1 percent and sometimes less than one-tenth or one-hundredth of 1 percent. This ownership interest can be compared to that of any shareholder of a company whose stock is listed on a national exchange—the right to vote but insufficient shares to affect the outcome. Members of large professional organizations may not automatically have goodwill.

The absence of professional goodwill in this situation is not foreign to the courts. In *In re Marriage of Slivka*, 183 Cal. App.3d 159, 228 Cal. Rptr. 76 (1986), the appellate court found substantial evidence to support the trial court's holding that the husband's partnership interest carried no goodwill value. The husband was a partner in the Southern California Permanente Group that provided medical services, under contract to the Kaiser Foundation Health Plan, Inc. The trial court found that, despite the fact that he was a partner, his situation most resembled that of an employee who has no ownership interest and who is paid for services rendered. Control over one's destiny and personal autonomy may become important in measuring the quality and quantity of professional goodwill. See also *In re Marriage of Aufmuth*, 89 Cal. App.3d 446, 152 Cal. Rptr. 668 (1979).

ATHLETES, CELEBRITIES, AND BUSINESS EXECUTIVES

There has been some discussion about the goodwill accruing to professional athletes, entertainment celebrities, and titans of the business world. A 1989 appellate case, *Piscopo v. Piscopo*, 232 N.J. Super. 559, 557 A.2d 1040 (1989), affirmed a finding that marital property included "celebrity goodwill" (see also *Golub v. Golub*, 139 Misc. 2d 440, 527 N.Y.S.2d 946 (1988)). Although most professional athletes receive salaries, a substantial number, such as boxers, tennis players, and golfers, are self-employed.

Because of their reputations, possibly earned during marriage, substantial income can flow from the sale of their likeness and their endorsements. Is this income stream an asset that is divisible upon marital dissolution? What about royalties from an autobiography written postseparation but marketable as a result of a reputation built during the marriage? What about security brokers who may receive large bonuses when moving from one firm to another—is this a measure of "employee goodwill"? A valuation expert facing this issue should become familiar with the discussions in "Community Property Interests in the Right Of Publicity: Fame and/or Fortune," 25 *UCLA Law Review* 1095 (1978). A similar question might be raised with respect to "golden parachutes" awarded after separation but resulting from efforts expended during the marriage. These and similar situations will inevitably come before an appellate court; the only questions are when and with what result. The vexing valuation problems may explain why no reported case exists. One would think that given the great risk associated with many of these occupations, only extremely conservative capitalization rates would receive court approval.

PROFESSIONAL EDUCATION AND LICENSES

Some cases have required valuing professional education and licenses. This area, like so many in the domestic relations arena, is changing constantly. The reader will find an excellent discourse on this subject in "When A Lawyer Divorces" (Gary N. Skoloff and Theodore P. Orenstein, American Bar Association (1986)). (Not to be ignored is an annual survey published in the Winter Edition of the *Family Law Quarterly* entitled "Family Law in the Fifty States," which analyzes current thinking in the various courts.)

Typically, a working spouse supports the family while the other spouse pursues an educational program or professional training, and the marriage dissolves prior to any meaningful economic benefit to the family. Here, the courts, charged with arriving at an equitable result, find themselves in a difficult situation. Little or no marital property exists to divide and the working spouse frequently cannot demonstrate a need for support, as she or he has an earning history and capacity.

Understandably, the courts initially rejected the valuation of such intangible and esoteric assets as an education. Lump sum alimony or spousal support was considered reasonable recompense (*Prosser v. Prosser*, 156 Neb. 629, 57 N.W.2d 173 (1953); *Daniels v. Daniels*, 185 N.E.2d 773 (Ohio App. 1961)). The leading case is *In re Marriage of Graham*, 194 Colo. 429, 574 P.2d 75 (1978) in which the Court found

> An educational degree, such as an M.B.A., is simply not encompassed even by the broad views of the concept of "property." It does not have an exchange value or any objective transferable value on an open market. It is personal to the holder. It terminates on the death of the holder and is not inheritable. It cannot be assigned, sold, transferred, conveyed or pledged. An advanced degree is a cumulative product of many years of previous education combined with diligence and hard work. It may not be acquired by the mere expenditure of money. In our view, it has none of the attributes of property in the usual sense of that term.

This major case has been followed by *Archer v. Archer*, 303 Md. 347, 493 A.2d 1074 (1985); *Helm v. Helm*, 289 S.C. 169, 345 S.E.2d 720 (1986); *Hodge v. Hodge*, 337 Pa. Super. 151, 486 A.2d 951 (1984); *In re Marriage of Horstmann*, 263 N.W.2d 885 (Iowa 1978); *Mahoney v. Mahoney*, 91 N.J. 488, 453 A.2d 527 (1982); *Stevens v. Stevens*, 23 Ohio St. 3d 115, 492 N.E.2d 131 (1986); and *DeWitt v. DeWitt*, 98 Wisc. 2d 44, 296 N.W.2d 761 (1980).

California recognized the issue in 1969 in *Todd v. Todd*, supra, but rejected the concept that professional education, when acquired with community property funds, could be community property. Before concluding that a major community property state has rejected the concept of professional education as a community asset, be aware that the *Todd* case did not present the fact situation that cried out for such a finding. In this case, the community had enjoyment of the investment in the professional education. But see *In re Marriage of Sullivan*, 134 Cal. App.3d 634, 184 Cal. Rptr. 796 (1982). Those cases in which there has been no such enjoyment have compelled the courts to find some value to the contribution made by one spouse to the professional education of the other spouse: *Greer v. Greer*, 32 Colo. App. 196, 510 P.2d 905 (1973); *Moss v. Moss*, 80 Mich. App. 693, 264 N.W.2d 97 (1978); *In re Marriage of Horstmann*, supra; *In re Marriage of Rubenstein*, 145 Ill. App. 3d 31, 495 N.E.2d 659 (1986); *Van Bussum v. Van Bussum*, 728 S.W. 2d 538 (Ky. App. 1987); and *Drapek v. Drapek*, 399 Mass. 240, 503 N.E. 2d 946 (1987).

Finally in 1979, the courts started to recognize that professional education may be marital property: *Inman v. Inman*, 578 S.W.2d 266 (Ky. App. 1979); *Hubbard v. Hubbard*, 603 P.2d 747 (Okla. 1979); *Wisner v. Wisner*, supra; and *In re Marriage of Lundberg*, 107 Wis.2d 1, 318 N.W.2d 918 (1982).

Because of that court's high standing in the area of equitable distribution, the New Jersey decision in *Mahoney v. Mahoney*, supra, which held that a professional education was not "property" to be divided but instead gave rise to a "reimbursement" of costs incurred in obtaining the degree to the working spouse, became an important stepping stone. The court, quoting *DeWitt*, supra, reasoned that despite the professional education, the recipient might not choose to practice the profession, may fail at it, or may not practice it successfully. In other words, the value of the education and training may never be enjoyed. (Compare with goodwill that also may never be realized by the owner for a variety of reasons such as lack of stability, disability, or death.) For a contrary holding, see *Cronin v. Cronin*, 131 Misc. 2d 879, 502 N.Y.S.2d 368 (1986).

Because of the risks involved and to avoid the costs of continued jurisdiction in these cases, the court decided against a finding of a property right subject to distribution. Mahoney clearly gave rise to the California case *In re the Marriage of Sullivan*, supra, which concluded, as did *Mahoney and Todd*, that a license or degree was not an asset. Mrs. Sullivan worked and had a child while her husband attended medical school and completed his internship and residency. They separated just prior to his commencing practice. *Sullivan* was appealed to the California Supreme Court which, seemingly, asked the legislature for guidance. The result was California Civil Code § 4800.3 that provided for, under "proper" circumstances, reimbursement to the community for the following:

1. Community contributions to education or training
2. Interest at the legal rate
3. Any loan taken out during marriage, the proceeds of which were used for education or training, shall be assigned, for repayment, to the benefited party

The Supreme Court remanded the case to the trial court for determinations in accordance with the newly enacted code section.

However, a law degree is an asset, said the appellate court in Michigan in *Woodworth v. Woodworth*, 126 Mich. App. 258, 337 N.W.2d 332 (1983) as is a medical license in New York, *O'Brien v. O'Brien*, 66 N.Y.2d 576, 489 N.E.2d 712, 498 N.Y.S.2d 743 (1985), and North Carolina, *Geer v. Geer* 84 N.C. App. 471, 353 S.E.2d 427 (1987).

THE "DOUBLE DIP"

No discussion of this subject would be complete without mentioning double counting, which is spoken of widely by valuation experts in this field but unrecognized by any reported case to date. This is the "double-dip" or "two-bites-of-the-apple" theory. In simplest terms, the theory questions the fairness of using the total value of the professional practice in both dividing the marital assets and counting the total income therefrom as a measure of the supporting spouse's ability to pay spousal support.

Components of income from a typical professional practice might be diagrammed as follows:

A. Normal earnings (average earnings of similarly educated and experienced practitioner)

B. Excess earnings (goodwill)

C. Investment earnings (earnings on employment of invested capital)

In determining the supporting spouse's ability to pay support, courts look to the total earnings, A B C.

Supporting spouses argue that they are charged for the benefits of components B and C in the division of the marital property when goodwill and invested capital are counted as components of marital property. Under these conditions spouses rightly argue that to count all of income in computing spousal support payments is to double count the benefits of the goodwill and the invested capital.

CONCLUSIONS

Professional goodwill, its existence and value, will be debated as long as marital dissolutions occurs. Courts will struggle to be equitable to the marital partners both in valuing marital property and in setting support orders. The accountant is to instruct the courts as to the current thinking regarding the existence and value of professional goodwill, both in equitable distribution and community property jurisdictions. The charge as professional accountants is to serve the courts honestly and with integrity and wisdom. In so doing, the profession grows in stature in the eyes of the courts and the laity. This suggests that anyone entering the field of domestic relations forensic accounting must stay abreast of the constant changes occurring in case law in all jurisdictions.

APPENDIX
INFORMATION REGARDING PROFESSIONAL PRACTICES AND GOODWILL

Law Practices

Altman & Weil — Annual survey
P.O. Box 472
Ardmore, PA 19003

The American Lawyer
American Lawyer Media, Inc.
600 Third Avenue
New York, NY 10016

National Law Journal
111 Eighth Avenue
New York, NY 10011
Local Bar Association

Occasionally state or local bar associations will conduct surveys of their members. These can be most useful because the major surveys are broad based in terms of geographical area.

Accounting Practices

State Societies — Annual Survey

A number of the major state societies conduct annual surveys. These are frequently broken down into smaller geographical areas. State society addresses can be obtained from the AICPA.

Medical Practices

American Medical Association — Annual Survey
Order Department OP22817
P.O. Box 10946
Chicago, IL 60610-0946

Medical Economics — Annual Survey
Box 55
Oradell, NJ 07649

This biweekly publication not only conducts an annual survey and publishes the results in a September issue, it also reports during the year on other financial factors of practices, occasionally dealing with specialties. This publication reports on specialties more extensively than does the AMA.

Local Medical Societies

Local societies may also have useful survey material.

Dental Practices

American Dental Association — Annual Surveys
211 E. Chicago Ave.
Chicago, IL 60611

The ADA has several publications that can be most helpful in valuing dental practices.

Local Dental Societies

Check for publications or surveys conducted by local groups.

Architectural Practices

Local AAA Chapters .
State or local chapters occasionally perform salary surveys of their members.

Engineering Practices

Associated General Contractors of America — Annual Survey
1957 "E" Street, N.W.
Washington, DC 20006

General Material

Davis, Muller, "Valuation of Professional Practices in Dissolution Cases," 74 *Illinois Bar Journal* 14 (September 1985), Illinois State Bar Association, Springfield, IL.

Dlugatch, H.E. and H. Olds, 'Goodwill Determination in Professional Practice Evaluation—Pursuant to a Marriage Dissolution," 4 *Glendale Law Review* 28 (1982), Glendale University College of Law, Glendale, CA.

Goodwill, American Jurisprudence, 5 *Proof of Facts Annotated* 505, Bancroft-Whitney Company, San Francisco, CA 1960.

Gerhardt, C.D., "Putting a Value on a Medical Practice," 7 *Family Advocate* 10 (Summer 1984). Section of Family Law, American Bar Association, Chicago, IL.

Habeeb, W.R., *Accountability for Goodwill of Professional Practice in Action Arising from Divorce or Separation*, 52 *American Law Reports* 3d, 1344, The Lawyers Co-operative Publishing Company, Rochester, NY 1973.

Hempstead, J.E., "Putting a Value on a Law Practice," 7 *Family Advocate* 14 (Summer 1984). Section of Family Law, American Bar Association, Chicago, IL.

Pratt, S., *Valuing Small Business and Professional Practices* (Homewood, IL: Dow Jones-Irwin 1986), 483 p.

LIST OF CASES

Archer v. Archer, 303 Md. 347, 493 A.2d 1074 (1985)
In Re Marriage of Asbury, 144 Cal. App. 3d 918, 193 Cal. Rptr. 562 (1983)
In Re Marriage of Aufmuth, 89 Cal. App. 3d 446, 152 Cal. Rptr. 668 (1979)
Austin v. Austin, 619 S.W.2d 290 (Tex. App. 1981)
Closson v. Closson, 30 Wyo. 1, 215 P. 485 (1923)
Cronin v. Cronin, 131 Misc. 2d 879, 502 N.Y.S.2d 368 (1986)
Cruttwell v. Lye, 34 Eng. Rep. 129 (Ch. 1810)
Daniels v. Daniels, 185 N.E.2d 773 (Ohio App. 1961)
Depner v. Depner, 478 So. 2d 532 (La. App. 1985)

DeWitt v. DeWitt, 98 Wisc. 2d 44, 296 N.W.2d 761 (1980)
Drapek v. Drapek, 399 Mass. 240, 503 N.E.2d 946 (1987)
Dugan v. Dugan, 92 N.J. 423, 457 A.2d 1 (1983)
In Re Marriage of Fenton, 134 Cal. App. 3d 451, 184 Cal. Rptr. 597 (1982)
Finn v. Finn, 658 S.W.2d 735 (Tex. App. 1983)
Matter of Marriage of Fleege, 91 Wash. 2d 324, 588 P.2d 1136 (1979)
In Re Marriage of Fonstein, 17 Cal. 3d 738, 552 P.2d 1169, 131 Cal. Rptr. 873 (1976)
In Re Marriage of Fortier, 34 Cal. App. 3d 384, 109 Cal. Rptr. 915 (1973)
In Re Marriage of Foster, 42 Cal. App. 3d 577, 117 Cal. Rptr. 49 (1974)
Geer v. Geer, 84 N.C. App. 471, 353 S.E.2d 427 (1987)
Geffen v. Moss, 53 Cal. App. 3d 215, 125 Cal. Rptr. 687 (1975)
Golden v. Golden, 270 Cal. App. 2d 401, 75 Cal. Rptr. 735 (1969)
Golub v. Golub, 139 Misc. 2d 440, 527 N.Y.S.2d 946 (1988)
In Re Marriage of Graham, 194 Colo. 429, 574 P.2d 75 (1978)
Greer v. Greer, 32 Colo. App. 196, 510 P.2d 905 (1973)
Hanson v. Hanson, 12 Fam. L. Rep. (BNA) 1596 (Mo. Ct. App. W. Dist. 1986)
Helm v. Helm, 289 S.C. 169, 345 S.E.2d 720 (1986)
Hertz v. Hertz, 99 N.M. 320, 657 P.2d 1169 (1983)
Hodge v. Hodge, 337 Pa. Super. 151, 486 A.2d 951 (1984)
Holbrook v. Holbrook, 103 Wis. 2d 327, 309 N.W.2d 343 (1981)
In Re Marriage of Horstmann, 263 N.W.2d 885 (Iowa 1978)
Hubbard v. Hubbard, 603 P.2d 747 (Okla. 1979)
Inman v. Inman, 578 S.W.2d 266 (Ky. App. 1979)
In Re Marriage of King, 150 Cal. App. 3d 304, 197 Cal. Rptr. 716 (1983)
Levy v. Levy, 164 N.J. Super. 542, 397 A.2d 374 (1978)
In Re Marriage of Lopez, 38 Cal. App. 3d 93, 113 Cal. Rptr. 58 (1974)
In Re Marriage of Lukens, 16 Wash. App. 481, 558 P.2d 279 (1976)
In Re Marriage of Lundberg, 107 Wis. 2d 1, 318 N.W.2d 918 (1982)
Mahoney v. Mahoney, 91 N.J. 488, 453 A.2d 527 (1982)
Mitchell v. Mitchell, 152 Ariz. 317, 732 P.2d 208 (1987)
In Re Marriage of Morris, 588 S.W.2d 39 (Mo. 1979)
Moss v. Moss, 80 Mich. App. 693, 264 N.W.2d 97 (1978)
Mueller v. Mueller, 144 Cal. App. 2d 245, 301 P.2d 90 (1956)
Nail v. Nail, 486 S.W.2d 761 (Supreme Ct. Tex. 1972)
Nehorayoff v. Nehorayoff, 108 Misc. 2d 311, 437 N.Y.S.2d 584 (1981)
O'Brien v. O'Brien, 66 N.Y.2d 576, 489 N.E.2d 712, 498 N.Y.S.2d 743 (1985)
Piscopo v. Piscopo, 232 N.J. Super. 559, 557 A.2d 1040 (1989)
Powell v. Powell, 231 Kan. 456, 648 P.2d 218 (1982)
Prosser v. Prosser, 156 Neb. 629, 57 N.W.2d 173 (1953)
In Re Marriage of Rives, 130 Cal. App. 3d 138, 181 Cal. Rptr. 572 (1982)
In Re Marriage of Rubenstein, 145 Ill. App. 3d 31, 495 N.E.2d 659 (1986)
In Re Marriage of Sharp, 143 Cal. App. 3d 714, 192 Cal. Rptr. 97 (1983)
In Re Marriage of Slater, 100 Cal. App. 3d 241, 160 Cal. Rptr. 686 (1979)
In Re Marriage of Slivka, 183 Cal. App. 3d 159, 228 Cal. Rptr. 76 (1986)
Spaulding v. Benenati, 57 N.Y.2d 418, 442 N.E.2d 1244, 456 N.Y.S.2d 733 (1982)
Stern v. Stern, 66 N.J. 340, 331 A.2d 257 (1975)
Stevens v. Stevens, 23 Ohio St. 3d 115, 492 N.E.2d 131 (1986)
Stolowitz v. Stolowitz, 106 Misc. 2d 853, 435 N.Y.S.2d 882 (1980)
In Re Marriage of Sullivan, 134 Cal. App. 3d 634, 184 Cal. Rptr. 796 (1982)
Todd v. Todd, 272 Cal. App. 2d 401, 75 Cal. Rptr. 735 (1969)
Van Bussum v. Van Bussum, 728 S.W.2d 538 (Ky. App. 1987)
In Re Marriage of White, 98 Ill. App. 3d 380, 424 N.E.2d 421 (1981)
Wisner v. Wisner, 129 Ariz. 333, 631 P.2d 115 (1981)
Woodworth v. Woodworth, 126 Mich. App. 258, 337 N.W.2d 332 (1983)

23

MARITAL DISSOLUTION: TRACING AND APPORTIONMENT OF ASSETS

Cathy Partmann Ravano, CPA
Donald L. Gursey, CPA

INTRODUCTION

Forensic accountants practicing in community property states are frequently asked (in conjunction with legal counsel) to characterize property acquired by a couple during marriage. This complex task is compounded by issues of property acquired prior to marriage and property acquired by gift during marriage. Furthermore, each state defines its own method of characterization in the state's statutes and case law. Readers must carefully research every characterization-related engagement; the case law addressing the issues discussed in this chapter changes often.

Property may be characterized as community (or marital), separate, both community and separate, and quasi-community property. The following definitions may help to clarify such confusing nomenclature:

Community Property

Property, both real and personal, acquired through purchase by a couple while married and while domiciled in a community property or marital property state. The philosophy from which this broad definition of community property descends is found in Ballinger's "A Treatise on the Property Rights of Husband and Wife under the Community or Financial System"[1] and is as follows:

> The principal which lies at the foundation of the whole system is, that whatever is acquired by the joint efforts of the husband and wife, shall be their common property; the theory of the law being, that the marriage, in respect to the property acquired during its existence, is a community of which each spouse is a member, equally contributing by his or her industry to its prosperity, and possessing an equal right to succeed to the property after its dissolution, in case one survived the other.

Separate Property

Property acquired through purchase (or inheritance and gift) that is not community property, with the exception of quasi-community property or some other form of concurrent ownership between the couple.

Quasi-Community Property

Mainly defined by California and Arizona, this is property acquired by a current California or Arizona resident, while a nonresident of those states. The property must qualify as community property in all other respects. This includes any property exchanged for property previously classified as quasi-community property. To classify property as quasi-community in a divorce proceeding, the spouses must reside in a state that recognizes quasi-community property, and the moving party must file for divorce in that state's court.

The portion of this definition that frequently results in litigation and that leads to tracing of assets is the interpretation of the term *acquired*. Traditionally, property purchased during marriage acquires a character identical to that of the funds that purchased it. Identifying the source of the original funds frequently requires tracing.

The "domicile" issue raises additional questions regarding jurisdiction and ultimately the possible recharacterization of property held by a married couple. Domicile is a legal issue that addresses the individual's residency in terms of both physical presence and the intent to continue living in that particular state. The couple's domicile at the time of purchase dictates which state's laws characterize the property; however, the couple's domicile at the time of a spouse's death or a divorce *could* reclassify the property. Individual state laws define domicile as it affects property held by a married couple, even when the couple has moved from one community property state to another.

Property does not need to be classified until a spouse dies or the couple seeks a divorce. At that time, the ability to create community property ceases. Problems that may arise from classifying property while both parties are alive and still married include creditor rights and the individual's liabilities, tax implications, management and control of property, personal injury proceeds, life insurance, property improvements, and postseparation increases in value.

TRACING, COMMINGLING, TITLE AND APPORTIONMENT: AN OVERVIEW

Tracing, commingling, and apportionment are case-driven judicial principles used to identify the separate or community portion of assets. these principles are usually invoked when simply applying legal presumptions leads to inequitable results.

This overview will assume that the property referred to has not been given to the other spouse as either a gift or pursuant to a contractual agreement. Having confirmed this qualification, the forensic accountant must ascertain the character of each property held by the two individuals, regardless of the form of the title and the accompanying presumptions. The procedures to ascertain the source of funds used to purchase the property are called *tracing*.

Separate property is usually acquired by exchanging other separate property so that the acquired property retains the original property's character. Likewise, exchanging solely community property for other property would characterize the newly acquired property as community property. There may exist a *rebuttable* presumption in community property states that classify property. When the source is traceable to separate property, the emphasis generally rests on the original source of the funds rather than the acquisition's timing—the "where" rather than the "when." Some states, however, do not always allow tracing to the original source to classify community property. Circumstances often obscure part or all of the original source of funds. In such a case, the forensic accountant emphasizes the acquisition's timing—the "when" rather than the "where."

If the separate property source is not identified and the purchase occurred during marriage, the court presumes a community property classification. Some states, however, either through statute or case law, allow reimbursement—to the extent of the investment—to the spouse who invested separate property in an asset that is classified as community property.

Separate property mixed with alleged community property creates *commingled property*. Identifying the separate and community portions of this property challenges any forensic accountant. The methods for treating alleged separate property interest that has been labeled as community property are varied, complicated, and receive different emphasis from each state.

States generally hold that the form of title at the time of establishing ownership is the determining factor regarding the property's characterization. Many states, however, have case law that considers substance rather than the form of ownership in dividing property. There, the burden of proof rests on the party claiming an ownership form differing from that listed on existing property records. In addition, the states do not uniformly regard the static nature of the property's original characterization. For instance, if property purchased before marriage is not encumbrance-free at the time of marriage and community funds reduce the encumbrance during marriage, the property's ownership includes an interest vested in the community regardless of the title's original form. Improvements made to the separate property from community property funds or community effort may also cloud the classification.

The theory of *apportionment* also offers potential problems in identifying the property's character. This theory recognizes not only separate and community funds or property used for initial purchase but also possible fluctuation in the proportionate separate and community ownership. The apportionment theory adjusts the ownership proportions to reflect separate and community funds used to reduce the original encumbrance; it also changes the proportions to reflect improvements or additions to the original property from either source.

COMMINGLING: PRESUMPTIONS

Commingling combines community property with separate property during marriage. Basic commingling rules can help ascertain at least the initial characterization of the commingled assets. One generally presumes that when separate and community property have been so extensively commingled that one cannot trace the separate property interest, the alleged separate property interest ceases to exist, thus characterizing the entire commingled property as community property (*Estate of Cudworth*, 133 Cal. 462, 65 P. 1091 (1901)). The basic commingling rule does not apply when the community property component comprises a small part of the total property. In such cases, the entire asset will be deemed as separate property.

FORM OF TITLE

Although an asset's character is set at acquisition, the form of ownership (title) does not prove conclusively that an asset is separate, community, or quasi-community. States such as Louisiana, Texas, and New Mexico allow the form of ownership at the acquisition date to become static unless title is changed by law, gift, or transmutation. This generally holds true regardless of improvements made to the original property and payments made on the original separate property from funds that are not the title holder's separate property. In many jurisdictions the commingling rules defer to title when the couple has taken title as community property or if they agreed (in writing or orally) that the asset was community property. The states vary as to whether the agreement must be written.

PROPORTIONATE OWNERSHIP

If one can establish (trace) the separate and community property interest, the community property presumption relating to the commingled property usually does not apply, and the established nature of each interest remains intact. This creates an ownership proportionate to the percentage of interest that each different asset used to acquire the asset in question bears to the total asset. Most of the states subscribe to this co-ownership form, but individual state's laws should be checked. Some states do not allow apportioning of certain types of commingled properties. The asset's appreciation and depreciation during ownership must be allocated to the community property and separate property components.

GAIN AND INCOME

Applying the proportionate ownership interest theory is further complicated by jurisdictional differences in the treatment of an asset's natural appreciation, its income, its purchase from the income of another proportionately owned asset, and an increase in the asset's value through the community's effort. Generally, community property states do not agree on changes in the proportionate ownership of an asset by a married couple. Also, federal and state tax laws' treatment of income does not agree with community property principles, although state laws usually dictate the community property or separate nature of income for federal tax purposes.

Theoretically, the community property states each have their own rules regarding community effort and separate property income. In practice, mathematically interpreting and applying these rules is laborious. Generally, the states provide guidance through case law. Texas, Idaho, and Louisiana create community income from some categories of income generated by separate assets during marriage, whereas other income categories may remain as separate property (*Arnold v. Leonard* 114 Tex. 535, 273 S.W. 799 (1925)). The remaining community property states allow income from separate property to retain its separate property character. This "American rule" stems from the 1860 California case, *George v. Ransome* 15 Cal. 322 (1860). The 1979 Arizona case, *Cockrill v. Cockrill* 124 Ariz. 50, 601 P.2d 1334 (1979) has more recently discussed this theory. Little attention has been given to separate property assets such as oil, gas, and timber that generate income that some states classify as community but whose principal value either decreases or is depleted during marriage.

Some uniformity does exist among the community property states, in the assumption that spouses' earnings while married are community property. Consequently, in many jurisdictions, the separate property's increased value attributable to community efforts generates a community interest in the separately owned property. This interest from community efforts is measured aside from any appreciation in the separate property attributed to natural causes. The community property interest equals the portion of the separate property appreciation attributable to the value of the community efforts relative to the separate property's total value. This chapter will discuss specific methods used to apportion the community property interest attributed to community effort in separate property.

TRACING

Finding its source in case law rather than statutes, tracing is a commonly used method to define an asset's original character or to separate or partition assets that have been combined (commingled) during the marriage. Some community property states do not always permit tracing to identify community property interest in separate property. Tracing, however, is the principal procedure to rebut the presumption that property acquired during marriage is automatically community property. Tracing is also used frequently to ascertain the taxability of income items and to distinguish an asset's nature vis-à-vis creditor's claims.

An assets' unmixed character is traceable to the character of the asset that was used for its acquisition. If the tracing process establishes that community assets were used to improve or increase separate property assets, a right of reimbursement may exist, such as that found in California (Civil Code §§ 4800.1 and 4800.2) and Louisiana statutes.

The two established tracing methods are *direct tracing* and *indirect tracing* (family expense method).

DIRECT TRACING

In *direct tracing*, one establishes the source of an asset by recreating the steps through which the asset progresses to its current ownership form. This includes analyzing sales, additional acquisitions, gifts, and the like. One uses tracing to prove that assets can retain their character as separate assets when they are commingled with or enhanced by community property assets. Even when sufficient separate funds were available in the commingled account from which an asset was purchased, it does not always follow that property acquired is separate. In the California case *Hicks*, 211 C. 2d 144 (1962), the court said:

> Separate funds do not lose their character as such when commingled with community funds in a bank account so long as the amount thereof can be ascertained. Whether separate funds so deposited continue to be on deposit when a withdrawal is made from such a bank account for the purpose of purchasing specific property, and whether the intention of the drawer is to withdraw such funds therefrom, are questions of fact for determination by the trial court.

Disposition of the separate funds and the other spouse's acknowledgment of a particular form of ownership may also be required to substantiate this claim.

The following lists some simple examples of postmarital acquired property that retain their character as separate property and rebut the community property presumption:

1. Premarital separate real estate property exchanged for another parcel of real property
2. Premarital asset (separate property) sold and another asset purchased with the same fund
3. Asset received by gift or inheritance by one spouse during the marriage and subsequently sold or exchanged for another asset
4. Income from separate property (in those states where it retains its separate nature) used to purchase an asset during the marriage

These are very elementary examples of the direct tracing of assets acquired during marriage in which one may overcome the presumption that characterizes an asset acquired during marriage in a community property state solely as community property. The examples do not include, however, complicating factors such as how title was held, transmutations, or gifts between spouses during marriage.

INDIRECT TRACING

Indirect tracing, also known as the family expense method, tries to offer as proof of a property's character the depletion of another class of property that the spouse held. For example, one might prove that all the community property funds had been spent on the family's living expenses. By deduction, the remaining property may be concluded to consist of a different property class than that which was dissipated, that is, separate property of one or both spouses. (Hence this tracing method is also known as the "family expense method.") To reiterate, if the court considers earnings as community property and assumes that family living expenses were paid first from these community earnings that have completely dissipated, then any assets acquired must have been acquired from separate property. The following discussion is found in the California case of *See v. See*, 64 Cal.2d 778, 415 P.2d 776, 51 Cal. Rptr. 888 (1966):

> The presumption (of community property) applies when a husband purchases property during the marriage with funds from an undisclosed or disputed source, such as an account or fund in which he has commingled his separate funds with community funds. (*Estate of Neilson*, 57 Cal.2d 773, 742, 371 P.2d 745, 22 Cal. Rptr. 1 (1962). He may trace the source of the property to his separate funds and overcome the presumption with evidence that community expenses exceeded community income *at the time of acquisition*. If he proves that at that time all community income was exhausted by family expenses, he establishes that the property was purchased with separate funds. (*Estate of Neilson*, supra, at p. 742; *Thomasset v. Thomasset*, 122 Cal. App. 2d 116, 127, 264 P.2d 626 (1953)). Only when, through no fault of the husband, it is not possible to ascertain the balance of income and expenditures at the time property was acquired, can recapitulation of the total community expenses and income throughout the marriage be used to establish the character of the property.

Note that in *See*, at p. 785, the court made a statement regarding a theory of reimbursement for community expenses paid from separate property:

> A husband who elects to use his separate property instead of community property to meet community expenses cannot claim reimbursement. In the absence of an agreement to the contrary, the use of his separate property by a husband for community purposes is a gift to the community.

Beam v. Bank of America 6 Cal.3d 12, 490 P.2d 257, 98 Cal. Rptr. 137 (1971) further limits the scope set forth in *See* to those circumstances when total family living expenses can be compared to total community income. the court in *Beam* stated that when excess community income was available and this income was commingled with separate income, assets purchased with those commingled funds are usually considered community assets.

COMMINGLED BANK ACCOUNTS

In addition to indirectly tracing funds through the community expense method, practitioners use other methods:

1. A chronological schedule of the deposits and withdrawals from the fund. This system applies the first-in, first-out theory to the funds analyzed.
2. The spouse who does not control the funds traces specific deposits to the commingled account. This would possibly set forth a separate property interest in the funds themselves.
3. The spouse without control of the funds establishes a claim against the funds by tracing funds directly through the account to the purchased assets. This may prove a separate ownership interest in the asset.

CREDIT PURCHASES

Borrower collateral, lender intention, and the source of payments are three areas that one should examine to establish separate or community property interests in an asset purchased using credit during marriage. As is true of other tracing methods, little consistency exists among the community property jurisdictions in treating such acquisitions. The signatures on the loan documents and the manner in which title is held are not always conclusive factors in establishing separate versus community ownership.

One complication occurs when separate property provides the down payment for an asset. The collateral used to secure the credit is separate property, but the loan payments come from community property funds. Some community property states do not recognize the payments made toward reducing the debt as establishing a community property interest but look solely to the assets' characterization when the original purchase occurred. Some of the more enlightened community property states, however, recently have used apportionment in these situations.

TRANSMUTATIONS

Transmutations are voluntary gift-related or contractual changes in the form of property ownership between spouses. This may apply to current assets or to future assets such as earnings. A transmutation of earnings for community property purposes does not change the federal tax treatment of those earnings (*Lucas v. Earl*, 281 U.S. 111 (1930)). Transmutations may change separate property of one spouse to separate property of the other spouse, separate property to community property, and community property to separate property of either or both spouses. As clear as this theory's application appears to be, the individual community property jurisdictions have inconsistently interpreted and imposed restraints on transmutations. The practitioner needs to know the laws of each community property state related to applying the transmutation doctrine.

APPORTIONMENT

The "inception-of-title" doctrine states that the property's title at acquisition does not change to reflect additional contributions or improvements made after the purchase. This underlying doctrine often forces the courts to consider the extensive commingling of separate and community funds used to purchase an asset and/or make payments on credit. Frequently, courts have had to take a position regarding improvements made to separate property assets through community efforts (service).

One must distinguish between apportionment and the right to reimbursement. When property is acquired from both community and separate property, the acquired property's ownership is proportionate. This *rule of apportionment* creates a dual ownership that fluctuates frequently during marriage. Conversely, the *rule of reimbursement* dictates that when improvements are made from one categorized property (i.e., community property) to property categorized in another manner (i.e., separate property), the party or parties making the improvements may be entitled to reimbursement of their funds so used.

DEFINITION

Apportionment establishes ownership by applying the percentage that the separate and community investments bear to the total investment. For example, if tracing established that the husband had $20,000 of separate property, the wife had $10,000 of separate property, and the community had excess receipts over expenses of $20,000, and all these funds were invested in an asset, the property would be owned as follows:

Husband's separate property	$20,000	40%
Wife's separate property	$10,000	20%
Community property	$20,000	40%
Total investment	$50,000	100%

Any additions to the investment after the initial purchase would alter the ownership percentages accordingly.

One of the most frequently litigated area in marital dissolution occurs when one spouse had separate property investments or a separate property business before marriage and the business or property value increased during marriage due to the personal efforts of either or both spouses. Under these circumstances, some courts try to establish a method of carving out a portion of the value increase for which the community should be compensated because of the services rendered. The major difficulty lies in measuring the value or worth of the community services versus the inherent increase in the investments or business value. The courts in community property states have addressed this problem and varied greatly in their findings, not only among the states, but also within each state.

California has had numerous cases that deal with apportionment. Two landmark California cases continue to be relied on both within and without the state: *Pereira v. Pereira*, 156 Cal. 1, 103 P.488 (1909) and *Van Camp v. Van Camp*, 53 Cal. App. 17, 199 P.885 (1921).

In *Pereira*, the court decided "to allocate a fair return on the (husband's separate property) investment (as separate income) and to allocate any excess to the community property as arising from the husband's efforts" (*Estate of Neilson*, 57 Cal.2d 733, 740 (1962)). This emphasized community labor's primary importance for the separate property's growth during marriage. Conversely, in *Van Camp*, the court concentrated on the original capital and its natural growth as the major factor in the growth of the separate business. Thus, assuming the community was fairly compensated for the working spouse's efforts, all appreciation would be separate.

As stated in *Tassi v. Tassi*, 160 Cal. App. 2d 680, 690, 325 P.2d 872 (1958), the court wanted "to determine the reasonable value of the husband's services. . ., allocate that amount as community property, and treat the balance as separate property attributable to the normal earnings of the [separate estate]." although the courts rely heavily on the first two formulas, even in California they are not obligated to use either formula. The courts of New Mexico, Nevada, and Arizona regularly and uniformly apply formulas specified in these cases. The following discussion applies the *Pereira* and *Van Camp* rules to a hypothetical scenario.

SCENARIO

The husband had a separate property corporation prior to marriage, with a value on the wedding date of $50,000. The marriage lasted 7 years, and at the separation date the business was worth $100,000. The husband had worked full-time in his business during the marriage and received an annual salary of $60,000. In the divorce proceedings, the wife includes in her alleged community property a portion of the business value increase during the marriage, claiming that the husband's labors in his business during the marriage were community property.

APPLICATION OF THE "*PEREIRA* RULE"

The theory behind the *Pereira* Rule rests on a principle of reimbursements and not on the estimated fair value of the husband's services to the separate property business.[2] Accordingly, the courts would apply a fair rate of return to the value of the husband's separate property business at the time of marriage without ascertaining whether the husband's salary during marriage had adequately compensated the community. Assuming a 6-percent rate of return on the corporation, the court would allocate as the husband's separate property $21,000 of the $50,000 value increase during marriage. The remaining appreciation of $29,000 would be attributable to the community efforts of the husband in the business during the marriage. The wife would receive one-half of this $29,000 community property interest, or $14,500.

APPLICATION OF THE "*VAN CAMP* RULE"

Under the *Van Camp* Rule, the court would place a reasonable or adequate compensation test on the husband's services to the corporation during marriage. If the husband was adequately compensated during marriage and/or did not contribute highly specialized skills to the business, all of the corporation's growth would be allocated to the separate property investment in the business. The community would have no interest in the increase in value during marriage.

ADDITIONAL POSSIBILITIES UNDER THE "*VAN CAMP* RULE"

Alternative 1

Assume that the court finds that the husband should have received an average annual compensation of $65,000. Because the husband received an average annual salary of $60,000, an underpayment of $5000 per year or $35,000 occurred. A court applying the *Van Camp* Rule—and believing that the husband could control his salary level—could allocate the $35,000 salary "underpayment" top community property. The wife's share would be one-half of the $35,000, or $17,500. the husband would claim as separate property $15,000 ($50,000 less $35,000) of the corporation's appreciation during marriage. This approach would allocate $14,000 less in separate property appreciation to the husband than he would have received under the *Pereira* Rule.

Alternative 2

Assume that the court finds that the husband should have received an average annual salary of $40,000. Theoretically, the community was overcompensated by an average of $20,000 per year for the 7 years of marriage, or $140,000. Because the community was more than adequately compensated for services during marriage, the growth in the business was generated from the husband's separate property investment. No precedent exists, however, for the separate property holder to claim reimbursement from the community for this excess compensation.

These apportionment principles derived from the landmark California cases, logical or not, have not been adopted by Texas or by Washington. Texas has chosen a system that individually categorizes income and gain items. These categories have evolved from case law. Once the items have been categorized, the Texas courts make an all-or-nothing determination as to rights of ownership. This approach completely ignores apportionment, although, in *Jensen v. Jensen*, 665 S.W.2d 107 (Tex. 1984), a theory of reimbursement has been set forth:

> . . . the reimbursement theory more nearly affords justice to both the community and separate estates. This theory requires adoption of the rule that the community will be reimbursed for the value of time and effort expended by either or both spouses to enhance the separate estate of either, other than that reasonably necessary to manage and preserve the separate estate in the form of salary, bonus, dividends and other fringe benefits, these items being community property when received . . .

Washington also generally does not apply the rules of apportionment unless the spouses have previously agreed to do so. If the separate property business is incorporated, Washington has ruled that the corporation's earnings remain separate property, expect for the salary paid to the working spouse or spouses (*Pollock v. Pollock*, 7 Wash. App. 394, 499 P.2d 231 (1972)).

APPORTIONMENT: SEPARATE DEBT PAID WITH COMMUNITY FUNDS

Frequently, a spouse brings to the marriage separate property with an accompanying encumbrance. Payments may be made on this debt during the marriage from the title holder's separate funds or from community funds. California case law has developed formulas that approach this situation in a commonsense manner.

In *In re Marriage of Moore*, 28 Cal.3d 366, 615 P.2d 208, 168 Cal. Rptr. 662 (1980), the wife purchased a residence shortly before marriage. The mortgage was paid both from her separate funds and from community funds during the marriage. To establish the community interest in the wife's separate property residence, the California Supreme Court applied the following formula:

Mortgage *principal* payments made from community property	÷	Total purchase price	=	Percentage of community interest

Any appreciation in the asset's value is multiplied by the percentage of community interest measured by this formula to calculate the community interest in the appreciation. this community interest in the asset's appreciation, when added to the community principal payments made (the numerator) results in the total community property value in the separate property assets. Note that this computation ignores interest payments, taxes, and any maintenance payments made by the community.

The 1982 case *In re Marriage of Marsden*, 133 Cal. App. 3d 426, 181 Cal. Rptr. 910 (1982) clarified the formula developed in *Moore*. (The additional clarification was needed because of the short time period that the separate property was held prior to marriage in *Moore*.) In *Marsden*, the court applied the formula's community interest percentage only to the appreciation during marriage. All appreciation before the marriage was allocated to the purchaser spouse's separate property interest.

REIMBURSEMENT

Three situations cause one spouse to seek reimbursement from the other spouse: the use of separate property to improve community property, the use of community property to improve separate property, and the use of one spouse's separate property to improve the other spouse's separate property.

Because most community property states lean toward community property status of asset, the use of separate property to improve community property had been most frequently viewed as a gift to the community. Amid much uncertainty and controversy, however, California adopted Civil Code § 4800.2 in 1983. This statute provides for reimbursement for any separate property expenditures made to acquire or improve a community property during marriage. The statute does not provide for interest or appreciation on this separate property. Several aspects of this statute have been and continue to be further defined by cases. Much of the controversy has centered around the timing of the rule's application. One must carefully research the current status of the section before applying the general rule. Other community property states may eventually readdress reimbursement as a result of this California legislation.

Improvement of separate property of one spouse with separate property of the other spouse falls outside the general community property rules. A transmutation of this nature has a strong presumption of being a gift in most community property states.

One spouse's use of community funds to improve his or her separate property falls under the reimbursement and apportionment theories.

CONCLUSION

State law identifies the principles to be applied when an issue exists as to the property's character. In most states that have apportionment, commingling and tracing issues, counsel must prove the property's character based on the principles that support the clients' contentions, whereas the duty to maintain meticulous books and records rests with the litigant claiming separate property.

The accountant has to apply the principles underlying state law and use the books and records of the litigants assisting counsel either to establish or rebut a claim of apportionment, commingling, or any form of transmutation. Whatever the result, no perfect or consistent method applies to every case.

NOTES

1. R.A. Ballinger, *Ballinger on Community Property*, Bancroft-Whitney, 1985.
2. The *Pereira* case provided for a simple interest rate of return pursuant to stipulation by the parties. Presently, the application of either a simple or a compound rate is up to the discretion of the court. Either method may be used in order to obtain substantial justice.

LIST OF CASES

Arnold v. Leonard, 114 Tex. 535, 273 S.W. 799 (1925)
Beam v. Bank of America, 6 Cal. 3d 12, 490 P.2d 257, 98 Cal. Rptr. 137 (1971)
Cockrill v. Cockrill, 124 Ariz. 50, 601 P.2d 1334 (1979)
Estate of Cudworth, 133 Cal. 462, 65 P. 1041 (1901)
George v. Ransom, 15 Cal. 322 (1860)
Jensen v. Jensen, 655 S.W.2d 107 (Tex. 1984)
Lucas v. Earl, 281 U.S. 111 (1930)
In Re Marriage of Marsden, 133 Cal. App. 3d 426, 181 Cal. Rptr. 910 (1982)
In Re Marriage of Moore, 28 Cal. 3d 366, 615 P.2d 208, 168 Cal. Rptr. 662 (1980)
Estate of Neilson, 57 Cal. 2d 733, 371 P.2d 745, 22 Cal. Rptr. 1 (1962)
Pereira v. Pereira, 156 Cal. 1, 103 P. 488 (1909)
Pollock v. Pollock, 7 Wash. App. 394, 499 P.2d 231 (1972)
See v. See, 64 Cal. 2d 778, 415 P.2d 776, 51 Cal. Rptr. 888 (1966)
Tassi v. Tassi, 160 Cal. App. 2d 680, 325 P.2d 872 (1958)
Thomasset v. Thomasset, 122 Cal. App. 2d 116, 264 P.2d 626 (1953)
Van Camp v. Van Camp, 53 Cal. App. 17, 199 P. 885 (1921)

24

MARITAL DISSOLUTION: PSYCHOLOGICAL ASPECTS

Melvin A. Schiller, CPA

INTRODUCTION

The accounting profession's expertise and discipline place CPAs in a unique role to assist legal counsel and their clients in obtaining an equitable apportionment of marital assets and liabilities. The practitioner's adherence to the independent and objective standards should be beyond reproach. An experienced forensic accountant in a marital dissolution action must also avoid emotional involvement in the competition between attorneys and the emotional distress arising from the end of a marriage.

Under the judicial system, marital dissolutions are adversary matters. The respective legal counsel enter the arena as advocates to fight for their clients' rights and interests. Unfortunately, this adversarial position causes emotional tension even between professionals.

In addition to the trauma created by the attorneys' actions, the principals are in emotional distress. The CPAs serve best by not adding fuel to the principals' disagreements and the competitive spirit between legal counsel.

Forensic accountants will necessarily encounter the nonclient spouse and legal counsel under adverse circumstance and may even experience conflicts with his own client. The ability to avoid participating in or aggravating the emotional problems increase with the experience gained in this specialty field.

The friendly divorce is myth and rarely occurs. Forensic accounting excludes the sorrows of child welfare or custody battles and instead centers on equitably apportioning the marital assets and liabilities and dealing with spousal and child support.

Not every marital dissolution engagement embodies all facets of the CPA's work program. This chapter describes possible encounters and recommended treatment of parties to avoid further impairing their relationship or adding to the existing discord.

INITIAL MEETING WITH ATTORNEY

The attorney becomes familiar with both the financial aspects of the marital estate and the emotional status of the parties prior to meeting with the CPA. The attorney's evaluation of the principals' personalities will materially assist the CPA in pursuing and completing the engagement. Conferences with the attorney should be purposeful and offer a sense of accomplishment and direction. The accountant should obtain explicit instructions and an understanding of the task at hand. The following issues should be covered at this time: scope of engagement, billings, timing of engagement, and discovery procedure.

The accountant should be conscientiously thorough without overworking the engagement. This initial meeting establishes the assignment's phases, which will be subsequently set forth in an engagement letter.

The accountant and attorney should agree as to the one billed and the one responsible for making payments. (A later section more fully addresses billing and collection.)

Attorneys seek the services of forensic accountants upon perceiving such a need. Experienced attorneys will immediately solicit such assistance to achieve a team effort.

The client should be informed of the potential benefits and costs incurred by the attorney to obtain expert help.

Be wary of an attorney's requesting priority services just before trial. Such tactics breed client discord, disruption of office routine, inaccurate findings, billing disputes, and disruption of other client and nonclient commitments.

The most efficient assignment for accountants employs formal discovery, via depositions, document production requests and, at times, interrogatories. Some attorneys prefer informal discovery whereby the accountants have more personal contact with the nonclient spouse and agents. The accountants must avoid creating animosities in such dealings and will have such informal contacts only under express instructions from the attorney.

An unduly extended discovery period can add to the parties' anxieties and probably result in unreasonably high fees. Accountants share an obligation with the attorney to use their expertise efficiently. Continuous contact with the client and attorney to obtain information and documentation needed to complete the engagement is a solution. An accountant accepting such an assignment should conscientiously start and finish it within a reasonable time period.

CLIENT MEETINGS

The accountant and the attorney, as professionals, have experience in other similar cases. One job ends and then the next one begins. This is not true of the client spouse. The interview will be with a distressed individual who has gone through a hellish period, possibly embodying recriminations, arguments, threats of economic deprivation, bodily harm, fear of a mental breakdown, and other worries. Suicidal tendencies sometimes accompany severing marital ties.

Avoid becoming engaged in emotional discussions. The attorney has responsibility to obtain properly designated medical professionals as warranted by the circumstances. The accountant should avoid these discussions entirely.

The CPA should explain fees to the client spouse. Some CPAs do not choose to bill for the initial interview, thus enabling the client and the accounting firm to make an impartial decision about retention without financial coercion related to such costs.

Avoid clients seeking to get even with the despicable spouse, regardless of cost. Those assignments often increase uncollectible fees receivable.

The client's state of mind and continuing mental turmoil must be considered during subsequent meetings. The client has acquired a team of experts and may view any grandiose promises as gospel. Guard against such tactics by adhering to the professional role of reporting unbiased facts and carefully rendering opinions. Financial and mental repercussions occur when clients realize that they were led down the primrose path by professionals promising more than could be delivered. It leaves the client with the stigma that the other spouse was the "winner."

MEETINGS WITH THE NONCLIENT SPOUSE AND/ OR AGENTS

During the case, the CPA will directly contact the other spouse or the spouse's agents, or both. This individual has a team of professionals ready to do battle and understand the accountant's adversarial role.

The painstaking process of severing marital ties eventually focuses on economics. One cannot be faulted for seeking maximum benefits and financial superiority over one's ex-spouse.

Naturally, the nonclient spouse may view the accountant's efforts with anger, suspicion, and hostility. Such emotional distress is expected, and accountants should not try to distort their client's position. A job well done will engender respect for the accountant's efforts.

Accountants must remain vigilant during any discussions with the nonclient spouse or attorney, and these conversations should occur only in the client–attorney's presence. The attorney may use random statements for impeachment at trial.

During discovery, the forensic accountants will probably confer on findings to decide where agreement or disagreement exists on financial issues. Comments against the client will be carried to the attorney and used at trial. Conversely, such conferences may offer opportunities to elicit tactical information for the benefit of one's client. In general, such meetings are not recommended and, in any case, should involve the opposing attorneys as well.

SETTLEMENT NEGOTIATIONS

Out-of-court settlements dividing the marital assets and liabilities and seeking agreements on other issues have emerged as more attractive than trials for reaching conclusion, allowing the principals to embark upon their new lives. This procedure avoids (1) lengthy and expensive trials, (2) the possibility of trial postponements due either to busy court calendars or a shortage of judges, and (3) the further delays of appeals from the court's decision.

The goal is to attain a reasonable settlement based on all known facts and opinions via negotiating on the strengths and weaknesses of respective positions. Experience teaches that in marital dissolutions a reasonable settlement is preferable to the emotionally destructive and expensive days of trial. A dispassionate but overworked judge of moderate intelligence may not render findings and decisions superior to those achieved by interested professionals and principals willing to negotiate a settlement.

Some attorneys have learned to complement their own skills with those of an accountant in negotiating. The team may practice beforehand, arguing the issues and even using a good-guy–bad-guy approach. Some attorneys request the accountant to assume leadership in conversation, freeing the attorneys to contemplate, evaluate, and prepare for the next strategic move.

Because settlement negotiations and discussions cannot be introduced at trial, forensic accountants can practice advocacy at this time without corrupting their status as expert witnesses at trial. Such advocacy statements, to be effective, must be tempered with good judgment, be constructive, and not conflict with a CPA's overriding ethical standards.

The settlement approach succeeds only when both parties and their agents deal in good faith. Settlement offers using scare tactics often lead to the courtroom.

The attorney and forensic accountant are outsiders, retained to recommend how former partners will permanently divide their worldly possessions and make future cash transfers between each other. The accountant should try to empathize with the parties and consider their inner turmoil raised by requiring professional outsiders to accomplish what they cannot.

How can the forensic accountant best serve the client in negotiations? The accountant will gather data and form opinions over weeks or months and will capsulize them for use by the attorney who pursues settlement on all issues over one or two days. The CPA and lawyer should attend to the following issues.

1. The attorneys should gather data about all assets and liabilities of the marital estate, regardless of materiality.
2. The attorneys should comprehend and discuss income tax ramifications.
3. The accountants should review the marital settlement agreement on financial issues to ascertain whether the written agreement conforms to the understanding.

RULE OF CONFIDENTIALITY

CPAs designated as expert witnesses do not have the right to keep materials confidential. The opposition can discover writings, workpapers, and conversations.

The CPA, retained as consultant rather than expert witness, is not subject to discovery. The loss of privilege probably is retroactive to the start of the engagement; if the role changes from consultant to expert witness, then all documents and conversations may become discoverable.

Accountants may unwittingly injure their client and their own credibility with written opinions or memoranda unsupportable by facts. Anticipate that the opposition will scrutinize all written documents.

INDEPENDENCE AND OBJECTIVITY

The forensic accountant must attend to professional ethics. Although lawyers and parties to the action are expected to maintain a bias favoring the client, accountants enhance their professional reputation by resisting the "hired gun" status. However, accountants owe no obligation to assist the nonclient spouse other than to divulge their findings at time of interrogation. The accountant is obligated to render opinions as an expert to assist the court in its determinations and not simply be the conduit for overzealous or overreaching attorneys or their clients.

Court judges who regularly hear marital matters discuss cases with one another and can filter out the biased accountants and their testimony. In one case, while under cross-examination, an accountant admitted that his client had instructed him to use a liquidation valuation, rather than a fair market value. The court struck all of his testimony from the record.

BILLING AND COLLECTING FEES

Marital dissolution engagements often present collection problems. Thus many CPA firms restrict their forensic accounting practices to commercial litigation. For those specializing in dissolutions, the following guidelines may enhance collections:

1. Meet the client and attorney at the beginning of the engagement to discuss the CPA's responsibilities relating to discovery and trial.
2. Explain the types of service fees and costs for which the client will be obligated to pay and set these forth in the engagement letter.
3. Clearly explain that CPA firms are prohibited from entering into contingency fee arrangements under Rule 402 of the AICPA Professional Rules of Conduct and that they are not financing institutions. Opposing counsel can claim advocacy, where large unpaid fees exist, to challenge the expert's credibility at trial.
4. The emotional turmoil affects clients immersed in the dissolution of a marriage. An accountant should explain all the potential costs and benefits of special tasks when laying out the scope of the engagement with the attorney and client. Discussions should include whether the results will justify the costs.
5. Plan to send monthly or biweekly itemized billings to inform the client on a current basis of the assignment's progress. (Such itemizations of services are discoverable.)
6. Insist on periodic retainers against billings, at least quarterly, but better yet monthly.

PART FIVE

DAMAGES

25

AN OVERVIEW OF THE ACCOUNTANT'S ROLE IN ASSESSING DAMAGES

John J. Costello, CPA
Vincent J. Love, CPA

Lawyers use experts to prove or disprove the amount of damages in civil law cases. Both the plaintiff and the defendant require expert advice, the plaintiff in constructing the damage claim and the defendant in evaluating the claim, identifying its flaws, and possibly devising an alternative amount based on different assumptions or methods.

Because of their experience with the financial aspects of business, accountants often fill the need for an expert on damages. Most cases can be handled by one or two accountants. Sometimes, however, the sheer volume of the damage calculations requires a large accounting firm because it can marshal staff all over the country. Consider the size of the IBM antitrust litigation of the 1970s or the AT&T divestiture proceedings of the 1980s. Quite often, large cases can require a team of experts to work on damage computations—economists, computer programmers, industrial engineers, statisticians, both practitioners and theorists.

Sometimes a case will call for an accountant who specializes in a particular industry. For example, cases involving mineral rights and production royalties often require specialized knowledge about the industry and its accounting practices. In natural gas production, for example, contracts often specify different royalty percentages for each of several end products, as each end product has different costs and a different level of profitability. A lawyer considering damage calculations in such a case needs a specialist who is familiar both with the complex cost techniques that are peculiar to gas production and also with the engineering matters of balancing the costs of producing each particular end product.

WHAT THE CPA DOES

Usually employed by the attorney, the CPA functions as a consultant or as an expert witness or both. Expert accountants learn to be expert witnesses by becoming familiar with court procedures and by getting practice in presenting complex ideas simply (see Chapter 5). The task of assessing damages is similar to examining a business operation—getting a picture of the whole environment, requesting the documents that provide the right data, and identifying the relevant information from the mass of data.

The lawyer figures out how to prove or disprove liability, whereas the CPA helps the lawyer calculate how much the liability is worth. The CPA also may help prove that the actions of one party did or did not cause damage to the other party, and CPAs who are experts in interpreting business facts can be of use, for example, in helping to establish liability, such as whether the defendant has engaged in predatory pricing. To show predatory pricing requires proving that a defendant's prices were below some stipulated legal definition of average costs. As experts in costs, accountants can offer lawyers help in measuring costs and in proving whether or not the defendant's prices fall within this definition.

The CPA who is establishing or rebutting a damage claim must not only analyze numbers but must also understand the assumptions that support those numbers. Expert accountants know what business documents contain information relevant to the claim.

Finally, the expert accountant can offer a lawyer an objective view of the case. Lawyers need to know both the strengths and the weaknesses of their client's positions before they go to court. Independent experts can provide an objective assessment of damage. The client's internal accountants can do the job, but it is harder for them to be objective. Independent accountants will have more credibility on the witness stand because of their independence.

THE BASICS OF DAMAGE COMPUTATIONS

The accountant can help the lawyer choose a strategy or an approach to assess damages that fits the particular case. There are some general methods but no set formulas.

Damage analysis involves expertise beyond that of the traditional audit engagement and relies heavily upon the imagination and creativity of the accountant. In a lawsuit, the usual paper trail is often nonexistent or incomplete. CPAs usually audit completed transactions, rather than deal with the "what-if" situations required in constructing or attacking damage claims. The expert will often have to develop figures that describe hypothetical situations: What might have happened if, for instance, prices had not been fixed, or if there had been no delay in the contract? The expert who is engaged to prepare a damage claim needs also to anticipate the approaches that the opponent's accountant is likely to use.

A good damage strategy requires imagination. There are some common methods of calculating damages, but they seldom will apply exactly to any particular case. The facts will determine the damage strategy. In formulating a damage strategy, one should try to push beyond the perceptual and conceptual blocks of habit.

Damage models attempt to measure losses. The alleged loss of a plaintiff can take many forms. Generally speaking, the plaintiff who wins a case can recover actual out-of-pocket losses, plus "reasonably foreseeable" or "but-for" losses to the business or property. That is, "but for" the actions of the defendant, the plaintiff would have made a specified "reasonably foreseeable" amount. These "but for" losses generally include any or all of the following: increased costs, lost profits, and decrease in the value of the investment. Often one of these methods for calculation of damages is used in conjunction with both or one of the other two.

Increased Costs

Increased costs often are at issue in price-fixing cases in which the defendant's actions caused the plaintiff to pay more for goods or services. Computing "increased cost" may be straightforward. First find the difference between the inflated price and the price that would have been paid had it not been for the defendant's actions. Then multiply the result by the quantity of items purchased.

Thus the formula is simply the difference in *price times quantity*. But in some cases, the volume of transactions involved can be quite large. Increased costs may not fully measure plaintiff's damages, if higher costs had led to reduced volume. A consideration of elasticities might lead to additional damages under the theory of lost profits.

Lost Profits

The plaintiff's loss is normal profit per unit times the number of units it would have sold "but for" the defendant's actions. There are three commonly used methods of calculating lost profits.

The Before-and-After Method. This method compares the plaintiff's profits (or units sold or prices) before the defendant's actions with its profits (or prices or units sold) after the defendant's actions. The information would come from the plaintiff's own business records. This method can fail to consider the possibility of increases in profits or units sold that exceed historic performance levels.

The Yardstick Method. Using as a "yardstick" a similar company, set of operations, or data series not affected by the defendant's actions, this method compares the yardstick's sales, profits, market share, or other relevant indicator during the relevant period with those of the plaintiff. Problems arise from the difficulties in establishing the validity of the comparisons because it is rare, for example, that any two companies are exactly alike.

The Market Share Method. This method calculates the effect of defendant's actions on the plaintiff's share of the market. A loss in market share is converted into the volume that would have been sold "but for" the defendant's actions. These market share effects, of course, may be difficult to establish.

Decrease in the Value of the Investment or Business

This aspect of damages measures the decline in the value of the plaintiff's business. The damages are the difference between the value of the business before and after the actions of the defendant. Although it may be easy to evaluate the business *after* the defendant's action, it is rare that the business will have been evaluated just before the defendant's action.

Evaluating Plaintiff's Damage Calculation

It is easier to critique a damage claim than to construct one. The more complicated the claim, the larger the likely number of assumptions and potential weak points. If one is constructing a claim, it pays to look at it critically, anticipating the arguments of the opposition.

Accountants are often asked to examine a plaintiff's damage calculation, either on behalf of the plaintiff or on behalf of the defendant. There are no formulas for evaluating damage calculations, and to do it well, an expert needs to have experience and imagination.

First, one must gain an understanding of the theory behind the method used. Is it sound? Are the assumptions reasonable?

Basically, the purpose of the evaluations is to see if the concept of the claim makes sense or to discover where it is flawed. It is often useful to study the history of the company's operations and to consider the calculation in the light of such economic elements as trends and statistics in the industry, the cost of labor, interest rates for borrowing capital needed to expand, and so on. It may help to compare the plaintiff's actual performance in the past with its own projections and forecasts. How good is the company's record at projecting future operations? If the plaintiff forecasted its expected profits before the event in question occurred, that forecast may have been relatively unbiased. How does the company's own forecast compare with the damages now claimed? In evaluating a damage claim, it is also valuable to examine the documents the plaintiff used in making its computation and to consult with other experts, such as economists, industrial engineers, investment bankers, and market researchers.

These are just examples, not an exhaustive list, of the ways to evaluate a damage calculation.

Estimating the Damages in Advance

The accountant may be able to help the lawyer by estimating the amount of the damages early in the case. For plaintiffs, the lawyer needs to know how much the case is worth to decide whether to bring suit and how much to estimate in litigation costs. For defendants, after the client has been found liable, the lawyer needs to know the least the client may be required to pay and what is the most the other side can reasonably claim.

This process can help the lawyer and the client choose a number to aim for and at what price. For instance, an expenditure of $10,000 more in legal and accountant's fees might be able to substantiate a number $150,000 higher. Or, if the accountants are working for the defense, they might be able to refute the claim entirely, given the time and the money to investigate the financial records in sufficient detail.

A plaintiff's damage figure should be one that more closely compensates for losses incurred and also can be defended well.

Tax Considerations

Taxes must be considered in all damage claims. The plaintiff prefers a settlement that is tax free. The defendant prefers a tax-deductible payment. Chapter 33 discusses the taxability of damage claims.

GUIDELINES FOR CREATING SUCCESSFUL DAMAGE STRATEGIES

Although each case deserves a fresh look, some guidelines have worked in the past for accountants, lawyers, and others who have developed damage strategies for complex commercial cases.

Keep It Simple

Successful damage strategies appeal to common sense. The simpler a damage calculation is to understand, the less vulnerable it is to challenges from the opposition. Conversely, the more complicated the calculation, the more there is for the opponent to attack and the more likely it will contain mistakes.

Be Reasonable

Frequently, large damages are awarded by courts. Although it might sound naive to advocate a reasonable approach, it is usually true that the more honest the claim, the more likely it is to succeed in court. Inflated claims make better targets for the opposition.

Brainstorm—and Be Creative about It

Before even getting down to dollars and cents, it it useful for the lawyer, the accountant, and the other experts to brainstorm about damage strategies as early in the case as possible. The aim is to think of every possibility that might arise, beginning with the most fundamental questions: Is there any damage? If so, will this be upheld in court?

There are times when the case is so weak that it is best to try to settle it as painlessly as possible. But even when the case is strong, it is helpful to play "devil's advocate," by pretending to be in the opponent's shoes. If one is working for the plaintiff, for example, one should pretend to be defending against one's own damage claim, thinking up the strongest possible arguments against it, then countering those arguments.

This is where creativity enters the picture. A good damage-strategy session requires imagination. Doing it well means looking at it from all angles, not following any formulas or prescribed methods.

Look at the Business

Learn about the business, including the industry, the competition, the setting, and so on, paying attention to what does and does not make sense.

Look at the whole situation in as broad a perspective as possible. All kinds of questions might be asked: What does the company have? What do they do? Does the claim make sense? Can the company produce what it claims it can? Do they have the right technology, sources of supplies, labor? What was their market share before the event?

Consider the case of a manufacturing plant that claimed millions of dollars in lost profits. The defendant's accountants decided to investigate the simple question of capacity. Could the plant actually have produced the number of widgets it claimed was possible? An industrial engineer sent to inspect the factory found it to be a garage. More often than not, it is a good idea to inspect the premises.

Another case involved a nursing home that was supposed to have been completed in the summer but was not ready to open until January. The plaintiff was able to recover damages for the entire winter after opening as well as the preceding summer and fall. The nursing home was located in the Midwest, and the plaintiff proved that few people in the Midwest move during the winter.

Get the Right Documents

It is valuable to have access to the right information. Accountants should advise the attorneys about document needs; otherwise they may be faced with an inadequate set of documents.

Typically, for example, a lawyer will get annual reports and invoices. Yet there could be more vital information in a company's internal budgets, sales forecasts, forecasts of profits, and interim reports.

The workpapers of the opponent's auditor can be valuable. In one case, for instance, a company sued a competitor for false and misleading advertising. The auditor's workpapers and management letter showed that the plaintiff had been losing money for many other reasons, never mentioning the alleged false and misleading advertising.

In another case in which a plaintiff was claiming millions of dollars in damages, the auditor's workpapers revealed that the company's inventory system was so chaotic that no one could possibly distinguish what any single product would cost to produce.

CONCLUSION

Accountants' training and experience prepare them for the tasks involved in assessing damages. The accountant can look at a business, sift through documents, ferret out the information that is relevant to the case, and use that information to help the lawyer develop the strongest possible damage strategy. Nevertheless, damage calculations stretch the limits of the usual activities of accountants. The "what-if" element that is characteristic of most lawsuits involves hypotheticals, not the actual histories accountants are accustomed to.

This particular application of accounting, then, calls forth imagination and creativity.

BIBLIOGRAPHY

Barkman, Arnold I., "Cost Defenses for Antitrust Cases," *Management Accounting* (April 1986), pp. 37–40.

Costello, John J., "Using Forensic Accountants," *The National Law Journal* (October 18, 1982), pp. 15–17.

Dobbs, Dan B., *Remedies* (St. Paul MN: West Publishing Co., 1935).

McCormick, Charles T., *Handbook on the Law of Damages* (St. Paul, MN: West Publishing Co., 1935).

26

BUSINESS VALUATIONS

O. Kit Lokey
Richard S. Braun
Sheryl L. Cefali

NEED FOR BUSINESS VALUATIONS IN LITIGATION

Valuing a business for litigation purposes is similar to valuing a business under any other circumstances. The appraiser must consider all the relevant facts, subject them to analysis and judgment, weigh them according to their importance, and develop a reasonable and supportable conclusion of value. An appraiser's skill in analysis and communicating clearly and convincingly will establish the appraiser's value as an expert witness for business valuations.

Companies and their components are frequently valued for litigation purposes because there is no clearly established, independent value for the assets to which all parties agree. This frequently occurs for a closely held business, regardless of its size, because typically there is no established market or arm's-length negotiated transactions in the company's stock. Transactions that may have occurred for gifts and other purposes may not have been conducted at "fair market value" (as defined later). Furthermore, these types of transactions are frequently sporadic and may have occurred at a time far removed from the relevant valuation date, when the value of the business may have been different.

Even if a company's stock is widely held and perhaps publicly traded, some question may exist as to whether its traded price is indicative of fair market value. When large blocks of the company's stock are not traded, or when public shares are thinly and infrequently traded, the traded price may not reflect fair market value. Such thinly traded stock may be discounted in value because of insufficient information available to shareholders or because of its limited marketability that could materially affect value.

Furthermore, even securities that are publicly traded in sufficient volume and carry no restrictions on sale may require discounts due to the size of the block of stock in question. A large block of stock cannot be marketed and converted to cash as readily as a few shares (the "blockage theory"). In other words, the offering of a large percentage of a company's stock in the market within a limited period of time could depress the price of these securities. If, however, the block of stock in question constitutes a controlling interest in the company, a premium for control may be applicable.

REASONS FOR VALUATION IN LITIGATION

Many litigation contexts demand a business valuation. Some examples of situations where a valuation may be required include marital dissolutions, dissident shareholder suits, or taxable transactions.

Marital dissolutions frequently give rise to the need for a business valuation. A business or professional practice may be the prime asset of a husband and wife, worth more than the house and other assets combined. Rules on the division of property in a divorce vary from state to state and sometimes complicate the appraiser's task. For instance, in California—a community property state—valuation of the underlying asset is only part of the assignment. The appraiser, for example, may be asked to calculate a reasonable return on assets held by one party prior to marriage, with any appreciation exceeding that return deemed as community property.

Dissident shareholders may sue as a result of a transaction in which a dispute arises over the proposed price to be paid for their shares. A corporation or partnership *dissolution* may require a valuation to determine an equitable allocation of value among the involved parties. Often, when a major shareholder leaves the business, the price for his shares must be established.

Taxable transactions sometimes require business valuations. A business owner who gives stock in a closely held company to a family member wishes to minimize its value for gift tax purposes. An owner making a charitable contribution wishes to maximize the stock's value for income tax purposes. Closely held stock must be valued for estate tax purposes. The value of any of these transactions may be challenged by the Internal Revenue Service (IRS) or other tax receiving authority. Hence, both the IRS and the taxpayer may require services of a business valuation expert for analysis and, ultimately, testimony.

Regardless of the valuation question, the appraiser must be careful to fairly represent the client while remaining independent and avoiding the role of advocate. It is not the appraiser's role to minimize his client's economic damage in litigation but to provide an objective and completely prepared appraisal that can be supported by expert testimony.

BUSINESS VALUATION TERMINOLOGY

One of the most widely recognized and accepted standards of value is "fair market value." *Fair market value* is the price at which an asset would change hands between a willing buyer and a willing seller, each having reasonable knowledge of the materially relevant facts, and neither under any compulsion to act (IRS Revenue Ruling 59-60 detailed at the end of this chapter). It is the value established for an asset between a buyer and seller negotiating at arm's length from a position of relatively equal strength. Three levels of fair market value exist: enterprise or controlling interest value, marketable minority interest value, and nonmarketable minority interest value.

Ownership of publicly traded securities typically represents a level of fair market value called *marketable minority interest* because the stock is liquid and may be easily converted to cash, but such ownership typically represents small block transactions that do not affect control of the company. Transactions that do affect control (acquisitions or leveraged buy-outs) are often consummated at a price that results in a premium above-the-marketable-minority-interest value. This premium paid for

EXHIBIT 26-1.

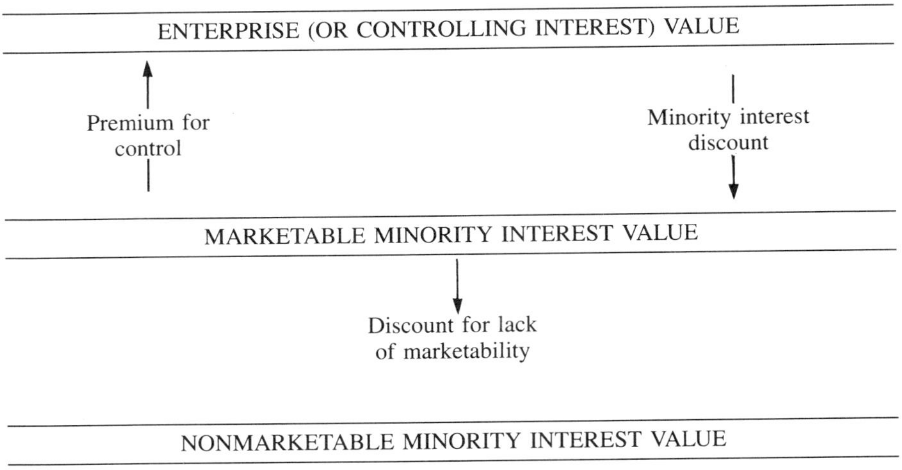

control can be measured and quantified. Conversely, securities without an active marketplace or with restrictions on their resale often transact at a discount reflecting the illiquidity of the securities.

Thus, the term *fair market value* has different meanings depending on the stock's liquidity and the size of the block of stock being valued. *Special purpose value* considers an asset's value to a particular buyer who may be willing to pay a premium over fair market value in exchange for a unique economic benefit or some special attraction of a noneconomic nature he may have to the asset. Examples of economic benefits include synergies and economies of scale that may benefit the special purpose buyer but that most other purchasers would not realize or be in a position to exploit. Noneconomic benefits, on the other hand, may be realized by the acquiror of a sports franchise, a newspaper, or a hotel, whose motivation goes beyond economic issues and may include fame and ego.

When valuing a business, one must distinguish *going-concern value* from *liquidation value*. Going-concern value assumes that the business is a viable economic entity and will remain as such in the future. This valuation basis acknowledges that an established business may be worth more than the value of its underlying net assets because of "economic goodwill." In addition to assets that a company may list on its balance sheet such as machinery, inventory, and real estate, a going concern may have valuable off-balance-sheet assets such as reputation, trained work force, and unique, internally developed products or services that would command a premium from the marketplace. Although one could value these assets individually, they are frequently included as a part of economic goodwill, which makes the value of the business as an ongoing enterprise worth more than the value of its tangible assets in liquidation.

Liquidation value, on the other hand, assumes the company will not remain as a going concern and its assets will be sold piecemeal. Usually, in a liquidation sale, some or all of the value reflected by economic goodwill will be lost because it is typically not an asset that has value separate and apart from the rest of the business. The assessment of liquidation value must consider the time needed to sell assets in an orderly fashion or the discounts associated with a "fire sale." Costs of liquidating assets, such as commissions, shrinkage of inventory and receivables, and ongoing operating expenses must be considered.

VALUATION DATES AND INDEPENDENCE

The effective valuation date can significantly affect value. As the stock market fluctuates, so does the value of most securities. Similarly, the value of a business does not remain static over time but changes in response to both internal and external conditions.

One should ignore events that occur subsequent to the valuation date. Only to the extent that a knowledgeable investor could reasonably anticipate, as of the valuation date, that a subsequent event would occur should the valuation reflect such an event. Conversely, an appraiser cannot ignore contingent assets or liabilities that exist as of the valuation date even though they may be difficult to quantify because of uncertainty surrounding the magnitude and likelihood of impact.

Finally, the appraiser should be "independent" in order to provide an unbiased—and therefore objective—opinion. Such independence and objectivity will enhance the appraiser's credibility as an expert witness in litigation. To establish independence, the appraisal fee should be fixed and not contingent upon the appraiser's conclusions or the litigation's outcome. Further, the appraiser should have no past or prospective material relationships with the client.

DISCOUNTS AND PREMIUMS

Discounts and premiums on valuation are usually expressed relative to a marketable minority interest value. Although there are many reasons why a particular security would sell at a discount from its marketable minority interest value, the most obvious is that there is no ready market for the stock or there are restrictions on the security's marketability. For example, one may have difficulty selling a small minority interest in a closely held business to an unaffiliated third party, and the stock would probably have to be discounted substantially to be sold. In demanding a discount, purchasers are acknowledging the difficulty they may have in finding a buyer when they want to sell. The appraiser can measure the appropriate level of discount for restricted stock by comparing the price paid for a private placement of restricted stock to the price paid for unrestricted stock of the same company trading on a public exchange. Other restrictions that affect selection of a discount include: restrictions on the ability to vote, buy/sell agreements, and "blockage" that may affect the ability of a large shareholder to sell all of his large block of stock in a reasonably timely fashion without negatively affecting the stock price.

A premium over marketable minority interest value may also be appropriate in some circumstances. For instance, the ability to control a company and affect its decision making is valuable and is typically not available to a minority shareholder. Therefore, one must usually pay a premium to minority shareholders to acquire a controlling interest in a company. The public marketplace provides a good measure of the premium that buyers are willing to pay. By comparing the preannouncement value of publicly traded securities to the price ultimately paid by acquirors in acquisitions, leveraged buy-outs, and similar transactions, one can quantify the types of premiums typically required to acquire control.

The appraiser should also consider additional factors in the valuation analysis, such as key employee risk, key customer or supplier risk, reputation, market share, and future growth opportunities. These factors can be quantified and may be reflected as a discount or premium to value; however, they are most frequently incorporated into the market multiples selected in the market comparison approaches, as described later.

QUALIFICATIONS OF AN APPRAISER

Currently no formal licensing procedures or other legal requirements exist to restrict someone from calling himself an appraiser or valuation consultant and offering services as an expert in valuation. As a practical matter, however, certain educational experience and professional criteria bear on the ability of a potential expert witness to provide valuation services.

A broad range of prior appraisal assignments in sufficient number and with reasonable frequency is helpful. One does not have to perform business valuations as a sole or even primary occupation, but no substitute exists for hands-on experience to sharpen skills and provide a broad base of experience from which to draw.

Membership in professional organizations may act as a screening mechanism to ensure a minimal level of competency and exposure to sound business valuation principles. The American Society of Appraisers, for example, requires years of relevant experience, interviews, and written examinations before an appraiser can use its "senior" designation. In addition, it requires continuing education, provides a code of ethics, and reviews complaints regarding competency as further checks on members. Although not a guarantee of competency, membership in such an organization may be helpful in identifying experts in business valuation services for litigation or other purposes.

Once the decision to hire an appraiser as an expert witness has been made, both the appraiser and client must agree on the scope of the assignment. Some of the key issues that should be agreed upon include:

1. The business entity or securities to be valued.
2. The valuation date or dates.

3. Other analyses, outside of the appraisal, that may be required.
4. The individual or team of individuals who will be working on the valuation engagement.
5. Any assistance to be provided by the company or other professionals that the appraiser may require.

The scope of the assignment becomes one of the key elements in the engagement letter that formalizes the agreement. In addition to the scope of the assignment, the engagement letter should discuss fees, limitations or restrictions of scope being placed on the appraiser, if any, and similar matters. This document can be valuable in the event of a future misunderstanding regarding services to be rendered and affiliated payment.

The engagement letter should specify who the client is and who is responsible for payment of fees. Frequently the client of record is the attorney who may protect the appraiser's workproduct under various legal theories. Alternatively, the client may be an individual shareholder, the company, or any party to the litigation. In any case, the client should sign the engagement letter acknowledging the agreement.

The engagement letter should specify fee arrangements. One can usually divide the engagement into an analytical stage and a testimony stage. It is often possible to quote a fixed fee for the analytical portion of the assignment including conclusions and the preparation of a report. Expert witness testimony in deposition or in trial is more difficult to quote on a fixed fee basis because the time required is generally not within the appraiser's control. Therefore, fees for testimony are typically based on an hourly or per diem charge. The letter can specify reimbursement allowed for out-of-pocket costs. Fees should never be contingent on conclusions or results obtained, because contingent fees call into question the appraiser's independence. Whenever possible, payment in full for the analytical portion of the engagement should be obtained prior to expert witness testimony.

DATA GATHERING

One of the most important steps in any appraisal process is data gathering. Because the proper analysis of an asset's value is dependent upon reasonable knowledge of the relevant facts, it is vital that the appraiser take steps to ensure the collection of such data. The appraiser should be allowed to rely on information received from informed sources that the appraiser believes to be reliable. Assumptions should be specified and limitations clearly indicated.

The amount and type of data will vary depending on the nature of the assignment and the type of business being valued. Although not all-inclusive, the following are documents that typically should be received.

1. Financial statements. An appraiser cannot analyze an established business without financial statements. If possible, one should obtain at least 5 years of annual data to track growth and other trends. Interim financial statements are often required, particularly when seasonality is an issue or when changes of a material nature have occurred since the last annual financial statement. A financial statement as of the valuation date is also desirable, but if one is not available, the appraiser should at least be informed of any material changes in the company's financial condition since the date of the last financial statement made available. Although audited statements are preferred, the appraiser can work with reviewed, compiled, or internally prepared statements as long as any significant deviations from generally accepted accounting principles are noted and taken into consideration. An appraiser should question management thoroughly regarding the content of the financial statements, how they were prepared, and particularly about atypical or unusual items.

2. *Tax returns.* These provide a good verification of the financial statements, especially when the statements are unaudited. Different accounting treatments for tax purposes versus financial statement reporting purposes may raise numerous questions and issues.

3. *Resumes of key personnel.* A company's prospects often depend on the quality of its management. Resumes will outline management's qualifications and credentials, including length of time they have been in their current positions.

4. *Stock agreements.* The valuation expert must know the rights, privileges, and restrictions of the particular class of stock to be valued as well as of all other classes of equity. This is vital when different classes of stock must be valued as part of the assignment.

5. *List of shareholders.* When valuing the stock of a business, particularly a closely held business, it is often important to know who owns the stock. This relates to the issue of actual or effective control and the premiums associated with control.

6. *Transactions in the company's stock.* Some of the best indications of value for a closely held business are actual transactions in the company's stock. Actual transactions that were conducted on an arm's-length basis and that were accomplished reasonably close to the valuation date merit serious consideration during valuation.

7. *Projections.* Companies are purchased based on expectations for the future, as opposed to past performance. Supportable and reasonable projections provide an important source of information in a business valuation. Small companies without a formal planning process are unlikely to have long-term projections, but even a 1-year projection may help the appraiser ascertain a company's direction.

8. *Other appraisals.* Prior appraisals of the company may also be useful. Real estate appraisals, for example, may indicate substantial value that does not appear in the financial statements.

9. *History and nature of the company.* The appraiser must have a historical perspective on the company, that provides a reasonableness check on the company's plans and projections.

10. *Significant contractual agreements.* If a company has a significant contractual agreement that could affect it materially, the agreement should be reviewed. Examples of such agreements include customer and supplier contracts with fixed prices, employment agreements, agreements between the company and officers or shareholders, and leasing agreements.

11. Product or service brochures. These can often help the appraiser better understand the company's products or services, especially complex or technical ones.

12. Offers for the company. An arm's-length offer for the company, made within a reasonable time period of the valuation date, can provide an indication of the company's value and should be considered in the valuation process.

13. Patents and other intellectual property. Legal monopolies that give a company an advantage over its competitors should be considered in determining the future prospects for the company.

In addition to receiving the kinds of information detailed, the appraiser should meet with company management and tour the company's facilities. A field visit allows the appraiser to interview management. A tour of company facilities can facilitate an understanding of the company's efficiency and organization and help the appraiser better understand how the business operates. In a litigation setting, the appraiser sometimes cannot meet with management if the client's interests differ from those of the company. Data collection and input from management may have to come from more formal procedures such as prior testimony, interrogatories, and depositions. Discussions with unrelated third parties familiar with the company and its operation, the industry, or other areas may also be desirable.

The nature of the appraiser's field visit questions will vary, depending upon the specifics of the case. However, the following are areas and issues that the appraiser could discuss in almost any assignment:

1. *Management.* Who are the company's key decision makers? What are their qualifications and experience? What is the nature and amount of their compensation? Is there any key employee risk? What is the breadth and depth of management in key areas? Has management done any succession planning?
2. *Customers and suppliers.* Do any customers or suppliers account for a large part of the company's business? Are there alternative sources of supply available? Are there unusual purchase or sales terms or other arrangements? What is their financial health? Are the relationships long-term or transient?
3. *Competition.* Who are the primary competitors? What are their strengths and weaknesses? What is their respective market share? How do their products and services compare to the subject company? If publicly traded, would they make good comparables?
4. *Nonrecurring gains or losses.* What is their magnitude and timing? What is their effect on value? To what extent should adjustments be made to reported earnings and cash flow?
5. *Intracompany and related-party transactions.* Are they conducted at arm's-length market value? Should adjustments be made for non-arm's-length transactions?
6. *Contingent assets and liabilities.* What is the estimated size and timing? What is the probability of gain or loss? Management should identify these contingencies to the appraiser.

7. *Nonoperating assets.* Does the balance sheet or income statement capture their value? What are management's plans for their use in the future? Should they be valued separately from the company's operations?
8. *Patents and copyrights.* What is their remaining legal life? Do they still have economic value? Has the company vigorously enforced their legal rights?
9. *Anticipated operating changes.* Does the company plan to purchase or sell assets? Does it plan changes in services, products, or facilities?
10. *Operations.* What is the status of labor relations? What is the current or potential effect of regulatory changes? Is there an existing or emerging product liability issue?

Naturally, the appraiser's questions will depend on the situation and the company under analysis. As the data collection and interview process continues, new issues will arise that the appraiser will want to pursue. The appraiser must be flexible and capable of moving from a fixed line of questioning in order to respond to issues raised during the interview process.

In addition to learning company specifics, the appraiser must understand the company's economic environment. The first step is to understand the outlook for the economy as a whole and the particular industry in which the company operates. Many companies are tied to business cycles. Few companies are immune to disruptive or beneficial changes in the economy as a whole. The effects of inflation, recession, interest rate changes, energy price changes, and other macroeconomic issues must be considered in the appraiser's analysis. Sources of such macroeconomic information include the *U.S. Industrial Outlook* and *Standard & Poor's Industry Surveys*, brokerage firm reports, economic reports from banks and other institutions, trade publications, and various newspapers and periodicals.

VALUATION APPROACHES

When valuing a business, there are a number of generally accepted valuation approaches typically utilized by business appraisers. They include the following:

1. Market comparison
2. Discounted future earnings and discounted net cash flow
3. Asset
4. Analysis of prior transactions
5. Comparable sales

MARKET COMPARISON APPROACH

The market comparison approach assumes that a company's value is based on investors' perceptions of the risks and rewards from an investment in the subject company relative to other investments. One can reasonably assume that companies in the same industry have risks and rewards that are more comparable than those of companies in different industries. Therefore, the market would generally perceive the risks and rewards of Ford and General Motors as more similar and comparable than those of Ford and IBM. Furthermore, an investor will not pay 10 times earnings for Ford and only 5 times earnings for General Motors unless it views Ford as less risky and/or potentially more rewarding in terms of profitability and growth and, therefore, a more attractive investment.

When valuing a business that does not have an active trading market, the appraiser cannot directly observe how investors value it. However, the appraiser can often identify publicly traded companies that resemble the subject company from an investor's standpoint. By comparing the subject company being valued to the comparable public companies on the basis of accepted risk and reward measures such as size, liquidity, leverage, profitability, and growth statistics, the appraiser can judge its relative financial and operating risk profile.

Other risk factors that the appraiser should consider are qualitative. The appraiser acquires qualitative information during visits to the company's facilities and in interviews with management. These qualitative factors include key customer or key supplier risk, key employee risk, diversity of operations, reputation, market share, and future growth opportunities. For example, both key customer and key employee risk would exist if an owner of a single-product company had a strong relationship with a customer that accounted for a significant portion of the company's revenues. If something happened to the owner or if the individuals' relationship with the company ended, the company could suffer severe financial consequences.

After analyzing the company's financial, operating, and qualitative risk profiles, the appraiser will ascertain the subject company's risk and potential reward relative to the selected comparable public companies. If the subject company has greater risk and less potential reward than that of the public comparable companies, one could reasonably expect that its relative value (all other things being equal) would be lower. Therefore, the appraiser would select a multiple (such as a price/earnings or price/cash flow ratio) that is lower than the comparative public companies' multiples to reflect the subject company's relatively greater risk and/or smaller potential reward.

CALCULATING MARKET MULTIPLES

Market multiples, such as price/earnings and price/cash flow ratios, are computed by dividing the mean stock price for the period immediately preceding the valuation date by earnings or cash flow (net income plus depreciation and amortization) per common share. The value derived from multiplying the subject company's earnings or cash flow by a price/earnings or price/cash flow ratio is the company's aggregate market value of common equity on a marketable minority interest basis.

When the company being valued has a significantly different capital structure relative to the comparative public companies used to generate market multiples, it is useful to apply debt-free approaches to valuation. Debt-free approaches measure the value that debt and equity holders together ascribe to the respective income and cash flow streams of a company. To calculate debt-free multiples for comparable companies, the total market value of debt is added to the market value of total equity on an enterprise basis (aggregate market value of equity plus a control premium) to compute total invested capital. The total invested capital is then divided by debt-free earnings or debt-free cash flow levels, such as earnings before interest and taxes (EBIT) or earnings before depreciation and amortization, interest, and taxes (EBDIT) to arrive at price/EBIT and price/EBDIT ratios, respectively.

Other accepted market comparison approaches include multiples of total invested capital to debt-free earnings (net income plus interest expense net of tax effects), total invested capital to debt-free cash flow (debt-free earnings plus depreciation and amortization), and total invested capital to revenue.

An appraiser often needs to use more than one market comparison approach. For instance, consider two companies with the same earnings potential, one with new equipment and one with old but serviceable equipment. The company with the newer equipment will have greater depreciation and consequently lower earnings. However, the company with older equipment and smaller depreciation will pay higher taxes and, therefore, generate less operating cash flow. An appraiser using only a multiple of earnings approach might conclude that the company with older equipment was worth more than the company with newer equipment, whereas reliance on only a multiple of operating cash flow approach could lead to the opposite conclusion. Using both the multiple of earnings and multiple of cash flow approaches, as well as other relevant approaches, helps to identify factors requiring judgment.

Not every valuation approach should be used in every situation nor given equal weight if included. The approaches and weight given to each in arriving at a conclusion will depend on the facts and circumstances surrounding each engagement. A multiple of book value, for instance, would be of little significance when valuing a service business with few fixed assets. Although the selection and weighting of approaches is subjective, it is not arbitrary. Decisions should be based on and supported by facts and reasonable interpretations.

After completing the risk assessment and selecting the appropriate multiples, the appraiser must select for the subject company the relevant earnings, cash flow, and other measures to be multiplied by the market multiples. Using earnings as an example, the appraiser must decide whether to use more recent earnings or consider earnings over a period of time. For instance, the earnings of a cyclical company can fluctuate greatly from year to year, sometimes even producing a loss. Simply selecting the most recent earnings will give a misleading picture of the company's true earnings potential if the company is at a peak or trough in its normal operating cycle. On the other hand, a noncyclical growth company is usually best analyzed using most recent earnings because the current nature of the company's operations most accurately reflects the company's earnings potential.

Complicating the selection of the appropriate base levels of earnings and cash flow are nonrecurring gains or losses and anticipated changes in operations. By definition, nonrecurring gains and losses are not expected to recur. Therefore, it would be inappropriate to apply the market multiples to an earnings level that was temporarily distorted by nonrecurring gains or losses. The same would be true of an anticipated change in operations. If a company has sold or purchased assets that are expected to materially affect earnings, it would not be appropriate to ignore the anticipated change. Other items that might require an adjustment include significant changes in compensation levels, loss or gain of product lines, loss of a key customer, and anticipated changes in operating costs. These types of changes may create a step function up or down in the company's earnings potential that the analysis must reflect.

The appraiser who has selected the proper earnings level and an appropriate risk-adjusted multiple can derive an indication of value. As a simplistic example, an earnings level of $1 million multiplied by a factor of 10 would result in a value indication of $10 million. The appraiser then needs to adjust for a control premium or nonmarketability discount from the marketable minority interest level of value, if appropriate. Other equity market comparison approaches, such as a multiple of cash flow or book value, should be handled similarly.

Because debt-free approaches arrive at a value indication for the total value of the company on an enterprise basis (debt plus equity), the value of debt must be subtracted once the debt-free levels of earnings or cash flow have been multiplied by the selected market multiples. Furthermore, the resulting equity value in debt-free approaches is on an enterprise or controlling interest basis, and a discount must be applied to derive a value indication on a minority interest basis. (A minority interest discount is the mathematical inverse of a control premium.)

DISCOUNTED FUTURE EARNINGS AND CASH FLOW APPROACHES

Discounting a company's projected earnings or cash flow to a present value is another approach to valuation. In theory, this is an important approach because investors are willing to pay only for anticipated future—not historic—cash flows. However, historical results are often indicative of what can be expected in the future. This approach suffers from the uncertainty regarding expectations. Forecasts or projections, when available, are usually provided by company management and should represent their best estimates regarding the future. Typically, projections are provided for a 5-year period. The appraiser usually has to ascertain what will happen after the projection period and then estimate an appropriate terminal value that adequately captures those expectations. Computing a value 5 or more years in the future is more difficult than computing a value for the company today. The terminal value estimate usually significantly affects the value indicated by the discounted projections method. A terminal value may be calculated using multiples derived in the market comparison approach discussed earlier, a perpetuity approach known as the Gordon Growth Model[1] (which assumes a constant growth beyond the projection period or, in some instances, a series of discrete annual growth rates), or other methods selected as appropriate by the appraiser.

The selection of the appropriate stream to discount will also affect the valuation. Although one can discount earnings or operating cash flow, free cash flow is most appropriate. Free cash flow is operating cash flow adjusted for required changes in working capital and net capital expenditures and taxes. Because free cash flow is net of cash needed by the business to meet its projection it is, therefore, theoretically available to shareholders as dividends. Investors are willing to pay only for the present value of future cash flows available to them for distribution, taking into consideration the timing of the flows and the perceived risk of achieving the flows. Therefore, discounting interim free cash flows plus the company's terminal value provides an important determinant of enterprise value.

Selecting an appropriate discount rate is also an important aspect of the discounted future earnings and cash flow approaches. No simple formula exists for selecting an appropriate discount rate. If the Company has debt outstanding, the interest rate on the debt provides one indication of investor risk. Because equity is more risky than debt, it should command a rate of return higher than the return on debt. Analytical techniques are available, such as the Capital Asset Pricing Model (CAPM)[2] to help the appraiser select a reasonable cost of equity and, where required, a blended or weighted average cost of capital (WACC).[3] A blended or weighted average cost of capital considers the cost of debt, the cost of equity, and the proportional amount of each in the company's capital structure.

No model, no matter how accurate, tells the entire story. If the company's projections are optimistic and a reasonable probability exists they will not be achieved, CAPM and other models will not capture this additional risk, will understate the appropriate discount rate and, therefore, overstate value. A premium should be added to the discount rate to reflect those company-specific items that CAPM does not consider. To ascertain the appropriate premium, the appraiser must review historical results as a reality check on the projections and question management regarding assumptions underlying the projections. If the company's revenues have been growing at 5 percent per year and the projections anticipate growth at 20 percent per year, the appraiser must understand why the company anticipates faster growth and feel comfortable with this assumption. If the assumption seems aggressive, a higher discount rate should be applied in the analysis.

An additional check on the reasonableness of company projections is a sensitivity analysis. By varying (reducing) some of the key assumptions in the projections, such as growth in revenues or profit margins, the appraiser can ascertain just how sensitive the projections are. Key assumptions can be identified and discussed with management. Once again, if the projection's key assumptions are aggressive (conservative), a higher (lower) discount rate may be required.

ASSET APPROACH

A third valuation approach is the asset approach. As the name implies, the asset approach looks at the underlying value of a company's assets to indicate value. Book value, based on historical costs rather than economic value, usually does not provide an accurate indication of value.

An adjusted book value approach considers the economic value of assets rather than their book value. This approach is most useful for companies with large investments in real estate and natural resources, where the income statements have not captured the economic value of such assets. An appraisal is completed for assets whose value may differ from book value, such as real estate that may have appreciated dramatically since purchase. The economic value substitutes for book value on the balance sheet, typically increasing owners' equity. An important component of the asset approach is the valuation of intangible assets. Patents and copyrights, trademarks, special licensing agreements, favorable raw material purchasing agreements, and special or unique computer software are a few examples of intangible assets the appraiser must identify and value in the adjusted book value approach.

One specialized version of the adjusted book value approach is the liquidation value approach. Liquidation value assumes the company will not remain a going concern and will sell its assets for their individual values. An orderly liquidation assumes that assets will be sold over a reasonable time period in order to realize their full economic value. A forced liquidation assumes assets will be sold quickly, with appropriate discounts taken to reflect the transaction's urgency. In either case, the analysis must include the costs associated with the sale of assets and the time value of money.

PRIOR TRANSACTIONS

Prior transactions in the subject company's stock can be important in determining current fair market value. In considering the relevancy of prior transactions, the appraiser must ascertain whether the sale was between unrelated parties, was negotiated in good faith, whether both the buyer and seller were reasonably informed as to matters relating to the company's investment merits, and whether any undue influence, duress, or compulsion was placed on the buyer or the seller. The appraiser must also consider the size of the block of stock previously sold and the proximity of the prior sale to the valuation date.

An arm's-length transaction of approximately the same size that was reasonably close to the valuation date would appropriately indicate value. Any differences noted in the circumstances of the prior sale and the contemplated transaction should be factored into the appraiser's analysis.

COMPARABLE SALES APPROACH

Comparable sales transactions provide another source of pertinent information useful in a business valuation. The sale of a business similar to the subject company indicates investor sentiment regarding such companies. The transaction must meet all the fair market value criteria previously described and should be adjusted for premiums and discounts where appropriate.

The difficulty in using comparable sales transactions is the typical lack of data regarding the transactions. Many such transactions involve closely held businesses where a transaction's terms are not generally available. The appraiser may be unable to obtain financial and other information to evaluate the relative risk between the comparable company and the subject company. Additionally, some transactions include stock, notes, other forms of consideration, or unusual payment terms, which affect the transaction's cash value.

When adequate information is available on comparable companies that have been sold relatively close to the valuation date, the appraiser should analyze those transactions in much the same manner as in the market comparison approaches. One should perform a financial and qualitative risk analysis comparing the subject company being valued to the company that has been sold. Furthermore, market multiples should be derived using the purchase price and the company's historical earnings and cash flow levels. After assessing the subject company's risk and potential reward relative to the comparable sale company, the appraiser would select investor multiples at levels either higher or lower than the implied transaction multiples as dictated by the risk analysis.

CONCLUSION OF VALUE

After the appraiser has applied the valuation methods described, and arrived at indications of value, he must reconcile these amounts to arrive at a conclusion as to value. The conclusion may be expressed as a range of value, but more typically it is expressed as a point estimate. In a perfect world the appraiser would expect all the valuation methods used to result in similar indications of value. This rarely happens.

The valuation indications will typically span a range of values, although indications from some approaches have a tendency to cluster. The appraiser should carefully consider how much weight to give indications that are distinctly different or are outliers either above or below the range. The appraiser should investigate outliers to ensure that no conceptual or mechanical errors occurred in applying the method.

No fixed procedure exists for assigning weights to various valuation indications. The appraiser may know that certain methods are more applicable than others for a given industry or situation. Asset holding companies, for example, are typically valued as a collection of their assets, which may be quite diverse and unrelated. Therefore, an asset-based approach in such a case may merit the greatest weight in the final analysis. On the other hand, service companies, whose tangible assets are relatively insignificant to their overall economic structure, are typically valued based on their ability to consistently generate earnings and cash flow. Therefore, an earnings or cash flow approach may receive the greatest weight. The weight given to each approach must be supported by the facts and circumstances of each case.

SUBSEQUENT EVENTS

Subsequent events generally can be classified into two categories: those that knowledgeable investors could have expected, such as increased operating costs or increased revenues, and those that could not have been reasonably anticipated as of the valuation date. These might include natural disasters that interrupt the company's operations or lawsuits resulting from undetected product flaws or major production accidents.

When an investor can reasonably anticipate the event prior to the valuation date, the appraisal must reflect the economic impact of such an event. Examples include an announced but not yet implemented increase in raw material prices, a liability resulting from a known toxic waste hazard for which the company is responsible, or the anticipated sale of an operating entity of the company.

NONOPERATING ASSETS

Many companies have assets on their balance sheet that can be classified for economic purposes as nonoperating. These assets do not contribute to the ongoing operations of the business. Examples include raw land or other real estate held for investment purposes, investment securities, or cash that exceeds normal working capital requirements. These assets may, as in the case of investment securities, generate income or, as in the case of raw land, generate losses.

Because these assets do not contribute to the ongoing operations of the business, the appraiser should remove their financial impact from the company's financial statements and value them separately. The value of the business enterprise would then be the sum of the value of its operations, as discussed above, plus the value of its nonoperating assets.

ALLOCATION OF VALUE TO VARIOUS SECURITIES

An appraiser's task frequently extends beyond establishing a value for the equity of a business as a whole. Many companies have more than one class of securities or may have other claims on the equity value. The appraiser must often value the individual securities of a business rather than the business as a whole.

After developing a value for the business as a whole, the appraiser must ascertain the rights, privileges, and restrictions of the various equity securities. Such securities take many forms but generally include multiple classes of common stock, preferred stock, convertible preferred stock, warrants, and other contingent equity claims such as stock appreciation rights, incentive stock options, and phantom stock.

Common shareholders have a residual claim on the firm's equity. This means their shares capture the value of the business less the claims of preferred stockholders and other senior equity claimants. For example, if a business worth $10 million has 1 million shares of common stock outstanding and no other claims on equity value exist, the common stock would be worth $10 per share. However, if other claimants have securities worth $6 million, then the common shareholders in aggregate have a claim on only the residual $4 million, and their stock is worth only $4 per share.

A company may have warrants or other contingent claims on the equity of a firm. A warrant is like an option except that it has a potentially dilutive impact on the value of other common shareholders. A warrant holder must pay a set exercise price per share for common stock received. A warrant will only be exercised if the stock price exceeds the exercise price. This causes dilution and has an impact on the value per share of common stock.

Warrants that are certain to be exercised because the common stock value is well above the exercise price and the time to exercise is about to expire can reasonably be viewed as equivalents to common stock for economic purposes. It would be appropriate to add the aggregate exercise price of such warrants to the aggregate common stock value and divide by the total number of warrants plus common shares. In other cases where the common stock value is below the warrants' exercise price, warrants may be valued through the use of analytical tools such as the Black/Scholes option pricing model, adjusted for anticipated dilution (Black and Scholes, 1973). The value established for warrants in this fashion should be subtracted from aggregate common stock value, and the remainder divided by the total common shares outstanding to establish a value per common share.

Many other possible forms of claims on equity value exist, such as participating preferred stock, constant dollar convertible preferred stock, convertible debt, and even different classes of common stock.

Preferred stock has a priority claim on a specified portion of the company's equity value. It is typically entitled to a fixed dividend that must be paid before dividends are paid to common shareholders. Preferred stock is also generally entitled to a preferential pay-out in the event of the company's liquidation. The company issuing the preferred stock frequently has the right to redeem the preferred stock at its liquidation value or some other predetermined amount.

VALUATION OF PREFERRED STOCK

Valuation of a preferred stock should begin with a thorough understanding of the nature of preferred stock as well as the typical preferred stock rights and privileges and their effects on value.

Unlike common stock, whose dividend rate often fluctuates with the level of corporate earnings, the dividend paid on preferred stock is generally fixed, either as a percentage of the stock's par (or stated) value or as a flat dollar amount. As such, higher grade preferred issues resemble long-term bonds in the sense that their values are interest sensitive. Common stocks, on the other hand, tend to be primarily earnings or cash flow sensitive.

Because preferred dividends are fixed, valuation should focus primarily on risk considerations. One aspect of risk is company-specific risk or that which relates to the ability of the subject company to meet its dividend and redemption commitments and provide for the preferred's liquidation preference in the event of liquidation. The most important company-specific risk is the reliability of future dividend payouts.

To assess the likelihood of future preferred pay-outs, the appraiser should use certain objective and quantifiable measures of company-specific risk to indicate the company's capability to meet dividend obligations. The prevalent measure of company-specific risk has been the pretax fixed charges coverage ratio, defined as the sum of pretax income plus interest expense (or, equivalently, earnings before interest and taxes, "EBIT") divided by the sum of interest expense plus pretax earnings required to pay after-tax preferred dividends. The higher the ratio, the greater the company's capacity to pay its preferred dividends and, therefore, the lower the risk and the required yield to an investor.

In addition to pretax fixed charges coverage, one can use other meaningful ratios that assess the subject company's ability to pay preferred dividends. One example is the cash flow to long-term debt ratio, which is defined as the sum of net income plus noncash charges (e.g., depreciation, deferred income taxes, etc.) divided by total long-term debt. Because interest on long-term debt is a fixed payment that is senior to any dividend pay-out, a higher ratio indicates a more favorable financial position to preferred stockholders. A similar measure of preferred dividend capacity can be expressed by the ratio of EBIT to the sum of total debt plus equity (at market value). A higher ratio indicates a more favorable financial position to preferred stockholders.

An objective measure of longer term dividend safety can be expressed by the subject company's debt to common equity ratio in which equity should be indicated on a fair market value rather than accounting basis. This ratio is especially important to a preferred shareholder because it measures the relative importance of claims on assets and earnings senior to the preferred shareholder (i.e., debt) versus those claims junior to the preferred shareholder (common equity). Thus, if the subject company has had poor recent performance, its various coverage ratios may indicate inadequate dividend coverage. However, if the same company also has a relatively low (or favorable) debt-to-equity ratio, it is more likely that preferred dividends can be maintained, or if dividends are in arrears, that sufficient corporate resources exist to cover arrearages.

Another important company-specific risk measure is the subject company's size, as measured by its common shareholders' equity as expressed on a fair market value basis. Larger companies tend to be more diversified than smaller companies because of multiple products or different markets. Thus any adversity that occurs to a larger company that could impair financial condition is likely to be more diffuse and affect earnings and dividend-paying capability to a lesser extent. In addition, larger size tends to be associated with increased financial strength and flexibility and, therefore, a somewhat lower overall risk of bankruptcy.

In addition to dividend protection, another important consideration in valuing preferred stock is protection of the liquidation preference. One measure that can be analyzed is that of total assets minus liabilities divided by the aggregate preferred liquidation preference. A higher ratio implies a greater protection of the shareholders' investment in the event of a liquidation of the company's assets.

None of the ratios by themselves directly imply either a fair dividend yield or a fair market value for the company's preferred stock. To conclude as to value, the appraiser should compare the company's ratios to similarly calculated ratios for a group of publicly traded preferreds having the same rights and privileges as that of the subject company.

If the ratio comparison shows that the subject company is a relatively greater investment risk than the group of public preferreds, the subject company's preferred should be assigned a correspondingly greater yield.

Ideally, the publicly traded preferreds should contain the identical rights and privileges as that of the subject company. However, closely held preferreds tend to have rights and privileges different from those commonly found in the public marketplace. When differences exist, the valuation should look at the individual rights and privileges of each individual security and assess their effect on the risk to an investor.

In addition to company-specific risk, another type of risk borne by the preferred investor is risk specific to the individual preferred issue. This type of risk is a function of the various rights and privileges of the particular preferred stock in question. Although numerous rights and privileges exist that could add to or detract from the value of preferred stock, the most common and relevant factors to valuation are cumulative dividends, voting rights, redemption privileges, and conversion rights.

Most publicly traded preferred stocks include a cumulative dividend provision. If dividends are noncumulative, a question exists as to the company's intention to pay dividends as they become due, and the investor faces additional risk not entirely related to the company's financial capability.

The right of preferred shareholders to influence company management varies with circumstances. Generally, voting rights can only add value to preferred shares, but the magnitude of the value enhancement varies. In most cases, preferred shareholders represent a negligible fraction of the total votes in a corporation and thus have little power to affect company policies. In a few cases, preferred shareholders as a group may have voting control, but the added value derived would depend, at least in part, on the cohesiveness of the preferred group. When dividends are noncumulative, voting rights would tend to be more valuable than when dividends are cumulative because the preferred shareholders can use their influence to compel the company to pay dividends.

Most publicly traded preferreds can be called by the company from the shareholder, at a specified price for a specified time period. This call option detracts from preferred value, but the amount of reduction in value depends on several factors.

One important factor that affects the call value is the length of time, if any, during which the company cannot call the preferred away from the investor. This is referred to as the *call protection period*. Another important factor is the price at which the company can call the preferred. A lower call price reduces value to the shareholder, both by increasing the probability that the preferred will be redeemed and by diminishing the proceeds to the shareholder upon redemption. Other factors to consider are the company's financial ability to cash out the preferred shares, as well as the company's track record of calling previous preferred issues.

There are many other possible forms of claims on equity value such as convertible preferred stock, participating preferred stock, constant dollar convertible preferred stock, convertible debt, and even different classes of common stock. All of these represent valuation challenges that go beyond the scope of this chapter but that need to be considered by the appraiser.

CONTENT OF REPORT

The appraiser usually documents the conclusions as to value in a written report. The report's length and format will depend on the valuation's purpose as well as the client's desires. Some items—including the following—should be included in any valuation report:

1. *Valuation date.* A valuation is relevant only as of a particular date. This date should be specified to avoid confusion.
2. *Nature of the asset or assets valued.* Identify the businesses or securities being valued; define whether the valuation is on a controlling, marketable minority, or nonmarketable minority interest basis.
3. *Purpose of the appraisal.*
4. *Scope of investigation.* State the documents reviewed, people interviewed, facilities visited, and assumptions relied upon. It is equally important to note limitations on the investigation, particularly those imposed by others.
5. *Restrictions on use of report.* Limit the use of the report and its conclusions to the specific parties and for the specific reasons that it was commissioned. A report intended for tax purposes may not be appropriate for other types of transactions or for litigation matters.
6. *Limiting factors.* No matter how extensive an appraiser's investigation, certain limitations are imposed by fees, time, and expertise. For instance, financial statements are generally relied upon without further investigation as representing the company's financial position in accordance with generally accepted accounting principles (GAAP), unless otherwise specified. Industry information derived from publications deemed reliable is generally accepted without further investigation. These limitations are important in defining the limits of the appraiser's responsibility.
7. *Detailed analysis.* Conclusions of value must be supported with a detailed, logical, and well-presented analysis. The description will enable the reader to ascertain the viability of the appraiser's conclusions relative to the facts presented. The description includes the analyses performed on the company and the application of the various valuation methods.
8. *Conclusions of value.* The valuation conclusion should be clearly stated and consistent with the facts presented. It should also reiterate the valuation date, any limitations placed on the appraisal, and the specific asset(s) being appraised.

The report may also include an industry review, a general economic outlook, a review of various valuation methods and why the approaches selected were deemed appropriate, a detailed risk analysis of the subject company compared to similar publicly traded comparable companies, and a detailed description of the comparable companies.

WORKPAPERS

Whatever the report's content, the appraiser must develop and maintain detailed workpapers to document the analysis and the information relied upon in arriving at the conclusions. Workpapers are important for the following reasons.

1. They provide a permanent record of the documents, interviews, correspondence, and analysis upon which the appraiser relied in rendering the opinion.
2. They establish a clear record of the scope of the appraiser's investigation.
3. The appraiser can use the workpapers as a check list to ensure that all necessary materials and documents for the analysis were received.
4. If a question or problem arises months or years later, the work papers provide an invaluable resource in refreshing the appraiser's memory and recreating the appraisal process.

To meet these goals, workpapers should include:

1. An administrative section containing billings, expenses, documentation of hours spent on the engagement, and similar matters.
2. A correspondence section.
3. A section containing the appraiser's notes of meetings and telephone conversations.
4. Information dealing with the company's industry and the general economic outlook.
5. Specific information on the company, such as product brochures.
6. An analysis section detailing the valuation methods used.
7. Information on the comparable publicly traded companies selected.
8. Financial statement information for the subject company.
9. A section on projections and business plans.
10. Other company documents such as articles of incorporation, and shareholder's agreement, etc.

One should ensure that workpapers do not contain superfluous or inconsistent materials, unanswered questions, and other items that might prove embarrassing and that may be irrelevant to the appraiser's analysis and conclusions. Remember, workpapers are to protect the appraiser—not to indict him.

REVENUE RULINGS AND COURT CASES

Appraisals, other than for establishing value for a transaction between related parties, are frequently performed to satisfy the particular requirements of a regulatory agency, such as the Internal Revenue Service or to comply with the provisions of a particular law. In such instances, knowledge of particular guidelines and relevant court cases can help the appraiser deal with controversial issues.

Appraisers dealing primarily with federal income tax matters should be familiar with the IRS pronouncements and revenue rulings as well as the relevant case law in this area. The following summarizes some of the more significant court cases and revenue rulings in this area.

Revenue Rulings

Revenue Ruling 59-60. Revenue Ruling 59-60 has served as a general guideline for the valuation of closely held securities since 1959. It remains the most widely used guideline in valuation today. The ruling specifically addresses stock valuations for gift and estate tax purposes. However, one can apply its principles to many valuation problems, including those related to employee stock ownership plans, stockholder buy/sell agreements, mergers and acquisitions, corporate reorganizations, marital dissolutions, and bankruptcies.

Revenue Ruling 59-60 states, in effect, that sound opinions of value must be based on all relevant facts and that no one formula can be devised that will be universally acceptable. Revenue Ruling 59-60 sets forth the following factors to be considered and analyzed in the valuation of capital stock:

1. The nature of the business and the history of the enterprise from its inception.
2. The economic outlook in general and the condition and outlook of the specific industry.
3. The book value of the stock and the financial condition of the business.
4. The earnings capacity of the company.
5. The dividend-paying capability of the company.
6. Whether or not the enterprise has goodwill or other intangible value.
7. Sales of the stock and the size of the block to be valued.
8. The market price of stocks of corporations engaged in the same or a similar line of business having their stocks actively traded in a free and open market, either on an exchange or over the counter.

Revenue Ruling 65-192. This ruling contains Appeals and Review Memorandum 34 (ARM 34). ARM 34 sets forth a formula to value the intangible assets of a business. The total value of the business is then concluded to be the net value defined as tangible net book value, plus the goodwill value as established by the ARM 34 formula.

Revenue Ruling 68-609. This ruling sets forth an approach often referred to as the "IRS formula" approach to valuation. The ruling can be applied as a general guideline for estimating the value of intangible assets and the value of a business enterprise. The method is based upon a capitalization of earnings process that allows an after-tax return on investment of 8 percent to 10 percent on net tangible assets and a return of 15 percent to 20 percent on intangible assets, depending upon the inherent risks associated with the investment. Revenue Ruling 68-609 states, however, that "the 'formula' approach may be used for determining the fair market value of intangible assets (and the business enterprise) only if there is no better basis therefore available."

Revenue Ruling 77-287. Revenue Ruling 77-287 amplifies Ruling 59-60 and sets forth valuation guidelines in computing discounts for lack of marketability for securities registered under SEC Rule 144. Because of the resale restrictions of Rule 144, Revenue Ruling 77-287 recognizes that the value of a restricted security is less than the value of its freely traded counterpart and provides guidelines in calculating this discount for lack of marketability.

The basis for Revenue Ruling 77-287 is the *Institutional Investor Study Report* published by the Securities and Exchange Commission in 1971. This study empirically examined discounts in transactions involving securities that are restricted under Rule 144. Based on more than 300 transactions, the SEC study found that the amount of discount allowed for restricted securities from the trading price of unrestricted securities generally relates to four factors:

1. *Earnings.* The higher the earnings level, the lower the discount.
2. *Sales.* The greater the dollar sales amount, the lower the discount.
3. *Trading market.* "According to the study, discount rates were greatest on restricted stock with unrestricted counterparts traded over-the-counter, followed by those with unrestricted counterparts listed on the American Stock Exchange, while the discount rates for those stocks with unrestricted counterparts listed on the New York Stock Exchange were the smallest."
4. *Resale agreement provisions.* Resale agreement provisions—such as "piggyback" provisions, registration provisions, and disclosure provisions—could have the effect of reducing the size of the discount.

Revenue Ruling 83-120. This ruling attempts to amplify Revenue Ruling 59-60 by specifying additional factors for valuing common and preferred shares. It reinforces Ruling 59-60 with respect to the key factors in valuing common stock, but details certain considerations important in valuing preferred stock. This ruling discusses yield, dividend coverage, and protection of liquidation preferences.

Court Cases

Bader v. United States, 172 F. Supp. 833 (S.D. Ill. 1959). The *Bader* case established that when determining the fair market value of a small, closely held corporation's stock, major factors to be considered should be book value, earnings power, and dividend-paying capacity. Furthermore, the valuation must be made as of a relevant date without regard to events occurring subsequent to this date.

Central Trust Co. v. United States, 305 F.2d 393 (Ct. Cl. 1962). In *Central Trust*, the tax court reaffirmed its position that when valuing stock for gift tax purposes, it is essential to obtain the most current information possible relative to the valuation date. The court also found that a company's past earnings trend, with adjustments made for any extraordinary or nonrecurring items, should be analyzed in arriving at a historical earnings level for use in determining the fair market value of a company's stock. Greater weight should be given to the most recent periods.

Woodward v. Quigley, 257 Iowa 1077 133 N.W.2d 38 (1965). Woodward v. Quigley found it appropriate to adjust earnings for liberal salaries received by officers who were also a corporation's majority stockholders. Specifically a company's value should not be based on a reduced level of net operating income attributable to excessive compensation to majority stockholders.

Estate of Kirkpatrick, 34 T.C.M. (CCH) 1490 (1975). The *Estate of Kirkpatrick* held that in determining fair market value of a minority interest in two closely held corporations, the respondent erred in placing primary consideration on the adjusted value of the corporations' underlying assets. Because the companies at issue were clearly operating companies, actively engaged in selling products and services to the general public, primary consideration should be given to their earnings and prospects for future profits as opposed to the value of their underlying assets.

Buffalo Tool & Die Mfg. Co. v. Commissioner, 74 T.C. 441 (1980). In *Buffalo Tool*, the judge rejected splitting the difference between extreme valuations prepared by each of the parties. Instead the judge supported the valuation with the most convincing argument.

Estate of Bright v. United States, 658 F.2d 999 (5th Cir. 1981). In *Bright*, the court ruled that no "control premium" should be attached to a minority interest block of stock even though the family unit controlled the corporation. In this case, the decedent's undivided one-half community property interest in a control block (55 percent) of stock was severed into two 27.5-percent interests. The court ruled that the control block was no longer a control block even though the decedent's husband held her interest as a trustee for the benefit of their children.

Andrews v. Commissioner, 79 T.C. 938 (1982). In valuing stock of four closely held corporations, the court rejected the valuations of both parties because they did not give appropriate relative weight to net asset value, earnings, and dividend-paying capacity. The court, however, applied minority interest discounts even though the decedent and his family collectively held all of the corporations' stock.

Department of Transportation v. Muller, 36 Cal. 3d 263, 681 P.2d 1340, 203 Cal. Rptr. 772 (1984). The courts ruled that the "excess income" method of measuring loss of business goodwill is a reasonable method of quantifying the loss even though other acceptable methods exist to value goodwill.

Harwood v. Commissioner, 82 T.C. 239 (1984). In valuing gifts of minority interest in a family partnership, the courts upheld discounts for minority interests and lack of marketability. The court held that a 50-percent discount was appropriate to account for the fact that the interests being valued were minority interests, were not publicly traded, and were subject to a restrictive clause in the partnership agreement.

Ronald v. 4-C's Electronic Packaging, Inc., 168 Cal. App. 3d 290, 214 Cal. Rptr. 225 (1985). The court found that price/earnings multiples of publicly traded companies may be used to assess the fair market value of a closely held corporation but should not be the only method used. This ruling emphasizes that a valuation should not rely solely on one method or approach to value but rather a combination of approaches.

Estate of Gallo v. Commissioner, 50 T.C.M. (CCH) 470 (1985). At issue was a minority block of stock (less than 2 percent) in a holding company, which held as its sole asset all of the capital stock of E & J Gallo Winery. This case is significant because the court placed most weight on the price/earnings ratios of comparable companies and it upheld a 36-percent discount for lack of marketability. The estate's valuation of the block was $341,620, the IRS valuation was $1,228,654, and the tax court decision was $279,186, which was lower than the estate's valuation.

OTHER VALUATION GUIDELINES

Many excellent books and articles have been written on how to value a business or its securities. Included in this list is the *IRS Valuation Guide for Income, Estate and Gift Taxes*. Although the IRS designed this guide specifically for training purposes and its contents cannot be "used or cited as authority for settling or sustaining a technical position," it nevertheless provides a useful guideline for valuation purposes. The guide includes chapters on methods and approaches to valuing closely held corporations, valuing preferred stock and discounts.

SUMMARY

Situations frequently arise during a litigation that require a business valuation. Valuing a business for any purpose requires a thorough understanding of the company and its operations, the industry in which the company operates, and the various valuation approaches that can be utilized. Because no single method or approach to valuation exists for unambiguously developing a company's value, the appraiser must be knowledgeable and experienced in all aspects of valuation methods and procedures and must have knowledge of ancillary areas of finance, economics, and accounting to effectively support the conclusion with a thorough and competent valuation. This is essential if the valuation is to withstand rigorous scrutiny often present in the litigation environment.

NOTES

1. The formula for the Gordon Growth Model is as follows:

$$V = \frac{D}{(K - G)}$$

Assuming the dividend (D) grows forever at a constant rate G, and G is less than the discount rate K, then V is the present value of the growing annuity stream (Gordon, 1959).

2. The Capital Asset Pricing Model is a framework for analyzing the relationship between risk and rates of return. The relationship between risk and return is known as the Security Market Line and is expressed by the following equation:

$$E(Ri) = Rf + B \times [E(Rm) - Rf]$$

where: $E(Ri)$ = the expected returns on Stock i
Rf = the risk-free rate of return
B = the beta coefficient for Stock i
$E(Rm)$ = the expected return on the market

3. The Cost of Capital is a weighted average of the firm's cost of debt and equity. The Cost of Capital can be determined with the following equation:

$$K_o = (D/V)(k_i)(1 - t) + (E/V)(k_e)$$

where: K_o = weighted average cost of capital
K_i = company's cost of debt
t = company's marginal tax rate
V = market value of the company's total invested capital
D = market value of the company's debt
E = market value of the company equity
D/V = proportion of debt to total invested capital
E/V = proportion of equity to total invested capital
K_e = company's cost of equity

BIBLIOGRAPHY

Black, F., and Scholes, M., "The Pricing of Options and Corporate Liabilities," *Journal of Political Economy*, 81 (May–June 1973), pp. 637–654.

Gordon, M.J., "Dividends, Earnings and Stock Prices," *Review of Economics and Statistics*, 41 (May 1959), pp. 99–105.

Modigliani, F., and M.H. Miller, "The Cost of Capital, Corporation Finance, and the Theory of Investment," *American Economic Review* (June 1958) pp. 261–297.

Samuelson, P.A., "Proof that Properly Anticipated Prices Fluctuate Randomly," *Industrial Management Review*, Vol. 6 (Spring 1965), pp. 41–49.

Sharpe, W.F., "Capital Prices: A Theory of Market Equilibrium under Conditions of Risks," *Journal of Finance*, Vol. 19, No. 30 (September 1964), pp. 416–422.

LIST OF CASES

Andrews v. Commissioner, 79 T.C. 938 (1982)
Bader v. United States, 172 F. Supp. 833 (S.D. Ill. 1959)
Estate of Bright v. United States, 658 F.2d 999 (5th Cir. 1981)
Buffalo Tool & Die Mfg. Co. v. Commissioner, 74 T.C. 441 (1980)
Central Trust Co. v. United States, 305 F.2d 393 (Ct. Cl. 1962)
Department of Transportation v. Muller, 36 Cal. 3d 263, 681 P.2d 1340, 203 Cal. Rptr. 772 (1984)
Estate of Gallo v. Commissioner, 50 T.C.M. (CCH) 470 (1985)
Harwood v. Commissioner, 82 T.C. 239 (1984)
Estate of Kirkpatrick, 34 T.C.M. (CCH) 1490 (1975)
Ronald v. 4-C's Electronic Packaging, Inc., 168 Cal. App. 3d 290, 214 Cal. Rptr. 225 (1985)
Woodward v. Quigley, 257 Iowa 1077, 133 N.W.2d 38 (1965)

27

LOST EARNINGS ARISING FROM PERSONAL INJURY, WRONGFUL TERMINATION, OR WRONGFUL DEATH

James H. West, CPA
Robert K. Athy, JD, CPA

This chapter discusses the information needed and approaches used in the computation of damages arising from wrongful terminations, personal injuries, or wrongful death. Most of the elements are identical regardless of the cause of action leading to the damages; however, there are some differences that are discussed first, followed by a section covering the information requirements and then a section on methodology. The chapter concludes with a discussion of special problems.

SIMILARITIES AND DIFFERENCES IN COMPUTATIONS

Personal injury, wrongful death, and wrongful termination cases all seek to quantify the economic loss of the plaintiff or the decedent's survivors.[1] The measured anticipated loss from date of incident reduced to its present value becomes the economic damages element of the settlement or award. In a wrongful termination case, the loss of earnings may be the only economic damages. In most wrongful death and personal injury cases, other economic damages occur (e.g. medical bills, home nursing care, funeral expenses). Of course, the period of time over which lost earnings are suffered also varies between the three types of cases. This chapter addresses only the lost earnings component. The other items are generally of an out-of-pocket nature and thus readily measurable.

Simply stated, the elements of the computation are the amount of earnings lost, the duration of the loss, and the present value discount factor. Each element may be computed in a variety of ways. Some jurisdictions require a particular method; others allow the expert to select the most appropriate method. This chapter considers each element and some of the variations.

Although the basic elements of the computation remain the same, some adjustments depend on the nature of the loss. In personal injury and wrongful termination cases, the plaintiff will usually be required to take reasonable steps to minimize ("mitigate") damages. In those cases the computation should be reduced by a reasonable estimate of the plaintiff's mitigation.

The period of loss in wrongful death cases is usually based on published worklife or life expectancy tables. The extent and duration of a disability resulting from personal injury or work interruption due to wrongful termination may be fixed before the loss is computed (if, for example, plaintiff has fully recovered or has been reemployed) but are more likely to be the subject of expert testimony.

In wrongful death cases, because the loss to the survivors or the decedent's estate is at issue, the loss is commonly reduced by the decedent's estimated personal consumption expenses. Similarly, in death and injury cases, an amount may be added to the claim to compensate for the lost value of the plaintiff/decedent's personal services to the household.

BASIC INFORMATION NEEDED

Biographical Profile

A biographical profile of the terminated, injured, or deceased party is the usual starting point. Often the attorney will have prepared a profile before an accountant begins work on the case. In wrongful death cases, interviewing surviving family members will often help. Personnel files kept by the decedent's employer may be an information source. The profile must reflect supported facts, rather than speculation, as it forms much of the basis for the expert opinion. In addition to the names of the plaintiff/decedent and immediate family members, the information should include at least the following.

Important Dates. The date of injury or date of death establishes the beginning of the loss period. Plaintiff/decedent's date of birth will be necessary to establish the correct age and to estimate life expectancies. In wrongful death cases, the date of birth of each immediate family member should be recorded. The dates at which a plaintiff has fully recovered from injuries or has been reemployed may signal the end of the loss period.

Health History. The accountant usually lacks expertise to give an opinion on medical aspects of the case; many jurisdictions, however, allow experts to base their opinions on information received from others or to assume the truth of such preceding testimony. In any event, the accountant should have enough information to understand how physical injuries and prior medical history may limit the plaintiff's ability to work. A plaintiff who had received a permanent disabling injury only a week before the accident at issue would have a weaker case for large damages. A decedent's prior medical history may provide information on limitations to worklife or life expectancy. Even the medical history of decedent's survivor can be significant if it would indicate that the survivor's life expectancy was shorter than the decedent's worklife expectancy.

Educational Background. Many jurisdictions consider lost earnings *capacity*, not simply lost earnings. The plaintiff or decedent may not need to have been employed on the date of loss. Accordingly, the injured party's entire educational and employment background is relevant. Moreover, where an obligation exists to mitigate damages, knowing the training the plaintiff has had that would qualify the plaintiff for substitute work will be relevant. Formal education, correspondence courses, on-the-job training, and even hobby experience may be relevant.

Income and Job History Data. A detailed personal income and employment history provides the starting point for the lost earnings computation. If the injured or deceased person was employed for a reasonable time prior to the loss, historical data will be a factor for projecting future loss of income. The obligation to mitigate damages, where applicable, requires post-injury or post-termination income to be included in the loss computation to calculate the actual net loss. Employment history is important to judge whether income would have likely changed with, for example, increasing responsibility.

Earnings is broadly defined to include all forms of compensation, commissions, bonuses, employer contributions to pension and profit sharing plans, and "perks" or fringe benefits. Do not overlook income from secondary jobs in personal injury and death cases. Income tax returns should disclose part-time work, consulting income, and military reserve income. Military reserve income further suggests the possibility of lost or reduced retirement benefits.

Personal Consumption Information. In wrongful death cases, the claim usually must be reduced by the deceased's personal consumption expenses, as these are expenditures no longer to be incurred by the estate. Although it would be ideal to construct a personal consumption history from the decedent's own records, sufficient records are rarely available to make a reconstruction. Studies discussed later in this chapter enable one to estimate consumption based on income and information about the number and type of household members. The deceased's relationship with each household member and any contribution to the household made by other residents may also be helpful information.

Applicable Law

Legal jurisdictions take varying approaches to computing lost earnings. Federal courts may not accept methods used in state courts. Some jurisdictions consider the impact of income taxes; others do not. Several methods exist to incorporate an inflation factor into the projection of future lost earnings, and each method requires a different treatment of the present value discount factor (see later discussion). The accountant should raise these issues with the attorney at the initial meeting and agree on the proper method to be used.

REFERENCE DATA

Local public, university, or law libraries contain necessary reference data. Computerized data bases may yield additional information or speed access to data. The accountant who computes lost earnings frequently will find certain references worth owning. The Bibliography section at the end of the chapter lists some recommended references.

PREPARING THE DAMAGE CLAIM

Computation of Undiscounted Future Earnings

This section deals with plaintiffs or decedents who had a recent history of earnings at the time of the loss. Special problems associated with claims of those not previously or not recently employed are treated later in this chapter.

Base Earnings. The first step is identification of lost "base earnings." Base earnings as used here includes the plaintiff's or decedent's total earnings at the time of the injury, death, or termination limited, however, in personal injury or wrongful termination to those earnings interrupted by the defendant's conduct. For example, assume that Paul Plaintiff is suing his previous employer, Ernie Employer, for wrongful termination. In addition to his work for Ernie, Paul held a regular part-time job and performed periodic consulting services for others. Absent additional information, Paul's lost base earnings would include only earnings from his employment with Ernie. If, however, Paul immediately found equivalent employment on condition that he drop the part-time job and all consulting activity, earnings from those sources would constitute lost base earnings. As noted in the previous section on income data, earnings are broadly defined. In addition to earnings from labor, base earnings may properly include items such as dividend income on securities and rental income if the wrongful conduct somehow interrupts those income sources.

Where the loss period is expected to be brief, perhaps because of quick recovery or good fortune in finding substitute employment, examining historic base earnings for a short period of time may be sufficient. A reasonable "rule of thumb" would be to use the same historic period as that of the stipulated or anticipated duration of the loss. Often, particularly in death cases, the loss period may span decades. A longer historical record should then be developed. Assuming the availability of reliable data, use at least 5 years of data.

History is often used to project future earnings. A consistent earnings record over the chosen historical period suggests that the same earnings level and trend would have continued into the future. Conversely, widely fluctuating historic earnings may suggest that history provides little insight into the future. At the least, identifying the reason for wide earnings fluctuations would be desirable. An effort should always be made to identify any reasons to suggest that future earnings would have deviated from historical earnings. For example, most employees see the greatest percentage increases in earnings in the early part of their careers with a tapering off of the rate of change as time goes on. The particular career track of the plaintiff/decedent and that of his peers should provide some guidance as to likely future income trends.

Employer records can suggest factors that would have affected income after the loss date, particularly if the plaintiff/decedent was one of several employees filling similar positions. Personnel records of career progress, including employee evaluations, may demonstrate the likelihood that plaintiff/decedent would have received promotions or merit increases. The same and other records (e.g., piecework or production records) may indicate, conversely, that plaintiff's productivity, and therefore earnings, was decreasing.

Sometimes available records will not provide a reasonable basis for estimating the path of earnings for a particular plaintiff or decedent. In those cases, one or more statistical methods may help.

One approach is to project average historical earnings into the future (inflation effects and adjustments are considered in a later section). Although the approach may be criticized as unsophisticated, it is easily understood by the jury and may be reasonable where the nature of future earnings was likely to remain consistent but the amount fluctuated historically. A statistical alternative is to fit a trend line to the historical data (after removing effects of historical inflation). Trend lines may be particularly appropriate where the historical data suggest a pattern of increasing or decreasing earnings.

Two types of trend lines are common: the least squares linear regression trend line and the judgmental trend line. Least squares is a mathematical method of fitting a straight line to the historical data, but the tool should be applied by an expert if the results are to be defensible. (Other chapters of this book describe the use of regression in litigation.)

The judgmental trend line is based on the expert's judgmental analysis of best fit, rather than on a mathematical analysis. The expert plots the historic data and then fits a line to it that appears to consider all available information, including facts not reflected by the numeric data. The judgmental trend line may draw criticism because of its subjective quality, yet it is easily understood and may be intuitively more acceptable than the mathematical methods.

The age-earnings profile, which compiles research data reflecting the actual earnings of a sample of workers of various ages at a given date, can be useful. The government periodically publishes age-earnings data, reflecting earnings in a specific occupation, an industry, or a given geographic area. The first consideration in using age-earnings profiles is whether the workers sampled are from the same "population" as the plaintiff or decedent. For example, the age-earnings profile of hourly factory employees will not apply if the plaintiff was an airline pilot because earnings in the two occupations change in response to different forces.

An age-earnings profile reflects only a cross-section of earnings at the time the data were gathered. It does not reflect the earnings of one worker or the same group of workers, over a period of time. One should not therefore use data from one age-earnings study to project future earnings.

The Value of Household Services

Wrongful death and personal injury cases customarily value the plaintiff/decedent's services that are lost to the household. If the case involves a homemaker's death or injury, this may be the major element of economic damages. Several methods are commonly used.

Whether the calculation is for the man or woman of the house, and regardless of which method is used, one must first identify the amount of time devoted to household services. Knowing something about the household helps to estimate time devoted to household tasks. Time varies with gender, size of the home, number and age of family members, number of wage earners, and other factors. Family members can provide this information. One should also combine hours devoted to household services with outside work hours to be sure the total is reasonable. Methods for estimating the hours devoted to household labor can become quite elaborate (See, for example, Kiker and Heath, 1987).

Ideally, one should allocate all the hours to the individual tasks performed and then "cost them out" based on market wages for each task (known as the specific identification method). Unfortunately, the market wages for each task may not be available. Alternatively, the total hours may be multiplied by the rate at which the plaintiff or decedent was paid for work outside the home (the opportunity cost method). Or the total hours may be multiplied either by the minimum wage or the market wage for household help (the replacement cost method). Each method neglects the fact that, in practice, more than one task may be performed simultaneously. The opportunity cost and replacement cost methods assume that all household tasks have the same value. The opportunity cost method further assumes that the same household services may have greatly different value depending upon who performs them. It is doubtful that either the minimum wage or plaintiff's own wage rate will reflect the cost of purchasing replacement services. These assumptions tend to defy reality.

In spite of its drawbacks, the most realistic method may be the replacement cost method used in conjunction with the local market rate for household help. Unless the remaining family members assume the tasks formerly performed by the plaintiff/decedent they will, after all, need to resort to the marketplace to fill the void.

Estimating the Loss Period

In quantifying damages, one must estimate the period of loss. In personal injury and wrongful termination cases, the period may be dictated by the facts or estimated by other experts. Medical or rehabilitation experts, for example, will usually testify regarding both the extent and period of disability. In wrongful termination cases, where the plaintiff continues to be unemployed or underemployed, employment specialists may testify.

In wrongful death cases, the loss period will most likely be fixed by the decedent's worklife expectancy as reflected in statistical tables. Sometimes, however, the life expectancy of the decedent's survivors or other facts may limit the loss period. Assume that Beth is the unfortunate victim of an automobile accident at age 39. Current worklife expectancy tables suggest that Beth, who was employed at the time of her death, would have worked an additional 16.1 years. Further assume that Beth's husband, Dave, is 65, or 26 years Beth's senior. According to life expectancy tables, Dave could be expected to live approximately 14.3 more years. Dave's loss can not be considered to extend beyond his own life expectancy. Thus the total loss period is 14.3 years (ignoring the complexities of joint probabilities) unless damages are also sought for Dave's and/or Beth's heirs.

Alternatively, consider the loss resulting from the death of a single parent whose youngest child is age 15. Absent some reason to assume an economic contribution to the child after age 18, it may be appropriate to limit the loss period to 3 years, that is, until the child reaches the legal age to gain employment or to the child's age at graduation from college if attendance at college was probable. Assumptions underlying the period of loss should be reasonable and supported by appropriate statistics, and that statistical information must be applied with an appreciation for the other facts. For our example of Beth and Dave, consider how the period of loss would differ if either had a terminal illness and had been given a maximum life expectancy of 6 months by his or her doctor.

Computation of Offsets to the Loss

Mitigation of Damages. As already mentioned, most jurisdictions require the plaintiff in personal injury and wrongful termination cases to take reasonable steps to minimize damages. In the context of computing lost earnings, this means that the claim should be reduced to the extent plaintiff finds or should be expected to find substitute income. The future value of substitute income is subject to the same projection techniques as those of lost income.

Personal Consumption Expenditures. Wrongful death cases commonly reduce the claim by the estimated amount the decedent would have spent on his or her own personal needs. In theory, to the extent decedent would have spent funds for his or her personal needs, that amount would not have been available for the survivors. The logic is less compelling when the suit is under a survival statute than when it is under a wrongful death statute. Nevertheless, most jurisdictions make the deduction.

Experts and jurisdictions differ on the best definition of "personal needs." Some include only basic needs such as food, clothing, and personal items. Some include all expenses necessary to maintain decedent's earnings stream. Others include everything that the decedent would have spent on his or her person during the loss period.

Consumption is frequently expressed as a percentage of income. Opinions also differ on whether the percentage should be applied to total household income, plaintiff's total base earnings, or only to what might be called plaintiff's "spendable" income (base earnings less fringe benefits and taxes). Obviously, the method used to derive the percentage factor usually will suggest the appropriate method for its application. As with other elements of the lost earnings computation, no one approach is best for all situations. It may be appropriate to present a range of outcomes, especially where alternative approaches appear equally reasonable.

When sufficient records are available, one should reconstruct household expenses for a year or more prior to the loss date. One can then allocate expenses among the household members for whose benefit they were made. Expenses such as utilities and housing costs may be treated as "family" or unallocable costs on the theory that heat and light, although enjoyed by each resident, are no less available to other family members.

Because of economies of scale, some costs do not drop ratably with the loss of a family member. Food expense is likely to follow this pattern. A reasonable way of handling these expenses is to treat the decedent as consumer of the last dollars spent by the household, that is, the marginal consumer. Under this theory, the decedent's consumption would be identified by comparing the pre- and postloss food expenses.

Personal and family data are often not available to support a reconstruction. In those cases, an estimate might be based on public data. The Department of Labor, Bureau of Labor Statistics, publishes periodic consumer data under various titles. Because some data are infrequently updated, opinions sometimes rely on studies made years earlier. Older information should be updated as best as possible, using perhaps consumer price index information.

Many experts have relied on consumption information developed by Earl Cheit (1961). Cheit's study suggests percentage consumption figures for heads of households based on family size. Although well respected, Cheit's study is dated from 1961, and there has been no study that attempts to determine whether through time or social changes the conclusions have become obsolete. Moreover, Cheit's figures do not vary with income level or other factors that today commonly are accepted as determinants of consumption.

Growth Rates and Discounting to Present Value

Once base earnings, the value of household services, and appropriate offsets are computed, some method of providing for inflationary growth of those factors is usually incorporated. Then, the entire inflation-adjusted future income stream is reduced to its present value. Much literature has been devoted to projecting inflation rates and determining proper present value discount factors. Relatively minor changes in the inflation and discount factors can produce widely different results, especially with a long loss period.

Several states have simplified the issue of inflation and discounting by simply requiring that they not be considered at all. A similar approach, taken most notably by Alaska courts, resolves the question by holding that the inflation rate and present value discount rate (market interest rate) fully offset one another. This approach is known as the "Alaska method" or as the "total offset" rule. In jurisdictions following either of these approaches, the computation, in effect, merely sums annual base earnings and household services figures reduced by projected personal consumption and other offsets, all stated in constant dollar terms.

Most jurisdictions permit expert testimony related to inflation projections and discount rates. The U.S. Supreme Court has held that the "Alaska method" may be appropriate where evidence is offered to support its validity, but it is not to be applied as a matter of law in actions based on federal law (*Jones & Laughlin Steel Corp. v. Pfeifer*, 462 U.S. 523 (1983)). Consequently, federal cases may admit expert testimony on projected inflation rates and appropriate present value discount factors. Most states have evolved a similar line of case law.

Historical inflation data are frequently based on *Consumer Price Index* information published by the U.S. Department of Labor, Bureau of Labor Statistics. In addition to the monthly CPI for all urban consumers, separate indexes are published less frequently for selected urban areas. Some argue that wage growth rates, not price growth rates, are the proper focus. A comparison of some long-term data suggests that, except for periods of high price inflation, wages have increased more steadily and slightly faster than consumer prices. Bear in mind that wage growth rates may differ by occupation.

The problem lies in selecting an historical inflation rate that will closely relate to future inflation. Some experts have used the current inflation rate (or wage growth rate). This approach seems flawed by the variability of both rates over time. Others have used an average of historical rates for a selected time period. The precision of any approach can be judged accurately only with hindsight.

Yet another approach has been to use a net discount rate. Proponents of this approach argue that, except during the early 1980s, interest rates on 3-year U.S. securities have tended to remain between 0 and 1 percent higher than the earnings growth rate (Corboy, 1984–85). Other studies suggest that the true rate of interest may be 3 percent. Therefore, experts following this approach will discount the projected real earnings stream to present value using a net discount factor of between one to three percent.

An appropriate discount rate (to be applied to a future stream that reflects expected inflation) generally applies the rate plaintiff can expect to earn on the sum awarded by the jury when it is invested in the "best and safest" investments (*Chesapeake & Ohio Railroad v. Kelly*, 241 U.S. 485 (1916)). Conservative investments are appropriate because the plaintiff should not be required to accept undue risk to maximize the return on the invested award. Interest-bearing U.S. Government securities are the most often selected vehicles, usually moderate to long-term Treasury securities.

SPECIAL PROBLEMS

In the case of a minor's wrongful death, there may be no work history to support an earnings projection. Estimating lifetime earnings then becomes a matter of determining what work level the minor would likely have been suited to and computing, based on governmental statistics, the lifetime earnings in selected occupations at that level.

The younger the decedent at the time of death, the more difficult the task becomes. High school aged children may have been tested for basic intelligence levels, psychological profiles, or even occupational preferences. Where specialized test results are not available, other school records may provide information to compare the child's academic and social skills, initiative, and so forth to those of classmates. Interviews with parents, teachers, and school counselors may provide invaluable information.

Especially where very young children are involved, establishing a profile of parents and siblings will be helpful. Absent special circumstances, a reasonable assumption may be that children can be expected to reach levels of occupational ability at least as high as their parents and commensurate with those of siblings. Children whose parents both obtained college degrees are more likely to obtain a college education.

Once the likely education level and, if possible, specific career probabilities are established, a wide variety of governmental data will assist in projecting lifetime income. The Departments of Labor and Commerce publish numerous sources to equate income with education, race, sex, and occupation.

If the decedent was a homemaker not employed outside the home, the focus will be on the value of household services. Occasionally the homemaker will have had an identifiable employment capacity. For example, the homemaker may have previously worked outside the home, had specific training, or even a marketable hobby skill. Such skills can be valued. The weight to be given such evidence may be for the jury, not the expert, to determine.

Self-employed decedents present different challenges. Net earnings and economic benefits provided by the business must be computed historically and projected to the end of the loss period. This requires an analysis of the business financial statements for a reasonable historical period, usually 3 to 5 years, at a minimum. Unusual and nonrecurring items affecting earnings of the business should be eliminated to avoid influencing the projection. In addition to examining the business itself, one should evaluate, if possible, the economic and industry conditions that might have affected the business. Generally, the approach resembles that taken in valuing a business for sale using the discounted future earnings approach.

NOTE

1. In various jurisdiction damages for wrongful death may be recoverable under either a "survival action" or a "wrongful death action." A discussion of the variety of forms taken by the two actions is beyond the scope of this book; in general, a survival action focuses on the decedent's loss and is brought on behalf of the decedent's estate. A wrongful death action focuses on the loss of the plaintiff's survivors and is usually brought by family members. Although the type of recoverable economic loss may differ depending on the nature of the action, this chapter assumes that the computation of lost earnings is the same in either case.

BIBLIOGRAPHY

Government Publications

Government publications may be ordered from the Superintendent of Documents, U.S. Government Printing Office, Washington, DC 20402. (202) 783-3238.

BLS Measures of Compensation. U.S. Department of Labor, Bureau of Labor Statistics, February 1986. Bulletin 2239.

Employment, Hours, and Earnings, United States, 1909–84. U.S. Department of Labor, Bureau of Labor Statistics, March 1985. Bulletin 1312–12. (Supp. July 1987).

Handbook of Labor Statistics. U.S. Department of Labor, Bureau of Labor Statistics, June 1985. Bulletin 2217.

National Center for Health Statistics: United States Life Tables. U.S. Decennial Life Tables for 1979–81. (Vol. 1, No.1) DHHS Pub. No. (PHS) 85-1150-1. (G.P.O. Aug. 1985)

National Economic Trends (monthly). Federal Reserve Bank of St. Louis.

National Survey of Professional, Administrative and Clerical Pay. U.S. Department of Labor, Bureau of Labor Statistics, October 1986. Bulletin 2271.

Statistical Abstract of the United States (Annual). U.S. Department of Commerce, Bureau of the Census.

Tables of Working Life: The Increment-Decrement Model. U.S. Department of Labor, Bureau of Labor Statistics, November 1982. Bulletin 2135.

U.S. Financial Data (weekly). Federal Reserve Bank of St. Louis.

Worklife Estimates: Effects of Race and Education. U.S. Department of Labor, Bureau of Labor Statistics, February 1986. Bulletin 2254.

Other

Cheit, Earl, *Measuring Economic Loss Due to Death and Disability* (Wiley & Sons, 1961).

Corboy, Philip. "The Impact of Economic Theory on the Determination of Damages in a Wrongful Death Case." 20 *The Forum* 606 (1984–85).

Kiker, B.F., and Julia Heath. "Evaluating Household Services: Additional Evidence." 1 *Journal of Forensic* Economics 19 (September 1987).

Parks, Richard. "The Evaluation of Earnings Loss in Alaska Courts: The Implications of Beaulieu and Guinn." 2 *Alaska Law Journal* 311 (1985).

Speiser, Stuart. *Recovery for Wrongful Death*, 2nd ed., 2 Vols. (The Lawyers Co-Operative Publishing Co., 1975. Supp. Sept. 1987).

Speiser, Stuart. *Recovery for Wrongful Death*, 2nd ed., *Economic Handbook* (The Lawyers Co-Operative Publishing Co., 1979. Supp. Feb. 1986).

Stein, Jacob. *Damages and Recovery, Personal Injury and Wrongful Death Actions* (The Lawyers Co-Operative Publishing Co., 1972. Supp. Oct. 1987).

LIST OF CASES

Chesapeake & Ohio Railroad v. Kelly, 241 U.S. 485 (1916)
Jones & Laughlin Steel Corp. v. Pfeifer, 462 U.S. 523 (1983)

28

LOST PROFITS

Neill W. Freeman, CPA
James A. Spielmann, CPA

OBJECTIVE OF A LOST PROFITS CALCULATION

Damages are a central issue in essentially all commercial litigation, both for plaintiffs seeking to prove them and for defendants seeking to disprove them. In many instances, the damages claimed by plaintiff are in the form of profits lost or foregone as a result of the defendant's alleged actions.

Profits are the excess of revenues over expenses for a specified time period. They can be for a specific transaction, for a class of transactions, for a business unit or for an entire entity. Lost profits occur when an entity is precluded from realizing a portion or all of those profits that would ordinarily inure, but for another party's action.

A lost profits calculation is used to ascertain the amount that will make the damaged party whole. In contract claims, the contract may limit the amount of the claim and the calculation method. In tort claims, the damages amount compensates the damaged party for losses proximately caused, whether anticipated or not. Another section of this book discusses in detail special classes of claims.

ELEMENTS REQUIRED TO BE PROVEN

Three elements must be proven for a lost profits claim to succeed: proximate cause, reasonable certainty, and foreseeability.

Proximate Cause

Recovery of damages for lost profits is subject to the general principle that damages must be proximately caused by the defendant's wrongful conduct. Proximate cause does not mean the only cause, but at least the major cause. The CPA as an expert may testify as to the cause-and-effect relationship. This may help establish the cause in fact. Whether a cause in fact constitutes a legal cause is reserved for the trier-of-fact—the judge and/or jury.

Reasonable Certainty

The second required element is that the damages must be proven with reasonable certainty. Uncertainty as to the fact of damages is fatal to the claim. Uncertainty as to the amount of damages is not fatal. The defendant cannot escape liability merely because the alleged action makes it difficult to calculate precisely the damages amount. The plaintiff need merely demonstrate a rational basis for the damages computation. It need not be the only basis. Plaintiff's proof, however flawed, is deemed sufficient if it is the best available, given the circumstances of the case. Training and experience almost invariably qualify CPAs to help calculate or refute damages for lost profits.

Foreseeability

The third required element is that the lost profits must have been foreseeable as the natural result of a breach of contract at the time the contract was made or the tort committed. This element is generally beyond the scope of the CPA's testimony unless the CPA is also qualified as an expert in the particular type of business or industry involved.

THE CPA'S ROLE

The CPA's role in lost profits calculations is generally within the lines discussed in Chapter 1. As a trial or testifying expert, the CPA will generally either sponsor or support the computation of the amount of damages or offer testimony as to the errors and/or omissions of the claim submitted. As a nontrial expert, the CPA helps counsel evaluate the amounts as calculated under various alternative theories, assists in the discovery required to obtain the information necessary to calculate or refute the amounts, and may help counsel select or prepare the testifying expert. In either role, the CPA may be required to comfortably employ concepts, developed by statute or precedent, that are not in accordance with, or even specifically prohibited by, generally accepted accounting principles.

THREE CONCEPTUAL AREAS

Lost profits damages claims fall, generally, into three conceptual areas: those in which a business suffers a relative reduction in income, but continues to exist; those in which a business is caused to cease or terminate its operations; and those in which a business never commenced operations.

METHODS TO CALCULATE LOST PROFITS

In contract claims, the contract may define the limits and methods of calculating lost profits damages. However, this is rarely the case. Usually one does not know with certainty what would have happened had the defendant's actions not occurred. Therefore, one must base lost profits on an understanding of the relevant business factors and projections of what one reasonably would expect to have occurred in the plaintiff's business environment.

The CPA can suggest three common, basic methods to calculate lost profits.

Before-and-After Approach

The CPA uses the periods before and/or after the alleged acts to calculate what the plaintiff's anticipated performance would have been during the period, or as a result, of the alleged acts. For example, during the damages period in a bid-rigging case, the market price for widgets, if no illegal behavior had occurred, might be expected to exhibit the same relationship to the market prices of Products A, B, and C, as it did both before and after the damage period.

Yardstick Approach

The CPA studies a similar company, industry, or market that was unaffected by the alleged acts to calculate what the plaintiff's performance should have been during the period of the alleged acts. For example, sales in the damaged market might be expected to have grown at the same rate relative to GNP (or other recognized indicia) as did a similar but unaffected market during the same period. Many government and private data sources and studies summarize the history and project the future of almost every industry.

Another variation measures the losses suffered by plaintiff based on the gains realized by defendant. The underlying theory is that the defendant's action transferred customers (or sales or market share, etc.) from plaintiff to defendant.

Sales Projections (Hypothetical Profits)

The CPA may create a model of the affected business by making assumptions based on how the plaintiff would have performed absent ("but for") the alleged acts. For example, in an antitrust case, "but for" profits could be measured in a microeconomic model of the affected market that would suggest how volume and prices might change in the absence of the alleged anticompetitive behavior. The plaintiff company's cost structure would be modeled and applied to this new volume and price.

ELEMENTS OF LOST PROFITS

Regardless of the approach or approaches used, the lost profits calculation requires revenues and costs that would have been earned or incurred in the "but-for" world. If the business is a continuing one or if only a portion of a business is affected, the revenues and costs generally should be the incremental revenues and costs of the affected lines or portion of the business. If the business is terminated, or unestablished, the revenues and costs generally should be total revenues and total costs. The CPA must first calculate the probable revenues that would have been achieved and the additional costs that would have been incurred to generate those revenues. Lost profits damages may also include a claim for incidental costs.

LOST REVENUES

The two key elements in calculating lost revenues[1] are volume and price. What quantity or volume would have been sold? At what price would the product or service have been sold?

Volume

To calculate lost revenue, the CPA must analyze the relevant market for the product or service and the volume that plaintiff could have attained but for the defendant's actions. Frequently, it may be useful for the CPA to analyze market behavior and the market share within that market.

Sometimes the market may be as broad as the total market for automobiles in the United States. Sometimes the market may not be so clearly defined (e.g., is the "market" for cellophane or for wrapping/packaging materials in general?). The market for Porsche autos may not be the same as that for Chrysler cars. Also, a Porsche dealer in Idaho has a smaller relevant market than a Porsche dealer in Southern California. There are fewer possible purchasers for luxury automobiles in Idaho, but Idaho may have a greater proportion of millionaires relative to the general population than does Southern California. To complicate matters further, Idaho purchasers are likely to travel much greater distances to the Idaho dealer than are Southern California purchasers. An analysis of the relevant market must consider, among other factors, whether geographic constraints to the market exist.

Industry statistics often are used in place of detailed analyses of relevant markets. However, the CPA must consider the risk that such statistics may be too broad to be meaningful. Sales of autos in Southern California are not likely to be a reliable predictor of sales of Porsches.

When a new product is involved, whether a market does or could exist is debatable. These cases may require a detailed market analysis. Computing the plaintiff's anticipated market share often can be addressed when analyzing the relevant market. An alternative to a detailed market analysis is to review the plaintiff's success in gaining market share in other markets or similar ventures. The success of other ventures in the same geographic area also may be a reasonable indication of potential market penetration.

A key factor to consider is whether the plaintiff's present or attainable capacity to produce and deliver the product or service is sufficient to achieve the projected sales volume. In addition to plant and equipment for production and personnel for delivery, the CPA may consider such factors as whether the financial capacity exists to fund required expansion, the adequacy of plaintiff's management talent, and the quality of its labor relations. Finally, the CPA will want to assess whether the plaintiff would be likely to have expanded its production capacity, assuming it had the capability. For example, if the expansion of production capacity would have required additional borrowings and plaintiff's board minutes indicate a strong aversion to assuming additional debt, then it might be unreasonable to assume that expansion would have occurred. Also, if the market is cyclical, a company may not expand its capacity to satisfy periodic unmet demand.

Price

The second element in calculating lost revenues is the price at which the incremental volume of the product or service would have been sold. Prices may be affected by many variables including market share, cost of production, competition, and regulatory environment. The key is to identify the most crucial variables and to calculate their potential effect under circumstances that would have existed in the "but-for" world. For example, the effect of regulation on the savings and loan industry was clearly greater a decade ago. Today, competition is probably the most important factor affecting price (i.e., lending rates) via its effect on the cost of funds. Similarly, some markets are subject to severe price erosion as a result of attempts to maximize throughput in the face of technological change. Computer memory chips that cost several hundred dollars each just a few years ago now sell for relative pennies.

The variables influencing price may affect not only incremental sales but also total actual sales. When calculating lost profits, care should be exercised in measuring the impact of charging a different price on total revenues. For example, suppose the plaintiff company actually sold 1000 units at $5 per unit ($5000 in revenues). In the "but-for" world, the plaintiff would have sold an additional 500 units, but the price would have been $4 per unit rather than $5 per unit. The incremental revenues are $1000. The company would have lost $1000 in revenues on actual unit sales because of the lower price [$5000 − ($4 × 1000) = $1000] but would have gained $2000 by selling more units (500 × $4 = $2000).

The focus may be on incremental profits of the entity as a whole rather than relating to a single product or product line because variables such as market share, price, productive capacity, and others often interact with each other. For example, the incremental sales of one product may increase the sales of another product (follow-on sales). If a manufacturer sells more fly rods, it may also sell more reels. Substitute products may bring about the opposite effect. If a milk distributor sells more low-fat milk, it may sell less whole milk.

Calculating incremental revenues is often the most complex element of calculating lost profits damages and is the element subject to the widest range of opinion and challenge. Some cases (such as antitrust matters) may apply econometric techniques. Regression analysis or other statistical methods to calculate revenues are often useful. Other cases require market studies. One may often compute incremental revenues using more than one of these approaches. Similarly, quantitative evidence may be used to calculate revenues, and qualitative evidence may be used to corroborate the result.

COSTS

Once lost revenues have been computed, the CPA must then ascertain what additional costs would have been incurred to generate those revenues.

Costs generally are considered to be variable, fixed, or semifixed (semivariable). Variable costs vary in some direct relationship or proportion to a change in production or sales.[2] Fixed or semifixed costs do not change over established ranges of production or sales but may change as certain thresholds are reached.

Generally, it is most appropriate to compare variable costs to incremental revenues in calculating lost profits. Costs that vary with activity are by definition incremental and may be incurred in production, selling, administration, or general management functions of the business.

Direct costs of production are typically variable and include materials and production labor. Overhead costs may or may not be variable. Care must be exercised to establish the elements of overhead that vary with changes in production levels.

Selling costs also often vary in some proportion to sales levels. Selling costs include salespersons' commissions, advertising, and marketing costs, distribution costs, and sales returns and discounts. One must distinguish between incremental and average costs. For example, the fixed salary component of an existing salesperson's total compensation would not be incremental, whereas the fixed salary component of a salesperson newly hired to sell the additional units claimed by plaintiff would be incremental. Total salesperson's costs would be components of average costs.

General and administrative costs must be analyzed to establish which of them are variable. These might include the home office costs related to purchasing materials, processing orders, financing additional working capital requirements, and collecting receivables (to include bad debt write-offs).

Most fixed costs are actually semifixed in that there usually is some capacity threshold that, when exceeded, will cause an increase in staff and/or facilities costs. When existing capacity is not sufficient to generate the incremental revenues claimed by plaintiff, then it is reasonable to include a factor for additional costs to expand capacity in the lost profits calculation. The relevant incremental costs to include may be the entire outlay or some fraction thereof based upon output, depreciation, or some other factor.

If existing management and administrative personnel cannot reasonably be expected to handle the assumed incremental sales revenues, then the lost profits analysis should include additional incremental staff costs.

INCIDENTAL COSTS

A lost profits damage claim may also include a claim for incidental costs. These are costs incurred as a result of the alleged acts, separate and apart from costs included in the lost profits calculations.

Incidental costs include, for example, penalties incurred on raw materials order cancellations or less than normal profit margins on the "fire sale" of inventories. Other examples include: expenses necessary to mitigate[3] the alleged damages; any out-of-pocket costs incurred as a result of the alleged acts, costs associated with any resulting excess capacity; costs incurred to complete contracts or commitments; and costs of personnel furlough or termination and plant closure costs. The expert should be sure not to double count these costs if already included in the lost profits calculation.

TIME VALUE OF MONEY

Historical and prospective lost profits must be adjusted to the approximate date of trial to account for the time value of money. Prejudgment interest, as a matter of law, varies among jurisdictions, and may differ between liquidated and unliquidated claims; counsel should guide the CPA. Regardless, the value of prior years' lost profits may be adjusted to their current value. Future lost profits should be discounted at an appropriate rate to their present value. Chapter 9 in this volume, "Time Value of Money," discusses the concepts of current value and present value.

TAXES

One should calculate lost profits before the effect of income taxes. Compensatory damages are almost always taxable to the plaintiff and deductible by the defendant. Therefore, to calculate lost profits on an after-tax basis, in most instances, would effectively subject the plaintiff to double taxation. Another view, with the same result, is that a reduction of lost profits for the effects of taxes would shift the penalty for the wrongful act to the government (which collects fewer taxes) from the defendant (who pays a lesser award.)

NOTES

1. The term *lost revenues* may refer to either total or incremental revenues.
2. "Variable costs" does not infer that costs maintain a linear relationship with sales (or other measurement base). For example, a 100% increase in sales does not necessarily imply a 100% increase in selling expenses.
3. If plaintiff fails to mitigate its damages, discuss with counsel the possibility of challenging those damages claimed that plaintiff failed to mitigate.

BIBLIOGRAPHY

Dunn, R.L., *Recovery of Damages for Lost Profits* (Lawpress Corporation, 1987).

Sims, R.S., and M.W. Haller, "Lost Profits: Covering All the Bases in the 'But For' World," *Inside Litigation* (February 1988), Vol. 2, No. 4, pp. 25–29. (Also appeared in *Computer Lawyer* (February 1988), Vol. 5, No. 2, pp. 11–15).

Wagner, M.S., and P.B. Frank, "Litigation Services," *AIPCA Technical Consulting Practice Aid 7* (1986).

29

COST ESTIMATION

Jeffrey H. Kinrich, CPA, CMC

INTRODUCTION

In many civil litigations, the plaintiff claims that, but for the defendant's actions, plaintiff would have earned a higher level of profits. These lost profits may have arisen from higher overall sales, from a particular sale, or from lower costs incurred in making the actual sales. All of these situations require an analysis of costs; in most cases this means estimating costs.

Need for Cost Estimation

Costs are relevant for several reasons. Damage claims are usually for lost profits, not lost sales. Only rarely can a business claim that lost profits equal lost sales. More often, a business that loses sales also avoids some related costs. Computation of lost profits usually requires computation of lost sales and the resulting avoided costs.

Costs may be relevant in relation to some other element of a claim. For example, the analyst may be interested in the profit contribution of a particular product line. In a patent case, the issue may be a reasonable royalty as a percentage of contribution margin. Each of these requires knowledge of the product's costs.

Sometimes plaintiffs are not claiming lost sales but instead extra costs incurred as a result of the defendant's conduct. Such cases also require the computation of costs.

Finally, some cases focus specifically on costs. For example, in a public utility rate case, the utility is geneally entitled to recover its costs of providing service. In an overcharge case, the plaintiff may try to show that the defendant earned an improperly large margin of profit over cost. In a predatory pricing case, the legal issue is the relationship between costs and prices. In all of these cases, it is essential to know the costs of the product or service.

From these comments, it is obvious that knowledge of costs is essential to many analyses. But why do we speak in terms of cost *estimation*? Why must costs be estimated, instead of known or computed with certainty?

Costs are rarely specifically known or knowable. Even resorting to the company's general ledger does not necessarily provide the analyst with an understanding of the firm's cost behavior. Although the general ledger contains all of the accounts that are used to develop the financial statements, these costs are not recorded on the basis of their fixed and variable components. Most often the analyst needs to estimate, for either all the accounts or for a selected number, which costs vary over time or with production.

Often, the analyst needs to know what costs *would have been* in some hypothetical situation. That is, the analyst needs to use historical data as a basis upon which to estimate "but-for" costs. Costs must be computed by applying analytic techniques and reasoning to the available information. These techniques and reasoning are what we mean by *cost estimation*.

On occasion, one needs to estimate quantities other than costs. These might include various revenue, asset, or liability accounts as well as nonfinancial quantities such as volume, capacity, or time. Many of the techniques described in this chapter, especially those in the section under allocation methods, may be useful in making these estimates. Despite this, for convenience, we will continue to talk about "costs" only. The reader may substitute other terms when appropriate.

Skills Required

Estimating costs requires substantial skill in three areas: cost accounting, economics, and statistics. Industrial engineering experience can also prove useful.

Cost accounting is the primary technical discipline used in cost estimation. Indeed, until a few years ago many would say that it was the only required skill. A cost accountant understands fixed and variable costs, capital expenditures, standard costs, budgets and budget variances, direct labor and materials costs, overhead costs and overhead allocation, contribution margin, incremental costs versus fully absorbed costs, and other topics. We discuss some of these concepts later in relation to cost estimation.[1]

In recent years, techniques of economics and statistics have been brought to bear in problems of cost accounting and estimation. Primary among these is regression analysis. Economics and statistics have provided the cost accountant with powerful tools. But to many cost accountants, these new tools are confusing. Acknowledging their power in solving problems, many practitioners are uncomfortable in knowing how to use the tools, when they are appropriate, and what problems to watch out for. This chapter explores some basic applications of economics and statistics to the problems of cost estimation.

Some areas of industrial engineering have relevance to cost accounting and cost estimation. Work measurement and job design, especially as they relate to the costs incurred in performing a task are useful techniques. These are considered to be less critical for the analyst to master, primarily because, to the extent they are important, they are often already in the cost accountant's "bag of tricks." The major lesson to be learned from industrial engineering is that understanding the underlying tasks and activities that generate the costs can help the analyst make informed judgments relative to cost estimation.

PURPOSE OF COST ESTIMATES

Within a litigation context, cost estimates may be required for:

- Total cost of a product or process
- Variable cost per unit of a product or service
- Fixed costs directly attributable to a product or service.

In selecting an estimation technique, keep the purpose of the estimate in mind. Some estimation techniques are more appropriate to one of the preceding types of cost than another. Often, total costs are easier to estimate than specific component costs. Sometimes the income statement or a separate management report provides total cost information. When total cost pool is not in dispute, relatively little analysis may need to be performed.

Other situations require some form of total cost analysis. The particular circumstances have a significant bearing on which technique should be employed. For example, a multivariate regression analysis may estimate total costs accurately but may be less precise in estimating the variable costs attributable to each causal factor. If the total cost is the quantity being estimated, the analyst may choose to stop the analysis at this point. If the relevant quantity is the variable cost per unit due to a change in a particular input, further work may be required.

If the purpose of the analysis is to estimate the fixed costs, then clearly one must understand the business operations before selecting an appropriate technique for measuring the costs. Both the magnitude and the types of costs that are considered to be fixed change over time. Also, when establishing the parameters of the analysis, the time frame must be scrutinized. Data from periods prior and subsequent to the period under examination may aid in understanding the behavior of costs over time, particularly in identifying changes in fixed costs.

Similarly, if the analysis concerns costs generated at a new production facility, analogies from other facilities may be appropriate. However, computing incremental costs at an existing plant may require an entirely different approach.

COST ENVIRONMENTS

A company's costs, reports, and information systems do not exist in a vacuum. A number of cost "environments" exist in the business world. Knowledge of these environments can aid the analyst in anticipating the types of reports that should exist, the types of questions to ask, and the types of analyses that the analyst should or could conduct.

Examples of cost environments include manufacturing (job cost and process cost), retailing, and service establishments.

Any business has certain cost "drivers," the causes of the most important costs and those most likely to change with volume. An understanding of the cost environment will enable the analyst to make preliminary judgments about the types of costs that may be important and thereby identify the questions to ask.

In a job cost manufacturing shop, costs may be collected for individual jobs, and the analyst can often consider the job to be the unit of analysis. When accounting records and supporting management reports disaggregate costs on a unit basis, the allocation of the fixed and variable components may require reexamination for purposes of the estimate.

The usual accounting for process costing environments collects costs and volumes in individual cost centers; the cost center, rather than the job, is likely to be the focus of the analysis. When costs are not identified with specific units of product, they are collected on a period basis in a work-in-process account. The total cost per unit could be estimated by dividing the total costs in this account by the units of production. In making such estimates, the analyst must match the time when the costs are accumulated with the period in which the units are produced.

Similarly, in some manufacturing businesses, direct labor may be an important cost driver, and the cost may be directly associated with the resulting product. In others, especially those making extensive use of capital equipment, direct labor may be almost insignificant; plant overhead may be the most important cost component.

A manufacturing company incurs significant nonmanufacturing costs, especially marketing and administrative costs. These costs are also prevalent in nonmanufacturing companies. Costs incurred to obtain customer orders and provide them with finished products are considered marketing. These costs usually include advertising, sales commissions and salaries, out-of-pocket expenditures to support the sales force (e.g., travel and entertainment), and the like. Administrative costs are those that support the organization such as executive and clerical salaries, data processing, and accounting expenses.

In retailing, the estimates of costs, particularly cost of goods sold, depend on how inventory is valued. Various accounting methods are available, and any independent cost estimate must consider the method used and the reasons why such a measurement was adopted for the particular firm.

Companies in a service industry need not measure inventory costs. Rather, service environments more closely resemble those in manufacturing where costs are accumulated by suborganizations or departments. Sometimes these costs are collected on a job or project basis; other times costs are accumulated by cost center. Costs are accumulated on the basis of work in process that represent the costs incurred but not yet billed or sold.

No matter what the cost environment, all but the smallest businesses are likely to have available certain standard types of reports supported by either a financial or managerial accounting system. The financial accounting system runs the gamut from invoices and other source documents to subledgers to trial balances and general ledgers. From this system, key internal and external financial reports and statements are produced.

The managerial accounting system is oriented toward management reporting rather than financial accounting. Such a system produces reports and information that enable those persons in control of the operations to plan, control, and make more rational decisions. The types of reports produced through the managerial accounting system include budgets, variance reports, standard cost analyses, departmental operating reports, product line financials, production schedules, and the like.

The combination of financial and managerial reports often provide the basic data required for estimating the costs at issue. Many times, available reports do not provide the required information. In these cases, the analyst must request special reports from the company's computer files or must gather needed data from source documents.

CONCEPTS

The overriding concept for approach cost estimation in litigation is that the analysis must fit the situation. Although such a statement could be directed at any application of cost estimation, it is particularly apt for litigation. In litigation, the types of analyses are oriented around the legal issues of the case and the facts of the dispute. For example, in a predatory pricing case where the plaintiff alleges that the defendant was selling below cost, estimating the company's total costs may not be as relevant as estimating the variable or incremental costs of a specific product or division.

Invariably, the data that an analyst faces are less than perfect. The issues of the case may require the analyst to estimate a complex set of costs for a particular situation different from those naturally accumulated in the accounting systems of the company. Rather, the analyst must rely upon the limited company data as well as outside information from industry, government, or competitors. An anlyst must recognize that having perfect data for the situation is an unreachable ideal; the burden on the analyst is to consider alternative sources of information and, where possible, different measurements for estimating cost. The rest of this chapter explores these different methods and the circumstances in which they may be employed.

Fixed and Variable Costs

A fundamental equation of cost accounting is:

$$\text{Total cost} = \text{Fixed cost} + \text{Variable cost per unit} \times \text{Number of units}$$

Fixed costs do not vary over time with different levels of production or activity, although they may vary for other reasons. Variable costs change with each additional unit of production. Costs can be viewed as semifixed or semivariable as well, but for this chapter we will assume that costs can be divided into fixed and variable components.

In many litigation cases involving lost profits based on a given level of lost sales, the variable costs become the critical cost components.

Short-Run vs. Long-Run Costs. A cost can only be called fixed or variable if a corresponding time frame is established. Over a long-enough time period, all costs are variable. Over short time periods, nearly all costs are be fixed. In measuring fixed and variable costs, the time frame is usually driven by the scope of the analysis. Rather than ask, "Which costs are fixed or variable?", the analyst better asks, "What would have happened to costs if actual sales had equalled forecasted (or 'but-for' sales?"

Increasing vs. Decreasing Sales. Costs often behave differently if sales are increasing than if they are decreasing. Typically, costs are "sticky," in that they may not increase as fast as sales increase nor decrease as fast as sales decrease. An analysis using increasing (or decreasing) sales and costs to make predictions in the opposite environment may be inappropriate.

Direct and Indirect Costs. In planning how to estimate costs, distinguishing direct and indirect costs can be useful. One could classify costs in a continuum from direct to indirect costs. Different estimation methods may be appropriate for different types of costs.

Direct costs are incurred solely and specifically in the production of a product or the delivery of a service. In the production process, direct costs usually consist of two elements—direct labor and raw material.

If direct costs represent one end of this continuum, in terms of their relationship with the production of the goods or service, then indirect costs represents the other. Indirect costs, including indirect labor, indirect material, manufacturing overhead, general and administrative costs, and selling costs are difficult to trace to the output of a specific good or service. Although these costs may be identifiable, estimating the proportion of them that is related to changes in the production process may be difficult.

Indirect costs need not be purely variable or fixed. The burden in litigation may not only be to defend the types of overhead costs included in the analysis but also to be able to specify what proportion of these costs—either in the aggregate or on an individual basis—may be variable.

METHODS FOR ESTIMATING COSTS

Costs can be measured in several ways. Among the methods that can be used are:

- Direct assignment
- Industrial engineering
- Accounting engineering
- Account analysis
- Cost accounting allocations (including statistical approaches).

These approaches overlap. In addition, different types of costs may be best analyzed by different methods.

Direct Assignment

Direct assignment of costs is used to relate a product to its directly related costs. For example, if the costs of a particular product are at issue, the direct labor costs of (people working specifically on the product) and direct materials (raw materials used specifically on the product) can be assigned directly. Typically, directly assigned costs are variable costs. When this method applies, it is usually simple and reliable.

Even if direct assignment is appropriate, the analyst must be wary of some accounting pitfalls. For example, inventory principles such as lower of cost or market or LIFO may affect financial statement presentation. The analyst should take these into account by making appropriate adjustments.

In analyzing direct costs, be sure to associate incremental costs with incremental volume. For example, if the average cost of raw materials inventory is different from the current cost, using historical financial records may be misleading.

Engineering of Costs

Industrial engineers often develop cost estimates for new plants, processes, or products. These techniques may be equally applicable to estimating "but-for" costs in a litigation context. In developing an engineering estimate, the costs are often developed "from the ground up," meaning that each cost is separately considered and measured, usually in some physical way (e.g., the number of board feet of lumber required would be calculated from blueprints). In litigation, this approach has the advantage of specifically identifying what costs will change and by how much. On the other hand, engineering cost estimates may be overly optimistic if not performed with great care. They may miss ancillary costs that change with incremental volume. Also, it is often difficult to estimate indirect and overhead costs using direct measurements.

An engineering cost study requires detailed analysis. It often involves substantial on-site work that may not be possible during the litigation. (The company may be out of business, or the analyst may not have access.) Accordingly, it is not surprising that engineering cost studies are rarely prepared for a litigation. However, an engineering cost study performed as part of a planning exercise, apart from and before the litigation commenced, may be useful.

A different type of engineering cost study is one based on similar experience with another location or a related product. The cost estimates are derived by analogy from the similar known situation. In many ways, this resembles accounting engineering (see later discussion) and may more readily apply to the litigation environment.

Accounting Engineering

In industrial engineering, the engineer identifies the particular processes and materials required, then estimates the costs based on direct measurements, labor rates, material costs, and the like. In "accounting engineering" (a nonstandard but descriptive phrase), the accountant estimates costs from experience with related products or services. Some standard costs may exist for various components. Historical data may also be available to validate the reasonableness of the standards. To the extent that historical data do not reflect current costs, adjustments should be made.

Account Analysis

Account analysis is the classic, simple method of identifying fixed and variable costs. The accountant reviews the detailed general ledger or chart of accounts and judges which costs are fixed and which are variable. For example, direct labor and materials may be judged to be 100 percent variable with production. Depreciation, rent, insurance, and legal fees may be judged to be fixed. If the variable cost per unit is desired, the costs judged to be variable are simply added up and the total divided by the number of units produced.

Although this approach is simple, it suffers from subjective accounting judgments. It does not distinguish semivariable or semifixed costs. Accordingly, it often works best when dealing with "clearly" fixed or "clearly" variable costs. Finally, it often gives results that can be challenged by looking at actual results. For example, another analyst can compare the incremental cost calculated via this approach with the actual incremental cost for some level of production at a different time period. The method is hard to defend without confirmation from one of the other approaches.

Cost Accounting Allocation

In many cases, especially for partially variable indirect costs, the approaches described are not feasible. Various allocation methods must be used instead. In some sense, these methods form the core of the discipline of cost estimation. There are three major categories of cost allocation methods: ratio analysis, graphical (nonstatistical) approaches, and statistical regression analysis.

Ratio Analysis. The most direct and simplest allocation method is to distribute cost by some unit of input or output. We call this a "ratio" approach. For example, if total overhead costs are known, overhead costs per hour of direct labor may be computed by simple division:

$$\text{Overhead costs per direct labor hour} = \frac{\text{Total overhead costs}}{\text{Total direct labor hours}}$$

In general, the total costs for a particular activity may be allocated proportionally to some other input or output by simple division. This enables us to compute, for example, costs per:

- Labor hour
- Machine hour
- Unit of raw material used
- Dollar of raw material used
- Unit of production
- Dollar value of production
- Unit of sales
- Dollar value of sales

These computations are straightforward and are often used to make quick analyses of costs. Because this method computes the average cost, it is most appropriate when the average cost is of interest. If, as is often the case, we are most interested in the marginal or incremental cost, these simple ratio estimates may be misleading. Only if the cost in question is almost a purely variable cost will the ratio correctly measure it. In using this approach to estimate incremental costs, the analyst should be comfortable that the numerator and denominator in the ratio vary together.

The ratio approach has other uses. For example, consider a situation in which some increased level of sales has been forecast, and the analyst desires to estimate the level of additional working capital required to support the increased sales level. One approach may be to compute the historical ratio of working capital to sales and apply the ratio to the sales forecast. Other balance sheet and income statement accounts may be similarly estimated.

In computing and using ratios for cost estimation, it is often important to compute the ratio over multiple time periods. For example, in computing overhead costs per labor hour, as in our example, we may compute the ratio monthly for the last 2 or

3 years. To examine the results, plot the ratios on a graph over time. Also, plot the ratios against total sales or costs to examine the relationship between the two.

This accomplishes two things. First, it enables us to examine trends, thus helping us judge what value should be projected into the future or applied to a particular period in the past. Second, it provides information about the stability or constancy of the ratio. If the ratio is nearly constant over a long time period, we may feel comfortable in projecting that value to continue, ceteris paribus. If the ratio exhibits large swings, the use of a ratio for a particular period may be less appropriate. If the ratio exhibits a pronounced trend over time or varies in proportion to some input or output measure (say, production volume), that might indicate that factors not accounted for by the ratio are affecting the cost. At a minimum, the range of values may indicate a range of possible estimates for the cost in question or may indicate that the cost behavior must be examined further.

Graphical Methods. Graphical methods occupy a middle ground between ratio analysis and statistical approaches. Ratio analysis proceeds from the assumption that the relationship between the two quantities in question is purely variable. Also, ratio analysis deals only with two quantities at a time. In most statistical methods (as discussed later), the specific relationship between the quantities is subject to analysis, and the relationship is not limited to two quantities.

By way of contrast, graphical methods need not assume that the costs in question are variable costs. However, we do not get the measures of accuracy and confidence obtainable from statistical methods. We are also limited, in most cases, to examining relationships between only two variables.

An analyst can use two general types of graphs to estimate costs: (1) cost versus time and (2) cost against some other quantity. These are graphical analogs of techniques discussed in previous sections. The first type of graph is a time series of, for example, general ledger or accounting costs. The second is a graph of the values that would be used in the numerator and denominator of a ratio analysis.

The first type of graph can be used visually and quantitatively to answer the questions: What is the typical amount of a cost? How much variability does it show over time? Are there any time trends in the cost?

Answers to these questions allow the analyst to judge whether the use of a recent or average value for a cost is appropriate. To the extent that costs are stable over time, the use of an average is supported.

The second type of graph helps identify the relationship between two quantities. For example, consider the problem of ascertaining the relationship between production volume and production cost. If we were using simple ratio analysis, we might compute the ratio "cost per unit." If we were to use this ratio, we would be assuming that cost of production was a fixed amount per unit, or equivalently, that costs varied directly with volume. This may or may not be true. We can use graphical analysis to help prove or disprove it.

To do this, simply plot production volume on one axis of a graphic (typically the X-axis) and cost of production on the other. Do this for a number of periods, often at least 2 years of monthly data or 4 years of quarterly data. Then study the resulting patterns.

Exhibit 29-1 shows some possible results. (Assume for simplicity that inflation is irrelevant. For a discussion of inflation, see the section on statistical methods.) Part (*a*) shows a clear linear relationship, with the points lying on a straight line passing through the origin. This graph shows that ratio analysis would be the appropriate method to use; costs are proportional to volume, and loosely speaking, no fixed costs exist.

In contrast, consider part (*b*). This graph also reveals a clear linear relationship, but in this case the line does not pass through the origin. Instead, the line extrapolates to show that there would be some costs even if volume were zero. This is the most typical pattern. In some circumstances (and with numerous caveats not discussed here), we can say that the value where the line intercepts the Y-axis is the fixed cost and that the slope of the line represents the variable cost per unit. The numeric values of these quantities can be computed statistically (see later discussion), or they can be estimated by eye using a ruler on the paper. Alternatively, we could simply read the graph by starting with the production quantity desired and finding the approximate corresponding cost.

If the data were as in Exhibit 29-1(*b*), the ratio analysis would have given an incorrect answer. Using ratios, we would have proceeded as if all costs were variable, thus ascribing too much cost to incremental production.

Exhibit 29-1(*c*) demonstrates another cost relationship. Costs, smooth and regular, do not have a linear relationship with volume. The incremental cost per unit is declining as more units are produced. In this case, neither ratio analysis nor linear regression analysis will give the proper result. The graph tells us that we must either use nonlinear statistical methods or simply use the graph itself to find costs for appropriate levels of production.

As we have alluded to and discuss more fully in the next section, statistical methods have become an important part of cost estimation. They are particularly useful when costs are influenced by two or more variables. Graphical techniques are used in conjunction with statistical methods. In comparison to statistical techniques, graphical approaches are often easier to understand for both the analyst and the audience (attorneys, judges, and juries). They can often be performed more simply, using paper, pencil, and a calculator rather than a computer. Graphics help to develop assumptions and to check the underlying assumptions of statistical approaches. And they may have a certain intuitive appeal.

On the other hand, graphical techniques may be less accurate than statistical ones. Even when the accuracy is comparable, statistical techniques provide additional benefits, such as confidence intervals and measures of variability, which graphs cannot provide. Because statistical and graphic techniques many times measure the same effect, it is often best to use the statistical technique to develop the "right answer" and a graph to present it to the audience.

Statistical Methods. In recent years, the combination of statistical methods and accounting has brought increased analytical power to the litigation analyst. However, this increased power requires the analyst to learn new and perhaps complex techniques. The analyst must then be able to communicate the relevance and results of the techniques to the client and the court.

EXHIBIT 29-1. COST BEHAVIOR

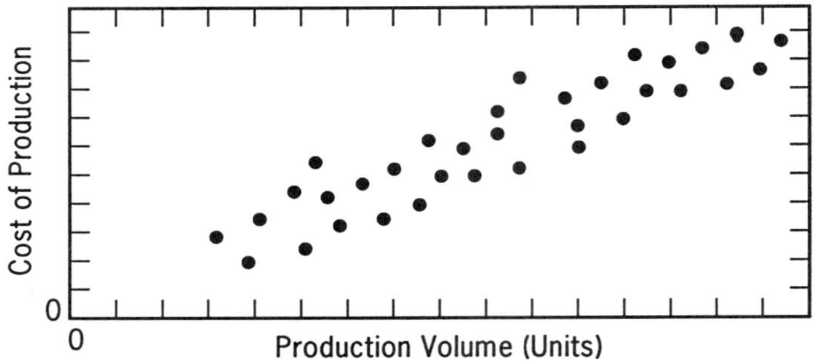

(a)

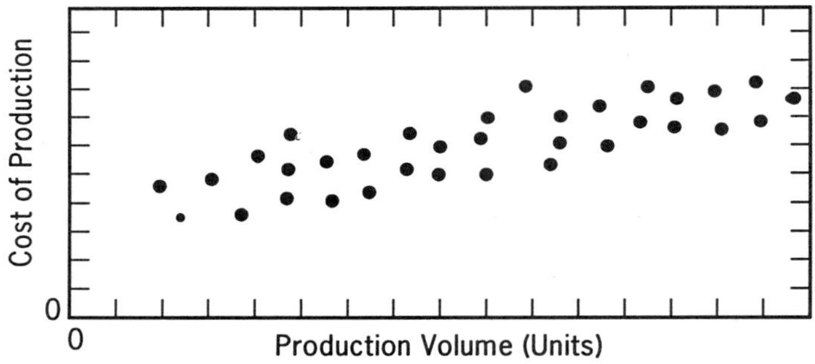

(b)

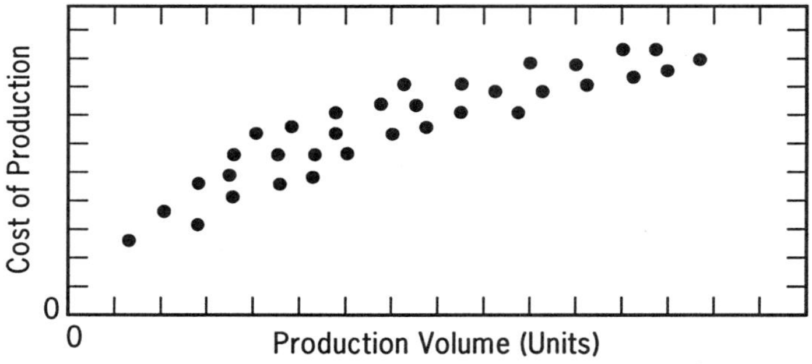

(c)

Foremost among these statistical methods is linear regression analysis, often simply called regression. This area is sometimes incorrectly referred to as time-series analysis; strictly speaking, time-series analysis is both narrower than regression (because regression does not require time-sequenced data) and broader than regression (because there are other techniques subsumed under the term *time-series analysis*). This section will focus on the basics of regression. Chapter 30 in this book discusses certain advanced topics in cost accounting and regression.

Common Situations in Cost Estimation

In preparing to estimate a particular cost, the analyst will often find one of the following situations:

1. Historical data on costs and related volumes are known, and we wish to estimate cost for some hypothetical alternative volume. For example, historical production costs and production volumes are known, and we want to know expected costs for some hypothetical production volume.
2. Historical data on a particular cost and other related costs are known, and we wish to estimate the particular cost given certain hypothetical levels of the related costs. For example, historical values for direct costs and overhead costs are known, and we want to know expected overhead costs for a given level of direct cost.

In each of these two situations, we may have two types of source data available. The first and most common type is time-series data, in which we have daily, monthly, or yearly values for the costs and volumes. Typically, these values are from the production facility under study.

Alternatively, information may be available as cross-sectional data, in which the data come from numerous plants, companies, and the line all at the same time. Sometimes the data are from other plants within the same company; other times the data come from industry studies involving numerous companies.

In any of these situations, we have data concerning two or more particular costs or volumes and desire to find a relationship that can predict one value given the others. Often we need to compute the incremental cost per unit for a given product. These are exactly the situations that regression attempts to address. The balance of this chapter introduces regression analysis as a tool for use in litigation cost estimating.

Regression Analysis

In simple terms, regression analysis attempts to find a relation between certain costs or volumes (called the independent variables) and a particular cost of interest (called the dependent variable). Regression is not limited to a relationship between one dependent variable and one independent variable; it can handle relationships between a dependent variable and numerous independent variables. A simple regression has only one independent variable. A multiple regression has more than one independent variable.

Regression usually requires a computer program. Numerous general statistics packages and specific regression packages exist for most computers. For a sample output of a regression program, see the sample regression output section.

In practice, most regression analysis is linear. The term *linear* refers to the fact that the measured relationship can be drawn as a straight line on a graph. (With more than one independent variable, the graph becomes difficult or impossible to draw, but mathematically the result is equivalent to a straight line.) Thus, to apply linear regression, the relationship between the independent and dependent variables in the relevant range should be approximately a straight line. This means, for example, that a one-unit change in production should have the same impact on costs when production is low as when it is high.

This restriction is not as onerous as it may seem. First, in practice, many costs are approximately linear. If they are not, often they are linear in some limited range of interest (see relevant range section or can be made linear through a mathematical transformation (see transformations section). In addition, a regression analysis provides diagnostic measures that enable the analyst to ascertain whether the assumption of linearity is reasonable in a particular instance.

In regression, a particular hypothesized relationship between dependent and independent variables is called a "model." A simple linear regression model is often shown as:

$$Y = aX + c$$

where Y is the dependent variable (say, costs), X is the independent variable (say units produced), a is the regression coefficient of X, and c is the constant term of the regression.

Consider a simple example. Suppose that we produce widgets. A production run costs \$100 to set up, and each widget costs \$2 to produce after set-up. The resulting equation is:

$$\text{Cost} = \$2 \times (\text{number of widgets}) + \$100$$

This is a simple linear relationship. A graph of this relationship is shown in Exhibit 29-2.

In regression, we simply turn the problem around. We would know, say, the number of widgets produced each month and the total monthly cost. We would hypothesize a model of the form:

$$\text{Cost} = a \times (\text{number of widgets}) + c$$

The goal of regression is to estimate values for a and c. This is done using a set of mathematical equations embedded in a regression computer program.

We are not limited to a single independent variable in constructing our model. For example, if on the same production line we produced both widgets and gizmos, the model might look like:

$$\text{Cost } a_1 \times (\text{number of widgets}) + a_2 \times (\text{number gizmos}) + c$$

In this case, a_1 is the incremental cost per widget produced, a_2 is the incremental cost per gizmo produced, and c is the constant (fixed) cost per period.

EXHIBIT 29-2. EXAMPLE OF LINEAR COST RELATIONSHIP

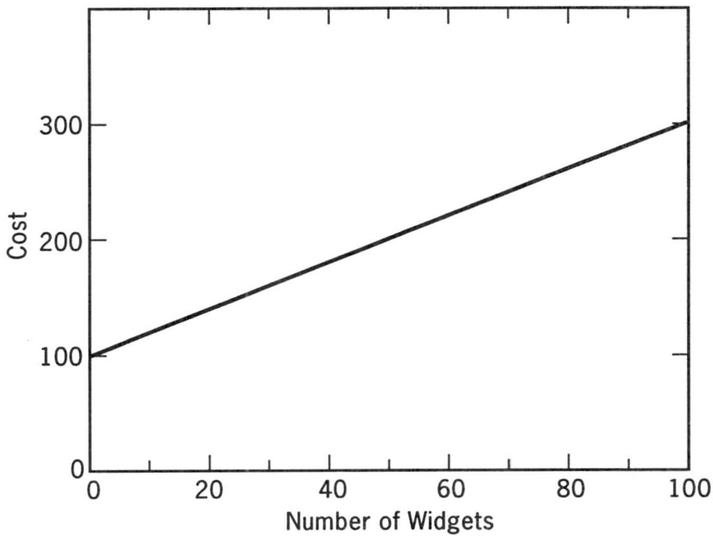

More generally, we may have any number of independent variables. The equation for the general linear model with n independent variables is:

$$Y = a_1X_1 + a_2X_2 + \ldots + a_nX_n + c$$

In applying regression analysis to cost estimation problems, the analyst must specify an explicit model for analysis. Many naive users of regression make the mistake of simply plugging data into a program and using the results. This can lead to misleading results. Recognize that whether a model is explicitly acknowledged or not, there is an underlying model. The careful analyst recognizes this fact and makes sure that the model describes the intended type of cost relationship.

In specifying a model, the analyst draws on knowledge of the economic and physical behavior of the variables involved. For example, as production volume increases, it may be reasonable to expect costs to increase directly, to increase but at a decreasing rate, to increase directly with a percentage change in volume, or to increase with the combined change in two or more different products.

Other possible issues are volume discounts, overtime costs, cost changes expected during expansion compared with changes expected during contraction, and technological change. Each of these implies a different model. The model must be specified to allow the contemplated relationship to be measured, or it will give inaccurate results. Sometimes the analysis needs to treat some aspects of the situation as a regression problem and apply different techniques (as discussed earlier in the chapter) to other aspects.

Building an explanatory model can be an iterative procedure. Early versions of a model should include those variables suspected of having an effect on the dependent variable. In subsequent iterations, the analyst can delete variables found to have a negligible effect or found to duplicate the effects of other variables and refine the model as necessary. However, a model should not include "everything but the kitchen sink." Including variables "just to see if they are significant," a practice sometimes called *data mining*, can lead to substantial errors in estimates of statistical significance. To avoid this problem, the analyst needs a "theory" of how costs behave before running regressions.

Volume Data

The preferred measure of production volume is "units." This is superior to sales (in dollars) because it avoids problems of price changes and inflation (see later discussion). When the sales dollar value of production is known but not the units of production, one might divide the dollar volume by the selling price, on a period-by period basis, to arrive at an estimate of units produced. Be careful to match costs to production volumes, not to sales volumes.

Inflation and Cost Data

Inflation has been part of the economy for decades and will undoubtedly remain so in the future. To obtain meaningful cost estimates, a regression analysis must separate the effects of inflation from those of changing activity levels. Typically, this is done by restating cost data to "constant" or "real" terms.

An inflation adjustment can be simple to do. First, choose an appropriate inflation index. The most common ones are the Consumer Price Index (CPI) and the Producer Price Index (PPI), both issued monthly by the U.S. Government. Then choose some base year into which all dollar amounts will be converted. The choice of base year will not affect the analysis, but it may make it easier to think about the magnitude of the results if the most recent year is chosen as the base year. Next, multiply each period's cost data by the ratio of the base year inflation index to the index for the year in question. (In this discussion, we talk about "years." The principle applies equally to monthly, quarterly, or other periodic data.) In equation form:

$$\text{Adjusted cost} = \text{Original cost} \times \frac{\text{Base year index}}{\text{Current year index}}$$

To see why this adjustment is necessary, consider an example. Assume production volume, costs, and inflation as shown:

Year	Units	Total Cost ($)	Average Cost/Unit ($)	Inflation Index (Yr 1 = 100)	Average Cost/Unit (Deflated $)
1	10	200	20	100	20
2	15	500	33	200	17
3	20	900	45	300	15

Without considering inflation, it appears that the average cost per unit increased from \$20 in Year 1 to \$33 in Year 2 to \$45 in Year 3. If we ran a regression with units as the independent variable and total cost as the dependent variable, we would find the resulting equation was:

$$\text{Total cost} = -\$517 + \$70 \times \text{Units}$$

The regression leads us to believe that the incremental cost per unit is \$70. This is an extremely misleading picture, as the last column in the tabulation shows. After adjusting for inflation, we find in fact that the average cost per unit is declining over time. The regression results on the adjusted costs yield the following:

$$\text{Total cost} = \$100 + \$10 \times \text{Units}$$

This indicates that in inflation-adjusted (Year 1) dollars, the incremental cost per unit is \$10. If we want to know the estimated incremental cost per unit in Years 2 and 3, we simply reinflate the estimate, getting an incremental cost per unit of \$20 in Year 2 and \$30 in Year 3. These results differ significantly from the \$70 measured without an inflation adjustment.

As a rule of thumb, an inflation adjustment should be considered whenever more than 2 years of data are involved, or whenever inflation exceeds 10 percent during the time span of the data. The inflation adjustment has three steps:

1. Make the inflation adjustment to deflate the data into constant dollars.
2. Perform the analysis.
3. Reinflate the results into current dollars of the time period(s) of interest.

Indicator (Dummy) Variables

The use of indicator (sometimes called dummy) variables is a valuable regression technique. An indicator variable is simply a variable set equal to zero for some observations and set equal to 1 for others. It serves as a "flag" to indicate that something is different about certain observations.

For example, consider a series of monthly data from accounting records spanning many years. In many accounting records, the entry in December may reflect year-end adjustments and so not reflect a typical month. Rather than ignore the December data, it is possible to create an indicator variable to attempt to capture the year-end effect. Set up a new variable with the value 1 in each December and 0 in all other months. The regression can then include this variable (along with the accounting data and other relevant variables). By considering the statistical relevance of indicator variable's coefficient (see later discussion below), the magnitude and importance of the December effect can be measured and extracted from the measurement of the other variables.

Other useful indicator variables may be:

- A variable that takes the value 1 for the "impacted" period and the value 0 otherwise

- A variable that takes the value 1 during an anomalous period (say, a fire or strike) and 1 otherwise
- A variable that takes the value 1 during a particular season of the year and zero otherwise.

This last example merits further mention. Dummy variables are good for capturing seasonality effects. One can use more than one indicator variable at once to measure effects of each season separately. To measure a quarterly effect, establish three dummy variables, each taking the value 1 for a different season of the year. Then put all three dummy variables into the regression equation. The resulting coefficients and statistics measure the effect of each season.

(In using dummy variables, we must define one fewer variable than there are possible situations, such as seasons. If *all* situations are assigned indicator variables, the model will be "overdetermined," and the regression computation will fail. The "unassigned" situation is uniquely identified by setting all the other indicator variables to zero.)

Transformations

A transformation is a mathematical manipulation applied to the data or the model before fitting the regression. Transformations convert the data into a form appropriate for the regression as specified. The transformation can be applied (1) to make the model amenable to analysis or (2) to make the data more suitable to the model.

To see an example of the first kind of transformation, consider an exponential model: $Y = aX^b$. This is not linear; it does not fit into the general equation previously enumerated. However, by use of a transformation, we can make it linear. We simply take the logarithm of both sides, getting

$$(\text{LN } Y) = (\text{LN} a) + b(\text{LN } X) .$$

By treating the variable "LN Y" as the new dependent variable, "LN X" as the new independent variable, and "LN a" as the new constant term, we have transformed the equation into one suitable for estimation by linear regression.

We have already seen an example of the second kind of transformation: the adjustments for inflation discussed. Other examples of transformations include:

- Multiplying two variables together
- Dividing one variable by another
- Raising a variable to a power
- Taking the logarithm of a variable
- Creating an indicator variable
- Computing the change in a variable from one period to the next.

These transformations allow the linear regression procedure to fit what would otherwise be nonlinear situations. As always, the analyst must think about the types of changes a transformation implies for the regression model before performing computations.

EXHIBIT 29-3. MONTHLY PRODUCTION AND COST DATA

Month	Units	Cost
January-86	42.3	3406.8
February-86	53.6	4367.4
March-86	51.6	3957.5
April-86	60.1	3659.4
May-86	41.5	2535.5
June-86	59.4	3685.7
July-86	59.1	3650.8
August-86	52.1	3863.7
September-86	58.4	4555.4
October-86	53.1	3871.5
November-86	50.4	2995.3
December-86	57.3	4490.8
January-87	70.6	5300.0
February-87	35.6	4287.8
March-87	49.5	3967.2
April-87	52.1	3573.2
May-87	63.2	4484.3
June-87	63.6	3760.2
July-87	63.2	4446.8
August-87	81.8	5600.0
September-87	73.8	4875.7
October-87	72.8	4378.7
November-87	81.3	5274.3
December-87	82.8	5276.1
January-88	74.0	4217.8
February-88	64.6	4938.0
March-88	65.1	5051.7
April-88	72.4	4397.4
May-88	88.8	4914.3
June-88	97.2	5852.3
July-88	95.1	6515.9
August-88	80.5	5250.9
September-88	101.4	5867.1
October-88	85.0	5331.0
November-88	81.0	4796.0
December-88	100.3	5886.3

Sample Regression Output

Exhibit 29-3 shows a sample set of data listing monthly production and cost data of widgets from the Widget Manufacturing Company for a 3-year period. A graph of the data is shown in Exhibit 29-4. The graph shows that the data are quite well-behaved and exhibit a linear relationship. Thus they are well suited for regression. (For a discussion of problems that may occur in data, see Chapter 30.)

A regression of the form Cost = $a \times$ Units + c was performed. An extract from the computer output is shown in Exhibit 29-5. At the top of the output, we see that the dependent variable is Cost. After some identifying information, we come to the regression results. The first column shows that two variables were

EXHIBIT 29-4. MONTHLY PRODUCTION AND COST DATA

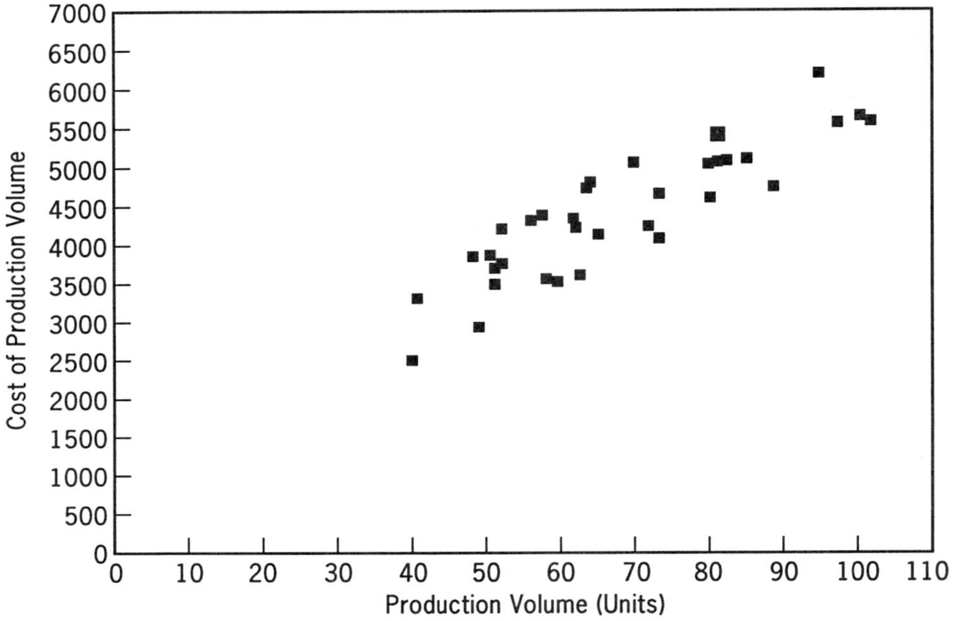

included in the regression: the constant (C) and the real variable Units. The next column shows the computed coefficients. Reading these values, we find that the resulting regression equation is.

$$\text{Cost} = \$47.90 \times \text{Units} + \$1{,}256.50$$

In other words, the incremental cost per unit is $47.90, and the constant term is $1,256.50. (The constant is often loosely interpreted as the fixed cost. Although this is true if the regression is relevant for values of the independent variable near zero, the analyst should be careful in making this assertion. See relevant range section).

EXHIBIT 29-5. SAMPLE REGRESSION RESULTS MONTHLY PRODUCTION AND COST DATA

Dependent Variable is COST
Number of Observations: 36

Variable	Coefficient	Std. Error	*T*-Statistics	2-Tail Significance
C	1256.50	308.82	4.07	0.00
Units	47.90	4.39	10.91	0.00

R-squared, 0.78; Adjusted R-squared, 0.77; S.E. Regression, 421.83; Durbin-Watson statistic, 1.78

The remaining output provides various measures of how well the regression fit the data. The following section discusses these measures.

Statistical Measures and Statistical Tests

One advantage of regression is that it not only provides estimates of the costs and other parameters but also measures the accuracy of those estimates. These measures fall into two groups:

- How well the model as a whole fits the data
- The importance of specific variables

The important measures in the first category are the square of the multiple correlation coefficient (R-squared or R^2), adjusted R^2, the standard error of the regression, and the Durbin–Watson statistic. In the second category, we find the standard error of each variable and the related t-statistics and measures of significance. Each of these is shown in the sample output in Exhibit 29-5. We briefly discuss each of these next.[2]

The square of the multiple correlation coefficient (*R-squared or* R^2) is a number that can range from 0 to 1.0. The larger the value, the better job of "explaining" the regression equation does. R^2 measures the percentage of total variation (of the dependent variable) from its mean *which is explained by* the regression equation.

If the regression equation fits the dependent variable perfectly, then $R^2 = 1$. If, on the other hand, the regression equation does not help at all, then the mean is the best estimator, and the predicted value just equals the mean. In that case, $R^2 = 0$.

A high value of R^2 leads us to say that the regression equation explains a large portion of the variation in the dependent variable fairly well. Thus, R^2 invites *the interpretation* that it measures the "goodness" of fit of a regression. This need not be so. In practice, it is difficult to draw firm conclusions about a regression from the value of R^2. There is no point where we can say that a particular R^2 is high enough to be explanatory. In some cases, an R^2 of .90 is not very good, whereas in others an R^2 of .10 may be sufficient. The answer depends on the alternatives and whether the relevant question is the prediction of the dependent variable or the coefficient of some independent variable. If the coefficient is of interest, the R^2 may be of lesser relevance. Interpreting R^2 requires experienced statistical judgment.

In our sample printout (Exhibit 29-5), the R^2 is .78, or 78%. That figure, combined with a look at the graph and the residuals (see later discussion), is fairly good, indicating that the regression equation predicts fairly well.

The *adjusted* R^2 is a simple variant of the R^2. In the basic formulation of R^2, adding any independent variable to the regression equation, even if correlated randomly with the dependent variable, cannot lower the R^2. The adjusted R^2 addresses this problem. In a loose sense, it indicates whether adding another independent variable is "worth it." Adjusted R^2 penalizes the computation for adding an uncorrelated variable. For this reason, adjusted R^2 is usually preferred to simple R^2. However, the adjusted R^2 makes an important difference only if the sample size is small. When the number of data points exceeds the number of independent variables by at least 20, the R^2 and adjusted R^2 are very close. In our example, the adjusted R^2 is 77%, almost exactly equal to the unadjusted R^2.

The *standard error (S.E.) of the regression* measures the size of the estimation errors made by the regression equation. Loosely speaking, the standard error of the regression measures the accuracy with which the dependent variable can be predicted for a given value of the independent variable. The units are the same as those of the dependent variable. It is analogous to the standard deviation of a variable; in fact, it is the standard deviation of the residuals. Because this value can be treated like a standard deviation, it is roughly true (if certain assumptions are met) that 95 percent of all predictions will be within two standard errors of the actual value. In our example, the standard error of the regression is approximately \$422. Thus approximately 95 percent of our estimates are within \$844 of the actual value.

In economic data, successive values of a variable are sometimes highly correlated. For example, quantity output or the inflation rate tends to change slowly over time, with successive months often close together. In statistical terms, this is called positive (first-order) serial correlation. (There is also negative serial correlation, but it is much less common.) Serial correlation can cause problems in drawing conclusions about regression results.

The *Durbin-Watson statistic* measures the extent of (first-order) serial correlation in the residuals. The statistic can range from 0 (perfect positive serial correlation) to 4 (perfect negative serial correlation). A value of 2 indicates no serial correlation. Interpreting the Durbin-Watson statistic requires looking up values in several tables. However, as a rule of thumb, if you have at least 50 observations and a few independent variables, a Durbin-Watson value below 1.5 or above 2.5 is reason to be concerned. (Correcting for a serial correlation problem and identifying higher order serial correlation are beyond the scope of this chapter.) In our example, the Durbin-Watson statistic is 1.78, indicating no problems with first-order serial correlation.

These statistics apply to the regression equation as a whole. We now turn to the second category of statistics, those that describe individual variables. As mentioned, the important statistics are the standard error of each variable and the related *t*-statistics and measures of significance.

The computed regression coefficient is subject to some degree of error because the data do not lie perfectly on a straight line. The *standard error* of each variable measures how accurately the variable's coefficient is known. In this way, the standard error is analogous to a standard deviation. Under the usual assumptions, confidence bounds for the coefficients can be constructed using a multiple of the standard error. For example, we can be roughly 95% confident that the true value of the coefficient is within plus-or-minus two standard errors of the computed value. In our example, an approximate 95 percent confidence bound for the coefficient of "units" is \$47.90/unit plus-or-minus approximately \$8.78/unit (i.e., two times the standard error of 4.39).

The *t-statistic* is a statistical test of the hypothesis that the true value of the coefficient differs from zero or some other specified number. (Usually the analyst tests to see if the estimated coefficient differs from zero, but other critical values are sometimes used.) It is unlikely (less then 5 percent chance) that the true value is zero if zero lies more than two standard errors away from the estimated regression coefficient. The value of the t-statistic is the number of standard errors between zero and the estimated value of the coefficient. It is computed as the coefficient divided by its standard error. In our example, the t-statistic for "units" is approximately

$$47.90/4.39 = 10.91$$

The value is compared to a standard table of t-statistics found in any statistics book. In general, if the t-statistic is greater than 2.0, we can conclude with 95% confidence that the true (unknown) value of the coefficient is not zero.

If the coefficient were truly zero, the corresponding variable would contribute nothing to the equation. Accordingly, a test of the hypothesis that the coefficient is zero is a test to see if the corresponding variable "matters" to the predictive power of the regression results.

Loosely speaking, the *level of significance* is the probability that zero (or some other specified critical value) is a plausible value for the true value of the coefficient. This is just the probability value (from the standard table of t-statistics) that corresponds to the observed t-statistic. (Significance level is usually measured as "two-sided" or "two-tailed," meaning that we are equally interested in whether the computed value is either above or below the true coefficient.) In our example (Exhibit 29-5), the "units" t-statistic of 10.91 corresponds to a significance level of 0.000, indicating that there is no chance (to three decimal places) that "units" is unrelated to the dependent variable.

Examination of Residual

The regression equation can be used to predict values for the dependent variable using the known value(s) of the independent variable(s). The differences between the predicted values of the dependent variable and the actual values are called the *residuals*. The pattern of the residuals can be an important diagnostic tool in ascertaining how appropriate the regression equation is.

Residuals are usually examined graphically. The residuals are plotted against other variables to see if any patterns exist. If the data have a natural sequence (e.g., they are time sequenced), a plot against time is most commonly used. Sometimes, the residuals are plotted against the estimated value of the dependent variable.

If the regression equation is properly specified, the residuals should just be the random errors inherent in the data. Accordingly, the residuals should not exhibit any particular pattern but should be distributed randomly (normally) around zero. (Mathematically, the average of the residuals must be zero.)

If the pattern does not look random, the regression may not be appropriate. Consider the patterns in Exhibit 29-6. In part (a), the residuals appear normal, and we are comfortable with the corresponding regression fit. This is the pattern we hope for.

EXHIBIT 29-6. EXAMINATION OF RESIDUALS

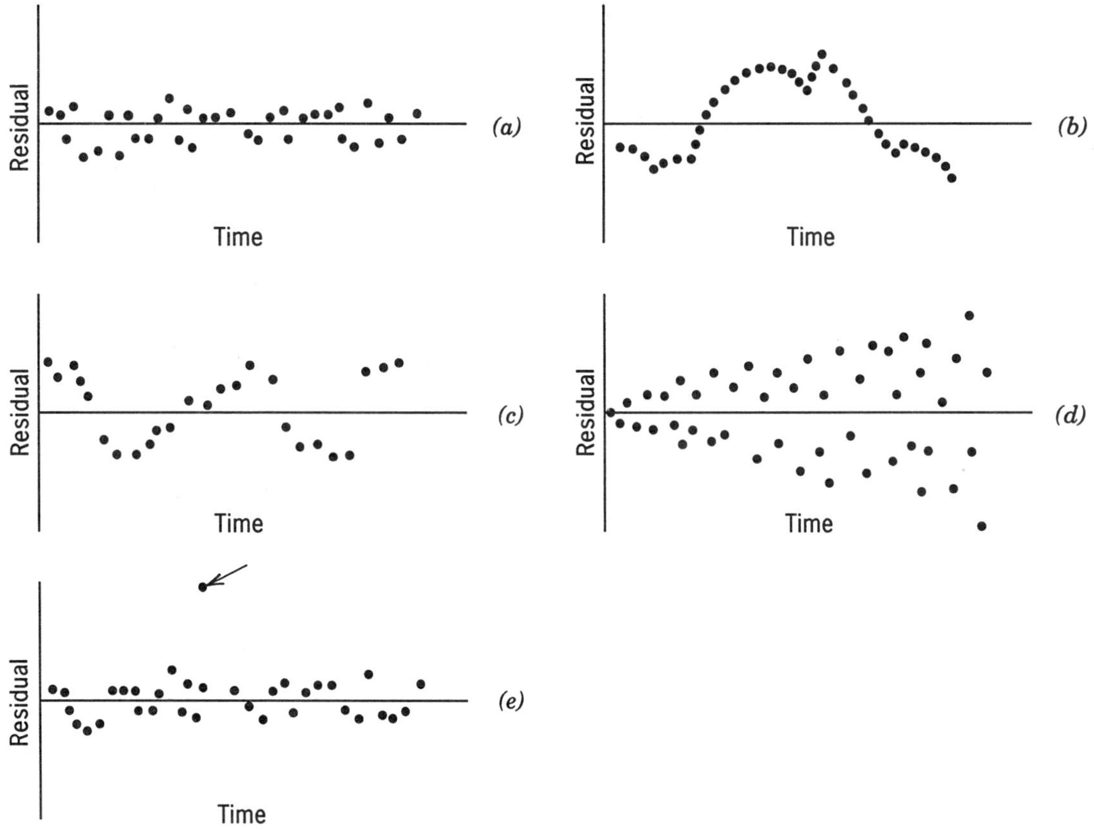

In part (*b*), the residuals begin negative, turn positive, and then become negative again. This pattern suggests that the data are not linear but rather curved. Fitting a straight line is not appropriate. The analysis should be redone with an appropriate transformation or nonlinear form.

In part (*c*), the positive residuals are likely to be followed by positive residuals and similarly for negative residuals. This indicates the presence of first-order serial correlation, meaning that one high value is likely to be followed by another high value. Appropriate corrective action should be taken; details are beyond the scope of this chapter.

In part (*d*), the variability of the residuals is growing over time. This problem is called heteroscedasticity. It may indicate that the regression results are not fully appropriate. Again, the solutions to this problem are beyond the scope of this chapter.

Finally, in part (*e*), we see that one residual value appears misbehaved. Analysts refer to this value as an outlier. This data point should be investigated. It may be an error. If not an error, it may include significant adjusting entries. (Commonly, the last month of the year is an outlier.) Possible solutions are to rerun the analyses without the offending point (if substantive reasons exist) to spread the year-end adjustment throughout the year, or to analyze the adjustment separately. If the outlier is of a recurring nature (every December, for example), it may be appropriate to use an indicator variable to measure the yearend effect. (See the previous section on indicator variables.)

Other Statistical Issues

Relevant Range. Any set of costs is collected from and applicable to a given range of production volumes. For example, over the last few years a particular factory may have produced from 5,000 to 10,000 units per month. This range is approximately the "relevant range." More precisely, the relevant range is the range of production volumes for which reliable extrapolations of cost can be made.

In our example, we would be fairly confident of conclusions about production in the range of 5,000 to 10,000 units per month. We would be less confident about extrapolating the conclusions significantly above or below this range, as we do not have statistical evidence that the behavior we observed would continue with the same cost relationship. Although the range of production is a reasonable estimate of the relevant range, ascertaining the relevant range is a matter of accounting and statistical judgment.

Often there is no choice but to extrapolate outside the relevant range; the required inference lies there, and no other reasonable approach presents itself. We recognize this often occurs and merely counsel caution. Other forms of evidence, including substantive judgments from personnel involved in the production process in question, should be used to validate the extrapolation.

As mentioned elsewhere in this chapter, the constant in a simple cost–volume regression is sometimes referred to as the estimate of fixed costs per period. This interpretation may be suspect when, as is usually the case, production volumes are always significantly greater than zero. This is because a production of zero units is outside the relevant range. (We do not say that this interpretation is wrong; merely that it should be made carefully and precisely.)

Nonlinear Cost Relationships. Not all costs, even within a relevant range or over a specified period, change linearly. In many operations a diminishing marginal cost of production exists where variable costs per unit may be lower, on a disproportionate basis, with each new level of production. In other operations, costs may increase at certain levels of production within the existing capacity of the facility. Cost analyses should not assume linear costs without reason.

Causation vs. Correlation. In regression, one of the measures of "goodness-of-fit" is the square of the multiple correlation coefficient, or R^2. This number measures how closely the dependent variable changes in sync with the independent variable(s). This is the concept called *correlation.*

This number does *not* measure causation. Simply because two variables are highly correlated, we cannot conclude that the changes in one cause the changes in another. From the mathematics alone, it is equally likely that the first variable causes changes in the second, that the second causes changes in the first, or that both are caused by some third unidentified variable. Accordingly, in reaching a conclusion about correlation, it is perfectly valid to say that the variables move together but not that changes in one cause changes in the other. Conclusions about causation generally come from nonstatistical analyses or a priori knowledge.

Number of Data Points Required. No hard and fast rule exists about the number of data points required for a regression. Certainly, the more, the better, provided that the expected relationship between the variables has not changed over time. A minimum of 15 or 20 data points is usually recommended. However, valid regressions can be run on as few as five or six points. If you use fewer than the recommended minimum, consult with a professional statistician to make sure your methods and conclusions are valid.

Multicollinearity. It is possible that two data series change almost in unison. If this is the case, we say they are highly correlated. In fact, the regression procedure itself uses the correlation between the dependent variable and the various independent variables to compute the regression equation.

However, in multiple regression, problems can occur if two independent variables are highly correlated. This is called *multicollinearity*.

Regression attempts to relate changes in the dependent variable to changes in the independent variables. The problem occurs if two (or more) independent variables are highly correlated. In that case, the regression formula cannot "figure out" which independent variable is causing the change in the dependent variable.

An example will clarify this problem. Consider sample data as follows:

	Independent Variable	
Dependent Variable	#1	#2
10	1	100
20	2	200
30	3	300
40	4	400

In this case, one possible equation would be

$$\text{Dependent variable} = 10 \times \text{Independent \#1}.$$

An equally valid choice is

$$\text{Dependent variable} = .1 \times \text{Independent \#2}.$$

If the analyst includes both independent variables in the regression, there is no mathematical way to figure out how to assign coefficients to the two variables. Instead, the regression algorithms usually are unable to compute anything at all.

Only rarely are two variables 100% correlated, as are the two independent variables in our example. If two variables are highly (but not perfectly) correlated, regression usually works and gives apparently correct results. However, because in some sense the technique "had trouble making up its mind" about how much weight to assign to each of the two variables, the user might be equally careful. Typically, correlations between two independent variables of over .80 should be considered a warning sign.

Multicolinearity can be detected in a number of ways. First, look for high correlations between two independent variables. If the variables vary together, it is unlikely that their effects can be separated. Second, look at the standard error of the varibles. If multicolinearity exists, the standard errors will be large, indicating that little confidence should be placed in the estimates. More advanced measures await the advanced student in other tests.

When multicolinearity exists, there is no way to perform the regression using the full set of independent variables. Two suggested solutions are (1) create a new variable by combining the highly correlated variables in some way (say, averaging, summing, etc.) or (2) delete all but one of the correlated variables, letting the remaining one be a surrogate for the common underlying cause.

In either case, be careful not to ascribe causation or correlation to one variable to the exclusion of the others. The interrelationships make such an attribution inappropriate, and the coefficient of the independent variable loses much of its desired meaning.

Changes in Cost Behavior over Time. An underlying assumption in regression is that the model describes the cost relationship. Consider a regression of the form:

Cost = $a \times$ Units + c. This equation asserts that the coefficients are constant over time. If a cost relationship shifts or evolves over time, the specified model is inappropriate.

Cost shifts can be gradual or sudden. Gradual shifts can result from a slow evolution in processes or inattention of management to slowly increasing costs. Inflation can also lead to a gradual shift in the relationship, but inflation can be handled separately as described. Sudden shifts can occur from the introduction of a new technique or process.

Statistical techniques can be used to identify if cost shifts exist. One technique is to explicitly include a "time" term as an independent variable. If the resulting coefficient is significant, there is evidence that some time trend exists. Typically, time itself is not causing the change; there is some underlying cause that moves with time. Whether it is necessary to identify this underlying cause or whether use of the time variable itself is sufficient depends on the requirements of the analysis. Inclusion of a time variable is usually not a substitute for making inflation adjustments.

Another technique to find cost shifts is to plot the residuals in time sequence. (See discussion on residuals.) A pattern in the residuals may indicate some cost shifts.

If a cost shift is suspected at a particular date, two alternative analyses are suggested. First, if sufficient data are available, the analysis can be performed using only the data before (or after) the shift. Second, an indicator variable can be used to pick up the effect of the cost shift. (See section on indicator variables.) A method for determining if a shift has occurred is described in Chapter 30.

Tests of Reasonableness. Any cost estimate, statistical or otherwise, needs to be confirmed as reasonable. Among the reasonableness tests are the following:

- Compare the results of applying more than one estimation method. If the results are reasonable, the methods should yield approximately the same results, or there should be good reasons for a discrepancy.
- Compare the results to reality. For example, compare estimated costs at historical volumes to historical costs. Compare results at an assumed "but-for" volume with historical results (at some other date) at roughly the same volume. The results need not be the same, but differences should be explainable.
- Compare the results to independent estimates of costs. For example, the company under study may have made cost forecasts as part of a business plan before the alleged liability acts occurred. Or there may be industry statistics that provide a useful baseline.
- Consider the intrinsic reasonableness of the results. Do costs increase with volume? Are costs appropriately behaved compared to changes in production capacity?
- Finally, apply a test called "interocular inspection." This is a tongue-in-cheek name for a real test, in which you stare at the results until the meaning hits you between the eyes. In other words, consider whether your results make sense.

Other Statistical Techniques

The statistical discussion in this chapter focused on regression analysis. Many other statistical techniques may be used in cost estimation. We mention some briefly; a detailed discussion is beyond the scope of this chapter. Consult a statistician for further information.

Time Series, ARIMA Models. Time-series analysis refers to the analysis of any data sequenced over time. The time order is an essential element of the analysis. Regression (using time as an independent variable) is one part of time-series analysis. Another approach to time series analysis is called ARIMA (autoregressive integrated moving average) modeling, sometimes termed Box–Jenkins analysis. This approach searches for recurring patterns in past history to forecast into the future.

Survey Research for Comparables. At times, the analyst needs information as to what is typical or average in an industry. A survey of the industry, of customers, or of the public may be appropriate to measure some factor. There are many rules and methods for conducting a statistically valid survey. Once the data is gathered, it is amenable to the sorts of analyses described in this chapter.

Statistical Sampling for Attributes. Statistical sampling is a way to estimate a characteristic of a population without observing every item. It is used when the cost of a complete enumeration is prohibitive. For example, if the average size of an invoice is of interest, it is probably sufficient to sample a statistically valid selection of invoices. There is no need to examine every one. Sampling is used frequently in the audit process; it is equally applicable to litigation.

CONCLUSION

Cost estimation is an essential part of the litigation analyst's work. Through the tools of cost analysis, including cost accounting, statistics, economics, and industrial engineering, the analyst can arrive at accurate and defensible estimates of cost. However, if the tools are applied by rote or without due thought, the results may be invalid and subject to attack. In cost estimation, as in any area of litigation analysis, careful thought and careful analysis are keys to success.

NOTES

1. For an introduction to cost accounting, see S. Davidson, M. W. Maher, C. P. Stickney, and R. L. Weil, *Managerial Accounting: An Introduction to Concepts, Methods, and Uses*, 3rd ed. (Hinsdale, IL: The Dryden Press, 1988), or another cost accounting test.
2. For a more complete but still simple discussion of regression, see Achen, *Interpreting and Using Regression*, 1982 (Series on Quantitative Applications in the Social Sciences, Number 29), or Schroeder, Sjoquist, and Stephan, *Understanding Regression Analysis: An Introductory Guide*, 1986 (Series on Quantitative Applications in the Social Sciences, Number 57). Both are published by Sage Publications, Beverly Hills, CA.

30

STATISTICAL ESTIMATION OF INCREMENTAL COST FROM ACCOUNTING DATA

William E. Wecker, PhD
Roman L. Weil, PhD, CPA, CMA

INTRODUCTION

Many litigation assignments require a computation of damages suffered by the plaintiff. Usually such damages reflect the incremental revenues and costs the plaintiff would have realized but for the actions or inactions of the defendant. This chapter focuses on advanced issues relating to the calculation of incremental costs for such damage cases.

The incremental cost is the additional cost of producing and selling additional units. Statistical regression analysis of accounting data may be used in some cases to estimate the incremental cost. When properly applied, regression analysis provides an estimate of incremental cost that can be accurate and reliable. When improperly applied, however, regression analysis provides an estimate of incremental cost that can be seriously biased and misleading. This chapter shows how a regression analysis of accounting data can produce a biased or misleading result.

ACCOUNTING DATA: USES AND LIMITATIONS

In estimating incremental costs for most firms under most circumstances, the analyst will have data from only a firm's accounting system. Such data are usually reliable, in the sense that they have been carefully gathered in the ordinary course of business and have been checked, if not audited. Nonetheless, such accounting data have serious limitations if mechanically used to measure incremental costs. This section describes the accounting data usually available and the difficulties they present.

The problem is to ascertain how much costs would have increased had production and sales increased by a specified amount.

Cost Behavior

Accountants and economists distinguish over 50 different terms involving the word *cost*. The Appendix presents a taxonomy for these terms and defines them.

This chapter focuses on incremental costs over either the long run or the short run. The time frame will depend on the specifics of a given assignment.

Long Run and Short Run. Long-run cost behavior differs from short-run cost behavior. Over sufficient time spans, all costs vary with changes in production: Plants can open or close; salaried executives can be hired or laid off; a business can shut down entirely. Over short time spans, essentially all costs are fixed. Therefore, estimating cost increases generated by given production and sales increases requires a statement of the time span over which the increases would have occurred.

Exhibit 30-1 illustrates this phenomenon. The line A-B shown in Exhibit 30-1 describes typical long-run cost behavior. If there is sufficient time, say several years, to adjust manufacturing processes to growth in production from Q0 to Q1, then costs will increase gradually along the line A-B from C0 to C1.

The line C-D describes short-run cost behavior. If production increases from Q0 to Q1 over a short time span, say 1 month, then costs will increase—from C0 to C2—more than they would over a long time span.

The greater cost increase for the short-run production increase occurs because firms do not add capacity as efficiently in a month as they do over several years. If capacity is to be added quickly, extra shifts may have to be added, involving overtime wages. Or less efficient manufacturing equipment may have to be brought out of mothballs and put back to work.

Expansion and Contraction. Similarly, when production decreases over a short period, costs decrease less than they do over a long period. If production decreases from Q0 to Q2 over a short time span, say 1 month, then costs per unit will decrease

EXHIBIT 30-1. LONG-RUN AND SHORT-RUN COST BEHAVIOR

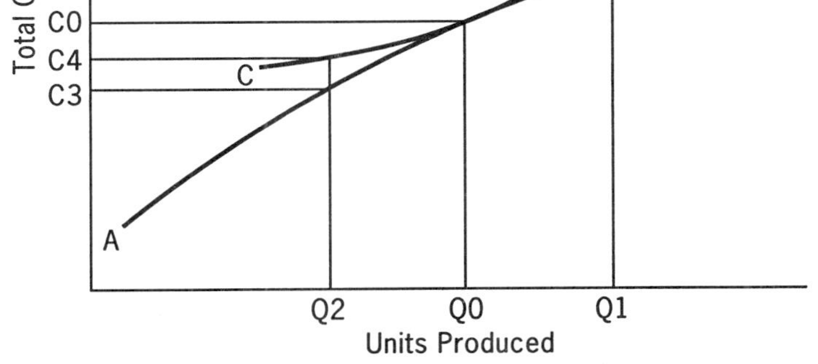

from C0 to C4 rather than from C0 to C3. The lower unit cost decrease for short-term contractions results from such factors as machinery put into mothballs or left idle, rather than sold right away. Or workers may remain on the payroll longer then otherwise necessary to maintain favorable labor relations.

Implications for Using Accounting Data. In estimating additional costs generated by additional production and sales, the analyst needs to distinguish two notions of additional costs: "marginal" costs and "incremental" costs. One accounting text states:

> The economist restricts the term marginal cost to the cost of producing one more unit. Thus, the next unit has a marginal cost; the next week's output has an incremental cost. If a firm produces and sells a new product, the related new costs would properly be called incremental, not marginal.[1]

In Exhibit 30-1, note that the initial cost increase from the point Q0 is, to the naked eye, indistinguishable on the short-run cost curve, C-D, from that of the long-run cost curve, A-B. Data in accounting records are not collected with the distinction between the long run and the short run in mind. Accounting records often obscure the difference between long-run and short-run cost behavior because the general ledger accounts do not distinguish costs incurred during periods of rapid growth from those of gradual growth. Nor do they distinguish costs incurred during periods of expansion from those of contraction. Thus a mechanical analysis of general ledger accounting data is unlikely to recognize the different economic eras that might underlie the costs.

A regression analysis that fails to distinguish long-run cost behavior from short-run cost behavior is unlikely to yield meaningful results. Similarly, a regression analysis that fails to distinguish costs occurring during expansions from costs occurring during contractions is unlikely to yield meaningful results.

Unadjusted General Ledger Accounting Data May Be Unsuitable

Accounting data collected from the ordinary books and records, the general ledger data, frequently reflect accounting estimates. These estimates, although correct for accounting purposes, may bias a statistical analysis of incremental costs.

Depreciation as an Example of an Incorrect Capacity Cost Measure. For both income tax and financial accounting purposes, new equipment is assigned depreciation schedules (generally different schedules for the two reporting purposes). The resulting amounts charged for depreciation will be recorded in the accounting records and, once recorded, will not be changed, even if the accountant later learns that the original estimate of useful life is incorrect.

Suppose equipment is expected at acquisition to have a useful life of 12 years and no salvage value. Assume straight-line depreciation is used and that at the end of the eighth year of use, market conditions change so that the equipment will be used for only 10 years, not 12.

Assume that depreciation accounting correctly measures plant costs. In retrospect, the plant costs over the 10 years during which the equipment is used should reflect one-tenth of the equipment cost each year. But the accounting data correctly accumulated in the general ledger under generally accepted accounting principles will reflect one-twelfth of the cost for each of the first 8 years and one-sixth of the cost for each of the last 2 years, Years 9 and 10.[2]

Thus, whenever the depreciable life of plant and equipment has changed during its life, the accounting data recorded for depreciation will not accurately reflect the year-to-year costs of using capacity. Whether accounting data can measure incremental costs of capacity is an open question not discussed here.

Salaries as an Example of Too Much Smoothing. Some manufacturing and sales employees are salaried, rather than paid on a piece rate (in manufacturing) or via commission (in sales). Such salaries are often quoted on an annual basis but charged into the general ledger accounts in equal monthly amounts. Sometimes, an accurate measure of additional costs associated with increased production (or sales) activity would require that the salaries be charged to months in proportion to effort during those months, rather than uniformly across months. Generally accepted accounting principles do not require that the monthly record of costs be adjusted at year end so that monthly amounts reflect monthly effort.

Thus, the general ledger data for such salaries, without adjustment, will show more uniformity (less variability) of costs through time than the effort to produce and sell additional units actually requires. The data in the general ledger accounts are too "smooth." Use of accounting data afflicted with this problem will underestimate incremental costs. Further difficulty arises from lags in the result from effort expended such that the increased output or sales may not occur in the same month as the increased effort.

Accounting Adjusting Entries as an Example of Too Little Smoothing. For other general ledger accounts, the data are not "smooth" enough. At the end of each accounting period, usually a calendar quarter but sometimes a year, the accountant makes adjusting entries.

Typical adjusting entries affect inventory valuation, bad debt expense, rent expense, insurance expense, and other items where charges for several months are recorded at a single time, usually when an expenditure covering several months is made.

Consider bad debt expense. Typically, once per quarter or once per year an accounting entry is made to recognize all bad debt expense for that period. Suppose the entry is made on December 31 for the fourth quarter sales. Then December's data will show three months' of bad debt expense, whereas October's and November's data will show none. Each month's general ledger accounts do not match the cost actually incurred each month; statistical analysis of such data may understate incremental costs.

Adjustments Must Be Made for Lags in Recording Costs. A supervisor may receive a lump sum, year-end bonus for extra effort. Unless adjustments spread the one-time bonus back to the periods when it was earned, costs for the overtime periods will be understated, and costs for the period of bonus payment will be overstated. Failure to adjust for this phenomenon will underestimate incremental costs derived in a statistical regression analysis.

General Ledger Data Omit Some Additional Costs. The accounting records do not include all costs of additional production and sales. An example is the added cost of carrying additional working capital to produce and sell additional units. As production and sales expand, a firm will need to carry more inventories and more accounts receivable. These items have a carrying cost that accounting usually does not recognize explicitly.

Additional Information Not Contained in the General Ledger Accounts

Factors Affecting Incremental Cost Relations. The accountant may be aware of a change that influences cost relations. For example, cost data may have been accumulated over a period when an important technology change occurred that altered the incremental cost of production.

Product-Specific Costs. The accountant may be able to exclusively associate certain costs (typically direct material and direct labor costs) with particular products. The statistical analysis may exclude such costs.

REGRESSION ANALYSIS OF ACCOUNTING DATA

To illustrate some pitfalls of a regression analysis of accounting data, consider a hypothetical firm that manufactures and sells widgits. Exhibit 30-2 shows a scatter plot of hypothetical monthly cost and production data for a 10-year period. Each point shown in Exhibit 30-2 represents the number of units produced (horizontal axis) and the total cost of production (vertical axis) in a month.

A regression analysis of the data begins by specifying the form of the relationship between the two variables. In this example the two variables conform to a straight-line relationship,

$$\text{Total cost} = a + b\,(\text{Units}) \;. \tag{1}$$

where the regression calculation will estimate the coefficients a and b of the straight line. The choice of a straight line is but one of many possibilities, and care must be used that the functional form chosen correctly represents the pattern that the data exhibit. To illustrate the point that a straight-line regression may not be the correct choice, consider the data shown in Exhibit 30-3. These data evidently do not conform to a straight-line relationship. We will show later how to perform a regression analysis of the data shown in Exhibit 30-3.

In addition to the assumption of a particular functional form, the regression analysis assumes that the costs in each month are influenced by random (unsystematic) factors that differ from month to month in their effect. These random factors represent "noise" in the data, which obscures the underlying relationship between the variables.

EXHIBIT 30-2. MONTHLY TOTAL COST VERSUS UNITS PRODUCED

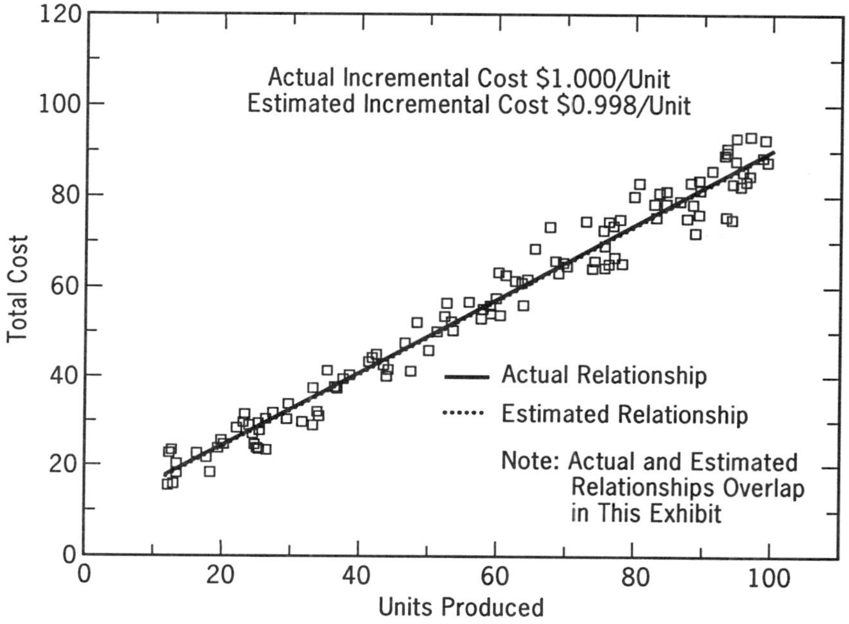

EXHIBIT 30-3. MONTHLY TOTAL COST VERSUS UNITS PRODUCED

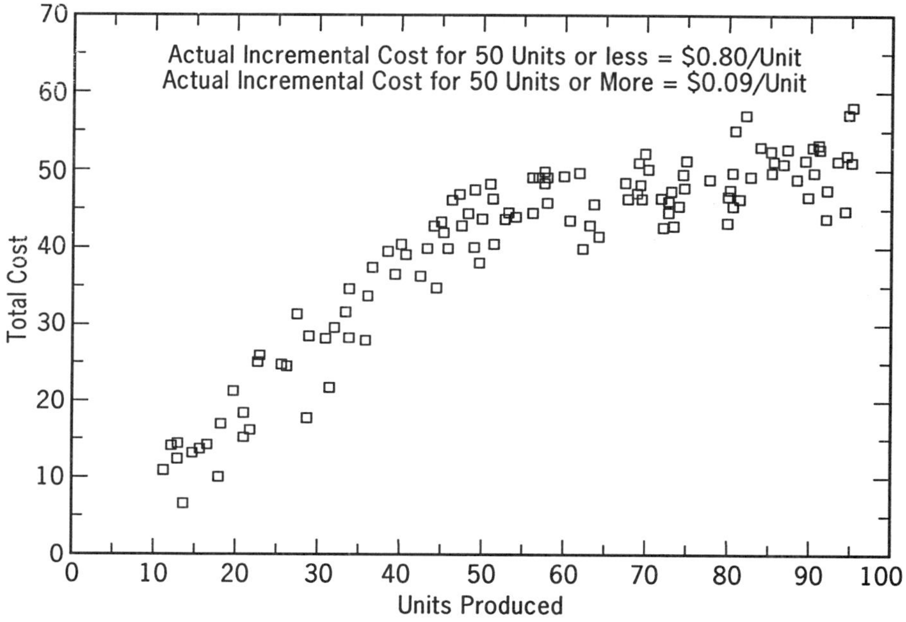

However, when the "noise" is systematic, as with accounting adjustments or short-run departures from the long-run cost function, the regression calculation will not produce reliable results.

The solid line in Exhibit 30-2 is the actual relationship between cost and units produced. The dotted line (which overlaps the solid line in this figure) was estimated by a regression calculation. Because the assumption of a straight-line functional form is correct in this example and because the "noise" is unsystematic, the regression line accurately measures the long-run incremental cost of producing an additional widgit.

Inaccuracies Arising from Accounting Allocations

To demonstrate the biasing effect of accounting allocations on regression estimates of incremental costs, we modified the data underlying Exhibit 30-2 by spreading 20 percent of each month's cost across the calendar year. This introduces systematic "noise" in the data in violation of regression assumptions. The modified data appear in Exhibit 30-4. A regression analysis of the modified data estimates incremental costs at .805, which estimate is biased downward by approximately 20 percent because of the accounting allocations.

EXHIBIT 30-4. MONTHLY TOTAL COST INCLUDING ACCOUNTING ADJUSTMENTS VERSUS UNITS PRODUCED

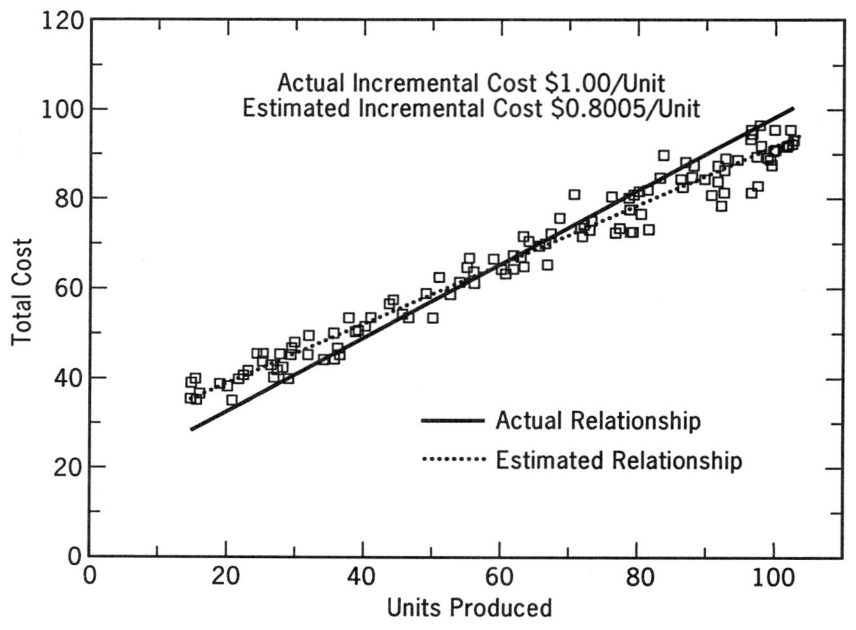

EXHIBIT 30-5. MONTHLY TOTAL COST VERSUS UNITS PRODUCED

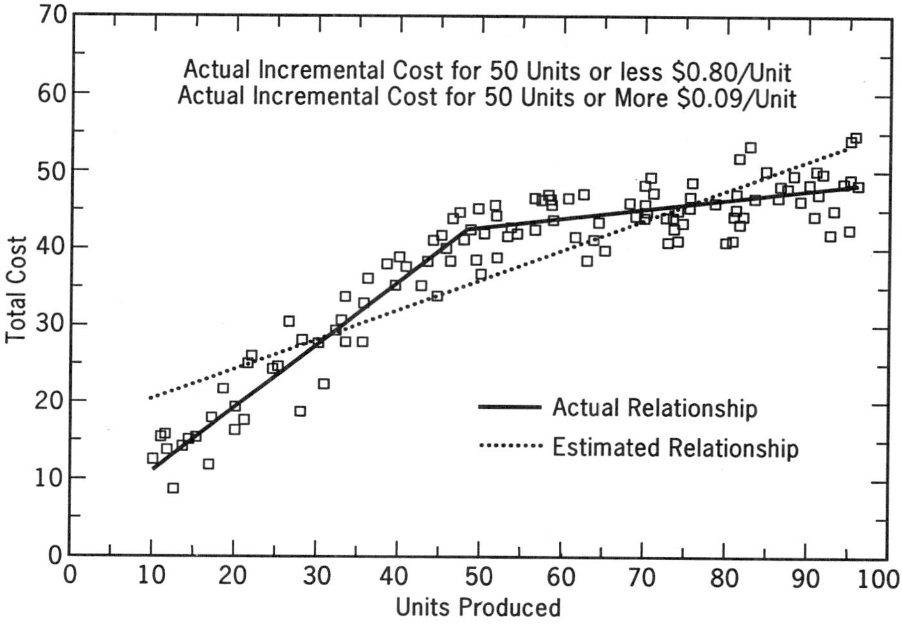

Inaccuracies Arising from a Changing Incremental Cost

In the sample shown in Exhibit 30-2, the incremental cost of production remains constant, and the relationship between total cost and units produced can be expressed in Equation (1) as a straight line. Sometimes the incremental cost of production does not remain constant and a straight-line regression as in equation (1) is not appropriate.

Economies of Scale as an Example of Changing Incremental Cost. Exhibit 30-3 shows hypothetical data on total cost and units produced where the incremental cost of production does not remain constant. The hypothetical data shown in Exhibit 30-3 exhibit lower incremental costs at higher levels of production—a common phenomenon termed *economies of scale*. The change in incremental cost results in a relationship between total cost and units produced that does not conform to a straight line. If this changing incremental cost is overlooked and a single straight-line regression is incorrectly assumed, the result is as shown in Exhibit 30-5. The straight line in Exhibit 30-5 underestimates incremental cost at low levels of production and overestimates incremental cost at high levels of production.

Some comfort may be gained from noticing that the linear regression estimate of incremental cost shown in Exhibit 30-5 is not wildly in error. The regression estimate of .338 lies between the actual values of .80 and .09 and perhaps may be regarded as a reasonable approximation to the correct values of .80 and .09 for

EXHIBIT 30-6. ERRONEOUS ESTIMATE OF INCREMENTAL COST RESULTING FROM MISSPECIFICATION

	Product 1	Product 2
Actual incremental cost first 5 years of data	1.0	1.0
Actual incremental cost second 5 years of data	0.9	0.9
Erroneous estimates based on regression using 10 years of data	0.4	1.6

some purposes. Unfortunately, this property cannot be relied on in general. Consider, for example, multiple linear regression. Multiple linear regression employs more than one independent (i.e., right-hand-side) variable and is used in cases where, for example, total cost data includes costs arising from more than one product. Equation 2 shows a multiple regression equation involving two independent variables.

$$\text{Total Cost} = a + b_1 \text{ (Units of Product 1)} + b_2 \text{ (Units of Product 2)} \quad (2)$$

For multiple regression, if the form of the relationship between total cost and units produced deviates from the assumed relationship, the resulting regression estimates may be totally meaningless. Consider the hypothetical example shown in Exhibit 30-6 that is similar in spirit to the example shown in Exhibit 30-3 and 30-5 but that employs two independent variables rather than one. The incremental cost is the same for each of two products for 5 years of monthly data and then changes slightly (from 1.0 to 0.9) for an additional 5 years of data. When a regression is performed assuming constant incremental costs as in Equation 2, the resulting estimates do not lie between the actual values of incremental cost and are instead seriously in error—0.4 and 1.6. This example illustrates that an apparent small change in incremental cost can have a large effect on the regression estimates if the change is not properly accounted for.

Changing Product Mix as an Example of Changing Incremental Cost. Another way the relationship between total cost and units produced can change occurs when a group of different products is treated as a single product. Exhibit 30-7 shows two products with different incremental costs that properly may be treated as a single product because the two products are sold in a constant proportion, here, two units of products for each unit of product. This is sometimes termed a constant *product mix*. A regression analysis of total cost versus total units produced (Product 1 and

EXHIBIT 30-7. TWO PRODUCTS SOLD IN A CONSTANT PROPORTION; TOTAL COST = \$1.0 × (UNITS PRODUCED PRODUCT 1) + \$0.5 × (UNITS PRODUCED PRODUCT 2)

Time Period	Units of Product 1	Units of Product 2	Total Units	Cost
1	10	20	30	\$ 20
2	20	40	60	40
3	30	60	90	60
4	40	80	120	80
5	50	100	150	100

EXHIBIT 30-8.

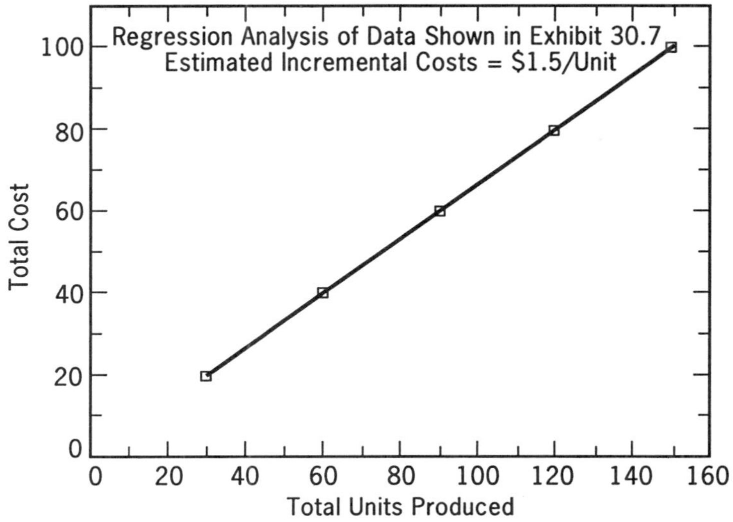

Product 2 combined) appears in Exhibit 30-8. The regression estimates incremental cost of $.67/unit as the correct average incremental cost per unit of one item of product 1 plus two items of product 2: $.67 = $2.00/3; $2.00 = $1 × 1 + $.50 × 2.

Exhibit 30-9 shows two products with different incremental costs that may not be properly treated as a single product because the two products are not sold in a constant proportion—the product mix changes. In this case the estimated incremental cost (shown graphically in Exhibit 30-10 that results from incorrectly treating the two products as a single product is $0/unit.

Inaccuracies Arising from Multicollinearity

A phenomenon termed *multicollinearity* occurs when the numbers of units produced of one product rises and falls in close synchrony with the number of units produced of another product. When the production data are collinear, it becomes difficult or impossible for a regression analysis to distinguish the influence on total cost of the

EXHIBIT 30-9. TWO PRODUCTS SOLD IN A VARYING PROPORTION; TOTAL COST = $1.0 × (UNITS PRODUCED PRODUCT 1) + $0.5 × (UNITS PRODUCED PRODUCT 2)

Time Period	Units of Product 1	Units of Product 2	Total Units	Cost
1	10	100	110	$60
2	20	80	100	60
3	30	60	90	60
4	40	40	80	60
5	50	20	70	60

EXHIBIT 30-10.

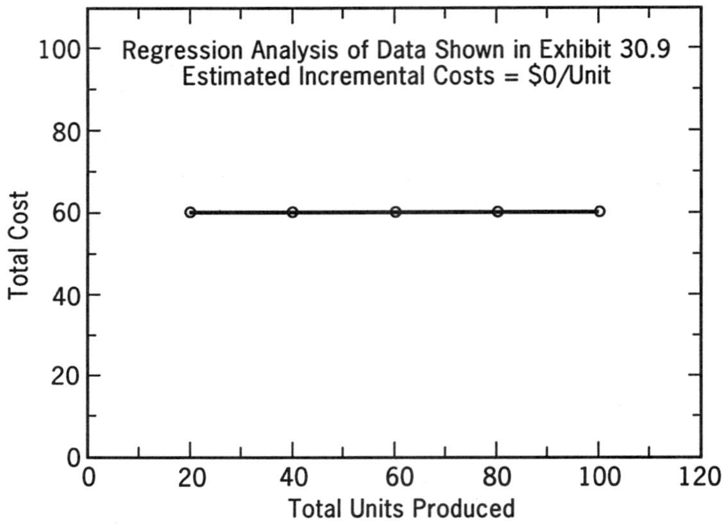

two products separately. To illustrate how multicollinearity can make it impossible to separately distinguish the influence on total cost of two products, consider the incremental cost of making a suit of clothes comprising one coat and one pair of pants. Suppose, if known, the incremental cost of making the coat is $60 and the pants $40 for a total cost of $100 per suit. Production data will show the cost of making 10 suits to be $1000 and 20 to be $1000, and a quick calculation will reveal the production cost of a suit to be $100. But from these aggregate data alone it is impossible to separate the $100 cost of the suit into its components—the $60 cost of the coat and the $40 cost of the pants.

The synchrony of production for the two products need not be a perfect lock step to render a regression analysis powerless to separate the incremental costs. A commonly cited rule of thumb suggests that a degree of correlation greater than .8 to .9 (correlation of 1.0 corresponds to perfect synchrony) may be sufficient to render a regression powerless to make the required separation.

DETECTING FLAWS IN A REGRESSION ANALYSIS

Informal Methods

Informal methods to critique regression analyses rely on subjective "impressions" gained usually from graphical displays of data. Despite their subjective nature, informal methods are important tools of the applied statistician. Moreover, the informal methods may be more intuitive and meaningful to laymen than a formal statistical test and therefore may be a more effective way to demonstrate to a layman an error in a regression analysis.

Exhibit 30-3 illustrates an informal method for checking the validity of a regression analysis. The visual impression gained from Exhibit 30-3 is that a curved rather than a straight line best describes the data. This visual impression can be further supported by applying a formal statistical test.

Formal Statistical Tests

Formal statistical tests detect violations of the underlying assumptions of a regression analysis. Many such tests exist, but they all use the same basic logic. A mathematical calculation is made of the probability of some feature of the data occurring (e.g., the chance of a fair coin landing "heads" 10 times in succession). The probability calculation is based on the assumptions that are being checked (e.g., the coin is fair). If the calculation yields a very small probability for an observed outcome, one of two possibilities exist:

- The small calculated probability is correct, in which case the data are simply extraordinary.
- The small calculated probability is incorrect, in which case one (or more) of the assumptions on which the calculation was based is violated.

When the calculated probability is sufficiently small (a commonly used standard is .05 or less) we are drawn to the latter of the two possibilities.

We illustrate the logic of a formal statistical test with a "coin flipping" example (because it is simpler than regression). Suppose a coin is flipped 10 times resulting in 10 heads and zero tails. Assuming a fair coin, the probability of such an occurrence is $(.5)^{10} = .00098$, or less than one chance in one thousand. Although such low probability events are possible, it is easier to believe that the coin is not a fair coin.

Some statistical tests are designed to be especially powerful at detecting specific violations of particular assumptions. These specialized tests are appropriate when a specific violation is suspected. Other statistical tests are less effective than the specialized tests at detecting any particular violation but have the ability to detect a broad range of violations.

The *F*-Test to Detect a Changing Incremental Cost

Exhibit 30-5 illustrates the idea of the *F*-test (sometimes called the "Chow" test). The data are divided into two portions and a separate straight-line regression is calculated on each of the two portions of data. If the data actually conform to a single straight-line regression (unchanging incremental cost), the difference between the two regression estimates of incremental cost will be small. If, however, the data exhibit a changing incremental cost, the difference between the two regression estimates of incremental cost will be large. One can calculate the probability of a dissimilarity as large as the observed dissimilarity occurring as a matter of mere chance, under the assumption that the actual relationship is that of a single straight line. In the case shown in Exhibit 30-5, the probability calculation shows that the difference in the two estimated incremental costs is too large to be explained by the change fluctuations in the month-to-month data and reveals instead a changing incremental cost. In the language of the statistician, the hypothesis of a single straight-line is rejected.

Tests of Reasonableness

In addition to the formal and informal methods, statisticians commonly test the reasonableness of regression results. If the regression results are at odds with experience and common sense, a healthy skepticism is appropriate. For example, a regression estimate showing a negative incremental cost or an incremental cost exceeding the product's selling price may indicate a violated assumption.

CONCLUSION

Regression analysis can be valid for estimating incremental cost. Unadjusted accounting data seldom conform perfectly to the assumptions of a regression analysis. Therefore, a regression analysis of unadjusted accounting data will most likely produce unreliable results. Formal statistical tests, informal statistical methods, and tests of reasonableness may detect and expose such unreliable results.

APPENDIX: COST TERMINOLOGY[3]

Distinguishing various concepts of cost often becomes important in litigation. The accountant should know the subtle distinctions between various cost concepts, particularly in responding to interrogatories and in deposition. The following distinctions have proved useful. (Synonyms appear in parentheses.)

The following pairs of terms distinguish the basis measured in accounting.

Historical Cost (Acquisition Cost) vs. Current Cost

A distinction used in financial accounting. Current cost can be used more specifically to mean replacement cost, net realizable value, or present value of cash flows. "Current cost" is often used narrowly to mean replacement costs.

Historical Cost (Actual Cost) vs. Standard Cost

The distinction between historical and standard costs arises in product costing for inventory valuation. Some systems record actual costs, whereas others record the standard costs.

The following pairs of terms denote various distinctions among historical costs. For each pair of terms, the sum of the two kinds of costs equals total historical cost used in financial reporting.

Variable Cost vs. Fixed Cost (Constant Cost)

Distinction used in break-even analysis and in designing cost accounting systems, particularly for product costing. See later discussion for a further subdivision of fixed costs and for an economic distinction closely paralleling this one.

Traceable Cost vs. Common Cost (Joint Cost)

Distinction arises in allocating manufacturing costs to product. Common costs are allocated to product, but the allocations are more or less arbitrary. The distinction also arises in segment reporting and in separating manufacturing from nonmanufacturing costs.

Direct Cost vs. Indirect Cost

Distinction arises in designing cost accounting systems and in product costing. Direct cost can be traced directly to a cost object (e.g., a product, a responsibility center), whereas indirect costs cannot.

Out-of-Pocket Cost (Outlay Cost; Cash Cost) vs. Book Cost

Virtually all costs recorded in financial statements require a cash outlay at one time or another. The distinction here separates expenditures to occur in the future from those already made and is used in making decisions. Book costs, such as for depreciation, reduce income without requiring a future outlay of cash. The cash has already been spent. See future versus past cost later.

Incremental Cost (Marginal Cost; Differential Cost) vs. Unavoidable Cost (Inescapable Cost; Sunk Cost)

Distinction used in making decisions. Incremental costs will be incurred (or saved) if a decision is made to go ahead (or to stop) some activity but not otherwise. Unavoidable costs will be reported in financial statements whether the decision is made to go ahead or not because cash has already been spent or committed. Not all unavoidable costs are book costs, as, for example, a salary promised but not yet earned that will be paid even if a no-go decision is made. The economist restricts the term *marginal cost* to the cost of producing one more unit. Thus the next unit has a marginal cost; the next week's output has an incremental cost. If a firm produces and sells a new product, the related new costs would properly be called incremental, not marginal. If a factory is closed, the cost saved are incremental, not marginal.

Escapable Cost vs. Inescapable Cost (Unavoidable Cost)

Same distinction as incremental versus sunk costs, but this pair is used only when the decision maker is considering stopping something—ceasing to produce a product, closing a factory, or the like. See next pair.

Avoidable Cost vs. Unavoidable Cost

A distinction sometimes used in discussing the merits of variable and absorption costing. Avoidable costs are treated as product costs, and unavoidable costs are treated as period expenses under variable costing.

Controllable Cost vs. Uncontrollable Cost

The distinction here is used in assigning cost responsibility and in setting bonus or incentive plans. All costs can be affected by someone in the entity; those who design incentive schemes attempt to hold a person responsible for a cost only if that person can influence the amount of the cost.

In each of the following pairs, used in historical cost accounting, the word *cost* appears in one of the terms where *expense* is meant.

Expired Cost vs. Unexpired Cost

The distinction is between expense and asset.

Product Cost vs. Period Cost

The terms distinguish product cost from period expense. When a given asset is used, is its cost converted into work in process and then finished goods on the balance sheet until the goods are sold, or is it an expense shown on this period's income statement? Product costs appear on the income statement as part of cost of goods sold in the period when the goods are sold. Period expense appear on the income statement with an appropriate caption for the item in the period when the cost is incurred or recognized.

Fixed (Historical) Cost

The following subdivisions of fixed (historical) costs are used in analyzing operations. The relation between the components of fixed costs is:

Fixed costs = Capacity costs + Programmed costs

Fixed costs = Semifixed costs + Fixed portions of semivariable costs + "Pure" fixed costs

Capacity costs = Standby costs + Enabling costs

Capacity Cost (Committed Cost) vs. Programmed Cost (Managed Cost; Discretionary Cost)

Capacity costs give a firm the capability to produce or to sell. Programmed costs, such as for advertising or research and development, may not be essential, but once a decision is made to incur them, they become fixed costs.

Standby Cost vs. Enabling Cost

Standby costs will be incurred whether capacity, once acquired, is used or not, such as property taxes and depreciation on a factory. Enabling costs, such as for a security force, can be avoided if the capacity is unused.

Semifixed Cost vs. Semivariable Cost

A cost fixed over a wide range but that can change at various levels is a semifixed cost or "step cost." An example is the cost of rail lines from the factory to the main rail line where fixed cost depends on whether there are one or two parallel lines but are independent of a number of trains run per day. Semivariable costs combine a strictly fixed component cost plus a variable component. Telephone charges usually have a fixed monthly component plus a charge related to usage.

The following pairs of terms distinguish among economic uses of decision-making uses or regulatory uses of cost terms.

Fully Absorbed Cost vs. Variable Cost (Direct Cost)

Fully absorbed costs refer to cost where fixed costs have been allocated to units or departments as required by generally accepted accounting principles. Variable costs, in contrast, may be more relevant for making decision, such as in setting prices.

Fully Absorbed Cost vs. Full Cost

In full costing, all costs, manufacturing costs as well as central corporate express (including financial expenses), are allocated to product or divisions. In full absorption costing, only manufacturing costs are allocated to product. Only in full costing will revenues, expenses, and income summed over all products or divisions equal corporate revenues, expenses, and income.

Opportunity Cost vs. Outlay Cost (Out-of-Pocket Cost)

Opportunity cost refers to the economic benefit foregone by using a resource for one purpose instead of for another. The outlay cost of the resource will be recorded in financial records. The distinction arises because a resource is already in the possession of the entity with a recorded historical cost. Its economic value to the firm, opportunity cost, generally differs from the historical cost; it can be either larger or smaller.

Future Cost vs. Past Cost

Effective decision making analyzes only present and future outlay costs or out-of-pocket costs. Opportunity costs are relevant for profit maximizing; past costs are used in financial reporting.

Short-Run Costs vs. Long-Run Costs

Short-run costs vary as output is varied for a given configuration of plant and equipment. Long-run costs can be incurred to change that configuration. This pair of terms is the economic analog of the accounting pair, variable and fixed costs. The analogy is not perfect because some short-run costs are fixed, such as property taxes on the factory, from the point of view of breakeven analysis.

Imputed Cost vs. Book Cost

In a regulatory setting, some costs, for example the cost of owner's equity capital, are calculated and used for various purposes; these are imputed costs. Imputed costs are not recorded in the historical costs accounting records for financial reporting. Book costs are recorded.

Average Cost vs. Marginal Cost

The economic distinction equivalent to fully absorbed cost of product and direct cost of product. Average cost is total cost divided by number of units. Marginal cost is the cost to produce the next unit (or the last unit).

Incremental Cost vs. Variable Cost

Whether a cost changes or remains fixed depends on the activity basis being considered. Typically, but not invariably, costs are said to be variable or fixed with respect to an activity basis such as changes in production levels. Typically, but not invariably, costs are said to be incremental or not with respect to an activity basis such as the undertaking of some new venture. For example, consider the decision to undertake the production of food processors, rather than food blenders, which the manufacturer has been making. To produce processors requires the acquisition of a new machine tool. The cost of the new machine tool is incremental with respect to a decision to produce food processors instead of food blenders, but, once acquired, becomes a fixed cost of producing food processors. If costs of direct labor hours are going to be incurred for the production of food processors or food blenders, whichever is produced (in a scenario when not both are to be produced), such costs are variable with respect to production measured in units but not incremental with respect to the decision to produce processors rather than blenders. This distinction is often blurred in practice, so a careful understanding of the activity basis being considered is necessary for understanding of the concepts being used in a particular application.

NOTES

1. See page 906, Sidney Davidson, Michael W. Maher, Clyde P. Stickney, and Roman L. Weil, *Managerial Accounting: An Introduction to Concepts, Methods, and Uses*, 3rd ed. (Hinsdale, IL: The Dryden Press, 1988). The Appendix reproduces this material. With permission.

2. Refer to Sidney Davidson, Clyde P. Stickney, and Roman L. Weil, *Financial Accounting: An Introduction to Concepts, Methods, and Uses*, 5th ed. (Hinsdale, IL: The Dryden Press, 1985). Pages 378–379 describe and illustrate the accounting methods for changing estimates of equipment life and pages 531–533 explain why these methods are a part of generally accepted accounting principles. With permission.

3. The material in this Appendix is taken from S. Davidson, M.W. Maher, C.P. Stickney, and R.L. Weil, *Managerial Accounting: An Introduction to Concepts, Methods, and Uses*, 3rd ed. (Hinsdale, IL: The Dryden Press, 1988), pp. 906–909. With permission.

31

SECURITIES ACT VIOLATIONS: COMPUTATION OF DAMAGES

Dale R. Hurd, PhD, CMC
Michael J. Wagner, JD, CPA, CMC

FEDERAL SECURITIES ACTS

The Securities Act of 1933 and the Securities Exchange Act of 1934 have generated a broad spectrum of judicial analyses and scholarly reflection.[1] This chapter summarizes these two acts and discusses the incorporation of "market effects" in a damage analysis.

The 1933 act deals with initial public offerings. This law requires that companies issue a prospectus that discloses required information to the public. The 1934 act addresses securities transactions that occur after the initial offering. The 1934 act requires that companies issue annual and quarterly reports.

Sections 9, 11, 12(1), 12(2), and 18 of the 1933 act and Section 10b of the 1934 act address damage computations. Rule 10b-5 of the Securities and Exchange Code enforces the regulation issued by the Securities and Exchange Commission (SEC) pursuant to § 10b of the 1934 act.

The major liability differences among the sections of the SEC code center on the plaintiff's burden of proof regarding plaintiffs reliance, scienter, privity, and causation. For reliance, the plaintiff must show that a misrepresentation factored substantially in the plaintiff's decision that resulted in a loss. For failing to disclose relevant information, the plaintiff must prove that a reasonable investor would consider the withheld facts important. For scienter, the plaintiff must prove that the defendant intended to deceive, manipulate, or defraud. In its broadest sense, *privity* refers to joint knowledge of a private matter. In SEC litigation, privity relates to a direct connection or successive relationship to a share of stock. For causation, plaintiffs must show that the alleged wrongful acts effected the loss.

The 1933 Act

Section 11. Under § 11, an initial purchaser—or under certain circumstances, an investor who acquired the registered security in the "after market"—has a claim if the prospectus and registration statement falsely stated a material fact or omitted a material fact required or necessary to make the statements forthright as of the effective date.

Plaintiffs must prove that the registration statement or prospectus contained a material untruth or omission when it became effective. The untruth or omission must relate to existing events when the registration statement became effective.

Plaintiffs do not have to prove causation, scienter, or privity and must prove reliance only if they purchased a security after the issuer publishes an earnings statement covering a 12-month period starting after the effective date.

The issuer, every person who signed the registration statement, every director, every underwriter, but not selling group members, and every professional expert who has been named (with his consent) as having prepared any part of the registration statement may all face liability charges.

Section 11 authorizes recovery of damages equal to the difference between the security's purchase price (not to exceed the offering price) and either (1) the security's selling price if sold before filing the complaint, or the greater of (2) the market value when the complaint was filed, or (3) the security's selling price if sold after the complaint was filed but before judgment. Exhibit 31-1 illustrates this relationship. Note that a plaintiff who purchased the security for more than the offering price cannot recover this increment under § 11. Also, a purchaser who holds the security after filing the lawsuit cannot recover additional price declines.

The statute of limitation runs 1 year after discovering the allegedly false statements or omissions or after such discovery should have been made by exercising reasonable diligence. Ultimate limitation is 3 years after the security was first "bona fide offered to the public."

Section 12. Sections 12(1) and 12(2) provide recovery rights to defrauded buyers. The plaintiff must prove that the prospectus or oral communications contained an untrue statement or omission of fact and that the plaintiff was unaware of this. For § 12(1) the plaintiff need not prove materiality, whereas section 12(2) requires materiality as a requirement of proof.

After the 1933 act was passed, the courts initially required strict privity between the buyer and seller to apply § 12. This ruling has evolved into a proximate cause

EXHIBIT 31-1. SECTION 11 DAMAGES

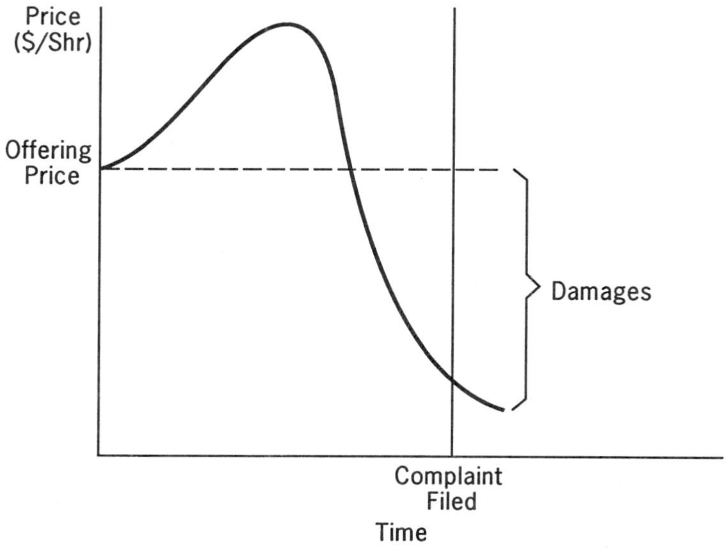

test that determines liability by examining the defendant's actions throughout the entire selling process rather than only at the transfer of title. The courts have further defined the proximate cause standard by requiring that the defendant's acts factored substantially in the specific sales transaction.

Section 12 authorizes damages recovery by "rescission": returning the stock plus any income received, such as dividends, in return for the full purchase price plus interest.

Section 12's burden of proof exceeds that required under § 11, but recoverable damages are much greater. Interest is not discretionary; the plaintiff automatically receives it.

The statute of limitations runs for 1 year after the injured party discovers the false statement or omission or after such discovery should have been made through reasonable diligence. Three years after the security's initial offering is the absolute limit, as under § 11.

Section 9. Section 9 relates to manipulative acts or transactions that cause false market signals, whether the transaction is a purchase or sale of securities. Privity, materiality, and reliance are not required as proof, only intent, and the defendant's influence on the stock price.

The court may impose either rescissionary damages or the losses incurred because of the manipulative acts, after factoring out market effects.

The statute of limitations runs for 1 year after discovering the false statement or omission or after such discovery should have been made through reasonable diligence. Three years after the security's initial offering is an absolute limit, as under § 11.

Section 18. Section 18 applies to anyone who makes a misstatement in a document filed with the SEC or causes such a document to be filed.

Under § 18, the plaintiff class may have either purchased or sold the securities. Plaintiff must prove reliance, materiality, and show the misconduct's effect on the security price.

Damages are limited to losses incurred by strict reliance on the material misstatement, after accounting for all other factors.

The statute of limitations runs for 1 year after discovering the misstatement or omission or after such discovery should have been made through reasonable diligence. Three years after the security's initial offering is an absolute limit.

The 1934 Act

Rule 10b-5. Section 10b of the 1934 act states that

> It shall be unlawful for any person, directly or indirectly, by the use of any means or instrumentality of interstate commerce, or of the mails or of any facility of any national securities exchange,
>
> a) To employ any device, scheme, or artifice to defraud,

> b) To make any untrue statement of a material fact or to omit to state a material fact necessary in order to make the statements made, in the light of the circumstances under which they were made not misleading, or
> c) To engage in any act, practice, or course of business which operates or would operate as a fraud or deceit upon any person, in connection with the purchase or sale of any security.

Under Rule 10b-5, the plaintiff must have either purchased or sold the security in question. For the defendant to be responsible for the plaintiff's loss, the plaintiff must prove certain facts: The defendant acted with scienter, the alleged fraud is material, the falsehood or omission injured the plaintiff, and the plaintiff relied on the material statement or omission. The reliance must be reasonable based on the plaintiff's sophistication and expertise, the existence of long-standing business or personal relationships, access to relevant information, or the existence of a fiduciary relationship.

Rule 10b-5 imposes an even greater burden of proof then that of §§ 11 and 12 of the 1933 act. Recovery, however, also includes the increment of price above the offering price for purchasers who bought in the open market when the market price exceeded the offering price. This creates a large exposure for defendants in 10b-5 cases. As explained later, the damages in such cases can greatly exceed the money that the defendant company received in an initial or secondary offering.

"FRAUD ON THE MARKET" THEORY

The requirement for proof linking the defendant's conduct to the plaintiff's injury is known as *reliance*. This causal link requirement prevents the securities laws from becoming "investors' insurance." The burden of proof concerning reliance has recently loosened from showing that the plaintiff relied directly on a defendant's communication.

The "fraud on the market" theory is a derivative of the efficient market theory. The efficient market theory proposes that market agents quickly assimilate all relevant information and initiate actions that change the securities' prices based on that information. Information includes world news events, annual and quarterly reports, press releases, and even insider trading. Astute traders quickly cause individual securities prices to change as new information becomes available.

Therefore, if information is fraudulent or omitted, traders cannot correctly value the security. The security's market value will either be understated or overstated depending on the nature of the withheld or fraudulent information. Simply stated, the market has been defrauded. Whether a particular investor knew or did not know of the fraudulent information does not matter. The individual investor relies on the market's efficiency to receive a fair price for the security.

Although some courts have adopted this fraud on the market theory, it deviates from the strict requirement that the investor relied on the fraudulent information.[2]

ALTERNATIVE MEASURES OF DAMAGES

Unfortunately, the law does not clearly address damages in securities litigation. Many theories have been advanced and accepted. The general rule for calculating damages in securities litigation has evolved into an out-of-pocket measure. To avoid difficult valuation issues, the courts have conservatively measured damages. The courts have only reluctantly allowed or estimated the lost expected return on a security. The courts also recognize the defendants' enormous financial exposure in class action securities litigation, another reason to conservatively calculate damages.

The following discussion summarizes several methods or theories used to calculate damages in securities litigation.

Rescission

One can broadly define rescissionary damages as the return to the investor of the value lost on the fraudulent transaction. Rescission unwinds the transaction. A defrauded buyer receives the price paid for the securities. A defrauded seller receives the security sold or its true value at the sale date. Of course, the plaintiff seeking rescission must return the value received from the fraudulent transaction; a defrauded buyer must return the securities (plus dividends or other income), or a defrauded seller must return the actual sales price received.

Rescission holds that if the investor had known the facts, the transaction would not have occurred. Therefore, to make the investor whole, one must unwind the transaction. Rescission is the basic method of computing damages under §§ 9 and 12(2) of the 1933 act.

Cover

The "cover" measure of damages awards to a defrauded investor who sold his stock an amount necessary to "cover" the difference between the investor's selling price and the cost of repurchasing the stock within a reasonable period after the corrective disclosure's release.

Benefit of the Bargain

The "benefit of the bargain" measure of damages considers the difference between the realized market value and the value that the defendant claimed would be realized when the transaction occurred. The courts have disfavored this method because, as previously discussed, damages include the investor's expected return.

Out of Pocket

The courts have variously interpreted how to calculate out-of-pocket damages. One approach to measuring out-of-pocket damages computes the difference between the price paid, or received, and the security's "true" value on the transaction date. The problem is in ascertaining the "true" value absent any fraud effects. The courts have recognized two methods to estimate this hypothetical value.

One method observes the price decline or increase immediately after the fraud's disclosure. If the security's price changes $10 upon disclosure, for example, the method assumes that this reflects the difference between the transaction price and the security's true value on the transaction date. This method has several problems. It assumes that the price's fraud component remains constant over time. This assumption may not be valid, depending on occurrences in the economy, the relevant industry, and the company. As the time lapse increases between the transaction date that the individual investor purchased or sold the security and the fraud's disclosure, the method becomes less reliable. Also, as discussed later, traders who bought and sold while the fraud was being perpetrated on the market presumably have no damages under this theory.

Another simplistic approach computes the difference between the price paid, or received, for the securities and the subsequent market price after the fraud's disclosure. Again, this approach is very direct because one readily can observe all values in question from market transactions. The damages are in fact the plaintiff's "out-of-pocket" losses. The underlying theory here assumes that the entire price change reflects the fraud increment. This approach ignores any industry or market conditions that also affected the security's price. The next section discusses a conceptually correct approach to estimating out-of-pocket damages.

Market Model

A specific security's price depends on many things, including the economy's business cycle, the current general market conditions, the industry's vitality, and events unique to the company. Because the business environment so profoundly affects observed security prices, damage estimates should focus only on the events unique to a company. Of necessity, damage calculations should segregate market effects from corporation specific events and estimate the affect of each on the observed market price.

The "market model" method of calculating damages in securities fraud overcomes the deficiencies of other methods. This method divides the observed market price into two components: (1) the security's true, underlying, or intrinsic, value that would be observed but for the fraud, and (2) the price's fraud component, which is the amount by which the market price deviates from the stock's intrinsic value.[3]

The market model measures damages as either: (1) the fraud component when the security was purchased or (2) the difference between the price's fraud component when it was purchased less the price's fraud component when it was sold.

Judge Posner comments on the market model with a hypothetical: "Suppose therefore that a misrepresentation in a prospectus for a new issue of stock leads brokers who read the prospectus to buy large amounts of the stock and to recommend that their customers do likewise . . . now consider what the measure of damages would be. At first blush it might seem obvious: It should be the losses of those who bought at a price inflated by the false prospectus, after eliminating [by means of the capital pricing asset model] other possible causes of the drop in the stock's price" (Posner, 1987, p. 423).

All individuals who purchase or sell the security after the alleged fraud but before the corrective disclosures are potential members of the damaged class (unless they are named defendants). The market model requires two distinct calculations for two types of shareholders: (1) those who still hold the security after the price fully reflects the corrective disclosure ("retention trader") and (2) those who sell the security before the market fully incorporates the corrective information ("in-and-out traders").

Retention. Retention traders purchase the security when the fraud component artificially inflated the market value and continue to hold the security after the fraud component was eliminated.

Because these traders still retain the security, what losses have they incurred? Have they lost the difference between the security's price when they purchased it less the price after the market has incorporated the corrective disclosure? Not necessarily because the corrective disclosure is not the only information that has affected the market price, and the intrinsic value may have changed notwithstanding the elimination of the fraud component.[4]

As indicated, the market theory defines damages as the difference between the fraud component of the security price when it was purchased less the fraud component when it was sold. For retention traders, who do not sell before the fraud component shrinks to zero (subsequent to the corrective disclosure), damages equals the entire fraud component of the security price at the time of purchase.

In-and-Out Trader. An in-and-out trader has both purchased and sold while the fraud was being perpetrated on the market. The ninth circuit recently ruled concerning in-and-out traders. In *Howard Wool v. Tandem Computers*,[5] the defense moved for summary judgment because Wool had bought and sold before any corrective disclosure was made; therefore Wool recouped any alleged price inflation upon his sale. In effect, the defense argued that the security's fraud component when Wool bought was the same as the fraud component when Wool sold because no corrective disclosure was made. The U.S. District Court for the Northern District of California granted the defendants' motion for summary judgment, whereupon the U.S. Court of Appeals for the Ninth Circuit reversed and remanded.

The decision to reverse the lower court recognizes that market forces may act upon the security's fraud component just as they do upon its intrinsic value. Consequently, no a priori reason exists for a constant fraud component throughout the damage period.

For example, consider the hypothetical firm Business Machines & Telecommunications (BM&T) that manufactures and sells geographically distributed data processing and telecommunications equipment, brand-named "Widgets." BM&T is a very stable company within a mature industry, and its security price has closely followed the industry trend over the past few years.

Upon BM&T's fraudulent announcement that it has begun engaging in oil exploration and has discovered oil in a previously unknown field with significant proven reserves, its security price suddenly jumps from $100 to $150. The security's intrinsic value, based on its Widget sales, remains $100. The fraud component consists of the increased market valuation, based on the fraudulent information about diversifying into the oil business, of $50.

Now consider the effect of the announcement of major declines in petroleum prices. As the market price incorporates this information, BM&T security's fall from $150 to $130. No change has occurred in Widget operations or industry conditions; the only change affecting BM&T's security is the anticipation of lower oil profits.

In this simple example, clearly, the intrinsic value has remained at $100, and the fraud component has fallen to $30 from $50. For an in-and-out trader who purchased at $150, damages equal $20 per share.

Now assume that BM&T lands a lucrative new contract selling Widgets to the government, and upon announcement of this news, its security price returns to $150. Note that if an in-and-out trader were to sell now, his apparent out-of-pocket loss would be zero, whereas his damages as calculated by the market model method remain $20 per share. This is because the true value is now $120, and the fraud component is $30. The $20 of damages equals the difference between the $50 fraud component when purchased less the $30 fraud component when sold.

Because the calculation of damages in the market model approach for in-and-out traders depends on when shares were bought and sold, ideally one should follow each individual share through its history of transactions. This is especially important because of the "ratchet effect" on damages when the security's fraud component may expand and contract several times during the damage period.

For example, suppose a security's fraud component expanded and contracted in a range of $5 to $15. If all purchases and sales occurred on the upward and downward phases when the fraud component was $10, then individuals who paid $10 too much when they bought the security also received $10 too much when they sold it. This situation would injure only the last buyers who held the security when the corrective disclosure was issued because the fraud component would quickly be eliminated. Consider the contrasting situation when all transactions occur at the cycle's peaks and valleys. Traders who buy when the fraud component is $5 and sell when it is $15 have no legal requirement to return this windfall. Traders who buy when the fraud component is $15 and sell when it is $5 incur damages for which the defendants are liable. Indeed, these circumstances could yield damages many times the total gains received by the defendants through their fraudulent acts. This "ratcheting" occurs when individuals do not have to disgorge their windfall profits when the fraud component expands, but when it contracts the defendants are liable for damages.

Judge Posner recently commented on this situation:

> But what about innocent people who profited from the fraud? Suppose that a person misled by the prospectus buys the security as its price is rising but unloads it at a profit before the bubble bursts. Unless he is forced to disgorge his profit, the corporation that issued the misleading prospectus will be made to pay damages in excess of the harm caused to defrauded buyers. As there is no legal or practical basis for forcing restitution by those shareholders who were unjustly but innocently enriched by the fraud, there is a danger of overdeterrence. (Posner, 1987, p. 423)

SEGREGATING THE FRAUD COMPONENT AND TRUE VALUE

As discussed, the total damages forthcoming from a 10b-5 action are based on the security's fraud component, changes in the value of the fraud component throughout the damage period, and the timing and magnitude of the transaction volumes (number of shares traded) during the damage period.

Because the defendant firm's security price performance is observed in a market environment that profoundly affects it, we can use the observed relationships between the security's true value during a period when fraud is not alleged and the performance of the overall market and/or market subsectors to help estimate the security's fraud component during the damage period. Exhibits 31-2 and 31-3 demonstrate that the observed relationships between a representative index and the broad forces affecting the market may help isolate the specific events affecting the defendant.

Control Period

To clearly observe the relationship between the intrinsic value of the defendant's security price and movements in the overall market, one must analyze this relationship during periods when the security price contains no fraud component. In periods without alleged fraud, the intrinsic value, on average, comprises the entire observed market price.

During these "normal" periods, the specific security price should react to the same general social, political, and economic news that affects the general market. Industry-specific information will also affect a security's observed market price.

EXHIBIT 31-2. RELATIONSHIP BETWEEN COMPANY AND INDEXES

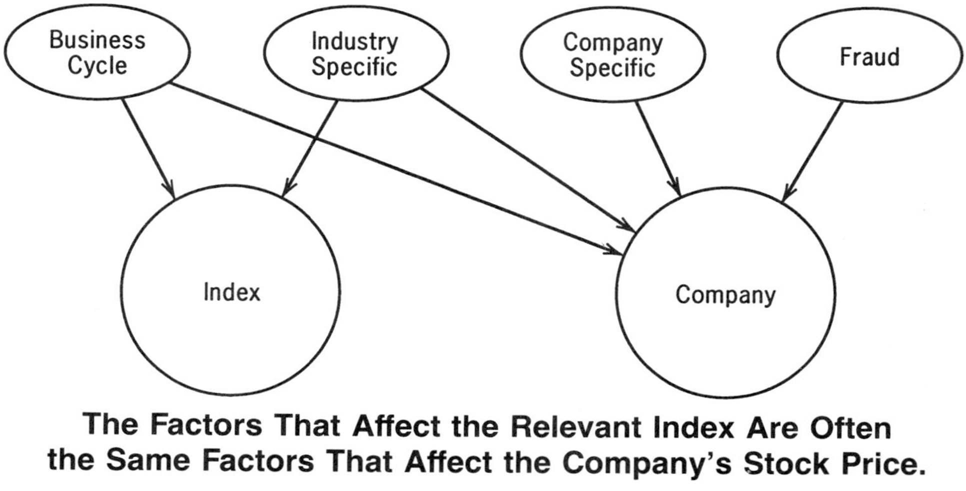

EXHIBIT 31-3. ISOLATING KEY FACTORS

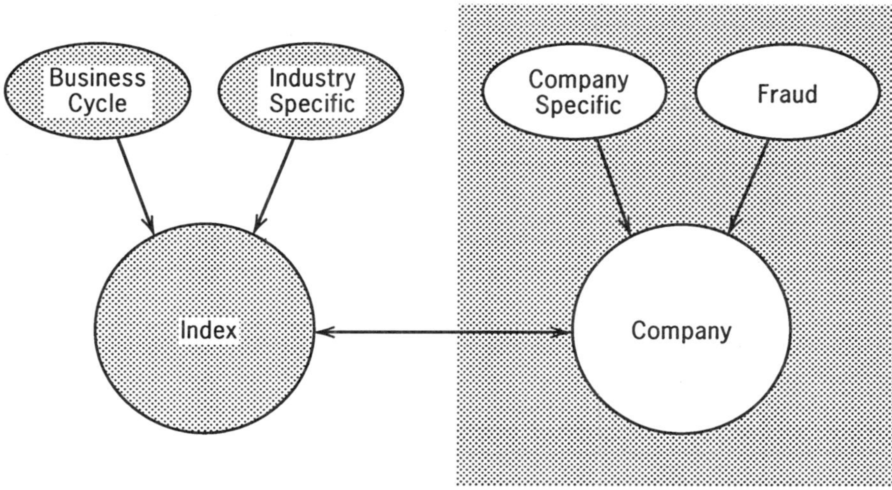

The Key Is to Isolate Those Factors That Affect Only the Company's Stock Price.

Sometimes, the industry-specific information incorporates the news affecting the general market, thus making the consideration of general market conditions superfluous if the industry-specific information is available.

Two choices exist for the control period: either before the alleged fraud or after all adjustments from the corrective disclosure have occurred.[6]

A control period preceding the alleged fraud is preferable (if available) because one does not have to ascertain the time required after the corrective disclosure to eliminate the fraud component.[7] Also, the market often overreacts, reducing the stock price to below the real intrinsic value until the price properly stabilizes. Finally, if the company faces litigation from the now disclosed misrepresentation, the stock price may continue its downward momentum.

Selecting the Appropriate Index

The damage calculations required are usually straightforward. The large data requirements and method for estimating the timing of trades, however, makes attention to detail especially important in implementing the market model.

Although the calculations in this method are mechanical, selecting the appropriate index to measure the defendant's security price performance against requires judgment and expertise.

General Market. At the fundamental level, using a broad-based index (such as the Wilshire 5000 or the S&P 500) will indicate the overall market effects on a particular stock issue. Undoubtedly, the market background influences a particular stock's price performance, but one can usually refine the analysis by employing market measures that more accurately discern among the myriad of currents and eddies present in the market dynamics. Using the market measures that bear most directly on the specific stock's price will greatly improve the model's accuracy.

Industry Index. Although an overall market index correlates with most firms, an analysis that includes an industry-specific index may yield a higher correlation and better estimate of true value. Sometimes the relevant industry index may not correlate well with the overall market index. In these situations, eliminating the general market from the analysis and relying wholly on the industry index will yield a better estimate.

But what of firms that engage in multiple lines of business? In these situations, one should consider multiple indexes corresponding to the firm's various industries. As explained later, these indexes may be either separate independent variables in a regression equation or combined into one independent variable that is a weighted average of the chosen indexes. Each selected index receives a weight based on the importance of the company's corresponding line of business; importance usually being determined by each line of business' contribution to gross profit.

For firms that change the relative importance of their lines of business during the damage period, the weight given each industry index that comprises the independent variable may vary to correspond to the firm's revised operations.

Most predefined industry indexes weight the components by some method. For example, the Standard & Poor's indexes are value weighted: The influence of the component corporations is proportional to the value of the shares outstanding (price per share times number of shares outstanding).

One major benefit of using predefined industry indexes is that they are (somewhat) immune to charges of "cherry picking" individual firms for inclusion in the index. The opposing side may still allege that one has selected industries that are beneficial for comparison. For firms that are clearly in well-defined industries, these charges can be refuted.

Peer Group. An alternative to using predefined indexes is to construct a "peer group" of firms selected for unique characteristics such that the group as a whole resembles the firm under investigation. In addition to "cherry picking" allegations, other problems emerge: which weighting scheme to use, changes in line of business (either of the firms in the peer group or of the firm under investigation), definitions of *similar*, and the proper number of firms to include in the peer group.

Peer group firms ideally should be in the same line of business, in the same geographic locations, approximately the same size (as measured by sales, assets, number of employees, or other criteria appropriate to the case), have similar capitalization, and be actively traded. One should also consider whether to include companies with pending allegations of SEC violations.

Security Splits and Dividends

Stock splits are troublesome because the market price of each of the new shares is initially inversely proportional to the degree of splitting. For example, in a two-for-one stock split, each new share is worth half the value of the old shares. To account for this phenomenon, one must express share values across time in terms of some "base date."

Similarly, if the facts mandate the consideration of dividends, one should incorporate them as described later *after* they have been adjusted for splits.

The Relationship between a Firm and the Market

Finance scholars have relatively recently explored the relationship between an individual firm's stock performance and the overall market's performance. This aspect of finance research has been applied by securities analysts, corporate portfolio managers, trust officers, and others charged with fiduciary duties.

CAPITAL ASSET PRICING MODEL

The capital asset pricing model (CAPM) is a familiar tool of security analysts and financial advisors. It is used to estimate an individual stock's risk vis-à-vis the risk inherent in the overall market. By comparing over an extended time period how the differential between the overall market rate of return and the risk-free rate of return correlates with the differential between the rate of return for the specific security and the risk-free rate of return, analysts can ascertain if a particular security is inherently more or less risky than the general market.

The model is specified as

$$R_s - R_g = a + b \times (R_m - R_g) + e$$

where

R_s = the rate of return on the stock analyzed.
R_g = the risk free rate of return.
R_m = the rate of return on the market.
a = the nonsystematic risk.
b = beta, the systematic risk of the stock; $b > 1$ is riskier than the general market, $b < 1$ implies less risk.
e = the error term of the regression.

The Market Model Formula

The market model closely relates to the capital asset pricing model, eliminating the risk free rate of return from the formula. Here we are not so much interested in the risk of the specific security, but only how its price performance correlates with that of the market. One market model specification is

$$R_s = a + bR_m + e$$

where

R_s = the rate of return on the stock in question.
a = intercept or estimate of the market independent rate of return. The average value of the "unsystematic" returns of the stock over time.
b = slope, or estimate of the proportion of the change in the market rate of return that is reflected in a change in this specific stock's rate of return.
R_m = the market rate of return.
e = the error term of the regression.

The presence or absence of dividend payments usually affects damages. The damage analysis must incorporate any material dividend payments during the time period of the analysis. One way of doing this is to include these dividends in the rate of return calculation.

The "wealth relative" procedure is analogous to compound interest calculations. This method assumes that dividends accruing through stock ownership are reinvested in the stock at the market price prevailing on the day of dividend distribution.

The "dividends-only" method resembles the wealth-relative procedure but does not assume that cash and stock dividends are reinvested. Note that this method does not require compounding; the analysis ignores dividends after they are received.

The "no-dividends" method is the simplest; the analysis considers only the stock price. This procedure is applicable only if the security has no dividend payments.

PROBLEMS IN TRACING SECURITIES TRANSACTIONS

Although one should know the timing of transactions when calculating damages in the market model method, in practice several problems exist in following the history of specific shares. We first discuss some of the problems encountered, then present a technique for estimating the timing of the trades.

Shares Owned in Beneficial Name

Securities are often held in a "street" name. This is usually the name of the brokerage house or other custodial institution that keeps its own ownership records. In these situations, one has to investigate not only the transfer agent's records but the accounts of the brokerage houses as well.

This process is further complicated because brokerage houses do not allocate any specific share to its clients' accounts but merely make accounting entries on the books to indicate ownership status. For sales of securities held in beneficial name, the transactions come from the pool of shares held by the brokerage house and are traceable only by going back to each of the individual accounts of the brokerage's clients.

Records Kept by Transfer Agent

Transfer agent practices also cause problems in tracing transactions. A lag often occurs between recording ownership cancellation and new ownership registration. Matching a particular certificate's seller and buyer becomes difficult because the transfer agents do not uniquely identify the shares and do not always record purchases and cancellations on the same day. The expert can use a flow assumption like those used in accounting for inventory at historical cost.

Intraday trades can complicate matters. Speculators or floor traders may take a position in the security lasting only a few hours. This is especially true shortly after an initial public offering (IPO) or a subsequent public offering (SPO). Specialists in the major exchanges or market makers in the National Association of Securities Dealers facilitate the transactions between buyer and seller, and the latter may count each share of a given transaction twice, once from seller to specialist and once from specialist to buyer. The NASD requires, for example, that if a market maker has a buy order in hand when he purchases a security in the market, then the transfer of that security from seller to buyer is one transaction. If, however, the market maker purchases the security and then receives the buy order, then each share transferred from seller to buyer would be counted as two shares traded in the volume statistics reported for that day. This overstates reported volume statistics.

LIMITATIONS OF THE MARKET MODEL APPROACH

The market model approach corrects many problems inherent in alternative methods but is not a panacea. In fact, if improperly implemented, this technique may introduce unique problems not encountered with other techniques. The following discussion highlights the major problem areas and suggested solutions.

Short-Interval Estimates of BETA

Estimates of beta (see section, Capital Asset Pricing Model) derived over short intervals may not adequately reflect the true relationships driving stock price performance and may unwittingly give undue weight to specific events unique to the time period in question.

Volatile Markets and Short-Interval Estimates

When short intervals are used for estimation in volatile markets, they tend to magnify the period's volatility. For example, a stock that swings wildly up and down within the day but ends the trading session much where it started at the opening bell would show markedly different rates of return (and beta) depending on the interval chosen to calculate these rates of return.

Separating Firm Specific Events. Although using the appropriate index helps to segregate firm-specific events from industrywide phenomena, it does not address the problem of further segregating the firm-specific events into legal and illegal components. To do this, one must carefully identify and measure (possibly with dummy or proxy variables) illegal and legal firm-specific activities. If legal and illegal information appear to be disclosed simultaneously, the market model cannot disaggregate the effects of each.

COMPUTING DAMAGES FOR AN INITIAL PUBLIC OFFERING

Initial public offerings present special problems because of the unique characteristics of a securities price performance when first introduced to the market. Exhibits 31-4 and 31-5 illustrate that IPOs have unique circumstances that require special consideration. One must use special techniques to isolate the company specific events that have affected the security's performance. To incorporate these special considerations into the analysis, one must choose an index or develop a peer group of corporations with an IPO date close to the defendant's IPO date.

"Hot Issue" Market Effect

A significant complication is the hot issue market effects.[8] In a hot issue market, IPOs tend to "outperform" more seasoned issues. This phenomenon continues until the new issues themselves become seasoned. This effect calls for a "seasoning" criteria when selecting a peer group. This usually means selecting comparables that went public within 1 year before or after the defendant firm's IPO date. Ideally, the peer group should include one firm that went public during each of the 25

EXHIBIT 31-4. RELATIONSHIP BETWEEN COMPANY AND INDEXES

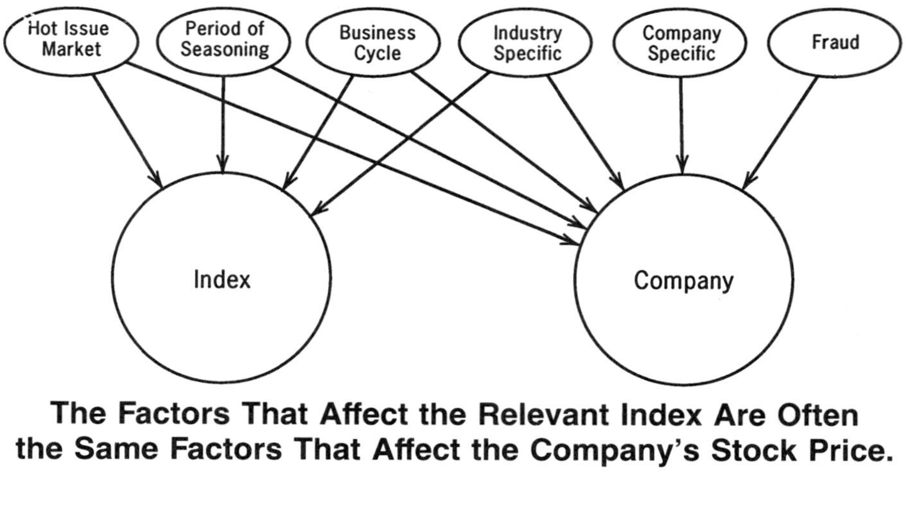

EXHIBIT 31-5. ISOLATING KEY FACTORS

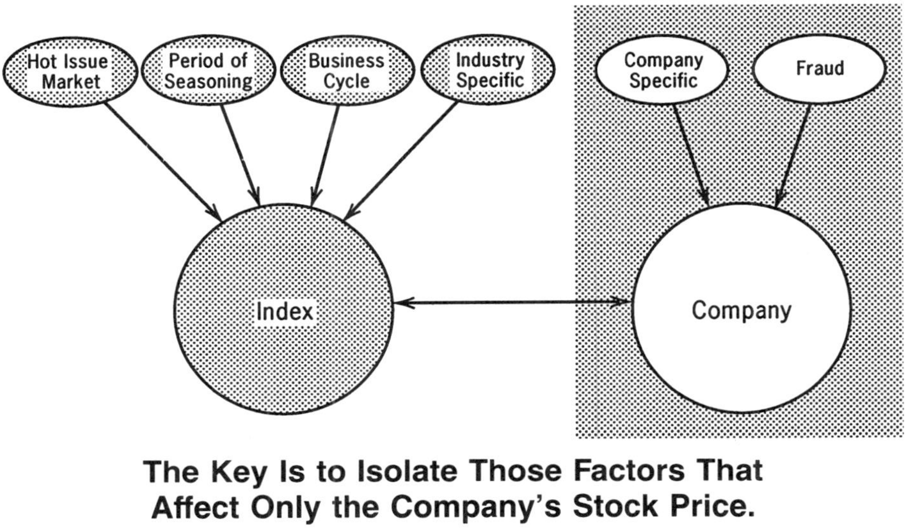

months covering this period. The following discusses this type of data and related analytical techniques.

Lack of a Control Period

Fraud allegations for an initial public offering pose special problems because no "before" period exists for benchmark comparisons; only the period after the corrective disclosure is available for investigating the "unaffected" relationships. Sometimes the "after" period also may not exist. The method described next functions even in those situations.

Developing an Initial Public Offering Index

The basic technique is the same as that described before: Identify companies in similar industries, of similar size, in similar geographic areas, and with similar capital structures. For IPOs, however, one must also screen for companies with an initial public offering relatively close to the defendant's IPO date. The selected peer group should have an IPO date in each period; the period intervals should be of sufficient duration to meaningfully estimate the defendant company's beta.

The following regression is then run for each period relative to the initial offering so that separate coefficients may be calculated for each period of seasoning:

$$R_{jt} = a_t + b_t R_m + e_{jt}$$

where

t = is the period of seasoning, held constant for each regression.
R_{jt} = is the return on security j during the tth period of seasoning.
a_t, b_t = are the regression intercept and slope coefficient respectively for period t.
R_m = is the period rate of return on the market as measured by an index such as the Standard & Poor's 500 or the Wilshire 5000; the measurement is taken during the same period as R_{jt}.
e_{jt} = is the regression random error term for security j during the tth month of seasoning.

For example, if $t = 1$, then the rate of return for the first period of seasoning for the peer group companies would be regressed on the market's corresponding rates of return. The estimates of a_1 and b_1 then provide information about the relationship of the peer group to the market for the first period of seasoning. One repeats this process for all periods during the damage claim to obtain estimates of a_t and b_t for each period. This creates a series of intercept and slope coefficients, each pair corresponding to a different period of seasoning during the damage period. These coefficients embody the average relationships between the market and peer group firms that went public around the time of the defendant firm's IPO date.

Expected periodic rates of return are calculated for the defendant firm using the estimated a_t's and b_t's for all damage claim periods. The rates of return may be transformed into expected security prices using the CAPM formulas. The difference between the actual security price and the expected security price measures the extent to which corporation-specific information has affected the security price. One may further decompose this component into legal and illegal components using the techniques explained.

NECESSITY OF ELIMINATING THE DEFENDANT'S TRADING

Because the named defendants are not members of the damaged class, to the extent possible, one should track their trading independently of all other traders. Clearly, one does not want to include in the damage calculations any losses suffered by the named defendants; however, their actions affect damages not only directly but also indirectly.

For example, the directors and officers may own securities that are restricted from trading until a specified date. In this situation, because zero probability exists of these shares trading before the trigger date, they should be removed from the "total shares outstanding" pool used to estimate the timing of trading activity. Including these shares would overstate the rate at which individuals enter the damaged class and understate the amount of in-and-out trading.

Although calculating damages using the market model may appear formidable at first, the application of these techniques is straightforward and clearly defined.

Applying modern financial theory to damages calculations contributes to enforcing the securities laws in a fair manner.

NOTES

1. The chapter's bibliography contains references related to damages under the securities acts.

2. See the recent Supreme Court ruling *Basic Inc. v. Levinson*, 485 U.S. 224 (1988).

3. Others use the term *intrinsic valuation* to refer to a general analysis of the company based on a true knowledge of the firm's assets, earnings, dividends, future prospects, and management competence. They label the stock price estimate obtained using the market model approach as *true value*. This chapter uses the terms *intrinsic value*, *underlying value*, and *true value* interchangeably. All refer to the nonfraud component of the stock price that is estimated in the most appropriate manner given the state-of-the-art. As financial analysis becomes more sophisticated, a superior estimation technique may supplant the market model approach. Currently, however, we believe the market model approach to be the most relevant.

4. Sometimes information related to the fraud, but not directly part of the fraudulent activity, will affect the stock's price. The market model analysis may be applicable in these instances, as explained later.

5. See *Wool v. Tandem Computers, Inc.*, 818 F.2d 1433 (9th Cir. 1987).

6. The distinction has been made (Finkelstein, 1983, p. 847) between a fraud that is fully reflected in the value of the stock on the date of the initial transaction (Type I fraud) and a fraud that is only fully reflected in the value of the stock some time subsequent to the initial transaction (Type II fraud). A complicating factor in Type II frauds is the effect of information that is related to, but not strictly part of, the fraud. As discussed later, in Type II frauds, one should use only the period prior to the fraud to estimate the firm's relationship to the market. Even then it may not be possible to use the market model to estimate the stock's fraud component after the market adjusts to related information.

7. Estimates in the financial literature range from a few hours to days. Some court cases have entertained periods of as long as 2 weeks.

8. For a more complete discussion of this phenomenon, see Hess and Frost (1982, p. 11), Ibbotson (1975, p. 235), and Ritter (1984), p. 215.

BIBLIOGRAPHY

Aharony, J., and I. Swary, "Quarterly Dividend and Earnings Announcements and Stockholders' Returns: An Empirical Analysis," *Journal of Finance*, Vol. 35 (March 1980), pp. 1–12.

Banoff, B.A., and B.S. Duval, Jr., "The Class Action as a Mechanism for Enforcing the Federal Securities Laws: An Empirical Study of the Burdens Imposed," *Wayne Law Review*, Vol. 31 (1984), pp. 1–134.

Barry, J.F., III, "The Economics of Outside Information and Rule 10b-5," *University of Pennsylvania Law Review*, Vol. 129 (June 1981), pp. 1307–1391.

Black, B., "Fraud on the Market: A Criticism of Dispensing with Reliance Requirements in Certain Open Market Transactions," *North Carolina Law Review*, Vol. 62 (March 1984), pp. 435–473.

Black, F., and M. Scholes, "The Capital Asset Pricing Model: Some Empirical Results,"

In J. Jensen, ed., *Studies in the Theory of Capital Markets* (Praeger, 1972), pp. 79–121.

Bridges, A.P., "Private RICO Litigation Based upon 'Fraud in the Sale of Securities'," *Georgia Law Review*, Vol. 18 (Fall 1983), pp. 43–82.

Brown, S., and J. Warner, "Measuring Security Price Performance," *Journal of Financial Economics*, Vol. 8 (September 1980), pp. 205–258.

Cho, D.C., and W.M. Taylor, "The Seasonal Stability of the Factor Structure of Stock Returns," *Journal of Finance*, Vol. 42 (December 1987), pp. 1195–1211.

Davis, K.B., "The Status of Defrauded Securityholders in Corporate Bankruptcy," *Duke Law Journal*, Vol. 1983 (February 1983), pp. 1–68.

Deakin, E.B., "Accounting Reports, Policy Interventions and the Behavior of Securities Returns," *The Accounting Review*, Vol. 51 (July 1976), pp. 590–603.

Devir, J.P., "Rule 10b-5 Damages: The Runaway Development of a Common Law Remedy," *University of Florida Law Review*, Vol. 28 (Fall 1975), pp. 76–101.

Easterbrook, F.H., and D.R. Fischel, "Optimal Damages in Securities Cases," *University of Chicago Law Review*, Vol. 52 (Summer 1985), pp. 611–652.

_______, "Mandatory Disclosure and the Protection of Investors," *Virginia Law Review*, Vol. 70 (May 1984), pp. 669–715.

Eastin, C.P., "The Use of Models in Litigation: Concise or Contrived," *Chicago–Kent Law Review*, Vol. 52 (1976), pp. 611–620.

Fama, E.F., "Efficient Capital Markets: A Review of Theory and Empirical Work," *Journal of Finance*, Vol. 25 (May 1970) pp. 383–420.

_______, "Risk, Return and Equilibrium: Some Clarifying Comments," *Journal of Finance*, Vol. 23 (March 1968), pp. 29–40.

_______, *Foundations of Finance* (Basic Books, 1976).

Finkelstein, J.T., "Rule 10b-5 Damage Computation: Application of Financial Theory to Determine Net Economic Loss," *Fordham Law Review*, Vol. 51 (April 1983), pp. 838–870.

Fischel, D.R., "Use of Modern Finance Theory in Securities Fraud Cases Involving Actively Traded Securities," *Business Lawyer*, Vol. 38 (November 1982), pp. 1–20.

Fischel, D.R., and S.J. Grossman, "Customer Protection in Futures and Securities Markets," *Journal of Futures Markets*, Vol. 4 (Fall 1984), pp. 273–295.

Fisher, F.M., "Multiple Regression in Legal Proceedings," *Columbia Law Review*, Vol. 80 (May 1980), pp. 702–736.

"Fraud on the Market: An Emerging Theory of Recovery under SEC Rule 10b-5," *George Washington Law Review* (May 1982), pp. 627–655.

Garth, B.B., I.H. Nagel, and S.J. Plager, "Empirical Research and the Shareholder Derivative Suit: Toward a Better Informed Debate," *Law and Contemporary Problems*, Vol. 48(3) (Summer 1985), pp. 137–159.

Grossman, S.J., and J.E. Stiglitz, "Information and Competitive Price Systems," *American Economic Review*, Vol. 66 (May 1976), pp. 246–253.

Grzebielski, R.J., "Should the Supreme Court Recognize General Market Reliance in Private Actions Under Rule 10b-5"?, *Baylor Law Review*, Vol. 36 (Spring 1984), pp. 335–374.

Hausfurther, A.M., "Securities," *Texas Tech Law Review*, Vol. 16 (1985), pp. 415–431.

Hess, A.C., and P.A. Frost, "Tests for Price Effects of New Issues of Seasoned Securities," *Journal of Finance*, Vol. 37 (March 1982), pp. 11–25.

Hillmer, S.C., and P.L. Yu, "The Market Speed of Adjustment to New Information," *Journal of Financial Economics*, Vol. 7 (1979), pp. 321–345.

Ibbotson, R.G., *Investment Markets: Gaining the Performance Advantage* (McGraw-Hill, 1987), pp. 294.

———, "Price Performance of Common Stock New Issues," *Journal of Financial Economics*, Vol. 2 (1975), pp. 235–272.

Ibbotson, R.G., and J.J. Jaffee, "'Hot Issue' Markets," *Journal of Finance*, Vol. 30 (September 1985), pp. 1027–1042.

Jacobs, A., "The Measure of Damages in Rule 10b-5 Cases," *Georgetown Law Journal*, Vol. 65 (June 1977), pp. 1093–1169.

———, *Litigation and Practice under Rule 10b-5*, 2nd ed., Vol. 5C (Clark Broadman Co., Ltd., 1988).

Jaffe, J.F., "The Effect of Regulation Changes on Insider Trading," *Bell Journal of Economics and Management Science*, Vol. 5 (Spring 1974), pp. 93–121.

Jensen, M.C., "Capital Markets: Theory and Evidence," *Bell Journal of Economics and Management Science*, Vol. 3 (Autumn 1972), pp. 357–398.

Joy, O.M., R.N. Litzenberger, and R.W. McEnally, "The Adjustment of Stock Prices to Announcements of Unanticipated Changes in Quarterly Earnings," *Journal of Accounting Research*, Vol. 15 (Autumn 1977), pp. 207–225.

Kennedy, P., *A Guide to Econometrics* (The MIT Press, 1986), p. 175.

Leas, P.J., "The Measure of Damages in Rule 10b-5 Cases Involving Actively Traded Securities," *Stanford Law Review*, Vol. 26 (1973–1974), pp. 371–398.

Long, L.C., "Treble Damages for Violations of the Federal Securities Laws: A Suggested Analysis and Application of the RICO Civil Cause of Action," *Dickinson Law Review*, Vol. 85 (Winter 1981), pp. 201–248.

Madeo, S.A., and M. Pincus, "Stock Market Behavior and Tax Rule Changes: The Case of the Disallowance of Certain Interest Deductions Claimed by Banks," *The Accounting Review*, Vol. 60 (July 1985), pp. 407–429.

Malatesta, P.H., "Measuring Abnormal Performance: The Event Parameter Approach Using Joint Generalized Least Squares," *Journal of Financial and Quantitative Analysis*, Vol. 21 (March 1986), pp. 27–38.

"Measurement of Damages in Private Actions Under Rule 10b-5," *Washington University Law Quarterly* (Winter 1968), pp. 165–179.

Mullaney, T.J., "Theories of Measuring Damages in Security Cases and the Effects of Damages on Liability," *Fordham Law Review*, Vol. 46 (November 1977), pp. 277–294.

Murdock, C.W., "Heard It through the Grapevine," *ABA Journal* (1 October 1987), pp. 100–108.

Polinsky, A.M., *An Introduction to Law and Economics* (Little, Brown & Co. 1983), p. 138.

Posner, R.A., *Economic Analysis of Law* (Little, Brown & Co., 1987) p. 666.

Rapp, R.N., "Rule 10b-5 and Fraud-on-the-Market—Heavy Seas Meet Tranquil Shores," *Washington & Lee Law Review*, Vol. 39, pp. 861–898.

Reder, B., "Measuring Buyers' Damages in 10b-5 Cases," *The Business Lawyer*, Vol. 31 (July 1976), pp. 1839–1854.

"Remedies for Private Parties under Rule 10b-5," *Boston College Industrial and Commercial Law Review*, Vol. 10 (Winter 1969), pp. 337–359.

Ritter, J.R., "The 'Hot Issue' Market of 1980," *The Journal of Business*, Vol. 57(2) (1984), p. 215–240.

Schlag, P., "An Appreciative Comment on Coase's 'The Problem of Social Cost': A View From the Left," *Wisconsin Law Review* (1986), pp. 919–962.

Schwert, G.W., "Using Financial Data to Measure Effects of Regulation," *Journal of Law & Economics*, Vol. 24(1) (1981), p. 121–125.

Schuller, D., "The Fraud on the Market Theory: Efficient Markets and the Defenses to an

Implied 10b-5 Action," *Iowa Law Review*, Vol. 70(4) pp. 975–993.

Sear, T.H., "Measure of Damages Crucial in Securities Fraud Actions," *The National Law Journal* (27 January 1986), p. 15.

Siegel, M., "The Interplay between the Implied Remedy under Section 10(b) and the Express Causes of Action of the Federal Securities Laws," *Boston University Law Review*, Vol. 62 (March 1982), pp. 385–442.

Soari, C.P., "The Efficient Capital Market Hypothesis, Economic Theory and the Regulation of the Securities Industry," *Stanford Law Review*, Vol. 29 (May 1977), pp. 1031–1076.

"The Fraud-On-The-Market Theory," *Harvard Law Review*, Vol. 95 (March 1982), pp. 1143–1161.

Thompson, R.B., "The Measure of Recovery under Rule 10b-5: A Restitution Alternative to Tort Damages," *Vanderbilt Law Review*, Vol. 37 (March 1984), pp. 349–398.

Verrecchia, R.E., "On the Theory of Market Information Efficiency," *Journal of Accounting and Economics*, Vol. 77, p. 77.

LIST OF CASES

Basic, Inc. v. Levinson, 485 U.S. 224 (1988)
Wool v. Tandem Computers, Inc., 818 F.2d 1433 (9th Cir. 1987)

PART SIX

INCOME TAX CONSIDERATIONS

32

MARITAL DISSOLUTION: TAX CONSIDERATIONS

Donald L. Gursey, CPA
Roseanna L. Purzycki, MSA, CPA

ALIMONY

Overview

The Income Tax Act of 1913 provided that alimony was not taxable to the recipient nor deductible by the payor. Congress recognized this as a financial hardship for the payor who had to pay alimony with after-tax income. Consequently, the 1942 Revenue Act permitted taxpayers to deduct certain types of payments and required the recipient to report the income. The law has changed numerous times with a significant change enacted by the Domestic Relations Tax Act of 1984 (DRTRA). The Tax Reform Act of 1986 (TRA of 1986) also modified the DRTRA rules.

Although one must know current law, one must also be familiar with the tax law just prior to the DRTRA changes. The pre-DRTRA law still applies to instruments executed prior to 1985. Instruments executed prior to 1985 may be subject to DRTRA if the instrument has been modified after January 1, 1985, to provide that § 71 of the Internal Revenue Code as amended shall apply.

Often the parties to a marital dissolution attempt to modify a final judgment. For example, the husband's income may have decreased, prompting a request to reduce alimony payments. The ex-spouses may want to change the original property settlement based on new information. The first questions for these modifications should be, "When was the final judgment executed? Has the final judgment been modified previously? Which set of laws apply to this case?"

Exhibit 32-1 summarizes the general requirements of pre-DRTRA, DRTRA, and the modifications of DRTRA by TRA of 1986. A discussion of current law as it applies to alimony follows:

DRTRA as Modified by the TRA of 1986—Statutory Requirements

Internal Revenue Code § 71 requires an individual to include in gross income all payments received as alimony or separate maintenance. Section 215 allows the payor to deduct the payments that have been included in the payee's gross income. Five general requirements must be met to qualify payments for this treatment.

EXHIBIT 32-1. REQUIREMENTS TO BE INCLUDIBLE/DEDUCTIBLE ALIMONY

Law	I. Pre-DRTRA (1954 Code)	II. DRTRA (TRA of 1984)	III. TRA of 1986
Effective Dates: Federal	Instruments Executed during 1954–1984	Instruments Executed during 1985–1986	Instruments Executed after 1986
General requirements	A. Obligatory. Payments must be made under an obligation to pay per written instruments (cannot be voluntary). B. For support. For support because of the marital or family relationship (cannot be compensation for a property interest). C. Periodic. Not defined in the code but has come to mean the following	A. Same as I(A), written instruments are defined in IRC § 71(b) (2). B. Payments must terminate at death. This must be expressly stated in written instrument. C. Designation as nondeductible alimony. Payments cannot be designated as not includible in gross income under § 71 and not allowable as a deduction under § 215.	A. Same as I(A). B. Instrument does not have to expressly state that payments terminate at death if termination occurs by operation of state law. C. Same as II(C). D. Same as II(D). E. Same as II(E).

(*Exhibit continues on p. 584.*)

EXHIBIT 32-1. *(Continued)*

Law	I. Pre-DRTRA (1954 Code)	II. DRTRA (TRA of 1984)	III. TRA of 1986
Effective Dates: Federal	Instruments Executed during 1954–1984	Instruments Executed during 1985–1986	Instruments Executed after 1986
	1. Indefinite in duration or amount 2. Contingent (a) Death of either spouse (b) Remarriage of recipient spouse (c) Change in economic circumstances 3. Paid over more than 10 years.	D. Cash payments. They must be made to the spouse or to third parties on behalf of the spouse. E. Separate households. If legally separated, parties cannot be members of the same household (not applicable to temporary orders).	
	D. Separate households. Parties must be separated and living apart by Reg. 1.71-1(b) (3) (even under temporary orders).		
Special rules		F. Minimum term of 6 years. G. Six-year recapture rule (only applied for first 3 years pursuant to TRA of 1986).	F. Minimum term is no longer required. G. Three-year recomputation rule.

Obligatory. A divorce or separation instrument must require the payments. The statute defines three classes of such instruments: (1) a decree of divorce or separate maintenance or a written instrument incident to such a decree, (2) a written separation agreement, or (3) a decree requiring a spouse to pay for the other spouse's support or maintenance.[1] The requirements for these types of instruments were the same under prior law.

Voluntary payments never qualify for alimony. The existence of a qualified written instrument does not guarantee deductibility. The instrument must specify the amount and time of the payments. Premature alimony payments may be classified as voluntary.[2]

Payments Must Terminate at Death. DRTRA required a divorce or separation instrument to *expressly* state that "there is no liability for any period after the death of the payor spouse to continue to make any payments which would otherwise qualify as alimony or separate maintenance."[3] The TRA of 1986 modified this provision so that the instrument need not expressly state the end of liability if the state law provides for termination.

Professionals must still be wary of instruments that provide for postdeath liability or "substitute" payment to the payee's estate. Where a payment continues after the spouse's death, the instrument may require payment to a trust or to alternate beneficiaries such as the children. Payments initiated at the payee's death would also violate the termination.

Such a postdeath provision will disqualify from tax deductibility similar payments prior to death. For example, an instrument requires alimony payments of $40,000 per year. Upon the wife's death, the husband must pay $15,000 per year into a trust for the children. Under these circumstances, $15,000 of the $40,000 annual alimony payments will be reclassified as nondeductible alimony payments per year because the $15,000 does not terminate at the wife's death.

The parties may negotiate the tax burden of the payment. This can be useful in the right economic circumstances. For example, suppose the wife is in a high tax bracket and the husband does not need additional deductions because of a net operating loss carryforward. The wife requires a higher alimony payment if the entire payment is includible in her gross income. The husband does not have additional cash to make a higher payment. Designating part of the alimony payment as excludible from the wife's gross income and nondeductible to the husband may be a solution. This should benefit both parties because the wife will not have to pay the tax, and the husband will not have to pay additional support to his former wife.

Payment in Cash or in Cash on Behalf of the Spouse. Alimony payments must be paid in cash to be deductible by the payor. Transfers of property will not qualify under §§ 71 and 215. This prohibits disguising a property settlement as deductible alimony.

In a departure from earlier law, payment does not have to be for the payee's support but only must be "on behalf of" the payee. Thus tuition, rent, mortgage, tax liabilities, or attorney fees paid by the payor for the payee's benefit qualify as deductible alimony.

Separate Households. Support payments will not qualify as deductible alimony if the husband and wife occupy the same household, even if they are legally separated. Physical separation of the spouses in the same dwelling unit they formerly shared will not constitute two separate households. The spouses will not violate this requirement if one of the parties is preparing to depart and does so no later than 30 days after the alimony payment is made.[4]

Only a decree of divorce or separate maintenance will legally separate the parties. Payments required by separation agreements or support decrees (pendente lite orders) may be deductible alimony, if they otherwise qualify, even when the parties occupy the same household.[5] This differs from the law before DRTRA where the parties had to maintain separate households even under temporary support orders.

Special Rules—Minimum Term Rule and Alimony Recapture

Six-Year Minimum Term Rule. The 1986 TRA of 1986 contains technical corrections to § 71 necessitated by the changes made 2 years earlier by DRTRA. DRTRA had mandated a so-called "minimum term rule" where, to be alimony, payment must be made in each of 6 postseparation years. Sec. 71(f)(6) defines the first postseparation year as the first calendar year in which the payor spouse paid alimony or separate maintenance payments to the payee spouse. A payment had to then be made in each of the 5 succeeding calendar years after the first postseparation year. The minimum term rule only applied to payments exceeding $10,000 during any calendar year. The rule was prospectively applied such that an instrument must require payment—even as low as $1—in each of the 6 postseparation years to satisfy the rule.[6] The 1986 TRA repealed this rule.

Six-Year Recapture Rule. DRTRA also sought to prevent property settlements disguised as alimony with its 6-year recapture rule. This rule required the alimony payor to recapture as income amounts that had previously been deducted as alimony when a payment fell short of a prior year payment by more than $10,000. The payee could deduct these recaptured amounts in the recalculation year.

The TRA of 1986 has replaced the 6-year recapture rule with a 3-year recomputation rule. Congress made this change to conform to the trend of state divorce law to require short-term support payments on the theory of "rehabilitative alimony."[7] The 6-year recapture rule still applies to decrees and agreements executed during 1985 and 1986 and for earlier agreements modified after 1984 to provide for DRTRA coverage. A special transitional rule in the TRA of 1986 shortened the recapture period for making alimony recalculations from 6 years to 3 years. Therefore, the old 6-year recapture rule is applied only for 3 years.[8]

Three-Year Recomputation Rule. The new 3-year recomputation rule is calculated in only the third postseparation year. A recomputation is not required for the second postseparation year or for any year after the third postseparation year. This makes the law much easier to apply than previously required by the 6-year recapture rule.

Although the code defines the first postseparation year as the year in which an initial payment of alimony or separate maintenance is made, the regulations clarify that payments under a temporary support order do not start the running of postseparation years.[9] No requirement exists that payments be made over the entire year. Thus, the actual payment period can be as short as 14 months, when the first payment is made in December of Calendar Year 1 and the last payment in January of Calendar Year Three.

The amount a payor must recapture in income (and the payee deduct) in the third postseparation year is a sum of two amounts computed in two steps. First, the payor must "recapture" payments made in the second postseparation year by the amount such payments exceed "the total of the payments made in the third post-separation year plus $15,000." Second, the payor must average the payments made in the second and third postseparation years reduced by the amount recaptured in Step 1. The payor must then "recapture" the amount by which the first year payments exceed "the total of the computed average plus $15,000." The cases in Exhibit 32-2 illustrate the recomputation required in the third postseparation year.

EXHIBIT 32-2. APPLICATION OF THE THREE-YEAR RECOMPUTATION RULES

Alimony Payments	Case #1	Case #2	Case #3	Case #4
Year				
1	45,000	45,000	20,000	40,000
2	45,000	40,000	30,000	32,500
3	0	5,000	40,000	17,500
Total Payments	90,000	90,000	90,000	90,000
Step #1				
Year #2 Payment	45,000	40,000	30,000	32,500
Less: Year #3 Payment plus $15,000	15,000	20,000	55,000	32,500
Amount Recaptured from Year #2	30,000 (A)	20,000 (A)	0 (A)	0 (A)
Step #2				
Year #2 Payment	45,000	40,000	30,000	32,500
Add: Year #3 Payment	0	5,000	40,000	17,500
Less: Amount Recaptured from Year #2	(30,000)	(20,000)	0	0
Subtotal	15,000	25,000	70,000	50,000
Divide by 2	2	2	2	2
Average	7,500	12,500	35,000	25,000
Year #1 Payment	45,000	45,000	20,000	40,000
Less: Average plus $15,000	22,500	27,500	50,000	40,000
Amount Recaptured from Year #1	22,500 (B)	17,500 (B)	0 (B)	0 (B)
Total Recapture (A) + (B)	52,500	37,500	0	0

Examples. The cases in Exhibit 32-2 point out how disastrous front-loading alimony payments can be. In each case, the alimony payments over 3 years total \$90,000. When payments increase each year (Case 3), no recapture will occur under the recomputation rule. However, for example, when payments decrease between Year 2 and Year 3 by more than the safe harbor amount of \$15,000, the payor will recapture some income in the third year.

The third year's alimony payment is key to avoiding or minimizing recapture.

A quick method exists to analyze whether income must be recaptured in the third year. Recapture is avoided if Year 2 payments exceed or equal Year 1 payments less \$7,500 *and* Year 3 payments exceed or equal Year 2 payments less \$15,000. The formula is as follows:

No recapture if,

$$Y2 \geq Y1 - \$7{,}500,$$

and

$$Y3 \geq Y2 - \$15{,}000$$

This guideline can be used to analyze instruments already executed or structure alimony payments in future agreements.

Three Exceptions to the Recomputation Rule. Recapture will not apply when payments cease due to either spouse's death or the payee's remarriage before the end of the third postseparation year.

The payor desiring large payments up front should consider temporary support payments. Temporary support qualifies as deductible alimony if it meets all general requirements of IRC § 71. The 3-year recomputation rule specifically does not apply to temporary support.

The third exception to the 3-year recomputation rule occurs when the instrument calls for "fluctuating payments not within the payor spouse's control." An arrangement qualifies if made pursuant to a continuing liability to pay for at least 3 years (a full 36 months) a fixed portion or portions of income from the earnings of a business, property, or services. The portions of the payor's income payable to the payee may vary as the payor's income varies, as long as the instrument specifies fixed percentages.[10] The 1986 TRA amended the fluctuating payment exception to clarify that it will apply when the fixed amount paid changes for different income levels. For example, the payor could be obligated to pay 30 percent of income up to \$50,000 and 20 percent of income between \$50,001 and \$100,000 and 0 percent over \$100,001. This type of arrangement clearly qualifies for the exception.

Tax Planning. The professional can easily avoid the recomputation rule by structuring alimony obligations in the divorce decree. However, recapture could inadvertently apply when the payor makes delinquent payments with currently obligated payments or prepays alimony. The client should be warned of possible recapture when payments are bunched and cautioned to fulfill all obligations as scheduled.

Even if the payor must recapture some income in the third postseparation year, a tax benefit could still occur. The payor can deduct the full amounts in Year 1 and

Year 2, even though recapture may occur in Year 3. Thus the payor derives benefit from the tax deferral. The declining tax rates in recent years make this even more advantageous. However, if tax rates should increase in the future, this advantage may be lost.

An important transitional rule in the TRA of 1986 applies to instruments executed in 1985 and 1986 that are subject to the 6-year recapture rule (which is applied for only 3 years). The 3-year recomputation rule may apply to these instruments if the instrument is modified on or after January 1, 1987, to provide that the 1986 TRA's amendments shall apply to the modified instrument. Obviously, one must get both parties to agree to modify the instrument.

ALIMONY TRUSTS

An alimony trust should be considered for spousal support in some marital dissolutions. The trust minimizes the risk of nonpayment and protects against a decreasing fluctuation in the payor's income. This alternative for spousal and child support may be warranted when the payor spouse is involved in risky business ventures or a bankruptcy risk exists.

The payor spouse may favor this alternative because it allows a transfer of the trust income with control retained over the trust corpus. Also, the recapture and recomputation rules do not apply to alimony trusts and *Lester* strategy (see child support section) of pre-DRTRA law that convert child support into alimony. A trust can be designed to reduce trust income according to the child's age or some other child-related contingency. This will not be grounds for treating a portion of the income as child support. The payor spouse, of course, may be reluctant to tie up capital for a long time and prefer simply to pay alimony from current earnings offset by a current deduction.

To qualify as an alimony trust, the trust must satisfy the general requirements of IRC § 71. The grantor spouse does not receive an alimony deduction for income reported by the payee spouse from the trust. However, the grantor is not taxed on any trust income unless the divorce instrument or trust agreement fixes an amount or portion of payments as child support. Thus the grantor spouse, by shifting the income to the trust, will achieve the same results as that of reporting income offset by an alimony deduction.

IRC § 71 Trust

Prior to December 31, 1984, IRC § 71 provided for an alimony trust created in contemplation of divorce or for a previously created trust used in the divorce to discharge the payor's support obligation.

This type of trust presented some disadvantages. First, transferring appreciated property to the trust could result in taxable gain to the grantor to the extent that the value of the assets transferred exceeded their cost basis. This occurred when the trust fully discharged the grantor's support obligations. Second, the payee spouse was taxed fully on the receipt of *any* trust distribution even when the trust lacked distributable net income ("DNI"), or the distribution was paid out of corpus.

Generally, DNI is the trust's taxable income before deducting distributions to beneficiaries and personal exemptions and excluding capital gains unless allocated to income under the trust instrument or local law.

The repeal of IRC § 71 trusts effective after December 31, 1984 and the concurrent passage of IRC § 1041 eliminated these problems.

IRC § 682 Trust

Subchapter J of the code governs a § 682 trust, which follows the normal trust rules. Prior to December 31, 1984, an alimony trust could be an IRC § 682 trust if it preceded any marital dispute and the recipient spouse was already a beneficiary. After December 31, 1984, this is the only type of alimony trust possible. IRC § 71 trusts predating December 31, 1984, may still exist when the spouses have not modified the divorce instrument or agreement to provide that IRC § 71, as amended by the 1984 TRA, shall apply to the modified instrument.[11]

A § 682 trust's advantage over a § 71 trust is that trust income taxable to the beneficiary spouse depends upon the presence of DNI, and income retains its character as capital gain, tax exempt, or ordinary. This helps the beneficiary spouse who will presumably report lower taxable income. Section 1041 also eliminates the grantor's taxation problems when appreciated property funds the trust. Exhibit 32-3 summarizes the alimony trusts.

CHILD SUPPORT

Child support provided for in a divorce agreement or decree is excluded from the payee's gross income and not deductible by the payor.[12] When payments total less than the required alimony and child support in a calendar year, the parties should apply the payments to child support first and then the excess to alimony.[13]

Curtailment of *Lester*

Prior to DRTRA, nondeductible child support payments had to be designated as child support in the underlying orders or divorce instruments. In *Lester*,[14] the parties agreed to reduce alimony payments by one-sixth whenever any of the three children married, became emancipated, or died. The Supreme Court found this indirect child support designation insufficient for tax purposes and considered all the payments as alimony. DRTRA narrowed the *Lester* holding by expanding the class of child support payments to include payments that decrease when a child-related contingency occurs.

One may still use the *Lester* strategy as long as alimony reductions do not violate the child-related contingency rules. This strategy is feasible when young children are involved in the divorce proceeding and alimony is scheduled to decrease before the children reach the age of majority.

EXHIBIT 32-3. ALIMONY TRUSTS

Type	IRC § 71 Trust	IRC § 682 Trust
Definition	A. Trust created in contemplation of actual separation or divorce or a previously created trust that is in discharge of an obligation imposed on the husband by a divorce instrument	A. *Prior to 12/31/84*—Trust that is in existence before a marital dispute arises and the recipient spouse is already a beneficiary. *After 12/31/84*—Trust established pursuant to a decree or agreement
Requirements	B. Must satisfy general requirements of IRC § 71	B. Must satisfy general requirements of IRC § 71
Availability	C. Only available under instruments executed prior to 12/31/84; § 71 trusts can be converted to § 682 trust by modifying the instrument	C. Only type of alimony trust possible after 12/31/84
Income taxability to beneficiary	D. Taxed fully on the receipt of any trust distribution, even when the trust lacks distributable net income or it is paid out of corpus	D. Depends upon the presence of distributable net income; income retains its character as capital gain, tax-exempt, ordinary (governed by Subchapter J)
Income taxability to grantor	E. No taxability of trust income unless the divorce instrument or trust agreement fixes a certain amount or portion as child support	E. No taxability of trust income unless the divorce instrument or trust agreement fixes a certain amount or portion as child support
Alimony deduction by grantor	F. No alimony deduction is available. However, income earned by trust is shifted to beneficiary.	F. No alimony deduction is available However, income earned by trust is shifted to beneficiary
Advantages under DRTRA	N/A	G. 1. Recapture rules do not apply 2. The $10,000/6-year rules do not apply 3. *Lester* strategy of old law can be used for converting shild support into alimony.

Clearly Associated Contingencies

DRTRA specified two child support categories. First, payments that are fixed or clearly earmarked in the divorce or separation instrument will be classified as nondeductible child support. Second, spousal support payments will be *treated as fixed* if the instrument specifies a child-related contingency that reduces the payments, thus converting these payments earmarked as alimony into nondeductible child support.

Child-related contingencies include, but are not limited to, attaining a specific age, marrying, dying, and leaving school.[15] The regulations add the child's attaining a specified income level, leaving the spouse's household, and gaining employment.[16] The payment reduction resulting from the contingency's occurrence will be reclassified as child support from the agreement's inception. For example, assume alimony payments are $2000 per month dropping to $1500 per month when the child becomes 18. Of *each* court-ordered payment, $500 will not qualify as alimony includible in the wife's gross income and deductible by the husband.

A contingency may be found to be child-related even though the instrument does not appear to include such a contingency. Two presumptions exist in which payments will be *presumed* to be reduced at a time "clearly associated" with the occurrence of a child-related contingency. The *6-month presumption* applies when alimony payments cease within 6 months of the child attaining 18, 21, or the local age of majority. The *multiple reduction presumption* exists when two or more payment reductions occur within a year (before or after) of the different children attaining any common age, between 18 and 24 inclusive.

An example from the regulations will help clarify the multiple reduction presumption. Assume that divorcing parents have two children. Child A was born on July 15, 1970, and Child B was born on September 23, 1972. A divorce decree dated July 1, 1985, orders payments of $2000 monthly until January 1, 1991, at which time they will decrease to $1500 per month until January 1, 1995, when they will decrease to $1000 per month.

The 6-month presumption does not apply, but the multiple reduction presumption does. First, there are two children and two scheduled reductions occurring between the ages of 18 and 24. The first reduction occurs when Child A is 20 years, 5½ months. Adding 12 months to this age totals 21 years, 5½ months. The second reduction occurs when Child B is 22 years, 3½ months. Subtracting 12 months from this age computes to 21 years, 3½ months. Thus the alimony reductions occur very close to a common age of the children after adding or subtracting 12 months. The service will presume that the reductions relate to child support and will reclassify $1000 of each $2000 payment from alimony to child support.

Both of these presumptions may be rebutted by showing a reason other than a child-related contingency for reducing alimony payments. For example, alimony may decrease when the wife sells the personal residence or upon the husband's retirement. Proof that the alimony reduction was motivated by a reason other than a child-related contingency should successfully rebut the presumptions.

DEPENDENTS

Before DRTRA, the rules for claiming dependency exemptions were confusing and often resulted in both parents claiming the exemption. The IRS was frequently involved in disputes with battling parents over support issues that generated little additional tax revenue. To minimize these problems, DRTRA amendments to § 152(e) sought to define the parent who would receive the exemption. The DRTRA amendments discussed next are effective for taxable years beginning after 1984.

General Rule

Generally, the parent with custody of the child for the greater portion of the tax year will be entitled to the dependency exemption. This rule applies to divorced or legally separated parents or to parents who have lived apart at all times during the last 6 months of the year. One or both parents must provide more than half the child's total support for the tax year. The custodial parent is treated as the parent who provided more than half the child's support even if in fact the custodial parent did not.

The most recent decree of divorce, separate maintenance, or custody usually determines which parent has custody. If no decree or written agreement exists, the parent with the physical custody of the child for the greater part of the year is considered the custodial parent. Additionally, if custody is uncertain due to legal actions pending at year end, physical custody will determine the custodial parent.[17]

Exceptions

Three exceptions exist to the general rule. It does not apply when a multiple support agreement is in effect[18]; when a decree or agreement executed prior to January 1, 1985, provides that the custodial parent has released his or her claim to the dependency exemption to the noncustodial parent[19]; and when the custodial parent relinquishes the exemption in accordance with Code § 152(e)(2).

Multiple Support Agreements

A multiple support agreement may be used when no one person provides over half the dependent's support. Over half of the support must be provided by a group that could have claimed the person as a dependent except for failing to meet the 50-percent support test. The group may agree that any one of the group who has contributed greater than 10 percent of the support may claim the exemption. The parties in the group who are not claiming the exemption must execute Form 2120, *Multiple Support Declaration*, agreeing not to claim the exemption for that year. This form must be attached to the return of the individual claiming the exemption.

Pre-1985 Divorce or Separation Agreements. For instruments executed prior to 1985, the prior law allows the noncustodial parent to claim the exemption. The noncustodial parent must provide at least $600 for the child's support during the year. If the parties want to apply the new law, they must modify the instrument to provide that that prior law does not apply.

Custodial Parent Releases Claim. The custodial parent may release the claim to the noncustodial parent. The custodial parent must sign Form 8332, *Release of Claim for Child of Divorced or Separated Parents* or a similar written statement stating that the custodial parent will not claim the child as a dependent. This form or statement must accompany the noncustodial parent's tax return. The custodial parent may agree to release the exemption a year at a time, for a number of specified years, or for all future years.

Other Dependency Provisions

Medical Deductions. A child's medical expenses may be deducted by the parent paying the expense regardless of who claims the exemption. The child must receive over half of his or her total support from the parents for this special rule to apply.[20]

Child Care Credit. The custodial parent may claim the child care credit for such expenses incurred so that the parent may work. The child must be under 15 or unable to care for himself or herself; must be in the custody of one or both parents for more than half of the year; and receive more than half of his or her support from the parents. The parent eligible to take the credit is the custodial parent who can claim the dependency exemption or the custodial parent who does not claim the exemption because of the exception to release the claim or due to the exception relating to pre-1985 instruments. The child will not be a qualifying individual for the noncustodial parent even though the noncustodial parent may claim the exemption.[21]

Exemption Phaseout

The personal exemption amount is $1900 for 1987, $1950 for 1988, and $2000 for 1989. After 1989, the amount will be indexed for inflation. The personal exemption amounts will be phased out for high-income taxpayers beginning in 1988. Parties negotiating a divorce should consider the phaseout when deciding who will claim the exemption to avoid giving it to a party who will not receive the full benefit.

Kiddie Tax

A common tax planning technique within the family unit has been to shift income from a parent in a high tax bracket to a child in a lower tax bracket. The TRA changed this technique by requiring that a minor's unearned income exceeding $1000 be taxed at the parent's highest rate. This provision applies to children under age 14.

The child has to compute his or her regular tax and share of "allocable parental tax" and pay the greater of the two computations. The allocable parental tax is that which the parent would have paid on the dependent child's unearned income if the parent had received the income.

This becomes complicated when the parents are divorced or separated. When the parents file a joint return, the child uses the total taxable income on the joint return. When the parents are married and file separately, the child must use the income of the parent with the highest income on the separate return. If the child cannot obtain the required information from the parents, the child may request that the IRS allow a disclosure or inspection of the parent's return under § 6103(e)(A)(iv).[22] When the parents are legally divorced or separated, the child uses the taxable income of the custodial parent as described in § 152(e) irrespective of which parent actually claims the dependency exemption.[23]

FILING STATUS

A married taxpayer may file a joint return, a separate return, or if certain requirements are met, may "be treated as unmarried" and file as head of household.

Marital status is determined as of the end of the taxpayer's year. Thus, if the taxpayer's year-end is December 31 and the taxpayer is divorced under a final decree on December 31, the taxpayer will be considered single for the entire year. State law governs whether an individual is considered married, divorced, or legally separated under a decree of separate maintenance. Marital status is recognized for filing a joint return even if the couple has not lived together for the entire year.

Married/Joint Return

Spouses filing a joint return are jointly and severally liable for tax payment obligations, plus penalties, additions to tax, and interest.[24] A spouse may obtain relief from joint liability under the innocent spouse rules of IRC § 6013(e). Filing a joint return results in an overall tax savings when one spouse has minimal or zero taxable income.

Married/Separate Return

Prior to the 1986 TRA, married taxpayers were usually discouraged from filing separate returns because the tax rates for this filing status were the most progressive. The tax rates are no longer more progressive after the 1986 TRA; however, a higher total tax will be paid by married couples filing separately when one spouse has minimal or zero taxable income. Some specific situations occur where a separate return could result in less overall tax, for instance, when both spouses have moderate income and one spouse has large medical deductions or a casualty loss.

Overall current tax savings may not be the primary factor in deciding to file jointly or separately. For example, assume the character of marital property is in dispute during a divorce proceeding, and a tax return must be filed by the spouses. The marital assets may be community property or separate property. Before the court adjudicates the property's character, the spouses agree to file jointly. The joint return computes the overall tax as zero because a business loss of $100,000 offsets other taxable income of $100,000. Later the court decides that the property generating the $100,000 of income was the husband's separate property and the business generating the $100,000 loss was the wife's property. Therefore, if the spouses had filed separately, the husband would have had taxable income of $100,000, and the wife would have had a net operating loss of $100,000. However, because a joint return was filed, the wife's net operating loss offset the husband's $100,000 of income, resulting in zero taxable income. For that year, the overall tax decreased, but the wife was deprived of the $100,000 net operating loss that could have been used against her future taxable income. In retrospect, the wife may not have elected to file jointly so that she could preserve the net operating loss for her future use.

Spouses often file a separate return for nontax reasons. One spouse may simply refuse to file a joint return to avoid becoming liable for the other spouse's tax liability. This often occurs when a divorce is pending or when one spouse is secretive about their personal finances.

Many special rules exist for taxpayers filing a married separate return. If one spouse itemizes deductions, the other spouse should itemize because a standard deduction will not be available to that spouse. Most often, neither spouse will be able to take the credit for child and dependent care.

For passive activity losses, an exception permits a deduction of up to $25,000 of losses that would otherwise be considered passive activity losses without regard to the passive activity loss limitations. These losses must be attributable to real estate rental activities in which the taxpayer actively participates.[25] If married taxpayers file separately and they live together for *all* or a *portion* of the taxable year, this exception does not apply, and zero losses can be claimed on either return. If the taxpayers file separately and live apart the *entire* year, each taxpayer may deduct up to $12,500 of losses.

On separate returns in noncommunity property states, the spouses must include their own income and deductions on their own returns. In a recent Tax Court case, *James E. Mahon*,[26] the taxpayers filed separate returns and split the husband's wages and retirement income evenly on each return. The court held that the husband was taxable on 100 percent of his wages and retirement income and that he, by himself, performed the services and earned the income.

In community property states, the spouses must divide community property income and deductions evenly on their separate returns and add these amounts to their own income and deductions from their separate property. IRC § 66, often called the "Abandoned Spouse Rule," protects a spouse who has not filed a joint return from imputation of community property income earned by the other spouse.

Changing the Election to File Jointly or Separately

Married taxpayers who file separately may change to a joint return any time within 3 years from the due date of the separate return(s) not including extensions. Taxpayers filing a joint return have only until the return's due date to change their status to filing separately for that year.

If a delinquent return was filed more than 3 years after the last date prescribed for filing a return, the IRS and courts routinely have required the taxpayers to file separately and would not accept a joint return.[27] The Tax Court in *Durovic* reasoned that the joint election could not be made after the 3-year limitation period. This position usually resulted in a higher overall tax on the delinquent returns. A recent Tax Court case overruled the finding in *Durovic* based on (1) the commissioner's own disavowal of the rule, (2) the intent of Congress as expressed in the legislative history of IRC § 6013, which allows married taxpayers to file a joint return, and (3) the statute's language. In this case, the court decided that IRC § 6013(b) applies only where a taxpayer seeks to change his filing status after having previously filed a return.[28] Thus, taxpayers filing delinquent returns may elect to file jointly.

Head of Household

Taxpayers qualifying for head of household status use lower tax rates than those filing as single or married filing separately. To qualify for this filing status, the taxpayer must be unmarried or considered unmarried on the last day of the tax year. The taxpayer is considered unmarried if:

1. The taxpayer files a separate return.
2. The taxpayer paid more than half the cost of maintaining a household for the tax year.
3. For taxable years beginning in 1985 and thereafter, the taxpayer's spouse cannot live in the household at any time during the last 6 months of the taxable year (before 1985, the spouse could not live in the house for the *entire* year).
4. The household must be the child's or stepchild's principal residence for over one-half of the year. The taxpayer must be able to claim the child as a dependent except that (a) by written declaration the noncustodial parent can claim the dependent or (b) the noncustodial parent provides at least $600 to support the dependent and claims the dependent under a pre-1985 agreement.

INNOCENT SPOUSE RULE

IRC § 6013(e) provides the most important exception to the entrenched principle that joint and several liability attaches to filing joint tax returns.[29] The so-called "Innocent Spouse" Rule is based on the premise that one spouse (the "innocent spouse") should not be responsible for unreported income or false deductions due to the other spouse's misconduct. This relief can be especially crucial when a couple later divorces and the innocent spouse is the more likely source of collecting unpaid taxes. DRTRA broadened this rule that was originally enacted in 1971 to include, among other things, protection from illusory deductions and unreported income.

A spouse may be relieved from joint and several liability if (1) the other spouse's *grossly erroneous* items cause a *substantial* tax underpayment; (2) the innocent spouse did not know or have reason to know of the underpayment; and (3) holding the innocent spouse liable for the deficiency would be inequitable. IRC § 6013(e) provides relief from the tax, interest, and penalties related to the understatement.

Grossly Erroneous Item. A "grossly erroneous item" is any omitted gross income item or any claim for deduction, credit, or basis unsupported by law or fact. Thus a deduction disallowed during an audit would not qualify unless the innocent spouse proves the deduction was bogus.

Substantial Underpayment of Tax. An understatement of tax due to omission of gross income must exceed $500 to be substantial. For a false claim of deduction, credit or basis, the underpayment must also exceed some percentage of the innocent spouse's adjusted gross income ("AGI") in the preadjustment year. If the innocent spouse's AGI is equal to or less than $20,000, then the underpayment must exceed 10 percent of AGI. If the AGI exceeds $20,000, then the underpayment must exceed 25 percent of AGI. The preadjustment year is the most recent tax year ending before the deficiency notice is mailed. If remarried, the innocent spouse's AGI must include the new spouse's income whether or not they file a joint return.

Knowledge of Understatement. Whether a spouse had reason to know of the understatement is often decisive in ascertaining "innocent spouse" status. Relevant cases have relied on the following considerations when evaluating the facts and circumstances: (a) spouse's involvement in family finances; (b) life-style of claiming spouse or family incongruous with income sources and amounts reported on the return; and (c) spouse's mental and physical health. Ignorance of tax consequences of known income sources will not support lack of knowledge. For example, a husband who knew of payments his wife received from her former husband and erroneously believed that such payments were excludible from income as alimony under IRC § 71(b) was denied protection under IRC § 6013(e).[30]

Inequitable Result. Prior to the 1984 amendment, IRC § 6013(e) required that the IRS consider the petitioning spouse's benefits from the understatement when determining the fairness of holding the innocent spouse liable for the deficiency. IRC § 6013(e) eliminates this explicit requirement, but the Tax Court has retained the "significant benefit" standard as a criterion of whether relief is justified.[31]

Where the claiming spouse or the family has received an "unusual" benefit (e.g., expensive jewelry, lavish family vacation) inconsistent with reported income, then "innocent spouse" status will be denied. Property transfers occurring in years subsequent to the understatement and pursuant to divorce have been deemed a benefit to an otherwise "innocent" spouse thereby precluding protection. Receipt of "ordinary" support, however, will not deny relief.

The *Internal Revenue Manual* states that a spouse will not have benefitted if the culpable spouse used the understatements solely for his or her own enjoyment (e.g., extramarital affair).

Community Property. Community property laws are disregarded while attributing understatement of earned income to a spouse. Income derived from property (e.g., rents), however, where neither spouse performs substantial services is considered the income of both spouses.

PROPERTY SETTLEMENTS

Nonrecognition of Gain on Spousal Transfers

Prior to DRTRA, the Supreme Court decided in *U.S. v. Davis*[32] that transfers of appreciated property pursuant to a divorce decree or separation agreement results in taxable gain to the transferor. The taxable gain amount equals the fair market value of the transferor's property or interest in the property less the cost basis. The transferee would then receive a step up in the property's basis based on the property's fair market value included in the transferor's gross income. DRTRA rescinded the *Davis* decision by passing IRC § 1041 that allows nonrecognition of gain or loss on any property transfer between spouses or between former spouses if the transfer is incident to a divorce.

Congress believed that spouses should be treated as a single economic unit and that taxing transfers within the unit would be inappropriate. The *Davis* rule frequently trapped the unwary; divorcing parties were surprised to find that equally dividing property believed to be jointly owned triggered gain recognition. Furthermore, the government often did not collect tax on the divided property's sale when it was eventually sold to third parties; the transferror frequently did not report the gain as the *Davis* rule requires, and the transferee claimed the step up in basis on the property's sale. IRC § 1041 remedied these problems.

IRS § 1041 has enormous scope. All property transfers between spouses or former spouses incident to a divorce receive nonrecognition treatment, including installment sale obligations,[33] life insurance contract transfers, and annuity contract assignments. The regulations state that nonrecognition treatment applies "regardless of whether the transfer is of property separately owned by the transferror or is a division [equal or *unequal*] of community property."[34] Also, such a property transfer does not trigger IRC Sections 1245 and 1250 recapture.

Carryover Basis to the Transferee

Because no gain or loss is recognized on the property transfer of a divorce settlement, it follows that the transferee will acquire a carryover basis in the property received. This occurs even when the transferred property has liabilities exceeding its basis.[35] The holding period also carries over.[36] This basis rule applies when a bona fide sale between spouses or former spouses occurs—the transferee cannot declare a step up in basis regardless of the consideration given.[37] As such, IRC § 1041 conveys the taxation on the property's appreciation from the transferror into the recipient's hands.

Generally, IRC § 1041 favors the taxpayer because most assets transferred in a property settlement are appreciated, and the parties to the divorce can postpone payment of tax on the appreciated value until sale to a third party. Good tax planning has the higher-tax-bracket spouse retaining property that has decreased in value to maximize the loss utilization.

Six-Year Rule

IRC § 1041 extends to all transfers between spouses and between *former* spouses if the transfer is "incident to the divorce." Incident to the divorce is defined as a transfer occurring "within one year after the date on which the marriage ceases, or is related to the cessation of the marriage."[38] Thus all transfers between spouses occurring within 1 year of the divorce are subject to IRC § 1041 regardless of the transfer's reason.

If the transfer occurs later than 1 year from the divorce date, then the transfer must be "related to the cessation of marriage" to qualify for IRC § 1041 treatment. The regulations provide that any transfer occurring within 6 years of the divorce date and pursuant to a divorce decree will be treated as related to the divorce.[39] Hence, any transfer occurring 1 to 6 years after divorce must be pursuant to a divorce decree to obtain IRC § 1041 treatment. The regulations specify that a divorce or separation instrument includes a *modification* to such an instrument.

A transfer occurring more than 6 years after the divorce is presumed unrelated to the divorce, and IRC § 1041 would not apply. The regulations suggest that this presumption may be rebutted by showing that the transfer occurred to divide the property owned by the parties at the time of divorce.

The rule's 6-year arbitrary time limit relates to DRTRA's 6-year recapture rules. The 1986 TRA repealed the 6-year minimum term rule and 6-year recapture, causing some to speculate that the final regulations will modify § 1041's 6-year rule.

Effective Date of IRC § 1041

Generally, IRC § 1041 applies to all transfers occurring after July 18, 1984.[40] Transitional rules apply to divorce instruments in effect prior to July 18, 1984. First, the former spouses may elect to have IRC § 1041 apply to all transfers occurring after July 18, 1984. Second, the former spouses may elect to have IRC § 1041 apply to *all* transfers occurring after December 31, 1983.[41] If neither of these elections are made for instruments in effect prior to July 18, 1984, then IRC § 1041 will not apply to property transfers made after that date.

These transitional rules continue to provide interesting tax planning opportunities to transfers between former spouses. In a recent Private Letter Ruling, a couple had divorced in 1982 with the husband retaining sole ownership of the personal residence while the wife occupied the home. Upon the residence's future sale, the divorce decree provided that the wife could keep the sale proceeds less an amount paid to her former husband equal to the federal and state taxes he would owe on the sale. In 1987, the parties wanted to modify their 1982 divorce decree to transfer the husband's interest in the residence to his wife along with an election to apply IRC § 1041. This transaction made the wife sole owner, allowing her to sell the house at any time and defer the gain if the house remained her personal residence.

The IRS agreed that the decree's proposed modification would qualify the transfer under IRC § 1041 if (1) they elected pursuant to the requirements in the temporary regulations to apply IRC § 1041; (2) they attach a copy of the IRC § 1041 election to the husband's return in the year of the transfer; and (3) both former spouses retain copies of the election.[42]

Frequently, decisions about property disposition between former spouses occur long after the final divorce decree. The parties should always consider the ability to use § 1041's nonrecognition treatment, even when the divorce instrument predates July 18, 1984.

RETIREMENT PLANNING

A marital division should consider the spouse's interests in various pension and profit-sharing plans, individual retirement accounts, and other employment-related plans including stock options, survivor benefit plans, deferred compensation plans, and other nonqualified plans. The nonemployed spouse could have a significant future interest in these assets based on the employed spouses services performed during the marriage. The division of these assets significantly affects the retirement planning of the divorcing spouses.

Individual Retirement Accounts

Alimony, includible in gross income pursuant to IRC § 71, is considered compensation for purposes of Individual Retirement Account (IRA) contributions.[43] This helps the spouse receiving alimony and who currently does not have any earned income. It could be the only tax-favored retirement savings vehicle available to that spouse.

Additionally, an IRA transfer by one spouse to a former spouse under a divorce decree or a written instrument incident to such divorce is not taxable. Thereafter, the account will be treated as maintained for the recipient spouse's benefit.[44] Thus the recipient spouse may receive distributions from the account without regard to the former spouse.

Other Retirement Plans

A retirement plan is any arrangement that accumulates funds for the future benefit of a retired or disabled employee or beneficiaries. Most plans are qualified plans that allow the employer to receive a current tax deduction for allowed contributions, do not tax earnings of the plan unless invested in certain assets, and do not tax the plan's participants on contributions made on their behalf until the participant receives a distribution from the plan. A nonqualified plan does not obtain these tax benefits.

Two basic categories of retirement plans are *defined contribution plans* and *defined benefit plans*. A defined contribution plan maintains a separate account for each plan participant. The participant's eventual distribution amount depends on the employer and employee contributions credited to the account; any forfeitures credited due to the termination of plan participants who are not 100% vested; and the income earned by the account. A defined benefit plan is one in which a participant accrues definitely determinable benefits payable at some defined time in the future. The employer contributes to the plan based on actuarial determined amounts necessary to fund the benefits of all plan participants.

Before deciding how to divide the retirement plan, one must ascertain the value of the plan assets or the present value of future benefits. The defined contribution plan can be valued in a straightforward manner because the plan maintains a separate account for each participant.

An actuary can value the defined benefit plan by estimating the present value of the future benefits based on statistical contingency charts for death, disability, employment termination, and other relevant calculations. Alternatively, depending on the plan's size, it may be possible to take the same approach used in defined contribution plans. That is, simply analyze the fair market value of the assets currently in the plan. This is particularly feasible for plans where most or all of the assets are to fund the divorced participant's retirement benefit. This is often encountered among professional employees who have personal service corporations such as physicians, attorneys, accountants, dentists, or people involved in the entertainment industry such as performing artists, producers, directors, and writers.

Alternatives for Division. Four basic alternatives exist for dividing the retirement plan assets. Frequently, the employed spouse retains all interest in the retirement plan and gives a comparably valued asset to the nonemployed spouse. One should use this alternative cautiously. A recent Private Letter Ruling concluded that cash payments to a wife in exchange for her community property interest in her husband's military pension represented payments for a right to future income rather than gain and therefore § 1041 does not apply. The ruling characterized the payments as ordinary income includible in gross income under § 61.[45]

The plan assets could also be divided by a "qualified domestic relations order" (QDRO) that assigns all or part of the participant's retirement benefits to the nonemployed alternate payee. The QDRO's alternate payee may be the participant's spouse, former spouse, child, or other dependent.[46]

Another method retains jurisdiction over the retirement plan until the employed spouse can receive retirement benefits. At that time, a computation of benefits due to the nonemployed spouse will receive benefits based on the percentage of funds resulting from the services performed during marriage.

Finally, in cases involving personal service corporations or closely held corporations, the parties could terminate the plan and distribute all the assets according to a mutually accepted property division. Each party can then roll over their distribution into an IRA thereby avoiding current taxation on the proceeds.

Advantages and Disadvantages. Several factors influence the decision as to which pension plan alternative to pursue. First, the client's immediate and future cash needs must be analyzed. Retaining 100% of the plan by the employed spouse in exchange for another asset depends upon the mix of assets available to divide. Suitable assets to use in trade may not exist, thereby forcing the couple to divide the retirement plan. If exchangeable assets exist, the nonemployed spouse may be left with no retirement funds on which to rely. This may not be a problem if the nonemployed spouse is relatively young and will resume a career accruing future pension benefits. An older, nonemployed spouse, however, may prefer retirement security. On the other hand, the nonemployed spouse giving up retirement benefits will receive present existing assets, when the assets may be needed most, to set up a new household, provide for current needs of children, and to pay for training to resume or start a career.

The employed spouse may prefer to retain 100 percent of the plan, thereby maintaining total control over the various retirement options. Also courts only reluctantly invade corporate pension or profit-sharing plans to benefit third parties. This could prove advantageous to a shareholder/employee of a risky business. Bankruptcy usually protects a corporate pension or profit-sharing plan.

Retaining the plan may benefit the employed spouse in other respects. In a recent case, the husband in a 25-year marriage exchanged other assets to retain the pension plan. The husband was the only employee of a personal service corporation involved in the entertainment industry, and the pension plan had assets of approximately $650,000. The husband agreed to pay alimony of $4000 per month to his former spouse. Shortly after the divorce, the husband's corporation could not generate any business, and he did not receive a salary. The husband went to court to reduce alimony payments based on his current income situation. The wife questioned whether the pension plan could be invaded to pay the required alimony, which the courts will probably not allow. Courts may be more willing, however, to invade a plan for the husband's child support obligation.

The advantages to dividing the plan by use of a QDRO include the following: (1) both parties share in the plan's retirement security; (2) both parties defer the payment of tax on the benefits until they receive the plan's proceeds; and (3) the nonemployed spouse will share in any increased retirement benefits attributable to changes in the plan and plan earnings.

Qualified Domestic Relation Orders. If the divorcing couple decide to split the retirement plan asset, a QDRO is generally required to ensure valid and enforceable assignment of the employee's benefits in a tax-qualified retirement plan. A court issues the QDRO to identify the alternate payee and specify the amount and timing of benefits to be paid.[47]

Payment of Benefits to the Alternate Payee. Generally, the benefits payable to the alternate payee begin when payments to the participant begin or would begin. All benefit payment options are available to the alternate payee that are available to the participant under the plan, except for joint and survivor annuities with respect to the alternate payee and his or her subsequent spouse.[48] Some retirement plans will distribute benefits to the alternate payee any time after a QDRO is issued. The plan cannot, however, force the alternate payee to accept an immediate distribution of an amount exceeding $3500.[49]

The earliest date on which an alternate payee may receive benefits depends on whether the participant has separated from service. If the participant is still employed by the plan's sponsor, then the alternate payee may receive benefits when the participant has attained the "earliest retirement age." This age is *not* determined by the retirement plan but by the Retirement Equity Act of 1984 (REA). The REA defines the participant's earliest retirement age as the earlier of (1) the date on which the participant is entitled to a distribution under the plan *or* (2) the *later* of age 50, or when the participant would be eligible for benefits if the participant had separated from service. If the participant has separated from service, the alternate payee can receive benefits only when the participant is entitled to receive them.

Plan Distributions

The plan's participant or alternate payee will receive distributions as an annuity or a lump sum distribution.

Annuity. Amounts received as an annuity are reported as ordinary income and may be reduced by a pro rata allocation of any employee contributions to the plan.[50] The alternate payee receives a portion of the payments in the form of employee contributions when payments are made pursuant to a QDRO.[51]

Lump Sum Distributions. A payment is considered a lump sum distribution if the recipient receives within 1 taxable year the entire balance credited to the individual's account from a qualified pension or profit-sharing plan, and it is payable on account of (1) the employee's death, (2) the employee attaining age 59½, or (3) the employee's separation from service or disability.[52] A lump sum distributee may qualify to compute tax on the distribution under a special 5-year averaging formula or, if certain transitional rules apply, under a special 10-year averaging formula. Alternatively, the distribution may be partially or totally rolled over into an IRA plan thereby escaping taxation until the IRA pays benefits. The distributee has 60 days after receiving the benefits to roll over the proceeds. A distributee electing this option should know that special averaging under the 5- or 10-year formulas are not available to IRA lump sum distributions.

MARITAL RESIDENCE

The tax consequences of the ownership, disposition, and interest payments on the marital residence is one of the most important aspects of a marital dissolution. A divorcing couple could easily decide on an ostensibly equitable or reasonable property settlement only to find that their arrangement has unintended tax results. The parties need to consider the tax rules applicable to a residence and fully understand the tax consequences of their decisions.

Sale of a Principal Residence

IRC § 1034 is a mandatory provision of the code that requires that gain realized on the sale of a principal residence be postponed or rolled over when certain conditions are satisfied. To apply this section, the taxpayer must sell his principal residence and reinvest the proceeds in a new residence within 2 years before or after the sale date. Part of the gain could be recognized if the old residence's total adjusted sales price is not reinvested.

When two parties own a residence (as is common with divorcing spouses), the statute allows each spouse to separately compute their gain and loss.[53] One spouse rolls over one-half of the gain when § 1034 is satisfied, whereas the other spouse does not qualify.

Property used by the taxpayer as a principal residence is a facts and circumstances test.[54] Generally, the taxpayer must physically occupy the principal residence.[55] Temporarily renting the property before sale will not exclude the new residence from consideration as the taxpayer's principal abode.[56] The taxpayer's intent is also an important factor. The extent to which the taxpayer has pursued selling the residence and whether the old residence has been abandoned as a principal residence will influence its characterization as a principal residence.

The principal residence issue often arises in divorce or separation situations. Compelling reasons usually exist for one party to move from the premises and live in other quarters during the dissolution proceedings. If the property is eventually sold, the spouse who has moved out will probably not satisfy the principal residence requirement and will not qualify for roll-over treatment of any gain on the property's sale. In *Young*[57] the taxpayer had to recognize a gain when he had not lived in the residence for over 2 years. The court concluded that the taxpayer moved from the residence when the divorce decree granted his wife and daughter exclusive use of the property.

In dissolution cases where the parties plan to sell the residence, the agreement should preserve the roll-over option for the spouses. Either the residence should be sold while it is still the principal residence of both parties, or in their property settlement, the spouse leaving the premises should consider transferring 100 percent ownership in the residence to the spouse remaining in the house.

One-Time $125,000 Exclusion of Gain

IRC § 121 allows taxpayers a one-time exclusion of up to $125,000 (as adjusted from time to time) of gain on the sale of the principal residence. To qualify for the exclusion, the taxpayer must have (1) attained the age of 55 at the time of the sale and (2) owned and occupied the residence for 3 or more years out of the 5-year period ending on the sale or exchange date. IRC § 121(b)(2) provides that the election will not be available if the taxpayer *or* his spouse has taken the election previously. Thus when a husband and wife exercise their right to the election, neither spouse may ever again exclude gain under this section.

Married taxpayers who jointly own a home may exclude a maximum of $125,000 of gain. If they file separately, they may exclude only $62,500 each. However, legally divorced parties who satisfy the IRC § 121 requirements may each exclude $125,000 of gain. Thus a divorcing couple eligible for this election would be wise to obtain the divorce decree prior to selling the residence.

Mortgage Payments

Four basic methods of joint ownership exist in real property: as tenants by the entirety, joint tenants with rights of survivorship, tenants in common, and community property. The property's co-ownership form dictates the tax results of mortgage payments.

In a divorce, the wife and children generally remain in the marital residence, with the husband obligated to pay the mortgage payment and taxes. If the property is held as a 50–50 tenancy in common, then the husband can deduct 50 percent of his payments on the residence as alimony (assuming the requirements of § 71 are satisfied). The remaining 50 percent of the payments will retain their character in the hands of the husband relating to his ownership of the property. One-half of the property taxes will be an itemized deduction. One-half of the interest expense will depend on the property's characterization in the hands of the husband.

IRC § 163(h)(3) allows a 100 percent deduction for qualified residence interest when certain requirements are met. This section defines the term *qualified residence* as the principal residence *within the meaning of IRC § 1034*. Because the husband no longer occupies the residence, he probably cannot deduct the interest as qualified residence interest. The remaining choices for deductibility are as consumer interest or investment interest. Both of these types of interest have limited deductibility. Classification as investment interest, however, would probably be preferable when the husband has investment income.

Property held in joint tenancy with rights of survivorship has a different tax treatment. The important factor is not the property's ownership but who has the mortgage liability. State law and the underlying documents must be consulted to ascertain the party or parties liable. In *Neely B. Taylor Jr.*,[58] the Tax Court held that the transferror was personally liable on the mortgage and the transferee was not. The recipient did not derive any economic benefit from mortgage payments and was not taxable on any of the payments as alimony. Presumably, the transferee would have to include 50 percent of the payments in gross income as alimony if the transferee had been 50 percent liable on the mortgage. The law in this area is complicated and should be reviewed before deciding on the property's ownership after the divorce and arranging for support through mortgage payments.

GIFT AND ESTATE TAX ASPECTS

An important and often overlooked aspect of the divorce involves decisions on gift and estate tax planning. Both parties must review and update their wills and trusts. After the divorce, the marital deduction for gift and estate tax purposes will no longer be available, and testamentary trusts set up for the spouse and children will have to be reconsidered.

Gift Tax

IRC § 2523 authorizes a deduction for gifts between spouses equal to the gift's value. For a gift of a life estate or other terminable interest received, no deduction is allowed. However, an election may be made for "qualified terminable interest property" (QTIP) given to the spouse that allows a full marital deduction against the donor's taxable gifts, provided the donee spouse includes the gift in his or her gross estate. Consequently, any gift tax problems with respect to gifts between spouses can be avoided during marriage.

IRC § 2516 provides that any transfers of property pursuant to a divorce made between spouses to settle marital and property rights and to support their children shall be considered exchanges for full and adequate consideration. Gift tax problems will be avoided pursuant to § 2516 when divorce occurs within 1 year before or 2 years after the settlement agreement date (for transfers made on or before July 18, 1984, the divorce had to occur within 2 years after the agreement). The divorce must occur within this time frame, but the actual property transfer may occur at any time as long as it follows the agreement.

These two code sections help divorcing spouses avoid most gift tax problems. Clients with a gift-giving schedule will want to consider gift splitting with their spouse in the divorce year but prior to the final decree date. The QTIP election could save taxes to the transferror spouse when transferring assets in trust to the spouse for life with remainder to the children. The transfer to the spouse may qualify under § 2516, but the remainder interest would be a gift of a future interest to the children without the benefit of the annual exclusion. The transfer spouse should consider the QTIP election on a transfer during marriage in this circumstance.

Estate Planning

Very basic estate planning decisions should be reviewed at the time of divorce. The client may want to change beneficiaries on retirement plans and life insurance policies on which ownership will be obtained pursuant to the settlement agreement. The current owner of a life insurance policy may wish to transfer policy ownership at the time of the divorce. This would remove the insurance proceeds from his or her estate (assuming survival of 3 years after the transfer) and provide continued support to the former spouse or to children after death. This arrangement would be preferable to an agreement whereby the payor spouse's estate continues to pay spousal support. Any such postdeath payment agreement would run afoul of the requirements for deductible alimony that must terminate at death.

Marital Residence. One must also consider the marital residence when planning for the estate. Divorcing spouses frequently wish to retain the residence for some time after the divorce is final. If the parties own the residence as joint tenants with right of survivorship, the death of one of the former spouses may trigger unintended results. If the decedent had provided most of the consideration for the residence, then the IRS could argue to include the entire residence in the decedent's gross estate without benefit of the marital deduction. To avoid this result, the parties may want to change title to ownership as tenants in common or as community property if possible. Alternatively, the divorcing spouses should consider transferring ownership entirely into the name of the spouse who will be residing in the residence.

QTIP Trusts. IRC § 2056(a) provides for an unlimited marital deduction to a decedent's gross estate thereby allowing a married couple to defer paying estate tax to the estate of the last spouse to die. The unlimited marital deduction may not be desirable, however, when it is advantageous to maximize the use of each spouse's $600,000 unified credit. Other considerations such as the possibility of the surviving spouse's remarrying, the surviving spouse's ability to manage financial responsibilities, and the desire to provide for the children of former marriages make the use of trusts in estate planning indispensable.

A trust, as a vehicle for a marital deduction bequest, offers the advantages of skilled management and asset investment and the protection of the beneficiary's interests from creditors. Since the 1981 Economic Recovery Tax Act ("ERTA"), most spouses with a substantial estate gave the surviving spouse a marital deduction bequest as is necessary to reduce the decedent's estate tax to zero, after applying the unified credit. The amount covered by the unified credit could be placed into a nonmarital trust, the income payable to the surviving spouse for life. If the surviving spouse does not need the income, the testator could make bequests directly to other family members.

Prior to ERTA, the most commonly used trust in marital deduction planning was the power of appointment trust that qualified for the IRC § 2056(b)(5) exception to the terminable interest rule. This trust qualified for the marital deduction when specific conditions were satisfied including the surviving spouse's ability to control the disposition of the trust corpus. This type of trust could pose a problem for a testator who wanted to provide a life income for his surviving spouse and reduce estate tax by using the marital deduction but who also wanted to direct the remainder interest to certain beneficiaries such as the children of a prior marriage.

ERTA created a new exception to the terminable interest rule that allowed a "qualified terminable interest trust" or QTIP trust. The QTIP trust and power of appointment trust differ in the grantor's or testator's ability to control the disposition of the remainder interest in the trust after the spouse's death. A QTIP trust allows the testator greater flexibility in arranging support for his survivors and control over asset dispositions along with the ability to save estate taxes through a marital deduction.

Gross Estate Deductibility of Obligations Pursuant to the Divorce. Prior to DRTRA, no counterpart to § 2516 existed in the estate area. Therefore, whether a decedent's postdeath obligation was deductible from the gross estate under § 2053 depended on the extent to which the obligations were supported by "full and adequate consideration in money or money's worth."[59] DRTRA added § 2043(b)(2) that allows an estate tax deduction for transfers pursuant to claims under a written separation instrument if the transfers satisfy marital or property rights and the agreement would have satisfied the requirements of paragraph 1 of § 2516. This amendment applies to the estate of a decedent dying after July 18, 1984.

NOTES

1. IRC § 71(b) (2).
2. *Moore v. United States*, 449 F. Supp. 163 (N.D. Tex. 1978).

3. P.L. 99-514, Act § 1843 (b).
4. Reg. § 1.71-1T (A-9).
5. Ibid.
6. Reg. § 1.71-1T (A-23).
7. Joint Committee on Taxation, *Explanation of the Technical Corrections to the Tax Reform Act of 1984 and Other Recent Tax Legislation*, May 13, 1987.
8. 1986 Act § 1881.
9. Reg. § 1.71-1T(d) Q-22.
10. Joint Committee on Taxation, *Explanation of the Technical Corrections to the Tax Reform Act of 1986 and Other Recent Tax Legislation*, May 13, 1987.
11. Reg. § 1.71-1T(e) (A-26, final paragraph).
12. IRC § 71(c)(1).
13. Reg. § 1.71-1(e).
14. *Commissioner v. Lester*, 366 U.S. 299 (1961).
15. IRC § 71(c)(2)(A).
16. Reg. § 1.71-1T(c) (A-17).
17. Internal Revenue Service, *Exemptions and Standard Deduction* (Publication 501, Rev. Nov. 1987).
18. IRC §§ 152(e)(3) and 152(c).
19. IRC § 152(e)(4).
20. IRC § 213(d)(5).
21. IRC § 21(e)(5).
22. Temp. Reg. § 1.1(i)1T, Q/A-22.
23. Temp. Reg. § 1.1(i)-1T Q/A-12.
24. IRC § 6013(d)(3).
25. IRC § 469(i).
26. *Mahon v. Commissioner*, 54 T.C.M. (CCH) 439 (1987).
27. *Durovic v. Commissioner*, 487 F.2d 36 (7th Cir. 1983).
28. *Phillips v. Commissioner*, 86 T.C. 433 (1986).
29. IRC § 6013(e)(3).
30. *Mass v. Commissioner*, 81 T.C. 112 (1983).
31. *Purcell v. Commissioner*, 86 T.C. 228 (1986).
32. *U.S. v. Davis*, 370 U.S. 65 (1962).
33. IRC § 453B(g).
34. Reg. § 1.1041-1T(d) Q-10.
35. Reg. § 1.1041-1T(d) Q-12.
36. IRC § 1223(2).
37. Reg. § 1041-1T(d) Q-11.
38. IRC § 1041(c).
39. Reg. § 1.1041-1T(b)(2) Q-7.
40. Reg. § 1.1041-1T(f) Q-15.
41. Reg. § 1.1041-1T(f) Q-16.
42. LtrRul 8707089.
43. IRC § 219(f)(1).
44. IRC § 408(d)(6).
45. Private Letter Ruling 8813023; 12/29/87, released 4.1.88.
46. IRC § 414(p)(8).
47. IRC § 414(p)(1) and IRC § 414(p)(2).
48. IRC § 414(a)(4)(A)(iii).
49. IRC § 411(a)(11).
50. IRC § 72(b).
51. IRC § 72(m)(10).
52. IRC § 402(e)(4)(A).
53. Rev. Rul. 74-250, 1974-1 C.B. 102.

54. Reg. § 1.1034-1(c)(3).
55. *Houlette v. Commissioner*, 48 T.C. 350 (1967).
56. Ibid.
57. *Young v. Commissioner*, 49 T.C.M. (CCH) 1002 (1985).
58. *Taylor v. Commissioner*, 45 T.C. 120 (1965).
59. F. Sander and H. Gutman, Tax Aspects of Divorce and Separation: A Detailed Analysis, *The Family Law Reporter*, p. 220 (1986).

BIBLIOGRAPHY

Arthur Andersen & Co., *Tax Reform 1986 Analysis and Planning* (Matthew Bender, 1986).

Asimow, Michael, "Alimony and Marital Property Divisions under the 1986 Act," *Taxes—The Tax Magazine* (June 1987), pp. 352–357.

Brown, William J., *Tax Strategies for Separation and Divorce* (McGraw-Hill Book Company, 1987).

California Continuing Education of the Bar, *Tax Planning for Marital Termination Settlements*, (September/October 1987).

Clemens, Bruce A., and Daniel J. Jaffe, *Employee Retirement and Deferred Compensation Plans on Dissolution of Marriage: Valuation, Distribution, and Tax Aspects*, California Continuing Education of the Bar, (October/November 1986).

Gursey, Donald L., *Family Law Symposium: Tax Consequences of Marital Separation and Dissolution*, California Continuing Education of the Bar, (November 1985).

Gursey, Donald L., and Roseanna L. Purzycki, "Alimony: A Taxing Situation," *Family Law News* (Spring 1987), p. 100.

Internal Revenue Service, "Tax Information for Divorced or Separated Individuals," Publication 504 (Rev. November 1987).

Internal Revenue Service, "Tax Information on Selling Your Home," Publication 523 (Rev. November 1987).

O'Connell, Marjorie A., *Divorce Taxation* (Prentice-Hall, Inc., 1985).

Poerio, Mark, "The Practical Side of Pensions and Qualified Domestic Relations Orders," *The Family Law Reporter*, Monograph No.1, (January 5, 1988), pp. 14, FLR 3001.

Randall, Gary C., "Practical Applications of the 1984 Domestic Relations Tax Bill-Trick or Treat?," U.S.C. Law Center Tax Institute, (Vol. 38, 1986), pp. 10–1 to 10–42.

Sander, Frank E.A., and Harry L. Gutman, *Tax Aspects of Divorce and Separation: A Detailed Analysis*, Updated for the Tax Reform Act of 1984 by Wicker, William C., Updated for the Tax Reform Act of 1986 by Blake, John F., and Pearle, Lynn K., *The Family Law Reporter*, The Bureau of National Affairs, Inc. (1987).

Van Houten, Margaret D., "Divorce Negotiations Carry Substantial Estate Planning Implications," *Estate Planning* (November/December, 1987), pp. 344–349.

LIST OF CASES

Commissioner v. Lester, 366 U.S. 299 (1961)
Durovic v. Commissioner, 487 F.2d 36 (7th Cir. 1973)
Houlette v. Commissioner, 48 T.C. 350 (1967)
Mahon v. Commissioner, 54 T.C.M. (CCH) 439 (1987)
Mass v. Commissioner, 81 T.C. 433 (1986)

Moore v. United States, 449 F. Supp. 163 (N.D. Tex. 1978)
Phillips v. Commissioner, 86 T.C. 112 (1983)
Purcell v. Commissioner, 86 T.C. 228 (1986)
Taylor v. Commissioner, 45 T.C. 120 (1965)
United States v. Davis, 370 U.S. 65 (1962)
Young v. Commissioner, 49 T.C.M. (CCH) 1002 (1985)

33

TAXATION OF SETTLEMENTS AND JUDGMENTS

Dan J. Hall

INTRODUCTION

Income tax rules affect business strategic planning and everyday decision making. Unlike the well-planned business transaction, litigation aims to recover damages or avoid liability. Knowledge of how taxes will affect a settlement or judgment may allow litigants to maximize their benefits or minimize their losses. Planning for these contingencies in the early stages of litigation, therefore, becomes as important as estimating damages themselves.

Typically, in litigation, the injured parties attempt to make themselves "whole" again. One cannot fully assess a litigation's economic realities, however, without consideration of taxes on the outcome. The economic benefit of an award can differ, for example, if the recipient's income is taxed as ordinary income or as a capital gain. Under certain circumstances, the award may be fully excludible from income and thus escape taxation altogether. The defendant's after-tax cost of the settlement will be significantly affected if the judgment is either fully or partially deductible than if it is wholly nondeductible.

Though the Tax Reform Act of 1986 reduced the benefits of capital gain treatment by eliminating the 60-percent exclusion from income of long-term capital gains, the distinction remains important. For example, capital losses may offset ordinary income up to $3000 for individuals, and any excess may be carried over to subsequent years. The taxpayer may offset capital gains equal to current capital losses plus any capital losses carried over from prior years. The distinction will also be important if Congress reinstates preferential capital gains treatment.

GENERAL RULE

The underlying claim that the judgment or settlement seeks to remedy usually determines a judgment's or settlement's tax effects.[1] Additionally, a settlement is taxed as capital gain only where a sale or exchange has occurred. The recovery is taxed in the same manner as the item for which it substitutes. The rationale is that any settlement received should be taxed as if the economic loss had not occurred. For purposes of taxability, it does not matter if the settlement concludes through informal agreement between the parties or through process of law. Thus tax considerations do not motivate litigants to choose one forum over the other or to settle a claim versus litigating a claim.

BUSINESS INJURIES

Lost Profits

Within a business context, to decide whether the underlying claim results from a loss from an interest in ordinary income producing assets, capital assets, or both may be difficult. If the underlying claim rests upon an asset that produces ordinary income, recoveries from such an asset should also be taxed as ordinary income.[2] Thus the recovery of lost profits is taxed as ordinary income. This is also true for recoveries resulting from insurance proceeds under a policy that protects against such loss.[3]

Damages to Capital Assets

If the recovery relates to damages sustained to an identifiable capital asset and if the sale or exchange requirement has been met, capital treatment should be afforded. Where direct damage or loss to a capital asset occurs and where the value is readily ascertainable, one can allocate the recovery between damages for lost profits and damages to capital assets. The recipient must demonstrate the portion of the recovery representing a capital item.

Damages to Goodwill

Taxpayers will often claim that a recovery reflects damages to goodwill and therefore should be treated as tax-free return of capital, rather than as ordinary income. Though damages in this context may represent lost profits, the underlying claim is that the destruction of business has occurred rather than just a temporary loss of income. The taxpayer, however, has the burden of overcoming the commissioner's presumptive correctness of determination that the entire amount recompenses for lost profits.[4] The taxpayer must also prove the basis in the asset destroyed.[5] Goodwill has tax basis only where it has been purchased as part of an ongoing business. Even then to allocate part of the purchase price to goodwill can be difficult. To the extent that basis can be shown in goodwill, amounts recovered will be treated as a return of capital. Any excess will be capital gain.

Where recovery is for damages sustained to a business asset and the amount received in excess of the asset's adjusted basis would have produced ordinary income had no injury occurred, ordinary income will result. An example is inventory. If, however, the asset is used in the taxpayer's trade or business (a § 1231 asset), the recovery in excess of basis will be taxed as capital gain, subject to the code's recapture provisions that require that gain attributable to previous depreciation deductions be taxed as ordinary income.[6]

Timing of Income

Litigants should also consider the timing of income for both accrual and cash basis taxpayers. Cash basis taxpayers generally recognize income upon receipt, whereas accrual basis taxpayers generally recognize income when their right to receive it is fixed or upon actual receipt, whichever is earlier. All other things being equal, it is better to recognize income later rather than sooner. A cash basis taxpayer will benefit, for example, from delaying a settlement so that cash is received early in the subsequent year rather than late in the current year. An accrual-based taxpayer might gain a similar benefit if a settlement is agreed upon just after rather than before year end.

Punitive Damages

Punitive damages received in a business settlement that are attributable solely to losses from business are generally taxable income to the recipient.[7] Punitive damages often result in antitrust cases, discussed more fully later.

PERSONAL INJURIES

General Rule

Internal Revenue Code § 104 provides a statutory exclusion from income for recovery of damages sustained from personal injuries. The rationale is that individuals should not be taxed on proceeds intended to make them whole again.

Types of Personal Injuries

Section 104 excludes from income amounts received under workmen's compensation, damages from personal injury or sickness, amounts received for injury sustained in the Armed Services or from terrorist attack. The regulations have expanded these rules to exclude from taxation recoveries based upon tort rights. Personal injury damages can stem from racial, age, or sex discrimination, emotional distress, and injury to reputation. For example, the Third Circuit affirmed a Tax Court decision that damages paid to a high-school teacher by the board of education for violating her right to free speech were tax free under § 104 even though the amount of the settlement was based on an injury to a personal right, not to a property right. The lost wages was an indication of the amount of damage but was not an independent basis for recovery.[8]

Awards or settlements resulting from actions on account of physical injury or personal damages fall within the scope of § 104 and are excluded from income. Injuries sustained by an individual in a business context may result in a recovery for personal or business interests. For example, a sole practitioner is slandered and consequently loses his livelihood. Has he suffered a personal injury through loss of reputation or a business injury in that he cannot practice his vocation? The answer depends upon the facts and circumstances.

Punitive Damages

The IRS has vacillated over the years as to whether punitive damages resulting from personal injury should be included or excluded from taxable income. In Rev. Rul. 58-418,[9] the service stated that the excludability of damages depended on whether they were compensatory or punitive. In Rev. Rul. 75-45,[10] the service reversed itself and held that all damages received for personal injuries were excludable from income. The IRS changed its mind again in Rev. Rul. 84-108,[11] revoking Rev. Rul. 75-45 and holding that recoveries representing purely punitive damages arising from personal injury are fully taxable.

Two courts have battled this issue with just as much inconsistency. In *Roemer v. Commissioner*,[12] the Tax Court held, in accordance with Rev. Rul. 58-418, that the punitive damages in a liable case related to compensation and that the compensatory damages were paid not for personal injury but for business injury. The court reasoned that the commissioner had included punitive damages in income in the same manner as compensatory damages, provided they arose from a personal injury, were taxable, and therefore the punitive damages were likewise includable in gross income. The Ninth Circuit reversed, holding that both the punitive and compensatory amounts of the damage award were nontaxable under § 104 because under California law defamation is a tort whether relating to business or personal life. The court referred to the service's own characterization in Rev. Rul. 75-45 that punitive damages in the area of personal injuries were excludable.

The Service in Rev. Rul. 85-143,[13] stated that it would not follow the Ninth Circuit's opinion in *Roemer* but instead would follow the Tax Court's opinion. However, the Tax Court in *Threlkeld v. Commissioner*,[14] reversed its own position in *Roemer*, holding that § 104 does not distinguish between damages received for injury to personal reputation and damages received for injury to business reputation. Thus the service can no longer rely on the Tax Court to support its position where a tort action gives rise to punitive damages.

ANTITRUST PROCEEDINGS

The antitrust laws comprise more than 30 federal statutes, including the Sherman Act,[15] the Clayton Act,[16] the Federal Trade Commission Act,[17] and the Robinson–Patman Act.[18] They prohibit monopolies, price fixing, and unfair competitive practices. These laws are enforced through fines and imprisonment, injunction suits, private suits for treble damages, and administrative proceedings.

Compensatory Damages

Antitrust recoveries can be either compensatory or punitive. The tax treatment of the compensatory portion depends upon the nature of the underlying claim, whereas the punitive portions are always taxable as ordinary income.

Compensatory damages generally fall into four categories:

1. Compensation for lost profits, which is ordinary income
2. Compensation for the destruction of a capital asset
3. Compensation for the destruction of a noncapital asset
4. Compensation for damages from overcharges on purchases.

With certain exceptions (discussed later), the amount received in an antitrust settlement is taxed as ordinary income. This treatment reflects the service's presumption that unless the taxpayer can establish the claim's origin, the amount received is treated as ordinary income. Where compensatory amounts can be shown to replace or restore the tax basis of property damaged, the recovery will not be taxable.[19] The taxpayer is allowed to treat the amounts recovered as a return of capital. Amounts received in excess of the tax basis will be taxable either as ordinary income or capital gain depending on the character of the assets damaged.

If the proceedings arise from excess charges due to price fixing, trade restraint, or other antitrust violations, compensatory amounts may be treated as a reduction of the purchase price of the property to which the violations relate.[20] As such, income recognition will be deferred until the assets are disposed of as if the correct price had been charged from the outset. For example, if inventory had been purchased under free market pricing conditions rather than pursuant to price fixing, the inventory would cost less. At inventory disposition, more income will be recognized because the cost of goods sold is less.

Punitive Damages

Section 4 of the Clayton Act provides that any person "injured in his business or property by reason of anything forbidden in the antitrust laws" may sue to recover "threefold the damages sustained, and the cost of suit including a reasonable attorney's fee."[21] Thus one-third of a recovery under § 4 of the Clayton Act will represent actual compensatory damages, and two-thirds will be punitive damages. The service has indicated in Rev. Rul. 67-33[22] that it will always treat the punitive portion of antitrust recoveries as ordinary income. This treatment stems from the Supreme Court decision in *Commissioner v. Glenshaw Glass Co.*[23] In this case, the Court assumed that the related compensatory damages were taxable as ordinary income. The court concluded: "It would be an anomaly that could not be justified in the absence of clear congressional intent to say that a recovery for actual damages is taxable but not the additional amounts extracted as punishment for the same conduct which caused the injury."[24]

The Court in *Glenshaw Glass* addressed the recovery of lost profits only. The Supreme Court reviewed this case in response to the lower court holding that the punitive portion was nontaxable. In this context, then, the Court's opinion is not necessarily authority that punitive damages are always ordinary income; this issue has never been addressed directly by any court.[25]

Deduction of Recoveries

Internal Revenue Code § 186 provides a deduction from income for certain recoveries with respect to compensatory injuries. Section 186 defines compensatory injuries as injuries from patent infringement, breach of contract or fiduciary duty, or an antitrust injury under § 4 of the Clayton Act. The deduction reduces the amount required to be included in income to the extent that the losses to which it relates did not previously give rise to a tax benefit. This is not an exclusion from taxes but rather a reduction or offset of the amount includable that may have to be reported.

The deduction is limited to the lesser of:

1. The amount received or accrued as damages for the recovery of such compensatory injury, or
2. Unrecovered net operating losses (NOLs) sustained as a result of the compensatory injury (reduced by losses and amounts previously allowed under Section 186).

The following example from the regulations, illustrates the application of § 186.[26]
Example:

(i) As of the beginning of his taxable year 1969, taxpayer A has a net operating loss carry-over from his taxable year 1966 of $550 of which $250 is attributable to a compensable injury. In addition, he has a net operating loss attributable to the compensable injury of $150 with respect to which the period for carryover under section 172 has expired without benefit to the taxpayer. In year four, he receives a $100 compensatory amount with respect to that injury and he has $75 in other income. Thus, A in 1969 has gross income of $175 and he is entitled to a $100 deduction (the compensatory amount received) under section 186(a) and this section (of regulations) since this amount is less than the unrecovered losses sustain as a result of the compensable injury ($250 + $150 = $400). No portion of the net operating loss carryover to the current taxable year attributable to the compensable injury is reduced under section 186(e) since the amount determined under section 186(e)(1) $100—does not exceed the amount determined under section 186(e)(2) $150. Therefore, A applies a net operating loss carryover of $550 against his remaining income of $75 and retains a net operating loss carryover of $475 to following years, of which amount $250 remains attributable to the compensable injury. In addition, he retains $50 of net operating losses attributable to the compensable injury with respect to which the period for carryover under section 172 has expired without benefit to the taxpayer.

PROOF REQUIRED TO SUBSTANTIATE CLAIM

As already mentioned, the Internal Revenue Service presumes that the recovered amounts are fully includable in income. The taxpayer has responsibility therefore to prove not only the recovery's classification but the basis of the damaged asset as well. For example, in *Raytheon Production Corp. v. Commissioner*,[27] the taxpayer did not prove basis in amounts recovered for the damaged goodwill. The First Circuit Court found no indication that the recovery was for lost profits, but with no proof of the basis of the goodwill damaged, had to find the entire recovery to be taxable. In another case,[28] the Tax Court held that the taxpayer lacked the evidence necessary to overcome the commissioner's determination that all amounts received represented lost profits. The taxpayer had negotiated a general release in an action to recover damages both from lost profits and from destruction of goodwill but failed to state on the release what amount was for destruction of goodwill.

The complaint should clarify whether the amounts sought represent lost profits, capital gain, or return of capital. In Rev. Rul 85-98,[29] the IRS reiterated its position that the complaint contains the most persuasive evidence of the recovery's character. For example, when the complaint seeks to recover for lost profits, the taxpayer will have a difficult time later claiming capital gain treatment.[30]

If remedy is received through judicial process, the judgment may allocate damages recovered to various components. The evidence brought to trial may support or deny the tax attributes when the taxpayer has to substantiate a position. Litigants should consider this when formulating arguments in favor of the tax treatment desired.

TREATMENT OF PAYMENTS BY PAYOR

General Rule under § 162

Payments made for compensatory damages are often deductible as ordinary and necessary business expenses under Internal Revenue Code § 162. Specifically, payments may be currently deductible or may have to be capitalized. Some amounts capitalized may not be depreciable or amortizable. The general rule that the underlying claim determines tax treatment also applies here: The defendant must capitalize payment to settle a claim relating to the sale of a capital asset, whereas the defendant may currently deduct settlement of a negligence claim.

The Seventh Circuit Court in *Anchor Coupling*[31] found that an amount paid to settle an alleged contract for the sale of the taxpayer's assets to be a nondeductible capital expenditure. In another case, the taxpayer's refinery caused severe damage to adjacent property, and he settled the suit by purchasing the property. The court ruled that the entire purchase price, including attorneys' fees, was a nondeductible capital expenditure.[32] In *Vermont Bank & Trust Co. v. United States*,[33] the Court found that payments to dissenting shareholders, who objected to a merger, were additional costs of the shares and, as such, were a nondeductible capital expenditure.

Punitive Damages Paid in Antitrust Cases

Punitive damage awards in an antitrust case are deductible under the general rules described above if no criminal proceeding under the federal antitrust laws is pending against the taxpayer or if the criminal proceeding is dismissed or ends in acquittal. Internal Revenue Code § 162(g) disallows, however, a deduction for the punitive portions of antitrust awards if a criminal conviction in a related case or a plea of guilty or nolo contendere either precedes or follows the payment. What constitutes a "related" case is a question of fact.[34]

Personal Injury Award

Payments made for settlements in personal actions are nondeductible. As a rule, all personal expenditures are nondeductible unless the code specifically identifies a deduction. The code does not provide a deduction for personal injury damage payments.

General Rule under Section 212

Section 212 provides for the deduction of expenses paid for the production of income; however expenses relating to capital assets must be capitalized. For example, in *United States v. Wheeler*,[35] a payment to settle a suit for the specific performance of a contract to sell stock was held to be a capital expenditure, which increased the basis of the acquired stock. The Court held the taxpayer settled in defense or protection of his title to the stock and the payment was, therefore, nondeductible. Where Code § 162 allows a business to deduct legal fees in connection with a litigation, an individual can deduct legal fees only to the extent they are for the production of income, providing they are not more properly characterized as capital expenditures. For example, expenses incurred in an action to recover damages relating to a personal automobile constitute personal expenditures and are not deductible. If, however, an action sought to recover losses to investments, the losses would be treated as capital losses, and the legal fees would be either deducted or capitalized.

The concept that the claim's origin controls the recovery's character was developed within the context of whether litigation expenses were deductible business expenses or nondeductible personal expenses. In *United States v. Gilmore*,[36] the taxpayer believed that if he lost the divorce proceeding, his controlling stock interest in his General Motors auto dealerships would be threatened and that the proceeding, by damaging his reputation, would endanger his ability to renew the General Motors franchise. The Court of Claims allowed 80 percent of the expenses to be deducted as business expenses, but the Supreme Court reversed the decision, ruling that the origin of claims test controlled. The origin of the claim in this case stemmed from a personal proceeding, divorce litigation, and not from an action in a business context. The litigation expenses were therefore ruled nondeductible.

EXHIBIT OF GENERAL RULES—TAX TREATMENT OF SETTLEMENTS AND JUDGMENTS

The following exhibit reflects the general rules regarding the tax treatment of settlements and judgments for recipients and payors.

EXHIBIT 33-1. GENERAL RULES—TAX TREATMENT OF SETTLEMENTS AND JUDGMENTS

	Ordinary Income	Capital Gain	Nontaxable
Tax consequences to recipient			
Business injuries			
Lost profits	×		
Damages to capital assets		×	
Damages to goodwill		×	
Punitive damages	×		
Personal injuries			
Compensatory damages			×
Punitive damages			×

(*Exhibit continues on p. 622.*)

EXHIBIT 33-1. *(Continued)*

	Deductible	Must Capitalize	Nondeductible
Tax consequences to payor			
Business injuries			
Lost profits	×		
Damages to capital assets		×	
Damages to goodwill		×	
Punitive damages, no criminal suit	×		
Punitive damages, criminal suit			×
Personal injuries			×

NOTES

1. *United States v. Gilmore*, 372 U.S. 39 (1963).
2. *Collins v. Commissioner*, 18 T.C.M. (CCH) 756 (1959).
3. Rev. Rul. 55-264, 1955-1, C.B. 11.
4. *Sager Glove Corp. v. Commissioner*, 311 F.2d 210 (7th Cir. Ill. 1963).
5. *Durkee v. Commissioner*, 8 T.C.M. (CCH) 701 (1949).
6. See IRC Sections 1245 and 1250.
7. See *Glenshaw Glass Co. v. Commissioner*, 18 T.C. 860 (1952).
8. *Bent v. Commissioner*, 835 F.2d 67 (3d Cir. 1987).
9. Rev. Rul. 58-418, 1958-2, C.B. 18.
10. Rev. Rul. 75-45, 1975-1, C.B. 47.
11. Rev. Rul. 84-108, 1984-2, C.B. 32.
12. *Roemer v. Commissioner*, 79 T.C. 398 (1982), rev'd, 716 F.2d 693 (9th Cir. 1983).
13. Rev. Rul. 85-143, 1985-37 IRB 7.
14. *Threlkeld v. Commissioner*, 87 T.C. 1294 (1986).
15. 15 USC §§ 1–7.
16. 15 USC §§ 12–27.
17. 15 USC §§ 41–58.
18. 15 USC §§ 13–13b, 21a.
19. *Durkee*, supra.
20. Rev. Proc. 67-33, 1967-2 C.B. 659.
21. 15 USC § 15.
22. Rev. Rul. 67-33, 1967-2 C.B. 659.
23. *Commissioner v. Glenshaw Glass Co.*, 348 U.S. 426 (1955).
24. Ibid, p. 431.
25. But see *Freeman v. Commissioner*, 33 T.C. 323, 328 (1959) where the Tax Court indicated in dictum that it agreed with the IRS that punitive damages are taxed as ordinary income.
26. Reg. § 1.186-1(f).
27. *Raytheon Production Corp. v. Commissioner*, 144 F.2d 110 (1st Cir. 1944).
28. *W. Walley, Inc. v. Commissioner*, 7 T.C.M. (CCH) 137 (1948).
29. Rev. Rul. 85-98, 1985-2 C.B. 51.
30. *Agar v. Commissioner*, 290 F.2d 283 (2d Cir. 1961).
31. *Anchor Coupling Co., Inc. v. United States*, 427 F.2d 429 (7th Cir. 1970).
32. *Clark Oil and Refining Corp. v. United States*, 473 F.2d 1217 (7th Cir. 1973).
33. *Vermont Bank & Trust Co. v. United States*, 296 F. Supp. 682 (D.Vt. 1969).
34. See Reg. Section 1.162-22(f), Examples 1, 2, and 3.

35. *United States v. Wheeler*, 311 F.2d 60 (5th Cir. 1953).
36. *Supra*, Note 1.

LIST OF CASES

Agar v. Commissioner, 290 F.2d 283 (2d Cir. 1961)
Anchor Coupling Co., Inc. v. United States, 427 F.2d 429 (7th Cir. 1970)
Bent v. Commissioner, 835 F.2d 67 (3rd Cir. 1987)
Clark Oil and Refining Corp. v. United States, 473 F.2d 1217 (7th Cir. 1973)
Collins v. Commissioner, 18 T.C.M. (CCH) 756 (1959)
Commissioner v. Glenshaw Glass Co., 348 U.S. 426 (1955)
Durkee v. Commissioner, 8 T.C.M. (CCH) 701 (1949)
Freeman v. Commissioner, 33 T.C. 323 (1959)
Glenshaw Glass Co. v. Commissioner, 18 T.C. 860 (1952), rev'd., 348 U.S. 426 (1955)
Raytheon Production Corp. v. Commissioner, 144 F.2d 110 (1st Cir. 1944)
Roemer v. Commissioner, 79 T.C. 398 (1982), rev'd., 716 F.2d 693 (9th Cir. 1983)
Sager Glove Corp. v. Commissioner, 311 F.2d 210 (7th Cir. 1962)
Threlkeld v. Commissioner, 87 T.C. 1294 (1986)
United States v. Gilmore, 372 U.S. 39 (1963)
United States v. Wheeler, 311 F.2d 60 (5th Cir. 1953)
Vermont Bank & Trust Co. v. United States, 296 F. Supp. 682 (D. Vt. 1969)
W. Walley, Inc. v. Commissioner, 7 T.C.M. (CCH) 137 (1948)

34

TAX FRAUD CASES

Marshall W. Taylor, JD
Howard R. Sheppard, CPA

INTRODUCTION TO THE LAW OF TAX FRAUD AND RELATED CRIMES

Tax Fraud Cases and the Accountant

The Internal Revenue Code provides both criminal and civil sanctions for tax fraud, together with civil penalties for negligence. In both a legal and ethical sense, the shading from tax negligence into tax fraud is often indistinct, leaving laypersons and experienced practitioners alike sometimes baffled by the IRS's choice of prosecution targets.

The Internal Revenue Service (IRS) cannot audit every return nor prosecute every tax violation. Consequently, in carrying out the enforcement mandate from Congress, the IRS attempts to apply its resources to maximize the objective of enhancing voluntary compliance.

Thus the Internal Revenue Service and Department of Justice (DOJ) appear to focus on perceived areas of chronic abuse, in hopes that prosecutions will deter others contemplating similar offenses. For example, in recent years, promoters of abusive tax shelters have been visible prosecution targets. Similarly, prosecutions of narcotic traffickers large and small have been intensified.

For many years, the government has selected well-known people as targets.[1] The IRS believes that the sight of the famous being prosecuted will create impetus for voluntary compliance by the general public.

The Internal Revenue Service usually assigns experienced special agents for pretrial preparation and court testimony in tax fraud prosecutions. These agents are well qualified and in most cases perform an outstanding job. The high success rate of convictions in tax fraud cases brought to court is evidence of the thorough preparation work by these government agents.

The accountant who is requested to assist counsel in the investigation or defense of a criminal tax fraud case should consider carefully the demands for time and specialized knowledge before accepting the engagement. Where a criminal investigation is ill-founded or a prosecuted case is based on incorrectly interpreted evidence, the forensic accountant can become the pivot point of the defense.

In a tax fraud criminal investigation, the accused's attorney should immediately engage a forensic accountant. The government should be persuaded, if at all possible, to abandon the investigation in the preindictment phase because even a successfully defended tax fraud prosecution can devastate the defendant's business and personal reputation. Consequently, this chapter focuses on litigation services not only for court testimony and related accounting support but also in a broader sense including administrative litigation. The substantive principles are the same, and the accountant is just as apt to find his services called for in the administrative arena as in court.

Most criminal tax investigations requiring accounting support work usually involve suspicion of one or more of four crimes: evasion, failure to file, false statements on returns, or aiding/abetting. The foundation of these will be accounting computations.

Tax Evasion: General Principles

Criminal and Civil Tax Evasion Cases. The most serious tax crime is tax evasion (I.R.C. § 7201). Tax evasion is also punishable with a civil penalty, which stands as of this writing as 75 percent of the portion of the tax deficiency attributable to fraud, together with interest on the penalty from the return's due date (I.R.C. § 6653(b)).

The legal criteria for either criminal evasion or civil fraud are the same: a tax underpayment accompanied by fraudulent intent. Fraudulent intent is the "intentional violation of a known legal duty."[2]

Criminal tax fraud matters are tried in the Federal District Court. The defendant may elect a jury trial.

Civil tax fraud cases may be tried in the Tax Court, or after assessment and payment in either the Federal District Court or the U.S. Claims Court. Jury trials, available for either civil or criminal tax matters, are permitted only in the Federal District Court. Choice of a forum in civil tax trials is entirely at the taxpayer's option because the taxpayer is the plaintiff or petitioner under both options.

Evidence of Fraudulent Intent. Fraudulent intent is almost invariably proven by circumstantial evidence falling into one of two categories: evidence of surreptitious behavior lacking reasonable and honest explanation and evidence of repeated pattern of understatement.

In *Spies v. United States*, 317 U.S. 492 (1943), the Supreme Court provided a sample list of suspicious practices from which one may infer fraudulent intent. These include dealing in cash where normal taxpayers would not do so, maintaining duplicate sets of books, making false entries on documents, destroying evidence, making evasive or false statements in audit, and hiding assets.

Because of the importance of pattern as circumstantial evidence, single-year cases are not preferred, unless the taxpayer has blatantly omitted income or claimed false deductions. Otherwise, the government prefers proof of significant understatements for 3 years or more. A pattern of noncompliance negates the defense of inadvertence and provides circumstantial proof of intent. Indeed, it has been held more than once that the government has a *prima facie* case on proof of pattern alone.

Obviously, therefore, accounting computations are the bedrock of tax prosecutions. Many cases can be defended effectively, especially at the preindictment phase, by accounting defenses that negate the existence of the 3-year pattern or undercut its circumstantial evidentiary usefulness. The defense focuses on the forensic accountant's work in such cases.

Where a 3-year understatement occurs, the defendant's accountant must carefully scrutinize the preparer's workpapers to ascertain whether any of the fault properly may be laid at the preparer's door.

Indeed, both sides consider the taxpayer's preparer to be a key player. The taxpayer will blame the preparer for all the ills of the tax return. The government will wish to call the preparer as a witness for two classes of testimony: first, that the client received clear instructions regarding proper accounting treatment of tax matters, thereby negating the defense of ignorance; second, to attribute any gaps on the return to the taxpayer's nondisclosure rather than the preparer's omissions or concealments. Nondisclosure to the accountant of secret cash transactions, additional bank accounts, sales of capital items, and the like are the grist of criminal tax prosecutions. The preparer's testimony removes the preparer as an intervening factor responsible for the underreporting on the return.

Of course, tax preparers may be culpable in tax fraud matters. See *United States v. Miller*, 529 F.2d 1125 (9th Cir. 1976), and *United States v. Burks*, 508 F.2d 672 (5th Cir 1975), where the tax preparer was convicted of preparing false tax returns.

Patterns of Evasion

General—Omission of Income. Though most tax evasion schemes fall into identifiable categories, many taxpayers' efforts to defraud the IRS bear the stamp of the individual taxpayer's personality.[3] Some will be brazen, some stupid, some intricate and clever. The most important of the classes of major tax fraud is omission of income through understatement of gross receipts. The schemes range from crude to exceedingly devious. Sometimes friends or trusted business associates or subordinates are in on the secret and other times not. As often as not, the IRS discovers the underreporting through disclosures from former friends or subordinates who know of the scheme.

Perhaps the most common tax fraud scheme, especially among retail merchants and some kinds of professionals, is the practice known as "skimming": taking some portion, sometimes all, of the cash receipts of a business enterprise and not reporting it to the government. Many taxpayers engaged in skimming leave behind damaging evidence in the form of duplicate books of account, one purporting to be true, and one "for the government." The duplicate books are frequently revealed to potential purchasers of the business. The government often discovers purported tax returns with seemingly inflated income figures that the taxpayer submits to banks in support of loan applications.

The cleverest skimming practitioners limit the practice to a percentage of the gross of the business that is small enough to avoid distorting other figures. Where the receipts of a business are all cash, the skimming would therefore be a small percentage of the total cash receipts. Where the business receives mostly checks and charge tickets, the skimming may be a substantial percentage of the cash received.

The government's attack on a well-conceived skimming scheme is difficult to launch. Of course, a taxpayer who brings the skimmed cash into the open by depositing it into bank or brokerage accounts, or by making large cash purchases of real estate, automobiles, or the like, simplifies the government's job. Many taxpayers are more devious, however, using the skimmed cash only as spending money for meals, trips, small luxury items, and the like. Tracing these expenditures is nearly impossible, and unless the government can secure customer lists or other evidence to reconstruct income directly, it is unlikely to prosecute for skimmed cash spent so discreetly.

Another device, more often used where the business receipts come in the form of checks, is to use dummy or foreign entities to receive diverted gross receipts. Such entities are particularly common for a business with foreign connections or operations. The practice of using dummy entities is difficult to detect. Once detected, however, these entities condemn a taxpayer because no legitimate explanation exists for this practice.

Many taxpayers with closely held corporations, apparently oblivious to the threat of criminal prosecution, will divert streams, in fact sometimes floods, of corporate gross receipts directly into their personal bank accounts and then fail to report the income at either the corporate or the personal level. Almost invariably the taxpayer with this problem claims that the tax preparer was fully aware of every relevant fact, had been provided personal bank statements, and had chosen not to report the diverted income stream. Naturally this claim is stoutly denied by the accountant, who faces felony charges if the taxpayer's assertions are true.

A variation on the foregoing arises where the taxpayer, claiming "sloppy recordkeeping," places the proceeds of occasional business sales (for example pieces of jewelry, automobiles, or other high-value items) into the personal bank account. Almost always, the taxpayer then tells the accountant that all the business income is deposited into the business account. The result is failure to report the bypass transaction.

Employee taxpayers often give employers false names or social security numbers for payroll purposes. The taxpayer receives wages either in the form of cash or establishes a bank account to cash the employer checks. Petty cleverness often trips up the participants because frequently the employer will withhold more income tax than is ultimately warranted, and the taxpayer then has difficulty claiming a refund for the excess withholdings.

A surprising number of professional people, including doctors, lawyers, and accountants—even those with specialized tax training—find themselves in a criminal tax investigation for unreported gross receipts.

Unreported Gross Income—Claimed Mistake. Most cases involving unreported gross receipts involve manipulation or secretiveness. Sometimes, however, the government will seek to prosecute taxpayers for unreported gross receipts that the taxpayer claims are arguably excludable, or at the least not reportable in the tax year in question. This type of case will often involve some speculation about the taxpayer's motives, thus making it a rather questionable vehicle for prosecution. The government's record in these cases is sporadic. Thus, in *United States v. Heller*, 830 F.2d 150 (11th Cir. 1987), the court of appeals overturned the conviction of an attorney who was prosecuted for failing to report gross deposits in his trust account that he argued were as yet unearned under his consistent method of accounting. In *United States v. Pomponio*, 429 U.S. 10 (1976), the government successfully prosecuted corporate shareholders for booking dividends as loans and for claiming corporate tax deductions on their personal returns.

We may see a decline in good faith controversies that materialize as tax fraud cases. The substantial understatement penalty under I.R.C. § 6661 provides a heavy disincentive for the taxpayer's taking aggressive positions without disclosure.

Should the return disclose the taxpayer's position, only remarkable circumstantial evidence would then subject the return to criminal prosecution.

Omission of Income from Sale of Assets. Frequently taxpayers omit income from major casual sales of assets. Sometimes this omission may arise from lack of sophistication in tax matters, ignorance, for example, of the requirement to report profit from sale of collector's items. Prosecuting such cases can become difficult.

On the other hand, consider a sale of a substantial asset, such as a piece of land held for profit by a taxpayer sophisticated in tax matters and that generates most of the taxpayer's available cash resources for the year. Failure to report such a transaction generates an almost prima facie criminal case. The government uses the "specific item" method to prove its case, alleging either evasion or false statements (I.R.C. § 7206(10)). If the government alleges false statements, it need not prove underpayment, only the failure to report.

Omission of Second Businesses and Casual Income. A favorite prosecution target is omitted second businesses. For example, the taxpayer may be fully employed as a gasoline station owner and have a second income from the sale of Halloween pumpkins that simply fails to appear on the tax return. The taxpayer's affairs are coherent, consistent, and fully explainable by only the primary occupation; the government will discover the second income only after considerable digging or with sheer blind luck. Deviousness of this kind, when discovered, is extremely damaging to the taxpayer later claiming to have innocently forgotten to report the business.

Casual cash income from hobby activities, swap-meet sales, handyman activity, and the like, the "gray market" of the American economy, no doubt generates staggering lost revenues for the Treasury. Problems with proving these violations prevent effective policing by the threat of criminal prosecution.

Fictitious Deductions. Fictitious deductions on personal returns present a problem in policing the compliance of wage earners. Such taxpayers frequently claim nonexistent charitable contributions, doctor bills, interest expense, child-care expenses, and the like. This is middle America's tax crime. The total of the false deductions on an individual return will not usually be considered appropriate for criminal prosecution, but the taxpayer frequently submits false substantiating documents in panic during an audit. This is a misdemeanor offense under I.R.C. § 7207 and has been frequently prosecuted, often for trivial offenses.

Two types of fictitious deductions are encountered in closely held corporations: (1) Corporate monies paid out for the owner's benefit—for example, expenditures labeled as repairs are in fact home remodeling for the company's owner. These expenditures are real and actually paid to third parties. They simply are not for the purposes claimed. (2) Corporate monies diverted to the owners for fictitious expenses, often to fictitious entities controlled by the owners. A variation of this occurs when trusted employees, not the owners, embezzle funds from the corporation by payments to dummy entities. In either case, the canceled checks create an audit trail to substantiate entries for taxable deductions, but they are necessary for executing fraudulent conduct. Unscrambling 2 or 3 years' of such activity can challenge even a sophisticated forensic accountant.

Other Tax Fraud Crimes: Failure to File, False Statements, Aiding and Abetting

In addition to felony evasion, the other crimes that taxpayers most frequently face are failure to file (a misdemeanor) and two other felonies—false statements on a tax return and aiding and abetting.

Failure to file, though a misdemeanor (I.R.C. § 7203), is a serious offense. The 1-year jail term possible for each unfiled return could result in a longer term of imprisonment than usually suffered by evaders. To obtain a conviction, the government need not prove a tax deficiency, though existence of an actual tax deficiency is strong circumstantial proof of intent. The elements of the crime are income sufficient to meet the minimum filing requirement, knowledge of the filing requirement, and intentional failure to file.

The perjury statute, I.R.C. § 7206(1), requires the "making" of a return (generally regarded as the taxpayer's duty, but also held to include a preparer's work as well), making a false entry on the return, and knowledge that the entry was false. This provision is often used as a proxy for evasion prosecutions where gaps in the government's knowledge enable the taxpayer to show reasonable doubt as to a tax deficiency. Because the sanction for false statements is almost as drastic as the sanction for evasion and the proof requirements are considerably more relaxed, prosecuting attorneys like this weapon. Often, the government is prepared to prove a tax understatement even when bringing the proceeding under the less rigorous requirements of § 7206(1) because proof of understatement is regarded as significant circumstantial evidence of motive for the false statements.

Aiding and abetting, principally a crime charged against preparers, falls under another subsection of § 7206, specifically subsection (2). Like subsection 7206(1), subsection (2) has comparative lack of rigor in the proof requirements. Again, this section requires no proof of understatement of tax, *Edwards v. United States*, 375 F.2d 862 (9th Cir. 1967), though, for the same reasons as with 7206(1), proof of understatement is often presented anyway. See *United States v. Hooks*, 848 F.2d 785 (7th Cir. 1988), where the appellate court, in affirming a conviction under § 7206(2), noted the size of the evaded tax deficiency in its opinion. Aiding and abetting has also been charged against the taxpayer where the taxpayer supplied false numbers to an unwitting accountant. See *United States v. Greger*, 716 F.2d 1275 (9th Cir. 1983).

The frequency with which the government tries to prove an understatement gives the accountant as significant a role in prosecutions under §§ 7203 and 7206(1) and (2) as occurs in cases brought under § 7201.

Defense Issues Common to Criminal Tax Cases

Taxpayer intent separates the hundreds of thousands of civil cases involving adjustments for increased tax from the few criminal cases prosecuted annually. Mistakes, negligence, even recklessness, do not in theory give rise to criminal liability.

Patterns of error can be strong circumstantial proof of guilt or innocence. Guilt is implied where errors consistently favor the taxpayer. Innocence is generally implied by random mistakes appearing both for and against the taxpayer. Patterns suggesting that expense items are omitted to divert attention from unreported gross receipts imply guilt. Demonstrated math errors, if not so repetitious as to be suspicious in themselves, are usually considered innocent errors. Any pattern that cannot be rationally reconciled with innocence, which consistently results in understatement and which cannot likely have arisen by accident, will be a very compelling indicator of guilt.

Deception and Concealment. Any demonstrable pattern of deception is damaging circumstantial evidence of fraud. Deception and concealment occurring during the tax year create overwhelming evidence. Deception during the audit phase is more ambiguous because the motive to deceive can arise from late discovery of innocent error. This is the "audit panic" defense seen in some criminal tax cases. The presentation of false statements and documents during civil audit can give rise to actionable criminal charges, but tax evasion (and civil fraud) is generally proven only if the taxable understatement arose from fraudulent intent at or before the time the return was filed. Subsequent evasive conduct is therefore not considered evasion, though it is frequently cited as circumstantial proof of evasion or evidence of a continuing course of conduct.

Mistake. Because tax fraud involves the intentional violation of a known legal duty, no taxpayer may, in theory, be convicted of mere mistakes.

Mistake of fact, for example, mistaken belief as to whether a taxable event had occurred, occasionally presents a fruitful area of dispute, but more interesting problems arise when the taxpayer claims to have misunderstood the requirements of the law. The courts have recognized that where the law was unclear, prosecution cannot follow from the taxpayer's having taken the more aggressive position.

Disagreement about what the law *provides* differs from disagreement about what the law *should be*. Tax protestors find no safe haven in the defense of mistake. Neither the individuals claiming that the taxing system is inherently illegal nor those who claim exclusion from tax because of conscientious objection can use the sincerity of their beliefs to bar prosecution.

Expert Advice. The defense of mistake closely relates to the frequent claim that the taxpayer's accountant has caused the problems on the return. The claim of accountant fault may fall into one of two classes. First, the taxpayer may claim that the accountant expressly advised a course of action later discovered to be illegal. Second, the accountant may be charged with carelessness—omitting disclosed material and the like. These claims are both effective defenses, if true. The government works very hard to deprive the taxpayer of this defense by an early visit to the accountant and a thorough interview or even sworn question-and-answer session. The constant threat of criminal charges compels many accountants to cooperate.

The defense of reliance on expert advice often terminates the investigation at an early stage.

If the government presses on, however, the taxpayer finds a hostile environment in court. The defense may need to prove that (1) the taxpayer gave the advisor all pertinent information bearing on the question; (2) the taxpayer relied on the advice; (3) the taxpayer had reasonable cause to believe the advice was accurate; and (4) the advisor was qualified to give the advice. (See *United States v. Samara*, 643 F.2d 701 (10th Cir. 1981); *United States v. Conforte*, 624 F.2d 869 (9th Cir. 1980).

Delegations of Responsibility. Delegation of responsibility will not avoid civil penalties such as the penalty for failure to file a tax return on time. For example, in *United States v. Boyle*, 469 U.S. 241 (1985), the court held that an executor, whether or not behaving reasonably in so doing, could not delegate the responsibility to file the estate tax return to an attorney and thus relieve the estate of liability for the 25-percent failure to file penalty.

This harsh rule does not apply to criminal tax law. Because criminal responsibility hinges on intentional violation of a known legal duty, delegation, no matter how ill advised, would normally relieve the taxpayer of criminal responsibility. This is true whether the delegated tasks relate to family or business accounting or to preparation of the tax return itself.

Special Characteristics of the Taxpayer. In general, personal characteristics that indicate sophistication and competence in tax matters will weigh against a taxpayer prosecuted for tax fraud. Because of the specific intent requirements of tax fraud, taxpayer characteristics that interfere with the ability to comply or that establish lack of personal sophistication tend also to attenuate criminal responsibility.

A good example of the increased care required of sophisticated taxpayers occurred in the case of a lawyer/CPA with a master's in taxation from New York University: *United States v. Diamond*, 788 F.2d 1025 (4th Cir. 1986). His protestations that the law was unclear on the deductibility of options losses were found not credible.

Taxpayers frequently claim that the failure to comply has arisen from chronic sloppiness, confusion, poor record keeping, and the like. Though this is theoretically an acceptable defense, it encounters deep skepticism among IRS special agents. If one anticipates chronic sloppiness as a realistic defense, it should be documented, if possible, by clear photos of the shambles in the taxpayer's business offices, together with notarized statements from fact witnesses at the earliest opportunity.

Disabilities or background elements tending to frustrate the taxpayer's honest efforts to comply will serve as effective defense arguments. Deep language deficiencies, illiteracy, emotional or physical ailments interfering with intellectual capacity typify such defenses. See for example, *United States v. Venuto*, 182 F.2d 519 (3d Cir. 1950), where the defendant proved that he was illiterate, able to read or write little beyond his own name, and that the entire task of his accounting and tax reporting was performed by an "itinerant bookkeeper" whose main business was selling insurance to merchants.

Burden of Proof in Civil and Criminal Tax Fraud Proceedings. In criminal prosecutions, the defendant has the presumption of innocence, and the government has a burden of establishing the elements of the offense beyond a reasonable doubt. In a jury trial, some judges instruct the jury that the government also has the burden of making its case intelligible.

In civil tax matters, the taxpayer, as in any other tax matter, has the burden of disproving the alleged tax deficiency. The government has the burden of proof (preponderance of the evidence) whether the fraud penalty applies. The government's principal task is to amass sufficient circumstantial evidence to demonstrate the intent to evade.

After a successful criminal prosecution, the government can usually use the legal concept of "collateral estoppel," which prevents previously decided matters from relitigation, to meet its burden of proof in a civil case without further evidence.

This result occurs even when the conviction has arisen from a plea bargain. Many practitioners attempt to avoid this result by offering a plea of no contest. Generally, the government will not accept such a plea.

Statutes of Limitations—Civil and Criminal

I.R.C. § 6531 sets the statute of limitations for all tax fraud criminal matters at 6 years from the date of the offense (generally the filing date, or if later, the return's due date). Within this time, an action must have begun, either by grand jury indictment, or, if the defense waives indictment, then criminal information (a simple pleading drafted by the prosecuting attorney). A special procedure, rarely utilized, also exists for filing a complaint to toll the statute of limitations.

The government has argued that when a taxpayer continues cover-up activities during the audit or investigation, the statute of limitations should be extended on the theory that the continuation of the offense prevents the limitations period from beginning to run. See for example, *United States v. Beacon Brass*, 344 U.S. 43 (1952). The government is understandably reluctant to rely on this theory because of its unpredictability.

On the civil side, no statute of limitations exists for the assessment of additional tax amounts (and the fraud penalty) where the tax understatement is attributable to fraud. (By comparison, the normal civil statute is 3 years from the filing date of the return, unless extended by certain statutory exceptions or an agreement between the government and the taxpayer.) Obviously practical limitations exist on the availability of documentary proof and useful witness memories in most cases beyond the 6-year criminal period.

Requests for Statute of Limitations Waiver. While a criminal tax matter is under investigation or prosecution, the government frequently approaches the taxpayer to extend the normal 3-year civil statute of limitations. A number of factors are relevant to the consideration of this question. Once the government has allowed the 3-year period to pass without mailing a deficiency notice, assessment of additional taxes is possible only if the government proves a civil fraud case against the taxpayer. The temptation to roll the dice and win all if the investigation is discontinued or unsuccessful prompts many to refuse the civil waiver. The government gives up a criminal case and possibly substantial tax deficiencies as well. This additional pressure may keep a marginal criminal case alive where it would otherwise be abandoned and will certainly result in the assertion of the fraud penalty in any later civil audit.

These concerns should generally prompt the taxpayer to sign the waiver. The later civil audit may eventually close amicably without the stigma of the fraud penalty. Furthermore, taxes involving the fraud penalty are nondischargeable in a liquidating bankruptcy should the taxpayer later need this remedy. With a signed waiver, the government examiner, unaware of this factor, may settle for less than the fraud penalty, causing the government to lose all in a subsequent bankruptcy proceeding.

DEALING WITH THE IRS DURING THE PREINDICTMENT PHASES OF A CRIMINAL TAX INVESTIGATION

Criminal Tax Procedure

The Players in a Criminal Tax Investigation. Most criminal tax fraud cases are developed through administrative investigations by commissioned special agents of the Internal Revenue Service. These special agents focus on developing evidence of tax crimes by interviewing witnesses and collecting documentary evidence.

A civil tax examiner called the "co-operating revenue agent" usually accompanies the special agent (*Handbook for Special Agents*, § 3(10)5.2.) The cooperating revenue agent prepares the accounting detail workup, controls the statutes of limitations on the returns under investigation, witnesses crucial interviews, researches technical questions of tax law, and controls the case for civil disposition of any resulting tax deficiencies after the criminal phase is completed.

The special agent may have legal counsel, a staff attorney from the chief counsel's office of the IRS. This attorney may play an advisory role on constitutional and legal problems relating to investigative techniques, may direct or suggest the nature and sources of evidence to be secured, or may suggest alternative legal theories for investigation. The attorney may also play a supporting role on technical matters in drafting administrative summonses and might interface with the Department of Justice should search warrants be needed. The taxpayer and the taxpayer's counsel would rarely be aware of the district counsel attorney's involvement in the investigative stages.

On rare occasions, the Department of Justice also involves a member of its staff, either in the Washington office or in the local office of the United States Attorney. This attorney would facilitate matters that involve district court presentations or to provide Department of Justice input into the investigative process.

The Phases of a Criminal Tax Investigation. The special agent performs the fieldwork to develop the case and recommends either to discontinue the investigation or to prosecute. An extended narrative report—called the Special Agent's Report (SAR)— supports the recommendation by setting forth the background of the case, offenses charged, and a summary of the evidence that supports the charges. Voluminous tabbed exhibits accompany the SAR. The SAR is zealously protected as confidential, as are the exhibits.

The taxpayer usually has an opportunity to protest the proposed prosecution by conference with the special agent's supervisor. Prosecutions are rarely dropped because of advocacy at the group manager level. These conferences are usually used as mechanisms for each party to secure a feeling for the other's case.

If the group manager affirms the decision to recommend prosecution, the matter is referred to the IRS's house counsel, the district counsel's office, for review of legal sufficiency of the prosecution. Another conference occurs at this level. As with the group manager conference, the parties use this opportunity to sound each other out. At this level, however, district counsel often recommends terminating the prosecution.

The district counsel's job is to review the file with two questions in mind. Does the reviewing attorney believe that the charged party is guilty? Does the attorney believe that the evidence in the file will support the burden of proof necessary for conviction? Because practitioners have blundered into supplying the district counsel with crucial missing evidence, this stage warrants great care.

If the district counsel decides to support prosecution, the case is referred to the Department of Justice for prosecution via a Criminal Reference Letter (CRL). If the district counsel regards the case as promising but flawed, he will refer the case back to the special agent for further development. If the case is regarded as hopeless, the matter is terminated through a Criminal Action Memorandum (CAM). The special agent or the agent's manager may protest adverse determinations through channels.

Cases referred for prosecution to the Department of Justice are reviewed in Washington, DC, by a staff trial attorney of the department. The taxpayer may request another conference at this juncture. The same opportunities and caveats apply to this conference as apply to those previously discussed. The conference probably has merit because the government's attorney may reveal something significant or useful to taxpayer's counsel, and cases are killed often enough in Washington to warrant the effort.

The decision to present all of the defense's accounting evidence should be made carefully. Certainly, if the evidence overwhelmingly demonstrates the taxpayer's innocence, the taxpayer should try to halt the case when it is still in the relatively private preindictment stages. But in questionable cases, it may well be more prudent to withhold a full presentation before trial because the revelation to the government of the taxpayer's strengths will present the government with ample opportunity to rework its case.

Sources of Criminal Tax Cases. Criminal tax cases, unless arising from grand jury investigations or unusual sources such as narcotics strike forces, usually arise from one of two sources: (1) a civil audit[4] or collection matter that indicates fraud and is referred from the IRS's Examinations or Collections Divisions to the Criminal Investigations Division (CID), or (2) tips from insiders, disgruntled employees, neighbors, former lovers, spouses, and so on. Many meritorious and not so meritorious cases are referred to CID and never opened or worked as criminal cases because of workload constraints. (See, generally, *Special Agents Handbook* § 3(10)3 et seq.)

Sources of Civil Tax Fraud Cases. During an audit, a civil examining agent who discovers indicia of fraud usually must forward the case to the IRS's Criminal Investigations Division (CID) for potential criminal investigation. Consequently, civil fraud audits do not spontaneously arise. A civil tax fraud case will almost always follow a successful criminal prosecution. Civil fraud cases may be investigated if the CID declines to investigate the matters because of workload or other constraints. Civil fraud cases may arise after substantial completion of a civil audit, where, the government decides that the audit's revelations warrant prosecuting a fraud action.

The Civil Aftermath of the Criminal Investigation. In the absence of the taxpayer's complete exoneration in the administrative investigation or at trial, a criminal tax investigation is almost invariably followed by a civil proceeding seeking to impose a tax deficiency and a fraud penalty. Because the criminal undertaking is the principal engine of the case, the mop-up work of the civil deficiencies often lacks the zeal that one might otherwise expect. This does not always benefit the taxpayer because a half-hearted workup can lose as much detail that would benefit the taxpayer as that benefiting the government.

In any civil tax deficiency proceeding, the government must usually satisfy the administrative and judicial requirements specified by I.R.C. § 6211 and subsequent related sections. These requirements are called the "deficiency procedures." The centerpiece of these procedures is the notice of deficiency, which the taxpayer must receive before any tax assessment and that allows the taxpayer to elect for mandatory prepayment judicial review in the U.S. Tax Court of the entire civil matter. A taxpayer convicted of evasion may not relitigate in the subsequent civil case the question of fraud, although he may litigate the size of the tax deficiency. On the contrary, a taxpayer convicted only of false statements may relitigate the elements of fraud other than willful intent.

I.R.S. Handbooks and Manuals. For further information regarding the internal procedures and case development methods of the special agent and the cooperating revenue agent, the accountant should become familiar with the provisions of the *Internal Revenue Manual* governing the Criminal Investigations Division. The public may obtain this immensely informative material, most notably the *Handbook for Special Agents*, through a loose-leaf service published by Commerce Clearing House. Of special interest are the extended examples and instructions for the methods of proof of unreported income. This chapter and the Appendix have incorporated certain portions of the Handbook.

Defense Strategies in the Investigative Phase

Summonses and Other Investigative Techniques—Early Investigative Phases. Usually the special agent opens a criminal investigation by simultaneously deploying a wave of investigative summonses and a surprise home or office interview of the target.

The special agent's first visit to the target can be devastatingly effective. The interview includes the *Miranda*[5] warning (not required by law but dramatic in its emotional effect on the target). The target may provide the special agent with a treasure-trove of admissions that unnecessarily complicate the defense during the investigation's later stages.

Compounding the shock of the special agent's home visit is the amazement and embarrassment when the target discovers that a blizzard of administrative summonses to produce documents has been served on banks, accountants, and business connections or customers. The taxpayer must be notified formally of summonses served on financial recordkeepers and has a mere 20 days to file a motion to quash this type of summons. Other summonses are served secretly and may only later come to light. Usually, the target does not have qualified criminal tax counsel with appropriate procedural knowledge. Often the client goes through several referrals before finding qualified counsel, by which time major procedural rights may have lapsed. Capitalizing on the initial confusion surrounding this potent opening assault, the special agent is apt to quickly collect, or at least secure access to, the bulk of the investigative database. Defense counsel must work intensively with a capable forensic accounting team to come to reliable conclusions about the nature of the defendant's problems and the appropriate strategies. Much of the accountant's work, even if the case goes to trial, will occur in the early weeks of the investigation.

The shift of momentum toward the taxpayer can come in various ways. Adroit counsel can frequently find ways to buy enough time for the forensic accounting team to do its necessary homework. For example, counsel may find appropriate grounds for court challenge to the administrative summonses. The court proceedings can delay the investigation. The examination of the special agent often produces helpful information. Counsel may secure a delay by persuading the special agent that the taxpayer will be able, after preparation, to present analyses to allay the agent's concerns.

During this phase, the defense team must keep abreast of the special agent's activities. The defense must obtain all documents and information that the special agent has received. The defense must approach summoned recordkeepers and request copies of all documents given to the government. Interviewed witnesses must be debriefed, but a word of caution is in order: Do not let the client or other people acting on the client's behalf interview any witnesses. Two people, including counsel for the defense and the accountant or some other observer, should attend each witness interview. Maladroit questioning, especially by the client, can lead to accusations of witness tampering in violation of 18 U.S.C. §§ 1503, 1505. Such accusations can result from seemingly innocuous actions as suggesting to witnesses that they rely on their Fifth Amendment rights.

Whether or not the defense attorney temporarily delays or slows the investigation, the accountant must analyze the taxpayer's affairs to provide the foundation of the defense's strategy. The accountant must have access to all of the taxpayer's documents that might relate to the investigation. The accountant's data must be updated with new information discovered from third parties as the investigation proceeds.

Identification of the Problem Areas. One of the most important tasks confronting the criminal tax defense team is to identify the targeted areas of principal concern to the investigating agents. An audit conducted with sufficient rigor to qualify as the basis for a criminal tax investigation will involve painstaking attention to detail. Because of the expense, the government focuses on preidentified areas of special interest. The accounting support to defend criminal tax investigations requires more effort than to prosecute.

If the criminal tax investigation has arisen from a civil audit, the context and flow of the interrupted audit proceedings may indicate the area(s) of special concern to the government. Constitutional limitations, supported by manual directives, generally require a civil agent, once confronted with evidence of apparent crime, to discontinue the work in progress and refer the case to the Criminal Investigations Division. Thus the subject last under inquiry when the audit was discontinued will often be the area of greatest sensitivity. The client sometimes informs the persons representing him in the audit when the examining agent is nearing sensitive material. Often, therefore, one can easily identify the problem in these situations.

For cases arising from tips from third parties, correctly identifying the problem areas frequently is more difficult. Many government agents seem concerned that if they reveal the true subject of their concern, the taxpayer will shred evidence, tamper with witnesses, and otherwise illegally obstruct the investigation. Often the most reliable technique for the professional to identify the government's areas of concern is a careful debriefing of the taxpayer and all third-party witnesses contacted by the government to ascertain the subjects explored by the special agent. The witnesses should painstakingly detail the interview in a memorandum as soon as possible, not only to ascertain the special agent's focus, but also to later clarify any misinterpretations by the special agent of what was said.

The Accountant's Role. During the investigative phase of a criminal tax case, the accountant must duplicate and check the technical tax accounting work of the special agent and revenue agent with the following objectives:

1. Identify the strengths and weaknesses in the taxpayer's affairs.
2. Review the preparer's worksheets to explain any error.
3. Produce rigorous analyses of income and deductions, as needed.
4. Understand the evidence, to place disclosures from the special agent or other government people in proper context.
5. Assist in the presentation of the taxpayer's case if full or partial cooperation at the agent level is chosen.

Many attorneys also will want the accountant to be the member of the defense team responsible for document management and control. Whoever assumes the principal duties in document organization, the accountant must have access to the entire document reservoir.

The Attorney-Client Privilege and the Retainer of the Preexisting Accountant. Rarely should the taxpayer's general accountant—especially the accountant for the periods under inquiry—perform the accounting support work on a criminal tax case. However, the taxpayer will often prefer, based in part on perceived cost savings, not to bring in a new person. This bias of the client should be resisted stoutly. First, the preexisting accountant is inevitably subject to a conflict of interest because of the ever-present potential for the examination to target the accountant as well. Second, preparing the accounting detail for criminal tax support work involves specialized techniques different from the experience and training of many accountants.

Another consideration is privilege. The accountant's work supporting a criminal tax investigation must be veiled by the lawyer's privilege. Unfortunately, the federal courts do not recognize an accountant-client privilege. Hence, to preserve the confidentiality of the accountant's workproduct, the accountant must be retained directly by the attorney.

An accountant who has done nonprivileged work for the client in the past or contemplates doing such work in the future will inevitably receive an inextricable blend of privileged and nonprivileged communications. Careful attorneys try to avoid this situation, which the government may more easily penetrate as to the privilege.

The taxpreparer not chosen as a target of the prosecution will often be a crucial witness for the government (See, e.g. *United States v. Popenas*, 780 F.2d 545 (6th Cir. 1985)).

Control of Document Turnover. One bedeviling issue for the defense is the control of document turnover to the government. Two principles are paramount.

Do not destroy evidence. This is a crime. If documents have been summoned or taken by warrant and if legitimate defenses exist against turning over documents, use all available administrative and legal means appropriate to the protection of sensitive material.

Do not offer material voluntarily until it is plainly asked for or required to be produced.

Tax Preparer's Workpapers and Records. The working papers of the taxpayer's preparer dating back to the period in question frequently become the focal point of the government's case. A cautious preparer, especially one who suspects trouble with the client and therefore diligently preserves the audit trail, frequently possesses evidence that, when understood, can be detrimental to the taxpayer.

Consider, for example, the typical claim made by a taxpayer: "I always deposit all of my business receipts into the First National Bank." For many businesses, the preparer would, in the absence of better information, construct gross business receipts by totaling the monthly deposits from the bank statements and would, after adjusting entries, use this total for taxable gross receipts. The careful accountant will preserve the audit trail deriving this data. If, in fact, the client uses two banks and deposits more than a minimal amount into a bank other than the First National Bank, the two sets of bank statements, together with the accountant's workpapers, are the skeleton of a criminal tax case. Without the workpapers, the mechanism by which the taxpayer underreported gross receipts would likely not be easily reconstructed and might be regarded as speculative. The presence of the work papers is the key to the government's proof of underreporting.

The accountant's workpapers are not confidential under any privilege claim recognized by the federal courts. (*United States v. Arthur Young*, 465 U.S. 805 (1984); *Couch v. United States*, 409 U.S. 322 (1973)). Taxpayers cannot assert a Fifth Amendment privilege respecting records in their accountant's possession (*Couch, supra; Fisher v. United States*, 425 U.S. 391 (1976)). The taxpayer's privilege against self-incrimination also does not cover the taxpayer's preexisting records because they do not constitute the taxpayer's compelled statements of self-incrimination. But the forced production of accountant workpapers, if demanded under a summons served on the taxpayer, can violate the taxpayer's constitutional privilege against self-incrimination under the theory that the implicit authentication of the document in response to the summons would be a nonverbal self-incrimination under the "act of production" doctrine (*United States v. Doe*, 465 U.S. 605 (1984)). The importance of accountant workpapers is so crucial to many tax fraud investigations that some taxpayers are tempted to cause the workpapers to disappear; however, the client should know that tampering with witnesses and the evidence of crime is itself a crime.

Amended Returns—Voluntary Disclosure. No practitioner can serve the public long without facing the question of whether to file amended tax returns correcting prior underreporting of tax. The accountant should almost invariably advise the filing of an amended return to correct an innocent error. True, agents acting with the wisdom of hindsight can misinterpret innocent circumstances. Nevertheless, as long as one can document the truth, preferably with contemporaneous notarized statements from fact witnesses, fear of prosecution should not restrain an honest taxpayer from clearing up the record.

Where a fraudulent tax return has been filed, the taxpayer may receive indication that the government is investigating *collateral taxpayer's returns* that may lead to an audit of the fraudulent return; accordingly, the taxpayer may file an amended return (see *Hirschman v. Commissioner*, 12 TC 1223 (1949)). Disclosure under these circumstances is at best only marginally voluntary. Filing an amended return was a common method of avoiding the fraud penalty or obtaining immunity when the Treasury Department had a voluntary disclosure policy. The department has abandoned that policy, and filing an amended return now offers substantially less assurance that a settlement of the civil liability will preclude criminal action. It is generally considered a good faith action when the taxpayer prepares and files a corrected amended return before any discovery of fraud by the Internal Revenue Service, but the government may use the amended return as an admission of greater tax liability and therefore, put the taxpayer in jeopardy.

Filing an amended return after the taxpayer is notified of a pending audit will not mitigate a fraud assessment (see *Bonucci v. Commissioner*, 39 T.C.M. (CCH) 179 (1979).

These considerations blend into the question of voluntary disclosure when fraud has occurred. Previously, the federal government had a written public policy against prosecuting taxpayers who voluntarily disclosed fraudulent errors on their tax returns. Today, voluntary disclosure is only one element to consider, among others, in the government's decision whether to prosecute.

The emphasis here is on the word *voluntary*. The disclosure must have been spontaneous, prior to any contact by the government, and it must have been truthful and complete. A true and correct amended return not prompted by government contact will usually go through the system without a ripple, putting the problem behind the taxpayer.

Once a government agent is assigned to the case, the considerations change. There is no such thing as a true voluntary disclosure at this stage. However, the government does appear to believe that soliciting tax returns, followed by criminal prosecution if the returns are filed, is a kind of entrapment. Therefore, complying with the demand of a revenue officer to file returns is usually safe.

Once a special agent is assigned, use care in deciding whether and when to file. During a criminal investigation, one probably should not file amendments because the returns are routinely used as evidence against the taxpayer as an admission of the tax deficiency arising from the fraud or failure to file. Some special cases may warrant the filing of returns even if a special agent in involved. For example, if the taxable income is zero in a failure-to-file situation, filing returns showing this may help. An equally effective, and safer, tactic would probably be to make a presentation to the special agent to this effect and file the returns after the criminal case closes.

To be assured that tax returns are filed on a timely basis or as of a specific date, mailing the returns by certified or registered mail is the safest way (*Walden v. Commissioner*, 90 T.C. 947(1988); Treas. Reg. § 301.7502-1(c)(2)).

Section 6501 of the code does not clearly define the term *Filed*, however, it is generally held that *Filed* is *delivered to* and *received by the IRS*. Section 7502(c) provides that for a return sent by registered mail, the registration is prima facie evidence the return was delivered to the IRS office to which it was addressed. Mailing the return by ordinary mail with sufficient postage and sufficient time for delivery by the U.S. Postal Service does not count if the Postal Service loses the return, it is burned in an air crash, or hijacked to a foreign country.

To be technically certain that the returns have been filed, do not rely on transmittal of the original documents to an IRS field employee (*Espinoza v. Commissioner*, 78 T.C. 412 (1982); I.R.C. § 6091 and Treasury Regulations thereunder).

In addition to mail registration or certification, a letter of transmittal with an extra copy of the return and self-addressed stamped envelope should be included with the return requesting an "IRS received stamp" be placed on the first and second pages of the copy of the return and that stamped copy returned to the sender. Another suggested practice is to photocopy the mailing envelope, stamped and addressed to the IRS office, and the certification documents all on the same sheet of paper by photo reduction process.

When the IRS Representative Comes Calling. The accountant may be visited by a special agent or by some other IRS person during the course of a criminal investigation or a civil investigation with criminal overtones. The accountant should not proceed without immediate contact with legal counsel because the visit to an accountant retained by counsel is likely to constitute an impermissible violation of the attorney-workproduct privilege. If such a visit occurs, the accountant ought to record the name of the individual, job title, badge or identification number, and office location. Specific data of potential later use include the name of the person's supervisor, the division and group to which the person is assigned, the person's job specialty, and whether the person is a member of any special team or on a special assignment, such as a narcotics task force. The accountant should note whether the taxpayer is a target of the investigation and what, if any, charges are being investigated.

If interviewed by the government, the accountant should debrief himself with a thorough written memorandum of the conversation, immediately afterward. This will help the accountant remember the details of the conversation and may prove useful later in impeaching inaccurate versions of the conference written up in special agents' memoranda of the interview. For an especially important conversation, accountants may consider notarizing their memorandum to establish the time of its creation that undercuts the charge of creating after the fact.

Etiquette and Pitfalls. Generally one should reply to all correspondence promptly, unless the attorney for strategic reasons directs otherwise. Similarly, the defense should furnish all requested information in the first response, unless the attorney decides to strategically meter the information. If the defense team decides to protect information by asserting privilege, then different considerations apply.

Send only photocopies of documents requested. Never release originals. If originals are placed under summons and a turnover of originals is contemplated, prepare and maintain clear photocopies of all material turned over to the government. Be aware that many documents have markings in colors (including notations made in magic marker). Assure that the retained copies of documents have distinctions sufficient to make out the material in pastel hues on the original. In some documents, the color coding is significant. These should never be turned over if an alternative exists. Never supply unrequested information unless it obviously helps your side.

Make careful judgments about whether the defense should provide information by correspondence or by oral interview. Correspondence has the virtue of an objective, written record. Interviews enable you to express complex thoughts more clearly and observe the effect of your information on the other side. You may also consider following up an oral presentation with highlights in written form or coming to the meeting with a letter explaining what you intend to say.

THE MECHANICS OF THE ACCOUNTANT'S WORK

Method of Proof: Omitted Income

To prove a fraud case that alleges that the taxpayer omitted income from his or her tax return, the government may use direct proof. This is evidence of actual specific items of income that do not appear on the return. Frequently direct proof will be missing, or the government cannot establish the failure to report a given transaction. In that case, the government will then use any of several methods of circumstantial or "indirect" proof of gross income. By measuring the circumstantially proven income against the reported gross receipts per the tax return, the government can show a reporting shortfall that is then attributed to fraudulent intent.

The indirect methods of proof, though imprecise, have been accepted repeatedly by the courts as the best that can be done in difficult situations. Several methods have become fairly standardized over the years. The IRS may combine these methods, resulting in a more complicated task for both the prosecution and defense's experts.

The IRS uses four traditional major indirect methods of proving unreported income[6]: net worth, expenditures, bank deposits, and the source and application of funds. Two lesser known specialized methods often used to corroborate other methods of proof, have been used. They are the percentage method and unit and volume methods. Each of the indirect methods is straightforward in theory but difficult to apply.

Specific Item Method. The specific item method, or direct method, uses proof of income-generating transactions that the return does not report.[7] Sometimes the specific item is one item, perhaps a large real estate sale or other substantial single revenue-generating event. Here the government proves the fraud by showing that the single transaction does not appear on the return. The prosecution attributes the omission, of course, to fraud. Sometimes the specific items may number in the dozens or hundreds, for example, all a lawyer's receipts for 3 years. In this case, more like the indirect reconstruction methods, the government will compare the results of the specific item buildup against the reported gross receipts, attributing any shortfall in reporting to fraud.

The government may sometimes use the taxpayer's records to prove the omitted specific items. Where the taxpayer's records are incomplete or nonexistent, the government will rely on outside sources of proof, such as canceled checks from customers, or public records, such as deed recordings for real estate transactions.

The specific item method is described in detail in the IRS *Special Agent's Handbook*.

Net Worth Method and Its Defenses. The net worth method is one of the indirect methods of proving unreported income. The term *indirect* means that the suspected income is estimated indirectly by its effect on the taxpayer's financial picture, rather than calculated directly by proof of its receipt. By the net worth method, the government attributes increases during the taxable year in the taxpayer's net worth to the receipt of taxable income. Because some income is spent as well as saved during the year, the net worth method normally requires a two-part calculation showing the increases annually in net worth, supplemented by expenditures made during each of the taxable periods.

The net worth approach has the following steps:

1. Calculate with "reasonable certainty" the net worth at the beginning of the period (*Holland v. United States*, 348 U.S. 121 (1954)). This opening net worth is the pivot point of the method. A weak opening net worth makes all the subsequent calculations suspect. Assets should be shown at cost. Assets carried over from beginning to end of the period should be included, to avoid distorting the percentages of net worth increase (*United States v. Dwoskin*, 644 F.2d 418 (5th Cir. 1981)).
2. Calculate the net worth at the end of each succeeding period.
3. Calculate the annual increases in net worth by subtracting the beginning net worth of each period from the ending net worth of each period.
4. Add to the increases in net worth the taxpayer's annual nondeductible expenditures (including living expenses) for each year. Do not duplicate expenditures for assets appearing in the net worth calculation.
5. Compare the income thus indirectly calculated to the reported taxable income to calculate the amount of unreported income for each period.

Holland v. United States, 348 U.S. 121 (1954) is the bedrock authority for the net worth method, a case that should be familiar to every forensic accountant contemplating a controversy involving the net worth method. In this case, the court expressed concern that use of the technique had been expanded to include ordinary persons with clearly disclosed sources of income. Nevertheless, the court approved the net worth method as used in that case, and in so doing, provided guidance important to this day on a variety of subjects, including the type of evidence required to establish opening net worth, the need for evidence of taxable sources, and the need for independent corroboration of willfulness.

The accounting defenses to the net worth method usually fall into one of several patterns, Many defendants assert that the government incorrectly calculated opening net worth, and that, therefore the apparent increases in net worth are illusory, being instead merely the surfacing of already owned assets. Other defendants claim that the increases in net worth arise from nontaxable sources. Finally, some taxpayers argue that the government's annual accounting calculations of net worth are technically erroneous.

Regarding the opening net worth calculations, probably the most frequently used defense (and often a very colorful one) is the "cash hoard" defense. Naturally, if the unexplained appearances of increases in wealth can be attributed to cash on hand at the beginning of the period, the government's case collapses. Because taxpayer's testimony respecting cash hoards is as difficult for the government to disprove as it is for the taxpayer to prove, many taxpayers are tempted to roll the dice with testimony regarding the existence of a cash hoard. If the special agents, early in the investigation, have had luck, the taxpayer in the initial interview will have denied the existence of a cash hoard, an assertion that comes back to haunt the defense when the decision is made to put on a cash hoard defense at trial. The unreliability of taxpayer admissions falls into the common law precept that uncorroborated admissions alone cannot convict. Thus a body of confusing case law has evolved regarding when, if ever, the taxpayer admissions regarding opening net worth need corroboration. (See *Smith v. United States*, 348 U.S. 147 (1954); *United States v. Calderon*, 348 U.S. 160 (1954); *United States v. Scrima*, 819 F.2d 996 (11th Cir. 1987)).

Probably the most important aspect of a cash hoard defense is to produce credible third-party evidence of the hoard's existence or at least evidence making its existence possible. (See *United States v. Rifkin*, 451 F.2d 1149 (2d Cir. 1971)).

Regarding nontaxable sources, the accountant must methodically exhaust every possibility of proving nontaxable sources. Inheritances, gifts, and loans (either received or repaid) are the most common.

One problem that the prosecution faces in the net worth method is in proving its case beyond a reasonable doubt. One might think that there is *always* reasonable doubt that net worth increases have taxable sources.

Holland provides solutions to this. First, the government may establish a "likely source" (taxable source) for the increased net worth. The taxpayer must then provide "leads" to the government to establish the income's nontaxable nature. Otherwise, the income will be presumed to be from the likely taxable source. *United States v.*

Massei, 355 U.S. 595 (1958) then established another alternative: The government could negate all likely nontaxable sources. This rather forbidding task is often accomplished by the special agents at the initial contact meeting where they closely inquire into leads and nontaxable sources. The taxpayer, unrepresented and without knowledge of the legal importance of the questions, will be tempted to bluff his way through this interrogation with answers that often are both knowingly false and damaging to the later efforts to defend the case.

Section 424.9 of the IRS *Handbook for Special Agents* contains the government's viewpoint on the taxpayer's defense in net worth cases. Exhibit 600-5 in the same source contains an example of the net worth method.

The Expenditures Method. The expenditures method is an alternative format for presenting net worth and expenditures information. This technique uses the taxpayer's annual expenditures, rather than net worth increases, as the principal measure of taxable income. Net worth increases become supplemental information. The *Handbook for Special Agents*, at para. 425.1 states that "the same items or accounts used in determining taxable income by the net worth method are also considered when the expenditures method is employed." The expenditures method is more likely to be used when the taxpayer expends income on living lavishly rather than acquiring assets.

The relation between income, expenditures, and the changes in taxpayer's assets (both up and down) are the same in the expenditures method and the net worth method. For example, the liquidation of assets can be as likely a source of spendable funds as is the receipt of taxable income. A weak opening net worth, especially one that fails to consider a cash hoard, can do just as much havoc to the government's case here as in the net worth method.

Nevertheless, the limited analytical effort shown in the *Handbook for Special Agents* and some case law[8] indicate that the expenditures method requires less care in preparing the net worth side of the computation than would be required by the net worth method. Perhaps because special agents tend to develop this side of the case less rigorously, the Department of Justice prefers the net worth presentation method. Consequently, the defendant's accountants should carefully look for flaws in the logic of an expenditures method case.

Defenses applicable to net worth cases apply generally to expenditures cases; and the principles of *Holland v. United States*, 348 U.S. 121 (1954) and its progeny also are regarded as generally applying.

The *Handbook for Special Agents* discusses the principles of the expenditures method of proving income and sets forth a sample summary schedule.

Bank Deposits Method. The last of the major circumstantial techniques for estimating taxable income is called the bank deposits method. More properly, this is the bank deposits and expenditures method. This method assumes that bank deposits and currency expenditures, unless demonstrated to have been made with nontaxable funds, arise from taxable income, if a likely source of the taxable income has been shown. One measures the year's taxable gross receipts by totaling the year's bank deposits and currency expenditures. Deductible expenditures must be subtracted from the bank deposits total to calculate taxable income.

As with other indirect methods, one should ascertain the cash on hand (currency) at the start of the period with reasonable exactness, at least if the deposits consist in whole or in part of currency.[9] Otherwise, the bank deposits may be explained as the surfacing of a preexisting cash hoard. On the other hand, the government has not been required to prove opening new worth.[10] In view of the strong likelihood that liquidated assets could have produced some portions of the deposits charged as income, it would seem that establishing opening net worth would logically be required. At the very least, cross examining the government's expert on this point may reveal logical weaknesses in the government's analysis.

The government must establish a likely source for the deposits in the form of an activity-producing taxable income. The likely source may be either legal or illicit activity. The deposits must be regular and recurring in nature and be of a type, amount, and timing that is consistent with the nature of the alleged income-producing activity. The classic model for this approach is *Gleckman v. United States*, 80 F.2d 394 (8th Cir. 1935) where the court stated:

> If it be shown that a man has a business or calling of a lucrative nature and is constantly, day by day and month by month, receiving moneys and depositing them to his account and checking against them for his own use, there is most potent testimony that he has income, and, if the amount exceeds exemptions and deductions, that the income is taxable.

By contrast, large deposits, standing alone, should not normally be included, because they are generally regarded as not supporting an inference that they arose from underreported taxable income.[11] Of course, if the government chooses to use specific item identification of such deposits, then they may be included as taxable if so established.

A bank deposits case should address the following technical issues:

All deposits into financial institutions must be considered, not just bank accounts. Thus deposits into other financial institutions such as brokerage accounts and checks negotiated directly as payment for other uses must be investigated. The total must include cashed checks.

Painstaking care must go into identifying transfers and redeposits, both of which are obviously nonincome items. For example, a withdrawal predating a deposit in another account may be a transfer.

A running account of currency withdrawals may help explain later deposits. Thus, for example, one may argue three $100 withdrawals over 3 weeks as a source for a deposit in the fourth week of $250. This conclusion would be enhanced if the taxpayer could logically explain the need for cash on hand and if analysis of the taxpayer's checking activity showed little need to deal in cash for personal expenditures.

Make adjustments for credit and debit advices, so that items such as bounced checks do not count against the taxpayer. Note any debit advices occurring after the close of the last taxable period in case deposited checks are nullified because they were charged back as NSF (nonsufficient funds) in a later year.

Checks in transit—items drawn in one period and cleared in a subsequent period—can sometimes perplex the government. These items can literally float without adequate testimony to tie them down to a specific year. The taxpayer should not shoulder the burden of establishing the correct year; the government must prove *its* case beyond a reasonable doubt.

If the government tries a hybrid of specific item and bank deposits analysis, the defense must ensure that the government does not double count by first tracking the income directly as a specific item and then indirectly as a portion of the undifferentiated bank deposits.

If the government supplements bank deposit information by an expenditures analysis, the cash expenditures are very likely sourced to cash withdrawals from bank accounts or from cashed checks. Consequently, a proper and logical cash expenditures analysis must not double count the taxpayer's income by first recording it as a bank deposit and then recording the same dollars as income when they show up later as a cash expenditure.

The government has an obligation to thoroughly investigate so as to identify nonincome deposits.[12] The taxpayer's accountant has an even more stringent obligation because the taxpayer's freedom may hinge on the adequacy of the effort to identify nonincome items. The duty on the defendant's accountant is so extreme that for practical purposes the defense of a bank deposits case may turn into a specific items case. Loans, insurance, gifts, exchanging checks for cash, and inheritances are all common nontaxable sources.

The accountant may have to examine the taxpayer's financial history in years before or after the prosecution period. Such an examination might reveal sources of taxable funds reported (or even unreported, as long as received) in prior years but deposited in the current year. Further review of earlier periods might reveal hard evidence of practices continuing into the prosecution period. An example might be exchanging cash for checks, a practice that creates the unwarranted appearance of deposit of taxable income. Introducing evidence from earlier years may fill in proof gaps in the later years' evidence.

The *Handbook for Special Agents*, in § 426 and Exhibit 600-6, discusses the bank deposits method that warrants close examination.

Other Methods. A variety of other techniques, not recognized as formal methods of indirect reconstruction, have been used on occasion as corroboration in criminal cases and sometimes as the principal method of proof in civil cases. The *Handbook for Special Agents* designates two such methods as the "percentage" method and the "unit" or "volume" method. These methods require the government to find some objective yardstick of the amount of business done by the taxpayer and apply either a percentage profit figure to gross dollar volume (the percentage method) or a dollar profit figure to the units produced or sold.

These techniques can be used for legitimate businesses, in which case industry sources may provide the dollar or percentage profit figures. The methods are also frequently used where the taxpayer is engaged in a criminal enterprise, in which case the profit figures may need to be derived from expert input by law enforcement officers or witnesses familiar with the profit data of that particular criminal activity.

In civil cases involving such indirect methods of proof, the government may use creative efforts to estimate gross receipts. In the case of a suspected illegal amphetamine manufacturer, the government obtained the utility bills for the taxpayer's residence, which showed industrial-sized consumption of electricity. The government, through expert input from chemists, calculated the kilowatt hours necessary to produce a given number of units of amphetamine. This allowed the agency to make a rough conversion from electricity usage to units of production, which were in turn converted into wholesale street value and a derived gross receipts figure. In another case, involving a suspected bordello, the government calculated the number of customers by reviewing the institution's consumption of clean sheets. With an average price per customer, the government was again able to produce a figure for gross receipts.

It should be apparent that the foregoing methods of proof, though perhaps adequate for estimating civil liability, are not sufficiently rigorous to satisfy constitutional standards for a criminal conviction. For this reason, in criminal litigation one will probably see these methods used only to corroborate one of the more widely accepted methods of proof.

The taxpayer's advisors should never overlook the probative value of percentage and unit data in the defense against inflated taxable income figures produced by the government. If objectively verifiable data from third-party sources—such as wholesale vendors selling to the taxpayer—can estimate the taxpayer's business volume, then standard markups or profit per unit figures may produce indirect evidence of the maximum possible level of income. Many information sources exist for percentage and unit data, including IRS statistics of income, *Dun & Bradstreet*, and *Financial Studies of the Small Business*.

Practical Pointers on Criminal Tax Accounting Support

Unreported income investigations are the most common of criminal tax matters. Because indirect methods are the most common way of proving these cases, the following details serve as practical approaches to such studies.

Finding the Evidence. The defendant's accountant in a tax fraud investigation focuses on refuting the harmful facts or implications alleged by the government in either a direct or indirect reconstruction case. The defendant's accountant probably will not reach the same conclusions as those of the government's analysts. In fact, even the government's own experts have differed widely in their conclusions. See *Gleckman v. U.S.*, 80 F.2d 394 (8th Cir. 1935).

Care and organization are the watchwords. The detailed work required can often involve the minute examination of literally hundreds or thousands of documents, including canceled checks, bank statements, ledgers, vendor invoices, sales records and notes, and scraps of paper generated or kept by the client over a period of years. Occasionally, the documents will be well organized, but the files usually consist of many boxes, of all different sizes, stuffed with papers without logical order. Frequently, the client may have discarded critical records. Usually, the client will have made no effort even to reconcile checking accounts or perform other minimal financial housekeeping.

The accountant, after having ascertained the investigation's probable focus, must decide early on what documents possessed by third parties must be secured for the required tasks. For example, bank records—such as bank statements, canceled checks, and deposit slips—are usually the starting point of the defendant's case. Unfortunately, many clients have mislaid or discarded their originals. When the defendant's accountant goes back to the bank for microfilm records of these documents, he faces hostility. Researching microfilm records is an unprofitable and time-consuming headache for the bank; many erect roadblocks to the request, including exorbitant search or copying charges, extended delays, or refusals to respond unless served with a subpoena.

Obtaining records from banks or other third-party organizations can be a race against time when the investigation focuses on older years. Banks, as well as many other organizations, have a specific schedule for discarding records; if recovery of older records is crucial to the case, vigorous efforts must be made to obtain the records as early as possible.

All Source Documents Must Be Retrievable. Once the documents have been recovered, they must be organized. Indirect reconstruction cannot begin until all pieces of evidence receive a sequential number or other unique identifying label or have been stored in a defined location. Each entry on the computerized summaries that the accountant will produce will need to be referenced to one, or more pieces of evidence which must be positively identified and easily recoverable from a logical organization.

The Accountant's Workproduct. The accountant's end product can be best visualized after describing the component parts. The basic assembly for the indirect reconstruction is a spreadsheet for each bank account for each year. The spreadsheet is captioned to identify the bank, the depositor's name, and the account number. Deposits are listed chronologically down the left side, showing the date and amount. Appropriate categories are set forth in vertical columns, such as "income deposits," "transfers," "other nonincome deposits," "unidentified," or any other category breakdowns suggested by the needs of the case. Each deposit is then logged into its appropriate category.

The bank account spreadsheets must also have columns for page references and for comments or narrative description. Each line item entry should then be referenced to one or more page references in the database of source documents to substantiate the categorization. The comments columns permit the reviewer to understand the nature of the transaction without consulting the primary source evidence.

The accountant prepares a similar spreadsheet for cash expenditures, listing the date, amount, and type of expenditure, together with categorization into columns showing the likely source of the cash from which the expenditure was made. The page references will show the evidence of the expenditure and its source.

Other spreadsheets may be required for deposits into brokerage accounts, mutual funds, and the like. Their format will resemble that described for bank accounts.

The separate spreadsheets for the individual accounts and brokerage accounts and the spreadsheet for cash expenditures are then summarized for each year. The summary sheets will list on the left side each bank account and then for that account spread the totals from the account sheet into columns ("gross deposits," "income," etc.). The columns on the summary sheet are then totaled to calculate the grand totals for each category. The accountant's final workproduct will thus be a (computer generated—usually a year to a page) schedule that sets forth the universe of deposits and cash expenditures. Each bank account will be allocated a separate line on the report, and a separate line will also show the aggregate cash expenditures. This summary sheet will give the reviewer an overview of the scope and nature of the transactions. At the same time, the reviewer may, by using the page references for every entry on the supporting schedules, ascertain the accuracy of any entry.

Approaching the Task of Reconstruction. At the beginning of the accountant's reconstruction task, many or most of the deposits will fall into the "unidentified" category. The accountant must remove as much as possible from the unidentified category because the bank deposits method regards unidentified deposits as income by default, unless the amount is so large as to be uncharacteristic of the asserted income source.

For criminal tax reconstructions, the accountant is entitled within reason to make every assumption in favor of the taxpayer, so long as the record contains arguable support for the accountant's choices. The prosecution must prove guilt beyond a reasonable doubt. So long as a reasonable possibility exists that a given deposit is nonincome in nature, the defense is entitled to the presumption that this is the case. But see *United States v. Samara*, 643 F.2d 701 (10th Cir. 1981), where the accountant went too far and usurped the province of the jury. Early in reconstruction, the accountant ought not, however, indulge in speculation but should confine any conclusions to those that can clearly be substantiated by direct proof.

The search for clues regarding the sources of deposits is both challenging and frustrating. Obviously, if the taxpayer keeps clear records of the amounts and sources of deposits, the accountant's job is merely compilation. The client should be aggressively questioned to produce any records, whether partial or complete, with which to cut the time spent in piecing together clues indirectly. Assuming the taxpayer has no such records, or that they are incomplete, then the accountant must take other steps.

The first cut at producing evidence of interaccount transfers is to compare each deposit with evidence of withdrawals from other accounts. Patterns will often quickly emerge. Transfers may always be in even-dollar amounts. Monthly transfers may occur to pay the mortgage. Certain accounts may always be the source of transfers into certain other accounts. Close consultation with the client will obviously assist in identifying such patterns.

For criminal tax reconstruction, if a withdrawal and a deposit of identical amount occur from the same or another account within a few days, it may be presumed that this is a nontaxable transfer or redeposit. Where transfers take the form of check deposits, the canceled checks showing the transfer of funds would be directly referenced as the proof of the transfer.

Sometimes large unidentified deposits whose source eludes the investigator predate a single check for a specific purchase such as a car or piece of real property. Often, under these circumstances the deposit is the source of the purchase money, and when the connection is made, the taxpayer will clearly remember the source of the funds. Thus the accountant will often find it fruitful to ask questions such as, "Where did you get the money to buy the Mercedes?"

Often the accountant will have to review several times other documents not having any clear or apparent connection to the bank deposit data itself. Thus the taxpayer may have a file on the probate of a parent's estate. Payoff dates in court accountings may coincide with the dates of large deposits into the taxpayer's accounts. Property closings similarly may be the obvious source of deposits once dates and amounts are matched up. Insurance files may produce proof of payments received during the year. Evidence of loans received by the taxpayer or repaid to the taxpayer will indicate nontaxable sources.

Whatever the evidence that the accountant relied upon, the accountant must reference by page number each document providing support for the position taken regarding a specific item. Because much of the detail on a large reconstruction is easily forgotten, no substitute exists for rigor in page referencing and intelligible narrative comments.

If the only evidence of a source of a deposit is a withdrawal revealed on another bank account statement, then the accountant needs to note only the page reference for the bank statement. On the other hand, if numerous documents piece together into the substantiation, they should each be separately listed. Where the conclusion is drawn from underlying calculations derived only indirectly from the substantiation, the calculations should be scheduled on a separate sheet that is assigned a page number; and the reference on the spreadsheet should be to this underlying schedule as well as to the substantiating source documents.

Other Sources of Evidence. The taxpayer's calendars or appointment books can be a fruitful source of evidence. These records may reflect notes about trips to the bank for appointments to discuss loans or loan applications. They may help refresh the taxpayer's memory about meetings with others concerning transactions concluded and reported in one year yet deposited in a subsequent year. They may disclose business trips and forgotten related expenses. Taxpayers often keep personal diaries of other information as well, such as records of living expenses, records of loan payments, etc. Scrutinize these, even if they are only partial records. Also, review any records which may produce information of casual sales of items such as cars, boats, household furniture, and valuables such as heirlooms, paintings, and objets d'art.

The taxpayer's correspondence files can also produce a wealth of useful information. They may contain corroborating evidence of nontaxable income or deductible expenses. Even if the taxpayer has not retained correspondence, the taxpayer may recall correspondence in the hands of others that may provide useful sources of leads or corroboration.

Obviously, bank files should be examined in great detail. However, not only may these files contain helpful information about nontaxable sources and other items of interest, they may also hold embarrassing information such as inflated net worth statements and phony tax returns provided to support credit applications. In a related vein, the accountant may find the data in the files of credit-reporting companies of value to provide clues for places to search for further information.

Stock records can be important. Corporation records of stock splits may prove where shares were acquired. Commercial publications such as *Moody's Dividend Record* will disclose portions of corporate distributions that are nontaxable or were taxable as capital gains. The possibility always exists that the government may have overlooked the nontaxable portion.

Escrow company files will provide information that may be of interest, such as detail on the cost basis of assets disposed of during the taxable year. Similarly, county property tax records can provide interesting information such as ownership history and records of deductible land taxes paid.

Legal records are important. Care should be used not to breach privileges, where they apply. The government frequently uses court records respecting the taxpayer's business and financial transactions and to find admissions or allegations about the taxpayer's personal wealth. This information may be used in favor of the taxpayer as well as against the taxpayer. Judgments may produce evidence of nontaxable cash receipts. Damage awards may be a business expense. Probate files may produce other evidence of nontaxable sources. Public records about incorporation and limited partnership filings can sometimes be productive.

Insurance records, whether of the taxpayer, the taxpayer's broker, or of insurance companies themselves can provide evidence of nontaxable sources such as casualty loss recoveries or medical reimbursements. The income may be nontaxable but sometimes offsets an otherwise deductible expenditure.

Credit card data, whether revolving charge or bank credit, contain useful information. Business expenditures may be thereby substantiated, and the fact and timing of business trips may be pinned down.

Telephone records, though falling into the general class of business expense substantiation, can also be of separate independent value, for example, to establish a circumstantial case of the business purpose of a trip. Similar observations may be made about travel records, whether from carriers or from travel agencies.

Other records of financial transactions such as petty cash fund records, accounting data on computer disks, and taxpayer-generated records can be found, often juxtaposed with seemingly irrelevant collections of data.

ACCOUNTING ISSUES AND THE ACCOUNTANT IN A CRIMINAL TAX TRIAL

Accounting Evidence: General Comments

Accounting evidence is the centerpiece of most criminal tax prosecutions. The government must prove a tax deficiency as a necessary element of an evasion case. Where possible, the government tries to prove a deficiency even for those tax crimes where tax deficiency is not an element of the offense. Consequently, the government almost always uses a summary expert witness who testifies to the tax accounting methodology and the accounting mathematics of the case and also provides an expert opinion regarding the tax deficiencies established by the evidence. The government's expert witness is usually a seasoned special agent with specialized government training on the special problems of reconstruction of income and other recurring issues in criminal prosecutions. The special agent summary witness may or may not have an academic accounting background that gives the agent special expertise on traditional accounting subjects.

Expert accounting witnesses can help the defendant's case. Many judgment calls are implicit in any indirect reconstruction. Many loose ends may be tied down by more diligent or skillful analysis than the government's summary witness has done. Rather than attempting to win the summary issues on cross-examination of the summary witness, counsel for the accused may prefer to rely more on an affirmative case presented by a specially prepared witness for the defense. Accounting evidence, not as expert opinion, but as part of the contemporaneous record of the transactions that are the subject of the government's accusations may also figure in many prosecutions. The meaning of such evidence, either in favor of the government or the taxpayer, may be explained by accountants as fact witnesses or by accountants as expert witnesses.

The Accountant and Preparation. Many attorneys, even those skilled in criminal tax defense, will rely heavily on the accountant to help develop the case and prepare for trial.

The core of the accountant's case preparation starts with a preliminary definition of the tasks at hand, followed by a personal review of the evidence. Staff may sort the documents into categories, but unless the volume of the data in the case reaches unmanageable proportions, the expert witness accountant should personally review every document, however briefly. Delegating this critical task to staff pulls the accountant away from the feel of the evidence and makes it harder, indeed probably impossible, to make the kinds of multiple connections (through instinct, intuition, or subconscious memory) in the later stages of case development that characterize the highest level of achievement in forensic accounting.

After reviewing the database, the accountant will then address other tasks; in criminal tax cases, this generally includes an indirect reconstruction of taxable income. The accountant must always maintain a thorough audit trail so that every number in a summary can be easily traceable to an underlying summary or source document through a coherent organization system. The summaries produced may well be the essence of the defense and provide the basis for much strategic planning in the case. Bad news on the tax arithmetic may suggest that the defense regroup and emphasize willfulness defenses. Good numbers may lead the defense to presenting an affirmative case on the question of the existence of a tax deficiency. Disputable items, perhaps areas of professional uncertainty under GAAP or some other standard, or year-end "floaters," uncertain as to proper year of inclusion, may suggest a defense structured principally on cross-examination.

To properly prepare complex accounting cases, especially those involving indirect reconstruction of income, the accountant will become immersed in the evidence, usually more so than the attorney. Poring over the myriad scraps of paper in the search of the patterns and interconnections of the taxpayer's financial transactions, the accountant will be reviewing, perhaps on multiple occasions, virtually every piece of evidence in the case. This places the accountant in a unique position to identify clues and evidence in the file that may bear on issues that do not directly relate to accounting. The accountant must always be current on the legal issues in the case and might volunteer new issues or new perspectives on issues as work progresses. The accountant should also be current on the problems in case development, such as finding missing witnesses or conflicting evidence. Stray marks, telephone numbers handwritten at the top of invoices, memos, and notes on the back of business cards—any of the foregoing and any of a multitude of other apparently trivial pieces of evidence may provide the clues to break open a case, and the accountant is likely to be the first person to see such material.

The accountant and the accountant's staff can also play the leading role in developing the document database from which the case may be tried. The assembly, organization, and computerization (where applicable) of the data may often be performed by the accountant. Both the accountant and the attorney should have access to the same fully organized, catalogued, and retrievable, unified document database.

Some attorneys will use accountants, especially those with prior IRS field investigation experience, to help develop the case through locating and interviewing witnesses and securing needed documents. If the accountant becomes so deeply involved, the attorney can lose the hands-on feel of the case. Therefore, this delegation should be used carefully. At trial no substitute exists for having had the attorney get the feel of the witnesses by conducting the preliminary interviews. The accountant generally should not conduct such investigations alone, though the accountant could accompany the attorney to ask questions and record the conversation.

The Accountant at Counsel Table. If invited to sit at counsel's table, the accountant can take careful notice of the evidence in the case as it develops. Lines of inquiry may suggest themselves to the accountant listening to the testimony. When the opposition's witnesses are under examination, the accountant should listen carefully and make clear, legible notes to pass on to the lawyer that suggest lines of inquiry. Some attorneys do not want even this assistance. Almost no attorney wants whispered advice or observations. Too much activity occurs in court to permit this kind of distraction.

The Accountant as a Defense Witness. Accountants are not invariably used as defense witnesses in the defense of criminal tax cases.

The accountant can testify as a rebuttal witness respecting technical errors in the presentation by the government's summary witness. The government usually chooses only seasoned veterans to testify as expert summary witnesses, and the defense is playing on the government's turf. Counsel may therefore decide not to undertake a direct attack on the summary witness through cross-examination but may instead seek to point out the weaknesses in the government's case without giving the government's expert a chance to explain his testimony while on cross-examination. The use of the defense expert as a rebuttal witness is an alternative. Unjustified assumptions, math errors, failure to give the benefit of doubt on ambiguous evidence, all of these can weaken or mortally wound the government's case. The means to bring these errors before the jury is through the testimony of the taxpayer's expert accountant.

The accountant may play a similar, somewhat related role if the government's case relies on disputed technical accounting matters. Here, however, the person whose professional activity is focused on forensic accounting may or may not be best qualified to opine on the pivotal technical issue. Counsel will need, therefore, to decide whether to use the forensic accountant or whether the technical issues may be better examined, and with greater authority, by an academic person or other expert professionally involved in the specific technical subject matter under scrutiny.

The accountant may also present an entire alternative summary and interpretation of the evidence. This presentation is made more persuasive with the use of bold, appealing, and understandable graphics. The accountant will probably testify as to the alternative's methods, assumptions, and conclusions, highlighting areas of disagreement with the government's figures.

The Accountant's Professional Responsibility. The accountant involved in preparing the defense of a client should scrupulously avoid the temptation to let professional judgment be clouded by the zeal to protect the client. Practical reasons exist for this. An accountant's presentation that is unimpeachable for bias is much stronger in its effect on both the government agents during the investigative stages and on the trier-of-fact in a criminal tax trial. In this regard, the accountant should review the pronouncements of the AICPA regarding professional judgment and duty to inform the government of errors in the tax return. See the *Statement on Responsibilities in the Practice*, AICPA, 1989 Revision.

CONCLUSION

For the accountant to perform his or her responsibilities in a civil or criminal tax fraud case, familiarity with legal precedent and methods of proof, an unrelenting search for documentation, and a skillful assembly of exhibits are all essential. If the accountant's summaries and workproduct tend to support the government's assertions that the taxpayer engaged in premeditated and willful efforts to evade taxes, the defense then may be required to shift to willfulness defenses or the exploitation of erroneous accounting methods on the part of the prosecution. In such a situation, the accountant may or may not be called as an expert witness. The potential availability of accounting defenses can never be tested until the work is done.

APPENDIX: BADGES OF FRAUD

The badges of fraud as set forth in the *Handbook for Special Agents* at § 940 are as follows:

(1) The taxpayer who knowingly understates income leaves evidence in the form of identifying earmarks, or so-called "badges" of fraud. Some of the more common "badges" of fraud are as follows:

(a) Understatement of Income

1. An understatement of income attributable to specific transactions, and denial by the taxpayer of the receipt of the income or inability to provide a satisfactory explanation for its omission.

a. Omissions of specific items where similar items are included. Example: Not reporting $1,000 dividend from Company A, while reporting $50 dividend from Company B.

b. Omissions of entire sources of income. Example: Not reporting tip income.

2. An unexplained failure to report substantial amounts of income determined to have been received. This differs from the omission of specific items in that the understatement is determined by use of an income reconstruction method (net worth, bank deposits, personal expenditures, etc.).

a. Substantial unexplained increases in net worth, especially over a period of years.

b. Substantial excess of personal expenditures over available resources.

c. Bank deposits from unexplained sources substantially exceeding reported income.

3. Concealment of bank accounts, brokerage accounts, and other property.

4. Inadequate explanation for dealing in large sums of currency, or the unexplained expenditure of currency.

5. Consistent concealment of unexplained currency, especially when in a business not calling for large amounts of cash.

6. Failure to deposit receipts to business account, contrary to normal practices.

7. Failure to file a return, especially for a period of several years although substantial amounts of taxable income were received. Examiners should not solicit delinquent returns where the taxpayer has willfully failed to file. A referral report should be submitted.

8. Covering up sources of receipts of income by false descriptions of source of disclosed income.

(b) Claiming Fictitious or Improper Deductions

1. Substantial overstatement of deductions. For example, deducting $5,000 as travel expense when actually the expense was only $1,000.

2. Substantial amounts of personal expenditure deducted as business expenses. For example, deducting rent paid for personal residence as a business rent.

3. Inclusion of obviously unallowable items in unrelated accounts. For example, including political contributions in Purchases.

4. Claiming completely fictitious deductions. For example, claiming a deduction for interest when no interest was paid or incurred.

5. Dependency exemption claimed for nonexistent, deceased, or self-supporting persons.

(c) Accounting Irregularities

1. Keeping two sets of books or no books.

2. False entries or alterations made on the books and records, backdated or post dated documents, false invoices or statements, other false documents.

3. Failure to keep adequate records, especially if put on notice by the Service as a result of a prior examination, concealment of records, or refusal to make certain records available.

4. Variance between treatment of questionable items on the return as compared with books.

5. Intentional under or over footing of columns in journal or ledger.

6. Amounts on return not in agreement with amounts in books.

7. Amounts posted to ledger accounts not in agreement with source books or records.

8. Journalizing of questionable items out of correct account. For example: From the Drawing account to an expense account.

(d) Allocation of Income

1. Distribution of profits to fictitious partners.

2. Inclusion of income or deductions in the return of a related taxpayer, when difference in tax rates is a factor.

(e) Acts and Conduct of the Taxpayer

1. False statement, especially if made under oath, about a material fact involved in the examination. For example, taxpayer submits an affidavit stating that a claimed dependent lived in his household when in fact the individual did not.

2. Attempts to hinder the examination. For example, failure to answer pertinent questions or repeated cancellations of appointments.

3. The taxpayer's knowledge of taxes and business practice where numerous questionable items appear on the returns.

4. Testimony of employees concerning irregular business practices by the taxpayer.

5. Destruction of books and records, especially if just after examination was started.

6. Transfer of assets for purposes of concealment.

(f) Other items

1. Pattern of consistent failure over several years to report income fully.

2. Proof that the return was incorrect to such an extent and in respect to items of such character and magnitude as to compel the conclusion that the falsity was known and deliberate.

(2) The following actions by the taxpayer, standing alone, are usually not sufficient to establish fraud. However, these actions with some of the "badges" listed above, may be indicative of a willful intent to evade tax:

(a) Refusal to make specific records available. (Examiner should note time and place records were requested.)

(b) Diversion of portion of business income into personal bank account.

(c) File return in different district. (This is weak but should be noted.)

(d) Lack of cooperation by taxpayer. Examiner should cite specific episodes, threats, etc.)

(3) The presence of one or more of these "badges" of fraud does not necessarily mean that the return is fraudulent. However, it should alert the examiner to this possibility and invite further and more probing inquiry.

NOTES

1. For example, Dominic Frontiere, husband of L.A. Rams Football team owner Georgia Frontiere, and band leader Skitch Henderson. See *United States v. Henderson*, 399 F.Supp. 508 (S.D.N.Y. 1975). In responding to Henderson's plea for leniency, the court stated, "The Biblical injunction applies: 'Ye shall Not Respect Persons in Judgment.' Deuteronomy 1:17."

2. *United States v. Bishop*, 412 U.S. 346, 360 (1973).
3. The Appendix lists some "badges" of fraud, taken from the *Handbook for Special Agents*.
4. The *Handbook for Special Agents* sets forth the following regarding Attitude and Conduct for the Taxpayer:

> "(1) The first symptom alerting the examiner to the possibility of fraud will frequently be provided by the taxpayer. Conduct during the examination may be indicative of the filing of improper returns. The examiner should be alert to the following actions:
> (a) repeated procrastination on the part of the taxpayer in making and keeping appointments for the examination;
> (b) uncooperative attitude displayed by not complying with requests for records and not furnishing adequate explanations for discrepancies or questionable items;
> (c) failing to keep proper books and records, especially if previously advised to do so;
> (d) disregard for books and records;
> (e) destroying books and records without a plausible explanation;
> (f) making false, misleading, and inconsistent statements;
> (g) submitting false documents or affidavits to substantiate items on the return;
> (h) altering records;
> (i) using currency instead of bank accounts;
> (j) engaging in illegal activities;
> (k) failing to deposit all receipts; and
> (l) quick agreement to adjustments and undue concern about immediate closing of the case may indicate a more thorough examination is needed.

5. In *Miranda v. Arizona*, 348 U.S. 436 (1966), the Supreme Court decided that suspects in custody must be instructed of their constitutional rights to silence and assistance of counsel. The special agent's visit to the taxpayer's home or office does not place the taxpayer into custody and thus does not trigger the constitutional mandate of *Miranda*. IRS manual policy requires *Miranda* warnings, however.
6. *Internal Revenue Service Handbook for Special Agents*.
7. "Specific items method" technically may also refer to the legion of cases involving false items of deduction, which of course must be disproved item by item just as the taxpayer's omitted items must be proven item by item under the method.
8. *Taglianetti v. United States*, 398 F.2d 558, 565 (1st Cir. 1968).
9. *United States v. Normile*, 587 F.2d 784 (5th Cir. 1979). However, the *Handbook for Special Agents* at para. 426.5(4) states that if the other requirements of the bank deposits method are met, the "lack of proof of the amount of cash on hand would not be fatal to the case."
10. *United States v. Stein*, 437 F.2d 775 (7th Cir. 1971).
11. *Paschen v. United States*, 70 F.2d 491 (7th Cir. 1934).
12. *Kirsch v. United States*, 174 F.2d 595 (8th Cir. 1949).

LIST OF CASES

Bonucci v. Commissioner, 39 T.C.M. (CCH) 179 (1979)
Couch v. United States, 409 U.S. 322 (1973)
Edwards v. United States, 375 F.2d 862 (9th Cir. 1967)
Espinoza v. Commissioner, 78 T.C. 412 (1982)
Fisher v. United States, 425 U.S. 391 (1976)

Gleckman v. United States, 80 F.2d 394 (8th Cir. 1935)
Hirschman v. Commissioner, 12 T.C. 1223 (1949)
Holland v. United States, 348 U.S. 121 (1954)
Kirsch v. United States, 174 F.2d 595 (8th Cir. 1949)
Miranda v. Arizona, 394 U.S. 436 (1966)
Paschen v. United States, 70 F.2d 491 (7th Cir. 1934)
Smith v. United States, 348 U.S. 147 (1954)
Spies v. United States, 317 U.S. 492 (1943)
Taglianetti v. United States, 398 F.2d 558 (1st Cir. 1968)
United States v. Beacon Brass, 344 U.S. 43 (1952)
United States v. Bishop, 412 U.S. 346 (1973)
United States v. Boyle, 469 U.S. 241 (1985)
United States v. Burks, 508 F.2d 672 (5th Cir. 1975)
United States v. Calderon, 348 U.S. 160 (1954)
United States v. Conforte, 624 F.2d 869 (9th Cir. 1980)
United States v. Diamond, 788 F.2d 1025 (4th Cir. 1986)
United States v. Doe, 465 U.S. 605 (1984)
United States v. Dwoskin, 644 F.2d 418 (5th Cir. 1981)
United States v. Greger, 716 F.2d 1275 (9th Cir. 1983)
United States v. Heller, 830 F.2d 150 (11th Cir. 1987)
United States v. Henderson, 399 F. Supp. 508 (S.D.N.Y.1975)
United States v. Hooks, 848 F.2d 785 (7th Cir. 1988)
United States v. Massei, 355 U.S. 595 (1958)
United States v. Miller, 529 F.2d 1125 (9th Cir. 1976)
United States v. Normile, 587 F.2d 784 (5th Cir. 1979)
United States v. Pomponio, 429 U.S. 10 (1976)
United States v. Popenas, 780 F.2d 545 (6th Cir. 1985)
United States v. Rifkin, 451 F.2d 1149 (2d Cir. 1971)
United States v. Samara, 643 F.2d 701 (10th Cir. 1981)
United States v. Scrima, 819 F.2d 996 (11th Cir. 1987)
United States v. Stein, 437 F.2d 775 (7th Cir. 1971)
United States v. Venuto, 182 F.2d 519 (3d Cir. 1950)
United States v. Arthur Young, 465 U.S. 805 (1984)
Walden v. Commissioner, 12 T.C. 947 (1988)

APPENDIX

MARITAL DISSOLUTION: SEPARATE PROPERTY AND MARITAL PROPERTY IN COMMUNITY AND OTHER EQUITABLE DISTRIBUTION PROPERTY STATES

Richard S. Wilkolaski, CPA
Richard Z. Schatz

INTRODUCTION

In the eighteenth century, after establishment of the U.S. Constitution, the legislators of the original 13 colonies attempted to define separate and marital property and establish their inherent rights. From those embryonic stages of family law to the present, each state jurisdiction has established its own definitions and characteristics of property in marriage and divorce. Initially, all tangible marital property and related property rights belonged to the husband. After the turn of this century and with the advent of women's rights, the wife began to vest ownership in property and obtain rights more equal to her husband.

OBJECTIVES OF THIS APPENDIX

For all 50 states and the District of Columbia, this Appendix addresses four property ownership categories (separate, marital, community, quasi-community) and division of property. This appendix discusses these categories within the following four equitable distribution systems:

1. *Marital property system*–In a marital property system, the court divides only property acquired during marriage that is not identified as "separate." The court will not divide, for example, property accumulated before marriage and that accumulated during marriage by gift or inheritance, normally referred to as "separate" or "individual" property.
2. *Community property system*—The primary difference between the marital property system and the community property system is the time when the marital interest attaches. The community property system gives each spouse a present, vested, one-half interest during marriage in all community property when it is acquired. Under a common law or marital property system, the marital property interest does not immediately attach when property is acquired during the marriage.
3. *Kitchen sink system*—The court may divide all property owned by either spouse at divorce, regardless of when or how it was acquired. In other words, the court, in ordering a property division, need not consider the separate and/or marital property aspects that may be inherent in a specific marital dissolution action.
4. *Hybrid system*—In some states, only marital property may be subject to division at divorce. Where a division of only marital property would be unfair, separate property may be included in the marital estate "balance sheet" and divided accordingly. This situation generally occurs under special circumstances and in limited instances. The "hybrid" system combines the "marital property system" and the "kitchen sink system." (A brief glossary accompanying this appendix more fully explains some of these terms.)

The following material represents an accountant's view, by state, as of early 1988. The user should discuss specific legal definitions and rules applicable to any specific matter with the attorney requesting services.

SUMMARY OF PROPERTY BY STATES

Alabama

Separate Property. All property acquired before marriage, all earnings received from third persons, and all damages that spouses may recover for injuries to their person or reputation are separate property and are not subject to each other's debts.

Marital Property. All property acquired by either spouse during marriage, except for separate property.

Community Property. System does not apply.

Division of Property. The court may order that separate property of one spouse be paid to support the spouse provided that such separate property was not acquired prior to marriage or by inheritance or gift. Any property used regularly for common benefit of parties during marriage may be awarded in a property settlement.

Alaska

Separate Property. Property and pecuniary rights acquired before marriage or by gift, devise, or inheritance and not subject to the other spouse's debts or contract.

Community Property. System does not apply.

Division of Property. In this marital property state, the court equitably divides property obtained during marriage. The court may, for equity, and under special circumstances, divide property obtained by either spouse before marriage.

Arizona

Separate Property. All property—real or personal—owned before marriage or thereafter acquired by gift, devise, or descent, and increase, rents, issues, and profits thereof is separate. Each spouse has sole management, control, and disposition rights of his or her separate property. Separate property of spouse is not liable for separate debts or obligations of other spouse, absent agreement to the contrary.

Community Property. All property acquired during the marriage that is not separate property.

Quasi-Community Property. Marital rights in property that was acquired elsewhere and that would have been community property if spouse was living in Arizona.

Division of Property. Court assigns each spouse's sole and separate property and equitably divides community, joint tenancy, and other property held in common though not necessarily in kind, without considering marital misconduct.

Arkansas

Separate Property. Property owned at time of marriage; property obtained by gift, bequest, descent, or transfer from any person; property acquired by trade, business, labor, or services carried on or performed on a spouse's sole or separate account. Income and proceeds from all such property shall, notwithstanding marriage, be and remain sole and separate property and may be used or invested and may be sold or transferred without spouse's interference. A spouse's separate property shall not be liable for the other spouse's debts, except as may have been contracted for support of spouse or children of marriage.

Marital Property. All property acquired by either spouse after marriage, except for separate property.

Division of Property. Each spouse is restored to undisposed property that she or he brought into marriage. All marital property shall be distributed one-half to each party unless court finds such division inequitable. When the court does not evenly divide marital property, it must explain why. The court may, at its discretion, consider federal income tax consequences of marital property division.

California

Separate Property. All real and personal property owned before marriage and that acquired afterwards by gift, bequest, devise, or descent, with rents, issues, and profits thereof is separate property and may be conveyed without the other spouse's consent. Personal injury damages comprise separate property in certain cases.

Neither the husband nor wife has any interest in the other's separate property, but neither can be excluded from other's dwelling, except in divorce, annulment, or separate maintenance proceedings, upon court order.

Community Property. All real property in California and all other personal property wherever located acquired during marriage while spouses lived in this state and certain property held in trust. Exceptions to this rule: (1) earnings of wife that husband has given or relinquished to her and (2) earnings of children living with or in custody of one spouse while living separate from the other spouse are the custodial parent's separate property. All real property in California and personal property wherever located, acquired during marriage that is not separate property, is community property.

Joint Tenancy. Property taken in names of husband and wife as joint tenants is not ordinarily community property but may be shown to be such according to the parties' intention. Joint tenancy in dissolution proceedings is presumed to be community property, but separate property contributions may be reimbursed under certain circumstances. Presumption may be rebutted by written evidence that it is separate property.

Transmutation. Beginning January 1, 1985, transfers from separate to community and community to separate must be in writing. Spouses may agree to transmute separate or community property with or without consideration, so long as it is in writing that expressly declares the consent of the adversely affected spouse. Third parties are not affected by transmutation of real property without notice, unless recorded. Gifts of tangible personal property, unless of substantial value, are generally excepted.

Quasi-Community Property. All real and personal property wherever heretofore or hereafter acquired (1) by either spouse while living elsewhere that would have been community property if the acquiring spouse had been living in the state or (2) in exchange for real or personal property wherever located that would have been community property if the acquiring spouse had been living in state.

Division of Property. Community property jurisdiction. Except upon the parties' written agreement or stipulation, the court must divide in kind or equally all community, quasi-community, and homestead property but may also award a particular asset to one party as deemed proper to equally divide the property. Personal injury damage proceeds shall be assigned to the party suffering injuries unless otherwise indicated by each parties' economic condition and needs, time elapsed since recovery of damages, and other factors. Property rights assigned in final judgment will not be reconsidered, absent fraud or other unusual grounds.

Colorado

Separate Property. Each spouse retains property owned at marriage, rents, issues, profits, and proceeds thereof and property obtained by descent, devise, bequest, or gifts from others.

Community Property. System does not apply.

Division of Property. Property is distributed upon dissolution or legal separation by giving each spouse his or her separate property and then dividing marital property as the court deems just. The court disregards marital misconduct and considers contributions (including contributions as homemaker), value of the property set aside for each spouse, increase, decrease, or depletion of separate property, and each party's economic circumstances. A written agreement executed before or during marriage but prior to filing the dissolution is generally enforceable as to property division.

Connecticut

Separate Property. Property acquired before marriage, or by gift, devise, bequest, or descent is separate. Also, married persons' separate earnings are their sole property. They may contract with their spouse or third persons, may convey and receive conveyance of real and personal property, may sue and be sued in their own name, and their marital property may be subject to attachment and execution.

Community Property. System does not apply.

Division of Property. Court may assign to either husband or wife all or part of the other's estate. Court may pass title to real property to either party or to third person or may order the sale of such real property, without any act by either husband or wife, when the court finds that it is the proper mode to effect the decrees. In fixing the nature and value of the property, if any, to be assigned, the court shall consider length of marriage, cause of dissolution, age, health, station, occupation, amount and sources of income, vocational skills, employability, estate, liabilities, and needs of each party and opportunity of each for future acquisition of capital assets and income. The court may further consider each party's contribution to acquiring, preserving, or appreciating the value of his or her respective estates.

Delaware

Separate Property. Real and personal property generally acquired before marriage or by gift, bequest, devise, or inheritance. A spouse holds all his or her property as a separate estate and may sell, convey, assign, transfer, devise, bequeath, encumber, or otherwise dispose of it without the other's consent.

Community Property. System does not apply.

Division of Property. Upon either party's request in a divorce or annulment proceeding, the court shall equitably divide all marital property without considering marital misconduct.

District of Columbia

Separate Property. A spouse may hold property separately and dispose and convey it as if unmarried. No spouse shall be liable because of any contract or tort in which the spouse has not directly or indirectly participated, except for debts incurred for necessities for either of them or their dependent children. Property acquired during marriage by gift, bequest, devise, or descent is separate property.

Community Property. System does not apply.

Division of Property. In absence of valid antenuptial or postnuptial agreements or decree of legal separation disposing of the property, each party receives the sole and separate property acquired before or during marriage, and all other property accumulated during marriage is equally distributed whether title is held individually or in form of joint tenancy or tenancy by entirety. This property shall be distributed after considering length of marriage, age, health, occupation, employability, assets, debts, and custody of minor children.

Florida

Separate Property. Real and personal property acquired before marriage, or by gift, bequest, devise, or inheritance. Married persons can manage and control their separate property without joinder or the spouse's consent.

Community Property. This system does not apply.

Division of Property. The court can adjudicate property rights only where they are properly placed in issue by pleadings. The court generally may not modify a valid property settlement agreement. Where parties cannot agree upon the property's disposition, the court can determine disposition, based on legal and equitable principles. The court recognizes special equities and equitable distribution doctrines. The court may also enforce any antenuptial agreement to arbitrate dispute.

Georgia

Separate Property. Property acquired before marriage remains separate; any property or salary acquired during marriage vests in and belongs to the acquiring spouse and is not liable for payment of the other's debt, default, or contract.

Community Property. System does not apply.

Division of Property. All real and personal property acquired during marriage is subject to equitable division. Property eligible for equitable division also includes personal injury claim and settlement for lost wages during marriage.

Hawaii

Separate Property. Real and personal property acquired before marriage or by gift, bequest, devise, or inheritance.

Marital Property. Community property first became possible by statute on July 1, 1945. Every existing marital community was dissolved on June 30, 1949, but this did not divest any interest in property that was acquired, established, accrued, or vested before that date. Also, except as otherwise provided, any right established or accrued and any action taken before June 30, 1949, is governed by the existing law when such right was established or accrued or such action taken.

Division of Property. The court can divide and distribute real, personal, or mixed estate of spouses, whether community, joint, or separate. Marital property may be divided in kind or in any other equitable manner that the court deems just.

Idaho

Separate Property. All money or other property owned before marriage or acquired afterwards by gift, devise, bequest, or descent is separate property, as is anything acquired with the proceeds of separate property. Spouses may, by written agreement, provide that all or specified property shall be separate property of one spouse. Real property conveyed by one spouse to the other is presumed to be separate estate of grantee, and grantor spouse only need execute and acknowledge conveyance.

Community Property. All property acquired after marriage, including the rents and profits of the separate property community, unless the instrument by which the property is acquired provides that rents and profits thereof be applied to that spouse's sole and separate use. Husband and wife have joint management and control of community property. Real property conveyed to revocable trust retains its community property character.

Quasi-Community Property. All personal property, wherever it is situated. Also, all real property in Idaho that was acquired while living elsewhere but that would have been community property if the acquiring spouse was living in Idaho at time of acquisition, plus personal and real property acquired in exchange for such property.

Division of Property. The court divides community property equally, in kind or as may be just. Laws of Idaho govern distribution and allocation of both separate and marital property.

Illinois

Separate Property. All real and personal property owned or acquired before marriage or by gift, devise, bequest, or inheritance thereafter is separate. A spouse may hold as such deemed separate real and personal property and dispose of it as if it were separate property.

Community Property. System does not apply.

Division of Property. All property acquired by either spouse subsequent to marriage, except certain nonmarital property (as described), whether title is held individually or in some form of co-ownership. Nonmarital property does not become marital where increase in its value arose from contribution of marital property, nonmarital property, or the spouse's personal effort. Where marital and nonmarital property have been commingled, contributing property is classified as newly acquired property that will be marital. The right to reimbursement exists, but contribution must be traceable by clear and convincing evidence. Transfer of marital property between spouses per agreement or by court order is not considered a taxable event. Court may set aside part of each spouse's property in separate fund or trust for support, maintenance, and welfare of child.

Indiana

Separate Property. Real and personal property acquired before marriage or thereafter by gift, devise, bequest, or inheritance.

Community Marital Property. System does not apply.

Division of Property. Court must divide parties' property justly and reasonably based on: (1) each spouse's contribution to acquisition, (2) extent of acquisition prior to marriage, (3) spouses' economic circumstances, (4) conduct of parties during marriage as related to property disposition, and (5) each party's earnings or earning ability. The court shall further consider tax consequences of property disposition with respect to each party's present and future economic circumstances. System of property distribution is common law.

Iowa

Separate Property. Married persons may own as their separate property and in their own right real and personal property and manage and dispose of it in the same manner as their spouse. The right of either spouse to a distributive sale in the other's realty cannot, however, be affected by a conveyance or mortgage in which he or she does not join.

Community Property. System does not apply.

Division of Property. Court may equitably divide property while considering children, property, and maintenance of the parties. When dividing property, the court must consider (1) whether distribution of property and assets is equitable under specific facts of case, (2) whether accumulated property is product of joint efforts of both parties, and (3) whether one party brought separate property into marriage. There need not be an equal or in-kind division.

Kansas

Separate Property. Spouses retain as their sole and separate property any property, real or personal, owned at time of marriage, or since acquired by descent, devise, bequest, inheritance, or gift. Separate property acquired by either spouse after marriage, whether held individually or in co-ownership, becomes marital property at time of commencement of marital dissolution action. Spouses' interests vest at commencement of action, with the court deciding the extent of vested interest. A spouse may carry on any trade or business and perform any labor or services for that spouse's sole and separate account, with those earnings and profits to remain as sole and separate property.

Community Property. System does not apply.

Division of Property. The court shall divide the real and personal property, whether either spouse owned it prior to marriage, acquired it in his or her own right after marriage, or both spouses acquired it by their joint efforts. The court may divide the property either in kind or by setting the same or a part thereof over to one of the spouses and requiring either to pay such sum as may be just and proper or by ordering a sale and division of proceeds therefrom. In dividing property, the court shall consider: age, length of marriage, property owned by parties, their present and future earning capabilities, time, source, and manner of property acquisition, family ties and obligations, allowance of maintenance or lack thereof, dissipation of assets, and other necessary factors.

Kentucky

Separate Property. Real and personal property acquired before marriage or thereafter by gift, devise, bequest, or inheritance. A married person's estate is liable for debts contracted or incurred before and after marriage. Spouses may acquire and hold separate property and may in their own name sell, encumber, and dispose of said separate property. Spouses are not liable for spouse's debts or responsibilities contracted before or during marriage, except to the extent that he or she has received property by virtue of the marriage. Otherwise, neither consort is liable for the other's obligations.

Community Property. System does not apply.

Division of Property. Written separation agreement between parties is encouraged, is binding upon the court, and will be enforced unless the court, after considering economic and other relevant evidence finds its provisions regarding custody and support unconscionable. Fault may still be factor in division although the law provides that marital misconduct not be regarded.

Louisiana

Separate Property. Property acquired prior to establishment of community property regime; acquired by spouse with separate or with separate and community assets when value of community assets is inconsequential; acquired individually by inheritance; acquired as damages from other spouse for breach of contract or fraud or bad faith in management of both separate and community property; and acquired as result of voluntary partition of community during existence of community property regime. Donation of interest in community property to other spouse transforms interest into separate property of donee. Personal injury damages are also separate property of spouse sustaining the personal injury; however, the portion of damages attributed to expenses incurred by community as result of injury or in compensation of loss of community earnings except that accrued after termination of community is community. Each spouse enjoys and disposes of separate property without concurrence of the other spouse. Spouse is liable with other spouse for family necessities. Except as provided by agreement, each spouse contributes to expenses in proportion to his or her means.

Community Property. Community property is that acquired during community through spouse's effort, skill, or industry or acquired with community things or with community and separate things—unless classified as separate property or donated to spouse jointly—or natural and civil fruits of community, or acquired for damages to community property, or all other property not classified as separate. A spouse may not alienate, encumber, or lease to a third person an undivided interest in community or particular thing thereof prior to the community's termination. A rebuttable presumption exists that things are community. One spouse may transfer separate property to the other, with the stipulation that it shall become community. Transfer by onerous title must be in writing and by gratuitous title must be by an authentic act. By such transfer, property is transformed into community property.

Division of Property. Spouse is entitled to one-half the value of community property used to satisfy the other's separate obligation or to acquire, use, improve, or benefit the other spouse's separate property. A spouse is also entitled to one-half of the value of separate property used to acquire, use, improve, or benefit the community and one-half of the enhanced value of separate property of the other spouse as a result of uncompensated labor or industry of spouses.

Maine

Separate Property. A married person may hold any property, real or personal, as separate property maintaining absolute control over it.

Community Property. System does not apply.

Division of Property. All property acquired during marriage is presumptively marital property unless otherwise shown. All rights in real estate are acquired by divorce decree when the decree or abstract thereof is filed in registry of deeds for county or registry district where the real estate exists. The nonowner spouse's claim to real estate as "marital property" does not affect the owner spouse's title until the nonowner spouse records in the appropriate registry of deeds either: (1) a copy of the divorce complaint, (2) a clerk's certificate of divorce complaint, or (3) a divorce decree or abstract thereof.

Maryland

Separate Property. Property owned at time of marriage and all other separate property that may be acquired or received during marriage is protected from debts of other spouse.

Community Property. System does not apply.

Division of Property. The court can make certain dispositions of property in cases filed after January 1, 1979. The Maryland court may exercise this authority after a foreign divorce if one spouse lived in Maryland when the foreign proceeding began and the foreign court exercised no jurisdiction over that spouse or property. When granting either divorce or separation, the court may order partition or sale of jointly owned personal property, but the court may not transfer ownership. When granting absolute divorce, the court shall value the "marital property" acquired during marriage other than by inheritance or gift and may grant monetary award as adjustment of equities of the parties' marital property. When granting separation or divorce, the court may decide which property is "family home" and "family use personal property," as defined, and may decide the use or possession of such property regardless of its title or ownership.

Massachusetts

Separate Property. Real and personal property acquired before marriage or acquired thereafter by gift, devise, bequest, or inheritance remain that person's separate property that the person may receive, hold, dispose of, and manage. Transfers of real and personal property between husband and wife are valid. Work and labor performed by wife for persons other than husband and children are presumed to be for her separate account.

Marital Property. Real and personal property acquired during the marriage that is not separate.

Community Property. System does not apply.

Quasi-Marital Property. A married person coming from another state or country into this commonwealth has all the rights, powers, and obligations given to married persons by laws of this commonwealth. Such a person retains all property acquired under the laws of another state or country, but future rights and liabilities are governed by the Commonwealth of Massachusetts.

Division of Property. May be ordered in addition to or in lieu of alimony, if certain factors apply. The property is subject to division irrespective of how the title is held or how it was acquired. In a divorce proceeding, the court cannot assign separate property of either husband or wife to a third party or to a minor child.

Michigan

Separate Property. Property brought into a marriage or thereafter acquired, except joint property, is separate, with right to manage and dispose of it alone, except that the husband's real estate is subject to dower. Separate property of either spouse is not liable for the other's debts.

Marital Property. Property held by the entirety or in such a manner that neither the husband nor wife individually has a separate property interest may constitute separate property of the husband and wife, as distinguished from community property. A married person may enter into a written contract jointly or severally with a third party. Unless otherwise provided, real property conveyed to the husband and wife is deemed to be held by the entirety, and personal property in the form of stocks, bonds, debentures, notes, mortgages, and other evidences of indebtedness to the husband and wife is considered jointly held with right of survivorship with same incidents as real estate held by entireties, but the presumption does not extend to bank deposits, land contracts, insurance, or other simple contracts.

Community Property. The statute establishing community property system was repealed May 10, 1948, with very limited protection of rights acquired prior to this date.

Division of Property. The court may restore to either party as it deems just and reasonable the separate real and personal estate. If the marital estate and effects awarded to either party are insufficient for suitable support and maintenance of either party and/or children, the court may further award such part of either party's real and personal estate as it deems just considering ability, character, station, and situation of parties and all other circumstances.

Minnesota

Separate Property. A married person may hold any property, real or personal, as separate. Nonmarital property is (1) any property acquired as gift, bequest, devise, or inheritance made by a third party to only one spouse, (2) acquired before marriage, (3) acquired in exchange for increase in nonmarital property, or (4) acquired after decree of legal separation or is excluded by a valid antenuptial contract.

Community Property. System does not apply.

Marital Property. The husband and wife, by their joint deed, may convey real estate of either, except homestead, subject to the other spouse's statutory right and either may, by separate conveyance, relinquish the rights in real estate so conveyed by the other.

Division of Property. The marital property distribution system applies. The court may equitably dispose of marital property without regard to marital misconduct. If the court finds that either spouse's resources or property—including a spouse's share of marital property—are so inadequate as to impose unfair hardship, it may also apportion to that spouse up to one-half of the other's nonmarital property, except property excluded by a valid antenuptial contract. All property, including vested pension benefits acquired during marriage, is presumed to be marital property unless shown to be nonmarital.

Mississippi

Separate Property. All property of a married person except the homestead—acquired before marriage, or by gift, devise, bequest, or inheritance is separate.

Community Property. System does not apply.

Division of Property. Property is distributed on the basis of title and special equity and the court's reasonable discretion.

Missouri

Separate Property. A spouse may hold as separate any property—real or personal—brought into the marriage and thereafter acquired by gift, bequest, devise, or descent or purchased with separate money or means, wages due from separate labor, wages due from any rights of action arising out of violation of personal rights, and all income, increase, and profits of any such property. Such property shall not be liable for the spouse's debts.

Community Property. System does not apply.

Division of Property. The court shall set apart to each spouse all separate property and shall divide marital property after considering relevant factors, including (1) each spouse's contribution to acquisition of marital property, including contribution of spouse as homemaker, (2) value of each spouse's separate property, (3) each spouse's economic circumstances when the property division occurs, including desirability of awarding family home or right to live therein for reasonable periods to the spouse having custody of any children, and (4) conduct during marriage.

Montana

Separate Property. Property brought into marriage or acquired thereafter by gift, devise, bequest, or inheritance is separate. Earnings during marriage are separate. Although neither husband nor wife is answerable for the other's debts, necessities for family and children's education are chargeable upon both's property. Separate property may also be held for a spouse's debts, if it is in that spouse's exclusive possession but only by those dealing in good faith with said spouse on the credit of such property.

Community Property. System does not apply.

Division of Property. Special equity system. The court shall equitably apportion property without regard to marital misconduct or recorded ownership and may protect children by setting aside a separate fund for their welfare.

Nebraska

Separate Property. Property brought into marriage and property that thereafter comes by descent, devise, or gift, or is acquired by purchase or otherwise is separate and is not subject to the spouse's disposal or liable for the spouse's debts. All property not exempt by law from sale on execution or attachment is liable for debts contracted for necessities furnished the family after execution.

Community Property. Law has been repealed.

Division of Property. Nebraska falls into the marital category of property division. The court may, at its discretion, include inherited property and retirement plans in the marital estate. Parties can enter into a written property settlement regarding support, maintenance, and property for themselves and any minor children. The agreement, except for terms relating to support and custody of minor children, is binding upon the court unless it finds the agreement unconscionable.

Nevada

Separate Property. All property brought into marriage and all property acquired afterward by gift, bequest, devise, or descent, or by an award for personal injury damages, with rents, issues, and profits thereof, is separate. If the husband and wife are living apart, the earnings of minor children—unless relinquished—are separate property of the spouse with custody or with whom the children are living. A spouse's written authority to the other to appropriate the spouse's earnings to his or her own use is deemed a gift and separate property.

Community Property. All property acquired during marriage, by either husband or wife, except separate property.

Division of Property. Nevada is a community property jurisdiction. The court may make an equitable disposition of community property and may also designate a portion of the husband's property for the wife's support or the wife's property for husband's support—if he is disabled or unable to provide for himself—or property of either spouse for their children's support.

Agreements settling property rights are favorably considered and usually approved. A property settlement agreement, made when divorce suit is pending or immediately contemplated, is not invalidated by a provision therein that it shall become effective only in the event of divorce.

New Hampshire

Separate Property. A spouse holds as separate all property at any time earned, acquired or inherited by, or bequeathed, given or conveyed to them—either before or during marriage—if such earning, acquisition, conveyance, gift or bequest were not occasioned by payment or pledge of the other spouse's property. Married persons have the same rights and remedies and are subject to the same liabilities regarding separate property as if they were unmarried.

Marital Property. Real and personal property acquired after marriage that is not separate property.

Community Property. System does not apply.

Division of Property. The court may distribute to the parties all or any part of the marital estate and may assign to both spouses any part of the marital estate as it considers just.

New Jersey

Separate Property. Real and personal property brought into a marriage or thereafter acquired by gift, devise, bequest, or inheritance is separate. The wife is entitled to her separate employment earnings and investments thereof. Separate property is not subject to the spouse's disposal nor liable for the spouse's debts. Suitable ornaments and apparel received from the spouse become separate property.

Community Property. System does not apply.

Division of Property. The court may equitably distribute certain real and personal property acquired by either party during marriage.

New Mexico

Separate Property. Property acquired before marriage or by gift, devise, bequest, or descent, or designated by written agreement of parties, or in deed concerning property held by spouses as joint tenants or tenants in common, or designated by court with all rents, issues, and profits thereof is separate. Neither spouse has any interest in the other's separate property, except that neither can be excluded from the other's dwelling. A woman's property acquired during marriage with a written instrument in her name alone—or in her name and the name of another party, not her husband—is presumed to be separate property if the instrument was delivered and accepted before July 1, 1973.

Community Property. All property acquired by either spouse during marriage, except for separate property, constitutes community property. Property acquired by either spouse during marriage is presumed to be community property.

Quasi-Community Property. Separate property acquired while in a common law jurisdiction and brought to New Mexico is divided according to the law of the state of origin on division of such marital property. Separate property acquired while living in New Mexico can be awarded to the other spouse only if justified as alimony.

Division of Property. On permanent separation, the court has the power to divide property with or without dissolution of marriage. Community property must be divided equally. After division, it is then separate property from which the court may award alimony.

New York

Separate Property. Property obtained before marriage, or thereafter by gift, devise, descent, or bequest is separate and is not subject to the spouse's control or disposal or liable for the spouse's debts. Married persons have all rights regarding real or personal property and acquisition, use, enjoyment, and disposition thereof and to make contracts in respect thereto with any person, including their spouse, and to carry on any business, trade, or occupation and be liable on such contracts and upon judgments, as if they were unmarried.

Community Property. System does not apply.

Division of Property. In proceedings begun after July 18, 1980, for divorce or annulment or for property distribution following a foreign divorce, the court shall grant respective rights of parties in separate and marital property and order disposition as follows: (1) Separate property shall remain such and (2) marital property shall be distributed equitably between parties, considering the facts of the case.

North Carolina

Separate Property. Real and personal property acquired before marriage, or by gift, devise, bequest, or inheritance.

Community Property. System does not apply.

Division of Property. In absence of separation agreement, either spouse may petition for equitable distribution of marital property. A married couple may execute a separation agreement consistent with public policy that will be legal, valid, and binding in all respects if the agreement is written and notarized.

North Dakota

Separate Property. Property acquired before marriage, in which the spouse has no interest; neither can be excluded from the other's dwelling.

Community Property. System does not apply.

Division of Property. The court shall equitably distribute real and personal property and may compel either party to provide for the children and to make such suitable allowance to the party for support during life or for a shorter period and may modify its orders from time to time. The court may assign homestead to the innocent party either absolutely or for a limited time. The court will consider age, earning ability, duration of marriage, marital conduct, station in life, circumstances and necessities of each, health and physical condition, financial circumstances as shown by property owned, its value and income producing capacity, and whether accumulated or acquired before or during marriage.

Ohio

Separate Property. Property acquired before marriage. Neither husband nor wife has any interest in the other's property, except right of support, dower, and to remain in the mansion house (family home) after death of either. Hence, either spouse may take, hold, or dispose of his or her separate property without joinder of other, though joinder is necessary to bar dower rights in real property.

Community Property. System does not apply.

Division of Property. Marital property type. The court equitably divides marital property.

Oklahoma

Separate Property. Property acquired by either spouse before marriage. A spouse's separate property is not liable for the other's debts contracted before marriage. Except as to the right of support, neither spouse has any interest in the other's separate property but may not be excluded from the other's residence.

Marital Property. Community property law became effective July 26, 1945, and was repealed effective June 2, 1949. The spouse whose property interest was affected by the law could, on or before June 2, 1950, record an agreement specifying the community property rights acquired by either party thereunder. After June 2, 1950, Oklahoma, as a common law jurisdiction, became an equitable property distribution state.

Division of Property. The court disposes of jointly acquired property as deemed reasonable regardless of legal owner. The spouse's interest in joint property acquired during marriage becomes vested upon divorce. The court may set apart a portion of a spouse's separate estate for child support where the other spouse has custody.

Oregon

Separate Property. Real and personal property acquired before marriage, in which neither spouse has interest in the other's property, except as to expenditures for family or education of children.

Marital Property. The Community Property Law of 1947 was repealed effective April 11, 1949. Prior rights are not affected. Community property may be converted into property held in common, by the entirety, or separate, by written agreement signed by both spouses. Oregon, as a common law jurisdiction, is now an equitable property distribution state.

Division of Property. The court must consider, as contribution to marital assets, the spouse's contribution as homemaker. A rebuttable presumption of equal contribution exists. The court must consider the tax consequences and other selling costs of assets reasonably anticipated by parties to be sold. The court may require that the custodian account for use of support. The court may not consider fault. The court may approve voluntary property settlement agreements providing for support.

Pennsylvania

Separate Property. Real and personal property acquired before marriage, or by gift, devise, bequest, or inheritance. A married person is not liable for the spouse's debts. A wife's separate earnings belong to her.

Marital Property. A community property law was repealed and deemed invalid under state constitution. Marital property is all property acquired after marriage, except that which is separate.

Division of Property. Marital property distribution prevails. Upon either party's request in divorce or annulment proceedings, the court must equitably divide all marital property as it deems just, without regard to marital misconduct. Real property conveyed or disposed of in good faith and for adequate consideration prior to commencement of divorce proceedings is not considered marital property. Marital property is subject to division regardless of how the title is held.

Rhode Island

Separate Property. Property acquired either before or during marriage remains separate property free from the spouse's control. Property inherited before, during, or after marriage is separate property and may not be assigned.

Marital Property. Property acquired after marriage, except for separate property.

Community Property. System does not apply.

Division of Property. In addition to or in lieu of alimony, the court may assign to a spouse a portion of the other's estate. Property is not assignable if it is separate and was held prior to marriage, but income derived therefrom may be assigned.

After filing of complaint for divorce from bed, board, and future cohabitation and until a decree of reconciliation, the court may permit either party to sell, mortgage, or otherwise dispose of the same free of dower or curtesy.

South Carolina

Separate Property. Real and personal property brought into the marriage or thereafter acquired by gift, devise, descent, bequest, or inheritance is separate property and not subject to the spouse's debts. Married persons have all rights to their separate property as if they were unmarried.

Marital Property. Property acquired during the marriage that is not deemed separate.

Community Property. System does not apply.

Division of Property. Marital property to be distributed regardless of title. The court equitably distributes property. The wife may claim contributions as homemaker as basis of special equity. Equitable distribution of marital property on divorce can take into account debts of both parties. Professional or other degree or license is not marital property. Improvements made to inherited property during marriage are subject to equitable distribution.

South Carolina

Separate Property. Real and personal property acquired before marriage, or by gift, devise, bequest, or inheritance. Except as to homestead, neither husband nor wife has an interest in the other's property, except their rights for support as provided by law, and neither can be excluded from the other's dwelling.

Marital Property. Property acquired after marriage that is not separate.

Community Property. System does not apply.

Division of Property. All property of spouses, including inherited property, regardless of which spouse holds title, is considered marital property to be divided between spouses, upon divorce at the court's discretion. The court considers length of marriage, property value, age and health, ability to earn a living, contribution to property accumulation, and income-producing capacity of each spouse's assets.
Fault must not be considered except if relevant to property acquisition during marriage.

Tennessee

Separate Property. Property owned before marriage or acquired thereafter by gift, devise, bequest, or inheritance.

Marital Property. Property acquired during marriage that otherwise is not separate.

Community Property. System does not apply.

Division of Property. Tennessee is a marital property state. The court shall equitably divide and distribute marital property, as defined by statute, without considering fault and may divest and reinvest title and—where necessary—order sale with proceeds to be divided between parties. The law does not affect the validity of antenuptial agreement or preclude incorporation into decree of property settlement agreement between parties. Court may award home and household effects to either party but must give special consideration to custodial parent.

Texas

Separate Property. All real and personal property owned or claimed by either spouse before marriage or acquired afterward by gift, devise, or descent, and any increase thereof is separate. Separate property is not subject to the other's liabilities unless both spouses are liable under law. Personal injury awards, except for loss of earnings, are separate property of the injured spouse. Bonus money and royalties payable with respect to oil and gas leases covering separate property are separate.

Community Property. All property acquired by either the husband or wife during marriage, except for separate property, is the spouses' common or community property. Rents, issues, and profits from separate or community property are community as are cash dividends from capital stock and interest on bonds. All property owned by husband and wife at dissolution of marriage is presumed to be community property unless otherwise proven.

Division of Property. The court may equitably divide property considering rights of each party and children.

Utah

Separate Property. Property acquired before marriage or acquired thereafter by purchase, gift, grant, inheritance, or devise remains separate.

Community Property. System does not apply.

Division of Property. Equitable distribution theory. The court may equitably divide the property.

Vermont

Separate Property. All real and personal property owned before or during marriage, except gifts from spouse. A spouse's separate property and the rents, products, and profits thereof, including any rights the spouse may have therein, are not subject to the other's liabilities, excepting those debts created for necessities for the family or for labor or materials furnished upon or for the cultivation or improvement of marital real property.

Marital Property. Property acquired during marriage, except separate property.

Community Property. System does not apply.

Division of Property. The court shall equitably dispose of property owned by parties separately, jointly, or by entirety, considering the merits of the parties and the condition in which the divorce shall leave them.

Virginia

Separate Property. Real, personal, tangible, or intangible property acquired before marriage and otherwise not deemed to be marital property is separate. The Premarital Agreement Act governs agreements entered into after July 1, 1986. Prospective spouses may enter into a premarital agreement regarding support, disposition of property, and other matters upon separation, marital dissolution, death, or other event. The agreement must be written and signed by both parties but is enforceable without consideration.

Marital Property. Includes real, personal, tangible, or intangible property acquired during marriage and not considered separate property including that portion of pensions, profit-sharing, or retirement plans acquired during marriage. The court may equitably distribute property of parties of divorce in foreign jurisdiction.

Community Property. System does not apply.

Division of Property. Property is divided by equitable distribution. The court may grant a monetary award, payable as a lump sum or in installments. In deciding the award amount, the court shall consider both parties as having an interest in marital property.

Washington

Separate Property. All real and personal property owned before marriage or afterwards acquired by gift, bequest, devise, or descent, or from the issues and profits of such is separate. Separate property is not subject to the other spouse's debts. Damages recovered in a personal injury suit are separate property of the injured spouse except to the extent of community interest, for example, lost wages.

Community Property. Property acquired after marriage by either husband or wife, or both, is community property, except for separate property.

Quasi-Community Property. Personal property and real property located in Washington, acquired during marriage by a spouse while living elsewhere—but that would have been community property had the spouse lived in Washington at time of acquisition—is quasi-community property.

Division of Property. The court may dispose of property as equal, just, and equitable without regard to marital misconduct. The relevant factors include the nature and extent of community and separate property, duration of marriage, and each spouse's economic circumstances at time of property division.

West Virginia

Separate Property. Real and personal property acquired before marriage, or thereafter by gift, devise, descent, or inheritance. A married person's rights with respect to property are those of a single person. The separate property is not subject to disposal by a spouse nor liable for a spouse's debts.

Marital Property. Property acquired during the marriage that is not deemed separate.

Community Property. System does not exist.

Division of Property. Absent valid prenuptial or separation agreement, the court shall equitably divide marital property. The court may consider the extent to which each party has contributed to acquisition, preservation and maintenance, nonmonetary contributions (i.e. homemaker services), and child care services. The court may also consider one party's contribution to the other's increased income-earning ability, including direct or indirect contributions to education or training for employment or other income-producing activity. The court may not consider fault or marital misconduct. The court may restore or distribute to a spouse property that the other controls.

Wisconsin

Separate Property. Property owned at marriage after December 31, 1985, is individual or separate property when the owner has a marital domicile in Wisconsin. Separate property also includes that acquired during marriage and after the later of marital domicile in Wisconsin, on January 1, 1986, and acquired as follows: (1) by gift or inheritance or distribution from trust created by a third party, (2) in exchange for or with proceeds of individual property, (3) from appreciation of spouse's individual property except to extent that appreciation resulted from substantial uncompensated efforts of either spouse, (4) by decree, marital property agreement, or reclassification, (5) as recovery for damage to spouse's property by other spouse, and (6) as recovery for personal injury except for loss of earnings and expenses paid from marital property.

Marital/Community Property. Effective January 1, 1986, Wisconsin adopted a modified form of community property and has become known as a marital/community property state. Wisconsin's marital property system is based on the Uniform Marital Property Act with variations. All property is marital except that which the statute classifies as otherwise. Income earned or accrued by a spouse during marriage is marital property. Substantial appreciation of property creates marital property if the appreciation results from substantial efforts of either spouse for which reasonable compensation was not received. Mixing marital property with property having any other classification reclassifies other property to marital unless other property can be traced.

Deferred Marital Property/Quasi-Community Property. Wisconsin's marital property system includes the concept of deferred marital property. Deferred marital property is property acquired during marriage and before the determination date (later of the effective date of the Wisconsin Marital Property Act, January 1, 1986, or establishment of Wisconsin domicile) that would have been marital property if acquired after the determination date.

Division of Property. Property acquired by either party by gift, bequest, devise, or inheritance, or from funds so acquired remains the separate property of such party unless the court finds that it would create hardship. Other property is presumed to be divided equally, but the court may alter this distribution after considering various specified factors, not including marital misconduct.

Wyoming

Separate Property. All property brought into a marriage or acquired during marriage in good faith by descent or otherwise, together with all rents, issues, increase, and profits thereof is separate. Such property is not subject to the spouse's disposal, control, or interference and is exempt from execution or attachment for debts if the property is not conveyed by the spouse in fraud of creditors. Necessary expenses of family and education of children are chargeable upon property of both husband and wife, or either of them, for which they may be sued jointly and separately. Married persons may transfer their separate property in the same manner and to the same extent as that of single persons.

Marital Property. Real and personal property acquired during marriage, except for separate property.

Community Property. System does not apply.

Division of Property. The court shall equitably dispose of property, considering the merits of the parties, the condition in which the divorce will leave the party that acquired the property, and burdens imposed on property for the benefit of either party or children. The court has broad authority in deciding "just and equitable" property disposition, which does not always reflect quantitative equality.

GLOSSARY

Bequest

A gift by will of personal property; a legacy. Disposition of realty in will is "devise."

Community Property

Property owned in common by husband and wife each having an undivided one-half interest by reason of their marital status. The following nine states have community property systems: Louisiana, Texas, New Mexico, Arizona, California, Washington, Idaho, Nevada, and Wisconsin. The remaining states are classified as common law jurisdictions. The difference between common law and community property systems centers around the property rights possessed by married persons. In a common law system, each spouse owns whatever he or she earns. Under a community property system, one-half of the earnings of each spouse is considered to be owned by the other spouse.

Descent

Hereditary succession. Succession to the ownership of an estate by inheritance or by any act of law as distinguished from "purchase." Title by descent of another acquires the real estate of the latter as his heir at law.

Devise

A testamentary disposition of land or realty; a gift of real property by the donor's last will and testament. Also, to dispose of real or personal property by will. (Disposition of personal property in will is "bequest.")

Equitable Distribution

No-fault divorce statutes in some states grant courts the power to distribute equitably upon divorce all property legally and beneficially acquired during marriage by husband and wife, or either of them, whether legal title lies in their joint or individual names.

Exist

To live; to have life or animation; to be in present force, activity, or effect at a given time, as in speaking of "existing" contracts, creditors, debts, laws, rights, or liens. To be or continue to be.

In-Kind Division

The asset is not divided, but rather both parties retain ownership as partners, tenants-in-common, or other form of joint ownership.

Marital Property

Property purchased by persons while married to each other and that, in some jurisdictions, on dissolution of the marriage is divided in proportions as the court deems fit.

Prevailing Party

The party to a suit who successfully prosecutes the action or successfully defends against it, prevailing on the main issue, even though not necessarily to the extent of the original contention. The one in whose favor the decision or verdict is rendered and judgment entered. The party ultimately prevailing when the matter is finally set at rest.

Quasi

As if; almost as it were; analogous to. This term is used in legal phraseology to indicate that one subject resembles another, with which it is compared, in certain characteristics, but that there are intrinsic and material differences between them.

Quasi-Community Property

As to family law matters, all real and personal property acquired by either spouse while living elsewhere that would have been community property if the acquiring spouse had been living in a community property jurisdiction.

Separate Property

Property owned by a married person is his or her own right during marriage. The real and personal property, including wages and earnings, of a woman that she owns at the time of her marriage, and the real and personal property, and the rents, issues, and profits thereof, of a married woman, which she receives or obtains in any manner whatever after her marriage, shall be her separate property as if she were single. In a community property jurisdiction, separate property is that which belongs entirely to one of the spouses. Generally, this property is acquired before marriage or acquired after marriage by gift or inheritance. For community property settlement, "separate property" is that which either party brings into the marriage, acquired during the marriage with separate funds, or receives by inheritance or particular donation.

BIBLIOGRAPHY

Black, H.C., M.A., *Black's Law Dictionary* (West Publishing Co., 1979).

California Family Law Reports, "*Family Law Roundup*" (CFLR, Fall 1986).

CCH Tax Law Editors, *1988 U.S. Master Tax Guide* (CCH, 1988).

California Society of Certified Public Accountants Education Division, *1987 Marital Dissolution Conference* (CSCPA, 1987).

CPA Foundation for Education and Research, *Understanding California Community Property* (1977).

Hogoboom, The Hon. W.P., and Justice D.B. King, *California Practice Guide Family Law* (The Rutter Group, 1987 and 1988).

Hogoboom, The Hon. W.P., Justice D.B. King, *Family Law Update 1986, New Legislation and Significant Cases* (The Rutter Group, 1986).

Krause, H.D., *Family Law in a Nut Shell* (West Publishing Co., 1986).

Losey, F.R., *Tax and Accounting Problems of Marital Dissolutions in a Community Property State* (CPA Foundation for Education and Research, 1977).

Martindale-Hubbell Law Directory (Martindale-Hubbell, Inc., 1987).

Oldham, J.T., *Divorce, Separation and the Distribution of Property* (Law Journal Seminars-Press, 1987).

TABLE OF CASES

Numbers in boldface refer to the page on which the case is mentioned.

INDEX